Financial Systems in Developing Economies

Financial Systems in Developing Economies

Growth, Inequality, and Policy Evaluation in Thailand

Robert M. Townsend

OXFORD
UNIVERSITY PRESS

OXFORD
UNIVERSITY PRESS

Great Clarendon Street, Oxford OX2 6DP

Oxford University Press is a department of the University of Oxford.
It furthers the University's objective of excellence in research, scholarship,
and education by publishing worldwide in

Oxford New York

Auckland Cape Town Dar es Salaam Hong Kong Karachi
Kuala Lumpur Madrid Melbourne Mexico City Nairobi
New Delhi Shanghai Taipei Toronto

With offices in

Argentina Austria Brazil Chile Czech Republic France Greece
Guatemala Hungary Italy Japan Poland Portugal Singapore
South Korea Switzerland Thailand Turkey Ukraine Vietnam

Oxford is a registered trade mark of Oxford University Press
in the UK and in certain other countries

Published in the United States
by Oxford University Press Inc., New York

British Library Cataloguing in Publication Data
Data available

Library of Congress Cataloging in Publication Data
Data available

Typeset by SPI Publisher Services, Pondicherry, India
Printed in Great Britain
on acid-free paper by
MPG Books Group, Bodmin and King's Lynn

ISBN 978–0–19–953323–7

1 3 5 7 9 10 8 6 4 2

Preface

The relevance of this book has been reinforced by recent events in US and world financial markets. Even in the popular press, parallels are being drawn between the current problems of emerging market countries in Eastern Europe and those of countries such as Thailand that went through—and in the case of Thailand served as the origin point of—the Asian financial crisis in 1997. Scholars such as Ken Rogoff have examined these Asian countries, and the many other countries around the world that have experienced historical financial crises, to try to get a sense through statistical analysis of the likely depth of the current recession and the likely rapidity of recovery, by sector. By focusing this book on historical Thai data and growth mechanics prior to 1997, we better understand not only the Thai crisis, but also the Thai recovery. As such, there are lessons to be learned for other countries, including those in trouble today. We also better understand the role of government policy, not only in the crisis but also in the Thai structural transformation prior to the crisis, a period of growth that helped make Thailand another Asian miracle. Government policy and its impact post crisis are also revealing in terms of post-Asian crisis micro-interventions, and the macro-interventions of 1997 and earlier credit crisis episodes.

Some of the parallels between today's Eastern European countries and the Asian countries of the 1997 crisis are false. Though both Eastern European countries of last year and Asian countries prior to 1997 all had very high growth rates, Asian countries were running fiscal surpluses, not deficits, for example. As Radelet and Sachs (1998) note, sovereign debt remained at prudent levels, savings and investment rates were high, and inflation was low. This caught the International Monetary Fund (IMF) by surprise and fueled the impetus for subsequent, post-Asian-crisis financial-sector assessment programs and early warning indices. On the other hand, both Eastern European and Asian countries share a common crisis symptom: euro- or dollar-denominated short-term loans associated with relatively large capital inflows, which, with a loss of confidence, bring capital flight and devaluations.

The consensus view of the Asian crisis is that it was, in large part, a run triggered by failing finance companies in Thailand. The Thai government had encouraged foreign capital inflow by maintaining attractive interest rates for apparently secure investments through offshore banks, all the while masking the underlying problem of non-performing loans in real estate with transfers from a relatively secret Financial Institution Development Fund. Rumors and occasional pressure on exchange rates were resisted until the Central Bank ran out of reserves. A serious recession followed the devaluation, though the onset took about six months. Despite the recession, the IMF argued for limited budget deficits and high interest rates to re-attract foreign capital. Some, such as Joseph Stiglitz, have argued that these actions amplified the recession. The US in the current recession has taken the opposite tact. In any event, Thai banks were not lending much at this time, and investment did not recover for several years. These ingredients are by now all too familiar to current observers of the US and other world economies.

But this book argues that, beneath the surface, Thailand remained in good shape. It is a picture drawn with much data and hard-nosed modeling. In essence, it is a tale of two financial sectors, the bad one associated with the crisis and the good one which fueled the growth before the crisis and facilitated recovery afterward. While foreign money flowing into commercial banks was fostering a real estate boom—an apparent bubble—there was a steady expansion of financial access on the domestic extensive margin, both before and after. That is, an increasing fraction of Thai households in towns and villages were gaining access to the formal financial system as new users of both savings and credit instruments. Accounting decompositions show that this increased financial deepening, along with improved education and occupation shifts, account for a non-trivial part of the observed improvements in per capita income, changes in inequality, and poverty reduction. One structural model put forth in this book uses this expansion of the financial sector as an exogenous policy change facilitating occupation shifts from subsistence agriculture to enterprise. The model delivers most of the observed movements in Thai productivity, that is, in total-factor productivity (TFP). Another structural effort models the expansion of the financial sector as endogenous and delivers almost exactly the observed long run, smoothed trend in financial access. Occupation shifts are domestic expansions. The same models establish that foreign capital inflows had little impact on growth. Put differently, the growth of Thai gross domestic product (GDP) was not spurious. It was much more than a bubble. This seems not to have been understood by foreign investors at the time.

The Thai government's Bank for Agriculture and Agricultural Cooperatives (BAAC) played a large role in the domestic expansion of the financial
sector, and hence in the increase in income and reduction in poverty over
the two decades prior to 1997. Unlike development banks in Latin America
and other countries, the BAAC was not making large losses and has been
judged by many to be largely free of corruption. Jacob Yaron shows that the
bank could have been making money with a relatively small increase in its
own lending rate, and some of the work presented in this book shows that
the BAAC was playing a relatively successful role not only in credit but also
in the provision of insurance. Unfortunately, the BAAC risk-contingent
lending system, with indemnities in the form of a system of flexible over-
dues, was mistaken by the IMF and World Bank in the Asian crisis as
symptomatic of yet another weak financial institution. External regulation
at that time was inappropriate. Outsiders did not understand the BAAC
system and the insurance role it was playing. Policymakers seemed prone to
jump to quick, inaccurate conclusions.

Of course, there were distortions, both micro and macro. On the micro
side, the same structural models show that while the BAAC was initially
more prevalent in the same areas as commercial banks—the industrialized
corridor stretching north out of Bangkok—it eventually expanded into the
outer provinces, targeting rural areas and those off the main roads. Meanwhile, for reasons that are somewhat speculative, commercial banks remained much more prevalent in the industrial corridor. Only a tiny
fraction of households in the Townsend Thai rural surveys shows up as
having commercial bank loans. So the model, which delivers a path of
costly but Pareto optimal financial deepening, under-predicts lending in
rural areas and over-predicts lending in towns. It is almost as if Thai policymakers, following a financial sector plan, had created a hole in parts of
formerly rural areas, now home to an increasing and unanticipated middle
class of entrepreneurs.

In any event, the interplay between the BAAC and commercial banks in
the end determined the actual financial landscape, and the next generation
of models will try to understand that interaction more deeply. This book
will try better to understand the policy motivation behind the observed
geographic expansion of BAAC branches. The Thai government maintains
a role in the continuing structural transformation and industrial organization models. Not-for-profit financial-sector participants are needed to understand that role, especially if one is to offer policy advice. Likewise, the US
is unlikely to re-emerge from crisis without a substantial government role,
inclusive in real estate, as with Fannie Mae (the Federal National Mortgage

Association) and Freddie Mac (the Federal Home Loan Mortgage Corporation). Indeed, the spread of mortgages to lower-income segments of the population is now understood by many to be a key part of the cause of the US financial crisis, in contrast to Thailand's history. Again, BAAC lending was driving TFP and growth. Ironically, though, the US does not have the panel data that Thailand does, namely the Townsend Thai data used in this book. These data can be used to create appropriate monitoring and evaluation systems of government and commercial financial institutions. There is a need to link the impact that financial institutions have on households and businesses to financial accounts for households and small businesses that can be created with collected micro-survey data. This process is well under way in Thailand, as described in the chapters to follow.

Distortions on the macro side are also apparent. Government involvement in the financial sector, though well-intended, can lead to repressions and, again, to crises themselves. We focus in Thailand not only on the 1997 crisis, but also on a revealing episode in the early 1980s. In those days, interest rates were fixed by regulation, both on deposits and loans. Oil price shocks led to inflation and negative real interest rates, *ex post*. Savings deposits left the banking system, while lending at existing fixed loan rates was inefficient. Eventually, financial institutions required intervention, with the government acquiring a large chunk of the banking system, both ownership via shares and a claim on resources, via government debt. One surmises that government finance of projects is not efficient, and a structural model, when calibrated with transactions costs and distortions around this observed extent of government involvement, delivers a period of stagnation at this time. Likewise, liberalization in late 1980 is associated with some growth and substantial welfare gains, though these are not evenly distributed in the population.

It takes models and data to judge whether government policy is helpful or harmful. After the 1997 crisis, with limited commercial bank lending and few finance companies left, the Thai government took a lead role in creating the financial infrastructure. In this case, it funded village-level savings and loans, at $24,000 per village in over 70,000 Thai villages, or 1.5 percent of GDP. This is in effect one of the world's largest micro-finance interventions, replete with joint-liability loans. As is illustrated in the chapters to follow, it can be evaluated using the essentially exogenous way the program was implemented, with varying numbers of households in villages. This million baht program increased consumption, overall lending, the frequency of investment, profits of those in business, and local wages, while at the same time raising interest rates and defaults. A structural model conveys the logic of the movement of these variables and the distribution of welfare gains. The larger point is that the Thai financial system is not yet perfect, and this is why government policies, in the presence of otherwise limited banking, can play a role. In this instance, the role is mostly positive, though an overall efficient design has yet to be determined. Further work is under way to understand the nature of the obstacles to trade which create these fine-tuned policy gains and losses, work which is illustrated in the closing chapters of this book.

There is an eerie similarity between the discussions today of what has gone wrong in the US, and elsewhere, and the discussion of causes and policy implications of the Asian crisis written between 1997 and 2000. In the case of Asia, there was an unsubstantial follow up as the world seemed to stabilize and memory dimmed. A deeper integrated understanding of the financial structure of emerging market countries, and advanced industrial-ized countries, is as relevant today as it was before. Achieving that goal is the motivation for this book.

Acknowledgments

I would like to thank my wife Pram for the loving encouragement to write this book.

The Townsend Thai data would not have been possible without Sombat Sakunthasathien, who helped launch the Thai project and continues to oversee data collection in Thailand. Anna Paulson, Tae Jeong Lee, and Mike Binford were all key, initial contributors to the Thai project.

Co-authors and PhD students whose work is the bedrock of this project include Christian Ahlin, Mauro Alem, Francisco J. Buera, John Felkner, Xavier Giné, Hyeok Jeong, Joseph P. Kaboski, Alex Karaivanov, Tee Weerachart Kilenthong, Yukio Koriyama, Gabriel Madeira, Edward S. Prescott, Esteban Puentes, Krislert Samphantharak, Samuel Schulhofer-Wohl, Suchanan Tambunlertchai, Kenichi Ueda, Sergio Samuel Urzua, James Vickery, Hiroyuki Yamada, Liu Yang, and Jacob Yaron.

Natalie Hoover El Rashidy coordinated and oversaw all aspects of the preparation of this manuscript. Pitsamorn Kilenthong provided invaluable help in research and Lenka Reznicek in editing and formatting. Akshay Birla and Brittany Piovesan diligently worked to track down original figures, permissions, and provided editing for the manuscript. While every effort was made to contact the copyright holders of material in this book, in some cases we were unable to do so. If the copyright holders contact the author or publisher, we will be pleased to rectify any omission at the earliest opportunity.

I would like to thank Aimee Wright at Oxford University Press for her patience and dedication during the sometimes frustrating process of preparing this book for publication.

This work has also benefited from the comments and suggestions of the participants at the 2005 Simon Kuznets Memorial Lecture Series at Yale University, the University College London Master Class, lectures at the University of the Thai Chamber of Commerce/University of Chicago joint research center in Bangkok, Thailand, as well as from my students at both the University of Chicago and MIT.

Finally, this material is based upon work supported by the National Science Foundation under Grant No. 0649302, the National Institute of Child Health and Human Development (NICHD) under Grant R01 HD27638, the John Templeton Foundation, and the Bill and Melinda Gates Foundation through the Consortium on Financial Systems and Poverty at the University of Chicago.

Contents

List of Figures

Note: Figures listed in **bold** also appear in the color plate section at the end of the book.

List of Tables

List of Tables

List of Abbreviations

BAAC	Bank for Agriculture and Agricultural Cooperatives
BC	Besley–Coate
BOT	Bank of Thailand
BREAD	Bureau for Research and Economic Analysis of Development
CARA	constant absolute risk aversion
CDD	Community Development Department
CDF	cumulative distribution function
CIRJE	Center for International Research on the Japanese Economy
CRRA	constant relative risk aversion
DCA	detrended correspondence analysis
DMP	debt-moratorium program
FDI	foreign direct investment
FGT	Foster–Greer–Thorbecke
GDP	gross domestic product
GIS	Geographical Information Systems
GJ	Greenwood–Jovanovic
GPP	gross provincial product
IMF	International Monetary Fund
IV	instrumental variable
JBIC	Japan Bank for International Cooperation
KS	Kolmorgorov–Smirnov
LEB	Lloyd-Ellis–Bernhardt
MLE	Maximum likelihood [parameter] estimation
NECTEC	National Electronics and Computer Technology Center
NESDB	National Economic and Social Development Board [of Thailand]
NICHD	National Institute of Child Health and Human Development
NSF	National Science Foundation

List of Abbreviations

OLS	ordinary least squares
PACAP	Pacific-Basin Capital Markets
PCG	production credit group
PPP	purchasing power parity
PTK	Paulson, Townsend, and Karaivanov
ROA	return on assets
ROE	return on equity
SDI	subsidy-dependence index
SES	[Household] Socio-economic Survey
SME	small and medium[-sized] enterprise
SR	Solow residual
TDRI	Thailand Development Research Institute
TEI	Thailand Environment Institute
TFP	total-factor productivity
TFPG	total-factor-productivity growth
TTP	time to progression
UTCC	University of the Thai Chamber of Commerce
VFCR	village-fund credit

Introduction

This book evaluates the financial system of Thailand, a prototypical developing Asian economy. Thailand is intended and considered within this work as a leading example of a developing economy, and the method of analysis developed here can be applied to emerging markets more generally. Specifically, the financial markets and institutions of this developing, emerging market economy are analyzed with applied general equilibrium models. The book then assesses the impact of the financial systems on growth, inequality, and poverty and also quantifies households and firm-level gains and losses to financial policy variation.

Within this work, the financial system comprises both the role of formal and informal financial sectors implicated in the intermediation of savings and credit and the allocation of idiosyncratic and aggregate risk. The book thus gauges the impact of specific financial institutions, markets for credit and insurance, and government policies on growth, inequality, and poverty at the macro, regional, and village levels. It delivers an analysis of the distribution of gains and losses to households and businesses from finance-induced growth and financial-sector policy variation. The methods used herein include parametric and non-parametric estimation, calibration, and model simulation, which are typically used in combination with one another. The data employed is drawn from the author's own Thai surveys, conducted since 1996 throughout Thailand, as well as secondary data assembled in a research database archive with Geographical Information Systems (GIS) functionality.

The fundamental premise of this work is: if markets and institutions were perfect and there were no policy distortions, then certain benchmark standards would be implied. Relative to these benchmarks there are many anomalies in the Thai economy, even for those using what are considered to be the safe and stable formal credit and savings instruments. Upon considering the data, it can be seen that initial wealth facilitates entry into business and facilitates investment for those already in business. Many households and businesses appear to be constrained in occupation choice, and estimated rates of return are high for occupation-constrained low-wealth households and low for unconstrained high-wealth households. Poor households and small to medium-sized enterprises (SMEs) are particularly vulnerable in consumption and investment to variation in income and cash flow, because some apparently insurable shocks such as movement in international rubber prices are not covered. This is but one example; there is other evidence of exogenously incomplete financial regimes which will be discussed in the coming pages.

Thus, various government program innovations and, conceivably, exogenous variations in access to intermediation have had a non-trivial impact on households and businesses. The new 1 million baht village funds program seems to have increased consumption, agricultural investment, and total borrowing beyond that of village-fund credit, while raising default rates and lowering assets and savings. Conversely, a Bank for Agriculture and Agricultural Corporations (BAAC) debt moratorium program has a neutral if not negative impact. Arguably, exogenous variation in village funds by policy (emergency services training, monitoring, pledged saving) and by type (rice bank, buffalo bank, production credit group, women's groups) implies variation in impact on asset accumulation, risk-sharing, occupation choice, and reliance on moneylenders. Instrumented variation in access allows an assessment of particular financial institutions such as commercial banks, BAAC, village funds, and the informal sector in providing a scorecard or rating system for their impacts on consumption and investment smoothing.

More generally, enhanced finance is established to be correlated with and, in the models evaluated here, causally related to the growth of GDP and to poverty reduction, though it has mixed consequences for the distribution of income. Macro total-factor productivity (TFP) is largely explained, and the TFP numbers make much more sense when we model the Thai economy based on its explicit micro foundations. Otherwise, TFP is negative for manufacturing during several sub-periods. Initially, an access–no access dichotomy is used. That is, there are some in the intermediated sector who have access and others in the same sector who do not, though the former group expands over time. Micro-Kuznet decompositions computed from socio-economic survey data examine the effects of increasing access to or use of the formal sector along with high and increasing income differentials. We find increased access accounts for a non-trivial part of the growth of per capita income, as well as increased inequality, albeit with other factors including education and sector shifts also playing a role. Financial access, occupation and sector choice, and education are consequently shown to play key roles in both the contemporary Thai economy and in Thai historical data. A model of occupation choice with an exogenous financial driver explains the upturn in the Thai economy at the moment of financial liberalization. In comparison, a model with en-dogenous financial access and no policy distortions delivers observed long-term historical trends but not that economic upturn. These same models are then used as we focus on areas of interest. Regional and village analysis employing these models reveals the impact of the government-operated BAAC expansion which targets credit and gaps in private commercial bank services. These indicate the potential political and economic impact of market segmentation. Variation over time is also important. The impact of the financial crisis, which restricted intermediation, and the subsequent increase in government participation in the financial sector, as well as its current impact, is again part of the analysis. Subgroups such as village networks and family-related conglomerates are also studied.

A repeated theme is the description of the Thai economy as an integrated micro–macro system, with the choices of diverse individual agents aggre-gated to explain group, village, regional, and macro variables. Choices are shown to be constrained by real obstacles to trade. Predetermined, low levels of wealth limit not only financial access but also occupation choice and the education of children. Indeed, transitions of households from farming and wage work to non-farm businesses, and the role of SMEs, are key ingredients in the Thai economy, not only in the past but also in the contemporary system. These factors are important because the dynamic evolution of the economy is determined by an evolving distribution of wealth. This discussion is featured in early parts of the book. Later additions include other obstacles. Upon consideration of the data, there seems to exist a moral hazard in entrepreneurial effort and project choice and ad-verse selection, such as the exclusion of safer customers from the loan market. Furthermore, there appears to be limited commitment problems, with loan size limited by collateral or wealth, and a tendency for strategic default limited by unofficial sanctions. Apparently there are transactions costs that vary with household and village characteristics, such as distance to a bank office. Each model has its blend of observable variables (e.g., wealth, distribution of wealth, division into collateral, roads, schooling) and unobservable variables (e.g., talent, latent firm size, heterogeneity in risk preferences, safe versus risky types, technologies). Tests distinguishing the models indicate that the mix of obstacles varies by region. Moreover, some of the transaction costs may pick up on the policy distortion of deliberately segmented markets. Finally, as noted earlier, contracts may be incomplete even beyond the revised benchmark standards that take these obstacles into account.

More generally, endogenous choices with impediments to trade and policy variation all play an important role in observed outcomes. Models of occupation choice that are limited by moral hazard, limited liability, or a combination of the two, make selection into entrepreneurship, investment, and rates of return all functions of wealth and talent. But the models take as a given which objects can be used as collateral, how much is required, the administered interest rates, the transportation costs associated with existing roads, and the bank's infrastructure. A model of endogenous access to formal credit and another model demonstrating a combination of formal and informal credit show how access choices are constrained by predetermined accumulated wealth, education and talent, the scale of potential enterprise, and current locations of the borrower. Again, these models take as a given transaction costs, the location of the bank, interest rates, and the legal system or collateral guarantees. An alternative model of whether to borrow and how much to borrow tests for adverse selection, taking as a given lender-imposed limits on loan size and opportunity costs related to individual and village characteristics. A model of this method of borrowing—i.e., individually with relative performance evaluations or as a group under joint liability—takes as a given pre-existing levels of wealth, inequality in the distribution of wealth, the covariance in project return, and the possibility within the economy of borrowing in these two different ways. Many of the variables should evolve over time as part of the optimal dynamics of the larger system, but there may be policy restrictions that are imposed. Models relating project risk to default test for moral hazard, strategic default, and adverse selection, taking as given interest rates, joint-liability co-payments, official penalties for default, screening and/or cooperation among joint-liability partners, the number of potential alternative lenders, and, again, the possibility of borrowing in groups. Many of these are policy decisions or control variables. Even given their limitations, both models described above offer insight into occupation choice and borrowing, by examining endogenous choices and their respective constraints.

There are thus non-trivial gains and losses to financial policy variation and, as previously discussed, consequences for growth, inequality, and poverty. Financial liberalization that facilitates access to intermediaries and weakens wealth constraints is shown under a variety of the models proposed here to encourage a distribution of gains which is particularly high for the talented poor. An evaluation of specific policy options shows that impact is a function of estimated impediments to trade. With transactions costs and limited commitment, enhanced collateral is more effective than the placement of the formal sector in villages or the availability of interest rate subsidies. When savings, and hence wealth, are endogenous, enhanced collateral and more-generous credit limits speed up life-cycle mobility. But the impact of wealth redistribution via subsidies and lowered interest rates can be large when moral hazard is a concern. Dominating, however, is movement on the extensive margin, the order of magnitude of gains for the poor who move from no access to limited access of some kind. The general equilibrium effect of changes in price from financial liberalization can cause losses for existing firms that hire unskilled labor. Domestic liberalization is the cause of a surge in growth and rising wages, and is associated with the fall in inequality. Augmented capital availability via foreign capital inflows could, in principal, be expansionary and welfare improving, but at estimated parameter values the effect is small; in any event, much of this seems to have been squandered. New roads and easier access to agglomeration synergies lower business-entry costs. This can even dominate the credit effect: new roads alter substantially the path of regional development. But, if credit markets are distorted by implicit government policy, there are gains to be made in their removal, shown in Thailand to be particularly high for the educated, rising middle class near main roads and towns. Further, wealth redistribution from the middle class to the relatively poor can slow down growth. In short, this book seeks to prove that the incompleteness of financial regimes, their evolution, and government policy can, through business formation and investment, alter growth rates, inequality, and poverty.

The Townsend Thai Data: Development, Extent, and Research Engendered

Given the ambitious tasks laid out above, it should come as no surprise that much work has gone into including analyses of all possible socio-economic data at micro, regional, and macro levels and uses, as well as data collected by the author in a relatively large long-term field research project.

The Townsend Thai data has its origin in initial field research in Northern Thailand. Townsend 1995b documents great variation in financial systems across villages relatively near one another. Informal structures and the use of family networks, quasi-formal village funds, and national-level financial institutions such as a Bank for Agriculture all seem to vary in the (small) sample, even holding the environment fixed. This puzzle led to the design of a large survey funded primarily by the National Institute of Health on Risk, Insurance, and the Family. This survey was a stratified clustered random sample of 192 villages in four provinces, two provinces in the industrialized/cash-crop region near the larger Bangkok metropolitan area and two provinces in the relatively poor and semi-arid Northeast, where subsistence rice farmers abound. The gradient from relatively rich to poor was a deliberate part of the design, with the hope that variation over space would be something like variation over time. Subsequent work has capitalized on this design. (Additionally, the four provinces chosen fulfilled another criterion—of having other secondary data, the Household Socio-economic Survey (SES), dating back to 1976; below we discuss further the use of overlapping, multiple data sets.)

The initial, relatively large survey carried out in April and May of 1997 covered 2,880 households, consisting of fifteen randomly selected in each of four villages for each of twelve tambons in each of the four provinces. This stratification of tambons was done to pick up key environmental variation documented in processed satellite imagery, as in Binford, Lee, and Townsend 2004. Topics in the household instrument covered include household composition, occupation, children living outside the household, residential patterns, household and agricultural assets, household businesses and landholding, and income and expenditures, as well as borrowing, lending, and savings. Additional survey instruments were delivered to 192 key informants, one for each village's headman, 262 joint-liability borrowing groups of the BAAC, 161 institutional surveys covering all village-level financial funds, and 1,920 soil samples. Data from each of these instruments are used in the research reported in the various chapters to follow. For example, Paulson, Townsend, and Karaivanov (2006) use the household survey; Ahlin and Townsend (2007b) use the BAAC survey; Kaboski and Townsend (2004) use the institutional and key informant survey, etc. Likewise, Giné (2001), Karaivanov (2003), and others have used these data in their PhD dissertations.

The Asian financial crisis occurred unexpectedly in July 1997, originating in Thailand with the devaluation of the baht. As the country headed into a deep recession, it became clear that there was an enormous—and important—

opportunity to track the impact of the crisis. With the timely help of the Ford Foundation, we fielded the first resurvey in 1997. These annual resurveys have continued with unbroken National Institute of Child Health and Human Development (NICHD) and National Science Foundation (NSF) support, and we now have ten years of panel data for households and key informants, a rare resource among developing countries. The resurvey rates are very high: 96 per cent to 97 per cent, making the data of great use to researchers. These data have been used in Alem and Townsend 2006 and Kaboski and Townsend 2007 to evaluate the role of financial institutions in credit and the allocation of risk, with instrumental or exogenous policy variation, and in Paulson and Townsend 2005 to document differences in the kinds of small businesses which were created in the crisis relative to their pre-crisis cousins. The research on enterprise formation and the evaluation of financial systems is funded by the NSF.

Unfortunately, the panel data cover only a subsample of the original 1997 survey: 960 households per year. However, more positively, as the surveys have gained recognition in Thailand, we have been supported by other sponsors and have extended the work. In cooperation with the BAAC, we added Prae in the North and Satun and Yala in the South, and with subsequent resurveys we now have a shorter yet regionally varied panel. Regrettably, the survey in Satun was interrupted by recent problems of terrorism and violence, and we have been unable to return safely, though in a sense this makes the initial survey there even more valuable. In 2005, the surveys in the other six provinces were extended to additional towns and cities in collaboration with the Ministry of Finance. We now anticipate offering an urban–rural contrast and an even more comprehensive account of the ever-changing financial system.

We were aware from the outset that certain activities and transactions would be difficult to measure accurately in annual recall data. Thus, in September of 1998, we began a detailed monthly panel. An initial baseline census covers all individuals and structures in sixteen villages, the four villages in one of the tambons in each of the four provinces of the original 1997 survey. The number of households in each village was increased from fifteen to forty-five, if there were sufficient households to do so, and other-wise the entire village is covered. We now have seventy-eight months for roughly 700 households who have been in the sample continuously for seven years (data for research at the time of writing). Topics in the monthly panel include household composition and occupational history, demo-graphic information on relatives not living in the household, interactions with relatives and non-relatives, information on household members' position in the village or tambon, financial and property assets, and detailed information on land holdings and use. Samphantharak and Townsend with Paweenawat and Pawasutipaisit create from the original data the income statement, balance sheet, and cash flow statements. Pawasutipaisit and Townsend are looking at case studies and success stories, and Paweenawat and Townsend are creating village-level product and balance and payment accounts.

All together, the Townsend Thai data is one of the longest panels in developing countries. A survey of similar scope is the 2002 follow-up of the 1982 Bangladesh Nutrition Survey which covered fifteen villages. This had a recapture rate at the individual level of 97 per cent. The NCAER ARIS-REDS Survey spans the period 1968–2006 in 6 rounds consisting of 250 villages, and is in the field now for the current round. It is a panel at the household level covering 10,000 households in the latest round. Additionally, Yale's Mark Rosenzweig reports their Economic Growth Center is embarking on two long-term panels. This project went into the field in Tamil Nadu in the fall of 2006 with a baseline including 5,000 households in 200 rural villages and 5,000 households in the urban population. The design is to follow the baseline individuals every three years, in perpetuity. These new collections of data are likely to become instrumental research tools in the developing countries which they examine, as the Townsend Thai data have been over the past twelve years.

Our survey and collection efforts in Thailand are supported by a variety of talented individuals and generous organizations. Khun Sombat Sakuntasathien is the Project Director of the surveys in Thailand. With his help, we have established the Thai Family Research Center, an organization we believe to be Thailand's premier data collection unit. At this date, we employ sixty-five staff in Bangkok and four regional offices. Some of the staff have been with us since the beginning, though data-collection methods have evolved with experience and the nature of the different surveys. A separate book by Sakuntasathien will provide a rich chronology of the data-collection efforts, of special interest to those doing long-term field research in developing countries. The monthly surveys have continued with the generous financial support from University of the Thai Chamber of Commerce (UTCC) in Bangkok.

Indeed, the University of Chicago and UTCC have founded a joint research center. This will house an increased number of secondary surveys: Household Socio-economic Survey (SES), Community Development Department (CDD), Bank for Agriculture and Agricultural Cooperatives (BAAC), Bank of Thailand (BOT), gross provincial product (GPP), Labor

Force Surveys, World Bank and Ajann Bank data, Pacific-Basin Capital Markets (PACAP), World Scope, and Japan Bank for International Cooperation (JBIC), among others. Various research papers featured in this book use multiple surveys. Lee, Kaboski, and Townsend use CDD and Townsend Thai data, Vickery and Townsend use SES and CDD, and so forth. The importance of comprehensive panel data and secondary surveys cannot be understated in research efforts, as the availability of multiple data sources is essential in developing microeconomic and macroeconomic models that can be combined.

The Larger Context: Literature in Review

The Thai economy represents the ideal of a successful Asian economy. Thailand's average growth of 4.7 per cent per year in real per capita household income, in combination with higher GDP rates for the two decades 1976 to 1996, garnered the country citations as the 'Next Newly Industrialized Country', following in the path of Taiwan, South Korea, Singapore, and Japan. GDP growth at over 12 per cent between 1987 and 1989 was among the highest in the world. The poverty rate fell from 46 per cent in 1976 to 9.8 per cent in 2002. The financial crisis and tsunami proved to be only small fluctuations around this long-term trend. As such, the Thai economy in 2003 had a growth rate second only to China and in 2004 a rate of 7 per cent.

The success of Asian Tigers feeds into a larger debate on the inevitability and desirability of growth both in the world economy and in specific countries. Here we briefly review the big picture, placing the book in this larger context.

Dollar and Kraay (2001) argue that dramatically increased incomes in 'globalizing' countries such as India, China, Vietnam, and Bangladesh have reduced world poverty. Others focusing on inequality disagree (see below). Related is growth club literature and a debate between Barro and Sala-i-Martin (2004) and Quah (1993) on convergence; the former suggest that some countries are able to join the club and catch up, but Quah argues that others remain left behind. Lucas (2003) argues that success stories could be told for most countries, were it not for internal restrictive policies or barriers to trade and financial flows. Aghion and Howitt (1995) agree that technological innovation and implementation, education, and competition are key forces for growth, but only for those countries on the technology frontier. For others off the frontier, the financial system and countercyclical government policy matter most.

In a debate with Galbraith and Pitt in *Foreign Affairs*, Dollar and Kraay (2002) also press the claim that growth among globalizing, formerly poor countries has caused world inter-country inequality to go down. In contrast, using both the now-standard decompositions that he has helped to foster and a somewhat larger sample, Bourguignon (1979) finds that world inequality increased from the beginning of the nineteenth century until the Second World War, driven by diverging cross-country incomes. More recently this trend in increasing inequality is weak, and other authors find it is now reversed. Both Bourguignon and Sala-i-Martin suggest that world inequality is driven now more by within-country inequality movements. Still, using cross-country evidence, Barro (2000) explains that the Kuznets curve, that of increasing and then decreasing inequality with growth, is not the dominant force in the data. His main finding is that equality is associated with growth in low-income countries, while high inequality is associated with growth in high-income countries. He then argues for and against redistributive policies, dependent on a country's relative income.

Many maintain a healthy skepticism about the ability to infer causality from correlations in the data, and all are aware of the issue. Rodrik (1999) argues further that the timing effects of globalization and liberalization policies are not consistent with the claims of Dollar and Kraay; he points out that India and China were growing before liberalization. Accordingly, there is now a literature distinguishing de facto versus de jure liberalization (e.g., Berglof and Claessens 2004). More generally, critics such as Rodrik take issue with cross-country work, worrying much about sample selection and the quality of the data. Others wonder as well about the standard linear specifications typically used in the empirical work. Indeed, Banerjee and Duflo (2003) take a non-parametric approach to the Kuznets curve in cross-country data and find that *any* change in inequality, in any direction, up or down, in one period, is associated with reduced growth in the next period.

Given concerns about cross-country data, controversies surrounding cross-country regressions, and the increasing relative importance in any event of within-country movements to world inequality and poverty, we turn next in this introduction to individual country studies.

Most are no less controversial. In the US, 'trickle-down economics' is a term often used by critics of growth policy in the popular press and in Congress, a phrase countered by the sentiment, 'a rising tide raises all boats.' The view that growth has beneficial consequences for the poor has professional economic antecedents dating back to Adam Smith (1776): to paraphrase, laissez-faire policies seemingly favorable to entrepreneurs, such as reduced taxes, promote growth in such a way as to reach less-wealthy individuals. The US debate continues, as various studies show that moderately high and sustained growth has benefited the relatively rich while leaving part of the middle class at lower real incomes. Juhn, Murphy, and Pierce, in a widely cited study (1993), document a fall in the average real wage and a rise in the returns to skill.

Other studies show great diversity over countries. Ferreira, Leite, and Litchfield (2007) show via decompositions that education plays a large role in the Brazilian inequality story, but they find that returns to education may be decreasing. Inflation also exacerbates inequality. Race and family type play a lesser role, and there seems to have been regional and urban/rural convergence. In Mexico, Orozco and Fedewa (2006) show that disintermediation after the 1992 financial crisis increased poverty and played a role in the movement in subsequent inequality. In other work for Mexico, a historical tendency toward convergence in incomes is now replaced with increasing concentration on the US border.

Others take a more theoretical approach. For example, Mookherjee, Banerjee, and Benabou (2006) focus on theories which make inequality a key factor in development economics. These authors are only beginning to examine the corollary empirical implications.

Many of the specific chapters to this book contribute directly to these debates. First, this close study of Thailand, a successful Asian Tiger, contributes to our understanding of the internal mechanics of growth. Second, the models included in this book make clearer the potential and actual mechanisms of trickle-down dynamics, as in Chapter 6. That is, we examine the often non-linear and sometimes complicated transitional dynamics of growth—and the heterogeneous impact of this growth with policy change on the Thai population. Third, Thailand displays a Kuznets curve, so we can study how a Kuznets curve can be generated in practice.

More specifically, Chapter 4 presents growth, inequality, and poverty decompositions for Thailand and enumerates key forces including education, occupation choice, and access to finance. These forces are associated with high growth, changing inequality, and a dramatic reduction of poverty levels. Viewing provinces and regions within Thailand as different countries, as in Chapter 3, we examine growth and inequality patterns as in the cross-country literature. There is convergence in part, but industrialization continues to make Bangkok an agglomeration hot spot, and a new agglomeration center has emerged in the North. Meanwhile relative poverty persists on the periphery. High growth regions tend to have high and increasing levels of within-region inequality, but the far South is an important and telling exception, given current political instability and terrorism, with low levels and high inequality of income. Chapter 4 also illustrates that there is more inequality across regions in provincial product than in household incomes. For example, in the relatively poor Northeast, migration with remittances is a substantial equalizing factor in overall welfare. In any event, the contribution of across-province income to inequality, while first increasing, is now decreasing.

On the macro policy side there is a variety of literature assessing policy and, in particular, the role of financial deepening and financial policy change. We begin with the evident controversy over globalization. Prasad, Rogoff, Wei, and Kose (2003) offer a recent, balanced appraisal bearing on the key question: does financial, capital account liberalization cause growth or instability? Their evidence is mixed. There seem to be countries which do benefit, but for others liberalization seems premature.

Cross-country correlations are used to argue that finance causes growth, as in the seminal paper of King and Levine (1993). In a comparative study of Mexico and Chile, Kehoe and Prescott (2002) find that the only reasonable explanation for higher TFPG in Chile versus Mexico post crisis and reform is that Chile had a better functioning financial system. Moving toward the use of instruments in cross-country micro data, Rajan and Zingales (1998) find that industrial sectors that are more in need of external finance relative to the US develop disproportionately faster in countries with more-developed financial markets. Beck, Levine, and Loayza (2000) find a very strong connection between the exogenous component of financial intermediary development and long-run economic growth. Using cross-country panels with more refined tests for exogeneity, Demirguç-Kunt and Maksimovic (1998) find that both banking system development and stock market liquidity are positively associated with high growth of firms; that is, a larger proportion of firms growing at an 'excess' level that requires access to external sources of long-term capital.

Within countries, Caballero, Hoshi, and Kashyap (2006) find that Japan stagnated due to an over-regulated and protected financial system, and Bertrand, Schoar, and Thesmar (2004) find that France grew at one point as a consequence of a financial liberalization. Burgess and Pande (2005) see poverty reduction in India as a direct result of increased access to credit via expanded bank branches in disadvantaged areas. Additionally, Banerjee and Duflo (2003) find that liberalized, then tightened, eligibility regulations for lending were associated with higher, then reduced, investment. Another within-country study is Guiso, Sapienza, and Zingales (2006), who find in Italy effects of differences in local financial development. For a larger review of this literature see Levine 1997.

That cross-country financial policy variation and within-country financial liberalization can have direct impacts on growth, poverty reduction, and inequality should not come as a surprise. There is a multitude of micro studies that find financial market anomalies or facts inconsistent with neoclassical, complete financial-market models. For example, real interest rates and internal rates of return are sometimes found to be quite high, as in Banerjee and Munshi 2004, Foster and Rosenzweig 1996, and McKenzie and Woodruff 2003. However, there are other instances in which high rates of return are not seized upon—for example, Goldstein and Udry 1999 and Duflo 2003. Further, high average internal rates of return and interest rates are dispersed and heterogeneous, implying that some inefficient projects are also undertaken. Indeed, dispersion of TFP across firms is taken as a measure of inefficiency, as in Abiad, Oomes, and Ueda 2004. For an excellent and more-comprehensive review of the development literature, see Banerjee and Duflo 2003.

Various chapters of this book make contributions to this literature. Introductory material in Chapter 1 notes the increased depth of the Thai financial system and changing government financial sector policies. After establishing that access to finance is a key force in growth and inequality decomposition, Chapter 5 describes in detail the historical and contemporary Thai financial system, including its informal markets. Tying to the work of Prescott, Caballero, and others, Chapter 6 uses a model with micro underpinnings estimated in the data to show that Thai TFPG is largely explained by arguably exogenous financial deepening, with the highest contribution in a liberalization period. Likewise, Chapter 4 argues that emerging market capital inflows were not the direct cause of growth and inequality dynamics within Thailand.

Chapter 7 documents the wide range of neoclassical anomalies in the Thai case—for example, high rates of return for low-wealth households and low rates of return for high-wealth households, better allocation of risk for higher-wealth households despite targeted credit programs, and investment and occupation choice related to wealth. Chapter 8 shows with micro data that financial-sector variation and government financial policies do have an impact on various outcome variables. There is natural policy variation across village funds promoted by different ministries, and, more recently, variation in per capita credit expansion in one of the world's largest microcredit interventions. Finally, the book integrates these reduced-form econometric assessments with explicit choice models, comparing instrumental variable (IV) estimates to the distribution of gains and losses to financial-sector policy change.

Embracing Multiple Approaches: Methodology and a Way Forward

The book does not shy away from measurement and the presentation of facts. We try not to force models onto data that would be inappropriate for that data. Still, some ordering of the data is needed, and measurement without theory certainly has its limits. So these summaries motivate, indeed anticipate, subsequent modeling choices. Similarly, both the micro and macro data are put into a unified (atheoretic) conceptual framework, a common framework for measurement purposes, as in Chapter 2. This is the framework of financial accounting and the national income accounts. They are, in fact, the same thing. This symmetric treatment of micro and macro data helps in consistency. A variety of techniques are used in analysis, from ordinary least squares (OLS) and IV regressions to non-parametrics, and on to structural estimation. This willingness to embrace multiple approaches, often in the very same context, seems to set the book apart from most professional literature. Of course, not all the models are entirely successful. Anomalies remain. These are fully reported and embraced as instructive for the next round of research. Indeed, this iteration is started here, as in Chapter 9, which articulates modified and new theories which link growth, inequality, poverty, and financial deepening. Subsequent research can be tracked on the author's website <http://cier.uchicago.edu/townsend_thai/townsendproj.htm>.

Still, the overall contribution of the manuscript is intended to be greater than the sum of the contributions of the individual chapters. As should be clearer from the earlier review of the literature, there is relatively little work that combines microeconomics and macroeconomics and equally little that combines both theory and data. In contrast, this book provides an overall conceptual framework that allows us to integrate both macro and micro data. The methods of the book have content in the sense that the various theories can, as noted, be rejected in the data, and again, fathering further rounds of the iterative research agenda. Finally, explicit frameworks allow the researcher to assess and quantify the heterogeneous impact of financial policy change at the levels of households and firms while being consistent with the facts of growth, inequality, and poverty.

There are relatively few contributions of this kind and, strikingly, practically none in developing countries. Banerjee and Duflo 2005 (see bibliography) travel down this road in their study of India, focusing as here on the financial system. Their theme is that the cross-country growth dynamics and TFP pioneered by Lucas (1993), among others, are hard to reconcile with an aggregated production function, as if the neoclassical framework were assumed to cover the micro data. Essentially, human-capital-adjusted worker-to-capital ratios imply TFP differentials between the US and India which would imply, in turn, an incredibly high interest rate in India. They find an average rate in India which, while relatively high, is only half the necessary order of magnitude. They also find, as noted, a large dispersion in interest rates. At the end of their book, Banerjee and Duflo thus begin the task of reconciling the anomalies with the macro evidence, moving toward a new micro-funded model with a small number of alternative technologies and varying fixed costs. They view their contribution as a preliminary attempt that is of interest primarily because there are few other studies which combine micro estimates with endogenous growth and inequality dynamics, as here.

Clearly, progress can be made, and has been made in other fields. Cunha and Heckman (2008) focus on human capital, the returns to schooling, and inequality in earnings in the US, as individuals with diverse talents and costs of selection maximize levels of education with limited information on ultimate returns. Much of this work is partial equilibrium and assumes complete markets, but Heckman, Lochner, and Taber 1998a and 1998b are a start on making the return on wealth and labor endogenous in the context of an aggregate production function. More explicitly, Cagetti and De Nardi (2005), and the literature they review, focus on wealth inequality in the US. The two begin with a representative-consumer, infinitely-lived construct, with a mechanical limit on credit, but they alter this to take into account heterogeneity—in particular, diversity in talent for wage-earning and setting up a business. High-wealth entrepreneurial individuals that value bequests to children and face uncertain lifetimes, seem to be a key to the concentration of wealth not only in the US but also in Sweden. The asset-pricing literature of Heaton and Lucas (2000) is solidly in this tradition. As usual, there are anomalies which fuel further work, but little of the literature provides models of transition and none deals with development and change in the financial system. This book can thus be seen as an attempt to unify fields under applied general-equilibrium modeling, bringing important, modified methods to emerging market countries.

1

Growth, Inequality, Poverty, and Financial Deepening

This chapter presents the salient facts related to growth, inequality, financial deepening, and policy variation. Described here are macro variables such as growth, which are often taken to characterize an entire economy as if it were composed of a homogenous collection of identical clones of a representative consumer. But inequality reminds us there is considerable heterogeneity, either initially or as the result of idiosyncratic shocks. Poverty is of special interest, but here distinctions are drawn among income, consumption, and wealth. Income is most transient, consumption is smoothed, and wealth moves slowly and most reflects underlying constraints. Financial depth is another key macro variable, but it also reflects policy changes that are at the heart of this book.

Growth has been relatively high for the past fifty years, with the exception of a sharp drop due to the 1997 financial crisis and the ensuing recession. The trend of long-term industrialization dominates the data, and it seems unwise to try to describe the contemporary Thai economy without understanding this history. Hence the focus in the models is on occupation choice and investment. Thailand has also gone through a demographic transition, with lower family size, increased longevity, increase in the number of inactive workers, and an increase in the number of female-headed households.

Inequality by almost all measures has been increasing since at least 1976, along with income, but, unlike the growth of income, inequality peaks and starts to decline in 1992, with some backtracking for the crisis. These movements in inequality are the focus of many of the models subsequently explored in later chapters, which pay particular attention to reconciling the theory of inequality with these observed facts.

Poverty measures have shown a steady decrease in the fraction of the poor, along with a decrease in the distance of the poor from the poverty line, with only a slight wobble in the crisis. Health and other measures of well-being have steadily improved over time, apart from HIV/AIDS. Poverty is shown in panel data to be a transient phenomenon, especially if the focus is on income, which responds relatively quickly to a variety of shocks in a variety of ways. Consumption is more stable, and wealth moves quite slowly. Thus, where wealth is the primary constraint on households, we would expect to see a more stubbornly persistent poverty, with constraints only attenuated in the long run. Many of the models focus on the relationships among wealth, underlying constraints, and endogenous choices.

Financial deepening in Thailand displays astounding trends relative to the US over the same period. Part of that can be attributed to a financial liberalization starting in 1986. Foreign capital inflows increased at the same time, so this needs to be sorted out with the subsequent models. By the 1990s, commercial bank regulation appears to have been increasingly deficient, and government transfers masked the distortion. Post crisis, the government's explicit involvement in the financial sector has increased.

1.1. Growth: Demographic, GDP, and the 1997 Crisis

The growth of GDP, 1950–2003, has been consistently high, at 6.2 per cent per year on average overall and 5.3 per cent on average on a per capita basis. There are exceptions—namely, negative growth in the early 1950s and more obviously the financial crisis of 1997. Though recovery from the crisis was slow, Thai growth by 2003 was the third highest in Asia, after China, India, and Vietnam. (At the time of writing, there had been an adverse impact from the 2004 tsunami as well as rising oil prices.) Of special note is the sharp upturn in growth in 1986, with per capita growth reaching 12 per cent, in contrast to the relatively sluggish period of the early 1980s. The lower per capita numbers early on reflect higher population growth prior to the demographic transition.

Indeed, the Population Census (see Table 1.1) shows a population growth rate of 2.2 per cent on average between 1919 and 2000. Though fluctuating decade by decade, population growth peaked at an annual rate of 3.15 per cent from 1947 to 1960 and has been on a steady decline ever since. The most recent rate, from 1990 to 2000, is 1.05 per cent (see Figure 1.1).

Over the last two decades, the demographic composition of Thai households substantially changed. Average family size dropped from 5.5 to 3.7, while the total population increased from 43 million to 60 million persons. Life expectancy at birth increased from 65 years to 74 years. The average age

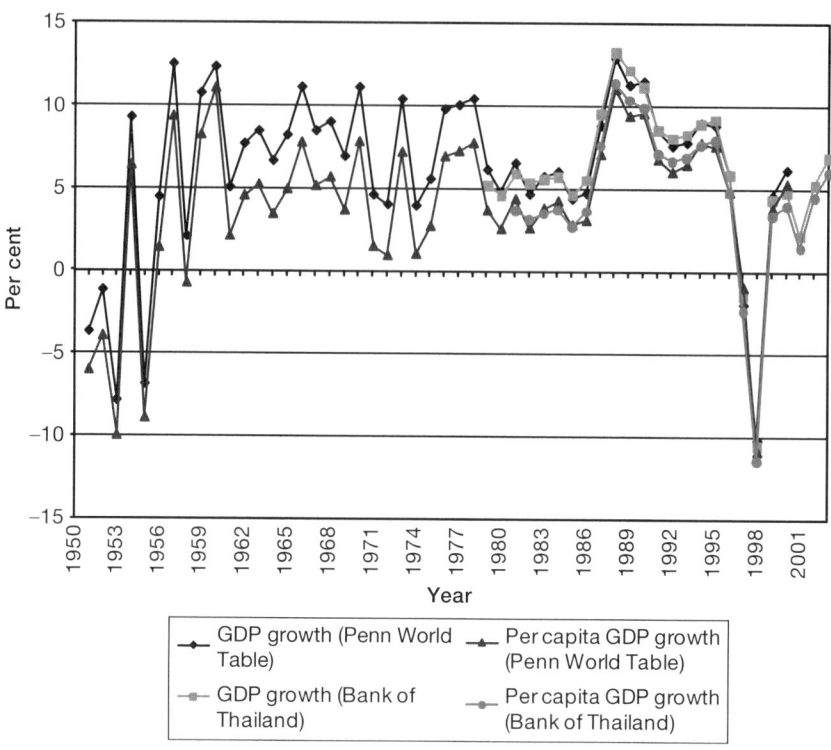

Fig. 1.1. *Annual growth rate of Thai GDP, 1950–2003*
Source: Compiled from Penn World Table and Bank of Thailand data.

Table 1.1. *Population of Thailand from 1909 to 2000*

Year	Population	Annual growth rate
1909	8,149,487	—
1919	9,207,355	1.22
1929	11,506,207	2.23
1937	14,464,105	2.86
1947	17,442,689	1.87
1960	26,257,916	3.15
1970	34,397,374	2.70
1980	44,824,540	2.65
1990	54,548,530	1.96
2000	60,606,947	1.05

Source: 2000.

of the labor force increased from 31 to 37. The proportion of households with a head more than 60 years old increased from 16 per cent to 22 per cent of the population. The proportion of female-headed households increased from 17 per cent to 24 per cent. The proportion of economically inactive households increased substantially from 10 per cent to 16 per cent.

The financial crisis of 1997 and subsequent recession has complicated much of the thinking about Thailand and Asian economies. It is not hard to find evidence of a dramatic slowdown, with domestic cement sales, construction, imported capital goods, and commercial car sales dropping to half of their previous levels, if not lower, according to Bank of Thailand estimates. Even as late as 2004, some indicators had not recovered (see Figures 1.2(a)–(d)).

But when viewed within a wider time frame, the crisis and recession have only modestly interrupted long-term trends (see Figure 1.3). The manufacturing share of GDP has increased more or less steadily, from 13 per cent in 1950 to 37 per cent in 2003, with agriculture declining from 37 per cent to 10 per cent. The agricultural series does go flat at about 1997, and the growth in manufacturing was attenuated at that time, but neither of these events is salient in the larger context. Clearly one cannot understand Thailand in the short or long term without understanding what lies beneath these trends.

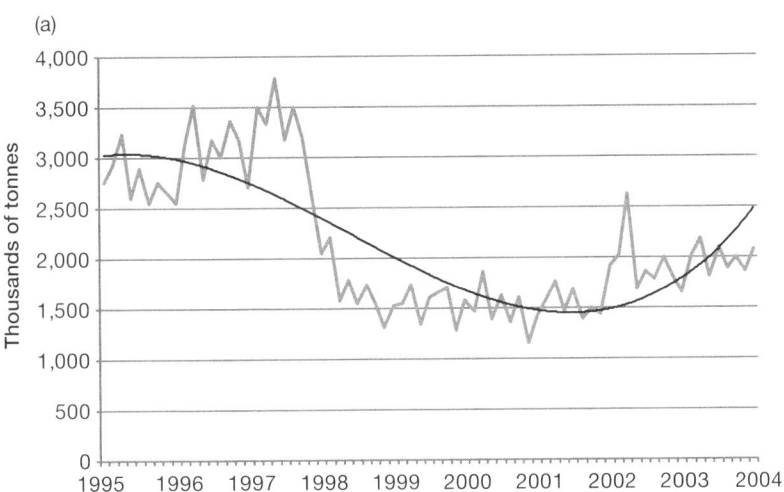

Fig. 1.2(a). *Private investment indicators with trends: domestic cement sales*
Source: Adapted from Bank of Thailand 2003.

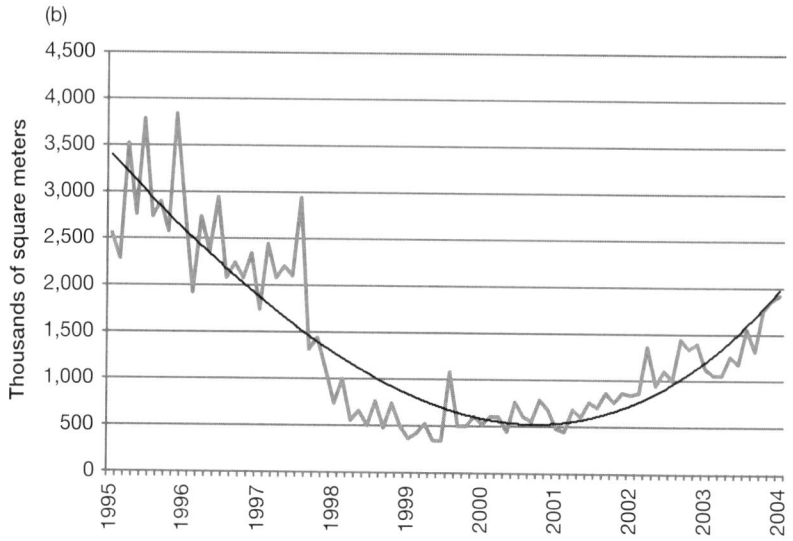

Fig. 1.2(b). *Private investment indicators with trends: construction areas*
Source: Adapted from Bank of Thailand 2003.

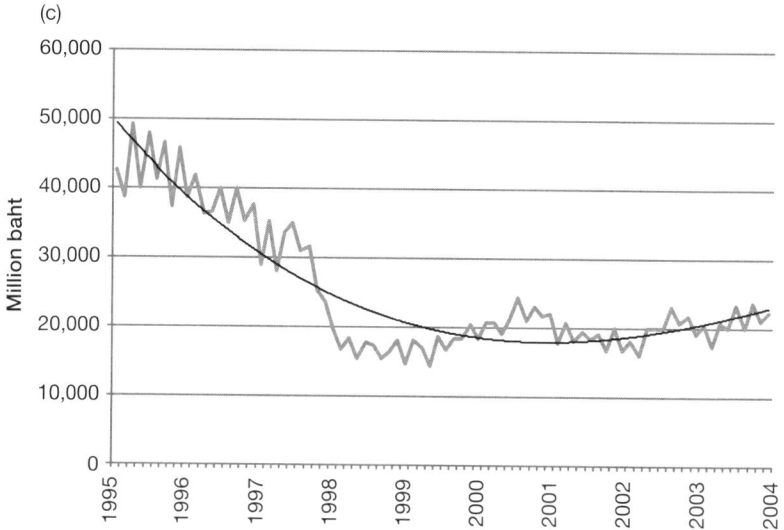

Fig. 1.2(c). *Private investment indicators with trends: imported capital goods (real terms)*
Source: Adapted from Bank of Thailand 2003.

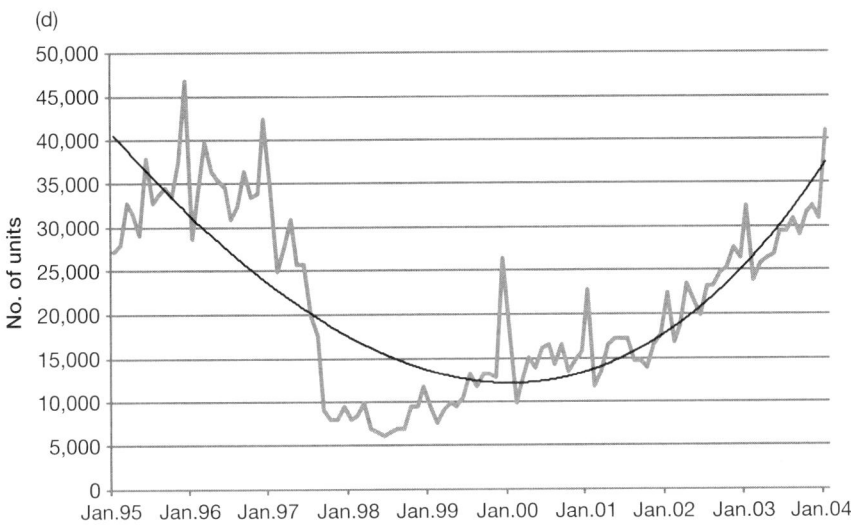

Fig. 1.2(d). *Private investment indicators with trends: commercial car sales*
Source: Adapted from Bank of Thailand 2003.

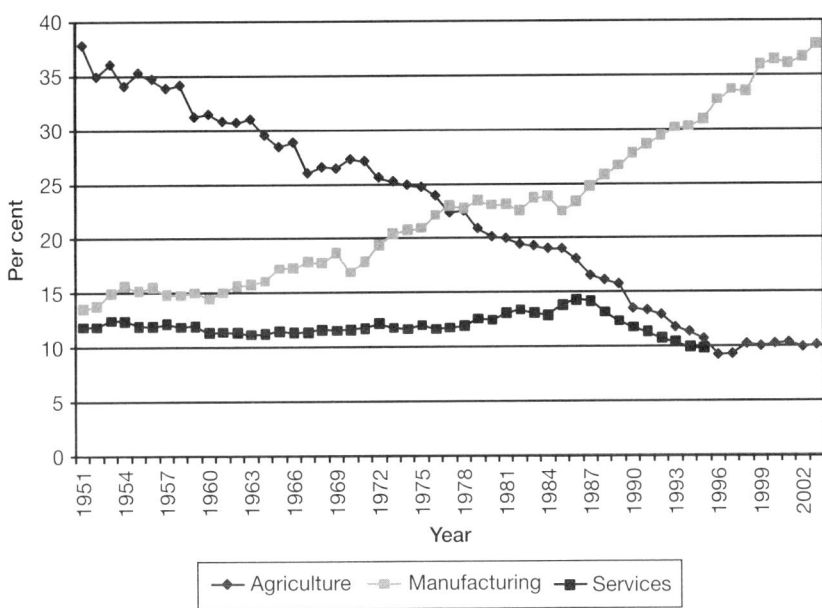

Fig. 1.3. *Agriculture, manufacturing, and services as percentages of real GDP, 1950–2003*
Source: Adapted from NESDB data.

1.2. Inequality

Accompanying long-term growth are movements in inequality (See Table 1.2). According to the Gini index, inequality rises from 0.436 in 1976 to 0.535 in 1992, before falling to 0.511 by 1996. The overall level of inequality is high for Asia and rivals the non-trivial levels of Latin America. Specifically, the average for East Asia and Pacific is 0.362, for Sub Saharan Africa it is 0.441, and for Latin America and the Caribbean it is 0.502 (see Jeong 2000).

Thai socio-economic data display the Kuznets curve. See Figure 1.4. Specifically, from 1976 to 1986 there is a period of increasing inequality with relatively flat growth. Then, from 1986 to 1992, inequality increases with relatively high growth. A small exception is the drop in inequality 1986–8. Inequality begins a longer-term decrease after 1992 while growth stayed relatively high.

The Gini is not the only measure of inequality, and indeed other measures such as the Theil entropy indices allow decompositions, as described below. But, with only one exception, every measure of inequality establishes 1992 as the peak. Other measures also pick up the more modest decline of 1986–8.

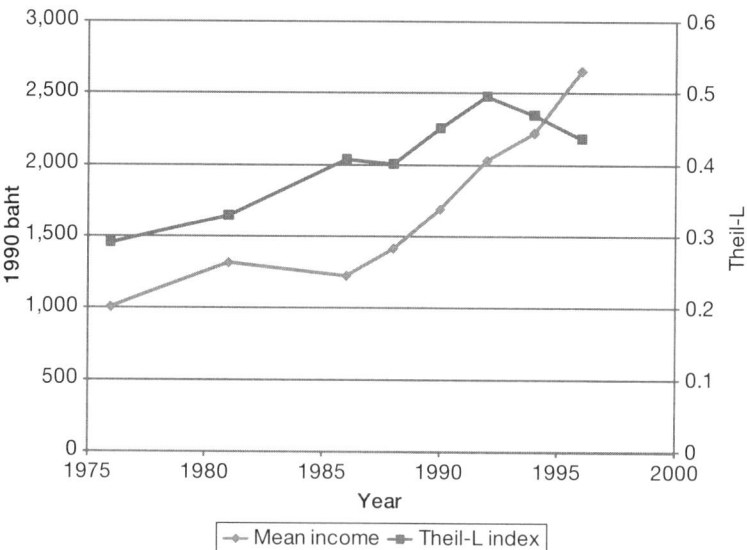

Fig. 1.4. *Average income and income inequality in Thailand*

Note: Kuznets curve: see stages marked as vertical lines.

Source: Jeong 2000.

Table 1.2. *Summary statistics for income in Thailand socio-economic survey*

Year	1976	1981	1986	1988	1990	1992	1994	1996	1976–96[1]
Population (million)	43.1	47.9	53.6	55.2	56.8	58.9	60.2	60.3	1.7%
Total income (billion)	43.5	63.1	65.8	78.2	96.2	119.7	133.9	160.4	6.7%
Mean	1,009.0	1,317.0	1,227.0	1,418.0	1,693.0	2,033.0	2,225.0	2,659.0	5.0%
Median	709.0	884.0	745.0	859.0	981.0	1,113.0	1,270.0	1,584.0	4.1%
Standard deviation	1,201.0	1,575.0	1,643.0	1,795.0	3,228.0	3,985.0	3,909.0	4,223.0	6.5%
Interquartile ratio	1.01	1.12	1.30	1.31	1.31	1.38	1.38	1.36	1.5%
Theil-L	0.292	0.330	0.408	0.402	0.451	0.496	0.470	0.437	2.0%
Theil-T	0.340	0.373	0.461	0.441	0.564	0.603	0.559	0.504	2.0%
Gini coefficient	0.418	0.443	0.489	0.486	0.512	0.535	0.521	0.503	0.9%
Coefficient of variation	1.191	1.195	1.339	1.266	1.906	1.960	1.757	1.588	1.5%
Atkinson index (e=1)	0.253	0.281	0.335	0.331	0.363	0.391	0.375	0.354	1.7%
Polarization	0.374	0.413	0.480	0.487	0.485	0.518	0.512	0.499	1.4%
Head-count ratio	0.483	0.359	0.446	0.365	0.307	0.256	0.205	0.130	−6.4%
Poverty gap	0.175	0.119	0.170	0.127	0.100	0.079	0.061	0.034	−7.8%
FGT P_2	0.083	0.054	0.085	0.060	0.044	0.034	0.026	0.013	−8.7%
Number of observations	11,356.0	11,880.0	10,895.0	11,044.0	13,174.0	13,458.0	25,208.0	25,110.0	

1. This column reports the annual average rates of change between 1976 and 1996 for each summary statistics.

Source: Jeong 2000.

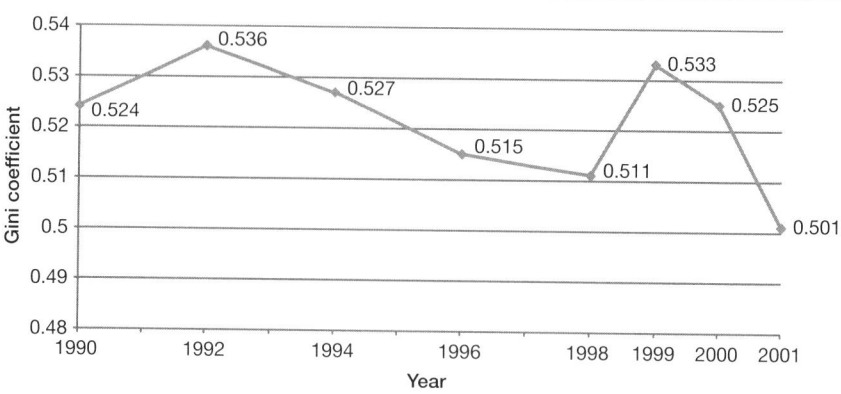

Fig. 1.5. *Gini coefficient of income distribution, 1990–2001*
Source: Adapted from Bank of Thailand data.

During the financial crisis, Thailand moved in reverse along the Kuznets curve, sliding back up the declining part of the line (see Figures 1.4 and 1.5). Not only did growth go negative, but inequality increased, by 1999 reaching the level it had been at between 1992 and 1994. One caution regarding the data is in order here. The SES is administered bi-annually in even years, with a few exceptions, so we have to interpolate for the odd years. Inequality appears lower in 1998 than in 1996, but one surmises that it had declined to a lower level in 1997 and increased thereafter to its 1998 level. In any event inequality seems to have resumed its downward trek after 1999, now reaching levels it had not displayed since the late 1980s.

1.3. Poverty and Well-being

The diversity and temporal movement in incomes is evident in the income histograms. Figure 1.6. shows kernel densities using the log scale, comparing 1976 to 1996, and shows a clear right-shift in the distribution. The fraction of the relatively poor, those on the left tail of the distributions, has diminished sharply over the years.

Hyeok Jeong's (2000) thesis shows with SES data that the fraction of impoverished households has declined from 48 per cent of total households in 1976 to 13 per cent in 1996. Jeong uses $2 a day as a widely accepted international standard, and converts this to Thai baht using the Penn World Tables purchasing power parity (PPP). The average distance

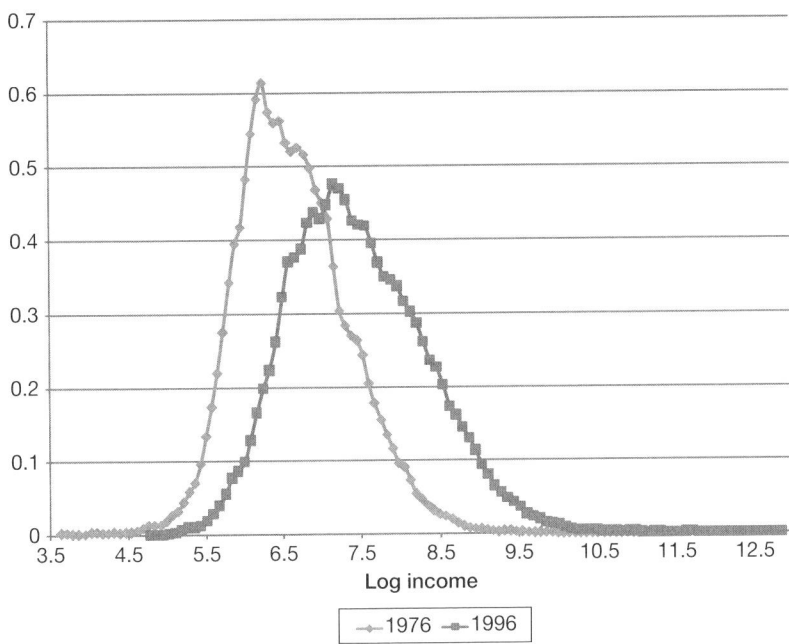

Fig. 1.6. *Kernel density estimates of income distributions*
Source: Jeong 2000.

between those of low income and the poverty line has declined from 17.5 per cent in 1976 to 3.5 per cent in 1996. Another widely used measure is the Foster–Greer–Thorbecke (FGT) measure, which adopts a squared-weighted scheme; and it shows similar movement (see Table 1.3).

The trend of decreasing poverty was slightly interrupted in the aftermath of the 1997 crisis, with the poverty rate rising from 12.5 per cent in 1998 to about 15 per cent in 2000. Shortly thereafter it achieved an all-time historic low, at 9 per cent, in 2002.

The decline in poverty is mirrored by improvements in other United Nations Development Programme (UNDP) indicators (see Figure 1.7). Thailand is classified by the UNDP as having a medium level of human development. The proportion of children suffering from malnutrition had been coming down in the 1990s, reaching 9.4 per cent in 2000. The longer-term, historical data are more dramatic. Infant mortality, deaths per 1,000, was 74 in 1970 and this dropped to 24 in 2002. By contrast, current rates are 87 in Laos and 96 in Cambodia. Life expectancy at birth was 61 years in 1970, and this has increased to 69 in 2000–5, compared with an increase from 40.4 to 54.5 in Laos and 40.3 to 57.4 in Cambodia.

Table 1.3. *Summary statistics of income in Thai Socio-economic Survey*

Poverty	1976	1981	1986	1988	1990	1992	1994	1996	1998	2000	2002
Head-count ratio	0.483	0.359	0.446	0.365	0.307	0.256	0.205	0.130	0.125	0.149	0.089
Poverty gap	0.175	0.119	0.170	0.127	0.100	0.079	0.061	0.034			
FGT P_2	0.083	0.054	0.085	0.060	0.044	0.034	0.026	0.013			
Sample size	11,356	11,880	10,895	11,044	13,174	13,458	25,208	25,110			

Source: Jeong 2000.

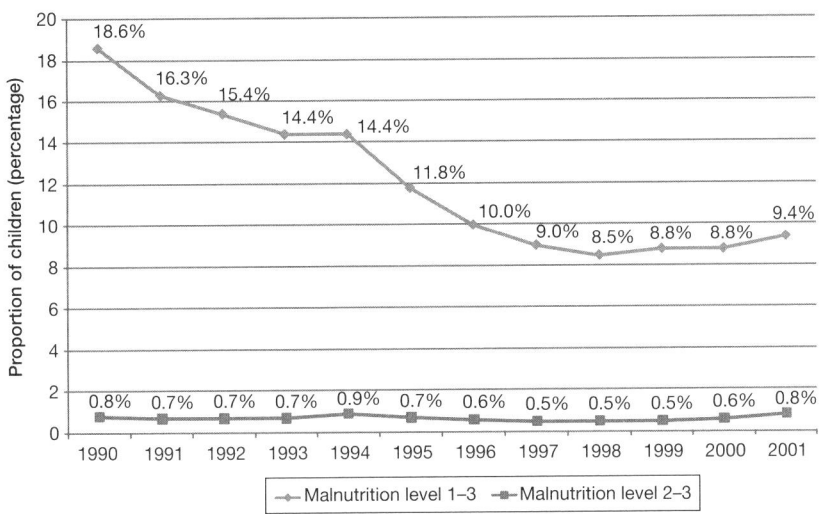

Fig. 1.7. *Proportion of children under the age of 5 suffering from malnutrition*
Source: Adapted from Thai Ministry of Public Health data.

Unfortunately, Thailand and other countries have had a problem with HIV/AIDS. The proportion of pregnant women infected reached 1.8 per cent in 1998, but this appears to have little to do with underlying growth process. The overall infection rate at 1 per cent in Thailand is low relative to many other countries.

The income histograms and poverty rate data might be taken to indicate that a small, if declining, segment of the population remains chronically poor. But such cross-sections can be misleading. The Townsend Thai Panel data of 1997–2003, show that households moved in and out of poverty. The number of years a household remained poor is only slightly tilted to the right: the fraction of those poor for one year only between 1997 and 2003 was 9 per cent, the fraction of those who were poor for four years was 12 per cent, and those who remained poor for all 7 years was 20 per cent (see Tables 1.4 and 1.5 for more details).

More revealing are tables reporting transitions in the panel across income, consumption, and wealth quintiles, comparing 1997 with 2003. Here 'poverty' is defined implicitly relative to the income levels of other households: 27 per cent of households stay in the lowest income quintile and 42 per cent in the highest income quintile. More typical are transitions into other groups. Indeed, 9.5 per cent of the population went from the lowest to the highest quintile, while 18.7 per cent fell down from the highest to the lowest quintile. The data clearly show that income is volatile.

Table 1.4. *Number of years household had been poor*

Number of years in poverty	Percentage
0	10
1	9
2	9
3	11
4	12
5	13
6	16
7	20
Total	100

Source: Townsend Thai Panel data.

Table 1.5. *Poverty transitions, 1997–2003*

Poor in 1997	Poor in 2003		Total
	No	Yes	
No	60.3	39.7	100
Yes	39.3	60.7	100
Total	48.9	51.1	100

Source: Townsend Thai Panel data.

Consumption may be a better measure of overall well-being and by that standard 44 per cent of the population remains in the lowest quintile, with 41 per cent in the highest. There are fewer transitions across the other quintiles as well. We may infer that households are attempting to smooth consumption from income fluctuations but are not completely successful in doing so.

Wealth is difficult to measure in most surveys, but crucial. When wealth is taken as a measure of well-being, things move slowly indeed. Approximately 70 per cent of the poor and rich stay in place and most of the mass is concentrated on the diagonal or adjacent categories. Wealth is, in some sense, a predetermined variable and is associated in the models with chronic constraints.

Two caveats, however: most households have gained in wealth, even more so than in income, and inequality in wealth seems to have decreased dramatically from 1977 to 1996. Wealth in the SES is not measured directly but indirectly through Jeong's principal components index of the ownership of key assets in the SES data. The right-shifted distribution of wealth and its smaller left tail are not reflected in quintiles such as those shown in Table 1.6(a)–(c).

Table 1.6. *Income, consumption, and wealth (a)–(c)*

(a) Transition by quintile of income (shocks)

Income quintile in 1997	Income quintile in 2003				
	1	2	3	4	5
1	27.4	29.2	17.3	16.7	9.5
2	19.4	25.5	29.7	13.9	11.5
3	17.8	23.1	17.8	24.9	16.6
4	16.5	15.9	22.6	25.6	19.5
5	18.7	9.6	10.8	18.7	42.2

(b) Transition by quintile of consumption (smoothing)

Consumption quintile in 1997	Consumption quintile in 2003				
	1	2	3	4	5
1	44.3	25.9	12.7	13.3	3.8
2	21.0	25.7	19.2	21.0	13.2
3	16.4	19.9	26.9	25.1	11.7
4	8.2	21.8	24.1	16.5	29.4
5	11.6	11.0	17.1	19.5	40.9

(c) Wealth quintiles in 1997 by wealth quintiles in 2003

Wealth quintiles in 1997	Wealth quintiles in 2003				
	1	2	3	4	5
1	69.9	22.2	5.2	2.6	0.0
2	24.6	42.3	23.4	8.0	1.7
3	9.6	22.6	37.9	26.6	3.4
4	0.6	11.1	22.8	42.7	22.8
5	1.2	1.2	8.2	18.2	71.2

Source: Townsend Thai Panel data.

1.4. Financial Deepening, Crisis, and Policy Change

The extent of intermediation, a standard measure of the depth of the financial system, is an aggregate money-to-GDP ratio. Thailand's M3/GDP ratio rose from 45 in 1976 to about 125 in 1997. As Figure 1.8 shows, Thailand passed the US level around 1987 and continued to climb thereafter, up until 2001. Only after 2002 does M3/GDP drop, and it remains well

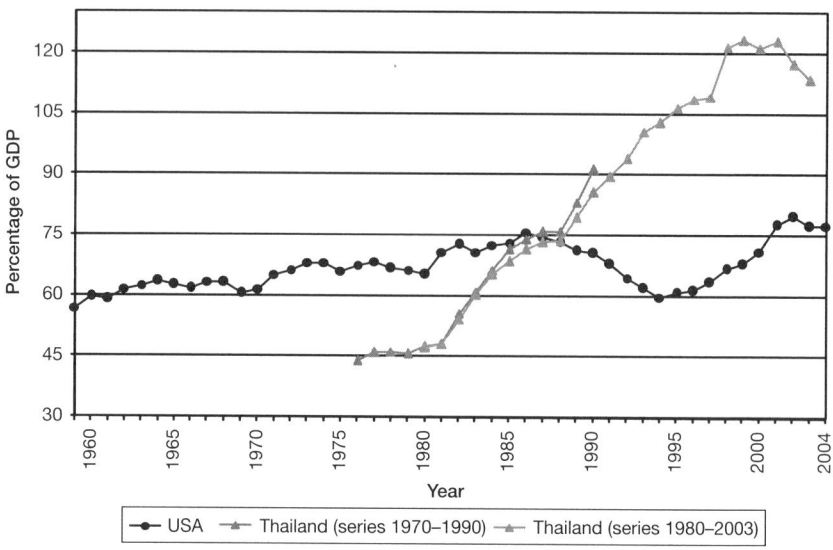

Fig. 1.8. *Thailand and the USA: M3 to GDP ratio, 1959–2004*
Sources: Adapted from Federal Reserve Bank of St. Louis, Bank of Thailand, and NESDB data.

above the US level, as is the case with other Asian economies. However, M3/GDP may also be taken as a measure of inefficiency, indicating the amount of money needed to support a given level of income; the jump in 1997 reflects an increase in the government's Financial Sector Development Fund and financial sector bailouts.

Other measures of Thai financial deepening from 1976 to 1996 display similar patterns. Figure 1.9 shows that total domestic credit and private credit relative to GDP both increased, with especially high rates of increase starting about 1988. Public credit, which had been increasing, decreased from that time onward. Another commonly used ratio, private-to-public credit, increased. Apparently, it was the private sector which expanded during the high growth period.

Expansion in the financial system took place on both domestic and foreign margins. The *S*-curve of expansion on the extensive domestic margin, shown in Figure 1.10, is computed as the fraction of households in the SES who had reported a saving or credit transaction with a formal intermediary in the previous month. The surge starting in 1986 is remarkable. Foreign capital inflows remained relatively small, but there was a substantial upturn at the same time, 1986. We will try to sort out and distinguish the impact of the models examined in subsequent chapters.

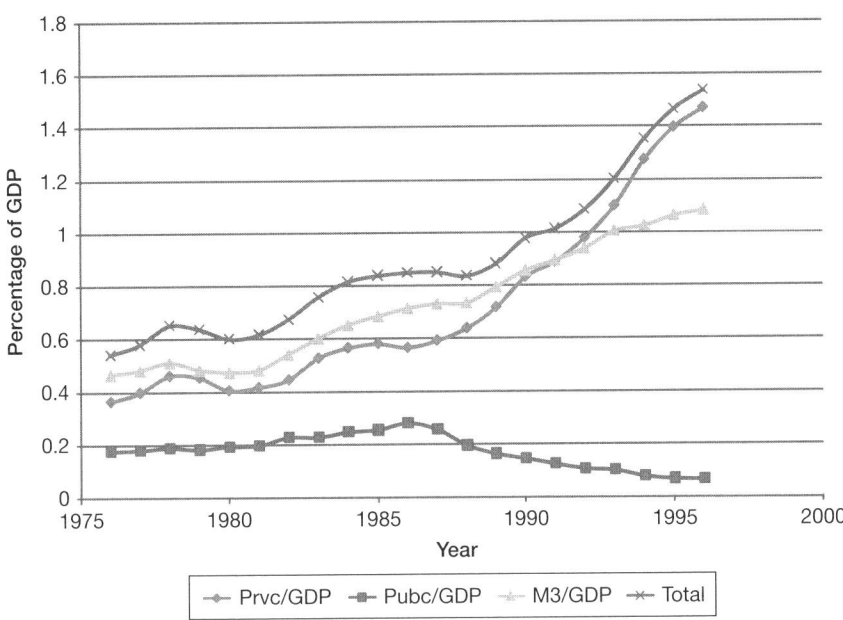

Fig. 1.9. *Macro-indicators of financial deepening in Thailand*
Source: Jeong and Townsend 2005.

The intimate link between the expansion of the financial system dating from roughly 1986 and deregulation and liberalization is evident in the chronology shown in Table 1.7. For example, in 1986 the government lifted interest rate ceilings on loans to designated priority sectors and reduced branching restrictions for newly merged finance companies. In 1988, smaller banks were allowed to open mini-branches and, in 1990, interest rate ceilings on saving were reduced. It seems likely that these changes in government policy had a positive impact, and this is analyzed below.

On the other hand, by the 1990s, problems with many of the commercial banks and finance companies had become increasingly evident, and the government and the regulatory framework proved incapable of responding adequately. Table 1.7 tells the tale. There was evident over-investment in the property sector; as property values fell, bank share prices fell too, yet reported capital adequacy ratios increased. Bank capital was overvalued, owing to insufficient provisioning and over-assessment of collateral values; the Bank of Thailand doubted it had the authority to intervene. Accrued

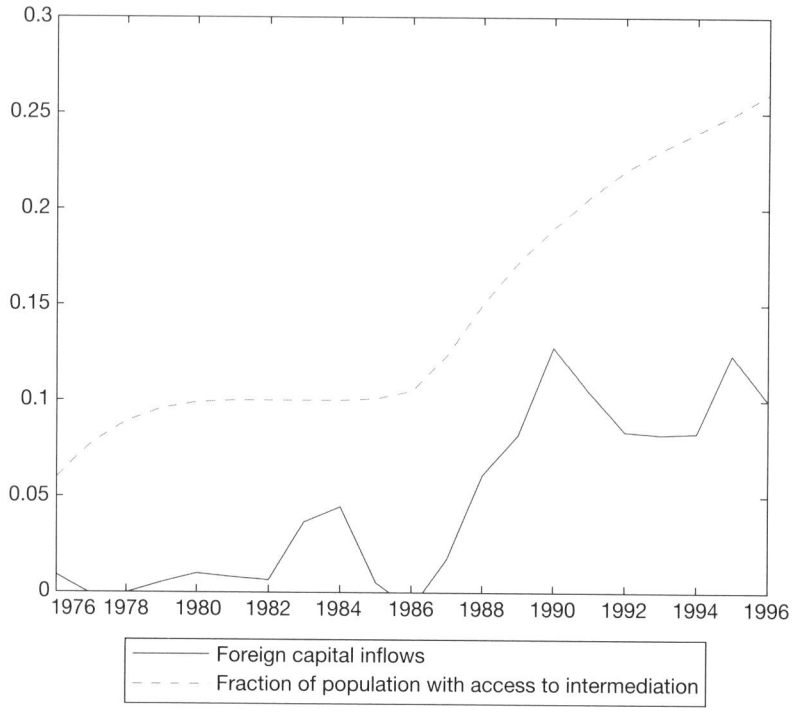

Fig. 1.10. *Foreign capital inflows and financial liberalization*
Source: Giné and Townsend 2004.

interest earnings on non-performing loans likewise inflated bank profit statements. Beginning with finance companies on the brink of failure, there was massive and secret support from the Financial Institution Development Fund, which reached $10 billon in 1997, about 8 per cent of GDP (see Figures 1.11 and 1.12).

The net effect of this episode, and contemporaneous government efforts to provide stimulus though the financial sector, is that the government's role in the credit sector has increased. Figure 1.13 shows that while the share of finance companies and commercial banks has decreased, state control over assets (loans as a percentage) was 10 per cent in mid-1997, and this reached 23 per cent by 1999. The new 1 million baht funds putting $25,000 in each of 75,000 villages alone sums to approximately 1.5 per cent

Table 1.7. *Chronology of major financial reform measures in Thailand since the second oil shock*

1975	• April. Securities Exchange of Thailand began trading (changed name to Stock Exchange of Thailand (SET) in 1991).
1979	• Repurchase market was established by the Bank of Thailand (BOT) to serve as instrument of open market operation, and to facilitate money market development by providing financial institutions with additional means of adjusting liquidity.
1980	• Ceilings on lending interest charged by commercial banks and finance companies were freed from the 15% limit imposed previously by the Civil and Commercial Code of 1924. This measure provided the BOT with more flexibility in adjusting interest rate ceilings in line with monetary policy stance and market force.
1984	• November. To facilitate informational trade and to improve Thailand's current account balance, the official exchange rate determination was changed from pegging the Thai baht solely to the US$ to pegging the Thai baht to a basket of major currencies. The Thai baht was also effectively devalued by 15% against the US$.
	• A joint private–public fund called the 'Small Industries Credit Guarantee Fund' was established to provide credit guarantee to small industries with fixed assets of less than 10 million baht. The Fund had been operated within the Industrial Finance Corporation of Thailand up until 1993, when it became an independent financial institution.
1985	• February. Imposing a 50-million baht limit on overdraft loan to any person. This was intended to improve the loan structure of commercial banks.
	• March. The BOT encouraged commercial banks to introduce the BIBOR (Bangkok Interbank Offered Rate) quoting system to facilitate money market transactions and to obtain benchmark money market rates.
	• May. Control on the opening of letters of credits was lifted.
	• November. The Financial Institution Development Fund (FIDF) was established within the Bank of Thailand to gain more flexibility in providing assistance to financial institutions in distress.
1986	• Separate interest rate ceiling for loans to priority sector was lifted.
	• To encourage mergers between finance companies, authorities relaxed branching restriction for newly merged companies, where the previous finance companies could operate only one branch office.
	• To enable credit foncier companies to mobilize funds from the public more efficiently, minimum maturity of promissory notes issued by credit foncier companies was reduced from 3 years to only 1 year, without early redemption.
1987	• The list of authorized businesses for commercial banks and finance companies was broadened to include the following: custodian service, loan syndication, advisory service regarding merger and acquisition, and feasibility study.
1988	• To help increase competitiveness of smaller banks, the BOT encouraged them to open 'mini-branches' in certain regions of the country to reduce operating cost.
1989	• June. Interest rate ceiling on commercial banks' time deposits of 1 year and over was lifted, marking the first step toward full interest-rate liberalization.
	• July. Prior approval from the BOT was no longer needed for outflow capital transfer regarding dividend repatriation and interest/principal payment on foreign debts.
1990	• March. Abolishing interest rate ceiling on commercial banks' time deposits of less than 1 year.
	• May. Phase 1 of exchange control liberalization began when Thailand formally accepted obligations under Article VIII of the IMF's Articles of Agreement, which resulted in complete liberalization of current account transactions and fewer restrictions on capital outflow.
	• November. Branch opening requirement for commercial banks to hold government bonds as a minimum proportion of total deposits was reduced from 16% to 9.5%.
	• Relaxing commercial banks' end-of-day net FX position limit from 20% to 25% of capital on net overbought, while the limit on net oversold remained at 20% of capital.

Source: Bank of Thailand.

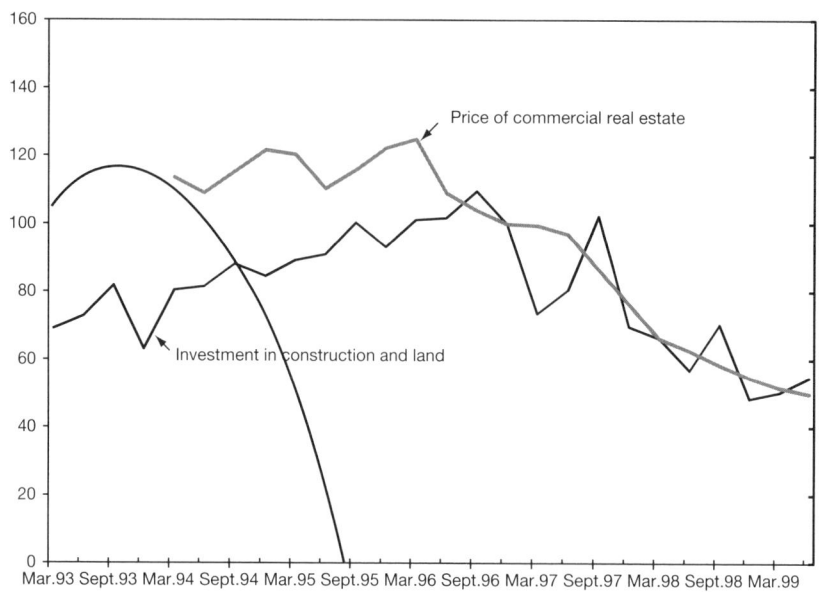

Fig. 1.11. *Property market indicators, 1993–9*
Dec. 1996 = 100.
Source: Haksar 2000.

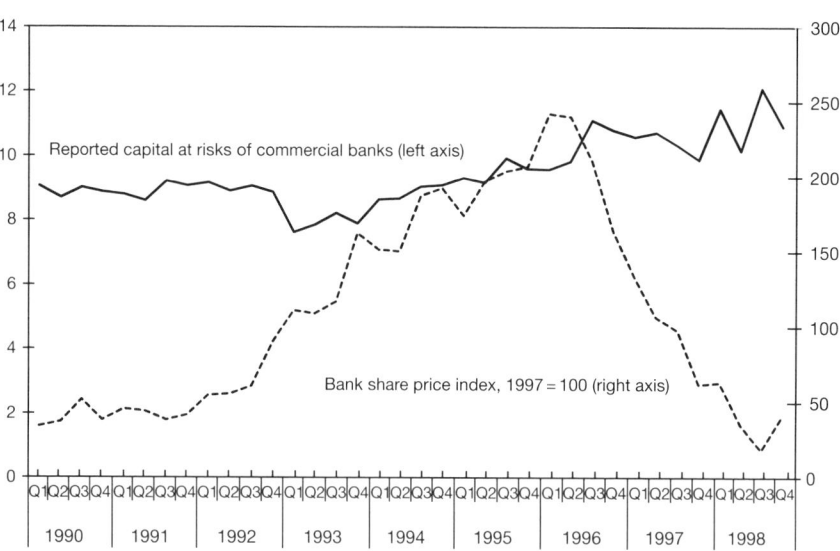

Fig. 1.12. *Commercial banks: reported capital adequacy and share prices 1990–8*
Source: Haksar 2000.

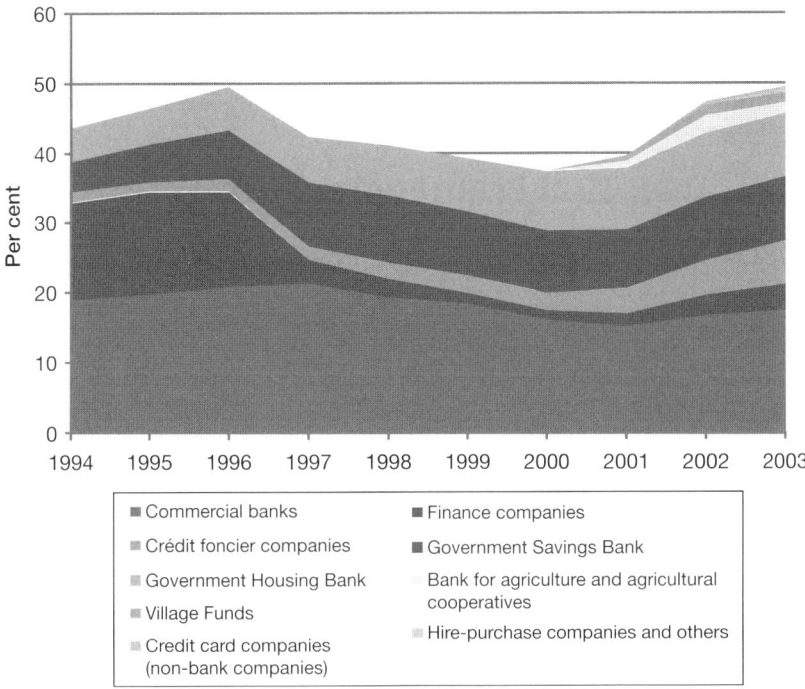

Fig. 1.13. *Formal sector household debt: regime shift in financial system*
Source: Annual Economic Report 2003, Bank of Thailand.

of GDP. There were new and expanded initiatives with the Government Savings Bank, Peoples' Bank, the BAAC, and SME Bank.

In sum, for better or worse, the government's role in the financial system has changed substantially over the years. This will be explored in what follows as we attempt to assess the efficiency of the financial system and the impact of policy change.

2

Conceptual Frameworks for Measurement

This chapter draws on standard accounting concepts to present a conceptual framework for measurement of stocks, such as assets and wealth, and flows, such as income and consumption, along with traditional decompositions. National income accounts are based on corporate financial accounts, so in the measurement there is a close and clean link between microeconomics and macroeconomics. These accounts distinguish assets and liabilities in the balance sheet, from (accrued) income (with saving as additions to net worth) and from cash flow as in a budget constraint. These accounts and the distinction between stocks and flows are drawn throughout this book, when discussing financial sector access/use, for example, and, of course, the models.

The unity of the accounts and measurement also means that, in principle, development economics, corporate finance, and macroeconomics all come together. Yet, in practice, the traditional accounting model of national income accounts and the associated 'circular flow' diagram envision little production in the household sector. For these and other reasons there are discrepancies between national income accounts and data from household surveys.

Still, even as estimated in the national accounts, non-farm proprietary income has been large relative to other factor payments. Non-farm proprietary income still dominates corporate profits, for example. Emphasizing the importance of domestic growth, private investment has the largest share of GDP and strongly tracks it. Data from an ongoing household survey and constructed balance sheet, income, and cash flow accounts show there is indeed much production in the household sector and the distinction between households and firms is blurred. The book emphasizes non-standard levels of aggregation, as well, such as kinships networks, villages, and family-related industrial conglomerates.

2.1. The Standard Accounting Model: National Income Accounts

The standard accounting model of an economy uses a 'flow of funds' concept, as illustrated in Figure 2.1, 'The Circular Flow'. In this model, households provide factors such as labor, land, and financing to firms which produce the economy's goods and services, paying back wages, rent, interest, and residual profits. In particular, financial markets and institutions mobilize savings and allow firms to invest. There is an obvious separation in this conceptualization between households as consumers and firms as producers, with rare exception.

Measures of GDP thus start logically with the accounts of firms; the balance sheet, income statement, and cash flow statement of corporate financial accounts form the basis for the construction of the national balance sheet and income and statements (Table 2.1(a)–(b)). Wages, interest, and rent in the income statement are among the cost of goods sold or goods produced for inventory. Retained earnings and dividends are a residual, adding to a firm's net assets or payment to its owners. Current assets and liabilities, real and financial, are listed on the balance sheet, with the difference as stockholders equity. Cash flows can be attributed to real activity, financing, or asset changes. The main difference between

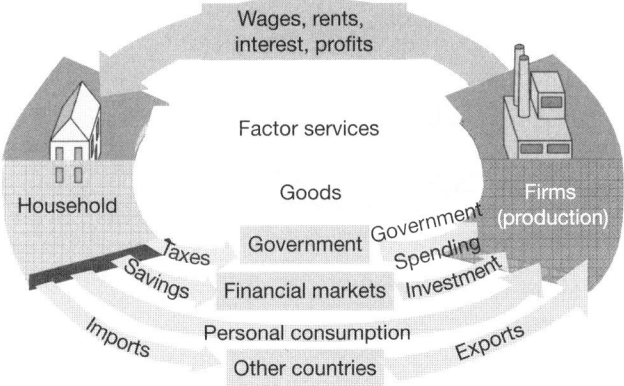

Fig. 2.1. *The circular flow*

The standard conceptualization of an economy is, as is summarized in the textbook, a flow of funds diagram. Households are imagined to provide factors such as labor, land, and financial accounts to firms who are imagined to produce the economy's goods and services, paying back wages, rent, interest, and residual profits. In particular, financial markets and institutions mobilize savings and allow firms to invest. There is an obvious separation between households as consumer and firms as producers, with rare exceptions.

Source: Colander 2004.

Table 2.1(a). *Balance sheet of a business firm 31 December 20___*

Assets	Liabilities and stockholders' equity
Current assets	Current liabilities
Financial assets	Loans
Cash and equivalent	Accounts payable
Accounts receivable	
Inventories	Bonds
Securities	Stockholders' equity
	Capital stock
	Retained earnings
Fixed assets	
Plant and equipment	
Less: Accumulated depreciation	
Land	
Less: Accumulated depletion	
Total assets	Total liabilities and stockholders' equity

Table 2.1(b). *Statement of income and retained earnings of a business firm for year ended 31 December 20___*

Sales, net of discounts
  Less: Cost of goods and services sold
      Purchased materials
      Purchased services
      Wages and salaries
      Depreciation
      Depletion
      Indirect business taxes
      Beginning inventory
      Less: Ending inventory

Equals: Operating income
  Plus: Interest and dividends received
  Less: Interest paid
  Plus: Gains (net of losses) on sales of fixed assets and securities

Equals: Net income before tax
  Less: Corporate income tax

Equals: Net income after tax
  Less: Dividends paid

Equals: Additions to retained earnings

Source: US Department of Commerce and Bureau of Economic Analysis 1985.

corporate and national accounting, beyond rearrangement categories, is the treatment of inventories. Goods produced but not yet sold are not counted as income in corporate financial accounting.

Inclusion of government accounts and foreign sector accounts, with remittances and investment abroad, completes the construction of the

Table 2.2. *Production, appropriation, and saving-investment accounts*

Business

Production account

Uses		Sources	
Wages and salaries	110	Sales	
Capital consumption allowances	10	To consumers	125
Net interest		To government	25
Interest paid		To business of plant and equipment	25
To households	6	To foreigners of goods and services	20
To government	2	Less: purchases from foreigners of goods and	
To foreigners	5	nonfactor services	10
Less: interest received		Change in inventories	5
From foreigners	3		
From households	4		
From government	1		
Indirect taxes	10		
Profits	55		
Charges against gross business product	190	Gross business product	190

Appropriation account

Uses		Sources	
Profits tax	20	Profits	20
Dividends paid			
To households	10		
To foreigners	5		

Households

Production account

Uses		Sources	
Wages and salaries	5	Sales to consumers	5
Charges against gross household product	5	Gross household product	5

Appropriation account

Uses		Sources	
Personal taxes	20	Wages and salaries received	
Purchases		From business	110
From businesses	125	From household	5
From households	5	From government	20

(continued)

Table 2.2. (Continued)

Business

Appropriation account

Uses		Sources	
Less: dividends received from foreigners	5		
Undistributed profits	25	Profits	55
Distribution of profits and saving	55		55

Saving-investment account

Uses		Sources	
Plant and equipment purchases	25	Undistributed profits	25
Change in inventories	5	Capital consumption allowances	5
Net acquisitions of financial assets	105		
Less: net increase in liabilities	100		
Gross investment	35	Gross saving	35

Households

Appropriation account

Uses		Sources	
Interest paid		Interest received	
To businesses	4	From business	6
To government	1	From government	4
To foreigners	5	From foreigners	5
Saving	15	Dividends received	
		From business	10
		From foreigners	5
		Transfer payments	10
Personal taxes, outlays, and saving	175	Personal income	175

Saving-investment account

Uses		Sources	
Net acquisitions of financial assets	39	Saving	15
Less: net increase in liabilities	24		
Gross investment	15	Gross saving	15

Source: US Department of Commerce and Bureau of Economic Analysis 1985.

national income accounts, as shown in Table 2.2. These include the production accounts, appropriations accounts, and saving-investment accounts, and they reflect the standard accounting model, with sector
accounts revealing the conceptualization of households as consumers and
not as firms, in consonance with the circular flow diagram.

2.2. Standard Decompositions in the Standard Model: Unincorporated Enterprise, Private Investment

Standard decompositions reveal some striking findings in the Thai national
accounts (see Figure 2.2):

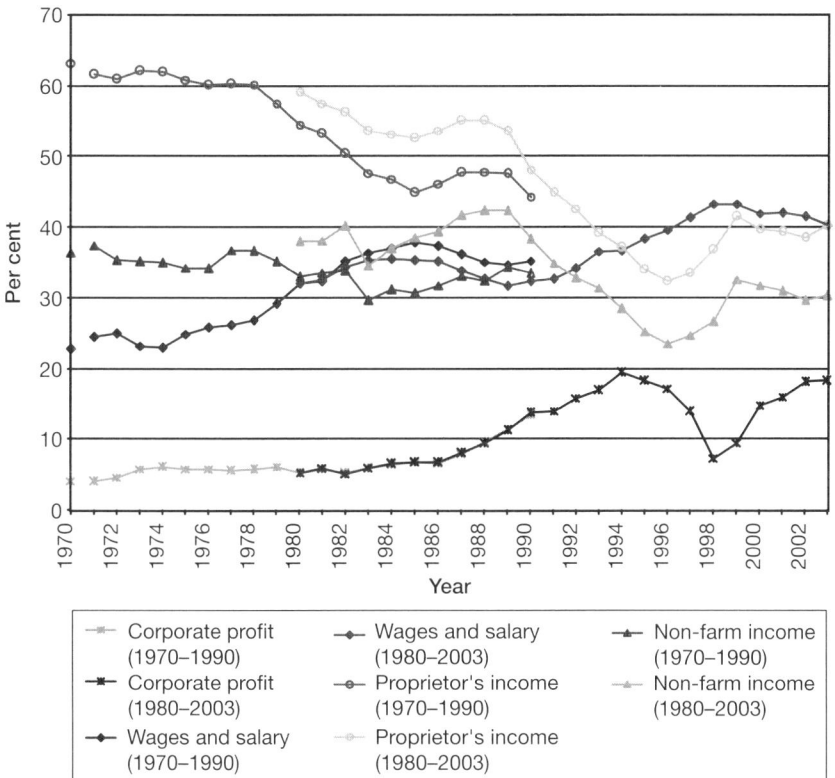

Fig. 2.2. *Thailand: distribution of national income, 1970–2003*

Source: Adapted from NESDB data.

2.2.1. Income Decomposition

- Farm and non-farm proprietary income in 1970 in Thailand was large, about 64 per cent of national income, and corporate profits was small, at only 5 per cent. This disparity, while less considerable, remains in the contemporary Thai economy, at 40 per cent and 18 per cent for proprietor and corporate income, respectively.

- Wage income at 22 per cent of all income in 1970 rose more or less steadily to peak at 45 per cent in 1997, equal to or exceeding proprietor income. Wages earnings have declined slightly since 1997.

- Non-farm enterprise has been at least half of all proprietor/enterprise income. Non-farm proprietor income peaked at about 43 per cent of all income in 1988, declined to 23 per cent in 1997, and then regained some of its former importance, rising to approximately 30 per cent in 2002.

- Non-farm enterprise is dominated only by wage earnings, at 40 per cent. All enterprise (farm and non-farm) is roughly equal to wages. All these exceed corporate profits, at only 18 per cent. In sum, non-farm enterprise has been and remains a pillar of the Thai economy.

2.2.2. Demand Decomposition

A demand decomposition of national product, Figure 2.3(a)–(d), highlights the related importance of investment.

- Consumption, as a percentage of GDP, has the largest share, at 75 per cent in 1957, though this has declined steadily, to about 55 per cent recently.

- Government's share is much lower, at around 10 per cent on average, with no obvious patterns.

- Investment share moves from 17 per cent in 1957 to over 40 per cent in the 1990s, with a subsequent decline in the crisis to 20 per cent, now rising slowly.

- Private investment tracks GDP quite closely, as illustrated in Figure 2.4. Deviations from trend in both series move almost in parallel since 1965.

Some of that investment was foreign direct investment (FDI). Prior to 1997, FDI in Thailand was approximately of the same order of magnitude as the current account deficit, which varied up to 8 per cent of GDP. The deficit moved to a relatively large surplus after the currency devaluation of 1997, though it has declined since then. The order of magnitude of FDI is

(a)

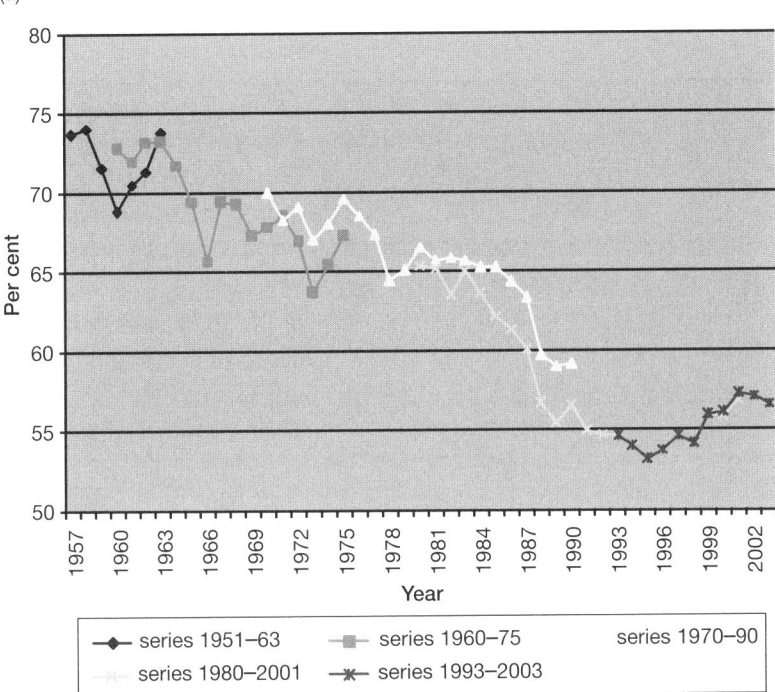

Fig. 2.3(a). *Private consumption share of GDP (current price)*

Sources: Adapted from NESDB data and Bank of Thailand data.

(b)

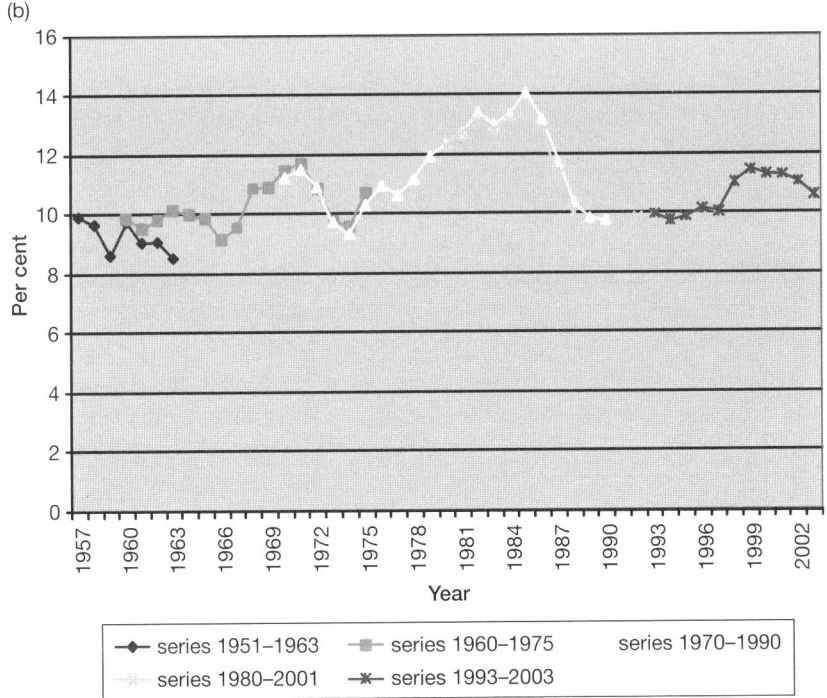

Fig. 2.3(b). *Government share of GDP (current price)*

Sources: Adapted from NESDB data and Bank of Thailand data.

(c)

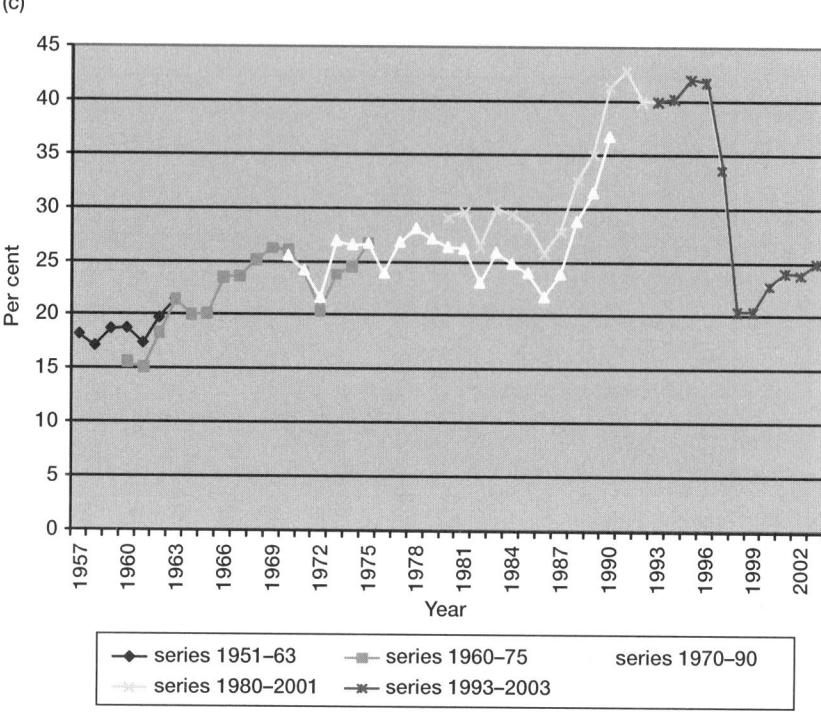

Fig. 2.3(c). *Investment share of GDP (current price)*

Source: Adapted from NESDB data and Bank of Thailand data.

(d)

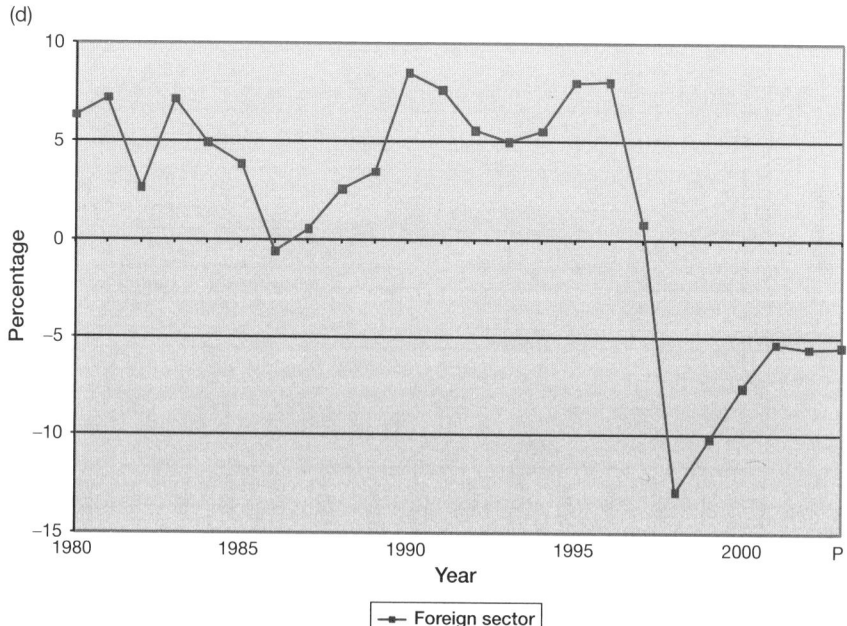

Fig. 2.3(d). *National current account deficit as percentage of GDP (current price)*

Source: Adapted from NESDB data and Bank of Thailand data.

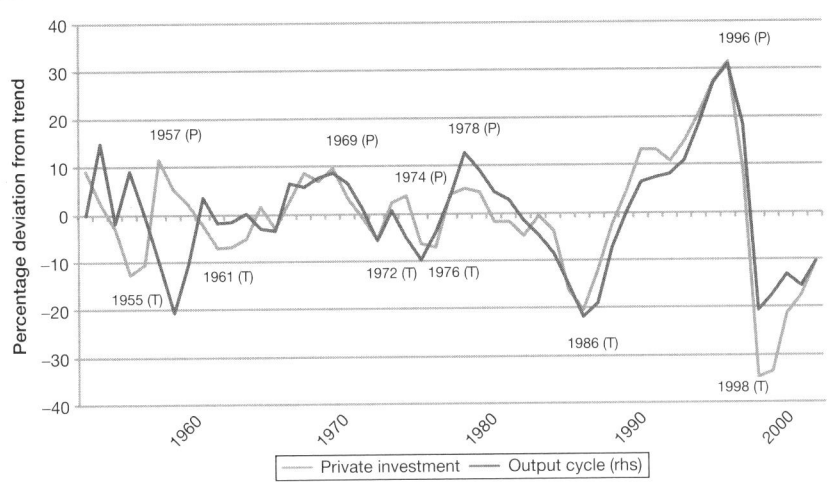

Fig. 2.4. *Investment cycles in Thailand, 1952–2002*
Source: Adapted from Bank of Thailand data.

displayed in Figure 2.5. The single largest type of FDI, as depicted in Figure 2.6, is in industry, followed by trade, though pre-crisis flows into real estate are evident. Within industry, as depicted in Figure 2.7, the primary sector moves from textiles, to electrical machinery and appliances, and then to machinery and transport equipment. Suehiro (1999) argues that foreign

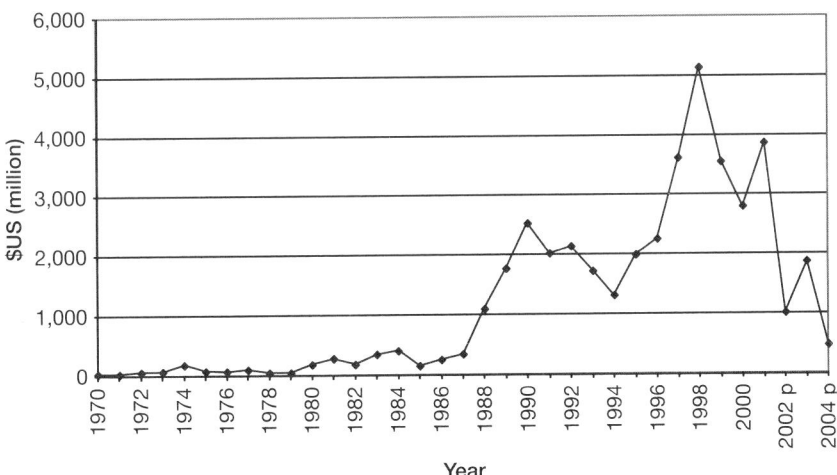

Fig. 2.5. *Thailand's net flow of foreign direct investment, 1997–2004p*
Source: Adapted from NESDB data.

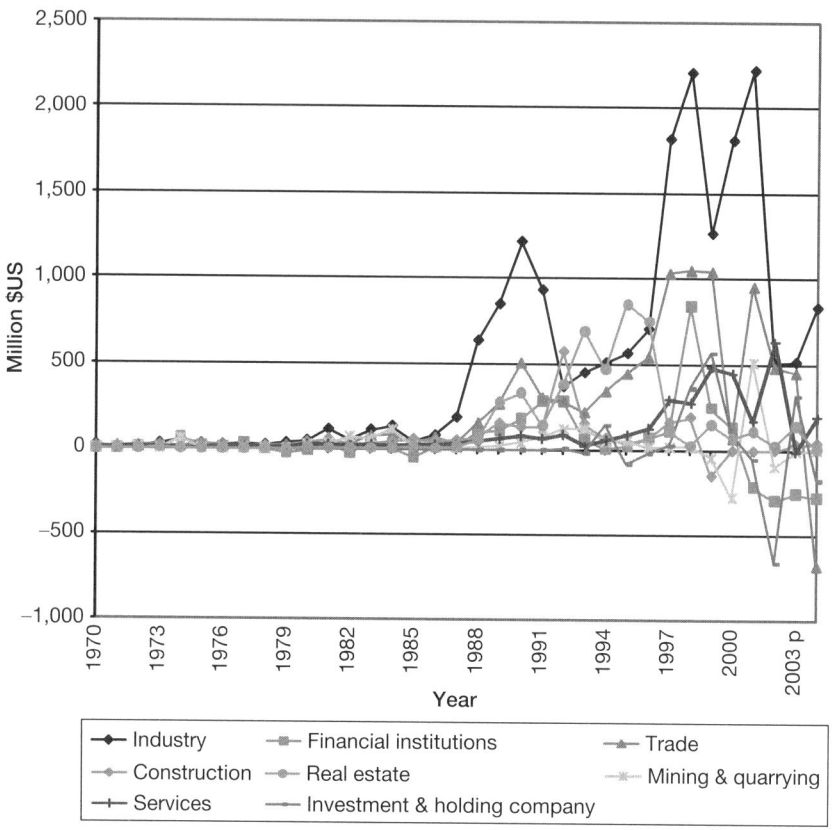

Fig. 2.6. *Net flow of FDI by sector, 1970–2004p (See color version at the end of the book).*
Source: Adapted from NESB data.

investment has been critical during various periods; for example, investment by Chinese nationals in small-scale enterprises such as hardware and weaving played an important role in the 1960s.

In sum, private investment seems closely correlated to movements in GDP. Much but not all of this is domestic investment. Factor payment data show that non-farm proprietorships play a large role in the Thai domestic economy, so investment in non-farm proprietorships has likely been substantial.

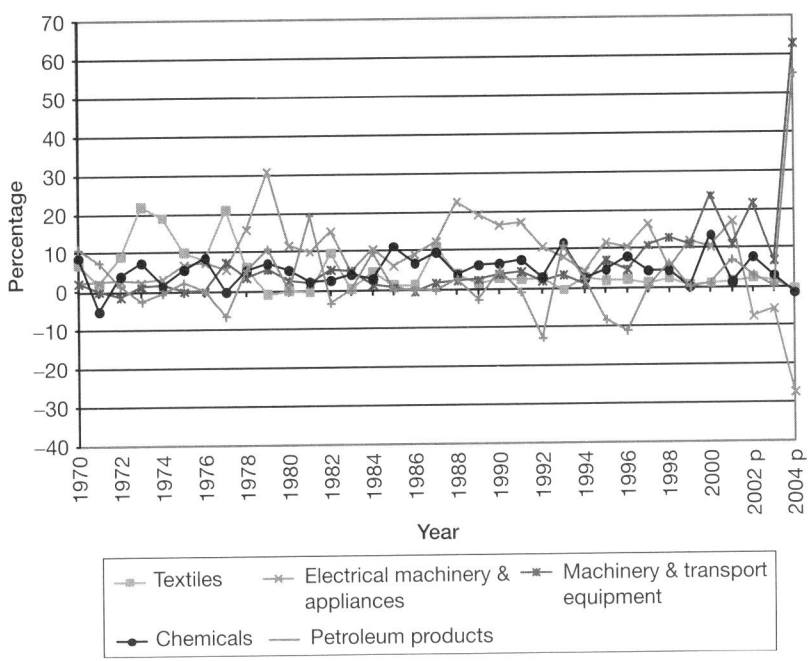

Fig. 2.7. *FDI in industry at disaggregate level (percentage of total FDI) (See color version at the end of the book).*

Source: Adapted from NESDB data.

2.3. Refining the Standard Accounting Model: The Construction of Households as Firms

We can refine the standard flow-of-funds accounting model by thinking of households as firms. For example, Samphantharak and Townsend (2009) provide an integrated view of households as producers. Given sufficient micro data of proper design, we can use standard accounting instruments to construct financial accounts for households as if they were firms engaged in production, and thereby enable measurement that cannot be accommodated by the standard conceptualization. Such accounts allow estimates of the contribution of households to national product through production and investment. Both household firms, and households running firms, can be viewed through the lens of these accounts and the measurements compared.

We model households as firms as follows. We use household surveys to obtain the necessary micro data; the Townsend Thai monthly data provide much of the necessary information for the construction of the balance sheet, income, and cash flow accounts. Household net worth can be viewed as equity, consumption as dividends, gifts as equity issue, and the household budget constraint as the firm cash-flow constraint. We distinguish between savings, a budget surplus, as in the cash-flow statement, versus savings as retained earnings as in the balance sheet. Net worth balances the difference between assets and liabilities. Changes in net worth from one accounting period to the next come from savings. Cumulative saving is the sum of historical retained earnings. Net savings is the change in overall retained earnings, and this must show up as an increase in assets or a decrease in liabilities.

The income statement reports revenues and costs from production activities (cultivation, livestock, business, labor) as well as interest income and expenses, capital gains, depreciation, and losses. Here, as with standard corporate accounts, income is reported on an accrual basis: expenses are subtracted as costs only at the time of the sale of product. (An exception is agricultural harvest which can be treated as goods sold and then repurchased to be put in finished good inventory.) Changes in work in progress inventory are one way to keep track of cash-flow expenses not yet subtracted. Net income, revenues less costs, is allocated into household consumption (dividend) and savings (changes in retained earnings).

The rate of return on total assets (ROA) measures a household's performance in using assets to generate earnings from all sources.

Cash flow is a much more volatile measure of 'income' than is net accrual income. Cash flows move with financing, consumption, and investment of course. But, more to the point, the remainder of cash flow, flow from production activities, fluctuates substantially more than net income.

An example drawn from the data will illustrate the technique as well as the potential complexity of the constructed accounts. We choose a relatively wealthy household, A, engaged in a small-to-medium-sized business enterprise, and a relatively poor household, B. The accounts are illustrated in Tables 2.3–2.6.

As can be seen from the balance sheet (Table 2.3), household A holds cash, inventory, and fixed assets, specifically milk cows, land, and household assets. This is consistent with the fact that the household's main economically productive activities are livestock and a retail store. The remainder of their assets consists of deposits at financial institutions and accounts receivable from trade credit. Liabilities consist of borrowing from other households and account payables to suppliers. The debt-to-asset ratio increases over time during the 48-month period, from 20 per cent to

Table 2.3. *Balance sheet of household A*

Month	5	6	7	8	9	10	11	12	13	14	15	16
Cash in hand	1,966,139	1,862,121	1,701,863	1,663,257	1,593,938	1,504,906	1,531,443	1,484,738	1,448,589	1,407,044	1,362,112	1,311,011
Account receivables	688,971	805,259	952,359	1,059,382	1,126,773	1,207,075	1,269,435	1,320,273	1,373,029	1,422,880	1,473,025	1,524,025
Deposits at financial institutions	167,271	167,969	168,094	156,799	157,474	157,469	189,549	201,194	240,759	240,304	240,249	240,194
ROSCA (net position)	33,000	37,000	41,000	11,500	16,050	20,600	25,150	28,450	7,750	10,750	16,750	23,750
Other lending	153,136	153,136	153,136	153,136	153,136	153,136	153,136	153,136	153,136	153,136	153,136	153,136
Inventories	1,346,939	1,440,729	1,576,481	1,697,413	1,842,527	1,986,251	2,111,673	2,238,242	2,356,958	2,486,177	2,609,586	2,744,157
Livestock	326,280	323,018	319,787	316,590	313,424	310,289	313,186	310,055	336,954	333,585	330,249	326,946
Fixed assets	967,342	973,759	970,949	968,151	965,365	962,591	959,828	957,076	954,336	951,608	948,890	946,185
Household assets	598,758	596,261	593,775	591,299	588,833	586,378	583,933	581,498	579,073	576,658	574,253	571,859
Agricultural assets	66,104	65,829	65,554	65,281	65,009	64,737	64,468	64,199	63,931	63,664	63,399	63,135
Business assets	2,479	11,669	11,620	11,572	11,523	11,475	11,428	11,380	11,332	11,285	11,238	11,191
Land and other fixed assets	300,000	300,000	300,000	300,000	300,000	300,000	300,000	300,000	300,000	300,000	300,000	300,000
Total assets	**5,649,079**	**5,762,991**	**5,883,669**	**6,026,228**	**6,168,687**	**6,302,317**	**6,553,400**	**6,693,163**	**6,871,511**	**7,005,483**	**7,133,997**	**7,269,404**
Total liabilities	1,132,310	1,280,270	1,425,465	1,570,660	1,715,855	1,861,050	2,116,245	2,260,056	2,403,867	2,547,678	2,679,744	2,827,946
Account payables	1,078,505	1,228,465	1,375,660	1,522,855	1,670,050	1,817,245	1,964,440	2,111,635	2,258,830	2,406,025	2,541,475	2,693,525
Other borrowing	53,805	51,805	49,805	47,805	45,805	43,805	151,805	148,421	145,037	141,653	138,269	134,421
Total household net wealth	4,516,769	4,482,721	4,458,204	4,455,568	4,452,832	4,441,267	4,437,155	4,433,107	4,467,644	4,457,806	4,454,253	4,441,459
Contributed capital (initial wealth)	3,439,250	3,439,250	3,439,250	3,439,250	3,439,250	3,439,250	3,439,250	3,439,250	3,439,250	3,439,250	3,439,250	3,439,250
Cumulative net gifts received	−6,664	−6,046	−6,357	−6,319	−7,576	−6,635	−7,233	−7,181	−6,774	−7,000	−6,335	−4,198
Cumulative savings (retained earnings)	1,084,182	1,049,517	1,025,311	1,022,637	1,021,158	1,008,652	1,005,139	1,001,038	1,035,168	1,025,555	1,021,338	1,006,406
Total liabilities and household net wealth	**5,649,079**	**5,762,991**	**5,883,669**	**6,026,228**	**6,168,687**	**6,302,317**	**6,553,400**	**6,693,163**	**6,871,511**	**7,005,484**	**7,133,997**	**7,269,405**

Source: Samphantharak and Townsend 2009.

Table 2.4. *Balance sheet of household B*

Month	5	6	7	8	9	10	11	12	13	14	15	16
Cash in hand	16,529	16,804	24,661	24,276	25,339	23,673	26,507	26,645	26,405	27,846	34,133	36,610
Account receivables	0	0	0	0	0	0	0	0	0	0	0	0
Deposits at financial institutions	120	140	160	180	200	220	240	260	280	300	320	340
ROSCA (net position)	0	0	0	0	0	0	0	0	0	0	0	0
Other lending	0	0	0	0	0	0	0	0	0	0	0	0
Inventories	3,772	5,878	444	0	0	0	0	350	2,478	1,238	1,418	7,540
Livestock	940	930	881	872	864	900	891	882	813	860	812	1,403
Fixed assets	14,918	14,866	14,814	14,763	14,712	14,661	14,610	14,560	14,510	14,459	14,410	14,360
Household assets	12,418	12,366	12,314	12,263	12,212	12,161	12,110	12,060	12,010	11,959	11,910	11,860
Agricultural assets	0	0	0	0	0	0	0	0	0	0	0	0
Business assets	0	0	0	0	0	0	0	0	0	0	0	0
Land and other fixed assets	2,500	2,500	2,500	2,500	2,500	2,500	2,500	2,500	2,500	2,500	2,500	2,500
Total assets	**36,278**	**38,619**	**40,960**	**40,092**	**41,114**	**39,454**	**42,248**	**42,697**	**44,486**	**44,704**	**51,092**	**60,253**
Total liabilities	7,800	7,800	4,500	4,500	4,500	4,500	4,500	4,500	6,140	6,140	6,560	5,640
Account payables	0	0	0	0	0	0	0	0	0	0	0	0
Other borrowing	7,800	7,800	4,500	4,500	4,500	4,500	4,500	4,500	6,140	6,140	6,560	5,640
Total household net wealth	28,478	30,819	36,460	35,592	36,614	34,954	37,748	38,197	38,346	38,564	44,532	54,613
Contributed capital (initial wealth)	26,580	26,580	26,580	26,580	26,580	26,580	26,580	26,580	26,580	26,580	26,580	26,580
Cumulative net gifts received	410	1,319	3,494	4,015	5,785	5,982	9,247	10,193	12,326	13,298	14,777	12,754
Cumulative savings (retained earnings)	1,488	2,920	6,386	4,997	4,249	2,392	1,922	1,423	−560	−1,314	3,175	15,279
Total liabilities and household net wealth	**36,278**	**38,619**	**40,960**	**40,092**	**41,114**	**39,454**	**42,248**	**42,697**	**44,486**	**44,704**	**51,092**	**60,253**

Source: Samphantharak and Townsend 2009.

Table 2.5. *Income statement of household A*

Month	5	6	7	8	9	10	11	12	13	14	15	16
Cultivation							3,200	11,676	11,676	11,676	11,700	
Livestock	30,485	27,753	26,180	21,780	26,730	28,050	39,000	39,600	79,600	39,600	33,000	31,900
Livestock produce	28,985	27,753	26,180	21,780	26,730	28,050	33,000	39,600	39,600	39,600	33,000	31,900
Capital gains	1,500						6,000		40,000			
Fish and shrimp												
Business	184,360	145,360	183,875	152,890	160,455	167,295	249,440	169,460	175,855	166,170	167,150	170,000
Labor	11,440	11,440	11,440	11,440	11,440	11,440	11,440	10,056	11,440	10,096	10,100	10,000
Others	6,000	3,000	6,000	6,000	6,000	6,000	6,000	6,000	6,000	6,000	6,000	6,000
Total revenues	**232,285**	**187,553**	**227,495**	**192,110**	**204,625**	**212,785**	**309,080**	**236,792**	**284,571**	**233,542**	**227,950**	**217,900**
Cultivation								1,468	1,468	1,468	1,468	
Livestock	31,944	30,281	27,642	22,813	21,715	19,225	20,371	25,573	27,787	30,064	28,059	27,048
Capital losses												
Depreciation (aging)	3,281	3,263	3,230	3,198	3,166	3,134	3,103	3,132	3,101	3,370	3,336	3,302
Other expenses	28,663	27,018	24,412	19,615	18,549	16,090	17,268	22,441	24,687	26,694	24,723	23,745
Fish and shrimp												
Business	220,176	167,323	199,933	150,300	159,472	173,440	262,931	182,317	186,649	173,751	174,006	177,608
Labor											150	100
Others												
Total cost of production	**252,120**	**197,604**	**227,575**	**173,112**	**181,187**	**192,665**	**283,302**	**209,358**	**215,905**	**205,283**	**203,684**	**204,756**
Interest revenue												
Interest expense	55	55	55	75	55	55	55	55	55	55	55	55
Other expenses	2,794	2,783	2,810	2,798	2,786	2,775	2,763	2,751	2,740	2,729	2,717	2,706
Depreciation of fixed assets	2,794	2,783	2,810	2,798	2,786	2,775	2,763	2,751	2,740	2,729	2,717	2,706
Insurance premium												
Extraordinary items												
Capital gains												
Capital losses												
Net income	**(22,684)**	**(12,889)**	**(2,945)**	**16,125**	**20,597**	**17,290**	**22,960**	**24,627**	**65,891**	**25,475**	**21,494**	**10,383**
Consumption	9,035	9,362	8,145	10,849	8,566	16,186	9,663	1,472	3,005	6,332	(2,399)	9,105
Savings	(31,719)	(22,251)	(11,090)	5,276	12,031	1,104	13,296	23,155	62,886	19,143	23,892	1,278

Source: Samphantharak and Townsend 2009.

Table 2.6. *Income statement of household B*

Month	5	6	7	8	9	10	11	12	13	14	15	16
Cultivation	110	3,590	5,100	130	90	160	100	110	130	330	200	9,160
Livestock												
Capital gains						45				155	40	600
Livestock produce						45				55	40	600
Fish and shrimp	500						500			100	70	
Business										960		
Labor	160	150	160	160	160	160	300	390	160	150	7,660	9,800
Others							250	250			160	180
Total revenues	770	3,740	5,260	290	250	365	1,150	750	290	1,595	8,130	19,740
Cultivation		800										2,660
Livestock	313	9	49	9	9	9	9	9	69	8	9	8
Capital losses	300		40						60			
Depreciation (aging)	13	9	9	9	9	9	9	9	9	8	9	8
Other expenses												
Fish and shrimp	574						24				108	
Business												
Labor												
Others											60	1,080
Total cost of production	886	809	49	9	9	9	33	9	69	8	177	3,748
Interest revenue												
Interest expense												
Other expenses	52	52	52	51	51	51	51	321	50	50	50	50
Depreciation of fixed assets	52	52	52	51	51	51	51	51	50	50	50	50
Insurance premium								270				
Extraordinary items												
Capital gains				6	342	116	74					
Capital losses				6	342	116	74					
Net income	−168	2,879	5,159	236	533	421	1,140	421	171	1,537	7,903	15,942
Consumption	2,432	1,447	1,693	1,856	1,290	2,309	1,610	919	2,154	2,291	3,414	3,839
Savings	−2,600	1,432	3,466	−1,619	−758	−1,888	−470	−498	−1,983	−754	4,489	12,103

Source: Samphantharak and Townsend 2009.

55 per cent. Average total assets over the 48 months is 9.57 million baht (0.23 million US$). Out of this value, the household's wealth accounts for 4.96 million baht (0.12 million US$).

On average, the primary source of revenue for household A is the trading of animal feed (75 per cent), recorded under business revenue. Other revenue comes from milk cows (16 per cent), recorded under livestock revenue, and from labor supply (4 per cent). The household also grows hay, used as livestock feed. Primary expenses are associated with the purchase of animal feed, which the household resells. Aging cattle are explicitly treated as a depreciation expense. Capital gains associated with the birth of calves and their maturation are also explicitly included. Capital losses are associated with premature death of an animal, at the current value, hence net of depreciation. Average total net income is 80,405 baht (2,010 US$) per month. The average savings rate out of net income is high (67 per cent). Cash flow for this household is different from accrual income, due primarily to changes in the animal feed inventory, changes in accounts receivable (trade credit), and depreciation.

Household B, the relatively poor household, has average assets and average wealth of 86,044 baht (2,151 US$) and 81,730 baht (2,043 US$), respectively. Its primary assets consist of cash and inventories. The only liabilities are loans from other households. Revenue comes from infrequent wages (36 per cent) and cultivation of rice (31 per cent). Costs of rice cultivation are high but also infrequent. The average total net income is 1,835 baht (46 US$) per month. Saving is frequently negative with the average over the 52 months around 45 per cent. The difference between cash income and accrual income is from rice inventory.

From Table 2.7 we see that the ROA of household A is considerably lower than the ROA of household B. This comes from a combination of two aspects of the data. First, household A is less productive relative to its Lop Buri counterparts: the ROA of 12.93 per cent is lower than the 15.32 per cent lower quartile in that province. Second, household B is more productive relative to its Sisaket counterparts: the ROA of 49.95 per cent is higher than the third quartile ROA in that province, 32.02 per cent. For both households, rates of return to equity (ROE) dominate ROA as if both households might consider borrowing more. The debt-to-asset ratio of the poor household B is quite low.

The variability of income and risk in the underlying environment is evident in many key variables. We emphasize first that cash flow for each household has a much higher coefficient of variation than does accrued net

Table 2.7. *Monthly average of annualized rates of return on assets (ROA), annualized rate of return on wealth (ROE), and their components*

	Household A [1st, 2nd, 3rd province quartiles]	Household B [1st, 2nd, 3rd province quartiles]
Rate of return on assets	12.93	49.95
(ROA) (%)	[15.32, 22.37, 32.11]	[14.63, 23.17, 32.02]
Profit margin ratio for ROA	21.13	52.22
	[−90.25, 30.87, 61.29]	[−42.02, 28.29, 59.34]
Asset turnover ratio	0.39	0.59
	[0.28, 0.38, 0.48]	[0.22, 0.33, 0.46]
Rate of return on wealth	15.95	52.85
(ROE) (%)	[18.24, 25.23, 37.05]	[17.96, 27.25, 44.76]
Profit margin ratio for ROE	21.10	52.22
	[−144.87, 25.81, 58.71]	[−90.74, 8.54, 51.73]
Asset turnover ratio	0.39	0.59
	[0.28, 0.38, 0.48]	[0.22, 0.33, 0.46]
Asset-to-wealth ratio	1.81	1.07
	[1.04, 1.13, 1.29]	[1.09, 1.20, 1.41]
Debt-to-wealth ratio	*0.81*	*0.07*
	[0.04, 0.14, 0.28]	*[0.09, 0.20, 0.42]*

Notes: Numbers in brackets below are the quartiles and median of the respective province; Lop Buri for household A and Sisaket for household B.
Source: Samphantharak and Townsend 2009.

income, specifically 2.98 versus 0.87 for household A and 2.88 versus 1.81 for household B. This was the guess which motivated the distinction and construction of the accounts from the outset. Relative to the province, household B has a relatively low variation of cash flow, while household A is closer to the median. Both households have relatively low coefficients

Table 2.8. *Coefficients of variation*

Variable	Household A [1st, 2nd, 3rd province quartiles]	Household B [1st, 2nd, 3rd province quartiles]
Cash flow	2.98	2.88
	[1.22, 2.25, 4.07]	[3.10, 4.01, 6.96]
Net income	0.87	1.81
	[0.91, 1.46, 2.25]	[1.86, 2.30, 2.95]
Consumption	0.65	0.46
	[0.53, 0.91, 1.39]	[0.56, 0.94, 1.76]
Consumption of	*0.30*	*0.60*
household production	*[0.30, 0.38, 0.48]*	*[0.51, 0.62, 0.69]*
Consumption	*0.66*	*0.64*
expenditure	*[0.56, 1.02, 1.60]*	*[0.88, 1.53, 2.75]*
Capital expenditure	4.78	—
	[3.63, 5.71, 10.35]	[4.14, 6.36, 10.92]

Notes: Numbers in brackets are quartiles and medians of the respective province.
Source: Samphantharak and Townsend 2009.

of variation of net income. More generally Sisaket appears to be a riskier environment than Lop Buri, consistent with the ordering of A versus B.

Consumption variability is in turn lower than the variability of net income, evidence of considerably smoothing, naturally enough. Consumption variability remains higher in Sisaket than in Lop Buri, but now the ordering of A and B is reversed, higher for A at 0.65 than for B at 0.46. One might infer the household B is smoothing better than its provincial counterparts. Variability of investment is large (see Table 2.8).

2.4. Discrepancies between Household and National Income

The construction of such household accounts clearly depends on the existence of data of sufficient quality and quantity. In principle, national accounts could be constructed from a complete census of such micro

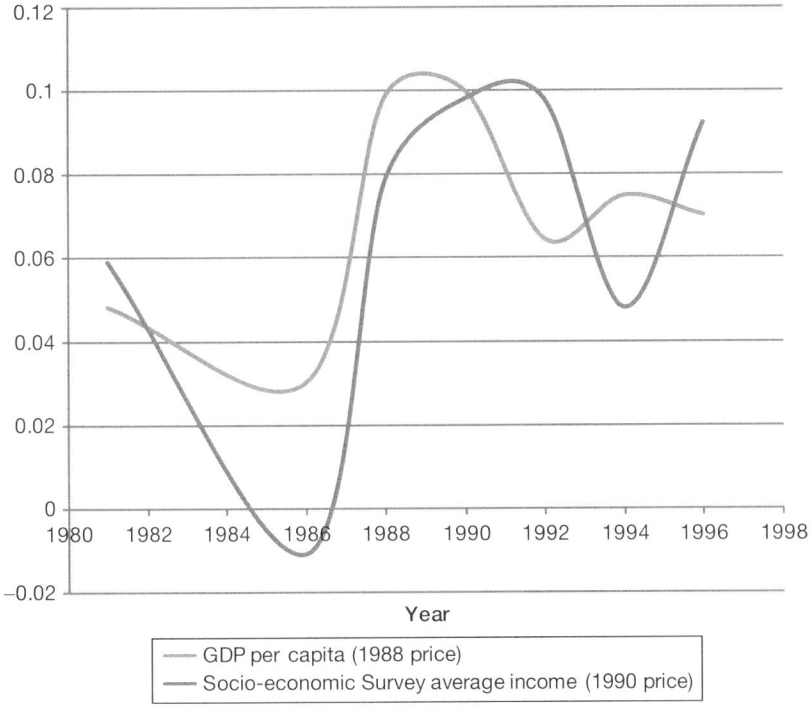

Fig. 2.8. *Annual growth rate of Thai per capita income*

Source: Jeong 2000.

accounts, but in practice there will be limitations to existing data. Proper survey design can provide reliable representative data, but even then we can expect to see discrepancies between measurements based on the macro data of national accounts and measurements based on accounts constructed from micro data. Thus, Thai GDP as measured in the national income accounts is not equivalent with household income as measured in socio-economic surveys, even accounting for the foreign sector. These income measures move roughly in parallel, but they are off in levels (see Figure 2.8).

According to national accounts, Paxson (1992) finds that the fraction of total household disposable income that was saved was approximately 15.5 per cent in 1975, 16.5 per cent in 1980, and 14.5 per cent in 1981; see also Figure 2.9 for other savings rates. In contrast, estimates of total national

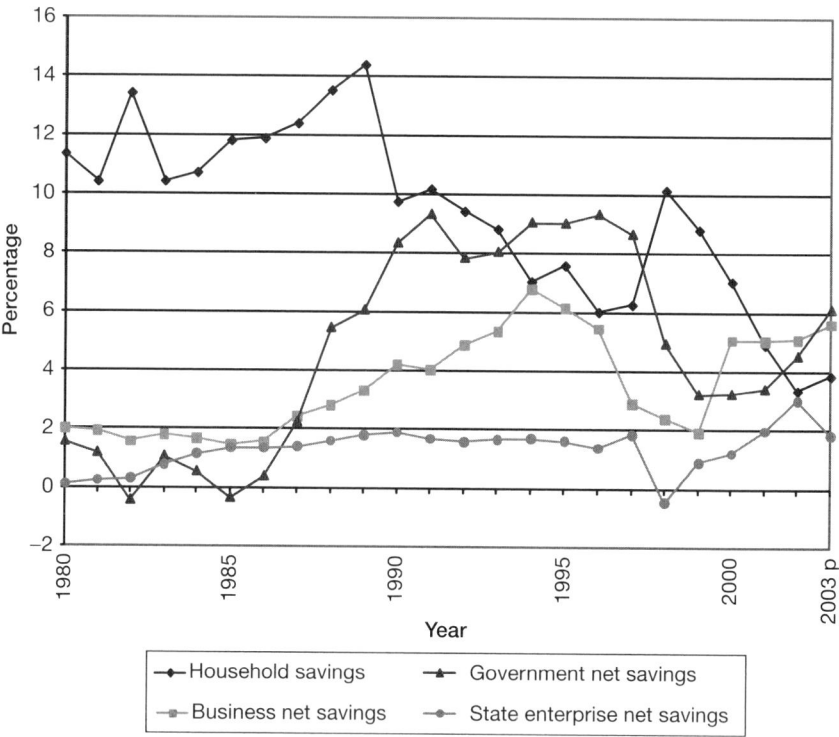

Fig. 2.9. *Household, business, and government saving as percentage of GDP (current price)*
Source: Adapted from NESDB data.

Table 2.9. *Savings rates by income quartile, using unadjusted and adjusted savings measures, 1981*

Quartile	SAVE1/income			SAVE2/income		
	Unadjusted	Adjusted	Difference	Unadjusted	Adjusted	Difference
Income less than 1,658 baht	−0.69	−0.61	0.07	−0.51	−0.44	0.07
Income between 1,658 and 2,850 baht	−0.24	−0.18	0.06	−0.09	−0.04	0.05
Income between 2,850 and 4,915 baht	−0.10	−0.05	0.05	0.04	0.09	0.05
Income greater than 4,915 baht	0.08	0.12	0.04	0.21	0.24	0.03

Notes: SAVE1 is income minus expenditure on all goods; SAVE2 is income minus expenditure on non-durable goods.
Source: Paxson 1992.

household disposable income and total household savings (using inflation-adjusted SAVE1, as in Paxson) constructed from SES data produces savings rates of 7.9 per cent in 1975 and 4.9 per cent in 1981. Even accounting for biases due to inflation, it still appears that households tend to under-report income relative to consumption (see Table 2.9).

A second caveat concerns accounting categorization. Household investment in income-producing activities needs to be conceptualized as savings allocated to real capital assets rather than consumption. For example, some consumer durables may be better classified as investment rather than consumption. The treatment of dividends (consumption) versus retained earnings (investment) in financial accounts reminds us this is an important distinction.

2.5. Aggregates: Elaboration of the Refined Model

In the standard flow-of-funds accounting model, firms and households occupy privileged positions, the former as producer and the latter as consumer. In section 2.3 we discussed the refinement of this accounting measurement framework to accommodate households as producers. In this section, we elaborate the refined model to accommodate unconventional aggregates, such as kinship networks, built on the foundation of household accounts. These aggregates are unconventional, in so far as they are not usually the subject of economic analysis, but the measurement framework remains that of conventional, standard accounting techniques.

Family Networks in Villages

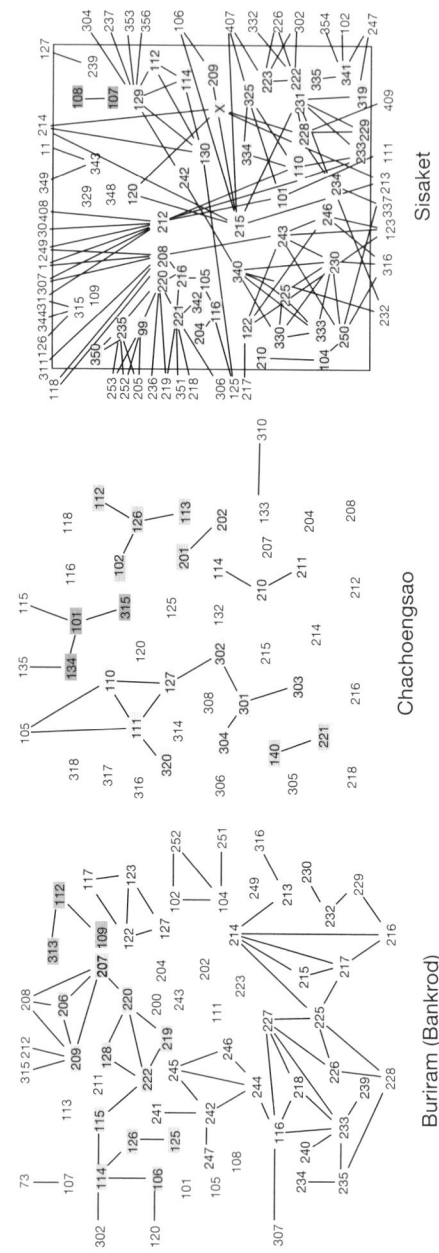

Fig. 2.10. *Family networks in villages (See color version at the end of the book).*

Sources: Townsend Thai data and Krislert Samphantarak.

Measurement and construction of financial accounts begin at the level of the individual household or enterprise. But these are social entities; they and their members are enmeshed in social and cultural networks of various kinds. They also exist in space, and are enmeshed in a geographic and ecological network of roads, waterways, fields, forests, and the like. Groups of households involved in common social and/or geographic relations can be conceptualized as economic units, just as households can be conceptualized as firms. The construction of household accounts as described in section 2.3 can thus be elaborated to support the construction of accounts measuring any of these aggregates. These constructions can in turn be aggregated, added up to portray the situation of any larger aggregate. Obviously one can stop short of aggregating all the way up to the national level.

Within Thai villages, for example, households may be related by blood and/or marriage to larger kinship groups. A typical village seems to have two or three dominant groups and a smaller number of disconnected households. But in some villages the groups are thin whereas in others virtually everyone is connected. Figure 2.10, depicting networks from Cha-choengsao, Sisaket, and Buriram illustrates these various possibilities. An arrow indicates a direct family connection across households in the

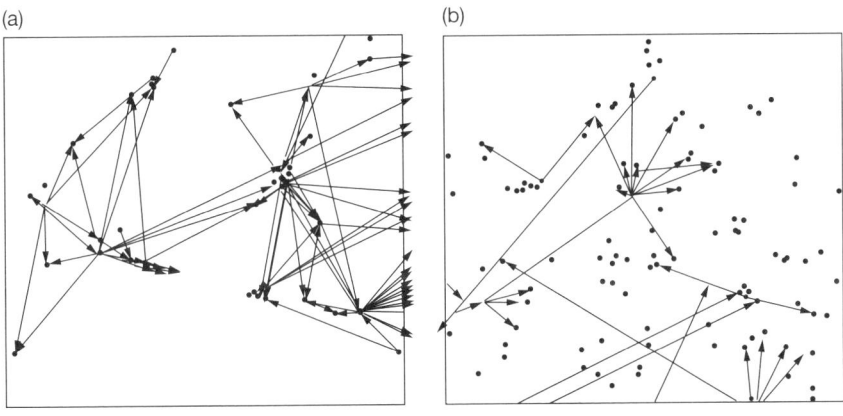

• Village location
N Arrows point to villages hiring tractors
    and from villages providing tractors

Fig. 2.11. *Tractor hiring network in two regions of Nang Rong*

K. Faust, B. Entwisle, R. R. Rindfuss, and Y. Sawangdee, 'Spatial Arrangement of Social and Economic Networks among Villages in Nang Rong District, Thailand', *Social Networks*, 21(1999), 311–37.

Source: Repr. from K. Faust, et al. 1999. Copyright 1999 with permission from Elsevier.

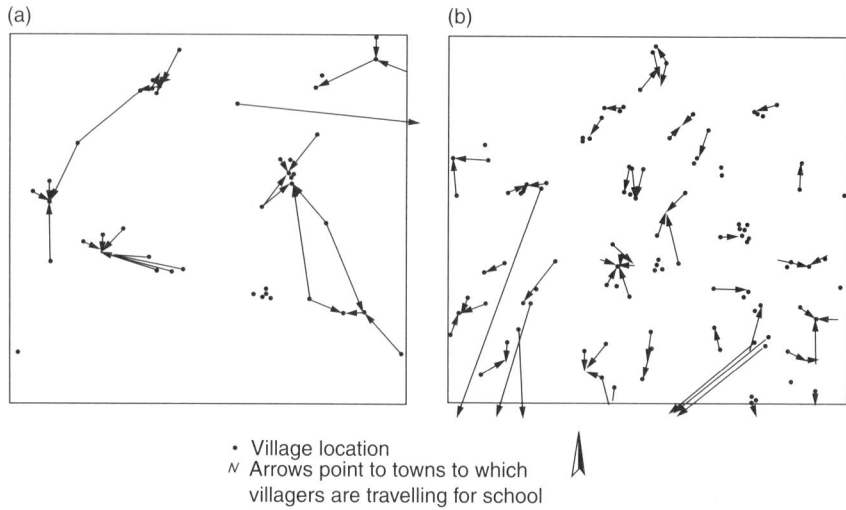

- • Village location
- ∾ Arrows point to towns to which
  villagers are travelling for school

Fig. 2.12. *Elementary school network in two regions of Nang Rong*

K. Faust, B. Entwisle, R. R. Rindfuss, and Y. Sawangdee, 'Spatial Arrangement of Social and Economic Networks among Villages in Nang Rong District, Thailand', *Social Networks* 21(1999), 311–37.

Source: Repr. from K. Faust, et. al. 1999. Copyright 1999 with permission from Elsevier.

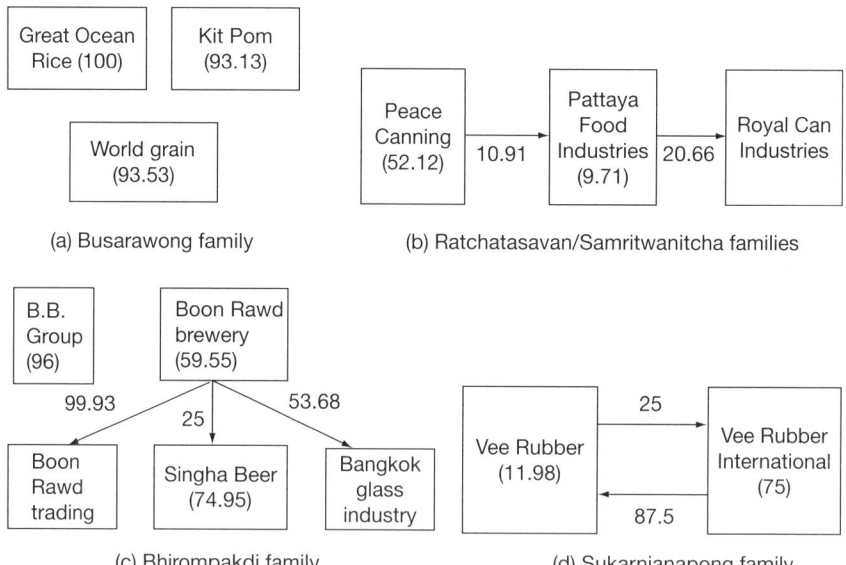

(a) Busarawong family

(b) Ratchatasavan/Samritwanitcha families

(c) Bhirompakdi family

(d) Sukarnjanapong family

Fig. 2.13. *Examples of simple group structures*

Source: Samphantharak 2002.

ongoing monthly Townsend Thai Survey or in the initial, one-time-only census (households outside the box). Colors indicate the different groups or dynasties. Subsequent analysis aims to see if the dynasty as a unit plays a social and economic role.

There may also be patterns in the relations across villages—for example, villages connected by labor- or tractor-market transactions, common elementary schools, or Buddhist temples, as illustrated in the GIS of the Faust, et al. (1999) Nang Rong project in Buriram: depicted in Figures 2.11 and 2.12.

Families may continue in importance even though villages may diminish in importance, as the country develops. Industrial conglomerates, including some of the largest firms in Thailand, are connected through family,

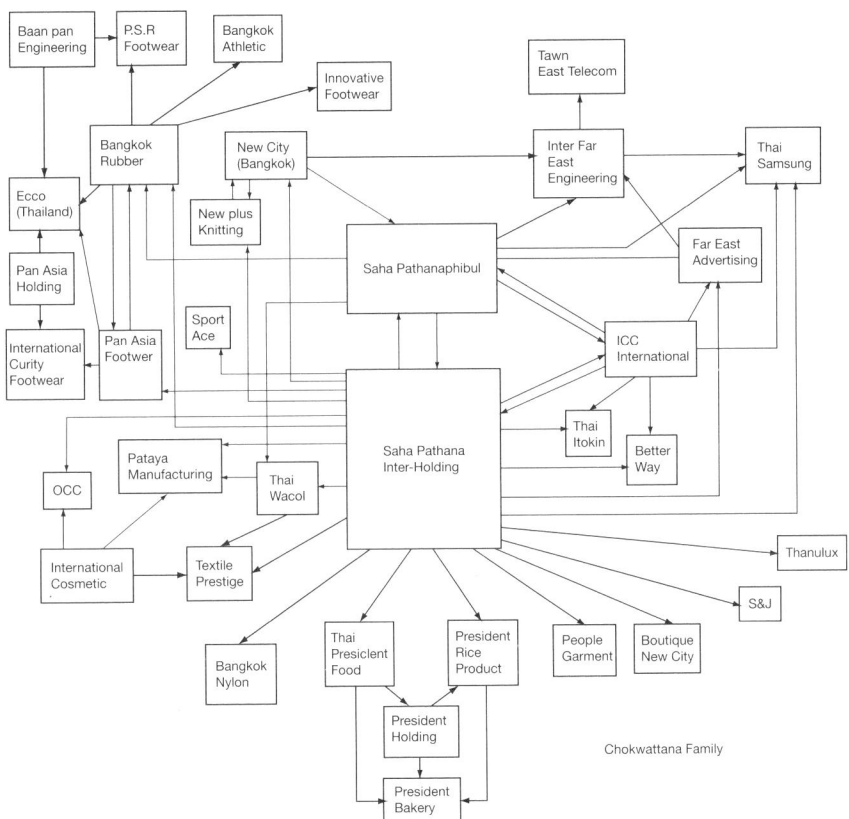

Fig. 2.14. *Example of groups with many chain shareholdings, many cross-shareholdings, and many pyramids*

Source: Samphantharak 2002.

marriage, and cross-shareholdings. Some of these structures are relatively simple; with a family holding a large number of shares in each of various units, vertically or horizontally. But, others are more complex, with chains of cross holdings—family connections are not well captured by simple indicators of shares directly held (cf. Figures 2.13 and 2.14). Again, the issue is whether a family-related conglomerate plays a role as a unit above and beyond the individual firms of which it is comprised.

3

Disparities among Regional Economies: Spatial (Dis)Aggregation

This chapter spatially disaggregates the national economy into provinces and then disaggregates further from counties (amphoe), to villages, to households, and even down to individuals. This is literally the physical representation of the macro economy built up from its micro foundations. Of course, no model should try to incorporate all aspects, and the models in the subsequent chapters take different actors as decision-makers: sometimes the household, sometimes an entire village, or, when aggregation permits, higher macro units. This chapter also reminds us that diversity in physical geography and locations is a source of economic heterogeneity.

Gross provincial product (GPP), which is analogous to GDP, displays great differences across provinces in wealth and in the relative importance of manufacturing versus agriculture. Moving across provinces within Thailand is akin to moving across countries. Poverty rates differ greatly across provinces, and the Townsend Thai Panel data are well placed to pick up this variation. The process of transition appears to have changed over time, with a greater tendency recently toward lack of convergence in provincial product across Thai provinces. The data also show signs of the kind of macro–micro discrepancy discussed in section 2.4—for example, variation in the manufacturing share of GPP across provinces is much greater than the variation in non-farm income attested in household surveys. Treating provinces as countries, we can use a simple model of endogenous household migration out of agriculture in the provinces to production and manufacturing in Bangkok, with remittances contributing to income back home in the province, to explain much of the apparent difference, just as foreign remittances can account for the distinction between product and income at the national macro level.

An overlap in the villages covered by the SES socio-economic database and Community Development Department (CDD) village data establishes via projections of the latter onto the former, with extrapolations, the spatial and temporal patterns of income growth at the county level (amphoes). There is initial concentration and then relatively dramatic convergence. Inequality across villages is strikingly high when the level of average income and development is low, drawing attention to across-village heterogeneity. Village-level data within provinces reveal unevenness of development, with concentrations in wealth and a variety of geo-spatial patterns. In later chapters, we will use a variety of models to interpret these data, to try to explain divergent growth given initial conditions.

At the household level, income change correlates weakly with macro/temporal shocks, even during the financial crisis. Clearly, occupation and geography play an important role in determining resistance to such shocks. Local satellite imagery picks up variation in ground cover, and this too helps to determine the timing of good and bad years. Townsend Thai Survey sampled tambons within provinces were selected in a stratified random sample, using that imagery. More generally, households are experiencing a variety of idiosyncratic shocks and common regional shocks—for example, deviations in rainfall and rubber prices from their historical average. There is some specialization in households and variation in diversification strategies, such as migration.

With all these shocks and sources of heterogeneity, it might seem there would be little that is systematic in the regional or national economies. Models will thus need to take into account variables at various spatial and temporal scales in order to provide a coherent, integrated macro–micro picture of the economy. But the heterogeneity we see in the various aggregate levels within Thailand mirror the patterns we see in the regional international economy. But, at the international scale, Thailand looks rich. Specifically relative to other nearby countries, the Northeast of Thailand has low poverty, low malnutrition, high deforestation, and much made-man irrigation. It differs dramatically from its Mekong basin, regional counterparts in Cambodia, Laos, and Vietnam. This raises the question of why these countries, adjacent to one another, differ so much, and motivates our choice of Thailand as a starting-point for studying the determinants of growth, inequality, and poverty.

3.1. Provincial Economies

A province can be thought of as a country, and, indeed, estimates of GPP are available from the National Economic and Social Development Board of Thailand (NESDB). One can see from Figure 3.1 the various regional patterns. Income/product is relatively high in and around Bangkok, the Central plains, and connections going north to Chiang Mai. Product is high also in much of the South, but not the provinces bordering Malaysia. Income/product is lowest in the Northeast. The ratio of the highest quintile of product per capita to the lower quintile is 3 to 1. The ratio of the highest province to the lowest is 25 to one. For comparison, the range of per capita GDP across countries in the Penn World Table is between those two.

Likewise, the fractions of product/income attributable to manufacturing and agriculture vary considerably and are more or less inversely related. The inter-quintile range of these percentages is from 7 per cent to 46 per cent, with extremes at 0.59 per cent and 77 per cent (see Figure 3.2(a)–(b)).

Poverty rates also vary across provinces. These range from 3 per cent or less in the lowest quintile of all provinces up to the 24 per cent to 50 per cent in the highest quintile. Rates are low in and around Bangkok, modest

Table 3.1.(a)–(b) *Transition of real per capita GDP, 1978–86 and 1989–98*

(a) First order, time-stationary (1978–86)
Grid (0, 0.5, 0.75, 1, 1.25, ∞)

	Upper endpoint				
Number	0.5	0.75	1	1.25	∞
174	0.9528	0.0410	0.0062	0	0
210	0.1090	0.8132	0.0778	0	0
105	0	0.3126	0.6256	0.0618	0
62	0	0.0224	0.2182	0.6101	0.1493
97	0	0	0	0.1400	0.8600
Ergodic	0.6156	0.2665	0.077	0.0198	0.0211

(b) First order, time-stationary (1989–98)
Grid (0, 0.35, 0.5, 0.75, 1.25, ∞)

	Upper endpoint				
Number	0.35	0.5	0.75	1.25	∞
156	0.9498	0.0502	0	0	0
155	0.0868	0.8596	0.0536	0	0
208	0	0.0501	0.9067	0.0432	0
102	0	0	0.0941	0.8645	0.0413
109	0	0	0	0.0439	0.9561
Ergodic	0.3639	0.2106	0.2251	0.1033	0.0971

Note: 1978–86: likely to move forward; 1989–98: forward and backward movement equally likely.
Source: Yang 2004.

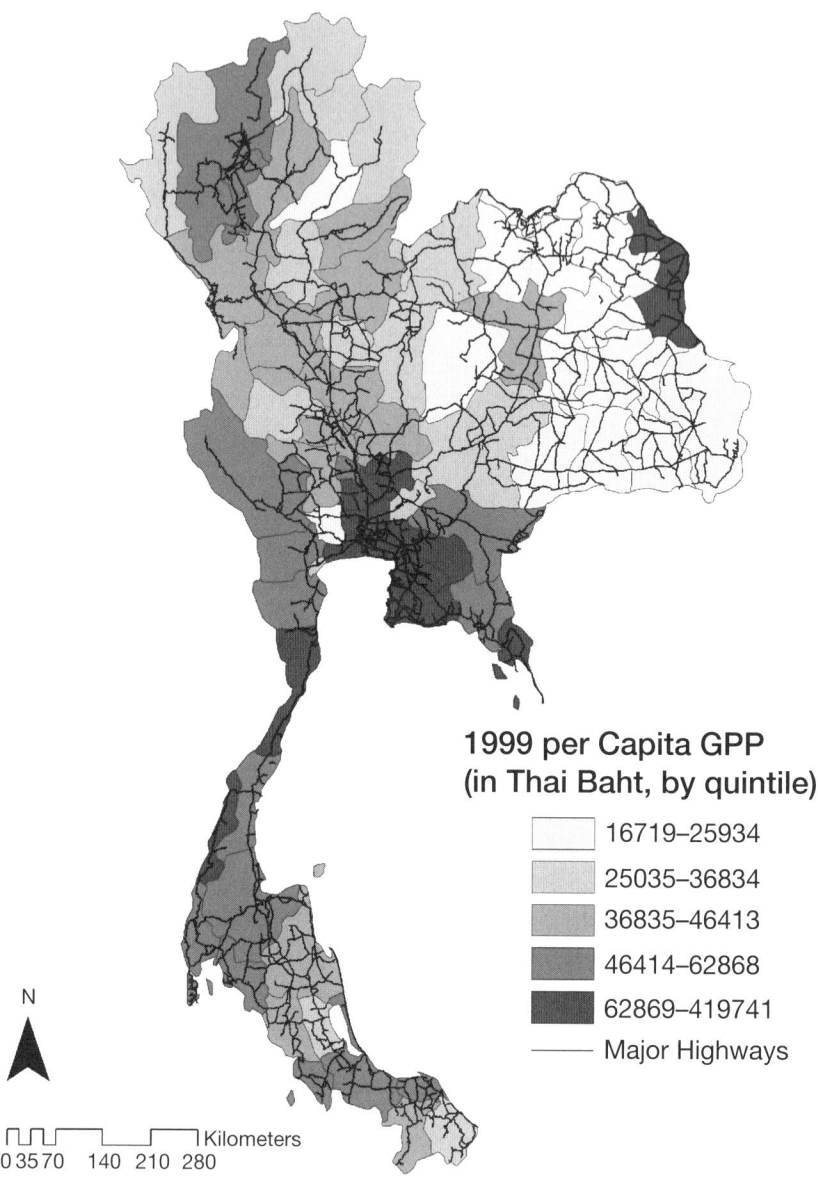

Fig. 3.1. *1999 Thailand per capita gross provincial product (GPP) (in Thai baht, by quintile) (See color version at the end of the book).*

Source: Adapted from NESDB data.

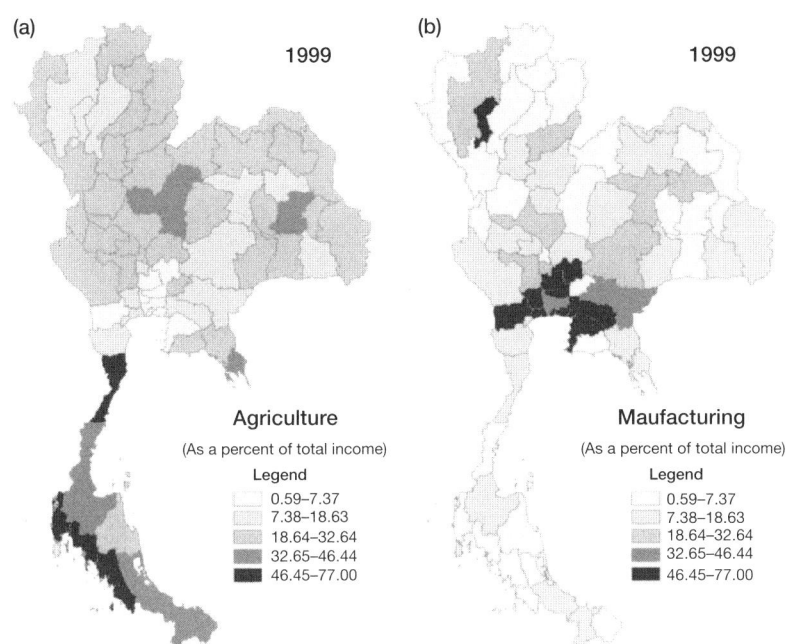

Fig. 3.2(a). *Agriculture in Thailand as a percentage of total income, 1999*
Fig. 3.2(b). *Manufacturing in Thailand as a percentage of total income, 1999*
(See color version at the end of the book).
Source: UNDP data.

near Bangkok and much of the South, but high in the Northeast, the Islamic provinces bordering on Malaysia, and some provinces bordering on Myanmar. Thus note that the Townsend Thai Project data span provinces with high and low poverty rates (see Figures 3.3 and 3.4, respectively).

A common characteristic of the literature on cross-country incomes is the search for evidence of convergence, with the lower-income provinces growing faster and catching up with the higher-income provinces. The same considerations apply to cross-provincial incomes in Thailand. Liu Yang's (2004) thesis uses the methods of Danny Quah (1993) to establish that there was a greater tendency toward convergence early on, from 1978 to 1986, than in the subsequent high growth period, 1989–98. That is, in the period of industrialization and financial deepening, a province is more likely to stay in its relative-income quintile. Table 3.1(a)–(b) at the top counts the frequency of annual transitions. Symptomatic of this, the 'steady state' ergodic distribution is relatively uniformly distributed,

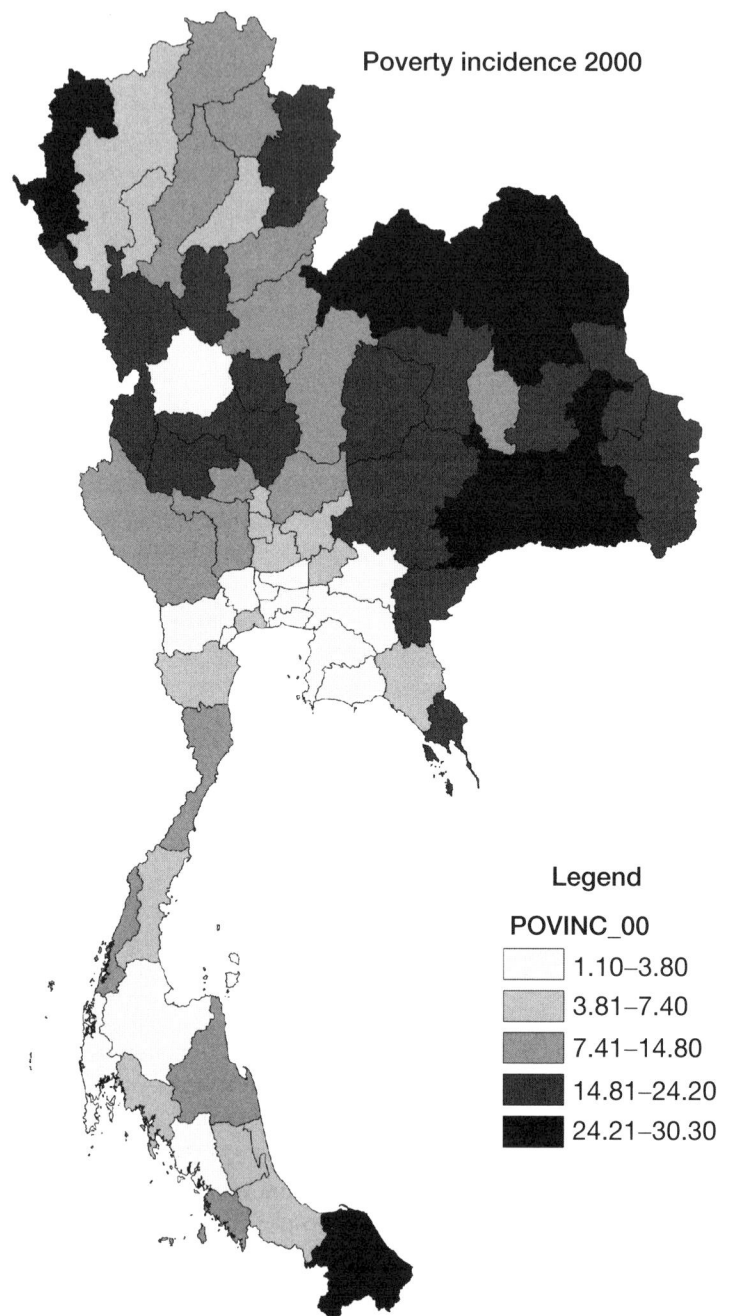

Fig. 3.3. *Poverty incidence in Thailand, 2000 (See color version at the end of the book).*
Source: UNDP data.

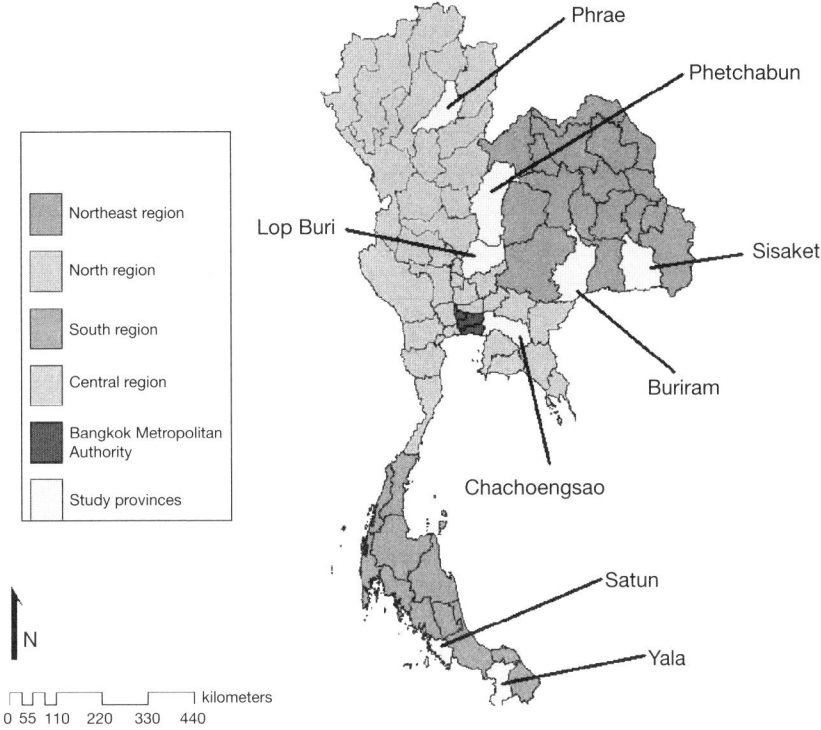

Fig. 3.4. *Thai geographic regions and study provinces*

Source: Adapted from NESDB data.

somewhat skewed left. In contrast, in the earlier period, a province with higher income is more likely to fall back to a lower category and the 'steady state' has a more concentrated distribution on the left.

3.1.1. Discrepancies between Provincial Product and Income: Migration and Remittances

Related to the measurement issue is the discrepancy between provincial product and provincial income. More specifically, as with growth and poverty, we can measure inequality at the cross-province level. The Theil-L index for provincial product is relatively high, at about 0.4, and displays the rising and falling pattern described earlier in the SES household data, hitting a peak in 1992. However, cross-province product-inequality levels are high relative to the cross-province contribution to inequality in the SES household income data (see Figure 3.5). The discrepancy is associated with product from manufacturing only. That is, the cross-province contribution

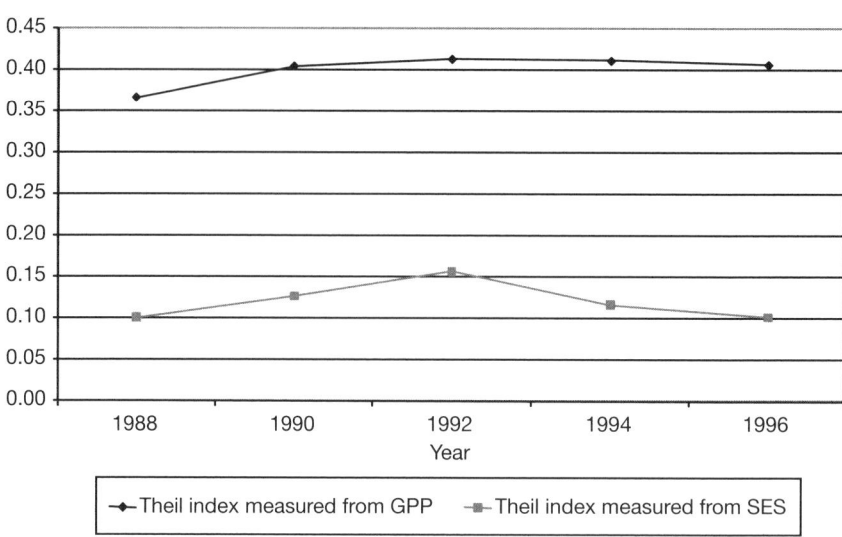

Fig. 3.5. *Cross-province inequality measured from GPP and SES data*
Source: Tang 2004.

Table 3.2. *Cross-province inequality (Theil-L index) in agriculture*

Data source	1988	1990	1992	1994	1996	1998	2000
GPP	0.159	0.125	0.164	0.189	0.187	0.197	0.202
SES individual earnings[a]	0.152	0.248	0.192	0.265	0.248	0.232	0.216
SES household income[b]	0.048	0.084	0.059	0.079	0.064	0.065	0.061

Notes: [a]Earnings measured as a sum of wage and farm profit, excluding remittances; [b]income measured as total monthly per capita income, including remittances.
Source: Yang 2004.

to inequality in agrarian product is similar to, if not less than, SES inequality in agriculture incomes (see Table 3.2).

The discrepancy is analogous to the discrepancy between national product and income and is consistent with a relatively simple model of migration out of provinces with 'foreign' remittances from migrants; which thus compensates for factors not located within the province. Yang (2004) first notes in the SES data that the fraction of households receiving remittances is large; it is 23 per cent in 1988, increasing to 34.5 per cent in 1999. Similarly, the income share of remittances for those SES households is large, 24.5 per cent in 1988 to 27.5 per cent in 1999. In CDD village-level data, the fraction of households with migrant laborers increases from 22.8 per cent in 1986 to 32.4 per cent in 1998, and as a fraction of all individuals,

Table 3.3. *Summary statistics, 1988–99*

	1988	1990	1992	1994	1996	1999
GPP dataset						
Number of provinces in sample	73	73	73	73	73	73
Mean percentage GPP in baht						
Whole sample (1988 prices)	28,710	34,864	39,840	46,605	52,727	47,135
Bangkok (1988 prices)	98,383	125,601	141,272	159,430	169,151	135,236
Sample without Bangkok (1988 prices)	20,183	23,532	26,871	31,528	36,833	34,687
Population of whole sample (1,000 persons)	54,330	55,839	57,294	57,514	58,780	60,549
Population of Bangkok (1,000 persons)	5,924	6,199	6,495	6,780	7,061	7,496
SES dataset						
Number of households in sample	11,045	13,177	13,458	24,583	24,433	7,580
Mean monthly per capita household income in baht						
Whole sample (1988 prices)	1,064	1,239	1,512	1,677	2,030	2,119
Bangkok (1988 prices)	2,506	2,922	4,162	4,081	4,673	4,794
Sample without Bangkok (1988 prices)	876	1,007	1,179	1,378	1,661	1,731
Fraction of households receiving remittances (percentage)	23.06	22.30	24.46	28.41	29.72	34.47
Share of remittances in household income percentage among households with positive remittances	24.55	23.49	23.83	27.05	27.92	27.55
CDD dataset						
Number of villages in sample	56,744	57,684	59,640	60,133	61,134	63,239
Mean percentage of households w/ migrants laborers	22.8	25.7	28.1	31.2	32.4	23.6
Mean percentage of out-migrants in population	8.1	9	10.3	11.6	12.1	9.8
Mean percentage of out-of-province migrants in population	5.4	6	7	7.9	8.2	6.2
Mean percentage of out migrants to Bangkok in population	3.7	4.6	5.7	6.5	6.7	4.7

Notes: From 1988 to 1992, population of whole sample in GPP dataset equals whole population of Thailand. From 1994 on, population of whole sample leaves out the part of three new small provinces, Sakaew, Nong Bualamphu, and Amnat Charoen. Mean percentage of remittances share (in gross income) is calculated by equally weighting households with different incomes.

Source: Yang 2004.

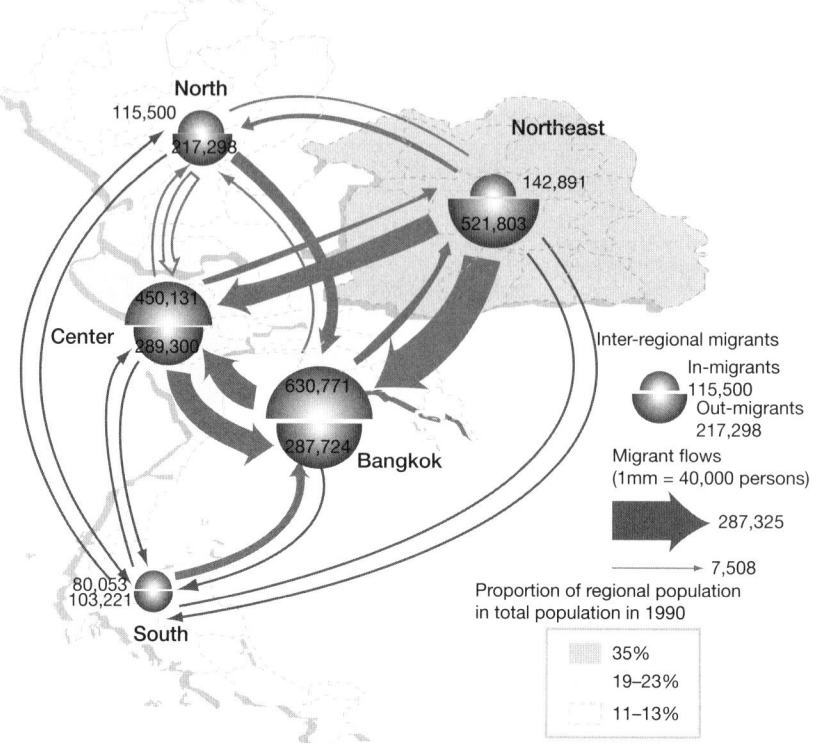

Fig. 3.6. *Inter-regional migrations, 1985–90 (See color version at the end of the book).*
Source: Kermel-Torres 2004.

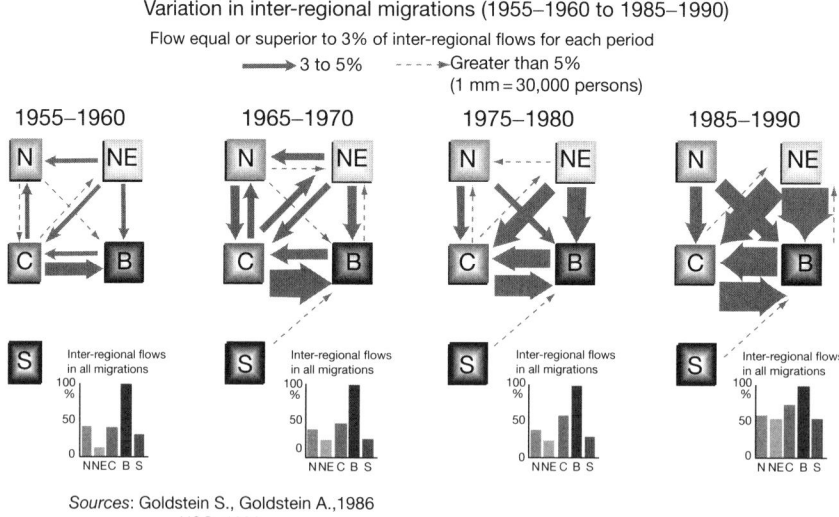

Fig. 3.7. *Variation in inter-regional migrations, 1955–1990 (See color version at the end of the book).*
Source: Kermel-Torres 2004.

from 8 per cent to 12 per cent during these years. Summary statistics are provided in Table 3.3.

The number of migrants and the fraction of migrants leaving their regions have increased over time, as shown by Figures 3.6 and 3.7. Migration was relatively limited in the early period of 1955–60, and a substantial amount of migration remained internal within the regions. From 1965 to 1970 intra-regional flows increased, and the largest intra-regional flow was from the Central region to Bangkok. By 1985–90, the largest intra-regional flows were from the Northeast to the Central region and to Bangkok, and also back and forth from Bangkok and the Central region. There has been little migration up from the South, and with the exception of 1955–60, even less in the reverse direction.

A mathematical model helps us think about the pattern more systematically. The simple model of Yang for the more recent 1988–98 period imagines that household j (as the representative consumer of household j) as a unit maximizes its total income at date t, $Y_{j,t}$, namely

$$Y_{j,t} = \max_{m_{j,t}}\{(1 - \theta m_{j,t})W_{j,t-1} + \theta m_{j,t} * W_{bkk,t-1} - C(\theta m_{j,t})\}, \quad (3.1.1)$$

Here, then, $Y_{j,t}$ denotes the expected household income of province j at the beginning of year t. Total labor supply of a household is normalized to one, $m_{j,t}$ denotes the proportion of laborers who migrate to Bangkok, and θ represents the mean work duration of an average migrant in Bangkok. In other words, $\theta m_{j,t}$ is the realized migrant labor supply, while $m_{j,t}$ is the observed incidence of migrants departing in year t. The relevant information on wage differentials is the wage earnings from the previous period. Variable $W_{bkk,t-1}$ denotes lagged wages earned by an average migrant household in Bangkok. Variable $W_{j,t-1}$ is alternative wages earned in the home province, j.

C is a convex function of migration cost. Assume $C(\theta m_{j,t})$ has the functional form of $Ce^{\gamma_2 d_2 + \gamma_3 d_3}D_j^{\gamma_1}(\theta m_{j,t})^\sigma$, where C is a scalar, d_2 is a dummy variable indicating the Northern region and d_3 is a dummy variable indicating the Northeastern region. D_j is the railway distance between Bangkok and home province j, measured in the GIS. As $C(\theta m_{j,t})$ is convex, $\sigma > 1$. Differentiation of objective 3.1.1 with respect to $m_{j,t}$ and taking logs,

$$\ln m_{j,t} = -\ln\theta - \frac{1}{\sigma - 1}\ln\sigma C + \frac{1}{\sigma - 1}\ln(W_{bkk,t} - W_{j,t-1})$$
$$-\frac{\gamma_1}{\sigma - 1}\ln D_j - \frac{\gamma_2}{\sigma - 1}d_2 - \frac{\gamma_3}{\sigma - 1}d_3. \qquad (3.1.2)$$

In equation 3.1.2, the proportion of migrant laborers $m_{j,t}$ is measured by the percentage of rural-to-Bangkok migrants in the rural population, by province. Five rounds of CDD survey data, every other year over the period from 1988 to 1996, are used in the estimation. Wage differentials are measured by the wage earnings in Bangkok (per capita GPP in Bangkok multiplied by the share of labor) minus per capita GPP of other provinces, assumed to be agricultural economies.

The estimated parameter values are: $\sigma = 2.15$, $\gamma_1 = 1.4$, $\gamma_2 = -3.1$, and $\gamma_3 = -3.9$. The values imply that migration cost is convex in the proportion of emigrants and increasing in the distance from Bangkok. But, a household in the Northern or, especially, Northeastern regions has lower migration cost compared with a household in the Southern or Central region, *ceteris paribus*.

Assume output in Bangkok is determined by a Cobb–Douglas production function:

$$Y_{bkk,t} = e^{\delta + \lambda t}K_{bkk,t}^{\alpha}L_{bkk,t}^{1-\alpha} \qquad (3.1.3)$$

where $Y_{bkk,t}$ denotes output, $K_{bkk,t}$ denotes capital stock, $L_{bkk,t}$ denotes total labor input, a is the share of capital compensation in output, δ is a constant, and λ is a technology shifter over time. Labor $L_{bkk,t}$ is $L_{bkk,t} = N_{bkk,t} + \theta\sum_{j} m_{j,t}N_{j,t}$, the sum of the labor supply, $N_{bkk,t}$, the stock of native labor supply in Bangkok plus migrant labor supply summing over all other provinces j—namely, $\theta\sum_{j} m_{j,t}N_{j,t}$ where $N_{j,t}$ is population in province j.

Per capita GPP of Bangkok in logs in given by:

$$\ln y_{bkk,t} = \sigma + \alpha\{\ln K_{bkk,t} - \ln(N_{bkk,t} + \theta\sum_{j} m_{j,t}N_{j,t})\} + \lambda t \qquad (3.1.4)$$

and wage earnings are proportional, i.e.,

$$W_{bkk,t} = (1 - \alpha)y_{bkk,t} \qquad (3.1.5)$$

The series of capital input, $K_{bkk,t}$, is constructed from Regional Gross Fixed Capital Formation Series released also by NESDB. Labor input series $L_{bkk,t}$ is constructed by combining the number of employed non-migrant laborers and number of employed migrants from the Reports of Labor Force Survey. Twelve years of data over the period 1985 to 1996 are used in the estimation.

The estimated share of capital, a, is 0.40 from the sample. The coefficient on the time trend, λ, is estimated to be 0.04, interpreted as an estimated annual productivity growth rate of 4 per cent. θ is not identified from the estimation because the whole term $\theta \sum_j m_{j,t} N_{j,t}$ is proxied by the number of employed migrants. In the analysis, θ is assumed to be 0.5—i.e., an average migrant works half a year in Bangkok.

We can derive the realized net income gain from migration from the entire household:

$$(1 - \theta m_{j,t}^*)W_{j,t} + \theta m_{j,t}^* * W_{bkk,y} - Ce^{\gamma_2 d_2 + \gamma_3 d_3}D_j^{\gamma_1}(\theta m_{j,t})^\sigma - W_{j,t}$$
$$= \theta(W_{bkk,t} - W_{j,t})m_{j,t}^* - Ce^{\gamma_2 d_2 + \gamma_3 d_3}D_j^{\gamma_1}(\theta m_{j,t})^\sigma \tag{3.1.6}$$

where

$$m_{i,t}^{*\sigma-1} = \frac{(W_{bkk,t-1} - W_{j,t-1})}{\theta^{\sigma-1}\sigma Ce^{\gamma_2 d_2 + \gamma_3 d_3}D_j^{\gamma_1}}, \tag{3.1.7}$$

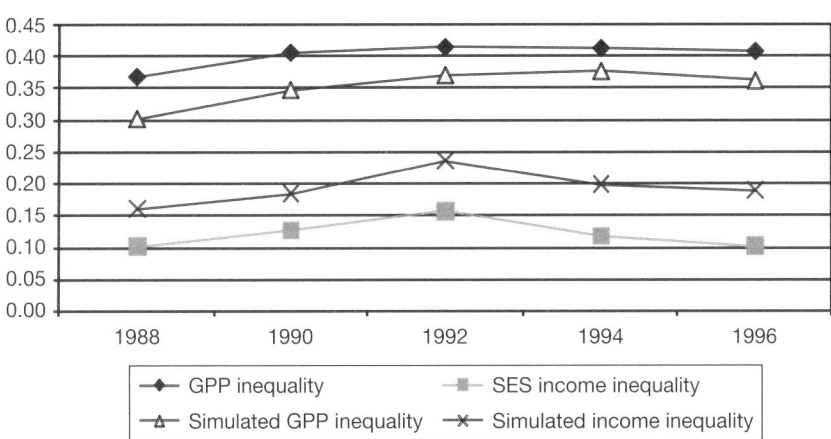

Fig. 3.8. *Cross-province inequality in production and income: data vs simulation results*

Notes: The calibrated parameter values for simulation are: $\mu=1$, $\theta=0.5$, $a=0.4$, $\sigma=2.15$. To simulate the Bangkok wage downturn during the financial crisis, it is assumed that productivity in Bangkok incurs a negative 20 per cent shock from 1996 to 1998. Inequality is measured by Theil-L index here.

Source: Yang 2004.

Table 3.4. *Comparison of simulated results vs sample data*

	1988	1990	1992	1994	1996
Simulated migrants population (1,000 persons)	1,242.60	1,359.70	1,748.90	1,971.40	2,277.00
CDD-estimated migrant population	1,287.80	1,596.60	1,951.50	2,191.20	2,348.10
LFS-estimated migrant population	400.60	433.50	624.60	509.50	718.40
Simulated Bangkok wage (1,000 baht)	51.90	67.33	77.67	86.90	92.98
Bangkok wage	59.04	75.36	84.78	95.64	101.52
Bangkok per capita GPP	98.40	125.60	141.30	159.40	169.20

Notes: Bangkok wage earnings are calculated by multiplying per capita GPP of Bangkok by the share of labor, which is set to be 0.6 for the benchmark case.
Source: Yang 2004.

and with other substitutions income and production inequality measures can be derived.

The model does well in tracking the CDD-estimated migrant population and Bangkok wage earnings (see Table 3.4). More to the point here, about half of the discrepancy in inequality of gross provincial product versus household income is explained (see Figure 3.8). Migration and remittances seem to be a big part of the inter-provincial, national economy. We learn from this as well that the informal financial system in the form of remittances is large and increasing.

Table 3.4 presents the aggregate level comparison of simulated migrant population and wage rates in Bangkok with those from the sample data. Overall, simulated results are a good approximation to the sample estimates.

3.2. County/Tambon Economies

Koriyama and Townsend, in 'Dynamic Poverty Mapping in Thailand: A Spatial Kuznets Analysis' (Koriyama and Townsend 2008) take advantage of an overlap between the randomly selected villages of the SES household expenditure and income survey and the virtually universal village-level CDD census. Specifically, per capita real income and consumption are regressed onto CDD variables stepwise with a truncation significance level of 5 per cent. Naturally, different variables are significant in different years, and there are some trade-offs between number of variables used and the percentage of the sample remaining. We then project income onto the remainder of the CDD sample. Maps at the tambon level distinguishing quintiles show a dramatic rise in income (see Figure 3.9(a)–(e)). At first this

(a)

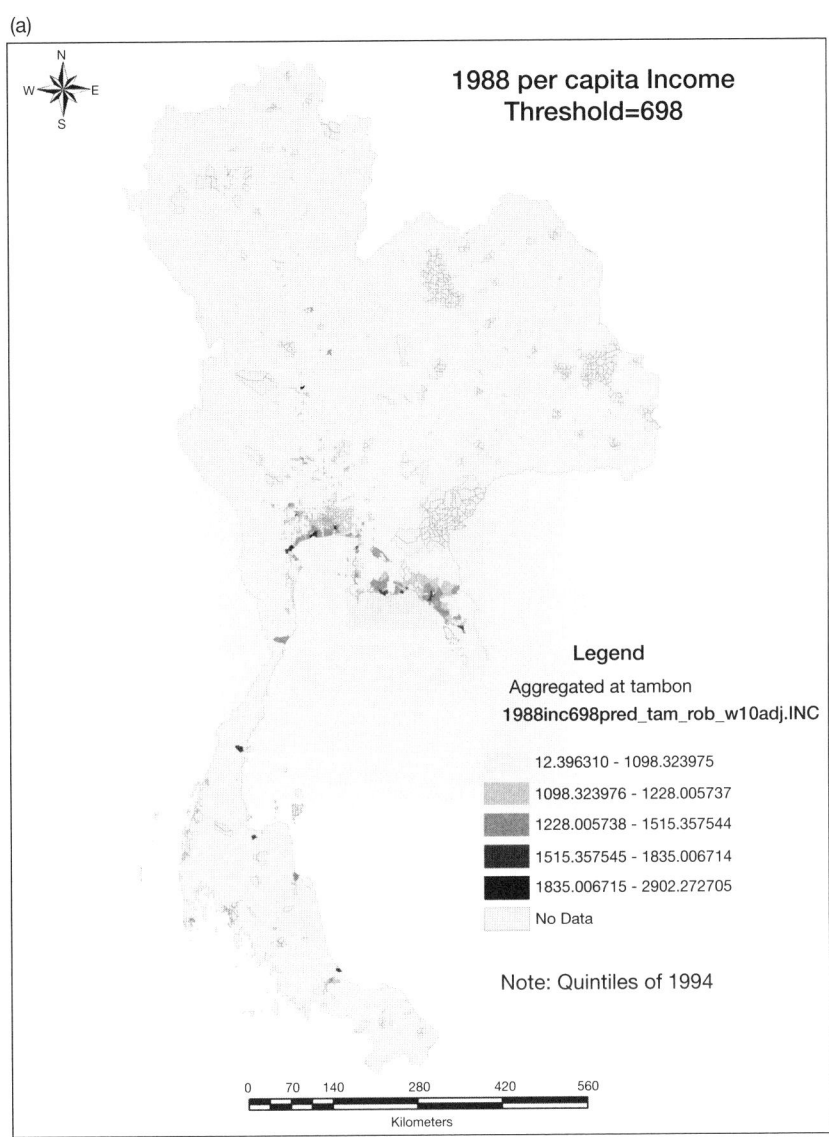

Fig. 3.9(a)–(e). *Per capita income, 1988–96 (See color version at the end of the book).*
Source: Koriyama and Townsend 2008, CDD data.

(b)

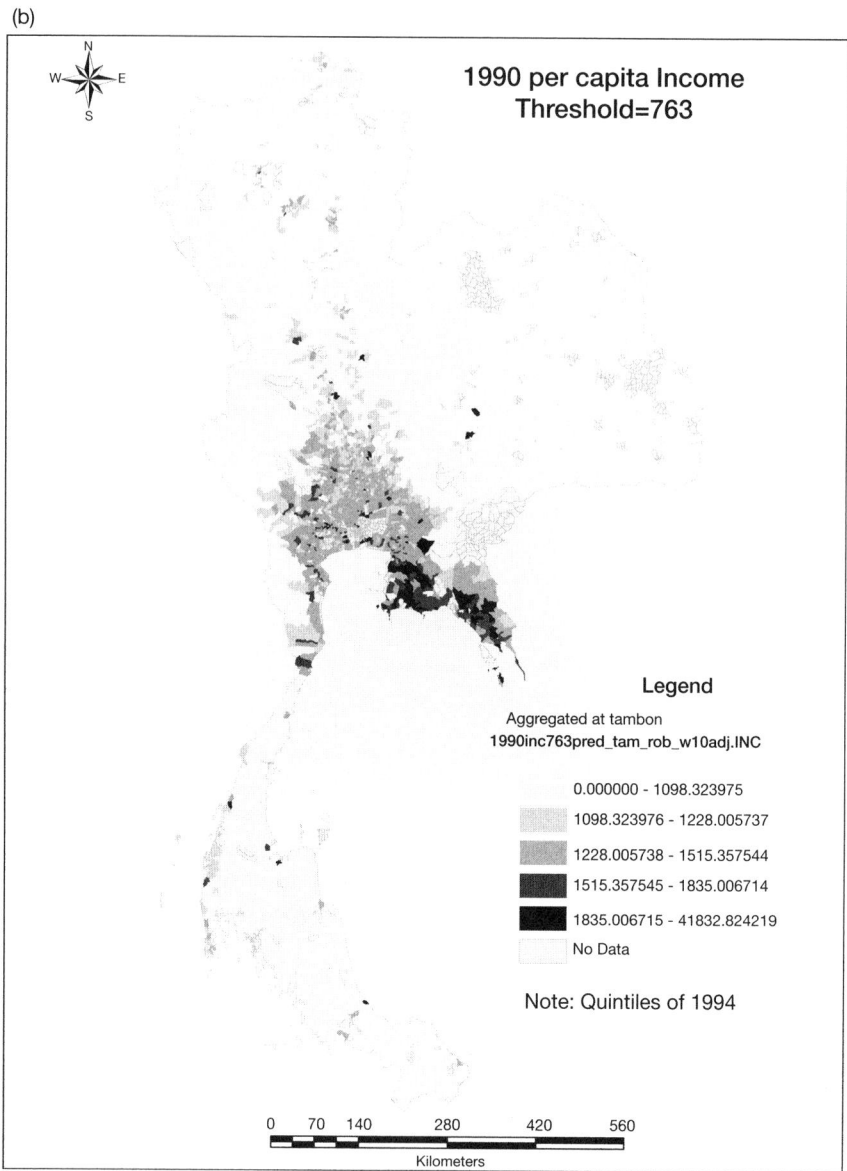

Fig. 3.9(a)–(e). *Continued*

(c)

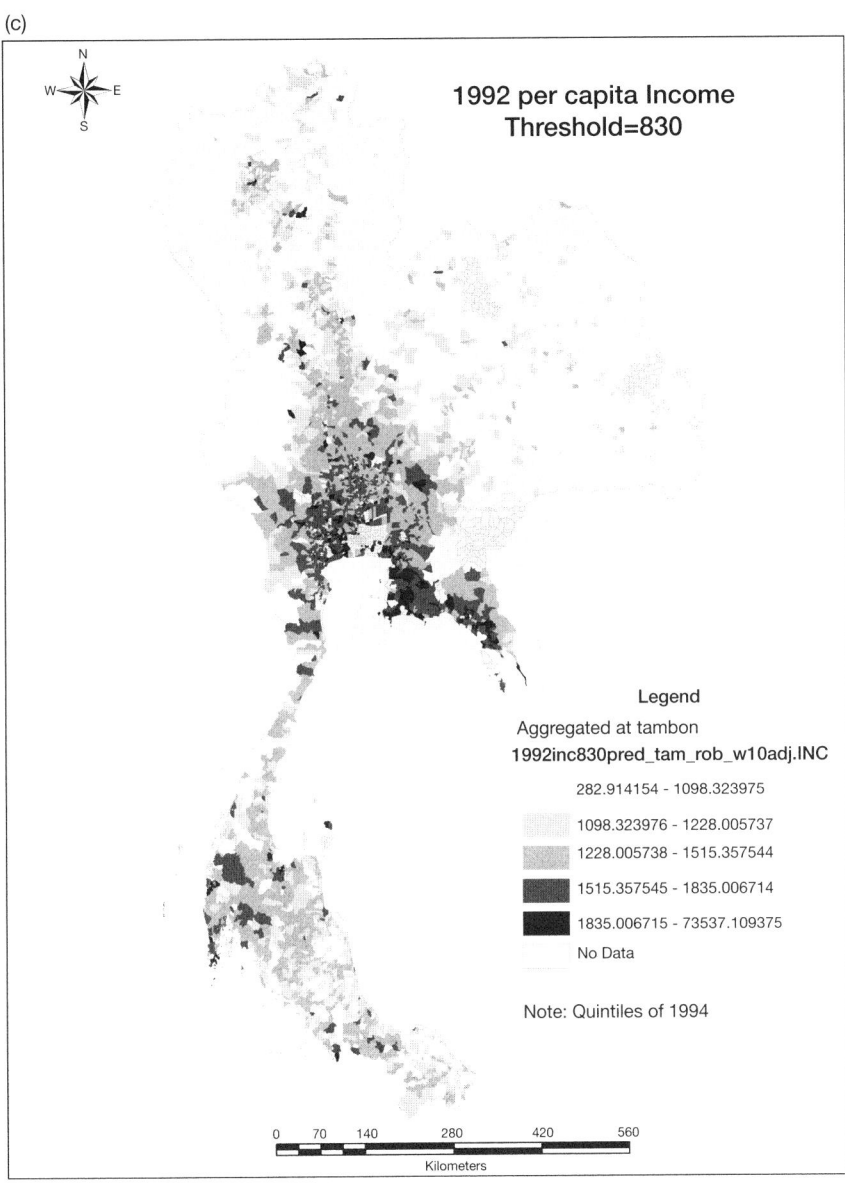

Fig. 3.9(a)–(e). *Continued*

(d)

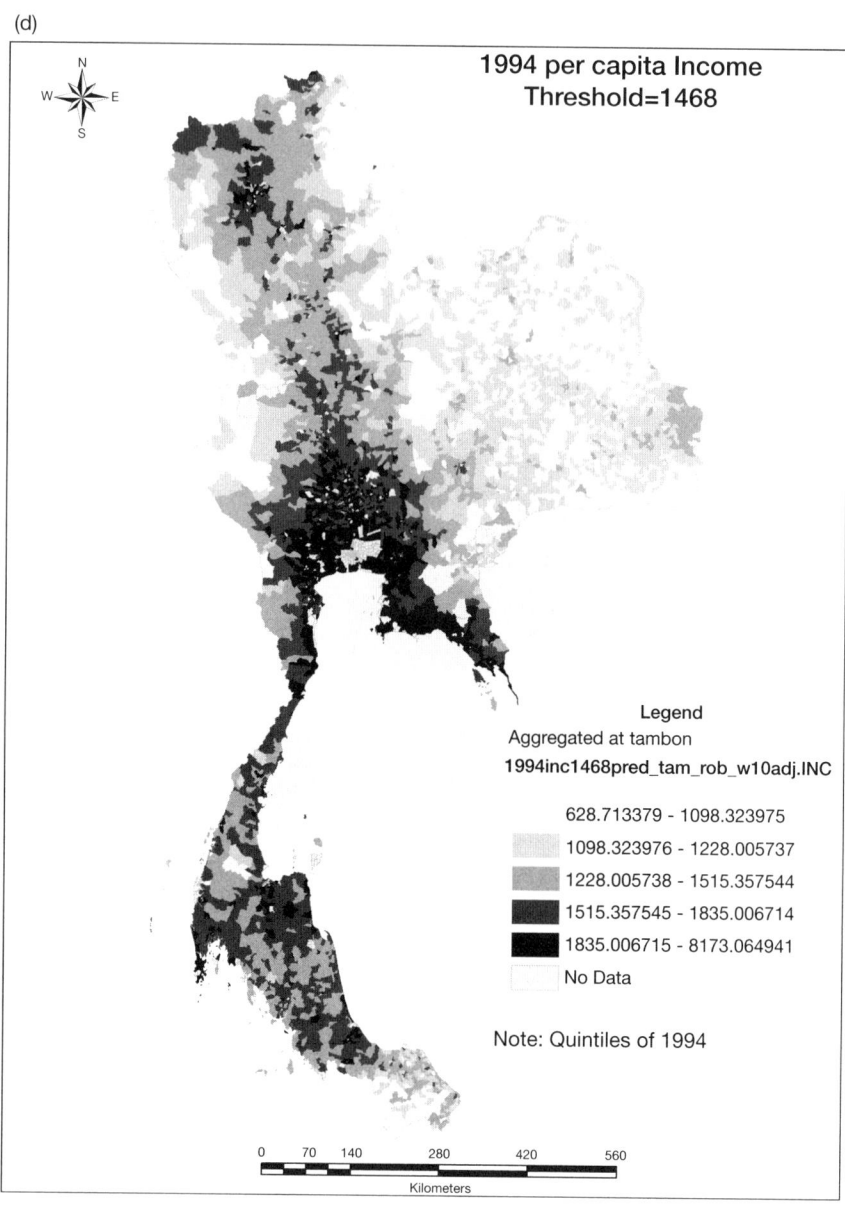

Fig. 3.9(a)–(e). *Continued*

(e)

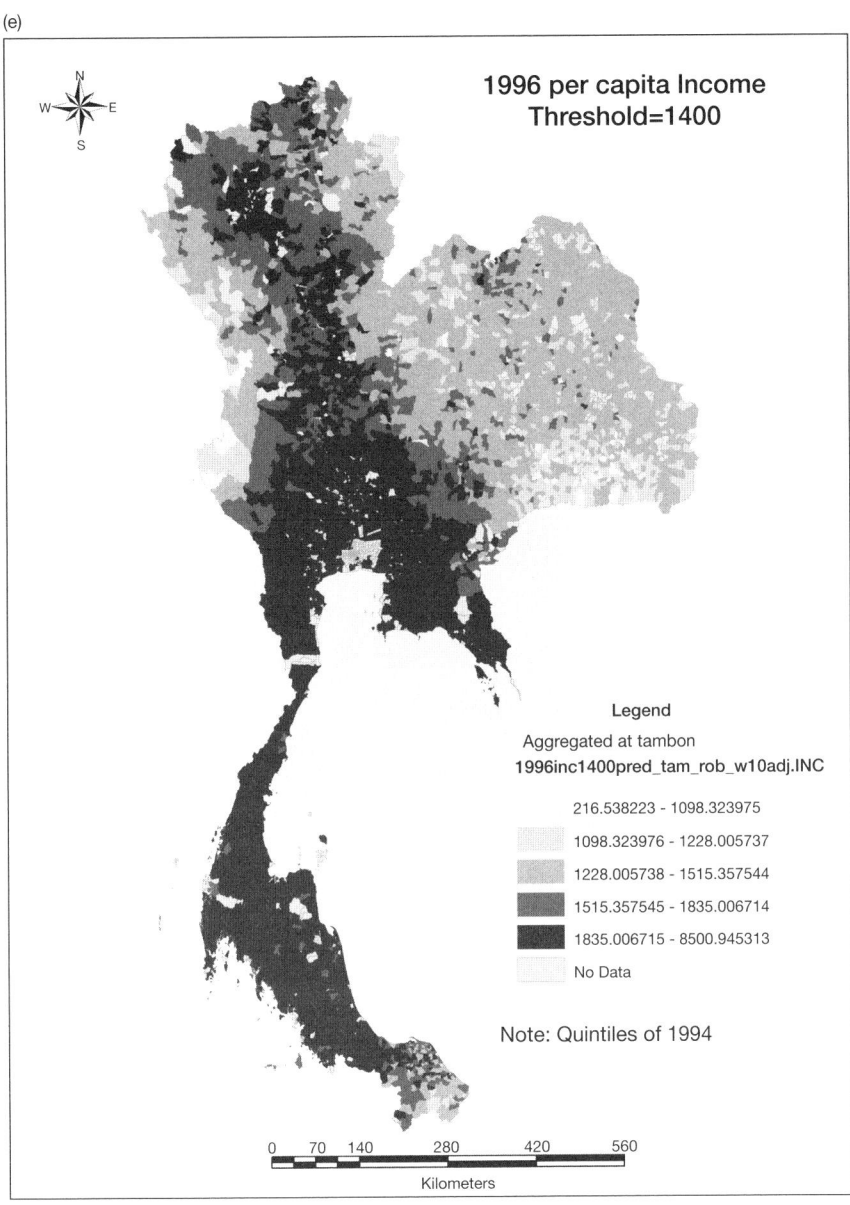

1996 per capita Income
Threshold=1400

Legend
Aggregated at tambon
1996inc1400pred_tam_rob_w10adj.INC

216.538223 - 1098.323975

1098.323976 - 1228.005737

1228.005738 - 1515.357544

1515.357545 - 1835.006714

1835.006715 - 8500.945313

No Data

Note: Quintiles of 1994

0   70   140   280   420   560
Kilometers

Fig. 3.9(a)–(e). *Continued*

(a)

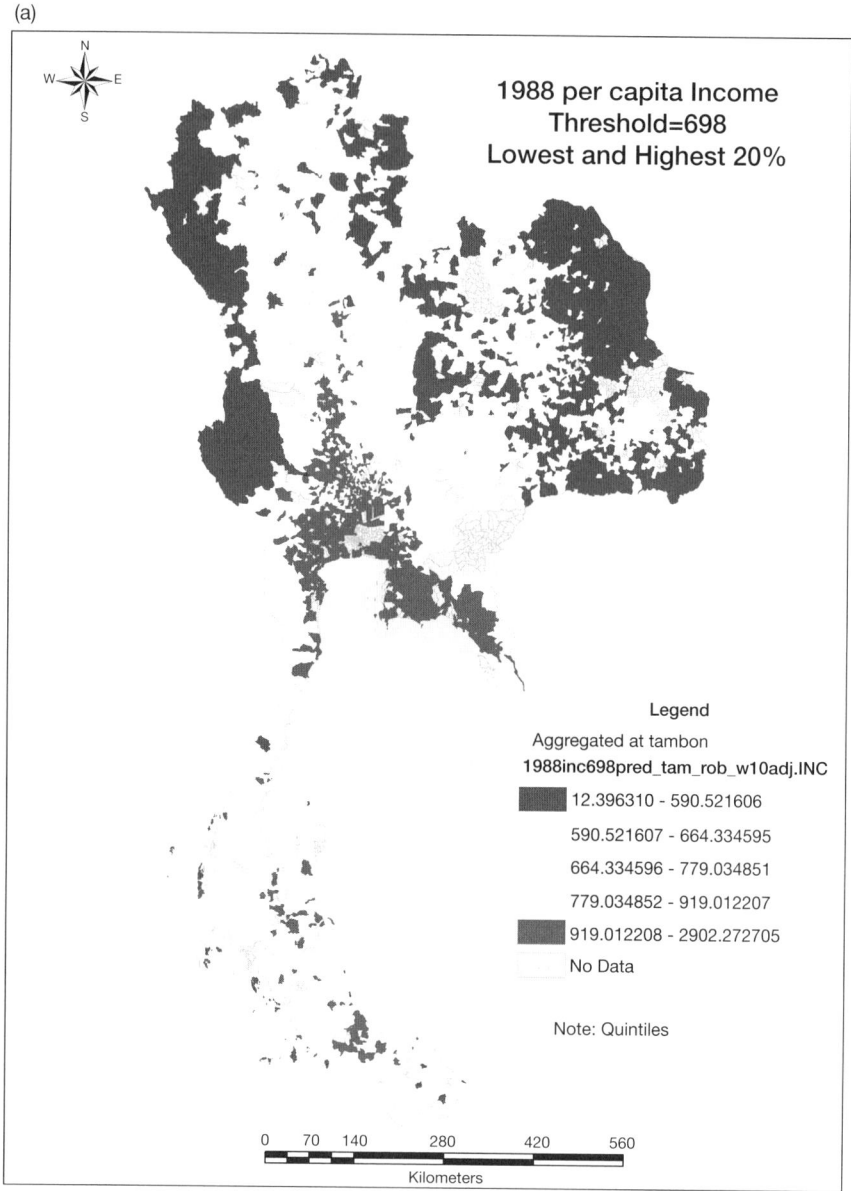

Fig. 3.10(a)–(e). *Wealth index, 1988–96, principal component of 3 assets (lowest 20 per cent) (See color version at the end of the book).*

Source: Koriyama and Townsend 2008.

(b)

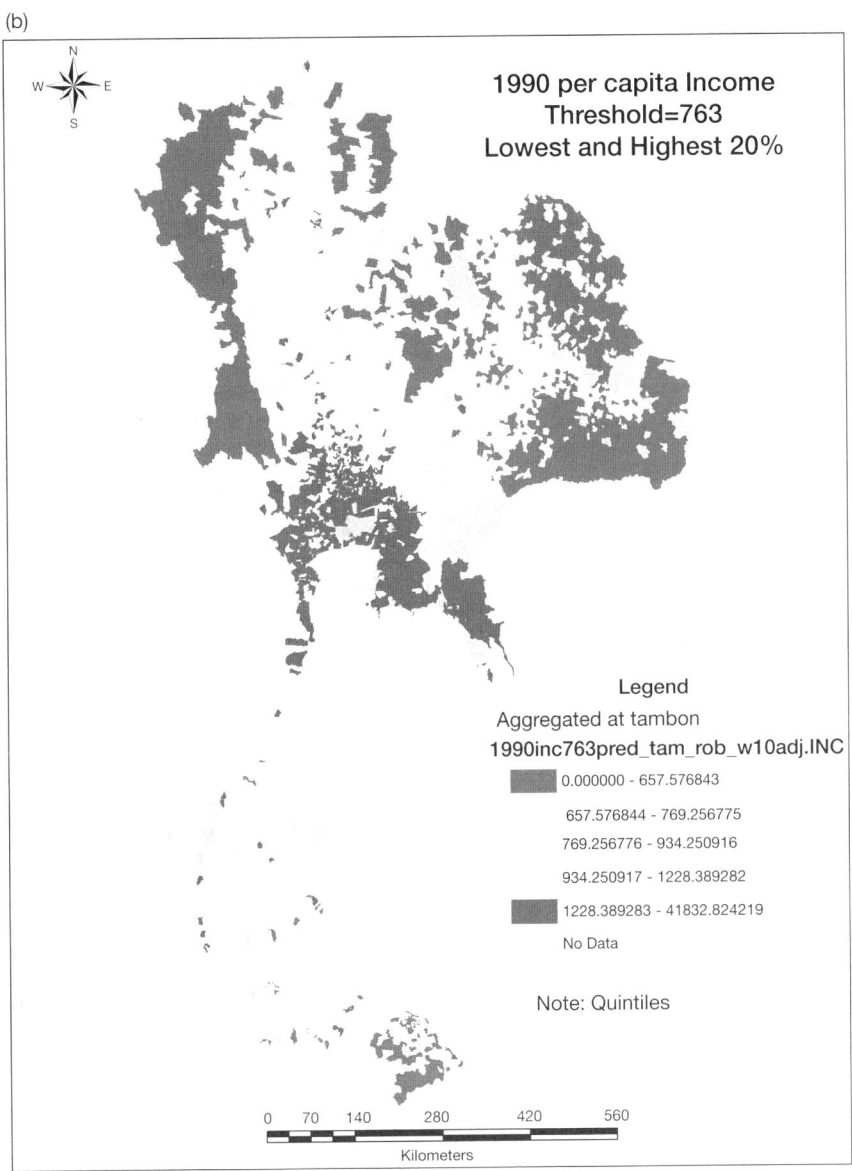

Fig. 3.10(a)–(e). *Continued*

(c)

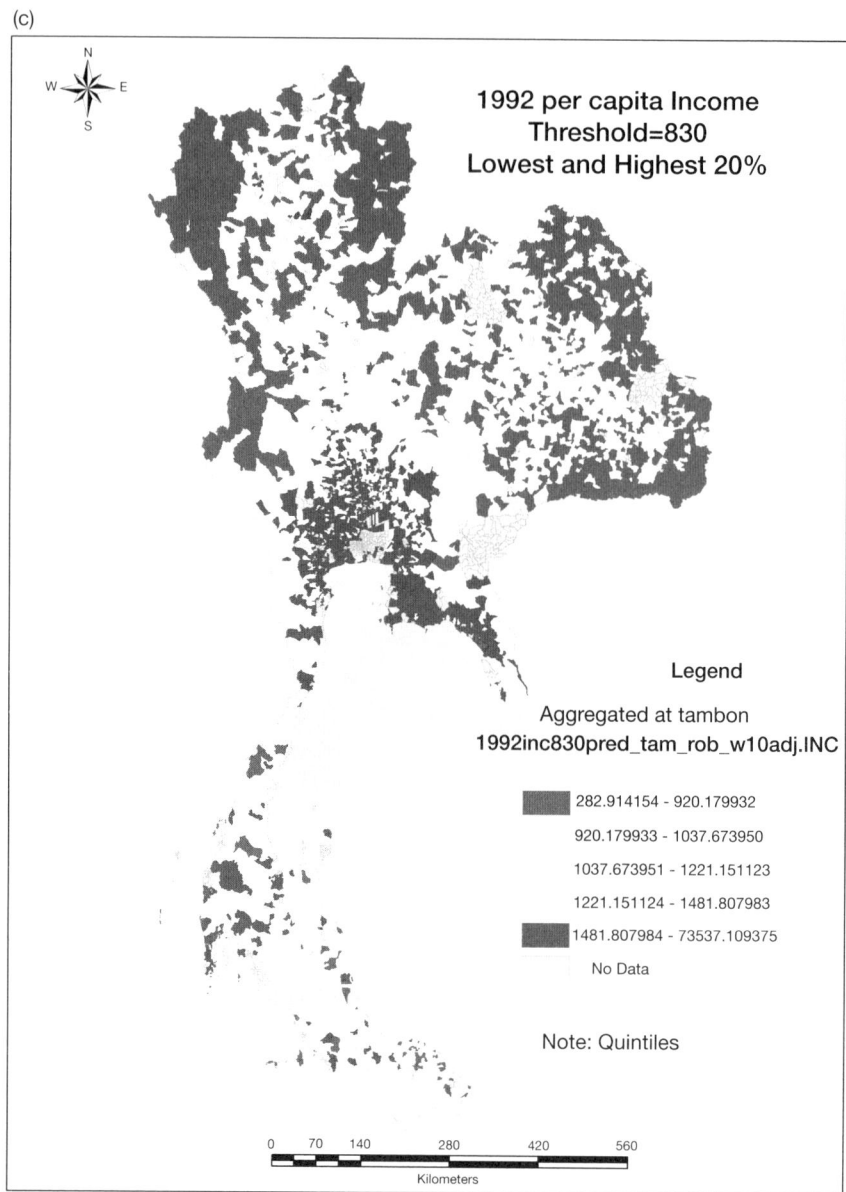

Fig. 3.10(a)–(e). *Continued*

(d)

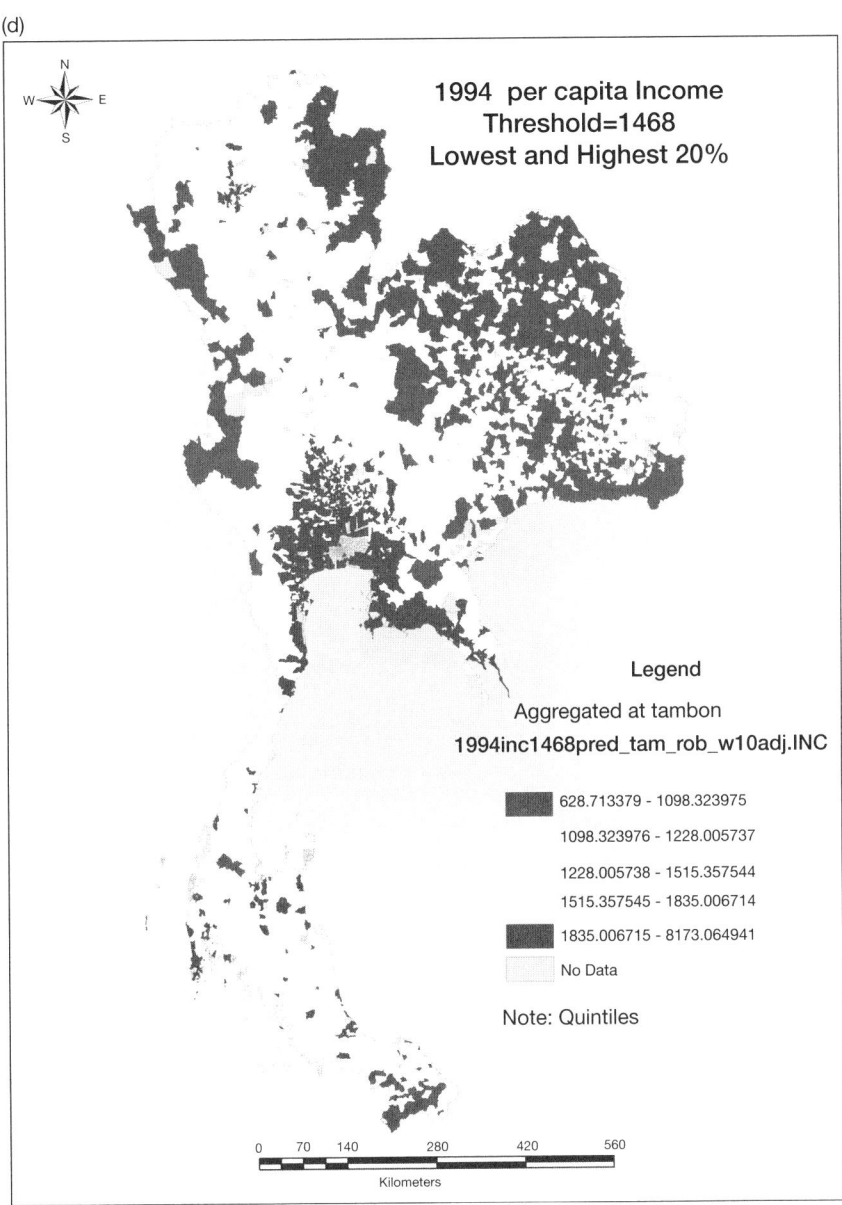

Fig. 3.10(a)–(e). *Continued*

(e)

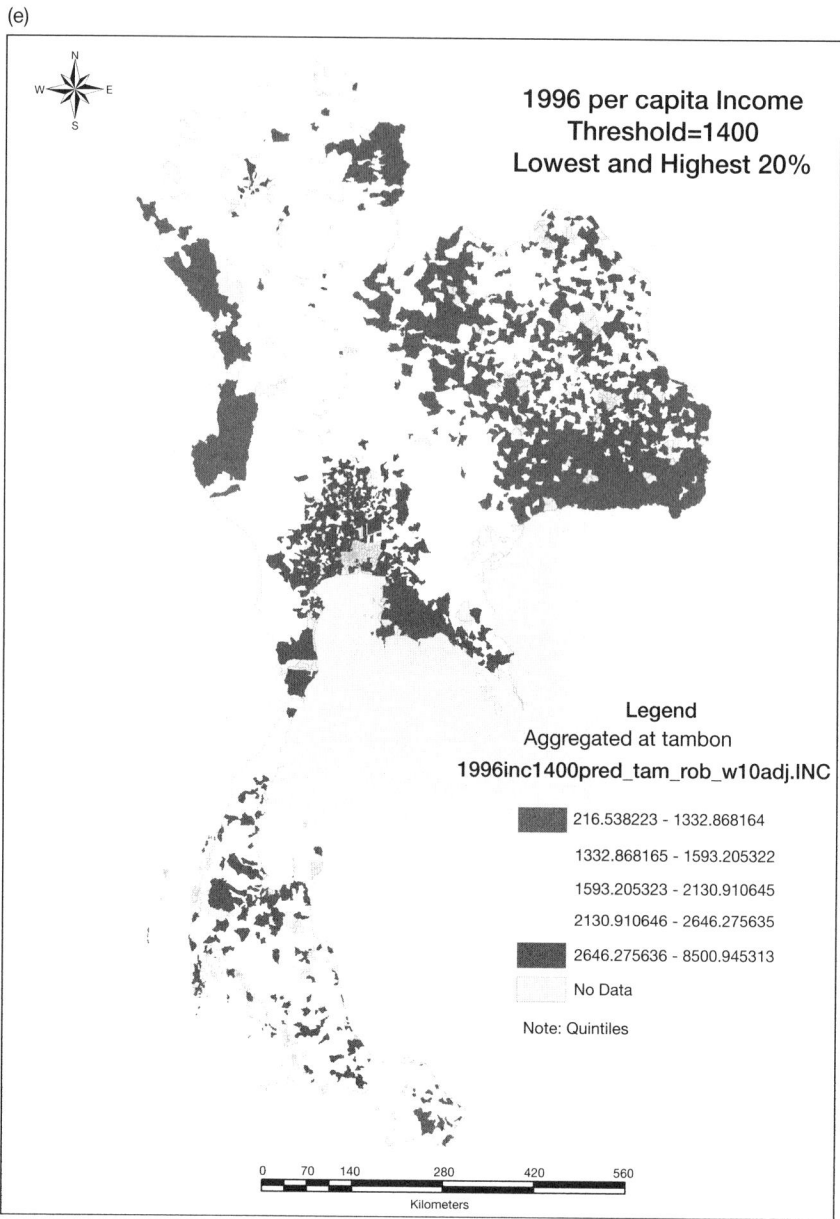

Fig. 3.10(a)–(e). *Continued*

(a)

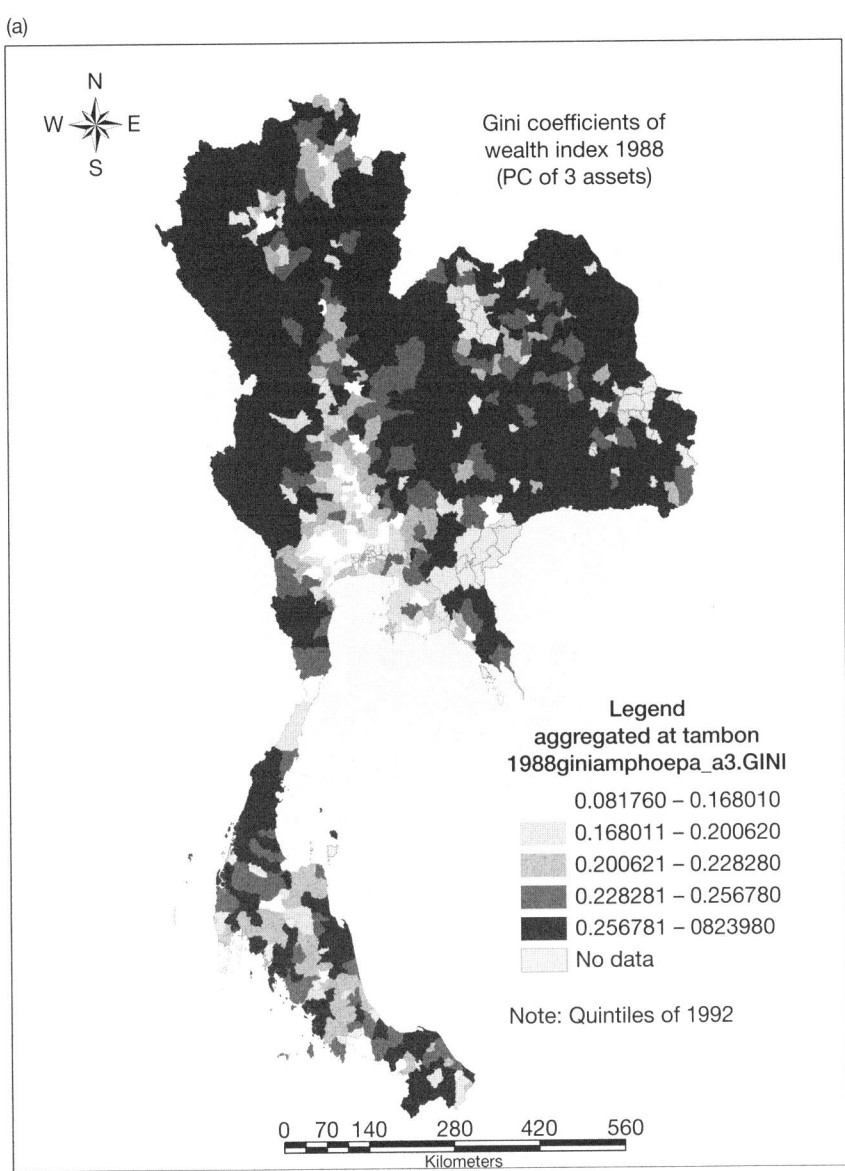

Fig. 3.11(a)–(e). *Gini coefficients of wealth index, 1988–96, principal component of 3 assets (See color version at the end of the book).*

Source: Koriyama and Townsend 2008.

(b)

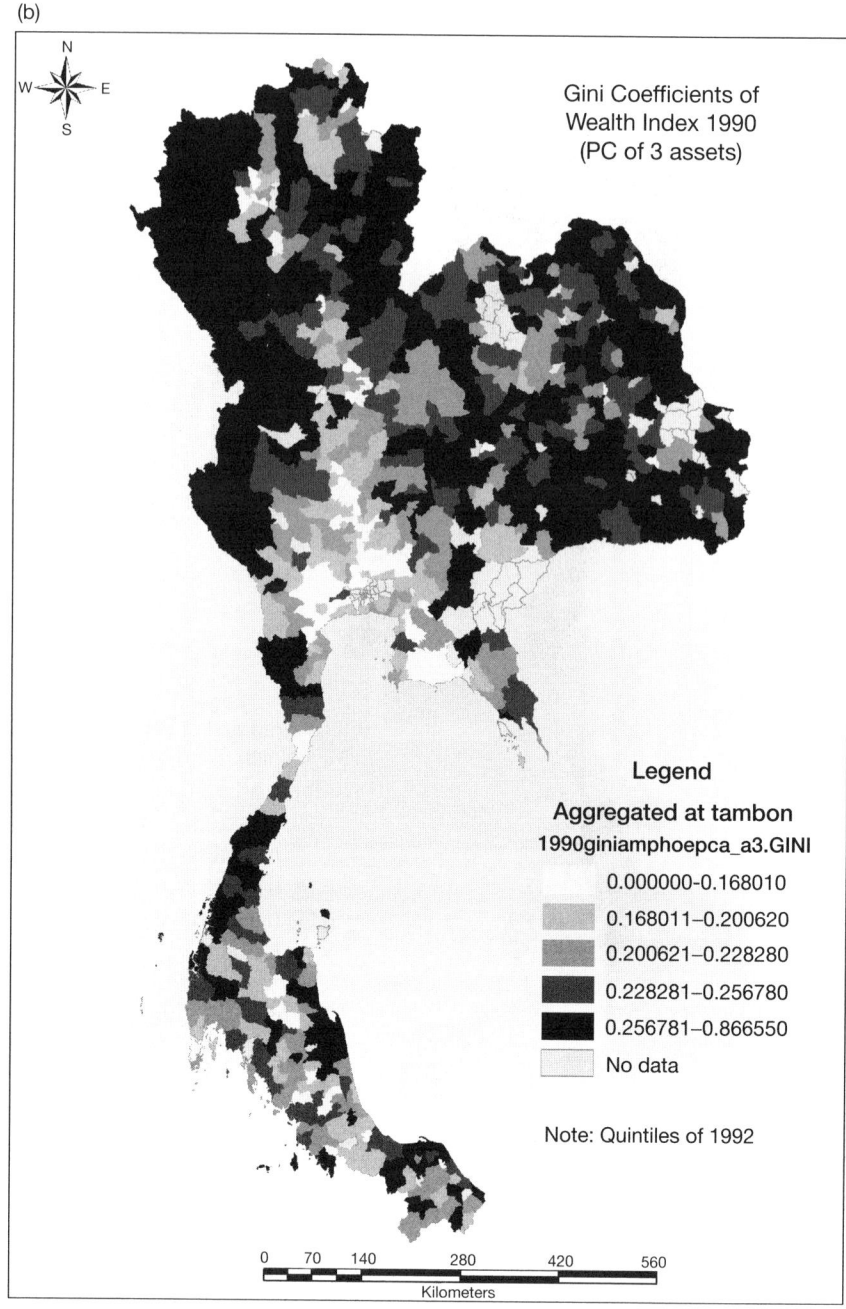

Fig. 3.11(a)–(e). *Continued*

(c)

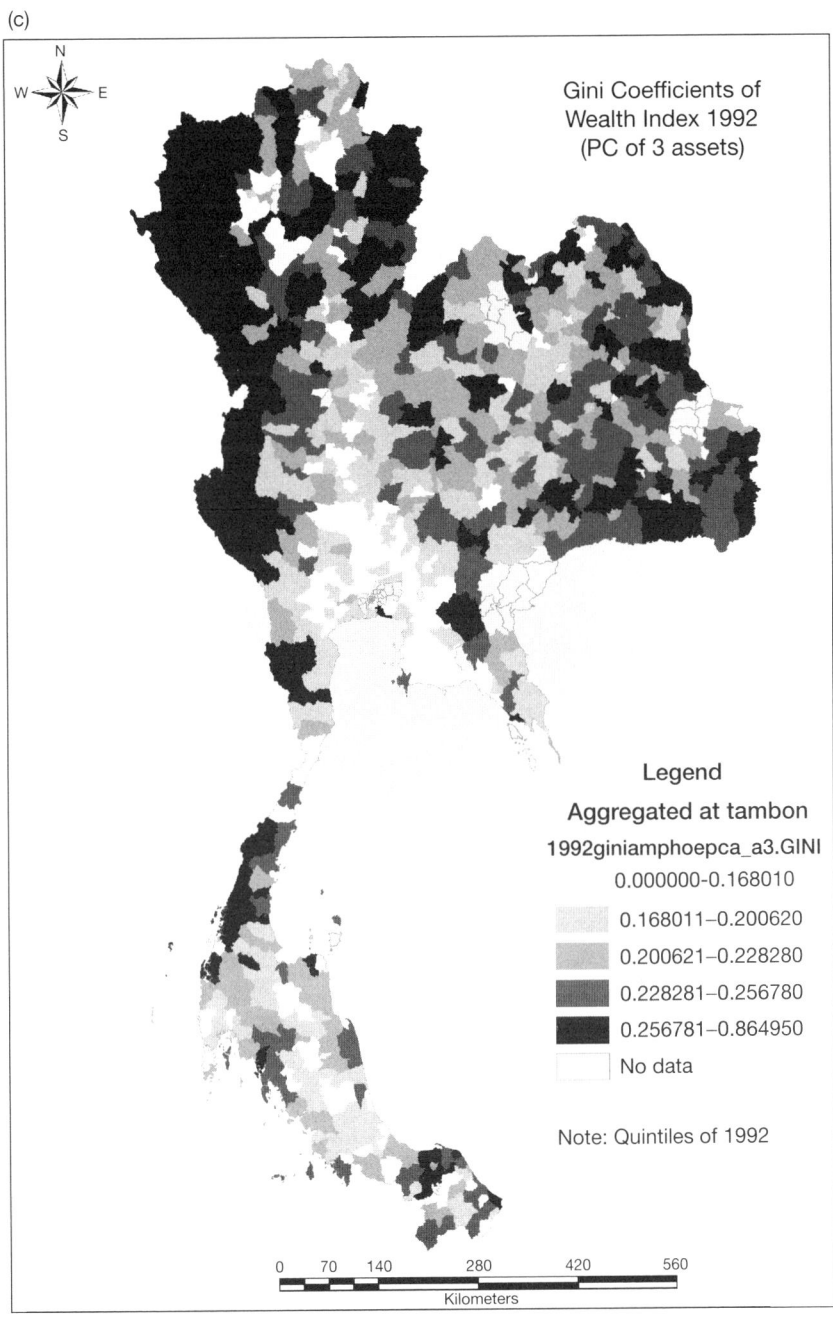

Fig. 3.11(a)–(e). *Continued*

(d)

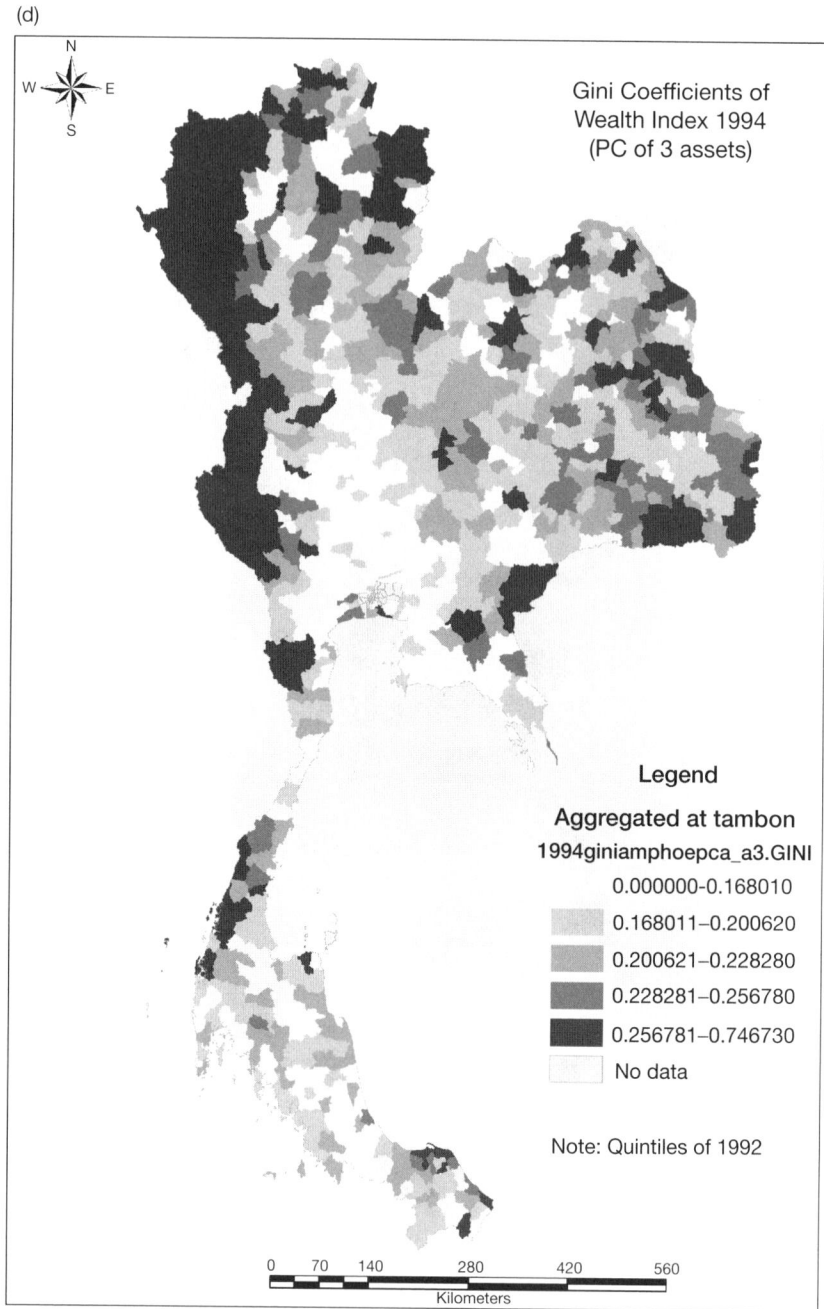

Fig. 3.11(a)–(e). *Continued*

(e)

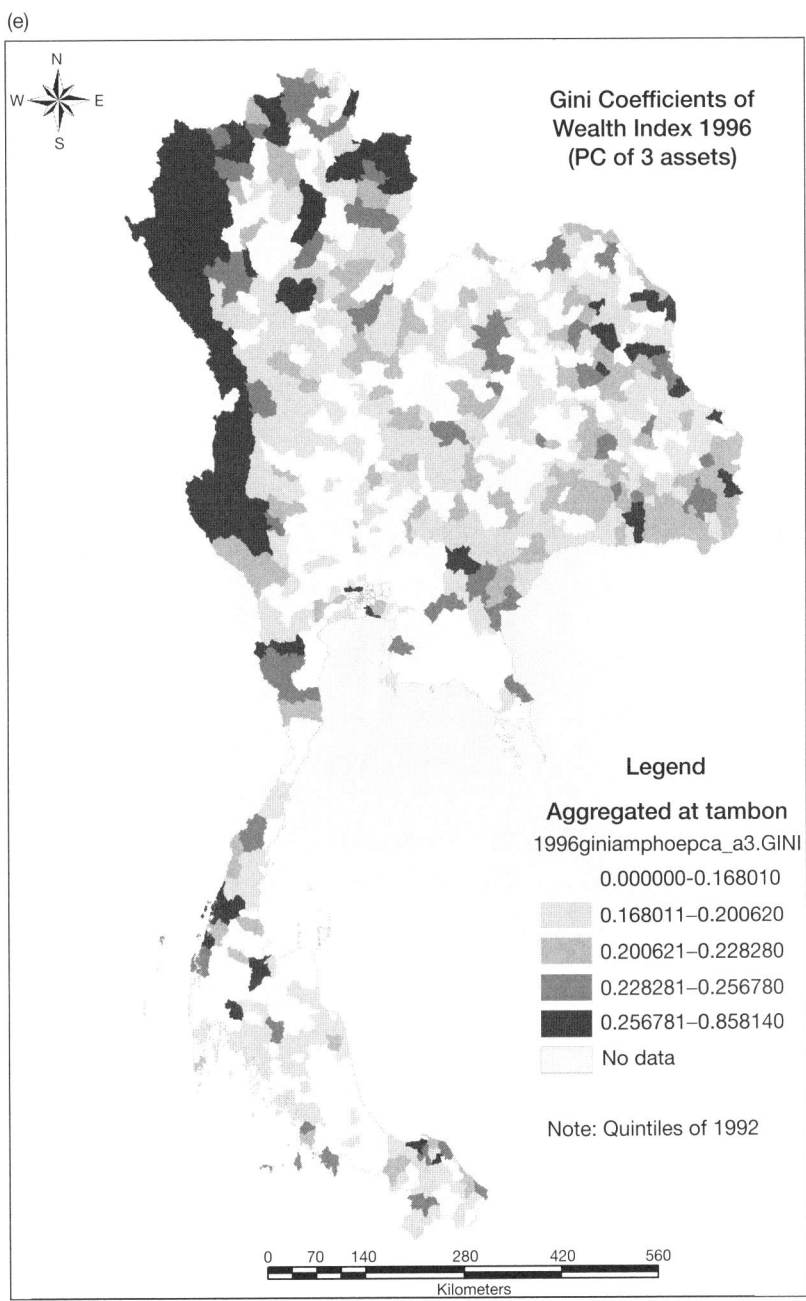

Fig. 3.11(a)–(e). *Continued*

(a)

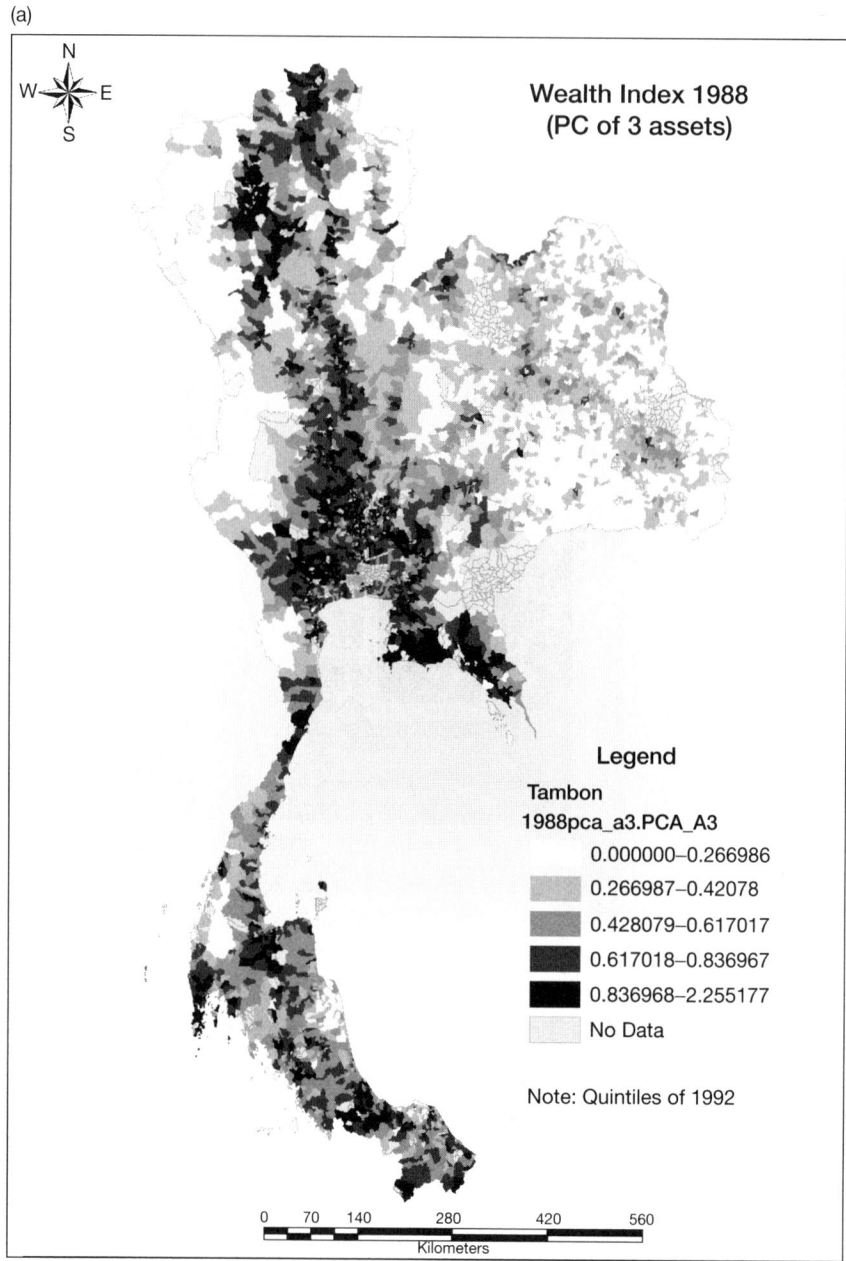

Fig. 3.12(a)–(e). *Wealth index, 1988–96, principal component of 3 assets (See color version at the end of the book).*

Source: Koriyama and Townsend 2008.

(b)

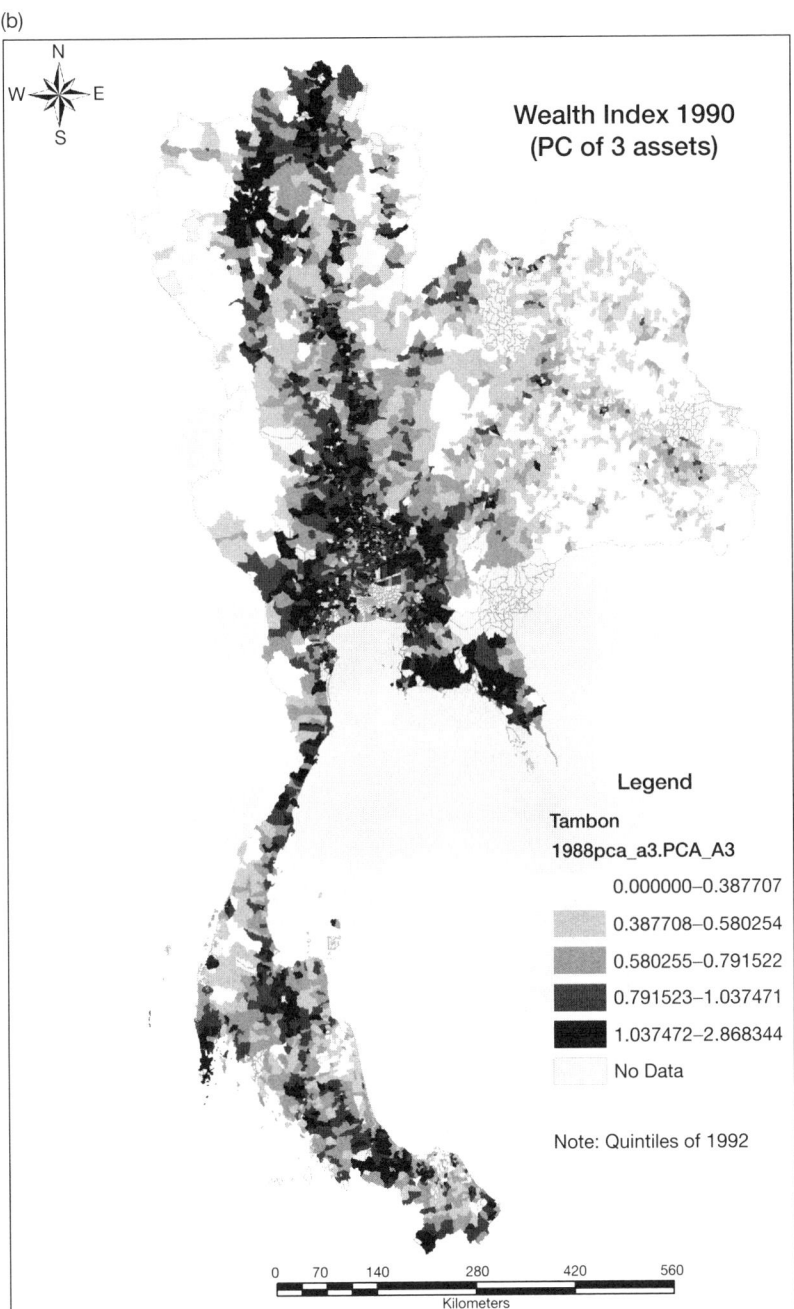

Wealth Index 1990
(PC of 3 assets)

Legend

Tambon

1988pca_a3.PCA_A3

0.000000–0.387707

0.387708–0.580254

0.580255–0.791522

0.791523–1.037471

1.037472–2.868344

No Data

Note: Quintiles of 1992

0   70   140   280   420   560

Kilometers

Fig. 3.12(a)–(e). *Continued*

(c)

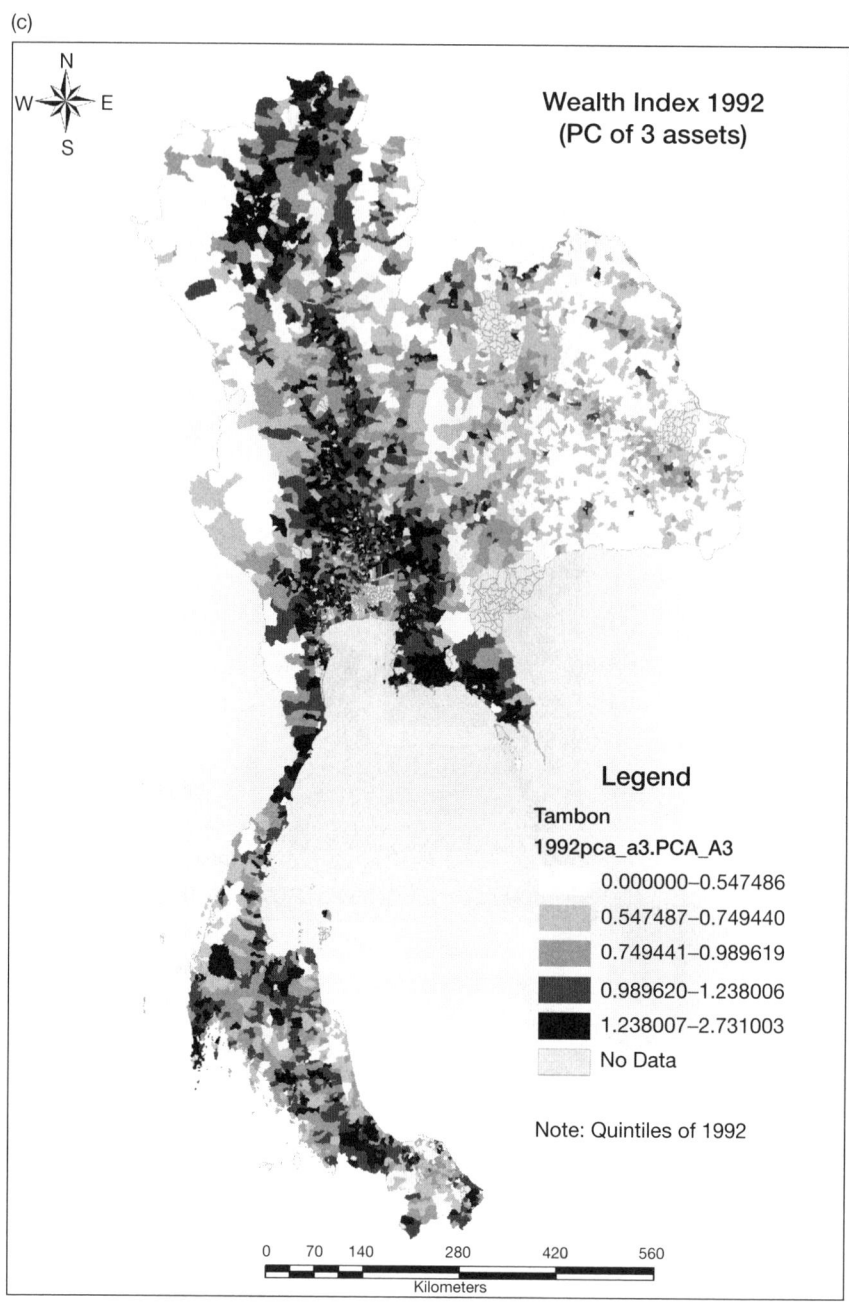

Fig. 3.12(a)–(e). *Continued*

(d)

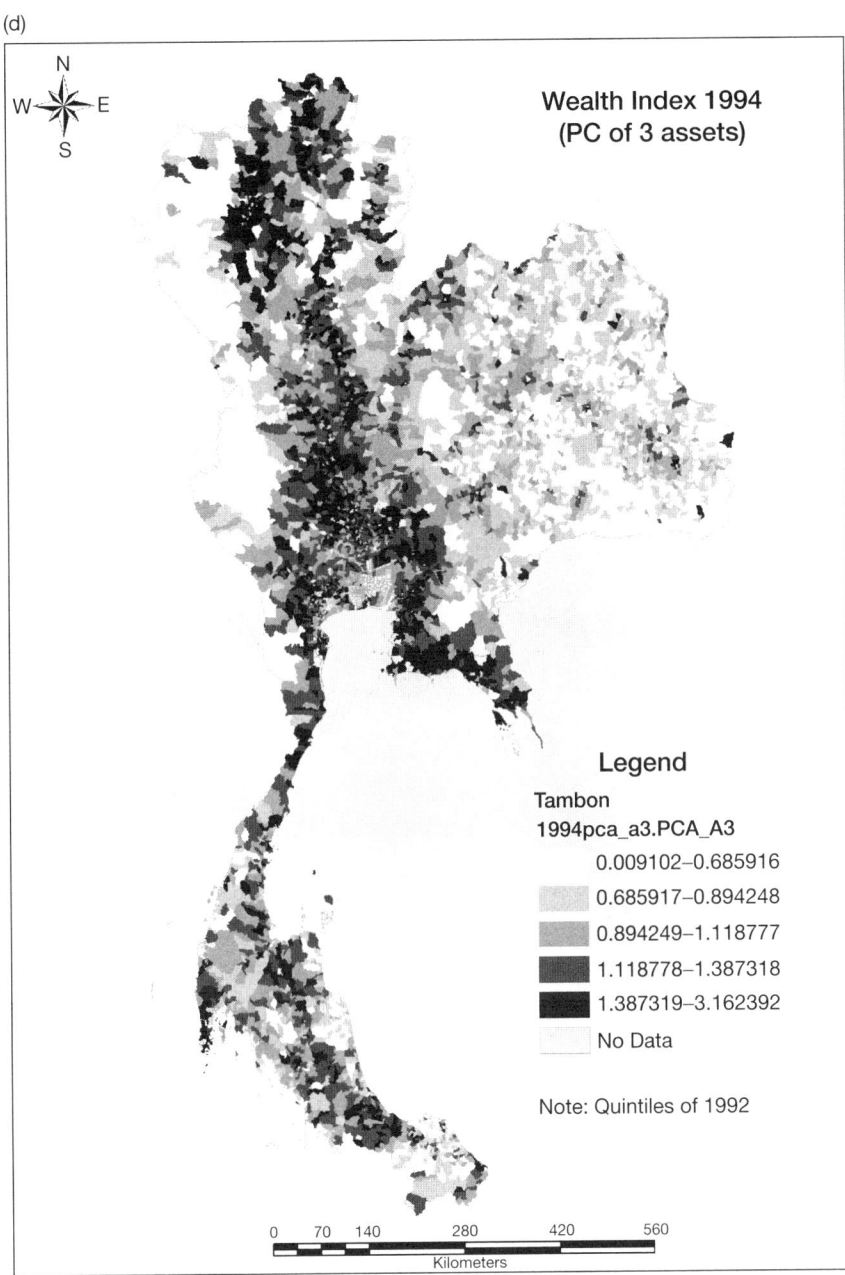

Fig. 3.12(a)–(e). *Continued*

(e)

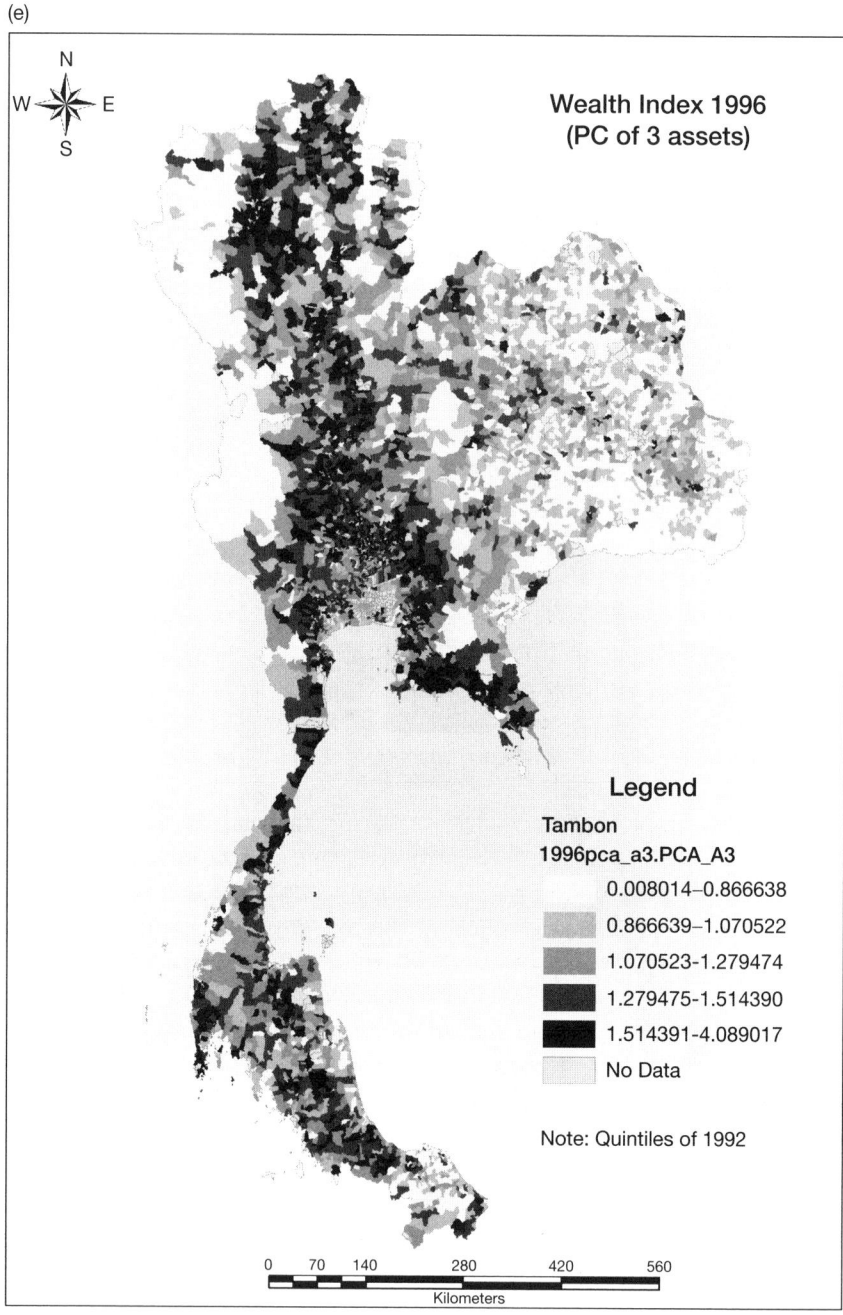

Fig. 3.12(a)–(e). *Continued*

is largely concentrated in and around Bangkok and the Eastern Seaboard, including the corridor stretching North and in parts of the South. But, by 1994, a convergent catch-up effect in household income is evident. Likewise, we can portray the incomes of the wealthiest and poorest tambons (see Figure 3.10(a)–(e)). As is displayed, relative poverty remains concentrated in the periphery of the country.

Finally, income across villages in each amphoe gives a measure of income inequality. Again, inequality increases until about 1992, and then decreases. The contribution of across-amphoe income levels to the total inequality starts to diminish even earlier (see Figures 3.11(a)–(e) and 3.12 (a)–(e)).

3.3. Village Economies: Within Provinces

The same techniques can be used to create a variety of perspectives on village economies. We used a GIS to vectorize the location of villages, amphoe district centers, and roads by type (see Figures 3.13 and 3.14). The GIS supports sophisticated geographic analysis—for example, we can compute minimum travel times between any two points, such as from a village to the intersection of two major highways or to a district center. All locations can be linked to existing secondary data (e.g., village points to the CDD village census data).

Within-province differences in income are striking. For example, the CDD can be used to create an index of wealth, based on principal components analysis of the holdings of TVs, WCs, pickup trucks, and motorcycles. A Moran index as in Figure 3.15 plots the concentration patterns—that is, villages with high wealth surrounded within a 10 km radius by villages of high wealth; low wealth surrounded by low; and the so-called high–low and low–high transition areas. The hot spots are in and around most provincial capitals and just off of highways and rail networks. One can also identify hot-spot spatial regimes, as in Figure 3.16—the north of Sisaket versus the south or the west of Lop Buri versus the east (not shown). There are also hot-spot areas related to agglomeration concentrations, as in Buriram (Figure 3.16). Some hot spots in 1986, such as eastern Lop Buri and Chachoengsao and northern Sisaket seem related to areas of early settlement (see Figure 3.17).

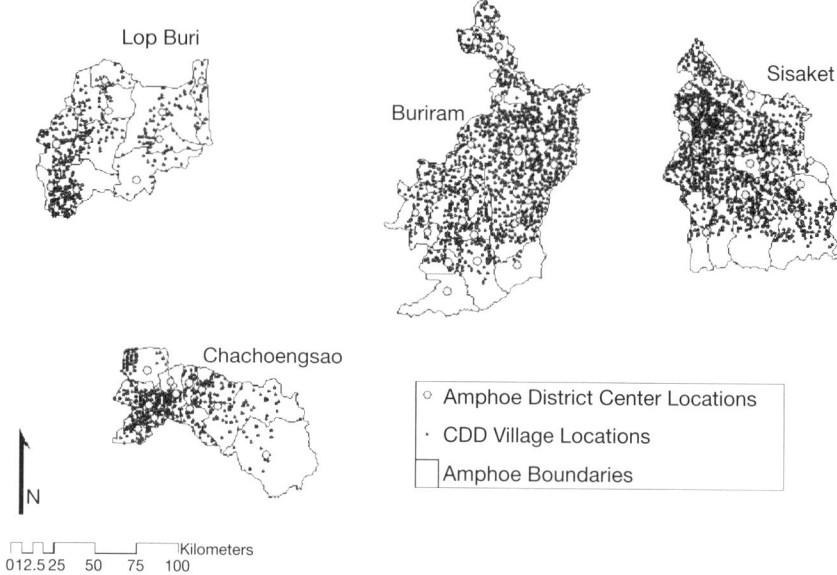

Fig. 3.13. *Community development department village and amphoe district center locations (See color version at the end of the book).*

Sources: Townsend Thai data and SES data.

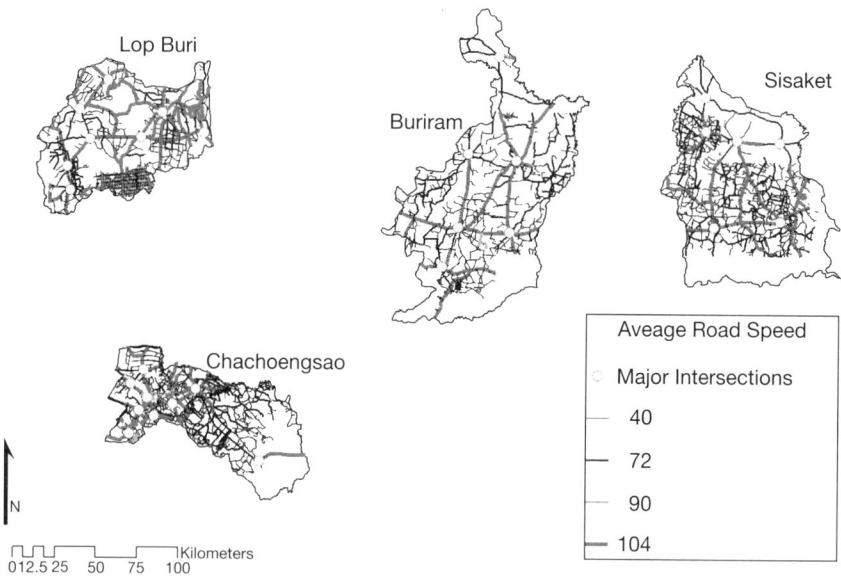

Fig. 3.14. *Road networks and major intersection locations, with average road speeds (See color version at the end of the book).*

Sources: Townsend Thai data and SES data.

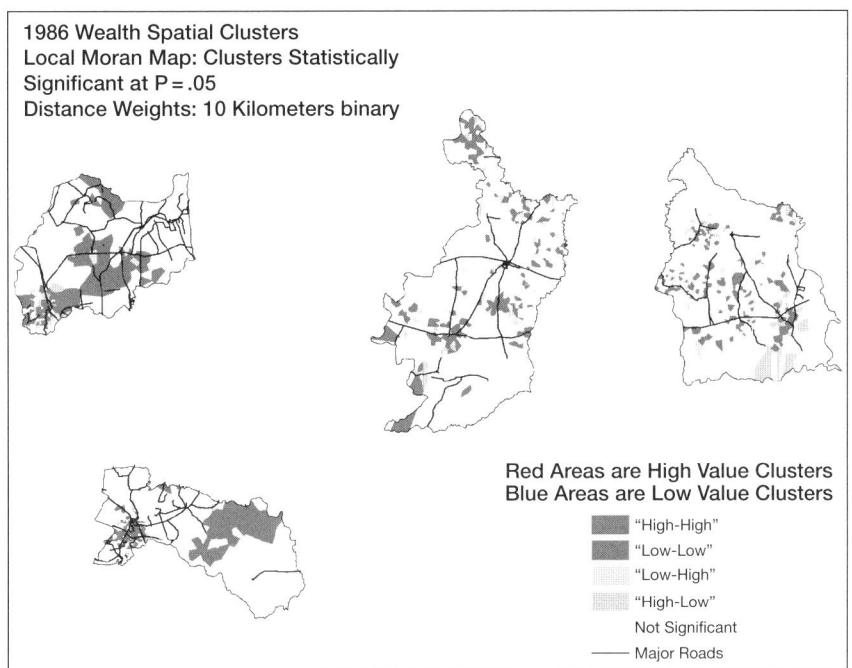

Fig. 3.15. *Wealth index, 1986 (See color version at the end of the book).*

Sources: Townsend Thai data and SES data.

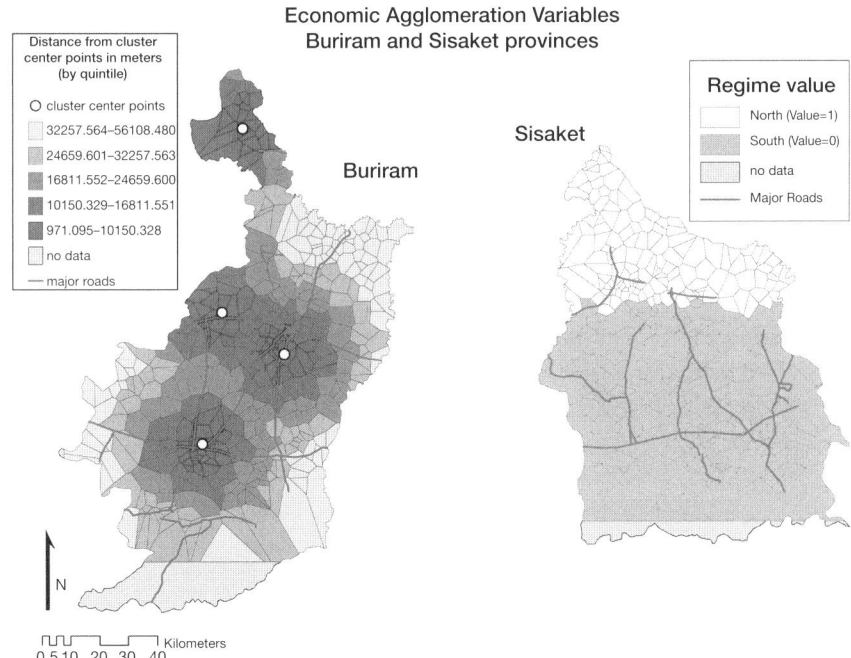

Fig. 3.16. *Buriram and Sisaket spatial heterogeneity variables (See color version at the end of the book).*

Sources: Adapted from Townsend Thai data and SES data.

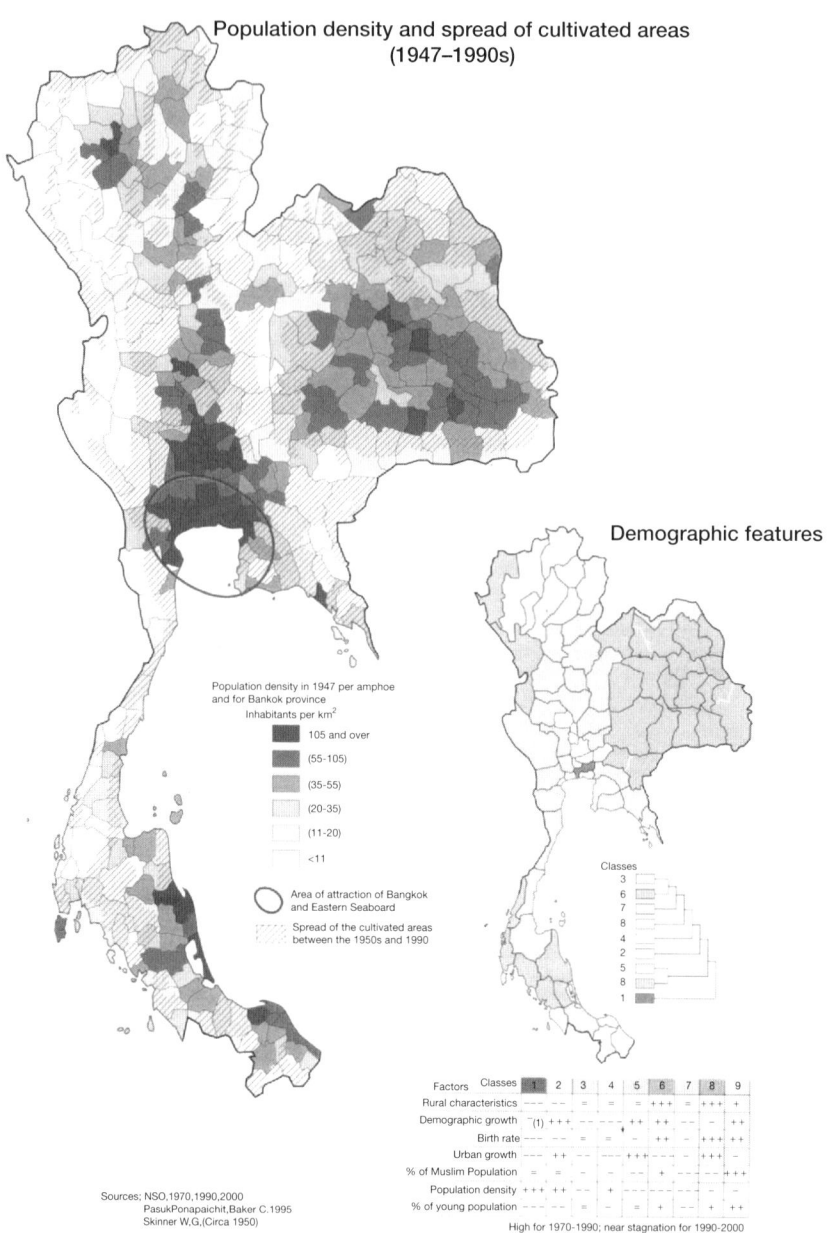

Fig. 3.17. *Population distribution and demographic features (See color version at the end of the book).*

Sources: Kermel-Torres 2004.

Table 3.5(a)–(c). *Aggregate versus idiosyncratic shock: regressions onto time-specific fixed effects*

(a) Regressing household income change onto time-specific fixed effects

Time dummies	All-sample		Central		Northeast	
	coefficient	P-value	coefficient	P-value	coefficient	P-value
			Townsend Thai Data			
1997–8	−1,120.1630	0.016	−2,516.8630	0.002	153.6520	0.754
1998–9	395.8540	0.392	−881.8360	0.269	1,596.7740	0.001
1999–2000	−1,800.5970	0.000	−2,099.4670	0.008	−1,512.0110	0.002
2000–1	603.1380	0.191	753.8640	0.342	459.2180	0.349
R^2	0.0054		0.0084		0.0091	
Prob > F	0.0001		0.0009		0.0003	
Obs	3618		1756		1862	

(b) Regressing household consumption change onto time-specific fixed effects

Time dummies	All-sample		Central		Northeast	
	coefficient	P-value	coefficient	P-value	coefficient	P-value
			Townsend Thai Data			
1997–8	−4,873.3240	0.000	−5,332.8760	0.000	−4,446.5960	0.000
1998–9	363.0010	0.374	1,480.4570	0.016	−694.5060	0.200
1999–2000	−905.690	0.026	−953.2730	0.117	−859.5240	0.114
2000–1	593.106	0.146	1,026.8040	0.091	167.8930	0.758
R^2	0.0382		0.0436		0.0349	
Prob > F	0.0000		0.0000		0.0000	
Obs	3623		1771		1852	

(c) Regressing household investment onto time-specific fixed effects

Time dummies	All-sample		Central		Northeast	
	coefficient	P-value	coefficient	P-value	coefficient	P-value
			Townsend Thai Data			
1997–8	3,860.0840	0.000	4,306.1290	0.000	3,422.4720	0.000
1998–9	−468.1280	0.153	−1,140.9260	0.024	186.3330	0.655
1999–2000	1,580.1150	0.000	1,628.2930	0.001	1,533.4460	0.000
2000–1	827.7850	0.011	780.0820	0.122	874.8860	0.036
R^2	0.0424		0.0443		0.0410	
Prob > F	0.0000		0.0000		0.0000	
Obs	3771		1864		1907	

Source: Alem and Townsend 2006.

3.4. Households in the National Economy: Temporal and Geospatial Variations

It is natural to ask how much of the variation in income at the aggregate, macro level or the regional level is detectable at the micro household level. A simple way to capture common macro shocks is to regress household income change in a panel onto common time effects, $\Delta y_{it} = \theta_t + \epsilon_{it}$ (see Table 3.5(a)–(c)). The 'explained' contribution to overall variance is low, indicating either a large degree of measurement error or little impact on households of what one might have presumed a priori to be a large influence from the macro economy. The signs are as expected—for example, negative in the 1997 crisis and positive in the subsequent recovery—but the orders of magnitude are not. The R^2s for consumption and especially investment are slightly higher, as the theory of risk-sharing below might imply. Stratification by region picks up regional shocks but only slightly higher explained variance.

Similarly, as a check, one can create a synthetic cohort from the cross-sectional SES data. We treat households as in a common cohort if they have the same levels of education and the same occupation type. The latter is what the SES refers to as socio-economic class. For each of the four provinces of the Townsend Thai Survey, there are 7×7 potential cohort groups

Table 3.6. *Creating a pseudo-socio-economic survey panel*

The construction of cohort is as follows (TTP-equivalent)
- Education: 7
    - →1: no formal education
    - →2: elementary (lower)
    - →3: elementary (higher)
    - →4: secondary (lower)
    - →5: secondary (higher)
    - →6: vocational education
    - →7: college and above
- Socio-economic class: 7
    - →1: farm operator, mainly owning land
    - →2: farm operator, mainly renting land
    - →3: entrepreneurs, trade and industry
    - →4: professional, technical and managerial
- Region: 4 (provinces)
    - →1: Lop Buri
    - →2: Chachoengsao (central)
    - →3: Sisaket
    - →4: Buriram (northeast)

Hence the maximum possible combination will be 196 (7*7*4)

Table 3.7. *Importance of idiosyncratic shocks: socio-economic survey data, rural regions*

	1996	1998	1999	2000
All				
Households (number)	1,246	1172	367	1,075
Average size of cell	11	9	5	9
Cohort included (number)	63	63	63	63
Central				
Households (number)	401	359	121	368
Cell/year (number)	50	58	35	59
Average. size of cell	8	6	3	6
Cohort included (number)	25	25	25	25
Northeast				
Households (number)	845	813	246	707
Cell/year (number)	63	67	43	66
Average size of cell	13	12	6	11
Cohort included (number)	38	38	38	38

Implies number of cohort in consecutive years

SES data	All		Central		Northeast	
1996–8	160.5989	0.472	−173.8037	0.350	186.5974	0.454
1998–9	−615.5994	0.007	−245.3791	0.189	−471.1660	0.061
1999–2000	329.4181	0.142	428.1347	0.024	229.2340	0.358
R^2	0.0505		0.0859		0.0264	
Prob > F	0.0186		0.0559		0.1795	
Obs	138		54		75	

Source: Alem and Townsend, unpublished.

(see Table 3.6). For comparability to the Townsend Thai Survey we restrict attention in the SES to those living in villages. In practice, it is not possible to create all cells, and the number of cells with sufficient data is even less. For example, in the comparable Central region in 1996 there are 401 SES rural households, 50 cohorts, with an average cell size of 8 households. The pseudo panel of 1996 and 1998 has 42 common cohort groups.

Limited as it is, regressions on this panel imply that aggregate, common time effects have slightly higher explanatory value, though obviously individual household variation is suppressed. There is some hint that geography matters: explained variance goes up to 0.086 when attention is restricted to the Central region alone (see Table 3.7).

There are other observable sources of heterogeneity that determine income change—for example, occupation helps to predict income, more so than common temporal effects per se, as in equation,

Table 3.8. *Level-change household income regressed on base period income by source*

	Chachoengsao	Lop Buri	Buriram	Sisaket
	Fish*	Fish*	Rentals	Government transfers*
	_Remittances	Government transfers	Financial	Rentals*
	_Government transfers	Remittances	_Remittances	Remittances
1997–8	_Wages*	_Wages*	_Wages*	_Agriculture*
	_Financial	_Agriculture*	_Government transfers	_Wages*
	_Agriculture*	_Financial*	_Agriculture*	_Business*
	_Business*	_Business*	_Business*	_Financial*
	_Rentals*	_Rentals	_Fish	_Fish*
Adjusted R²	.45	.52	.43	.37
	Financial	Government transfers*	Government transfers	Fish*
	Remittances	Remittances	Fish	Rentals*
	_Rentals	Financial	Remittances	Financial
1998–9	_Fish	_Wages*	Financial	_Wages
	_Wages*	_Agriculture*	_Wages*	_Remittances
	_Agriculture*	_Rentals	_Rentals	_Agriculture*
	_Business*	_Business*	_Agriculture*	_Business*
	_Govt transfers	_Fish	_Business*	_Govt transfers
Adjusted R²	.32	.25	.24	.22
	Rentals	Remittances	Rentals*	Fish
	Remittances	Govt transfers	_Wages	Remittances
	_Wages*	_Wages	_Financial	_Wages
1999–2000	_Business*	_Agriculture*	_Agriculture*	_Government transfers
	_Financial	_ Financial	_Remittances*	_Rentals
	_Agriculture*	_Rentals	_Government transfers	_Agriculture*
	_Fish*	_Business*	_Business*	_Business*
	_Government transfers	_Fish	_Fish	_Financial*
Adjusted R²	.27	.29	.25	.27
	Rentals	Business*	Rentals*	Fish
	Fish	Agriculture	Government transfers	Rentals
	Business	Financial	_Remittances	Remittances*
2000–1	Financial	_Wages	_Wages*	Business*
	_Wages*	_Remittances	_Agriculture*	Government transfers
	_Agriculture*	_Rentals	_Business*	_Wages
	_Government transfers	_Fish	_Financial*	_Agriculture*
	_Remittances	_Government transfers	_Fish	_Financial*
Adjusted R²	.14	.08	.16	.13

Notes: _ indicates Negative coefficients, *significant at 10%, coefficients are ranked in descending order. Agriculture: rice, corn, vegetable, or orchard farming and other crops, raising chicken/ducks, or pig/cow/buffalo and other livestock; fish: raising fish or shrimp; wages: wages and salaries; business: rice mill, store, mechanic/repair shop, hair salon/barber, restaurant/noodle shop, trading, and other business; rentals: payments from land or other rentals, roomers/boarders; financial: interest on savings, income-loan repayment, proceeds from ROSCA and dividends; government transfers: government assistance, scholarships or grants and retirement compensation; remittances: remittances from relatives or friends and gifts. Tambon fixed effects are included.

Source: Alem and Townsend 2006.

Table 3.9. *Changes (levels) of real income of households regressed on fraction of income by source, by changwat, including tambon fixed effects*

	Chachoengsao	Lop Buri	Buriram	Sisaket
1997–8	Agriculture Wages Business Financial Rental	Rental Financial * (−) Business *** Wages *** Agriculture	Wages Financial (−) Business *** Agriculture ** Business	Financial Wages (−) Business *** Agriculture Rental
Adjusted R²	0.68	0.92	0.57	0.7
1998–9	Agriculture Financial ** Wages ** Business Rental ** (−)	Wages Business Rental (−) Agriculture	Rental Financial * Wages (−) Business *** Agriculture	Rental Agriculture Wages Business (−) Financial
Adjusted R²	0.34	−0.08	0.56	−0.04
1999–2000	Rental ** Financial (−) Business Wages ** Agriculture	Agriculture Rental Wages Business	Wages Agriculture Business *** Financial * (−) Rental	Financial Wages (−) Business Agriculture Rental
Adjusted R²	0.14	−0.72	0.27	−0.49

Notes: (−) negative coefficients; * significant at 10; coefficients are ranked in descending order.
Source: Socio-economic Survey data.

$$\Delta Y^j_{t,t+1} = \beta D_{t,t+1} + \sum_i \xi_i Y^j_{0,i,t} + \varepsilon^j_{t,t+1}. \qquad (3.3.1)$$

That is, one can regress household j specific income change $\Delta Y^j_{t,t+1}$ onto the amount of income Y^j_t of j from various occupations *i* in the base year *t*, along with common tambon fixed effects $D_{t,t+1}$. Explained variation in Table 3.8 now reaches higher levels (e.g., from 0.08 to 0.52). We can see by the rank ordering of coefficients from high to low that households with wage earnings and those with remittances in the base year suffered lower income change than might have been anticipated in the crisis, while those in business suffered sharp declines. To an extent, the situation is reversed by the end of the panel, in the recovery. Reassuringly, the SES cohort analysis, Table 3.9, yields conclusions similar to the Townsend Thai Panel data.

Evidently, both geography and occupation play a role in income shocks. Using the SES, Townsend (1995) regressed the difference between amphoe (*a*) income growth and the regional (*r*) average income growth onto time difference and community *c* (urban, rural, sanitary district) fixed effects, as in the equation,

Table 3.10. *Region-, year-, and community-type patterns in income and consumption growth rates*

F test for	Different Occupation Groups**								Different Measures of Income and Consumption**			
	All Households		All Farmers		Rice Farmers		Entrepreneurs		All Income	No In Kind	Wages	Food
	Y	C	Y	C	Y	C	Y	C	Y	Y	Y	C
1 N: 75–81												
2 N: 81–6			••									
			••	•	••	•						
3 N: 86–8	••		•		•				••		•	
			••	•	••	•						
4 N	••		•		•				•			
5 NE: 75–81											••	
6 NE: 81–86												
			••	•								
7 NE: 86–88	••	•	•		•		•		••	••	••	••
8 NE	••	••					••		••	••	••	
9 C: 75–81												
10 C: 81–86												
			••	•	••	•						
11 C: 86–88	••	•	•		•				••	••		••
			••	•	••	•						
12 C	••		•		•				••	••		
13 S: 75–81												
14 S: 81–86			••									
15 S: 86–88			••		•		••	•				
16 S			••									
17 B: 75–81			••									
18 B: 81–86												
19 B: 86–88			••									
20 B			••									
21 U: 75–81												
22 U: 81–86												
			••	•		•						
23 U: 86–88			•		•							••
			••	•		•						
24 U			•		•							
25 SD: 75–81												
26 SD: 81–86												
					•							
27 SD: 86–88	••		•		•		••	••	••	••	•	•

Notes: Note that many fixed effects in income disappear in consumption. N = north, C = central, S = south, B = Bangkok, U = urban, SD = sanitary district; Y= year; C = community
•• = significant at 5% level, ¼ significant at 10%
** = significant at C (community types) and Y (years)
[Table 3.4.5. Region, Year, and Community Type Patterns in Income and Consumption Growth Rates. Note that many fixed effects in income disappear in consumption.
Note: N = north, C = central, S = south, B = Bangkok, U = urban, SD = Sanitary District. (**=significant at 5% level, * = significant at 10%) .

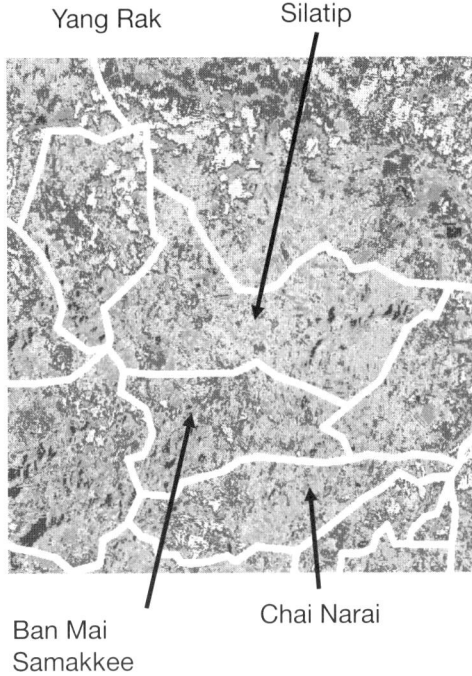

Yang Rak   Silatip

Ban Mai
Samakkee   Chai Narai

Fig. 3.18(a). *Variation in land cover in Lop Buri (See color version at the end of the book).*

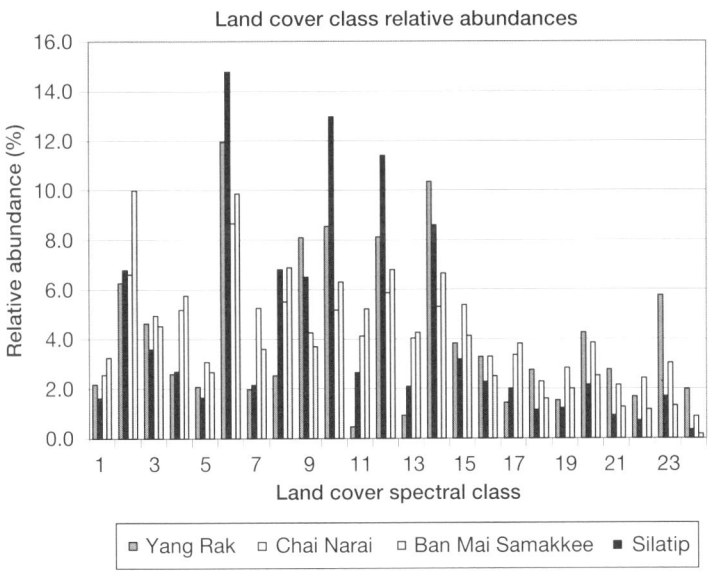

Fig. 3.18(b). *Histogram of land-cover class-relative abundances for 4 tambons in Lop Buri (See color version at the end of the book).*

Sources: Binford, Lee, and Townsend 2004.

$$\frac{\overline{\ln y_t^a} - \overline{\ln y_t^a}}{t - \tau} - \frac{\overline{\overline{\ln y_t^a} - \overline{\ln y_t^a}}}{t - \tau} = \chi \delta_{t,\tau}^{r,c} + \varepsilon_{t,\tau}^{a,r,c} \qquad (3.3.2)$$

where $\frac{\overline{\ln y_t^a} - \overline{\ln y_t^a}}{t - \tau}$ denotes the amphoe average, $\frac{\overline{\overline{\ln y_t^a} - \overline{\ln y_t^a}}}{t - \tau}$ denotes the regional average, and $\delta_{t,\tau}^{r,c}$ denotes the community/time fixed effect. Similarly for consumption,

$$\frac{\overline{\ln c_t^a} - \overline{\ln c_t^a}}{t - \tau} - \frac{\overline{\overline{\ln c_t^a} - \overline{\ln c_t^a}}}{t - \tau} = \theta \delta_{t,\tau}^{r,c} + \varepsilon_{t,\tau}^{a,r,c} \qquad (3.3.3)$$

This was done for each primary occupation group one at a time. There are many statistically significant fixed effects, especially for farmers; less so for rice farmers, and few for entrepreneurs (see Table 3.10 for an example of the results).

Even within amphoes, and smaller areas, there is important variation. For example, land cover varies across tambons. Satellites provide 7-dimensional readings of light reflectance. Each pixel, 30-meters square, can then be grouped into classes, such as the 23 classes depicted in Figure 3.18(a), for

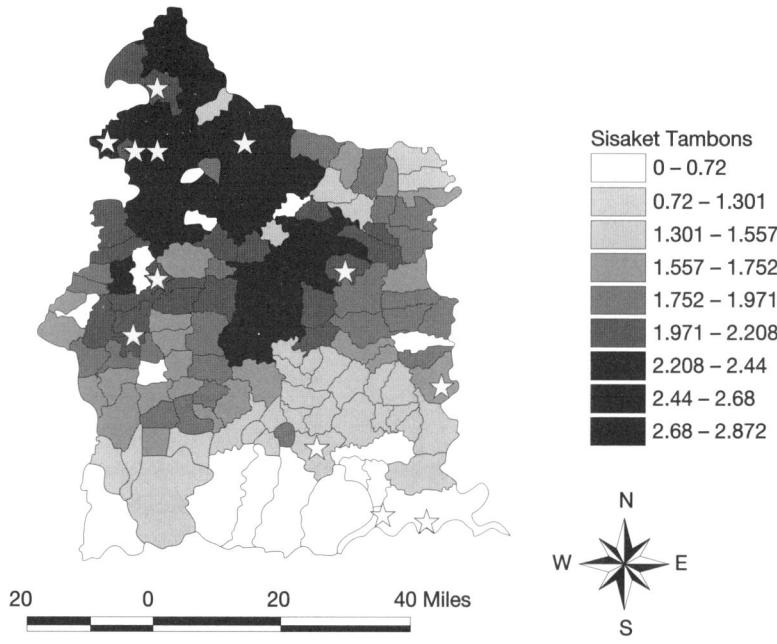

Fig. 3.19(a). *Sisaket tambon detrended correspondence analysis scores (See color version at the end of the book).*

Note: Stars indicate geographic location of sampled Townsend Thai Survey tambons.
Sources: Binlord, Lee, and Townsend 2004.

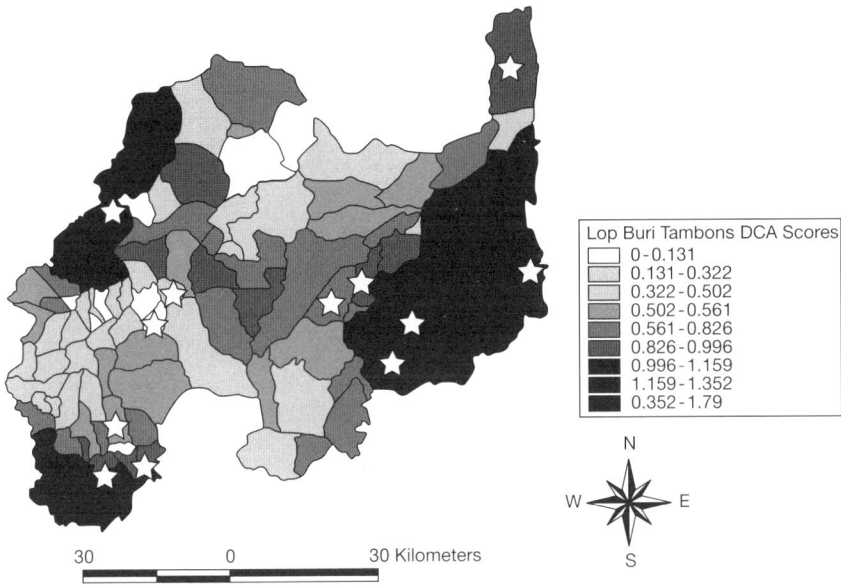

Fig. 3.19(b). *Lop Buri tambon detrended correspondence analysis scores (See color version at the end of the book).*

part of Lop Buri. By construction, there is low variation across pixels within a class, and high variation across pixels across classes. The histogram of abundance of the 23 spectral classes and the associated ground cover imagery for four tambons in Lop Buri are displayed again in Figure 3.18 (a)–(b). A principal components analysis then delivers low-dimensional factors or indices which account for the distribution of land classes within tambons. Two factors explain 70 per cent to 76 per cent of the variation.

The maps in Figure 3.19(a)–(b) reveal the distribution of (the first) factor score, varying from low to high as one moves in Sisaket from south to north. The Townsend Thai data were stratified so that random selection would pick up this salient variation. Subsequent analysis with the annual panel indicates that the likelihood of the timing of good and bad years varies with the factor scores. That is, in a given year, one is likely to have some tambons with high factor scores having high incomes and others with low factor scores having low income, and, much to the point, the reverse in other years. This is ideal for testing of theory of the optimal allocation of risk.

Households respond both in the SES and in the Townsend Thai Surveys to questions about whether the past twelve months constituted a good or bad year and, if bad, the cause. One can see not only the macro, regional,

Table 3.11. *Idiosyncratic shocks*

	Chachoengsao	Lop Buri	Buriram	Sisaket
11 Flood	17 (10.63%)	0	18 (10.71%)	56 (28.72%)
13 Drought	83 (51.88%)	17 (10.76%)	27 (16.07%)	107 (54.87%)
15 Pests	9 (5.63%)	44 (27.85%)	3 (1.79%)	11 (5.64%)
17 Other reason low crop yield	40 (25%)	49 (31.01%)	27 (16.07%)	100 (51.28%)
19 Fire	0	0	0	10 (5.13%)
21 Low price of output	52 (32.5%)	58 (36.71%)	85 (50.6%)	29 (14.87%)
23 High input price	49 (30.63%)	19 (12.03%)	12 (7.14%)	20 (10.26%)
25 Education expenses higher	8 (5%)	3 (1.9%)	2 (1.19%)	6 (3.08%)
27 Need extra money for ceremony	5 (3.13%)	0	0	10 (5.13%)
29 Lower income due to retirement	0	0	0	0
31 High investment costs	12 (7.5%)	12 (7.59%)	5 (2.98%)	13 (6.67%)
33 Expenses due to illness	4 (2.5%)	4 (2.53%)	4 (2.38%)	6 (3.08%)
35 Building expenses higher	0	0	0	4 (2.05%)
37 Death in family	0	0	0	0
39 Worked fewer days	23 (14.38%)	29 (18.35%)	7 (4.17%)	13 (6.67%)
41 Bad year for household business	48 (30%)	10 (6.33%)	10 (5.95%)	14 (7.18%)
43 Lost money from gambling	0	0	0	0
45 Unable to repay debts	4 (2.5%)	3 (1.9%)	10 (5.95%)	8 (4.10%)
Other	8 (5%)	18 (11.39%)	3 (1.79%)	9 (4.62%)

Source: Alem and Townsend 2006.

and occupational shocks but also idiosyncratic shocks such as expenses due to illness. The questions differ on the two survey instruments, and so the response rates and the apparent importance of distinct shocks are not identical. But, the overall picture is consistent: not all households have a bad year at the same time and the cause of bad years varies across the households (see Tables 3.11 and 3.12(a)–(b)).

One can summarize the temporal-, occupational-, geographic-, and household-specific shocks by equations capturing income processes. The well-known permanent income hypothesis postulates that income $y_{i,a,t}$ of household i at age a and date t is as follows,

$$Y_{i,a,t} = Z'_{i,a,t} + P_{i,a,t} + v_{i,a,t}$$
$$P_{i,a,t} = P_{i,a,t-1} + \varepsilon_t$$

, where $v_{i,a,t}$ is MA. (3.3.4)

Table 3.12(a)–(b). *Incomes, 1998 and 1999*

(a) Comparison between 1998 and 1999

	All	Central	Chapchoen	Lop Buri	Northeast	Buriram	Sisaket
			(from 1999 survey)				
Worse than 1998	46	11	10	1	35	27	8
	(35.38)	(22.00)	(31.25)	(5.56)	(43.75)	(47.37)	(34.78)
Better than 1998	12	5	5	0	7	7	0
	(9.23)	(10.00)	(15.63)	(0.00)	(8.75)	(12.28)	(0.00)
Unchanged income	72	34	17	17	38	23	15
	(55.38)	(68.00)	(53.13)	(94.44)	(47.50)	(40.35)	(65.22)
Number of households	130	50	32	18	80	57	23

( ) : ratio of HH, %

(b) Reason for bad income: number and percentage of households 1998–9

	Chachoengsao	Lop Buri	Buriram	Sisaket
Job loss	2 (6.25)	0	5 (8.77)	0
Reduced wages	0	0	8 (14.04)	2 (8.70)
Price/cost of agricultural production increased/ decreased	0	0	3 (5.26)	1 (4.35)
Drought/flood	0	0	1 (1.75)	0
Income from business decreased	5 (15.63)	0	14 (24.56)	3 (13.04)
Declined remittance/ assistance from government	0	0	4 (7.02)	0
Declined remittance/ assistance from person outside household	2 (6.25)	0	2 (3.51)	4 (17.39)
Decreased property income	0	1 (5.56)	1 (1.75)	0
Other	2 (6.25)	1 (5.56)	2 (3.51)	1 (4.35)

Source: Adapted from Townsend Thai Socio-economic Survey 1999, special SES survey.

Table 3.13. *International rubber prices*

	Percentage shock dissipated after 1 year	half-life of shock (months)
Rubber	18	43
Copper	10	80
Timber	43	15
Coffee	10	80
Rainfall	≈ 100	≈ <3

Source: Vickery and Townsend 2004.

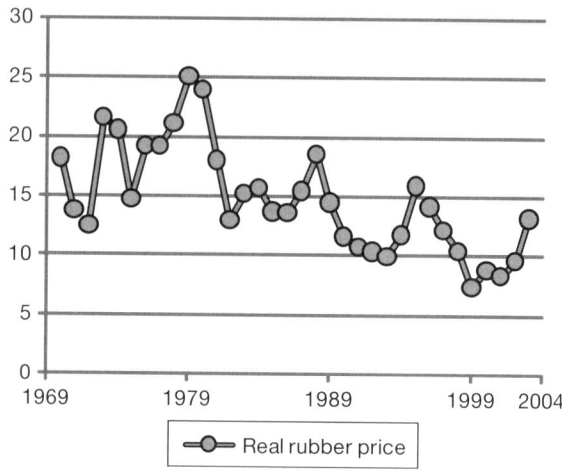

Fig. 3.20. *Real rubber price in 1996 Thai baht/kg (*1/100)*

Thus, $y_{i,a,t}$ is the sum of household characteristics $Z'_{i,a,t}$, occupation or location—for example, a permanent auto-regressive or random walk process $P_{i,a,t}$, with independent shocks $\varepsilon_{t,i}$, and transitory shocks $v_{i,a,t}$ following a moving average process. In some specifications in the literature, such as Paxson (1994),

$$y_{i,t} = \underbrace{y_{i,t}^{P}} + \underbrace{y_{i,t}^{T}} + \varepsilon_{i,t}. \tag{3.3.5}$$

Here, transitory shocks $Y_{i,t}^{T} 2pt\alpha_0 + \alpha X_{i,t}\ \alpha_2 E_{i,t} R_t$ consist of the product of a measure of exposure $E_{i,t}$—for example, land devoted to rice, and some regional/local shock, such as rainfall R_t. Another potential shock could be prices.

International rubber prices follow a slow-moving process. The half-life of a shock, deviation of the price from its long-term average, is 43 months (see Table 3.13). That is, only 18 per cent of the shock is dissipated after one year. In effect, a rubber price has a transitory and highly persistent component.

Evident from Figure 3.20, real prices have drifted downward on average over the sample period, driven in substantial part by increasing competition from synthetic rubber substitutes.

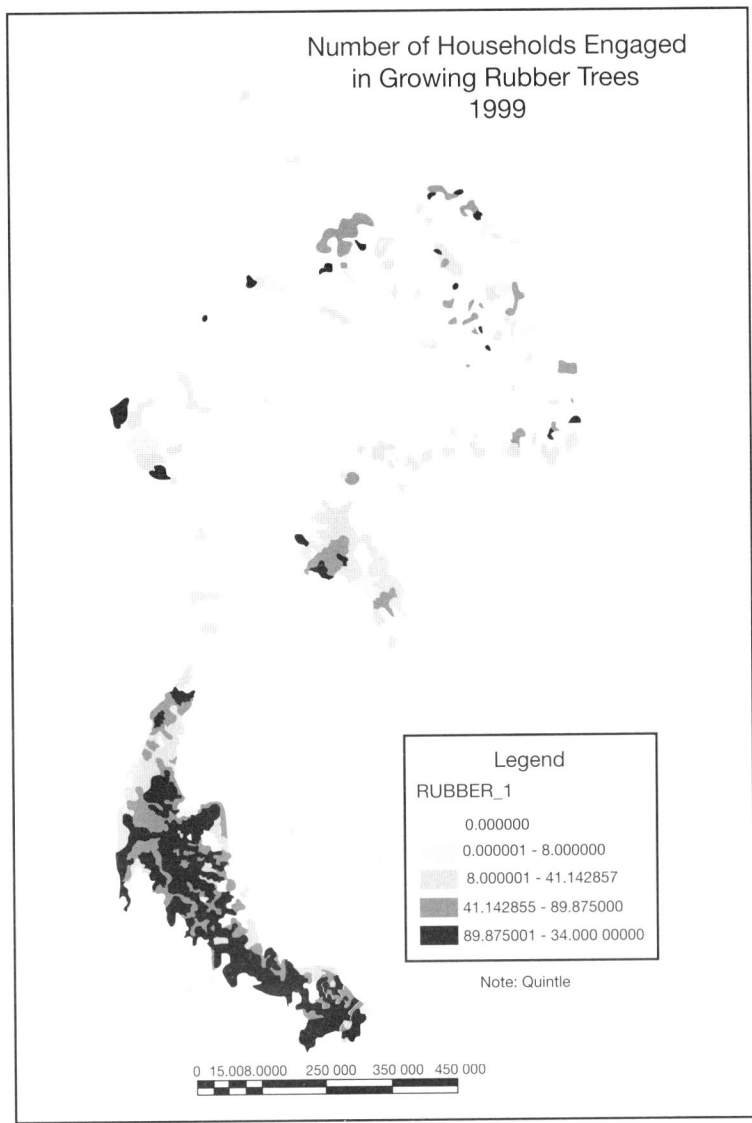

Fig. 3.21. *Number of households engaged in growing rubber trees, 1999 (See color version at the end of the book).*
Source: Townsend and Vickery 2004.

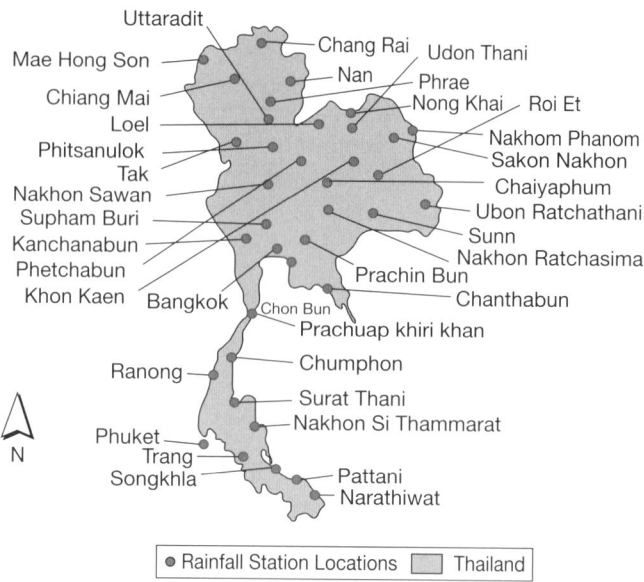

Fig. 3.22. *Thai rainfall station locations for 1951–85 monthly data (55 stations, 37 of them geo-located here)*

Source: National Electronics and Computer Technology Center (NECTEC) and Thailand Environment Institute data.

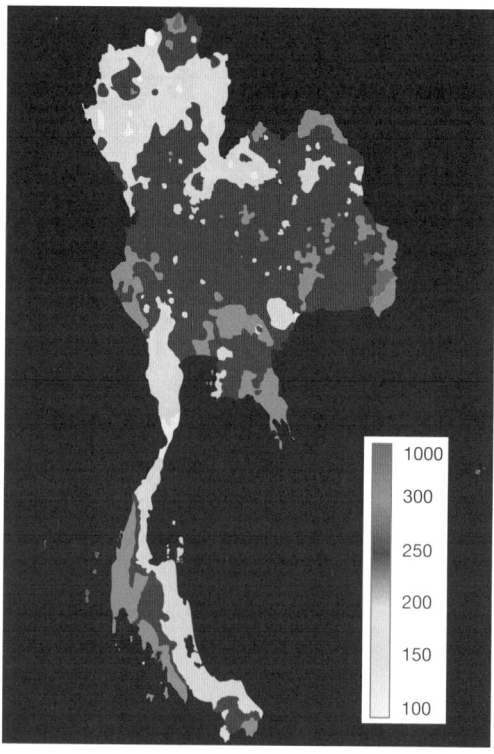

Fig. 3.23. *Average rainfall in Thailand (See color version at the end of the book).*

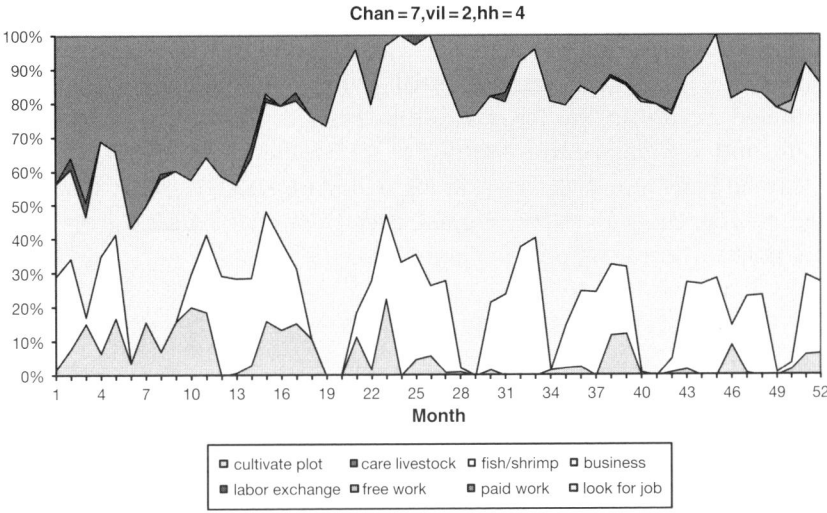

Fig. 3.24. *Within-household diversification*

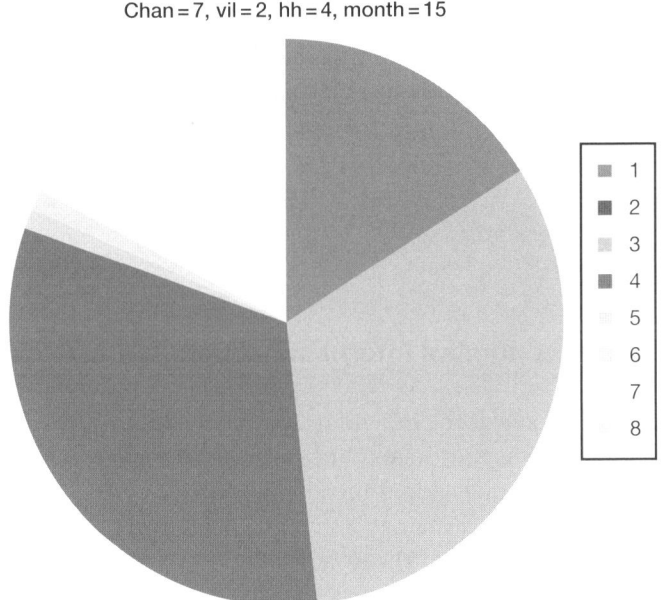

Fig. 3.25. *Within-household diversification*
Source: Townsend Thai data.

Exposure to rubber price shocks is captured in the GIS with the CDD village data measuring the percentage of households in a village growing rubber. Figure 3.21 displays substantial spatial variation, with rubber concentrated mainly in the lower two-thirds of the South, the Eastern Seaboard, and now parts of the Northeast.

Rainfall is measured by Thai stations, with data going back fifty years (see Figure 3.22). One can easily compute average rainfall for each gauge, and interpolate over the map, as in Figure 3.23.

3.5. Individuals in the Household

There is diversity even within households. That is, individuals within a household often work at distinct occupations. From the monthly micro time allocation data we create a measure of the extent of household diversification, or its inverse. Though atypical, the household depicted in the time series and the pie chart below, Figures 3.24 and 3.25, respectively, allocate the time of its members to labor supply, fish/shrimp, business, and agriculture, among other things. The average value of a diversification index is non-trivial. Thus, in a sense, we should treat households as multi-division firms, presumably balancing risk, productivity, and utility of its members. Likewise, a typical household has an individual or individuals that have migrated out of the village, 40 per cent of all individuals have left the village at some time. Migration is a topic we have considered earlier. This is a key aspect of within-household heterogeneity which shows up in national level statistics.

3.6. Mekong Economies: International Comparisons

The plethora of shocks at the individual (or local) level in a given year, and the earlier analysis, suggest there is little relation in a given year between a household's income, or regional income, and macro GDP. But, over the long haul, the impact of sustained and high GDP growth can be dramatic. In an ongoing project, the Northeast of Thailand—its relatively poor area— is compared to neighboring countries in the Mekong basin, specifically Laos, Cambodia, and parts of Vietnam.

Proportion of people living below the consumption-based poverty line

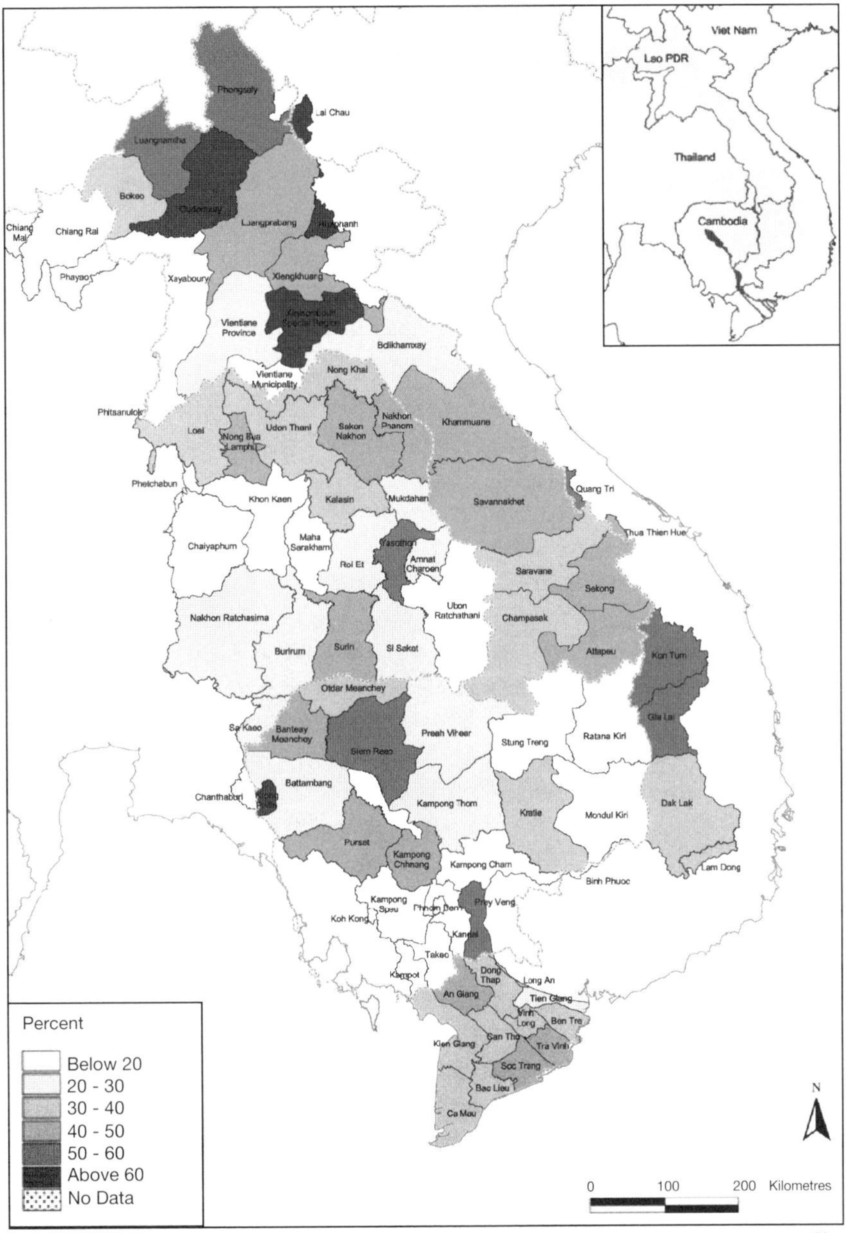

Fig. 3.26. *Proportion of people living below the consumption-based poverty line (See color version at the end of the book).*

Source: Hook, Novak, and Johnston 2003.

Proportion of children underweight for age

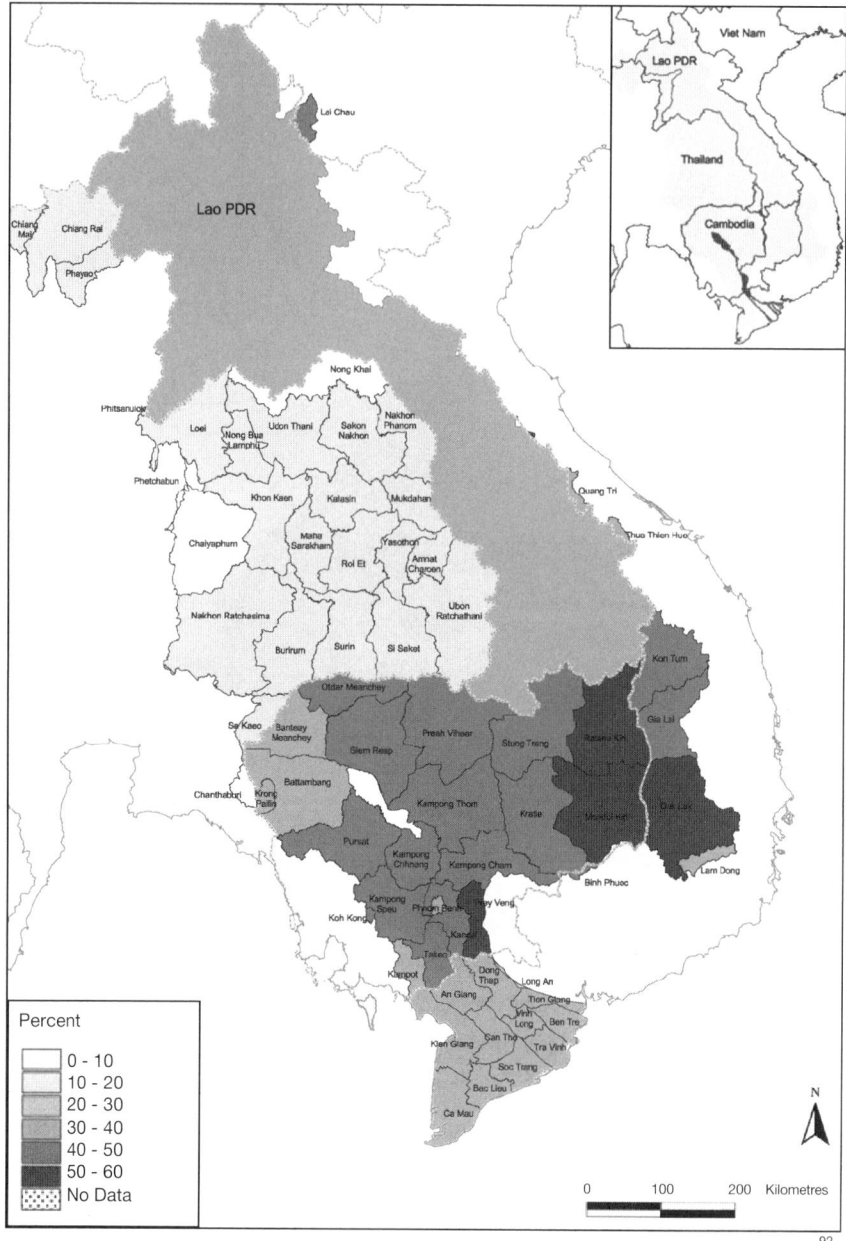

Fig. 3.27. *Proportion of children underweight for age (See color version at the end of the book).*

Note: Province names and boundaries are not shown where national or regional data are used.
Source: Hook, Novak, and Johnston 2003.

118

Major land cover categories

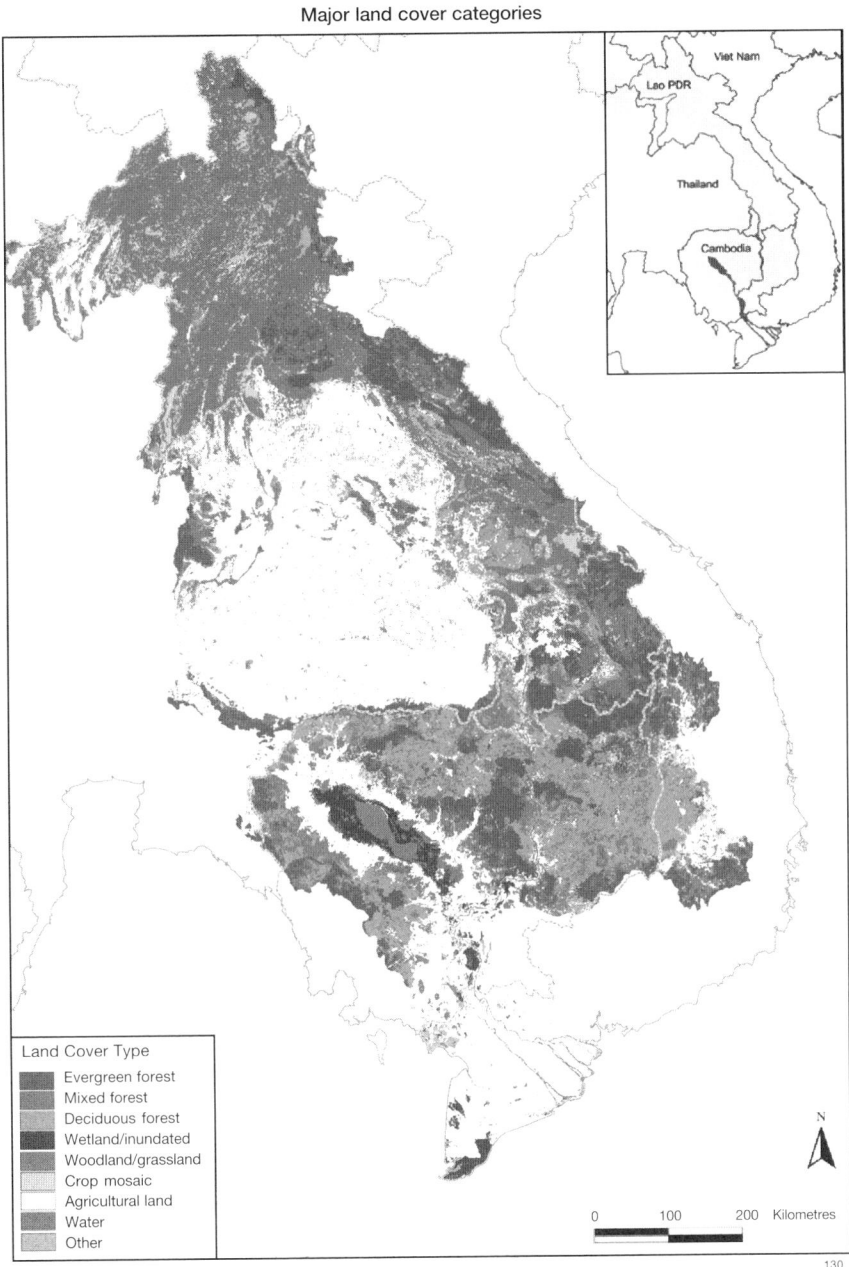

Land Cover Type
Evergreen forest
Mixed forest
Deciduous forest
Wetland/inundated
Woodland/grassland
Crop mosaic
Agricultural land
Water
Other

0   100   200   Kilometres

130

Fig. 3.28. *Major land cover categories (See color version at the end of the book).*

Source: Hook, Novak, and Johnston 2003. Repr. with permission of the Mekong River Commission.

119

Size of irrigation areas

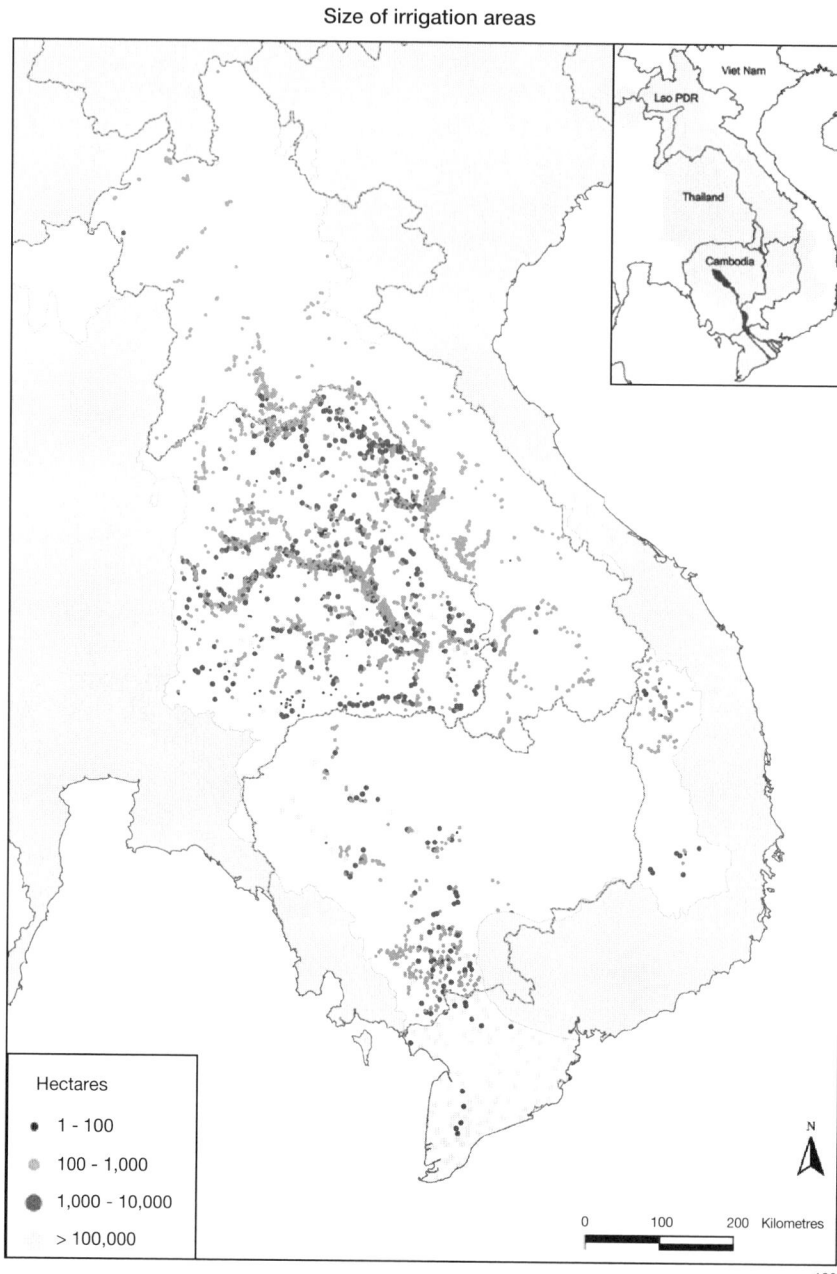

Fig. 3.29. *Size of irrigation areas (See color version at the end of the book).*

Source: Hook, Novak, and Johnston 2003. Repr. with permission of the Mekong River Commission.

120

One can plot the average distance to the poverty line by province, comparing across provinces and countries (see Figure 3.26). The entire Northeast of Thailand is no more than 5 per cent below the poverty line while rates in Laos and Cambodia are significantly higher, reaching 15 per cent to 20 per cent in various areas and occasionally above 25 per cent. Rates of children under weight by age are similarly striking (see Figure 3.27), at 10 per cent to 20 per cent of the population in the Northeast of Thailand, but 34 per cent to 40 per cent in Laos and 40 per cent to 60 per cent in much of Cambodia.

Deforested areas closely follow geo-political boundaries (see Figure 3.28). Virtually the entire Northeast is converted to agricultural use, in contrast to standing evergreen and deciduous forests or woodland/grass land in much of Cambodia and Laos. There are some exceptions: cleared agricultural land in Laos near Vientiane, in Cambodia around Lake Ton Lae Sap, and the Mekong drainage basin.

Related, of course, is the size of irrigation areas, with vast amounts of water control in the drainage basins of the Northeast (see Figure 3.29). In this case, however, Laos has significant irrigated areas, as does Cambodia around the Lake. The Mekong drainage basin in Vietnam is even more dramatic.

By and large, economic, health, and environmental variables have all been transformed in the process of fifty years of economic growth. It is important to understand what lies beneath this growth and transformation process.

4

Micro Kuznets and Macro TFP Decompositions

This chapter provides a transition from measurement and the assemblage of facts to a documentation of key underlying drivers of the Thai economy. The decompositions here are atheoretic but standard. More to the point, they provide us with a consistent, micro and macro sense of the key variables behind movements in income, inequality, and poverty.

More specifically, macro TFP decompositions of GDP growth and micro Kuznets decompositions of household income, inequality, and poverty establish the consistent, macro/micro importance of education, financial sector, occupation/sector transitions, and, again, geography. Much of the growth of GDP is attributable to factor accumulation, capital in particular. The residual—TFPG—is highly correlated with income change. Still, there are anomalies. Within-sector TFPG is negative for manufacturing and services, for example, and positive for agriculture. Distinguishing time periods, TFPG is negative except for the acceleration of income in the late 1980s. Decomposition by credit access in a model below will reconcile these anomalies.

Consistent with this, a micro decomposition of average income change into changes within sectors/groups and population shifts from low- to high-income groups shows the importance of financial access as well as education, occupation shifts, and urban to rural movements. Likewise, Kuznets decompositions using the Theil index show that inequality change is attributable to diverging average incomes across groups, especially for occupation and sector categories, and populations shifts across groups, especially for education and financial access. Poverty reduction can be attributed to the very same variables. Various models of household decision-making in the chapters below will be estimated and/or calibrated and then compared to these Kuznets decompositions. The macro models used to explain TFP and the micro model used to explain inequality are exactly the same. That is, we use macro models built up from micro foundations.

4.1. A Macro TFP Decomposition

The standard macro decomposition of growth distinguishes growth of factors—that is, land, labor, and capital, weighted by their respective factor shares, from the growth of productivity. The latter is the residual between weighted factor growth and actual growth. As in Young (1995), consider, for example, the translogarithmic value added production function:

$$
\begin{aligned}
Q = \exp \Big[& \alpha_0 + \alpha_k \ln K + \alpha_L \ln L + \alpha_t t + \frac{1}{2} B_{KK} (\ln K)^2 \\
& + B_{KL} (\ln K)(\ln L) + B_{Kt} \ln K \cdot t \\
& + \frac{1}{2} B_{LL} (\ln L)^2 + B_{Lt} \ln L \cdot t + \frac{1}{2} B_{tt} t^2 \Big]
\end{aligned}
\tag{4.1.1}
$$

where K, L, and t denote capital input, labor input, and time, and where under the assumption of constant returns to scale, the parameters α_i and B_{jk} satisfy the restriction:

$$
\alpha_K + \alpha_L = 1, \qquad B_{KK} + B_{KL} = B_{LL} + B_{KL} = B_{Kt} + B_{Lt} = 0. \tag{4.1.2}
$$

First, differencing the logarithm of the production function provides a measure of the causes of growth across discrete time periods:

$$
\begin{aligned}
\ln \left(\frac{Q(T)}{Q(T-1)} \right) = & \; \bar{\Theta}_K \ln \left(\frac{K(T)}{K(T-1)} \right) \\
& + \bar{\Theta}_L \ln \left(\frac{L(T)}{L(T-1)} \right) + TFP_{T-1,T},
\end{aligned}
\tag{4.1.3}
$$

where

$$
\bar{\Theta}_i = [\Theta_i (T) + \Theta_i (T-1)]/2
$$

and where the Θ_is denote the elasticity of output with respect to each input i or, equivalently, assuming perfect competition, the share of each input in TFPs. The translog index of TFP growth ($TFP_{T-1,T}$) provides a measure of the increase in output attributable to the time-related shifts in the production function.

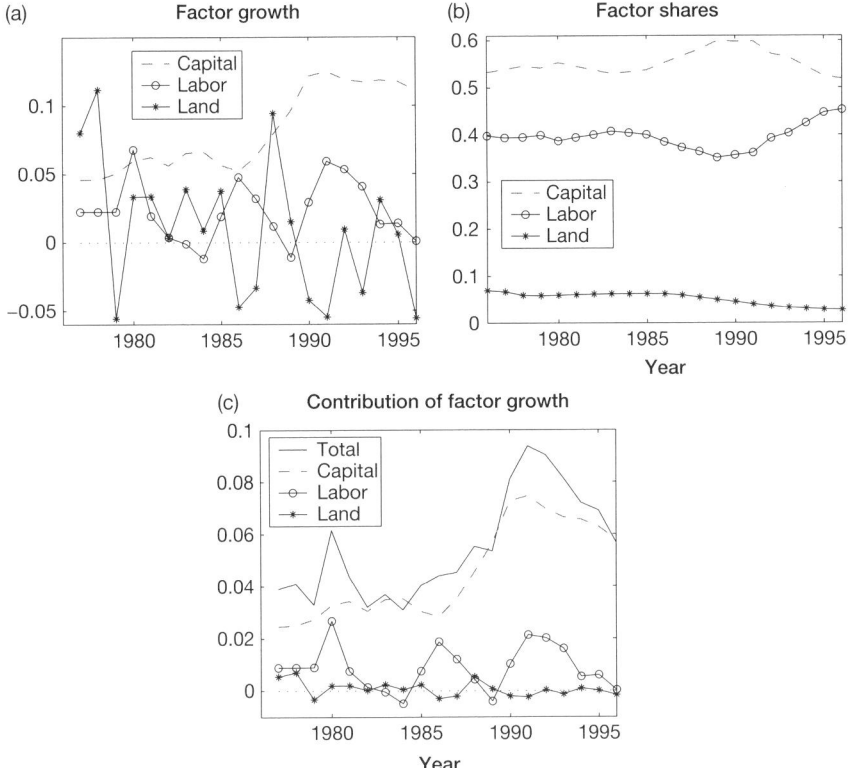

Fig. 4.1(a)–(c) *Decomposition of factor growth in Thailand*
Source: TDRI report, Tinakorn and Sussangkarn 1998.

Fig. 4.2 *Standard growth accounting in Thailand*
Source: TDRI report, Tinakorn and Sussangkarn 1998.

In a widely used TDRI report from Tinakorn and Sussangkarn (1998), the dominant factor for Thailand has been capital. As in Figure 4.1(a) and (b), it has the largest single share and the highest measured rate of growth. Note in (c) that its contribution to factor growth is only slightly below and moves closely with total factor growth. Total-factor-productivity growth (TFPG) is a non-trivial residual in Figure 4.2, about half the size of total GDP growth on average and moves closely with it.

Still, decompositions by sector beg questions. TFP from 1981 to 1985 separately for manufacturing, industry inclusive of manufacturing, and services ranges from only 4 per cent to 10.5 per cent of sector growth, and this goes negative when labor is adjusted for quality via the education/earnings numbers (see Table 4.1). Among all sectors, only agriculture has a relatively high TFPG, at 25 per cent and 35 per cent of total agriculture output growth, with and without labor adjustment, respectively. Likewise,

Table 4.1. *Sources of growth by sector, 1981–95 (based on 1988 prices)*

	Agriculture	Manufacturing	Industry (including manufacturing)	Service
1. Growth rate of output	3.71 (100)	10.35 (100)	10.50 (100)	7.83 (100)
2. Total-factor input				
Without labor-quality adjustment	2.42 (65.23)	9.26 (89.47)	10.08 (96.00)	7.39 (94.38)
With labor-quality adjustment	2.78 (74.93)	10.47 (101.15)	11.17 (106.38)	8.23 (105.11)
2.1 *Labor*	0.05 (13.48)	4.18 (40.38)	3.97 (37.81)	2.93 (37.42)
Employment	0.14	2.97	2.88	2.09
Quality changes	0.36	1.21	1.09	0.84
2.2 *Capital*	2.24 (60.38)	6.29 (60.77)	7.20 (68.57)	5.30 (67.69)
2.3 *Land*	0.04 (1.08)			
3. Total-factor productivity				
Without labor-quality adjustment	1.29 (34.77)	1.09 (10.53)	0.42 (4.00)	0.44 (5.62)
With labor-quality adjustment	0.93 (25.07)	−0.12 (−1.15)	−0.67 (−6.38)	−0.40 (−5.11)

Notes: Numbers in parentheses indicate percentage contribution to growth
Source: Tinakorn and Sussangkarn 1998: 34 (table 17).

in Tables 4.2 and 4.3, disaggregating into key time periods, TFPG for sectors such as industry and services is negative for the 1981–5 and 1991–5 periods, positive only for the high-growth-spurt, 1986–90 period.

On the other hand, a decomposition which takes into account access/ use of financial services yields a TFPG number which more closely tracks the aggregate (see Figures 4.3(a)–(e) and 4.4(a)–(b)). This is a preview of coming attractions. The model which generated the graph will be featured below.

4.2. A Micro, Kuznets Decomposition

A more micro, Kuznets decomposition keeps track of group incomes, typically groups with low income, l, and high income, h, and population shifts Δp^h from low to high across the groups, where Δ is a time-difference operator. Thus, average per capita income, $\mu_t = p_t^h \mu_t^h + p_t^l \mu_t^l$, or simply a population-weighted average, using population proportions p_t^l and p_t^h, of groups average incomes, μ_t^l and μ_t^h. Thus the growth or change of income is approximately

$$\Delta \mu = \{\bar{p^h} \Delta \mu^h + (1 - \bar{p^h}) \Delta \mu^l\} + (\bar{\mu^h} - \bar{\mu^l}) \Delta p^h. \tag{4.2.1}$$

or more generally with categories $k = 1, 2, \ldots K$,

$$\Delta \mu = \sum_k \bar{p}^k \Delta \mu^k + \sum_k \bar{\mu}^k \Delta p^k. \tag{4.2.2}$$

The first terms in the above two equations are the components of growth within subgroups, and the final term the growth due to population shifts. Likewise, the Theil-L inequality index I is defined as

$$I \equiv \frac{1}{n} \sum_{i=1}^{n} \log\left(\frac{\mu}{y_i}\right) \tag{4.2.3}$$

as the sum over households i of the log difference between average income μ and household i income y_i. Distinguishing again groups $k = 1, \ldots K$, the index I consists of a within component WI and an across component AI, $I = WI + AI$, where

Table 4.2. *Contribution of input and total-factor productivity to growth: industry*

| Period | GDP growth | Contribution from inputs | | | Total-factor productivity | |
| | | Capital (K index) | Labor | | Unadjusted | Adjusted |
			Employment	Quality adjusted		
1981–5	6.47	5.58	1.81	2.76	-0.92	-1.87
1986–90	14.42	7.07	3.5	3.83	3.85	3.52
1991–5	10.62	8.97	3.34	5.3	-1.69	-3.65
1981–95	10.50	7.20	2.88	3.97	0.42	-0.67
(Percentage contribution)	(100.00)	(68.57)	(27.43)	(37.81)	(4.00)	(-6.38)

Source: Tinakorn and Sussangkarn 1998: 31 (table 14).

Table 4.3. *Contribution of input and total-factor productivity to growth: services*

| Period | GDP growth | Contribution from inputs | | | Total-factor productivity | |
| | | Capital (K index) | Labor | | Unadjusted | Adjusted |
			Employment	Quality adjusted		
1981–5	5.33	3.99	1.81	2.79	-0.47	-1.45
1986–90	10.01	5.22	1.89	3.26	2.90	1.53
1991–5	8.15	6.71	2.58	2.73	-1.14	-1.29
1981–95	7.83	5.30	2.09	2.93	0.44	-0.40
(Percentage contribution)	(100.00)	(67.69)	(26.69)	(37.42)	(5.62)	(-5.11)

Source: Tinakorn and Sussangkarn 1998: 33 (table 16).

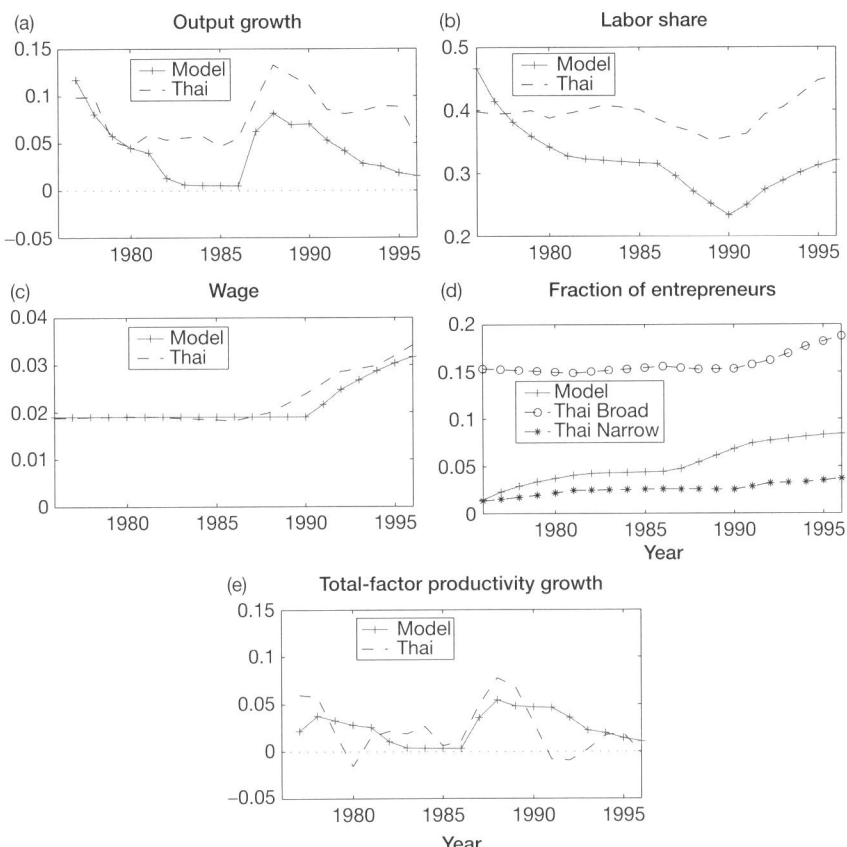

Fig. 4.3(a)–(e). *Total-factor productivity aggregate growth dynamics*
Source: Jeong and Townsend 2007.

$$WI = \sum_{k=1}^{K} p^k I^k \text{ and } AI = \sum_{k=1}^{K} p^k \log\left(\frac{\mu}{\mu^k}\right). \qquad (4.2.4)$$

Here, within category *WI* is simply the p^k population-weighted sum of inequality indexes I^k within groups k, and the across component *AI* is simply the population-weighted log difference between average per capita income μ and the group k average μ^k.

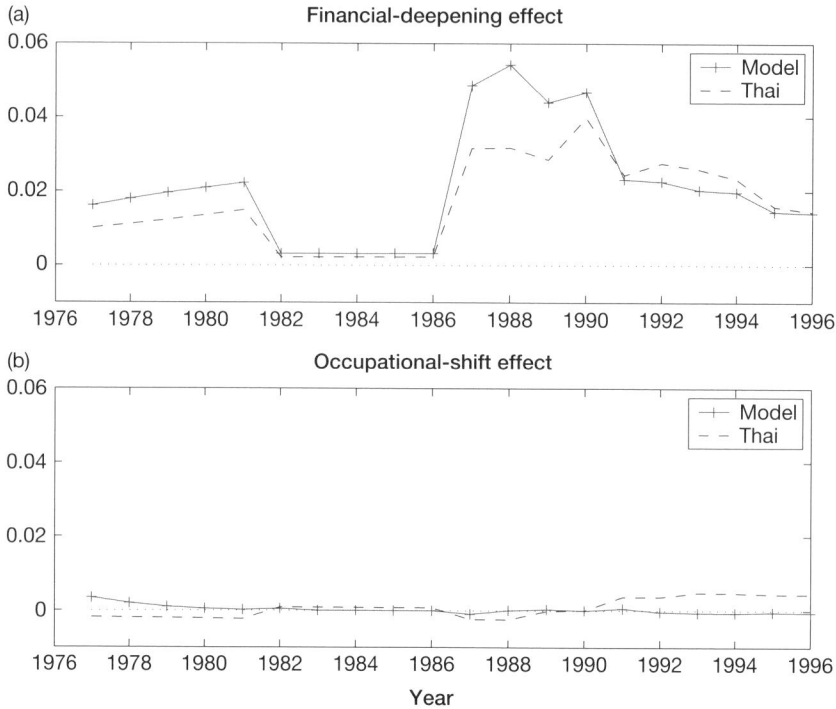

Fig. 4.4(a)–(b). *Total-factor productivity growth from financial-deepening effect and occupational-shift effect*

Source: Jeong and Townsend 2005.

Taking first differences over time, $\Delta I = \Delta WI + \Delta AI$, where both the within and across measures of inequality change have an easy interpretation. The change in the within measure is much as in the earlier per-capita income growth equation 4.2.2, that is, here

$$\Delta WI = \sum_k \bar{p}^k \Delta I^k + \sum_k \bar{I}^k \Delta p^k \qquad (4.2.5)$$

the sum of $\bar{p}^k$ population-weighted change in inequality indices ΔI^k and a composition effect, intuitively, the shift Δp^k, from low to high inequality groups. The change in the across measure

$$\Delta AI = \underbrace{\sum_k \bar{p}^k \left[\frac{\bar{\mu}^k}{\mu} - 1\right] \Delta \ln \mu^k}_{Divergence} + \underbrace{\sum_k \left[\frac{\bar{\mu}^k}{\mu} - \ln \frac{\bar{\mu}^k}{\mu}\right] \Delta p^k}_{Kuznets} \qquad (4.2.6)$$

consists of a divergence term capturing the change in income differences within groups $\Delta \ln \mu^k$ at fixed population proportions $\bar{p}^k$, and another, famous Kuznets composition effect, the change in inequality due to shifting population Δp^k across groups k with incomes different from the average. Note that a given population shift may either increase or decrease inequality, depending on the number of households in a group and how far group income is from the population average. The Kuznets curve refers to a tendency for this term to be positive at first, contributing to an increase in inequality as only a 'lucky' few have high incomes, then negative, as many people are in the high income group and the economy is moving toward equality at the higher income level.

For Thailand, we learn much from Jeong's (2000) thesis. The growth of average income in the SES, 1976–96, as seen in column 1 of Table 4.4, can be attributed to population shifts across occupations or production sectors, changes in financial participation, and increasing education, with contributions ranging from 18 per cent to 25 per cent. All three factors jointly account for 39 per cent of the total income change. Rural to urban shifts account for 7 per cent.

Table 4.4. *Composition effects on average income growth*

Characteristics	Overall	Stage 1	Stage 2	Stage 3
Age	0	3	0	0
Gender	2	5	1	4
Community type	7	17	2	12
Production sector	18	33	13	21
Occupation	21	39	17	30
Financial participation	20	23	27	18
Education	25	45	20	24
Joint three	39	66	38	38
Total growth	4.96	1.98	8.78	6.94

Notes: The numbers indicate percentage shares of income growth due to compositional changes out of total income growth.

Source: Jeong 2008.

Table 4.5. *Decomposition of inequality change*

Characteristics	Within-group inequality		Across-group inequality	
	Intra-group	Composition	Income-gap	Composition
Age	101	−2	1	0
Gender	97	0	2	1
Community Type	67	−1	24	10
Production Sector	58	9	25	8
Occupation	59	2	32	7
Financial Participation	59	12	2	27
Education	54	−7	5	47
Joint Three	28	2	19	51

Source: Jeong 2008.

By time period, or stages of growth described earlier, production sector/occupation is large in the first and last sub-periods, 1976–86, and 1992–6. In contrast, financial participation is high at 27 per cent in the high-growth, financial liberalization period. Education is high at 45 per cent in the first sub-period. Rural to urban population shifts are high in the first sub-period at 17 per cent, and non-trivial in the last sub-period also. Note that demographic effects (age, gender) are not accounting for much here.

As for inequality, in Table 4.5 column 2, the change in inequality within groups is the part that is not well explained. This is the intra-group effect. This remainder ranges from 41 per cent to 46 per cent for the same three factors: production sector/occupation, financial participation, and education—community type also matters. Interestingly, the Kuznets composition effect in column 4 is large at 27 per cent and 47 per cent for financial participation and education, respectively (a second within composition effect is contained in financial deepening, at 12 per cent), less so for sector and occupation. In contrast, income divergence effects are large at 25 per cent to 32 per cent for sector/occupation. Income divergence effects are non-trivial at 24 per cent for urban/rural community groups, though there is a 10 per cent population shift, composition effect, in addition.

Focusing on inequality and these sub-periods in Table 4.6(a)–(c), the occupation effect is coming primarily from an income divergence effects in all three sub-periods, with divergence in the first two sub-periods and

Table 4.6 (a)–(c). *Income divergence effects in 3 sub-periods*

(a) Stage 1

Characteristics	Within-group inequality		Across-group inequality	
	Intra-group	Composition	Income-gap	Composition
Age	102	−1	−1	0
Gender	95	0	4	1
Community type	57	−1	37	7
Production sector	43	7	35	15
Occupation	40	5	46	9
Financial participation	80	3	7	10
Education	61	−5	17	27
Joint three	48	4	28	20

(b) Stage 2 (total change per annum = 1.472)

Characteristics	Within-group inequality		Across-group inequality	
	Intra-group	Composition	Income-gap	Composition
Age	98	0	2	0
Gender	103	0	−3	0
Community type	48	−2	47	7
Production sector	44	9	50	−3
Occupation	35	5	54	6
Financial participation	24	13	28	35
Education	38	−3	27	38
Joint three	2	6	34	58

(c) Stage 3 (total change per annum = −1.481)

Characteristics	Within-group inequality		Across-group inequality	
	Intra-group	Composition	Income-gap	Composition
Age	99	1	0	0
Gender	100	1	0	−1
Community type	20	−2	91	−9
Production sector	24	−13	75	14
Occupation	4	−7	85	18
Financial participation	52	−10	72	−14
Education	46	2	80	−28
Joint three	−4	−2	99	7

Notes: The numbers indicate percentage shares of Theil-L index changes due to each component dynamics out of total change in Theil-L index: 'intra-group' for intra-group inequality change, 'income-gap' for divergence or convergence in income levels across income-status groups; 'composition' under 'within-group inequality' for composition effect via within-group inequality; and 'composition' under 'across-group inequality': for composition effect via across-group inequality. Negative number for Stage 3 indicates increase in inequality while positive number indicates decrease in inequality since the total inequality decreased for this period.

Source: Jeong 2005.

convergence in the last. (The sign is positive if it is consistent with the overall change in inequality.) The financial access/use composition effect is particularly large in the second high-growth, liberalization period, as anticipated, at 35 per cent. There are divergent income effects as well, as those with access have faster growing incomes, contributing to inequality. The income convergence effect lowering inequality is obvious for financial participation in the last sub-period, but this appears for virtually all types of subgroups. In contrast, a negative sign in the table indicates a tendency to increase inequality while the overall inequality index goes down, as in the bottom table, with the composition effect in education, financial participation, and community type.

The income effect in education appears more prominent now in Table 4.6 (a)–(c) in each sub-period than in the earlier overall decomposition in Table 4.5. The income effect for geography, urban/rural status is also now high, one of the largest numbers in all tables, but it moves consistent with the overall national trend, contributing to increasing inequality at first, and then decreasing inequality.

Poverty changes can be similarly decomposed into growth and inequality effects, as reported in Table 4.7. As could have been anticipated from the figure of shifting histograms, growth tends to shift income distributions to the right, reducing poverty, as there is less mass on the left tail. But an increase in inequality can fatten the left tail, raising poverty. Jeong (2000) shows that the growth effect dominates the inequality effect in the first two sub-periods. In the third sub-period inequality goes down so the growth and inequality effect work in the same direction. This is the reason why some of the earlier change maps were so dramatic. Jeong decomposes growth and inequality effects

Table 4.7. *Decomposition of poverty reduction into growth and inequality change*

	Overall	Stage 1	Stage 2	Stage 3
Growth effect	−2.28	−1.28	−3.82	−2.72
Inequality effect	0.36	0.68	0.86	−0.89
Total change	−1.71	−0.37	−2.90	−3.27

Notes: The numbers indicate the changes in head-count ratio in percentage terms due to income-growth effect (first row), effect of change in inequality (second row), and total change (third row). Negative numbers suggest reduction of poverty while positive numbers suggest increase in poverty since the base of the decomposition is a negative number, the poverty reduction. The difference between the sum of growth effect and inequality effect and total change is due to the residual term.

Source: Jeong 2008.

Table 4.8(a)–(d). *Composition effects on poverty reduction*

(a) Overall

Characteristics	Growth	Inequality	Total
Occupation	33	3	29
Financial participation	30	−10	14
Education	36	−11	18
Joint three	62	−12	39

(b) Stage 1

Characteristics	Growth	Inequality	Total
Occupation	103	−8	73
Financial participation	62	−27	24
Education	116	−49	46
Joint three	186	−59	92

(c) Stage 2

Characteristics	Growth	Inequality	Total
Occupation	21	1	21
Financial participation	32	−10	20
Education	24	−9	14
Joint three	48	−12	33

(d) Stage 3

Characteristics	Growth	Inequality	Total
Occupation	28	3	28
Financial participation	18	−10	6
Education	22	−11	9
Joint three	35	3	33

Notes: The numbers indicate the percentage shares of change in head-count ratio due to compositional changes in given characteristics via income-growth (first column), income-inequality change (second column), and combined effect (third column). Here positive numbers suggest reduction of poverty while negative numbers suggest increase in poverty since this table reports the shares, not amount, of corresponding effects to the total poverty reduction. The difference between the sum of 'growth' and 'inequality' columns and 'total' column is due to the residual term.

Source: Jeong 2008.

on poverty reduction into the familiar factors: occupation, financial participation, and education—with orders of magnitude that can be anticipated
from the earlier discussion. Here, however, the occupation effect
stands out more as the main driver of the reduction in equality (see Table
4.8(a)–(d)).

5

Driving Forces: Occupation, Financial Access, Education

This chapter examines each of the key driving forces of the Thai economy in more detail, first in the contemporary economy and then historically. Geography and space are incorporated within each topic. Many of the details here will turn out to be of considerable consequence for the modeling efforts below. We address in turn occupation, financial access, and education.

Many industries are concentrated in and around Bangkok, though not exclusively—food/beverage/tobacco are concentrated in the Northeast. The point is that occupation and business enterprise matter in virtually all regions of the country. Most firms are small in terms of numbers of employees. SMEs account for over 95 per cent of all firms, and about 50 per cent of employment and capital. There is thus an overlap of the firms found in a Ministry of Industry registry, on the one hand, many with a capitalization of 10 million baht or less, with the larger firms of household surveys, on the other. This was a point discussed earlier, that non-farm enterprise is significant in the national accounts. The real point is that the use of household data to understand the macro economy is not strained but natural. Historically, there is a steady movement of households out of agriculture and into self-employment or employer categories. The latter have higher incomes and greater within-group inequality. These will be incorporated into and/or compared with the predictions of the choice models below. Satellite imagery shows the corresponding urbanization and deforestation, and the village/regional models will be used to understand these patterns. Initial household wealth seems to facilitate subsequent household transition into business, and the assets of a new business are lower if the household is not borrowing. Thus prior wealth, if it is low, appears as a constraint, a key feature to be incorporated into models with constrained selection.

At an aggregated level commercial banks seem to dominate access, credit extended, and number of branches. These typically are presented as key facts in country financial sector assessments, such as those conducted by the International Monetary Fund (IMF). Often they are all we have to go on. But the aggregates can be misleading. In rural household data the Thai government's agricultural development bank, the BAAC, is the largest formal lender. So the formal sector needs to distinguish urban vs rural actual/potential clients and ideally to distinguish the financial provider. The informal sector is quite significant in household and SME surveys— though at the aggregated formal level this sector is not measured at all. The role and impact of the informal sector will be assessed through the models below. In the Northeast many transactions are within the village, among relatives and non-relatives, whereas in the Central region out-of-village transactions rise in importance. The village may be an important entity, but its importance may decline over time. More generally, the mix of lenders varies by region, and this is a key feature in the determination of obstacles to trade.

Some portion of household/businesses do not borrow at all. This motivates so-called dual-sector models which feature autarky vs interme-diated sectors, and also work in the subsequent models which retain autarky as a viable choice. Loans among households and SMEs vary in size, interest rate, collateral (joint liability, asset-backed, nothing), and default consequences. Several of the models will allow variation on the supply side and/or demand side along some of these dimensions. Savings are in both financial accounts and rice. The latter is especially important in the Northeast, indicative of the low level of intermediation in the area.

Debt/asset ratios, the stocks, are relatively low, and typically rise with firm size or household wealth. This may be indicative of which kind of constraints are prevalent, through the models below. Use of funds for consumption smoothing and investment/finance, the flows, seem to vary with financial-sector provider. Some aim for clientele at the middle or low wealth group. The various providers do have distinct policies. For example, the BAAC has a risk-contingency system in which loan repayment can be deferred or partially forgiven, though provisions are not charged appropri-ately. Village funds differ by policies, shown in the data to be correlated with success and failure in membership, saving, and lending growth. There appear to be gaps in services, and this historical and cross-sectional variation is a key to preliminary financial sector assessment of impact below.

Historically, financial deepening is most obvious for the BAAC which operates now in most villages, least obvious for village funds which, until recently, blink on and off with success and failure, and mixed for commercial banks, which spread like contagion in nearby areas. By household, preexisting wealth facilitates entry into the formal financial sector, as does education. Income differentials and inequality vary by access/no-access groups. The distribution of wealth is higher for those with commercial bank access, lowest for those who borrow informally, and concentrated in the middle for the BAAC. Evidently, there is a positive relationship between prior wealth and financial access, especially formal access, and so, again wealth as a constraint looms large.

Education levels vary over space, both across provinces and within provinces by proximity to major roads or towns. Secondary school are scattered, and many households have relatively low levels of education. Thus, varying levels of education should be taken into account in occupation choice and financial use, at least. The education of children still varies with parental wealth. Educational outcomes as part of constrained choice need to be studied further. Education is certainly a key variable in income, inequality, and poverty decompositions, as mentioned earlier. Income differentials have increased over time, and illiteracy has declined substantially. Inequality in income remains higher for the low education groups.

5.1. Occupation/Industrialization

5.1.1. The Contemporary Situation

The contemporary picture of industry shows that manufacturing of metal machinery and equipment is concentrated in the greater Bangkok areas but with non-trivial number of factories in the provinces (e.g., the corridor to the North, parts of the South, the Eastern seaboard, and the Northeast 'arc' swinging up from Nakorn Ratchasima to Ubon). In contrast, food and food processing are concentrated in the Northeast generally.

Food and beverages, fabricated products, non-metal products, and transportation are among the largest manufacturing sectors in having a combination of all three criteria: number of factories, capital, and employment (see Figure 5.1). The single largest type by number of factories is agroindustry (which includes small rice mills), followed by fabricated products.

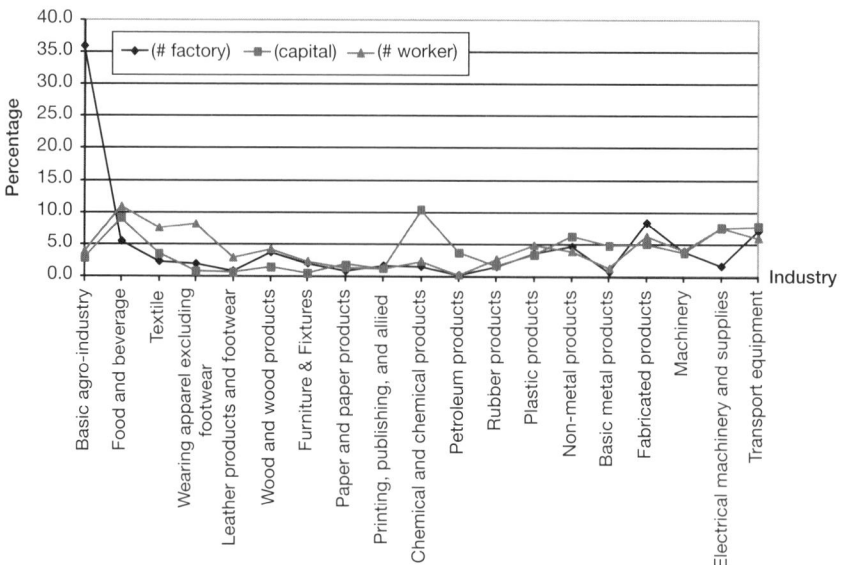

Fig. 5.1. *Industry share in total number of factory, total capital, and total workers, 2003*
Source: Office of Industrial Economics, Thai Ministry of Industry.

The largest by employment are food/beverage, textiles, wearing apparel, and electric machinery and supplies. The largest in terms of capitalization are chemical and chemical products, food/beverage/tobacco, and transport equipment (Table 5.1).

In Thailand, firms with 200 or fewer employees are termed SMEs (small and medium-sized enterprise) (see Table 5.2). As of 1996, these constituted 97.9 per cent of all establishments, employed 50.4 per cent of the employee workforce, and had 52.0 per cent of the registered capital. There is relatively little variation by sector. Virtually all rice mills are SMEs (excluded from the

Table 5.1. *Distribution of small and medium-sized enterprises by industry*

	Firms		Employees		Registered capital	
	N	share (percentage)	N	share (percentage)	million baht	share (percentage)
SMEs	124,771	97.9	1,605,815	50.4	1,218,856	52.0
Large enterprises	2,631	2.1	1,580,588	49.6	1,125,111	48.0
Total	127,402	100.0	3,186,403	100.0	2,343,967	100.0

Source: Japan Bank for International Cooperation.

Table 5.2. *Major products and their markets*

	Total	
Main products	N	percentage
Final product	450	70.1
Intermediate output	180	28.0
Both	19	3.0
Base all respondents	642	100.0

	Total	
Sales source	N	percentage
Domestic sales 100%	342	53.3
Domestic sales >50%	139	21.7
Domestic sales 50%: Export 50%	13	2.0
Export 51–100%	148	23.1
Base all respondents	642	100.0

Notes: Multiple answers.

Source: Japan Bank for International Cooperation.

above totals already). On the other hand, a lower 88 per cent to 89 per cent of the number of firms in textiles, foot ware, and petrochemicals are SMEs.

According to a Japan Bank for International Cooperation (JBIC) survey, non-trivial numbers of SMEs are connected to international markets. Sales via exports exceed 50 per cent of all sales for 23.1 per cent of all SMEs, though 53.3 per cent do rely on domestic sales only (see Table 5.2). Likewise, in Table 5.3, from 5.6 per cent to 32.1 per cent are prime contractors for multi-national and local companies, respectively.

Table 5.3. *Subcontracting relationships with multinationals or local firms*

	Prime contractor of		Subcontractor of			
	Foreign/ multinational producers	Local companies	Foreign/ multinational producers	Local companies	Neither	Base all respondents
N	36	206	33	90	286	642
percentage	5.6	32.1	5.1	14.0	44.5	100.0

Note: Multiple answers.

Source: Japan Bank for International Cooperation.

Table 5.4. *Fixed assets and number of employees*

Fixed assets	Total	
	N	percentage
Less than 10m BHT	240	37.4
11–50m BHT	157	24.5
51–100m BHT	44	6.9
101–200m BHT	41	6.4
NA	160	24.9
Base all respondents	642	100.0

Employees	Total	
	N	percentage
Less than 10 employees	137	21.3
11–50 employees	266	41.4
51–100 employees	114	17.8
101–200 employees	125	19.5
Base all respondents	642	100.0

Notes: As of June 1999, at cost.

Source: Japan Bank for International Cooperation.

Important for the argument which follows is the size of the SMEs' assets (see Table 5.5). No less than 37 per cent of all SMEs have assets less than 10 million baht (a more refined histogram is not available). For subsequent reference, 21 per cent have fewer than ten employees and another 41 per cent have between ten and fifty employees. Thus, the bulk of SMEs are small by most measures. Indeed, the Ministry of Industry's registry of firms uncovers many with fewer than ten employees and registered capital of 50,000 to 1 million baht (see Table 5.6 for an example).

One can also uncover firms in standard household surveys. The Townsend Thai data find 23 per cent of households in 1997 with non-trivial business assets (not featured in a table). Table 5.7 shows the average costs of household business assets for households that have businesses. The highest tercile has 261,000 baht in assets, 417,000 in assets in Chachoengsao. As reported in Table 5.8, transport and construction firms in the Northeast have 855,000 in initial business investment. (Total household assets reach 1.18 million baht in Chachoengsao.) There are in fact some households in the monthly data with business assets from 1 to 9 million baht (see example in Table 5.9). Clearly, the mid to high end of household enterprise is firmly co-mingled with the lower to mid range of the SMEs. We can thus use the household survey data to study with some confidence the establishment of non-farm enterprise.

Table 5.5. *Example from Ministry of Industry registry, Lop Buri*

Name	Capital	Manpower	Horsepower
Entrepreneur 1	550,000	4	61.35
Entrepreneur 2	6,500,000	81	—
Entrepreneur 3	1,601,000	10	40.36
Entrepreneur 4	362,000	3	26.02
Entrepreneur 5	3,970,000	27	636.83
Entrepreneur 6	200,000	5	9.00
Entrepreneur 7	1,250,000	10	33.54
Entrepreneur 8	190,000	5	—
Entrepreneur 9	210,000	1	10.66
Entrepreneur 10	735,000	9	51.86
Entrepreneur 11	200,000	4	—
Entrepreneur 12	292,000	2	44.11
Entrepreneur 13	750,000	2	11.00
Entrepreneur 14	380,000	7	30.75
Entrepreneur 15	450,000	4	35.81
Entrepreneur 16	55,000	8	47.26
Entrepreneur 17	142,000	2	12.25
Entrepreneur 18	50,000	7	10.04
Entrepreneur 19	234,000	217	39.09
Entrepreneur 20	25,000,000	69	14323.07
Entrepreneur 21	167,000,000	88	7180.00
Entrepreneur 22	70,000,000	100	11126.17
Entrepreneur 23	15,500,000	42	1415.7
Entrepreneur 24	81,500,000	42	1425.89
Entrepreneur 25	205,400,000	70	—
Entrepreneur 26	—	33	8230.5
Entrepreneur 27	492,000,000	151	6069.91
Entrepreneur 28	3,800,000	62	20.75
Entrepreneur 29	8,500,000	20	258.75
Entrepreneur 30	100,000	2	25.88
Entrepreneur 31	1,150,000	7	16.50

Source: Thai Ministry of Industry

Table 5.6. *Average costs of household business assets*

Income tercile	Whole sample	Chachoengsao	Lop Buri	Buriram	Sisaket
All households	175,824	260,492	118,817	121,898	59,379
Low	75,785	62,172	129,224	88,428	25,867
Medium	90,792	133,348	30,643	76,060	62,794
High	260,556	416,846	154,447	167,904	70,780

Notes: Values are in baht, nominal values not adjusted for inflation or depreciation. At the time of data collection, 1,000 Thai baht ≈ US$ 40. Table presents the results only for households that own businesses.

Source: Townsend Thai Survey 1997.

Table 5.7. *Median initial investment by region and business type, 1,000s of 1997 baht*

Business type	Whole sample	Northeast	Central
Shrimp/shrimp and fish/fish	50	9	51
Shop	16	16	16
Trade	21	21	23
Restaurant/noodle shop	7	32	6
Transport and construction	278	855	181
Sewing/silk/embroidery	10	5	17
Mechanic/repair shop etc.	31	23	84
Rice threshing	47	59	12
Services (haircut, laundry, etc.)	20	25	14
Other	45	34	68
Total	32	19	38

Source: Anna L. Paulson and R. M. Townsend, 'Entrepreneurship and Financial Constraints in Thailand', *Journal of Corporate Finance*, 10 (2004), 229–62. Copyright 2004; reproduced with permission from Elsevier.

Table 5.8. *Households with largest business asset in each province*

Village	Asset (baht)	Type of business
70737	1,680,000	shrimp farm, concrete factory
270230	9,065,612	construction equipment, construction job, gas station
490416	841,000	dig the well
530131	546,350	shop, rice mill, (small) bus

Source: Townsend Thai Monthly Survey.

5.1.2. History

Historically, there is a salient transition out of agriculture and into wage work and non-farm enterprise. The table from the SES, 1976–96, indicates the decline in small farmers, from 44.5 per cent to 23.8 per cent of the population. Large farmers also declined from 6.3 per cent to 2.5 per cent, as did the few in fishing. There is a steady rise in the number of production workers, from 5.9 per cent to 15.2 per cent, and service workers, from 8.0 per cent to 13.6 per cent. The number of non-farm self-employed is relatively flat, first falling and then, after 1990, rising. More telling perhaps is the more or less steady increase in the number of non-farm employers from 1.3 per cent to 3.2 per cent. Related would be the increase in professional workers, from 4.1 per cent to 6.6 per cent. The number of households on 'assistance' rises from 3.5 per cent to 12.1 per cent. The models below will begin by aggregating some of these categories, again featuring the choice between wage and non-farm enterprise (Figure 5.2).

The skills of these various categories of workers should be reflected in part in earned incomes (see Table 5.10). Small farmers, farmer workers, and general

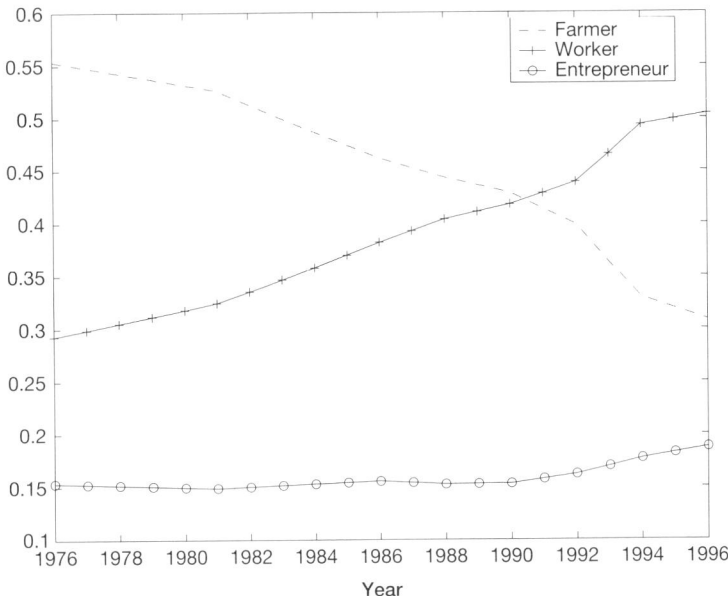

Fig. 5.2. *Trend of occupational composition in Thailand*

Source: SES data, Jeong and Townsend 2007.

Table 5.9. *Composition of income status groups (percentage)*

	1976	1981	1986	1988	1990	1992	1994	1996	76–96[1]	76–86[2]	86–92[2]	92–6[2]
Occupation												
Small farmer	46.1	45.8	39.4	38.6	36.9	34.8	27.9	26.2	−19.9	−0.67	−0.77	−2.16
Fisher and other farmer	2.0	1.7	1.3	1.2	0.9	0.7	0.9	0.7	−1.3	−0.08	−0.10	0.01
Big farmer	7.6	6.7	7.1	5.0	5.4	4.8	3.0	3.0	−4.6	−0.05	−0.40	−0.43
Non-farm self-employed	13.2	11.3	11.4	11.4	11.3	11.4	12.5	13.3	0.1	−0.18	−0.01	0.48
Non-farm employer	1.4	2.6	2.5	2.6	2.6	3.1	3.2	3.5	2.1	0.10	0.11	0.10
Own-account professional	0.1	0.1	0.1	0.0	0.1	0.2	0.3	0.2	0.0	0.00	0.01	−0.01
Farm worker	4.7	5.7	6.6	6.8	6.2	6.0	6.3	5.5	0.8	0.19	−0.10	−0.12
General worker	5.0	1.6	3.9	3.8	3.8	3.9	3.7	3.0	−2.0	−0.11	0.00	−0.24
Production worker	5.9	7.7	8.7	8.5	10.4	11.3	14.1	15.5	9.6	0.28	0.42	1.06
Service worker	7.4	7.9	8.3	9.7	10.7	11.1	12.3	12.8	5.4	0.10	0.47	0.40
Professional worker	3.7	4.4	4.6	5.3	5.0	5.2	5.8	6.2	2.5	0.09	0.10	0.25
Assisted	2.2	3.6	5.3	6.3	6.0	6.5	9.4	9.4	7.1	0.31	0.20	0.72
Rentier	0.5	1.0	0.7	0.8	0.8	0.9	0.7	0.7	0.2	0.02	0.05	−0.05
Financial participation												
Non-participant	93.5	89.8	89.3	84.7	80.4	78.1	75.5	73.4	−20.1	−0.41	−1.86	−1.19
Participant	6.5	1.02	10.7	15.3	19.6	21.9	24.5	26.6	20.1	0.41	1.86	1.19
Education	18.3	12.5	8.6	7.6	7.1	6.9	6.2	5.6	−12.7	−0.97	−0.27	−0.34
No formal	73.1	76.1	78.6	77.4	76.4	74.9	73.2	71.8	−1.3	0.55	−0.63	−0.78
Primary	5.4	6.3	6.1	6.9	8.3	8.9	10.3	11.4	6.0	0.07	0.47	0.63
Secondary	2.2	3.6	4.0	4.5	4.2	4.6	5.0	5.3	3.1	0.18	0.09	0.18
University or higher	1.1	1.5	2.7	3.6	4.0	4.8	5.3	6.0	4.9	0.17	0.34	0.31

1. Total change in population fraction between 1976 and 1996.
2. Annual average change in population fraction for corresponding periods.

Source: Townsend Socio-economic Survey data; Jeong 2008.

Table 5.10. *Average income profile (1990 baht)*

Occupation	1976	1981	1986	1988	1990	1992	1994	1996	76–96[1]	76–86[2]	86–92[2]	92–6[2]
Small farmer	637	799	649	749	844	911	1,069	1,309	3.7	0.2	5.8	9.5
Fisher and other farmer	875	1,221	798	1,305	1,472	1,982	2,833	2,370	5.1	−0.9	16.4	4.6
Big farmer	1,090	1,361	1,064	1,425	2,037	1,546	1,743	2,379	4.0	−0.2	6.4	11.4
Non-farm self-employed	1,421	1,645	1,485	1,654	1,956	2,244	2,391	2,961	3.7	0.4	7.1	7.2
Non-farm employer	3,422	3,629	3,525	3,637	5,647	6,223	6,607	6,979	3.6	0.3	9.9	2.9
Own-account professional	2,536	2,108	2,455	7,427	2,843	13,517	10,851	7,257	5.4	−0.3	32.9	−14.4
Farm worker	715	748	616	676	753	833	942	1,147	2.4	−1.5	5.2	8.3
General worker	766	893	720	685	800	1,056	1,117	1,391	3.0	−0.6	6.6	7.1
Production worker	1,217	1,470	1,388	1,532	1,674	1,957	1,787	2,078	2.7	1.3	5.9	1.5
Service worker	1,521	2,055	2,122	2,244	2,498	3,115	3,231	3,711	4.6	3.4	6.6	4.5
Professional worker	2,245	3,082	3,389	3,837	4,557	6,127	6,008	6,964	5.8	4.2	10.4	3.3
Assisted	1,233	1,917	1,645	1,842	1,796	2,050	1,942	2,299	3.2	2.9	3.7	2.9
Rentier	1,372	2,238	2,311	2,125	4,504	4,301	4,250	3,774	5.2	5.3	10.9	−3.2

1. Total change between 1976 and 1996.
2. Annual average change for corresponding periods.

Source: Townsend Socio-economic Survey data; Jeong 2008.

Table 5.11. *Inequality profile by Theil-L index*

Occupation	1976	1981	1986	1988	1990	1992	1994	1996	76–96[1]	76–86[2]	86–92[2]	92–6[2]
Small farmer	0.180	0.179	0.217	0.216	0.230	0.229	0.275	0.288	10.8	0.37	0.20	1.48
Fisher and other farmer	0.216	0.395	0.253	0.377	0.381	0.514	0.887	0.467	25.1	0.37	4.34	−1.15
Big farmer	0.236	0.239	0.296	0.285	0.504	0.326	0.334	0.400	16.4	0.60	0.51	1.84
Non-farm self-employed	0.251	0.258	0.265	0.262	0.294	0.297	0.290	0.285	3.4	0.14	0.54	−0.32
Non-farm employer	0.325	0.366	0.392	0.398	0.584	0.512	0.513	0.465	14.0	0.68	1.98	−1.17
Own-account professional	0.183	0.344	0.379	0.728	0.294	1.372	0.932	0.349	16.6	1.95	16.56	−25.58
Farm worker	0.133	0.161	0.207	0.163	0.160	0.201	0.191	0.189	5.6	0.74	−0.10	−0.30
General worker	0.120	0.156	0.179	0.164	0.143	0.166	0.195	0.169	4.9	0.59	−0.21	0.06
Production worker	0.173	0.219	0.243	0.247	0.247	0.272	0.247	0.250	7.6	0.69	0.50	−0.56
Service worker	0.172	0.213	0.229	0.231	0.254	0.263	0.274	0.250	7.8	0.57	0.57	−0.33
Professional worker	0.166	0.200	0.208	0.202	0.221	0.316	0.277	0.287	12.2	0.42	1.80	−0.71
Assisted	0.313	0.325	0.405	0.408	0.382	0.451	0.374	0.330	1.7	0.92	0.77	−3.03
Rentier	0.415	0.530	0.607	0.423	1.007	0.700	0.602	0.510	9.4	1.91	1.55	−4.75

1. Total change between 1976 and 1996.
2. Annual average change for corresponding periods.

Source: Townsend Socio-economic Survey data; Jeong 2008.

workers earn roughly the same amounts and are on the low end. On the high end are non-farm employer, own account professionals, and professional workers. The latter two have the largest increases in income over the twenty years. In between these high and low income groups lie non-farm self-employed, earning more than twice that of workers and about half that of employers and/or professionals. Some of the models below act as if wage work and subsistence agriculture are equivalent in income, and this is not far from the actual facts of the data. The income differences between self-employed and employer categories may have to do with the scale at which constrained households can operate, as in the models below.

Inequality is roughly correlated with the level of income (see Table 5.11). The lowest inequality groups are small farmers, as well as farm, general, production workers (though professional workers and own account professionals have low inequality in income, an exception). The highest inequality groups are non-farm employers and non-farm self-employed (but inequality is high for farmers, an exception).

The occupation shifts out of farming and into other occupations is reflected in satellite imagery depicting deforestation and urbanization. The forests of eastern Chachoengsao (Figure 5.3) and southern Sisaket are now largely gone. Industrialization and construction along the corridor going from Bangkok to the eastern sea board in Chachoengsao and around Sisaket city are evident, in red, on the map. We shall try to explain these patterns, subsequently.

The transition from agriculture into non-farm occupations is often direct. By far the single most common movement in the Townsend Thai data, 1992–7 retrospective, is out of the rice farmer category, into construction and business/skilled trade, shrimp, and other crops, for a total of 37 per cent of the rice-farming population (see Table 5.12). Those farming other crops also make some such transitions, 28 per cent in total. Movement into business and skilled trades is relatively large, and farmers also tend to switch crops.

Despite the prominence of SMEs in the contemporary Thai economy, firms were historically even smaller. A 1980 study from the Ministry of Industry, even excluding rice and saw mills, ice-making, and printing, finds that 63.3 per cent of firms had between one and nine employees, with an additional 30.2 per cent at between ten and forty-nine workers (see Table 5.13). This is clearly a left-shifted histogram relative to the previous more contemporary 1996 data. Suehiro (1989) compares the size distribution between 1963 and 1970 and again finds the distributions shifts left as one goes deeper into the past, even within those seven years. The number of establishments with 10–49 workers was 62.5 per cent in 1970 and increases to 84.3 per cent as one goes back to 1963. The proportion of

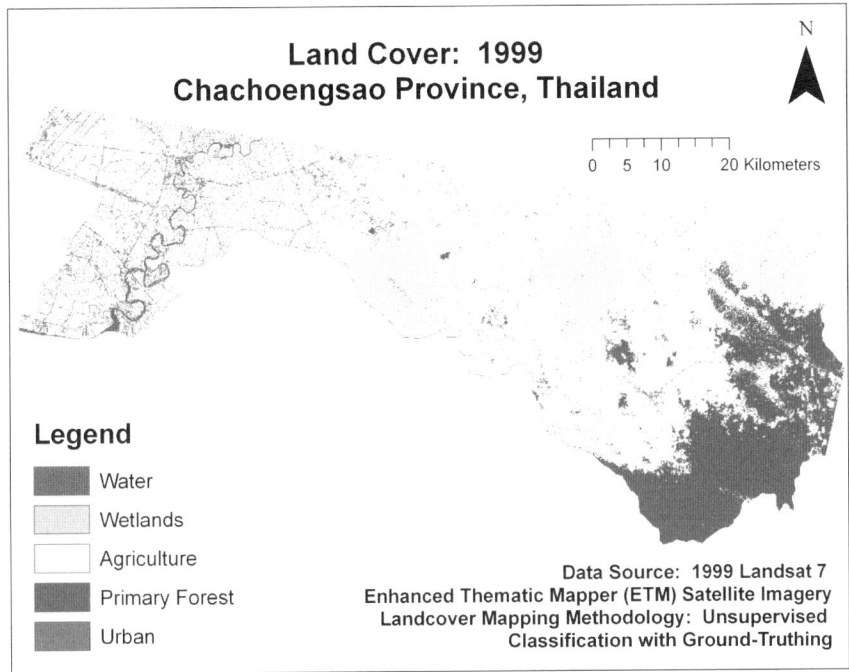

Fig. 5.3. *Satellite view of the industrialization of Thailand (See color version at the end of the book).*

Source: Felkner 2000.

small establishments contributing to employment, value added, and wages and salaries likewise shifts left as one goes backward in time.

The distribution of establishments (by type) in the most developed, Bangkok/Thonburi Areas in 1960 is listed in the table (see Table 5.14). Apart from matches and cement, most establishments are quite small, including those run by Chinese, where the average employment overall is 8.5 workers.

One surmises from NESDB data that, early on, the food and beverage sector was among the most important. However, it has been in decline since 1950. Textiles and wearing apparel peaked in the mid-1980s. Transportation and petroleum have increased over time, but with cycles (see Figures 5.4(a)–(e) and 5.5)).

Despite non-trivial income gaps, movement of households into higher income categories has come slowly. The Townsend Thai data measure occupation transitions, as noted earlier, and also retrospective wealth. Non-parametric regressions reveal that the 1992 wealth of those still in farming helps to predict the fraction that makes a subsequent transition out of the farm and into other enterprise, 1992–7. Standard errors do not

Table 5.12. *Percentage distribution of occupational changes over past six years*

New occupation of household head = >	Rice farmer	Farmer, other crop	Shrimp farmer	Construction	Business/ Skilled trade	Professional/ Administrative	General worker, Cleaner/Janitor	Other	Total
Old occupation of household head									
Inactive/no occupation	0.0	0.0	0.0	0.0	0.0	0.0	0.0	0.2	0.2
Rice farmer	0.2	7.1	7.3	6.7	7.9	0.8	4.7	2.8	37.5
Farmer, other crop	1.4	15.4	2.8	1.0	3.9	0.2	1.8	1.4	27.8
Shrimp farmer	0.0	1.2	2.0	0.2	0.6	0.0	0.0	0.2	4.1
Construction	0.2	0.6	0.4	0.2	1.0	0.2	0.4	0.4	3.4
Business/Skilled trade	1.4	1.2	2.0	0.8	4.9	0.4	1.2	0.6	12.4
Professional/Administrative	0.0	0.6	0.0	0.0	0.6	0.4	0.4	0.4	2.4
General worker, Cleaner/Janitor	0.8	1.8	1.0	1.8	1.6	0.0	0.8	0.6	8.3
Other	0.8	1.0	0.0	0.2	1.2	0.0	0.4	0.4	3.9
Total	4.7	29.0	15.4	10.9	21.7	2.0	9.7	6.9	100.0

Source: Jeong, unpublished.

Table 5.13. *Number of factories classified by size of employment and regions, 1980*

Size of employment	Bangkok	Central	Northern	Northeastern	Southern	Total	Percentage for each size
1–9	10,019	4,935	1/602	2,415	1,526	20,497	63.3%
	(48.9%)	(24.1%)	(7.8%)	(11.8%)	(7.5%)	(100.0%)	
10–49	4,145	2,410	932	1,257	760	9,774	30.2%
	(45.2%)	(24.7%)	(9.5%)	(12.9%)	(7.8%)	(100.0%)	
50–199	507	663	169	281	112	1,732	5.3%
	(29.3%)	(38.3%)	(9.8%)	(16.2%)	(6.5%)	(100.0%)	
200 and over	118	118	43	32	18	399	1.2%
	(29.6%)	(47.1%)	(10.8%)	(8.0%)	(4.5%)	(100.0%)	
Total	15,059	8196	2,746	3,985	2,416	32,402	100
	(46.5%)	(25.3%)	(8.5%)	(12.3%)	(7.5%)	(100.0%)	

Notes: Excludes rice mills, sawmills, ice-making, and printing firms.

Source: Ministry of Industry, Factory Control Division.

Table 5.14. *Establishments in the Bangkok–Thonburi area, 1960*

Type of business	Numbers of establishments			Number of employees	Employees per establishment
	Total	Thai	Foreign[a]		
Hardware	1,024	285	739	5,926	5.8
Printing, book binding	530	290	240	5,014	9.5
Sawmilling	317	89	228	4,771	15.1
Weaving with handlooms[b]	382	15	367	4,527	11.9
Rice-milling	149	92	57	2,625	17.6
Candles, joss sticks	111	34	77	2,148	19.4
Machinery repairing	283	122	161	2,096	7.4
Weaving with machines	185	16	169	2,052	11.1
Spinning	62	9	53	1,586	25.6
Pharmaceuticals	228	85	143	1,562	6.9
Flour-milling	196	32	164	1,448	7.4
Matches	4	1	3	1,283	320.8
Garments[c]	29	8	21	1,116	38.5
Aerated water	47	14	33	1,005	21.4
Tobacco	94	23	71	825	8.8
Shellac	24	7	17	558	23.3
Soap[c]	13	2	11	550	42.3
Cement	1	0	1	521	521.0
Ice	43	24	19	510	11.9
Liquor	6	5	1	218	36.3
Total[d]	7,302	2,233	5,069	62,264	8.5

Notes: [a]Mostly the Chinese group.
[b]Establishments with five looms or more.
[c]Establishments with five employees or more.
[d]Includes other businesses.

Source: Suehiro 1989.

overturn this conclusion, especially on the low end of wealth. It would thus seem there are barriers to entry, for example, imperfect credit markets. This is a key feature of the constrained household choice problems below.

Related, for those in a new business, one year old or less, the distribution of business assets is shifted to the right if the household is able to obtain formal borrowing, relative to those in financial autarky, who neither borrow nor save. (Interestingly, those with savings only are asset poor—see below for a model which rationalizes this conclusion.) See Figure 5.6(a) and 5.6(b).

However, for those starting business in the 1997 financial crisis, the picture is cloudy if not reversed. It is as if either a restricted financial system took its toll or the incentives to enter business shifted with changing

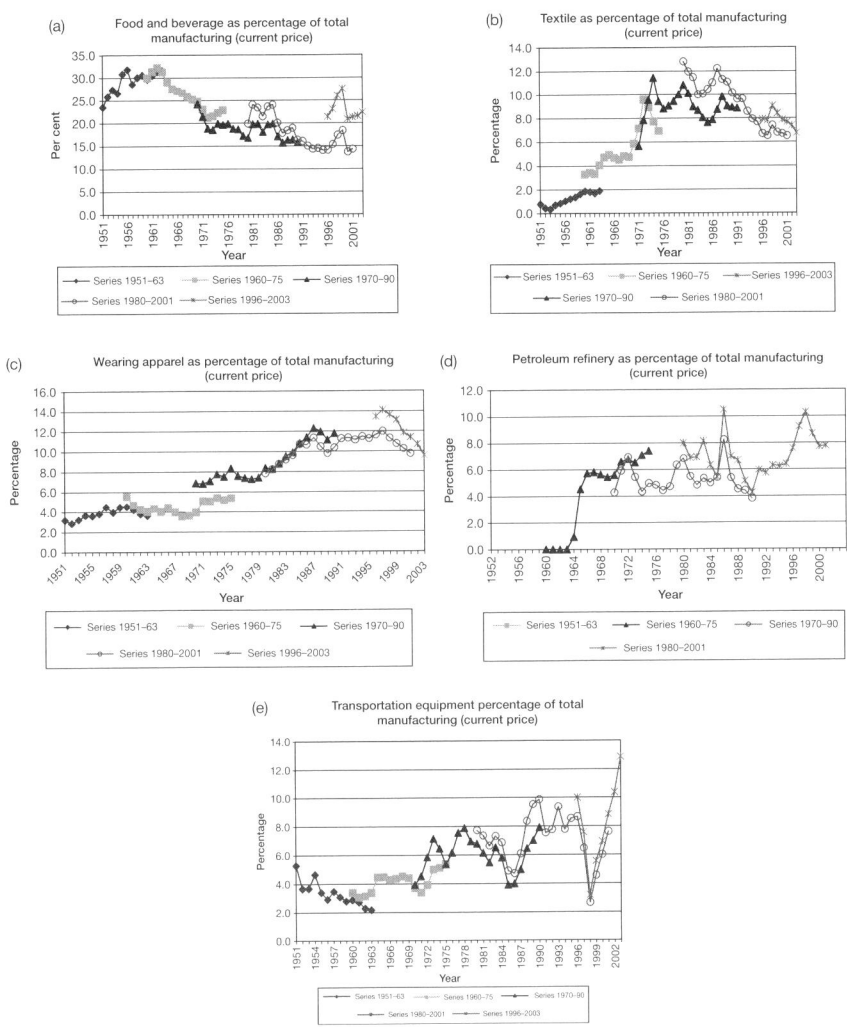

Fig. 5.4(a)–(e). *Manufacturing in Thailand, 1951–2003*

Source: Adapted from NESDB data.

income differentials. Paulson and Townsend (2005) find that start-up in-vestment was smaller than normal in this period, and households were less skilled. In short, these businesses may have been a substitute for wage employment. Over the longer history and in the contemporary situation, that is not the typical case.

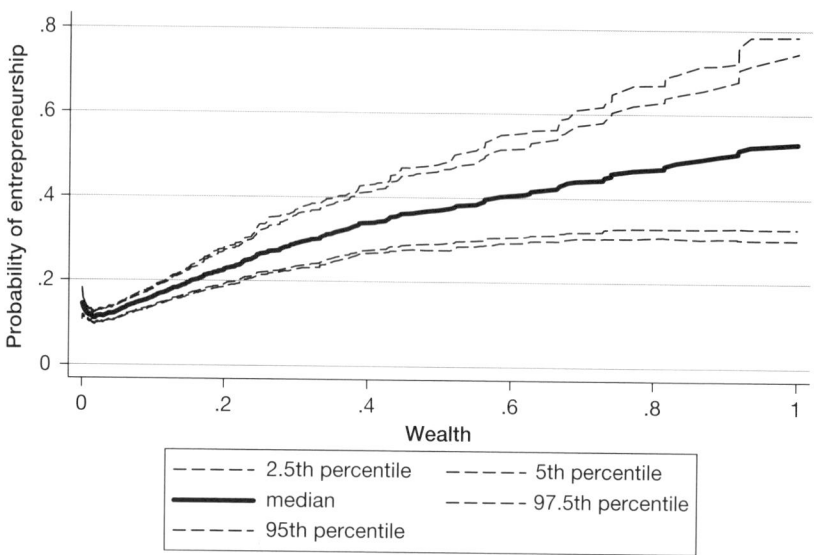

Fig. 5.5. *Non-parametric relationship between starting a business and wealth*

Note: y-axis indicates probability of starting a business (1992–7), x-axis indicates prior wealth in 1992. Dashed line indicates 90 percent confidence interval, dotted line $=\pm 2\sigma$.

Source: Paulson, Townsend, and Karaivanov 2006.

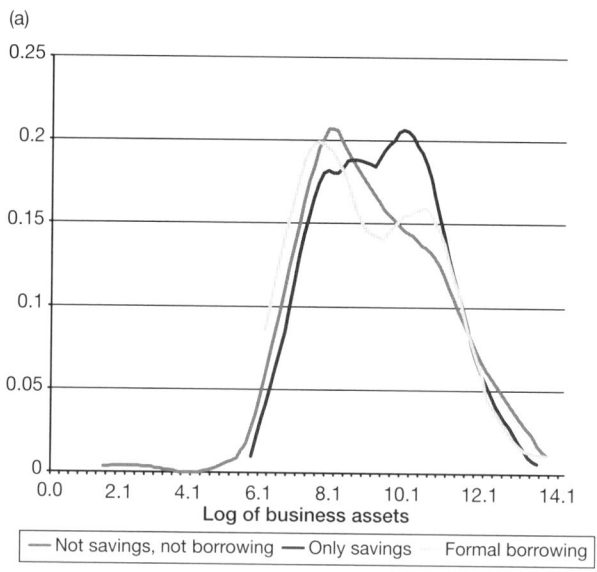

Fig. 5.6(a). *Business less than one year old before 2002*

Source: Townsend Thai data.

(b)

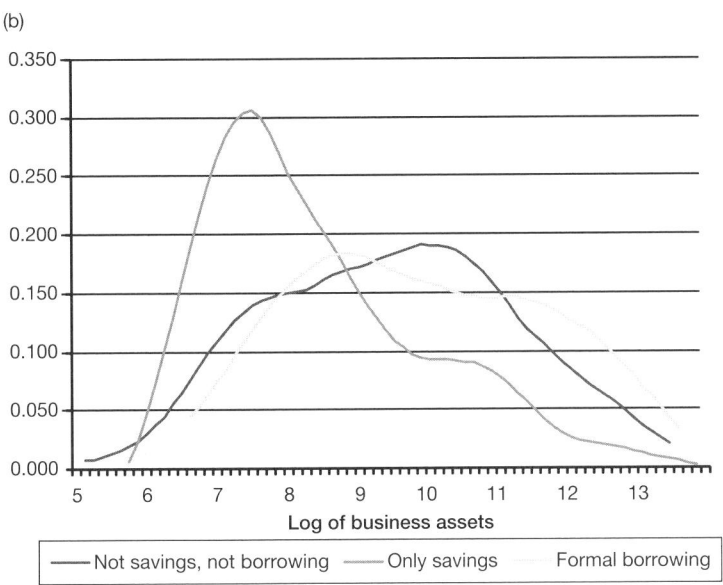

Fig. 5.6(b). *Business less than one year old after 2002*

Source: Townsend Thai data.

5.2. Drivers: Financial Situation (Contemporary Picture)

A table summarizing the formal financial system shows that commercial banks in 1996 had four times the funds mobilized, and about the same multiple of the liabilities, as their nearest competitors, finance companies, and three times the level of assets. The Government Savings Bank (GSB), Government Housing Bank, and the Bank for Agriculture and Agriculture Cooperatives (BAAC) constitute the next largest group, though each is quite small in comparison. For example, the GSB had at best 33 per cent of the funds mobilized by finance companies, and the BAAC lent about 12 per cent relative to finance companies (see Table 5.15).

But, household surveys in rural and semi-urban areas portray the opposite picture. In the Townsend Thai data, as in Table 5.16(a)–(b), commercial banks in 1997 have only 3.4 per cent of all loans, or 15.8 per cent by value. Much of this is the Central region, at 15 per cent to 26 per cent, rather than the Northeast, at 5.0 per cent to 6.4 per cent. The BAAC has 34.3 per cent of all loans, 28.6 per cent by value. This reaches 39.9 per cent in the Northeast. The informal sector, missing of course from the previous Bank of

155

Table 5.15. *Key statistics of Thai financial institutions at end of 1996*

Financial institutions	Number	Number of branches	Assets[1]	Funds mobilized from households[1]	Credits extended[1]
Commercial banks	29	3171	5,626,661.2	2,642,854.2	4,825,056.5
Finance companies[2]	91	71	1,811,937.6	661,016.4	1,488,187.8
Credit foncier companies	12	0	8,517.7	6,151.6	6,742.3
Mutual fund management company	8	195 funds	216,240.7	na	na
Government Savings Bank	1	543	237,442.2	205,374.2	56,256.7
Government Housing Bank	1	169	211,444.2	59,370.7	198,499.5
Bank for Agriculture and Agricultural Cooperatives (BAAC)	1	628	212,067.1	57,239.3	165,621.5
Industrial Finance Corp of Thailand (IFTC)	1	23	143,802.8	—	103,234.3
Small Industry Credit Guarantee Corporation (SIGC)	1	0	607.7	—	—
Small Industry Finance Corporation (SIFC)	1	1	1,887.6	—	698.4
Export-Import Bank of Thailand (EXIM bank)	1	2	34,623.8	—	30,744.6
Savings cooperatives	1127[3]	0	254,400.0[4]	181,750.0[4]	212,600.0[4]
Agricultural cooperatives	2832[3]	0	34,180.0[4]	17,150.0[4]	23,290.0[4]
Life insurance companies (including composite company)	13	1216	145,172.9	116,738.9	31,847.2

1. Unit: million baht.
2. Including finance and securities companies.
3. End of 1995.
4. Estimated.

Source: Bank of Thailand.

Table 5.16(a). *Lender distribution by number of loans.* **(b)** *Lender distribution of total credit.*

(a)

Lender	All	Chachoengsao	Lop Buri	Buriram	Sisaket
Neighbor	7.8	8.6	7.8	8.4	6.5
Relative	15.9	16.9	14.2	17.2	15.0
BAAC	34.3	28.3	25.1	39.0	41.2
PCG	1.4	1.2	1.5	0.6	2.2
Commercial Bank	3.4	5.5	5.8	2.2	1.4
Agricultural Cooperative	10.0	14.0	13.3	5.1	9.6
Village Fund	1.0	0.6	0.5	1.6	1.0
Rice Bank	0.4	0.0	0.0	0.5	0.7
Moneylender	10.1	5.9	12.0	12.2	9.0
Storeowner	4.1	4.8	5.1	4.0	2.9
Supplier	0.2	0.3	0.4	0.0	0.3
Landlord	0.1	0.0	0.0	0.4	0.1
Purchaser	1.2	1.1	3.7	0.0	0.3
Other	10.0	12.4	10.5	8.5	9.6
Total	100.0	100.0	100.0	100.0	100.0

(b)

Lender	All	Chachoengsao	Lop Buri	Buriram	Sisaket
Neighbor	2.4	2.7	2.1	2.9	1.3
Relative	14.3	25.6	6.2	8.4	7.4
BAAC	28.6	25.1	22.2	39.9	38
PCG	1.2	0.2	0.9	0.1	7.4
Comm. Bank	15.8	15.9	26.2	6.4	5
Agricultural Cooperative	8.8	12.5	7.8	3.0	8.8
Village Fund	0.2	0.1	0.2	0.3	0.2
Rice Bank	0.0	0.0	0.0	0.1	0.1
Moneylender	6.0	3.6	7.2	8.3	7.5
Storeowner	6.9	6.4	5.4	12.8	2.7
Supplier	0.1	0.2	0.0	0.0	0
Landlord	0.0	0.0	0.0	0.2	0
Purchaser	2.9	0.3	9.2	0.0	0.3
Other	12.6	7.4	12.7	17.6	21.4
Total	100.0	100.0	100.0	100.0	100.0

Sources: Townsend Thai Survey 1997; Kaboski and Townsend 2007.

Thailand table, is quite large, constituting 34 per cent of the total, and even larger in total number of loans, as loan size can be small. The informal sector consists of a variety of players: neighbors, relatives, moneylenders, storeowners, input suppliers, landlords, and output purchasers. Note that one should not confuse the informal sector with stereotypical money-lenders as they are only part of the story. Of some interest, the variety of non-trivial lenders, formal and informal, is greater in the Central region—we might anticipate that intermediation seems to work differently there.

The percentage of households not borrowing is 32 per cent of the surveyed population of the Townsend Thai 1997 data (see Table 5.17). These households either lack access or choose not to borrow. This is lower in the Northeast, at about 23 per cent, though in a TDRI study the estimate is about 40 per cent. The BAAC has a large role in the Northeast. Evidently, though, financial autarky is important (to be imposed exogenously or modeled below). Of those borrowing, the percentage of households using formal credit only is 62 per cent to 70 per cent of the borrowing population, according to a variety of surveys reproduced by the Bank of Thailand, in Table 5.18. Those using the informal only are estimated at 6 per cent to 17 per cent. Of those in business, 34 per cent self-finance while 36 per cent use commercial banks/BAAC/formal, 17 per cent moneylender/informal only, and 13 per cent the

Table 5.17. *Loan distribution, by changwat*

	All	Chachoengsao	Lop Buri	Buriram	Sisaket	Korat	Nan
Percentage with loans	68.0	57.0	60.6	76.9	77.7	57.3	59.8
Total number of loans	3467	661	817	1045	944	—	—
Not borrowing	32.0	43.0	39.4	23.1	22.3	42.7	40.2

Sources: Thailand Development Research Institute data; Giné 2001; and Townsend Thai data.

Table 5.18. *Shares of formal vs informal credits*

	By number of households			By amount of outstanding credits
Percentage of households with debt	Household Attitudes toward Debt and Savings (HADS)(2004)	National Statistical Office (NSO) (2002)	National Statistical Office (NSO) (2004)	Household Attitudes toward Debt and Savings (HADS)(2004)
Formal credits only	70.0	71.0	70.0	62.1
Informal credits only	9.0	17.0	15.0	5.6
From both sources	21.0	12.0	15.0	32.3
Total	100.0	100.0	100.0	100.0

Source: Bank of Thailand estimates.

Table 5.19. *Borrower distribution, by changwat*

Borrower	All	Chachoengsao	Lop Buri	Buriram	Sisaket
Relative in village	30.3	24.8	25.6	31.9	36.8
Relative not in village	15.2	24.2	20.4	8.5	11.4
Non-relative in village	39.7	31.7	35.5	47.2	40.8
Non-relative not in village	12.6	19.3	14.0	8.9	10.5
Business partner	0.3	0.0	1.2	0.0	0.0
Other	2.0	0.0	3.5	3.4	0.5
Total	100.0	100.0	100.0	100.0	100.0

Sources: Kaboski and Townsend 2004; Townsend Thai data.

Table 5.20. *Size, duration, interest rate, percentage of loans at zero, interest of loans lent, by borrower*

Borrower	Average loan size (in 1000s)	Average duration (months)	Average interest rate (annual) (per cent)	Percentage of loans at zero interest
Relative in village	14	17	13	64.8
Relative not in village	58	15	19	70.9
Non-relative in village	13	12	46	50.8
Non-relative not in village	74	14	57	44.3
Business partner	40	12	10	50.0
Other	12	19	30	26.7

Source: Townsend Thai data.

combination of formal and informal. One may note the variety and combination of lenders, anticipating further analysis in the models below.

The variety in the informal sector, by region, is reflected in the Townsend Thai data in Table 5.19 in a number of ways. The largest categories of transaction partners in the Northeast are relatives and non-relatives in the village, whereas relatives and non-relatives not in the village rise in importance in the Central region. Non-relatives in the village are the single largest category in both regions, however, 33 per cent to 43 per cent.

Interest rates vary, with large fractions at zero interest for relatives in and out of the village (see Table 5.20). Likewise, duration is longer for relatives in villages. In sum, the village, or the family within the village, may constitute an important entity in finance risk-sharing networks. This will be tested in the work reported below. Average interest rates, even when positive, vary accordingly: low for relatives in the village and high for non-relatives out of the village. Loan size is lowest for relatives in the village and highest for those not in the village, especially non-relatives. It seems the informal sector may change as the economy develops, toward larger loans at higher interest but of shorter duration.

Among SMEs in the JBIC survey, commercial banks in 1996 were the dominant source of credit, for 58 per cent of survey respondents, and 'informal' the dominant source for only 6.7 per cent (see Table 5.21). This seems substantially different from the household numbers (though the questions were asked differently). Sample selection and the behavior of commercial banks require further investigation.

Collateral, as in Table 5.22, is often required for most household borrowing from commercial banks and also for many households borrowing from the BAAC and moneylenders. Land is the most common asset used, at 77 per cent, 32 per cent, and 22 per cent for these providers, respectively. Physical collateral-to-loan ratios are high, at 15 overall. One guesses that land deeds cannot be subdivided even for small loans. It would thus seem from these data that default (and collateral) is a potential problem. The most common collateral alternative to physical collateral is some kind of joint guarantee, either with a single guarantor or with a group, at 29 per cent overall and 50 per cent of BAAC customers. 21 per cent of those borrowing from village funds have group-guaranteed loans.

But 41 per cent of the sample of borrowers claims to have not needed collateral at all. This is especially true for loans from the informal sector, including moneylenders, but also from village funds. Enforcement may not be an issue in these cases. Distinguishing the informal sector from the formal sector is a task that lies ahead.

A surprisingly large number of loans to SMEs seem to be absent physical collateral (see Table 5.23). For example, in 1996, 87.4 per cent for loans less than 6 months in duration, 46 per cent for loans 12 months or longer. Land, inventory, and some equipment provide the collateral for those needing it (see Table 5.24). Thus, relative to the household survey, physical collateral is less often required. Unfortunately, we know little about those borrowing in other ways. The best guess is that there are individual or personal guarantees of some kind, but more information is needed.

One measure of default is a binary dummy from the BAAC survey, which equals one if the BAAC has ever, in the group's history, raised the interest rate as a penalty for late payment. 27 per cent of groups responded affirmatively. This relatively high figure should not be taken as a mark against the BAAC lending program. Annual default rates are much lower, whereas this measure of default is over the entire history of the group (median group age is ten years). Further, imposing an interest rate penalty is one of the first remedial actions in a dynamic process the BAAC uses with a delinquent group.

Table 5.21. *Sources of credit, 1996*

	Working capital				Capital investment			
	1996	1997	1998	1999	1996	1997	1998	1999
Public financial institutions	3.6	3.4	3.7	3.7	2.5	2.6	2.6	2.2
Commercial banks incorporated in Thailand/abroad	58.7	58.6	57.5	56.9	41.3	40.0	36.9	36.6
Finance companies	1.2	1.1	1.1	1.1	1.7	1.6	1.4	1.4
Informal financing	6.7	7.6	8.3	8.4	4.0	4.7	5.8	5.1
Overseas/offshore financing	1.2	1.2	0.9	1.4	2.2	1.9	1.2	1.6
Other lending institutions for factoring, leasing	0.5	0.6	0.6	0.3	0.6	0.9	0.9	0.5
Sales proceeds	45.5	45.6	47.0	48.11	17.6	17.6	20.2	20.4
Company's internal reserves	20.6	21.2	23.2	23.4	15.0	15.0	15.6	15.4
Head office	3.3	3.1	3.0	3.0	3.3	3.3	3.0	3.0

Source: Japan Bank for International Cooperation.

Table 5.22. *Sources of collateral*

Lender	None	Land-borrower use	Land-lender use	Savings guarantee	Future crop guarantee	Other collateral	Single guarantor	Multiple guarantor	Other	Total
Overall	41.5	21.8	1.3	0.1	0.3	3.9	2.7	26.6	1.7	100
Neighbor	85.5	7.5	2.6	0.0	0.0	1.5	1.1	1.5	0.4	100
Relative	93.1	3.1	0.9	0.0	0.0	0.9	0.5	1.1	0.4	100
BAAC	9.8	31.9	1.0	0.2	0.2	4.1	2.0	48.4	2.5	100
PCG	36.2	6.4	2.1	6.4	0.0	2.1	10.6	36.2	0.0	100
Commercial Bank	1.7	77.1	2.5	0.0	0.0	9.3	5.9	0.9	2.5	100
Agricultural Cooperative	8.9	38.3	2.0	0.0	0.3	4.9	1.2	44.4	0.0	100
Village Fund	72.7	6.1	0.0	0.0	0.0	0.0	0.0	21.2	0.0	100
Rice Bank	63.6	0.0	0.0	0.0	9.1	0.0	0.0	9.1	18.2	100
Moneylender	62.8	21.6	2.0	0.0	0.9	3.5	3.8	2.9	2.6	100
Storeowner	72.7	4.9	0.7	0.0	0.7	5.6	9.8	4.9	0.7	100
Supplier	100.0	0.0	0.0	0.0	0.0	0.0	0.0	0.0	0.0	100
Landlord	100.0	0.0	0.0	0.0	0.0	0.0	0.0	0.0	0.0	100
Purchaser	48.7	10.3	0.0	0.0	2.6	35.9	0.0	0.0	2.6	100
Other	39.7	6.7	0.6	0.0	0.3	4.1	5.8	39.7	3.2	100

Sources: Townsend Thai Survey 1997; Kaboski and Townsend 1998.

Table 5.23. *Collateral requirement by loan period*

Duration of loans	Yes		No		n/a		Total
	N	%	N	%	N	%	N
				1996			
Less than 6 months	71	11.1	561	87.4	10	1.6	642
6 months or longer	87	13.6	544	84.7	11	1.7	642
12 months or longer	337	52.5	295	46.0	10	1.6	642
				1997			
Less than 6 months	92	14.3	540	84.1	10	1.6	642
6 months or longer	96	15.0	536	83.5	10	1.6	642
12 months or longer	316	49.2	316	49.2	10	1.6	642
				1999			
Less than 6 months	100	15.6	532	82.9	10	1.6	642
6 months or longer	92	14.3	540	84.1	10	1.6	642
12 months or longer	301	46.9	331	51.6	10	1.6	642

Source: Japan Bank for International Cooperation.

Table 5.24. *Form of collateral*

	1996		1997		1999	
	N	%	N	%	N	%
Land and building	307	79.7	295	81.7	284	80.7
Machinery and equipment	57	14.8	97	26.9	100	28.4
Stocks	87	22.6	105	29.1	101	28.7
Others	6	1.6	6	1.7	7	2.0
NA	4	1.0	6	1.7	7	2.0
Base all respondents	385	100.0	361	100.0	352	100.0

Notes: Multiple answers.

Source: Japan Bank for International Cooperation.

Households are asked about the consequences of default, and the responses vary by lender (see Table 5.25). For commercial banks, 'land is repossessed (or other)' is the answer for 35.1 per cent of the respondents, and 'the borrower would not be able to use that lender again' for 49.3 per cent. No consequences to default are reported for loans from relatives, at 44 per cent, and from suppliers, at 50 per cent, though 'cannot borrow from that lender again' is about equal in importance. Of great interest, 'cannot borrow from any lender' is a common response for loans from BAAC, production credit group (PCG) village funds, and also moneylenders, ranging from 7 per cent to 18 per cent. This answer may be an indicator of villages' level sanctions for the potential loss of village reputation.

Table 5.25. Consequences of default distribution by lender

Default Consequence	Neighbor	Relative	BAAC	PCG	Commercial Bank	Agricultural Cooperative	Village Fund	Rice Bank	Moneylender	Storeowner	Supplier	Landlord	Purchaser	Other
None	18.5	44.0	3.7	0.0	2.5	6.2	0.0	0.0	14.5	14.1	50.0	0.0	15.4	9.4
Cannot borrow from lender	61.9	45.7	47.1	63.0	42.0	49.3	43.8	81.8	48.4	38.0	37.5	0.0	53.8	48.8
Cannot borrow from anyone	3.1	1.3	13.2	15.2	10.9	9.4	18.8	0.0	7.0	2.8	0.0	100.0	2.6	6.4
Other (including land repossession)	16.5	9.0	36.0	21.7	44.5	35.1	37.5	18.2	30.1	45.1	12.5	0.0	28.2	35.4
Total	100.0	100.0	100.0	100.0	100.0	100.0	100.0	100.0	100.0	100.0	100.0	100.0	100.0	100.0

Sources: Townsend Thai Survey 1997; Kaboski and Townsend 1998.

Table 5.26. *Reasons for saving by income tercile*

Reason	Income Tercile		
	Low	Medium	High
Bequests (Life-cycle)	11.52%	13.08%	16.05%
Emergencies (buffer/insurance)	54.97%	54.66%	*51.97%
Business investment (future investment)	3.21%	2.90%	**6.35%

* indicates significance at 0.05%; ** indicates significance at 0.01%

Source: Townsend Thai data.

Evidently, loss of physical collateral is not the only sanction, both for formal and informal loans. This will be taken up in the models below.

Borrowing is of course only half of the intermediation picture. The other half is saving. Households report emergencies, bequests, and business investment as motives for savings (see Table 5.26). These motives are implicitly assumed in the models below, featuring finance/business, risk-sharing, and overlapping generations. By value, as in Table 5.27, 56 per cent of savings are in commercial banks and 13 per cent in BAAC accounts. Many respondents report having cash, jewelry, and/or gold in the house (though we do not have values). Rice in storage is a dominant mode of savings, reaching 47 per cent by value in parts of the Northeast. In sum, savings takes place in formal and informal ways, and formal intermediation appears quite limited in some places.

One can measure the extent of intermediation by stocks or by flows. A revealing number is the debt-to-asset ratio, easily computed from balance sheets, if available. The medians of this ratio across provinces in 1997 are close to zero, rising from 0.03 to 0.05 by 2003. Though increasing, these are low numbers, indicative of limited credit on the supply and/or limited demand. Histograms (Figure 5.7) reveal a relatively high concentration of the population at or near zero debt, virtual financial autarky, though the latter has diminished over time. Means are somewhat higher, rising from 0.08 to 0.20. The difference between the means and medians reveals the existence of a few relatively large debt-holders. There is some regional variation, offering interesting exceptions: the debt-to-asset ratio is higher in the Northeast and lower in the South. The former may reflect BAAC outreach/targeting (see Table 5.28).

In the JBIC SME data, 37 per cent of the firms have debt-to-asset ratios below one (see Table 5.29(a)–(b)). For firms in the Ministry of Industry data, debt-to-asset ratios increase with the size of the firm (gross assets), especially so when one eliminates from the sample bankrupt (negative equity) firms and controls for industry effects (see Table 5.30). These ratios for

Table 5.27. *Where savings are held*

| | Where savings are held, for the whole sample | | | | | Saving institutions by value: differences in changwats from overall sample (percentage)[1] | | | |
Institution	By account (percentage)	By value (percentage)	By account (percentage)	Account size	Average change	Chachoengsao	Lop Buri	Buriram	Sisaket
Commercial Bank	12.88	55.59	22.70	74,201	19,314	+11	+16.5	−32	−41
Agricultural Cooperative	4.55	3.28	8.02	12,521	2,264	—	—	−2.5	—
BAAC	13.22	15.32	23.30	19,838	2,177	+3	−9.5	−9.5	+17
PCG	3.27	2.84	5.76	14,888	4,190	−2.5	+4.5	−2.5	—
Rice Bank	0.92	0.23	1.62	4,461	1,120	—	—	—	—
Jewelry	14.64	—	—	—	—	—	—	—	—
Cash	28.63	—	—	—	—	—	—	—	—
Rice Storage	18.50	14.41	32.61	13,176	−84	−9	−12	+33	+24
Government Savings	1.06	1.14	1.87	18,143	5,128	—	—	—	—
Insurance	0.22	0.46	0.39	41,415	8,050	—	—	—	—

1. Values are listed only if they are greater (in absolute terms) than 1%.

Source: Townsend Thai data.

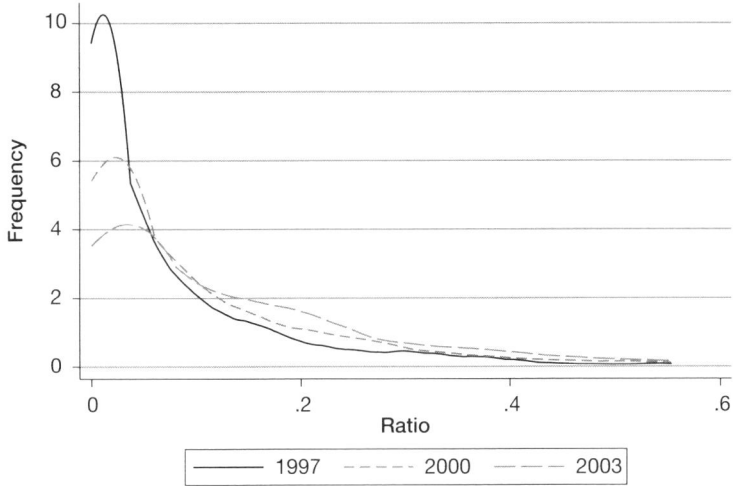

Fig. 5.7. *Debt-to-assets ratio, central northeast Thailand*

Source: Townsend Thai data.

Table 5.28. *Mean debt-to-asset ratio*

Changwat	1997	1998	1999	2000	2001	2002	2003
Chachoengsao	0.0796	0.0509	0.1011	0.1326	0.1388	0.1624	0.1791
Buriram	0.0742	0.2910	0.1361	0.1492	0.1715	0.2014	0.2425
Lop Buri	0.0855	0.0955	0.1914	0.0929	0.1564	0.1682	0.2167
Sisaket	0.0935	0.1246	0.2578	0.1828	0.1762	0.1888	0.1894
Total CNE	0.0832	0.1405	0.1730	0.1403	0.1614	0.1810	0.2075
Satun							0.1597
Yala							0.0781
Total South							0.1191

Source: Townsend Thai data.

firms are larger than those for the household rural survey. The point is that in measures that use stocks, the financial system appears quite skewed, with levels of debt increasing more than proportionately with household assets and with firm size. Still, there are exceptions by region and sector. In several of the models below debt-to-asset ratios and how they move with wealth are revealing of underlying constraints.

Flows are consistent with a less-skewed picture. The excess of consumption over income must be financed, or a surplus saved. Likewise, investment must be covered by cash flow from operations, or financed. The

Table 5.29. *Summary statistics by size of the firm, 2001*

(a) Capital structure

	First quartile	Fourth quartile
All observations		
Number of observations	1,022.00	1,021.00
Total Assets (millions)		
Mean	5.46	286.00
Standard deviation	3.89	743.00
Debt to Asset Ratio		
Mean	1.25	0.71
Standard deviation	13.01	0.62
Liabilities Nominated in Baht (percentage of Total Liabilities)		
Mean	99.78	90.54
Standard deviation	2.88	21.14
Truncated sample (only firms with positive equities)		
Number of observations	843.00	881.00
Total assets (millions)		
Mean	5.45	285.00
Standard deviation	3.82	738.00
Debt to Asset Ratio		
Mean	0.41	0.55
Standard deviation	0.35	0.26
Liabilities nominated in baht (percentage of total liabilities)		
Mean	99.73	90.36
Standard deviation	3.19	20.84

Notes: Size = total assets; total number of observations = 4,086 firms.

Sources: Thai Ministry of Industry and Townsend and Sauphantasak calculations.

(b) Regressions of debt-to-asset ratio on firm's size

Dependent variable: debt-to-asset ratio		All Firms		Truncated sample (only firms with positive equities)	
Total assets (million baht)	Not significant (p = 0.997)	Not significant (p = 0.82)	–	$2.68*10^{-12}$** (p = 0.05)	–
Total asset quartile (1, 2, 3, or 4)	–	–	−0.16* (p = 0.10)	–	0.04*** (p = 0.00)
Industry fixed effects	Not controlled	Controlled	Controlled	Controlled	Controlled
Number of observations	4,081	4,081	4,081	3,444	3,444

Notes: Significance levels * = 10%, ** = 5%; and *** = 1%.

Sources: Thai Ministry of Industry and Townsend and Samphantharak calculations.

Table 5.30. *Debt-to-equity ratio*

	1997		1998		1999	
	N	percentage	N	percentage	N	percentage
3.0 or more	56	8.7	55	8.6	54	8.4
3.0–2.5	21	3.3	26	4	26	4
2.5–2.0	29	4.5	27	4.2	27	4.2
2.0–1.5	35	5.5	45	7	36	5.6
1.5–1.2	71	11.1	66	10.3	63	9.8
1.2–1.0	119	18.5	107	16.7	112	17.4
1.0 or less	236	36.8	246	38.3	254	39.6
n/a	75	11.7	70	10.9	70	10.9
Base all respondents	642	100.0	642	100.0	642	100.0

Source: JBIC

Townsend Thai annual panel stratified by wealth and lender/mechanism reveals in Table 5.31 that formal borrowing from the BAAC and from Agricultural Cooperatives and rice stocks are most used by the relatively poor. Notably, the poor have greater use than the rich of the formal financial system as far as the BAAC is concerned. The number of borrowers from commercial banks is too limited to allow an assessment, but this speaks for itself. Loans from informal sector and savings in commercial banks are more used by the middle and upper segments of the surveyed population. This belies the stereotypical picture of the informal sector as most prominent for the poor. Borrowing from relatives is an important informal exception. As might have been anticipated from the earlier discussion of provincial economies, remittances and government transfer are helpful for most categories of borrowers.

5.2.1. BAAC: Operating Systems and Imposed Regulation

To understand the use and impact of a financial institution it is necessary to understand its operating system. We use here BAAC as a primary example as we have much more relevant information for this financial-sector provider.

The BAAC has a system under which farmers can be granted relief via loan extension, interest reduction, or even principal forgiven. Until recently, loans could be delayed or restructured up to three times without penalty if the borrower were judged not to be in willful default. Occasionally, the government will pay off part of the loan for the farmer. In effect, this system is capable of providing insurance to farmers who experience *force majeure*

Table 5.31. *Partial correlation coefficients of consumption and investment deficit with frequency of use*

	Consumption				Investment			
	All	Poor	Middle	Rich	All	Poor	Middle	Rich
Rental/Financial income	.057***	.053	.040	.050	.016	.015	.017	.025
	(.001)	(.011)	(.160)	(.131)	(.370)	(.644)	(.544)	(.456)
Government transfers	.212***	.070**	.145***	.266***	.042**	.085***	.061**	.043
	(.000)	(.034)	(.000)	(.000)	(.017)	(.011)	(.033)	(.192)
Remittances	.091***	.3062*	.101***	.090***	.028	.048	.051*	.024
	(.000)	(.062)	(.000)	(.006)	(.112)	(.145)	(.076)	(.468)
Formal borrowing	.038**	.104***	.022	.034	.043**	.366***	.002	.042
	(.029)	(.002)	(.456)	(.304)	(.014)	(.000)	(.930)	(.209)
BAAC	.027	.047	.009	.029	.004	.091***	.011	.016
	(.124)	(.158)	(.762)	(.380)	(.845)	(.007)	(.707)	(.623)
Agricultural Cooperatives	.020	.083**	.004	.009	.003	.340***	.017	.011
	(.272)	(.013)	(.889)	(.792)	(.885)	(.000)	(.565)	(.746)
Commercial Bank	.012	dropped	.024	.020	.004	dropped	.029	.007
	(.479)		(.410)	(.557)	(.824)		(.316)	(.828)
PCG	.067***	.024	.034	.099***	.031*	.006	.053*	.031
	(.000)	(.439)	(.242)	(.003)	(.082)	(.858)	(.066)	(.348)
Informal borrowing	.063***	.008	.060**	.031	.138***	.011	.050*	.129***
	(.000)	(.807)	(.038)	(.347)	(.000)	(.739)	(.083)	(.000)
Moneylender	.053***	.017	.103***	.017	.024	.014	.062**	.022
	(.003)	(.606)	(.000)	(.604)	(.170)	(.688)	(.031)	(.517)
Neighbor	.004	.023	.011	.035	.003	.020	.014	.003
	(.819)	(.489)	(.701)	(.300)	(.865)	(.558)	(.635)	(.927)
Relative	.035**	.056*	.046	.017	.028*	.008	.033	.033
	(.051)	(.097)	(.112)	(.604)	(.093)	(.822)	(.253)	(.327)
Store Owner	.052***	.008	.017	.030	.179***	.054*	.030	.185***
	(.003)	(.803)	(.566)	(.374)	(.000)	(.105)	(.308)	(.000)
Lending	.026	.035	.040	.037	.028	.042	.020	.025
	(.141)	(.286)	(.170)	(.260)	(.112)	(.210)	(.489)	(.442)

(continued)

Table 5.31. (Continued)

	Consumption				Investment			
	All	Poor	Middle	Rich	All	Poor	Middle	Rich
Formal savings	.032*	.008	.034	.061*	.039**	.011	.037	.041
	(.075)	(.810)	(.232)	(.067)	(.028)	(.731)	(.193)	(.222)
BAAC	.005	.020	.005	.007	.005	.027	.027	.002
	(.782)	(.554)	(.874)	(.844)	(.775)	(.423)	(.346)	(.948)
Agricultural Cooperatives	.001	.065**	.014	.008	.016	.068**	.005	.020
	(.962)	(.051)	(.620)	(.820)	(.382)	(.042)	(.869)	(.557)
Commercial Bank	.058***	.017	.060**	.119***	.069***	.051	.012	.067**
	(.001)	(.608)	(.034)	(.000)	(.000)	(.128)	(.679)	(.045)
PCG	.013	.040	.022	.063*	.013	.033	.030	.004
	(.455)	(.233)	(.441)	(.061)	(.466)	(.328)	(.309)	(.897)
Informal savings rice	.011	.063*	.063**	.039	.013	.019	.044	.033
	(.523)	(.058)	(.029)	(.239)	(.481)	(.565)	(.127)	(.320)
Household assets	.056***	.060*	.051*	.027	.001	.101***	.069**	.010
	(.002)	(.070)	(.077)	(.415)	(.952)	(.002)	(.017)	(.769)
Livestock	.043**	.092***	.080***	.007				
	(.015)	(.006)	(.006)	(.823)				
Productive assets	.011	.050	.043	.035				
	(.526)	(.133)	(.133)	(.297)				

Notes: Frequent use is a dummy variable indicating whether the household had a particular type of transaction in 3 out of the 4 years in the panel; P-value in parenthesis.
Source: Alem and Townsend 2006.

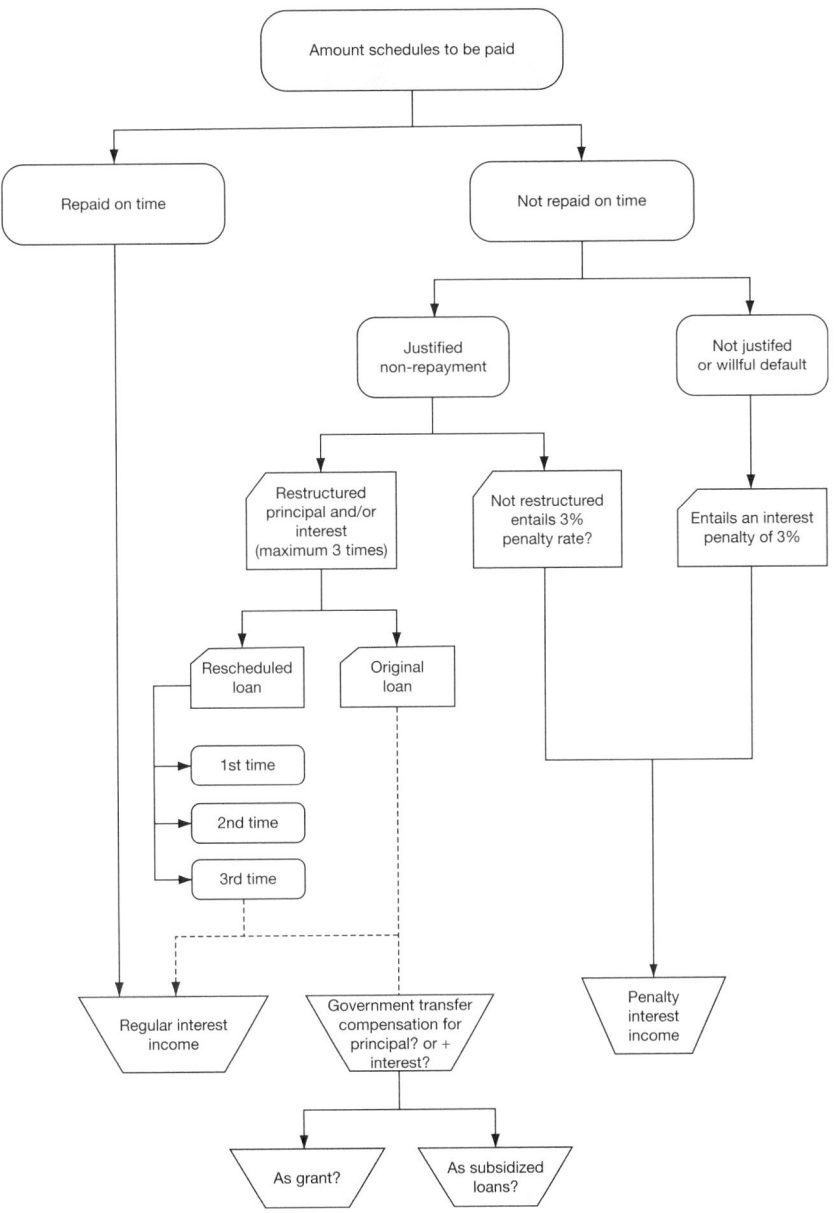

Fig. 5.8. *Bank for Agriculture and Agricultural Cooperatives operating procedures*

Source: Townsend and Yaron 2001. Originally pub. by the Federal Reserve Bank of Chicago in 'The Credit Risk Contingency System of an Asian Development Bank', *Federal Reserve Bank of Chicago Economic Perspectives*, 25 (2001), 31–48.

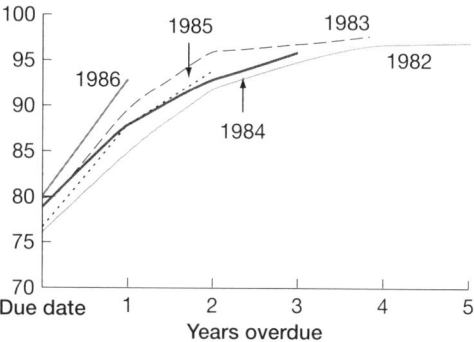

Fig. 5.9. *Percentage of original loan amount paid on time and belatedly against original maturity*

Source: Yaron, Benjamin, and Piprek 1997.

events. The net present value of loan repayment is a function of idiosyncratic shocks. The magnitude of the impact on clients will be assessed below.

The percentage of BAAC loans paid on time starts at a relatively low 75 per cent to 80 per cent, based on 1980s data, but arrears history reveals that repayment rates rise to a relatively high 95 per cent or over. Thus, based on experience, the BAAC should not provision linearly, as was recommended (more or less), and implemented, during the financial crisis (see Table 5.32). There of course should be an immediate provision as soon as the loan is overdue, and then the rate of residual, augmented provisioning should increase over time as it is less likely the loan will be repaid.

Of course, provisions also need to take into account the possibility of adverse macro shocks (see Table 5.33). The amount one year in arrears was 4,488 million baht in 1997 and this falls with repayment to 2,669 million baht two years in arrears in 1998. Then, reflecting the crisis, the entire

Table 5.32. *Bank for Agriculture and Agricultural Cooperatives provisioning for loan losses*

Age of principal overdue	Loan loss provision rate (percentage)
< 1 year	10
> 1–2 years	30
> 2–3 years	50
> 3–4 years	70
> 4 years	100

Source: Townsend and Yaron 2001. Orig. pub. by the Federal Reserve Bank of Chicago.

Table 5.33. *Changes in arrears by age, Bank for Agriculture and Agricultural Cooperatives, 1997–9*

Years in arrears (age)	Amount in arrears, 1997	Percent change 1997–8	Amount in arrears, 1998	Percent change 1998–9	Amount in arrears, 1999	Average percent change 1997–9
1	4,488	−40.53	6,272	−49.35	3,938	
2	1,246	−22.95	2,669	−25.03	3,177	
3	509	−22.00	960	−20.10	2,001	−33.23
4	295	−22.71	397	−20.40	767	−21.54
5	224	−20.98	228	−19.74	316	−21.21
6	73	−20.55	177	−17.51	183	−21.24
7	45	−17.78	58	−17.24	146	−19.27
8	29	−17.24	37	−18.92	48	−18.91
9	15	−16.56	24	−17.33	30	−18.35
10	136		126		124	−17.00
Total	7,060	55.07	10,948	−1.99	10,730	23.28
Outstanding from FY 1997	7,060	−33.77	4,676	−22.69	3.615	−28.44
Outstanding from FY 1998	—	—	10,948	−37.96	6,792	—

Notes: Amounts are baht in millions.

Source: Townsend and Yaron 2001. Orig. pub. by the Federal Reserve Bank of Chicago.

schedule shifts up: the amount one year in arrears in 1998 was 6,272 million, and this falls with repayment to 3,177 million two years in arrears in 1999. Aggregate shocks need to be taken into account in insurance arrangements.

Provisioning enters as a cost on the BAAC income statement. This is covered by revenue in the line marked 'other income' (income recompense plus other government transfers). In effect, the government is paying the premium for a mandatory insurance fund which benefits BAAC farmers' clients. Ideally, this would be administered as a lump sum transfer to branches (or even the farmers) who would then be allocated credit and insurance based on incentives (see Table 5.34).

Indirectly, BAAC clients are receiving the subsidy. More generally, the BAAC does lend at below market rates and does rely on a transfer from the central government. But we would like to know the magnitude of the subsidy and the benefits received by farmers. For costs, Townsend and Yaron (2001) use market prices for all sources of funds, including funds lent at concessionary rates. The costs should include appropriate provisions as noted.

The models below also use an outside market interest rate as the true cost of funds. Yaron's subsidy dependency index at 35 per cent indicates the amount of an increase in the average on-lending rate that would have been necessary

Table 5.34. *Bank for Agriculture and Agricultural Cooperatives profit and loss statement*

	31 March 1999		31 March 1998		31 March 1997	
	baht	per cent	baht	per cent	baht	per cent
Revenues						
Interest earned on loans to client farmers	19,768	82.33	21,187	86.98	19,704	79.88
Interest on loans to farmers' institutions	1,497	6.23	1,723	6.34	1,191	4.83
Interest on deposits with other banks	32	0.13	143	0.53	124	0.50
Interest on government bonds and promissory notes	542	2.26	2,266	8.34	2.040	8.27
Other income[1]	2,173	9.05	1,850	6.81	1,607	6.52
Total revenues	**24,011**	**100.00**	**27,170**	**100.00**	**24,665**	**100.00**
Expenses						
Salaries, wages, and fringe benefits	3,291	13.87	3,123	11.58	3,177	13.64
Interest paid on deposits	6,055	25.52	10,035	37.21	9,325	40,04
Interest on commercial bank deposits	–	–	261	0.97	280	1.20
Interest on borrowing and promissory notes	3,987	16.80	5,321	19.73	5,221	22.42
Loan expenses	31	0.13	27	0.10	163	0.70
Travel and per diem expenses	126	0.53	120	0.44	133	0.57
Provision for doubtful accounts	5,665	23.87	4,833	17.92	2,751	11.81
Bad debts written off	7	0.03	9	0.03	27	0.12
Other expenses	1,179	4.97	1,287	4.77	1,054	4.52
Depreciation on assets and leasehold amortization	592	2.50	616	2.29	600	2.57
Losses due to exchange rate fluctuation	1,983	8.36	550	2.04	557	2.39
Total expenses	**23,731**	**100.00**	**26,967**	**100.00**	**23,289**	**100.00**
Net profit	**280**		**203**		**1,377**	

1. Other income includes government transfers among other items.
Notes: Amounts are baht in millions. Columns may not total due to rounding.
Source: Townsend and Yaron 2001.

Table 5.35. *Summary of significant correlations between relevant institution types/policies and growth/failure*

Correlations with membership growth		Correlations with savings growth		Correlations with lending growth	
Positive	Negative	Positive	Negative	Positive	Negative
Offer lending services	Saving is optional	Require minimum initial deposit	Standard savings accounts	Provide agricultural training	Institution is a buffalo bank
Require minimum initial deposit		Have membership application forms	Time deposit savings	Make cash loans	Make rice loans
		Pledged savings accounts	Only villagers can be members	Amount of savings used as evaluation criteria	
		Provide non-agricultural consultation or advice			
		Provide emergency assistance			

Notes: Other policies that were tested include, among others: collateral required, guarantors required, payment frequency of six months or less, monitoring frequency of six months or less, borrowers who default can not reborrow, and all borrowers are monitored. These did not have significant relationships with growth.

Source: Kaboski and Townsend 2005. Copyright 2005 European Economic Association.

for the BAAC to cover all costs, assuming no substitution in borrower behavior. Lending below that rate creates a distortion. The lending rate and overall subsidy are two variables that can be considered in the subsequent analysis in computing the distribution of gains and losses to policy change. An important point here is that Yaron's subsidy-dependence index (SDI) for the BAAC is not large. It is lower than for state-owned financial institutions in most other countries. The subsidy and burden on Thai taxpayers may not be high. It is also likely given the risk-contingencies in its loan contracts that the BAAC is providing considerable net benefits to farmers. Other financial institutions may not offer complete substitutes, in which case financial sector assessment should show a positive risk-sharing gain.

The configuration of policies across the financial institutions operating in a given economy is likely to be different. Sometimes policies vary even among financial institutions of the same type. The example here is drawn from Kaboski and Townsend (2004). Village funds in Thailand vary considerably in whether or not they offer lending services, whether there is a required minimum initial deposit, if members fill out application forms, if savings must be pledged, if non-agricultural consultation is provided, and whether or not there is an emergency service. These policies are associated in the data with positive intermediation: the growth in members, increases in savings mobilized, and/or in funds lent. On the other hand, village funds that make rice or buffalo loans (not cash), offer optional or standard savings accounts, and restrict membership to villagers only are funds that are likely to shrink or fail. In short, there is (unnatural) variation in intermediation across various funds with distinct policies, and this will be exploited in assessing impact below. Indeed, policies which promote intermediation will be shown to be having a positive impact on customers and bad policies a negative one (see Table 5.35). (Unfortunately, we do not have the information in Thailand to do this for some of the other financial-sector providers.)

5.2.2. Financial Deepening: The History

The aggregated M3/GDP movement and other statistics presented in earlier chapters can be presented here at the institutional level. There are telling contrasts across the various providers, indicative of (potential) supply-side variation.

The BAAC expanded dramatically in the 1980s and 1990s. The map from the BAAC annual report indicates new branches opened in 1994 alone. The analogue for M3/GDP for the BAAC would be private deposits to agricultural output, or total liabilities to agricultural output. Both increase over time, with an accelerated expansion starting approximately in 1988 (there is no drop in the financial crisis). This expansion could bring increasing benefits to farmers, if the operating system functions as envisioned. On the other hand, village funds reported to be operational in CDD data prior to 1997 blink on and off over the years with little geographic pattern. Ironically this may help to identify impact, as noted (see Figures 5.10 and 5.11).

Between the expanded and now virtually universal BAAC and the (previously) thin and erratic village funds lie the commercial banks. In the CDD data commercial banks are seen to expand over time and space via evident clustering. Commercial banks remain limited in many areas as late as 1994. Note in particular the relatively limited commercial bank access/use in the Northeast and far South in 1994. On the other hand, the expansion at the village level in the Central area province of Chachoengsao is evident (see Figures 5.12(a)–(b) and 5.13(a)–(b)).

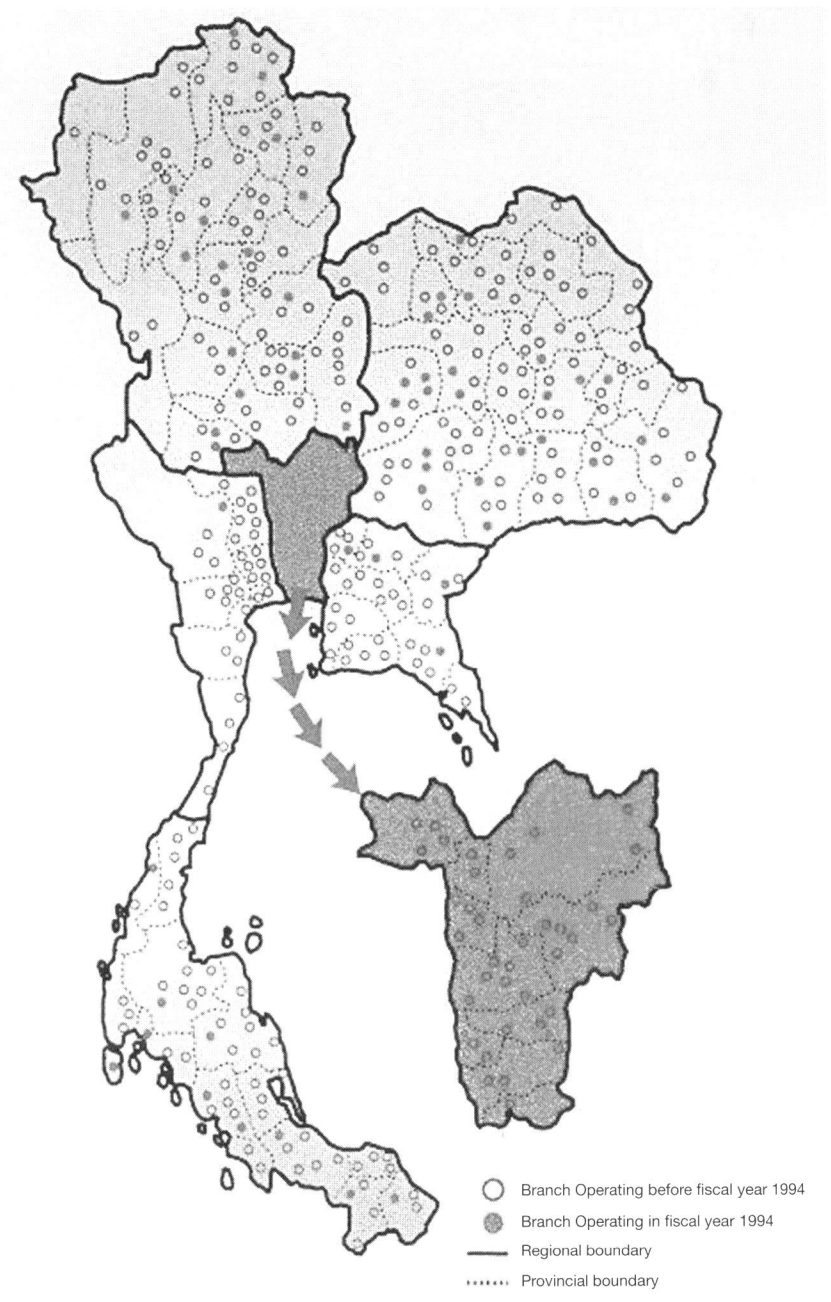

Legend:

○ Branch Operating before fiscal year 1994
◉ Branch Operating in fiscal year 1994
── Regional boundary
······· Provincial boundary

Fig. 5.10. *Bank for Agriculture and Agricultural Cooperatives operating area*

Source: Adapted from Bank for Agriculture and Agricultural Cooperatives (BAAC) Annual Report 1994.

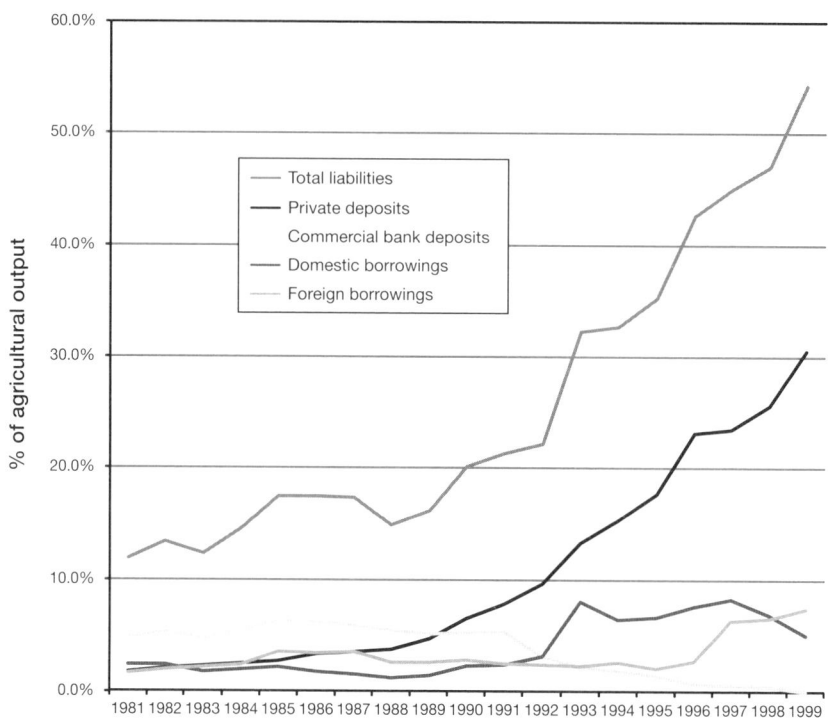

Fig. 5.11. *Bank for Agriculture and Agricultural Cooperatives liabilities composition*

Source: Adapted from Bank for Agriculture and Agricultural Cooperatives (BAAC) Annual Report 1994.

In summary, there are striking differences over space and time (in Figure 5.14(a)–(b)) between the expansion of the government-operated BAAC and private sector/regulated banks. Initially, in 1986, the BAAC is more prevalent in the Central region, but the growth rate for the BAAC is higher in the Northeast. By 1996, BAAC prevalence in the Northeast is equal or greater than in the Central region. (This was noted in the Townsend Thai 1997 data.) In contrast commercial bank prevalence is not only higher in the Central region in 1986, the expansion there over subsequent years to 1996 is higher as well.

The contrasting spatio-temporal dynamic paths of the BAAC and commercial banks are evident locally, within provinces. Figures 5.15(a)–(d), from Assunção, Mityakov, and Townsend 2008 display non-parametric graphs of the spatial correlation of the change in BAAC and commercial bank-use.

(a)

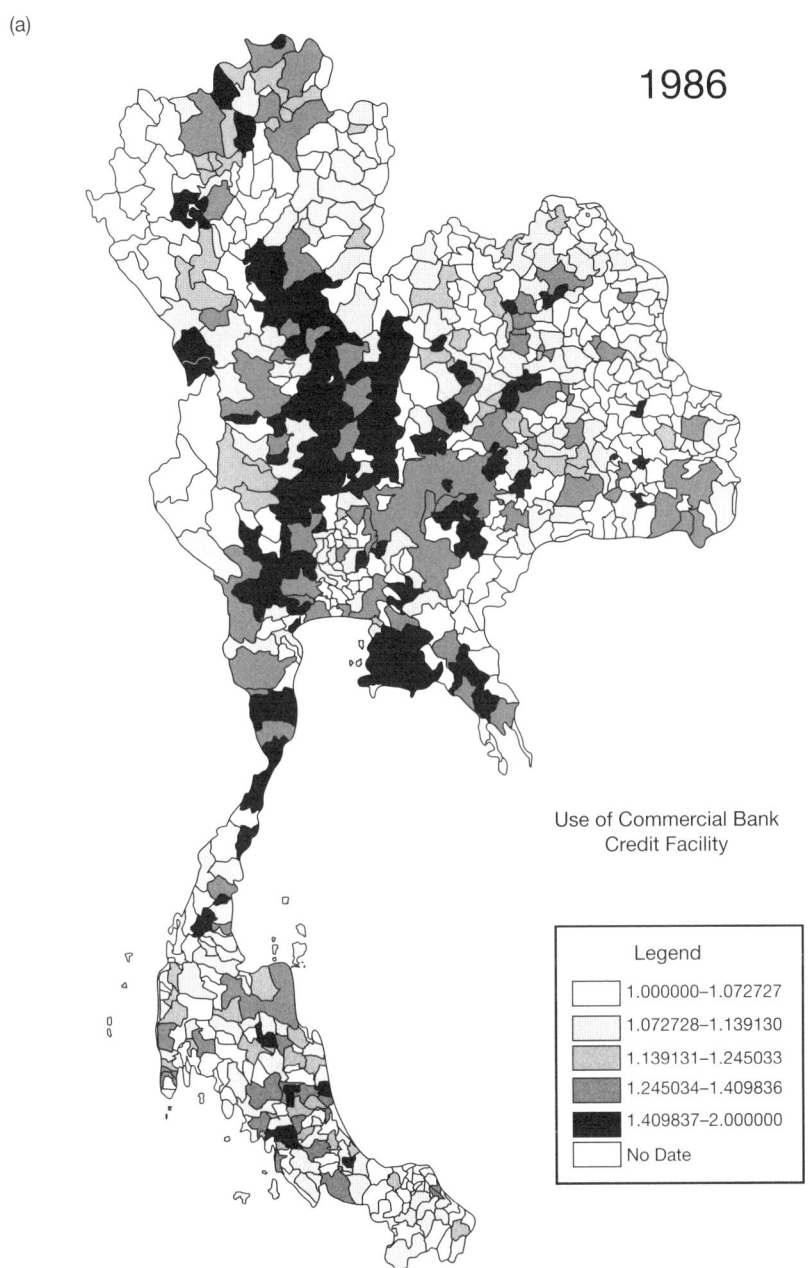

1986

Use of Commercial Bank
Credit Facility

Legend	
	1.000000–1.072727
	1.072728–1.139130
	1.139131–1.245033
	1.245034–1.409836
	1.409837–2.000000
	No Date

Fig. 5.12(a)–(b). *Use of commercial bank credit facility, 1986 and 1994 (See color version at the end of the book).*

(b)

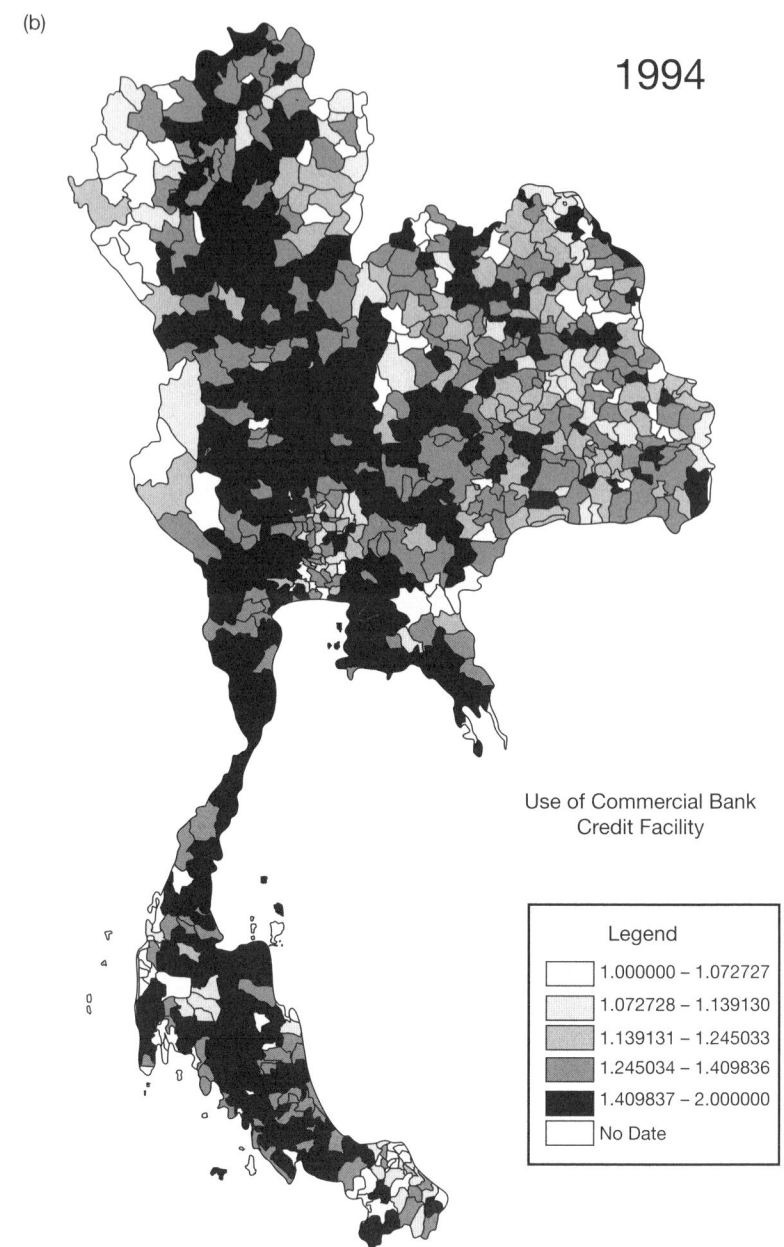

1994

Use of Commercial Bank
Credit Facility

Legend

	1.000000 – 1.072727
	1.072728 – 1.139130
	1.139131 – 1.245033
	1.245034 – 1.409836
	1.409837 – 2.000000
	No Date

Fig. 5.12(a)–(b). *Continued*

(a)

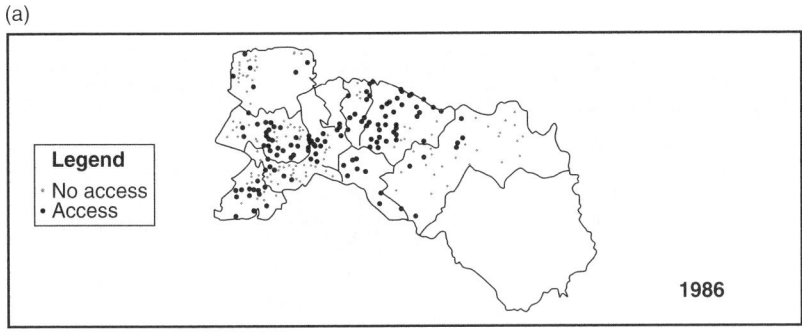

(b)

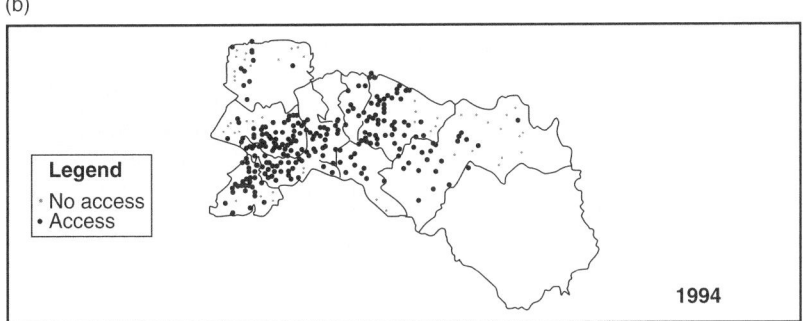

Fig. 5.13(a)–(b). Village-level increase, Chachoengsao, 1986 and 1994

Source: Adapted from community development department data.

Let $D_{i,j}$ an exogenously defined distance function between villages i and j. For example, it can be considered simply as $D_{i,j} = \|s_i - s_j\|$, where s_i is the location of village i. A general spatial autoregressive model of change variable y_i is given by:

$$y_i = \sum_{i \neq j} g(D_{i,j}) y_j + \beta' x_i + u_i. \qquad (5.2.2.1)$$

Figures show that expansion is flat for the BAAC, indicating that new customers are likely to fall anywhere in the province, but quickly decreasing to zero for commercial banks, indicating the contiguous, adjacent expansion of commercial bank access.

The SES, cross-sectional household surveys dating back to 1976 show an expansion in the fraction of households having a savings or credit

(a)

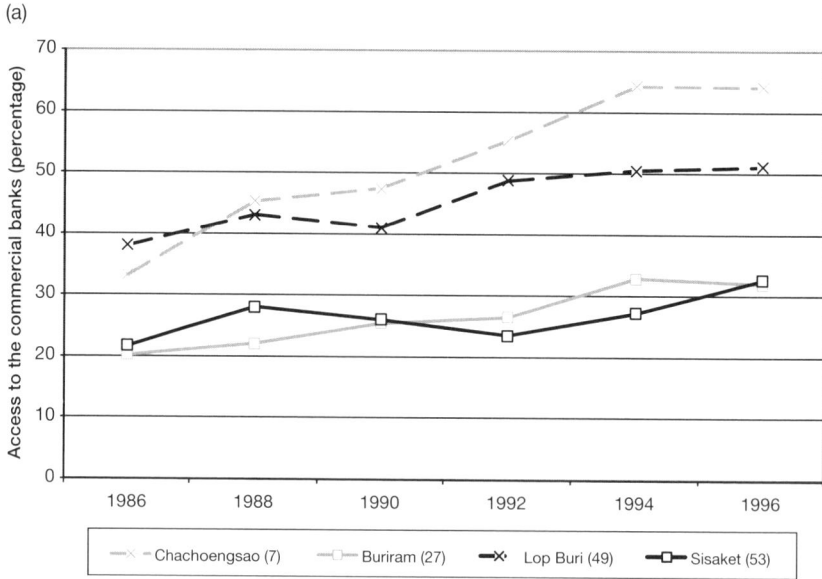

Fig. 5.14(a). *Percentage of villages with access to commercial banks, 1986–96*

Source: Adapted from community development department data.

(b)

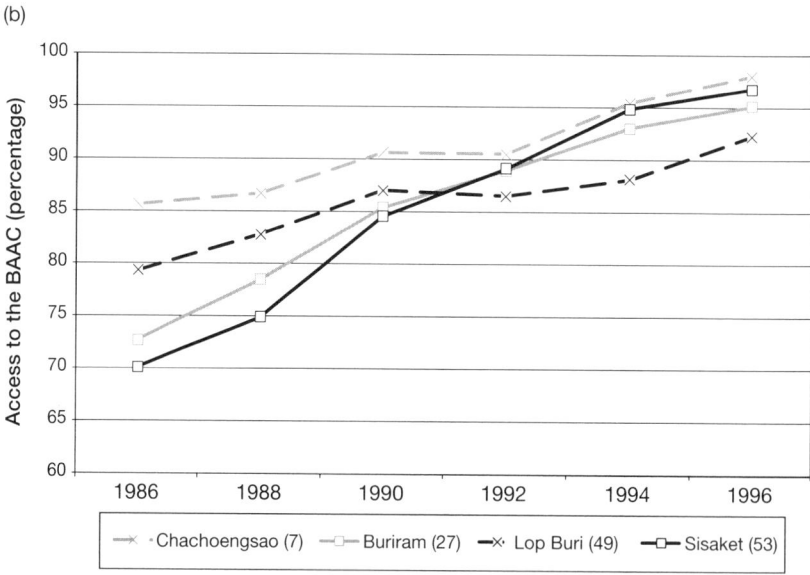

Fig. 5.14(b). *Percentage of villages with access to Bank for Agriculture and Agricultural Cooperatives, 1986–96*

Source: Adapted from community development department data.

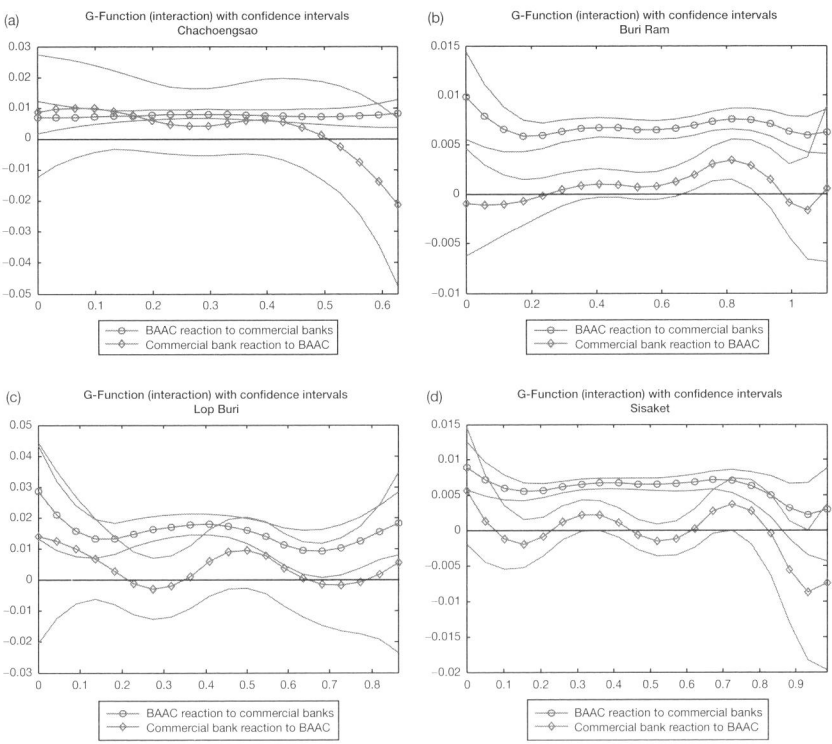

Fig. 5.15(a)–(d). *Geographical interaction of the change in the access to the Bank for Agriculture and Agricultural Cooperatives and commercial banks in selected provinces*
Source: Assunção, Mityakov, and Townsend 2008.

transaction with a formal financial-sector intermediary (BAAC, commercial bank, credit foncier). As described earlier, the percentage with access rises from 6.5 per cent in 1976 to 26.6 per cent in 1996 (see Table 5.36). The associated income differential of those with access over those without is over two to one and increasing, except after 1992. This is what accounts for the contribution of the financial sector expansion to the growth of per capita income and, via the Kuznets effect, to an increase in inequality. Inequality is also higher among the participant group, so there is an additional composition effect to the increase in inequality that comes with the increase in financial access.

Behind the scenes of growth with increasing inequality lie the reduced-form participation schedules (see Figure 5.16). For most education groups,

Table 5.36. *Composition of income status groups (percentage)*

Year	1976	1981	1986	1988	1990	1992	1994	1996	76–96	76–86	86–92	92–6
Financial participation												
Non-participant	93.5	89.8	89.3	84.7	80.4	78.1	75.5	73.4	−20.1	−0.41	−1.86	−1.19
Participant	6.5	10.2	10.7	15.3	19.6	21.9	24.5	26.6	20.1	0.41	1.86	1.19

Average income profile (1990 baht)

Year	1976	1981	1986	1988	1990	1992	1994	1996	76–96	76–86	86–92	92–6
Financial participation												
Non-participant	943	1189	1079	1209	1296	1490	1678	2043	3.9	1.4	5.5	8.2
Participant	1956	2446	2464	2575	3327	3973	3912	4357	4.1	2.3	8.3	2.3

Inequality profile by Theil-L index

Year	1976	1981	1986	1988	1990	1992	1994	1996	76–96	76–86	86–92	92–6
Financial participation												
Non-participant	0.266	0.298	0.362	0.346	0.341	0.366	0.361	0.353	8.8	0.96	0.07	−0.32
Participant	0.358	0.327	0.415	0.423	0.480	0.521	0.498	0.434	7.6	0.58	1.75	−2.16

Source: Jeong 2008.

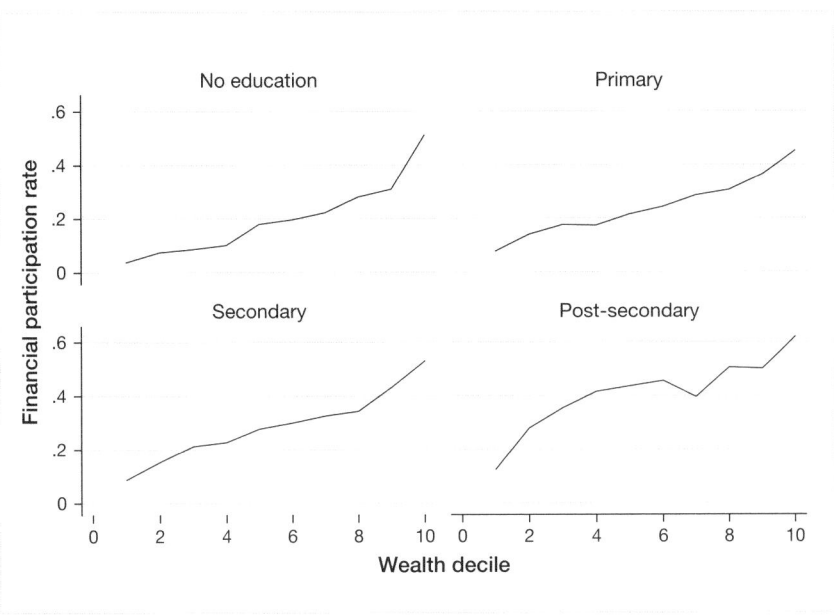

Fig. 5.16. *Financial participation rate over wealth by education level*
Source: Jeong 2000.

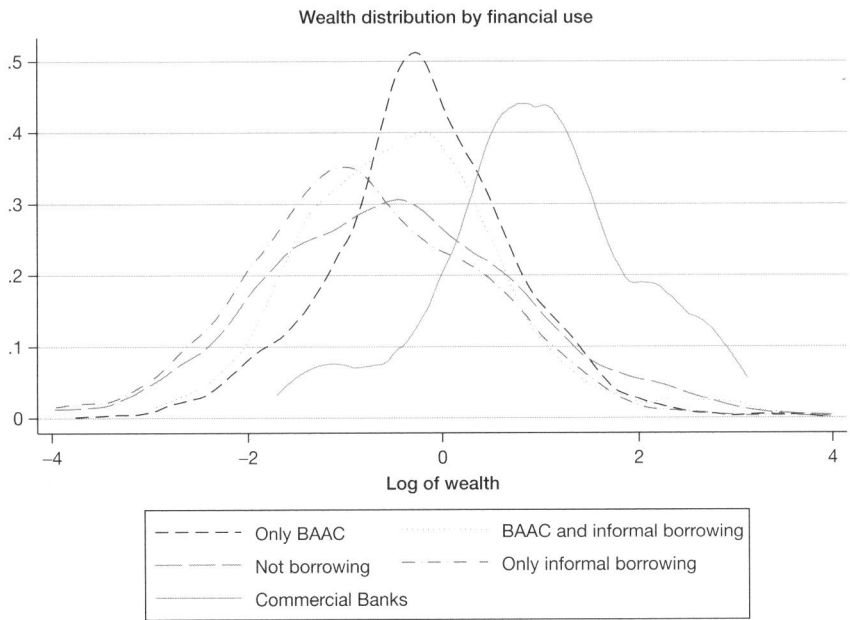

Fig. 5.17. *Household wealth distribution by sources of borrowing, 1997–2004*
Source: Townsend Thai data.

access/use is increasing with wealth, though, for the most part higher, the higher is education. Thus, *ceteris paribus*, increases in wealth and education would increase financial access. These participation schedules and the economy-wide dynamics are a key feature of the models below.

Related, those borrowing from commercial banks have higher levels of wealth than those borrowing from the BAAC, which in turn have higher levels of wealth than those not borrowing at all. But, the lowest levels of wealth are those borrowing from the informal sector, lower than those not borrowing at all. The choice of borrowing methods, whether to self-finance, and the relation to wealth, are subjects to which we shall return subsequently (see Figure 5.17).

5.3. Education

There are obvious differences in the level of education by region, with the greater levels of Bangkok metropolitan area outpacing the rest. Migrants to Bangkok, and for the most part migrants to the other regions, have higher levels of education than non-migrants.

There are evident differences in the level of education locally, across and within provinces (see Figures 5.18 and 5.19). Education levels are lower in the Northeast, and the percentage completing advanced secondary education is higher for those near urban areas and living near major road systems. This distance to secondary schools does vary by village, with evident clustering (see Figure 5.20 (a)–(b)).

The determination of education at the household level has yet to be studied in detail, but evidently predetermined wealth of the parents and parents' education levels play roles in the education of the children. Those with greater wealth (e.g., refrigerators) are more likely to have children in more-advanced schools (see Table 5.37).

The bulk of the Thai population (by household head) have relatively low levels of education. The more highly educated constitute a larger, but still relatively small part of the population even by 1996. See histograms in Figure 5.21. As in Table 5.38, the fraction of the population with no formal education drops from 18.3 per cent in 1976 to 5.6 per cent in 1996. The fraction with secondary education increases from 5.4 to 11.4 per cent, vocational from 2.2 to 5.3, and university/higher from 1.1 to 6.0. The income differential between the lowest and highest groups was over 4 to 1 in 1976, and this increases to almost 6 to 1 as the growth of income is

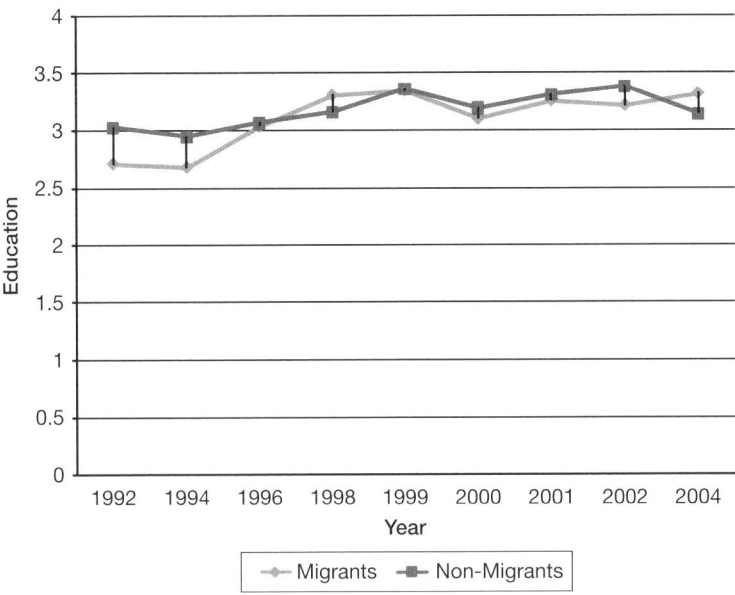

Fig. 5.18(a). Weighted level of Education for migrants and non-migrants (SES code: mobility=8,9: BANKOK)

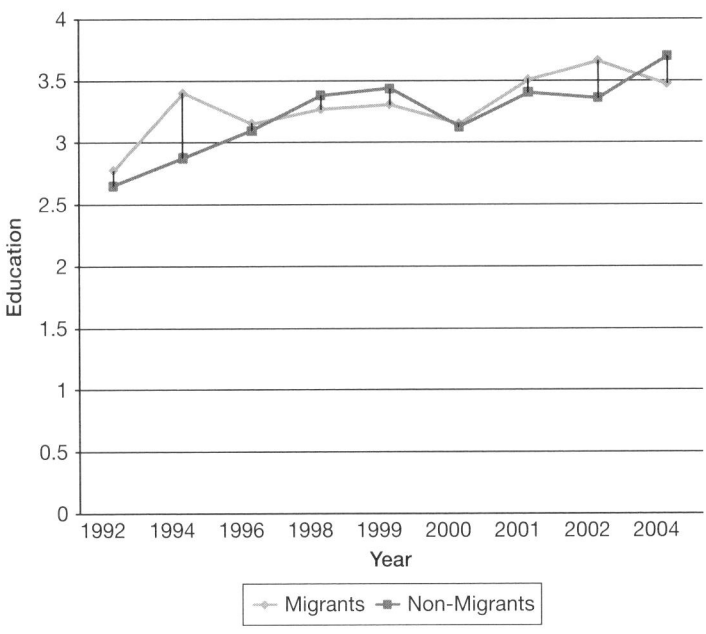

Fig. 5.18(b). Weighted level of Education for migrants and non-migrants (SES code: mobility=8,9: NORTH)

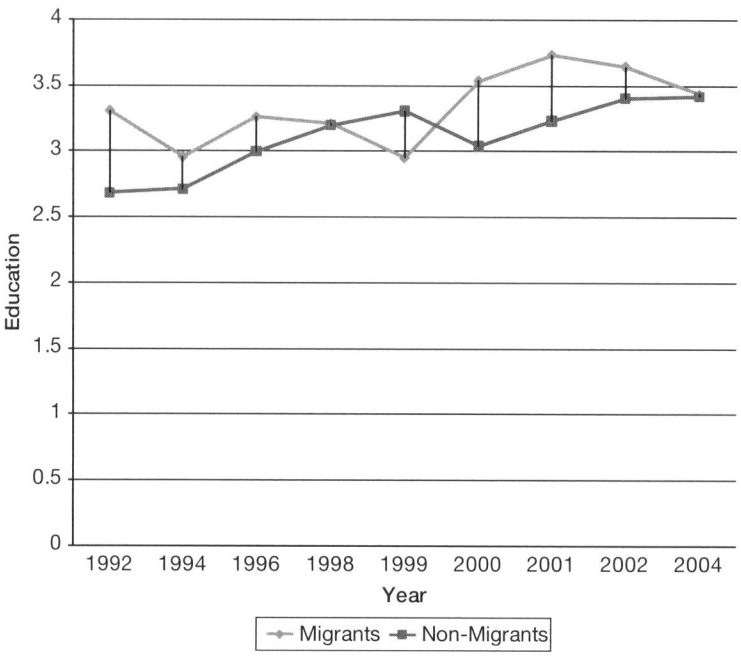

Fig. 5.18(c). Weighted level of Education for migrants and non-migrants (SES code: mobility=8,9: NORTHEAST)

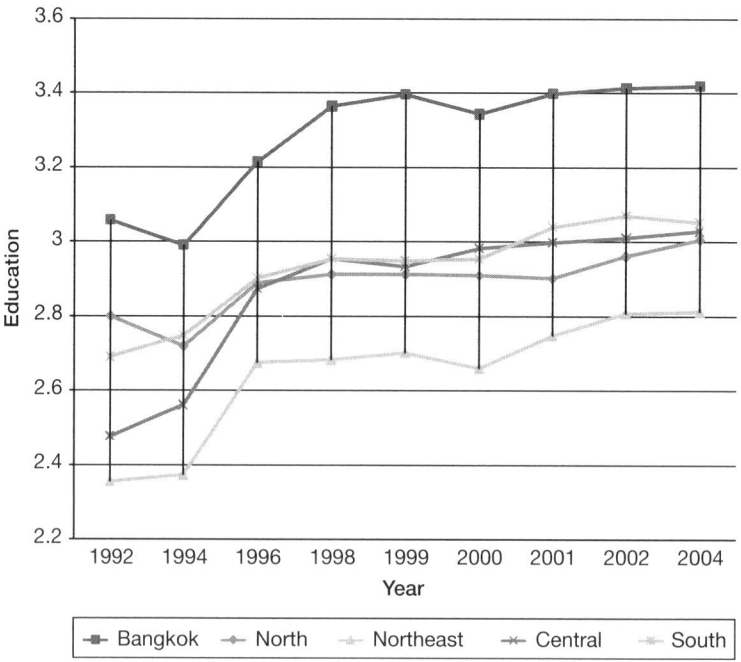

Fig. 5.18(d). Weighted level of education across regions

Source: Adapted from Townsend Socio-economic Survey data.

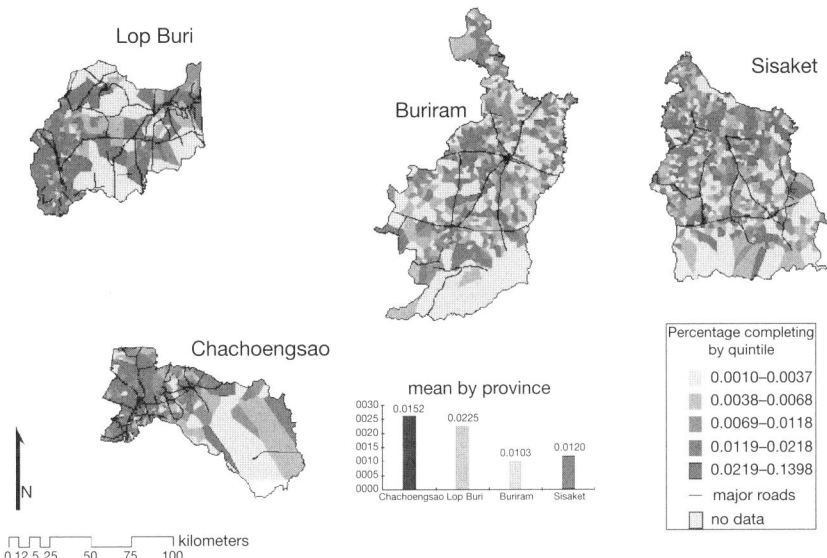

Fig. 5.19. Percentage completing advanced secondary education, 1986

Source: Felkner and Townsend 2007.

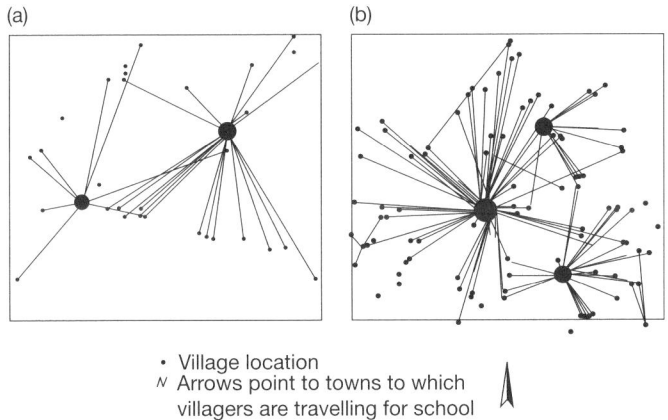

Fig. 5.20(a)–(b). *Secondary school network in Nang Rong*

Note: The mean distance between all pairs of villages within Nang Rong district is 19.41 km.

Source: Repr. from K. Faust, B. Entwisle, R. R. Rindfuss, and Y. Sawangdee, 'Spatial Arrangement of Social and Economic Networks among Villages in Nang Rong District, Thailand', *Social Networks*, 21 (1999), 311–37. Copyright 1999 with permission from Elsevier.

Table 5.37. *Results from simple regressions on the determinants of schooling attainment*

	(1)	(2)	(3)	(4)
	ASch	PSch	MSch	InSch
Age	−0.019	0.016	0.005	−0.052
	(11.044)**	(6.48)**	(2.63)**	(35.68)**
AgeSq	0.002	−0.001	−0.001	0.005
	(10.522)**	(3.42)**	(3.93)**	(25.35)**
Female	−0.012	−0.106	0.048	−0.043
	(0.263)	(1.94)	(1.26)	(1.29)
FemaleAge	0.002	0.011	−0.004	0.005
	(0.763)	(3.53)**	(1.87)	(2.56)*
FemaleAgeSq	−0.003	−0.015	0.005	−0.007
	(1.180)	(3.80)**	(1.79)	(2.99)**
Female head	0.001	−0.001	0.000	−0.001
	(1.132)	(1.02)	(0.25)	(0.89)
OwnLand	−0.004	−0.044	0.020	0.008
	(0.378)	(1.85)	(0.97)	(0.49)
PlotArea	0.000	−0.004	0.002	0.002
	(0.172)	(0.93)	(0.66)	(0.88)
PlotDistance	0.001	−0.002	0.002	0.000
	(1.719)	(1.96)	(0.99)	(0.44)
HaveFridge	0.009	−0.071	0.050	0.048
	(0.819)	(3.09)**	(2.60)**	(3.13)**
HaveMotorCycle	−0.009	0.014	0.011	−0.028
	(0.925)	(0.66)	(0.59)	(2.07)*
Household has non-householder males	0.004	−0.002	−0.004	0.010
	(1.158)	(0.21)	(0.55)	(2.04)*
Household has non-householder females	0.001	0.006	−0.004	−0.007
	(0.146)	(0.71)	(0.69)	(1.29)
Chachoengsao	−0.032	−0.034	0.042	−0.005
	(3.120)**	(1.25)	(1.86)	(0.31)
Lop Buri	−0.026	0.051	0.002	−0.022
	(2.139)*	(1.98)*	(0.07)	(1.27)
Sisaket	−0.023	0.008	0.083	0.067
	(2.003)*	(0.32)	(3.95)**	(3.91)**
Constant	0.411	0.357	0.095	1.263
	(11.176)**	(7.75)**	(2.80)**	(41.83)**
Observations	2783	2783	2783	2783
R-squared	0.229	0.14	0.04	0.62

Source: Townsend research note.

substantially higher for the more educated groups. This is what accounts for the contribution of education to the growth in per capita income, and via the Kuznets effect, to an increase in inequality. On the other hand, within-group inequality is higher for the least-educated groups, so the secondary composition effect lowers inequality.

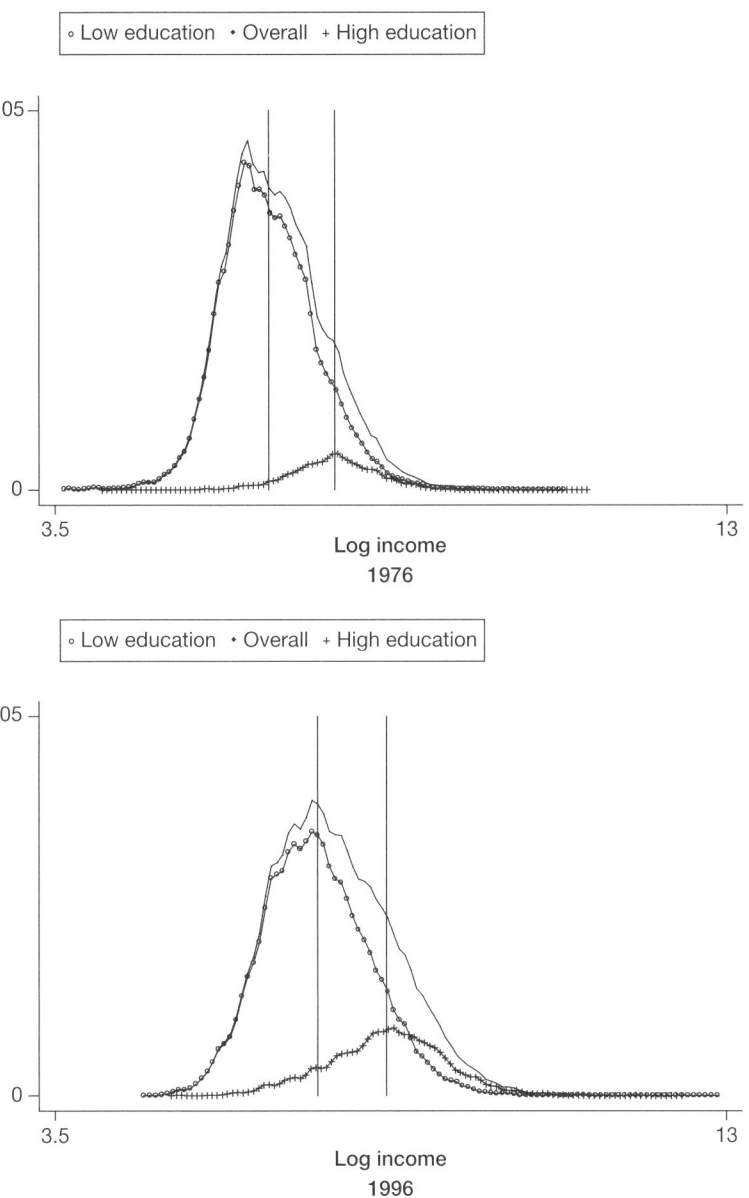

Fig. 5.21. *Composition of aggregate distribution by education, 1976 and 1996*
Source: Jeong 2000.

Table 5.38. Composition of income status groups (percentage)

Year	1976	1981	1986	1988	1990	1992	1994	1996	76–96	76–86	86–92	92–6
Education												
No Formal	18.3	12.5	8.6	7.6	7.1	6.9	6.2	5.6	−12.7	−0.97	−0.27	−0.34
Primary	73.1	76.1	78.6	77.4	76.4	74.9	73.2	71.8	−1.3	0.55	−0.63	−0.78
Secondary	5.4	6.3	6.1	6.9	8.3	8.9	10.3	11.4	6.0	0.07	0.47	0.63
Vocational	2.2	3.6	4.0	4.5	4.2	4.6	5.0	5.3	3.1	0.18	0.09	0.18
University/Higher	1.1	1.5	2.7	3.6	4.0	4.8	5.3	6.0	4.9	0.17	0.34	0.31

Average income profile (1990 baht)

Year	1976	1981	1986	1988	1990	1992	1994	1996	76–96	76–86	86–92	92–6
Education												
No Formal	851	1111	890	994	1063	1153	1187	1420	2.6	0.4	4.4	5.3
Primary	908	1131	982	1116	1297	1445	1604	1945	3.9	0.8	6.6	7.7
Secondary	1861	2312	2253	2445	2970	3239	3369	3604	3.4	1.9	6.2	2.7
Vocational	2261	2825	3030	3268	3971	4614	4768	5209	4.3	3.0	7.3	3.1
University/Higher	3753	4802	4402	4525	5366	7816	7398	8299	4.0	1.6	10.0	1.5

Inequality profile by Theil-L index

Year	1976	1981	1986	1988	1990	1992	1994	1996	76–96	76–86	86–92	92–6
Education												
No Formal	0.270	0.310	0.355	0.330	0.331	0.408	0.365	0.356	8.59	0.85	0.88	−1.28
Primary	0.249	0.276	0.318	0.312	0.341	0.340	0.336	0.320	7.0	0.69	0.37	−0.52
Secondary	0.201	0.256	0.300	0.328	0.419	0.356	0.381	0.338	13.7	0.99	0.93	−0.45
Vocational	0.191	0.161	0.240	0.210	0.294	0.319	0.298	0.255	6.4	0.49	1.32	−1.61
University/Higher	0.187	0.209	0.180	0.204	0.243	0.320	0.248	0.253	6.6	−0.08	2.34	−1.67

Source: Jeong 2005, unpublished.

6

Integrated Micro–Macro Models with Dual Financial Sectors

This chapter presents the first two micro–macro dual-sector models, based on some of the findings of the initial chapters. These first models emphasize occupation/activity choice, with the financial sector either expanding exogenously in one model, imitating the data, or chosen endogenously and growing in a second. Occupation/sector and financial access were key variables as established earlier. Both these models are applied at varying geographic scales: from the macro-aggregate economy to regional and village economies and then to households, as anticipated. Success and anomalies are documented.

The first model emphasizes the transitions of households from subsistence agriculture or wage work into the establishment of non-farm enterprise. For the sector without intermediation, this transition is facilitated by predetermined wealth. Thus, those without wealth will be constrained. The transition into business is also facilitated by talent, which lowers the fixed costs of establishing business. Talent could be related to education. Wealth and talent are the sources of heterogeneity, with measured and unobserved components. Micro, cross-sectional, or retrospective data from those not participating in the financial sector allow estimation and identification of the key underlying parameters of the production function and talent distribution. Note the use of micro data to estimate the micro underpinnings. A second sector allows perfect intermediation at an equilibrium interest rate, so that talent, time, and factor inputs are used optimally. Unrestricted migration across the two sectors is allowed at an equilibrating wage.

The intermediated sector is given increasing weight over time, exactly as observed in actual participation data. The savings rate and cost-of-living parameters are calibrated. Then, given an estimate of the initial distribution of wealth, as observed in cross-section data, the model is simulated over time, delivering an endogenous interest rate and wage rate, the evolving distribution of wealth, GDP growth, labor share, and the fraction of entrepreneurs. Simulations illustrate the importance of financial liberalization to observed growth spurts and deliver simultaneously the distribution of gains and losses to liberalization in the population. This is the first assessment in the book of the impact of financial policy variation, here through the lens of this structural model. Similar counterfactual model experiments show that foreign capital inflows were not the big driver of growth. Similarly, the informal sector adds little. A decomposition of TFPG using the explicit micro underpinnings shows that financial deepening explains much of that widely used macro residual.

A second model emphasizes the information and risk-sharing advantages of the formal financial sector, imagined again to be perfect for those with access but quite limited for those without access, not inconsistent with the data. Fixed and marginal transactions costs yield a wealth threshold below which households remain in autarky, smoothing idiosyncratic and aggregate shocks with accumulated wealth, diversifying into risky and safe activities. Wealth again is a key variable determining who is constrained, but the predicted path is Pareto optimal given transactions costs. Rates of returns, the range of shocks, risk aversion, the preference discount rate, and transactions costs are either calibrated or estimated, with the scale of fixed costs determined by the initial distribution of wealth and participation data. Note again the use of micro data to estimate underpinnings. Simulations of growth, inequality, and financial participation establish that the model can explain well the observed trends in the featured macro facts, but not the spurt in the growth rate at the time of financial liberalization. Incorporating financial-sector policy as a prior distortion allows an estimate of the distribution of gains to liberalization: these favor the middle class. This is the second assessment of the gains to financial-sector liberalization, again through the lens of a structural model. Related, the model tends to over-predict financial deepening for the educated and urban population, as if there were policy restrictions with unintended consequences. Note the use of the model with micro data to assess financial sector distortions.

Both these dual-sector models are estimated and simulated at the village level, for the four provinces of the original Townsend Thai Surveys. These provinces display interesting patterns in the concentration of wealth, enterprise, bank access, and transportation infrastructure as noted earlier. Both models do well with temporal trends. The occupation-choice model also does well with spatial and reduced forms patterns if the cost of business entry is inversely proportional to distance from 'hot-spot' agglomeration centers. New roads have a large impact on regional development. The endogenous financial participation model allows estimation of entry costs which vary across space and by financial provider. But costs are estimated to be lower for those far from main roads and lower for those using the Bank for Agriculture, revealing again an apparent distortion and/or targeting. Wealth redistributions can slow down growth in urban centers.

The occupation-choice and financial-access-choice models are estimated again with the SES income and expenditure cross-sectional survey and taken to the growth and inequality decompositions featured in the introductory chapters. The models, though occasionally off in levels, do well with temporal trends and do well qualitatively with the decompositions. Aspects of the end-of-period simulations match well the observed distributions of income. But the models overemphasize the financial access or occupation dichotomies relative to the data, which have much more within group diversity and less of a difference across sectors. In the data, there is more co-movement across occupation, wage/firm groups and across financial-access/no-access groups than in the models. The models also overdo the financial dichotomy: there are more firms in the data in the non-intermediated sector than a dichotomous model would imply, and likewise less risk-sharing in the data in the intermediated sector than the model would imply. The access/no-access dichotomy will be further scrutinized below.

6.1. Occupation Choice: Financial Sector Exogenous

6.1.1. Review of the Key Facts

To review, Thailand experienced relatively rapid growth between 1950 and 1997. This is associated with an increase in inequality countered by an eventual rise in the wage and labor share, even for the low skilled. There has been a steady exit from agriculture into non-farm wage employment and non-farm enterprise. Wealth seems to constrain the relatively poor away from non-farm enterprise. Many enterprises operate on a small scale. There is a high if not increasing level of savings. The financial system has expanded, as measured by traditional macro ratios and micro-access surveys. Measured TFPG has contributed, apparently, but TFPG is often negative in time and sector decompositions.

6.1.2. The Model

The basic building block of the model at the micro, household level is the choice of occupation. A household has income γ in subsistence agriculture, wage w in (unskilled) employment, and profits π in non-farm enterprise. The last is determined by choice of hired unskilled labor l and utilized capital k.

$$\pi(b, x, w) = \max_{k,l} f(k, l) - wl - k$$
$$s.t. k \in [0, b - x], l \geq 0$$

Specifically, let $f(k, l) = \alpha k - \frac{\beta}{2}k^2 + \xi l - \frac{\rho}{2}l^2 + \sigma lk$. Then $l(b, x, w) = \frac{\sigma k(b,x,w) + (\xi - w)}{\rho}$ and $k(b, x, w) = b - x$ if constrained or $k(b, x, w) = \frac{\rho(\alpha - r) + \sigma(\xi - w)}{\beta\rho + \sigma^2}$ otherwise.

Note that there is no access to credit; also capital must be self-financed, that is, $k \leq b - x$ where b is initial, beginning-of-period, predetermined wealth and x is a fixed set-up cost for going into business. The last is imagined to be unobserved to the econometrician/analyst, but known to be distributed in the population according to density $h(x, m)$. Each household has to know its own x before choosing, so x along with wealth b is the key pair of state variables. Wage w is vital and also exogenous. The cumulative distribution of x in the population is:

$$x \sim H(x, m) = (1 - m)x + mx^2.$$

When $m=0$, this distribution is uniform, when $m<0$ it is tilted to the left, and $m>0$, tilted to the right.

End-of-period resources consist of earnings from a chosen occupation, plus what is left of initial wealth, so that

$$W(b, x, w) = \begin{cases} \gamma + b & \text{if a subsistence worker,} \\ w - \eta + b & \text{if a wage earner,} \\ \pi(b, x, w) - x - \eta + b & \text{if a firm} \end{cases}$$

is the array of choices. Here η is an additional disutility cost of leaving subsistence agriculture. End-of-period utility $U(C,B)=C^{1-\omega}B^{\omega}$ is maximized by choice of consumption C and savings B for next period. That way, ω is the saving rate out of end-of-period wealth.

The original model is taken from Lloyd-Ellis and Bernhardt (LEB), but it is representative of occupation-choice models in the literature. See Banerjee and Newman 1993, Matsuyama 2001, Aghion and Bolton 1997. It is modified by Giné and Townsend 2004. Again, the key beginning-of-period state variables capturing heterogeneity for the household are initial wealth b and

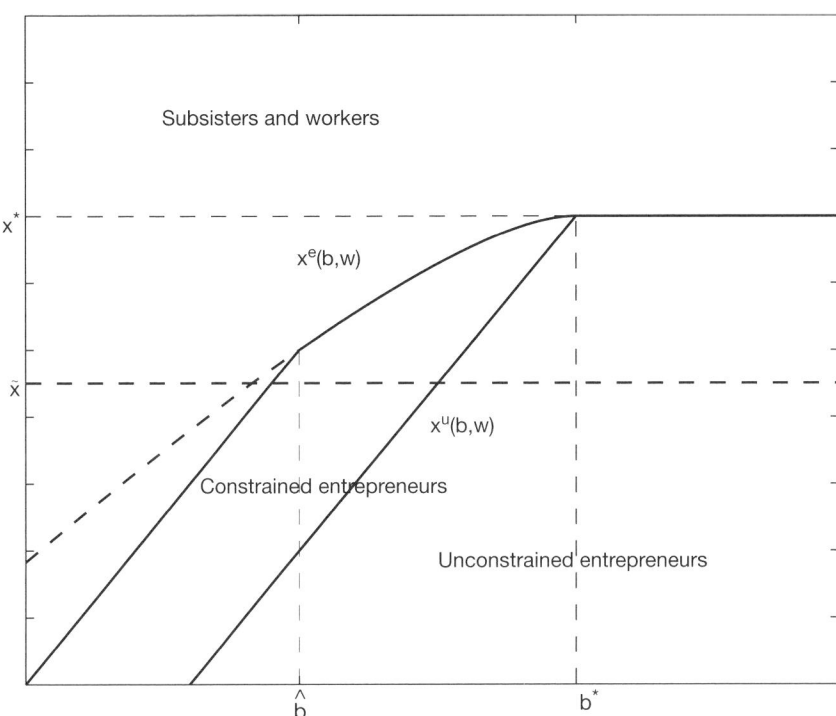

Fig. 6.1. *Occupation choice map*

Note: Wealth facilitates entry into business, facilitates investment of existing businesses (ROA).

Source: Repr. from X Giné and R. M. Townsend, 'Evaluation of Financial Liberalization: A General Equilibrium Model with Constrained Occupation Choice', *Journal of Development Economics*, 74 (2004), 269–307. Copyright 2004 with permission from Elsevier.

set-up cost x (see Figure 6.1). Intuitively, there is a region of high-cost and low-wealth households who choose to be subsistence wage earners. Note that in equilibrium, with some population left in subsistence agriculture, $w-\eta=\gamma$, and thus we can collapse the wage and subsistence sectors into one: households will either be indifferent or the entire subsistence agricultural sector will be depleted. On the other extreme, there is a region of low cost, $x<x^*$, high wealth, $b>b^*$, households who will be running firms at the scale l^* and k^* as if they can hire labor and utilize capital at wage w and implicit zero net interest rate, $1+r=1$, the rate at which resources at the beginning of the period can be carried over in the back yard to resources at the end of the period. There is also a region of constrained firms with wealth and set-up costs such that $k=b-x<k^*$. These firms hire a limited number of workers, if any, and have limited capitalization. They would also appear to have high

rates of return as measured by the average yield $\frac{y}{k}$, or ROA. The 'curve of indifference' $x^e(b,w)$ marks the combinations of wealth and cost pairs under which a household is indifferent between subsistence/wage work and profits from enterprise, and $x^u(b,w)$ marks the margin at operating at unrestricted scale k^*. It is important to note that most firms will not be indifferent—that is, will have profits π over and above the opportunity cost of foregone earning w.

If there were perfect credit markets—that is, a market clearing interest rate r at which households and firms could borrow and save as much as they wanted—then occupation choice would not depend at all on initial wealth b. This is a typical, neoclassical result. There would be complete separation between the production and consumption activities. Firms operated by households maximize profits, as would any firm. Here, without other sources of heterogeneity in production by type or sector, all firms operate at a common scale $k^*(w,r) = \frac{\rho(\alpha-r)+\sigma(\xi-w)}{\beta\rho-\sigma^2}$, and hire identical labor $l^*(w,r) = \frac{\sigma k^*+(\xi-w)}{\rho}$. All have marginal ROA=$r$, that is, rates of internal and external returns are equated, at a common market clearing interest rate. There would be a critical level of cost $\tilde{x}(w,r) = \frac{f(k^*,l^*)-wl^*-rk^*-w}{r}$, below which all households would be entrepreneurs. Thus, only talent matters in occupation choice, not initial wealth, and only talented households are running firms. In comparison to the non-intermediated sector, low-wealth households are more likely to be firms, but high-wealth low-talent households are more likely to be savers, to put their money in the bank rather than operate an inefficient enterprise.

What we see in a cross-sectional retrospective Townsend Thai Panel is the initial wealth b of households in 1992, and whether they choose to enter business in some specified interval of time, between 1992 and 1997. The occupation diagram with costs x uniformly distributed—that is $m=0$—tells us in a straightforward way the fraction of households which are predicted to enter business. According to the model, those entering business at initial wealth b are those with costs less than $x^e(b,w)$. This is just the vertical distance from zero up to the $x^e(b,w)$ curve of indifference. Note this probability is increasing in wealth b, for example. Less obvious from the diagram, the curves shift up when the wage w decreases.

More formally, let $y_i=1.0$ denote the binary choice of household i for setting up an enterprise, or not. The probability that $y_i=1$ is $\Pr\{y_i=1\}= \Pr\{x_i \leq x^e(b_i,w)\}$. The log likelihood for a sample of n households is then written as:

$$\log L = \sum_{i=1}^{n}\{y_i \ln[\Pr\{x_i \leq x^e(b_i,w)\}] + (1-y_i)\ln\left([1-\Pr\{x_i \leq x^e(b_i,w)\}]\right)\}$$

where

$$\Pr\{x_i \le x^e(b_i, w)\} = (1 - m)x^e(b_i, w) + mx^e(b_i, w)^2$$

In cross-sectional SES data we imagine we are seeing (estimated) wealth at the beginning of the period and occupation choice at the end of the period, on the assumption that wealth moves slowly with the life-cycle, as in the data. That is, the wealth/enterprise profile is meant to have an implicit causality running from initial wealth to subsequent enterprise and not the other way around.

If there is variation in the wage rate over time, or alternatively the North-east and Central regions of Thailand are not well linked by migration, as if self-contained regional economies, then there are two sets of curves in the occupation-choice diagram and all the underlying parameters of technology can be identified from the micro data. We also need to estimate a scale parameter which converts Thai baht into model units.

Parameters such as the cost of living η, savings rate ω, and potentially exogenous growth in subsistence income γ_{gr} are not obtained from micro data but rather are calibrated. The model is simulated as below, getting

Table 6.1. *Maximum likelihood [parameter] estimation (MLE) results: estimation from two data sets*

	Townsend socio-economic survey data		Townsend Thai survey	
	Coefficient	Standard error	Coefficient	Standard error
Scaling factor				
s^1	1.4236	0.00881	1.4338	0.03978
Subsistence level				
γ	0.02744	0.00119	0.01538	0.00408
Fixed cost distribution				
m	−0.5933	0.05801	0.00559	0.17056
Technology				
α	0.54561	0.06711	0.97545	0.00191
β	0.39064	0.09028	0.0033	0.00013
ρ	0.03384	0.00364	0.00966	0.00692
σ	0.1021	0.02484	0.00432	0.00157
ξ	0.2582	0.03523	0.12905	0.04146
Number of observations	24,433		1272	
log-likelihood	−8233.92		−616.92	

1. The parameter value and standard error reported are multiplied by a factor of 10^6.
Notes: Calibration values from Jeong: $\gamma = .0190$, $\alpha = 1.1111$, $\beta = .0610$, $\rho = .0063$, $\sigma = 0.00$, $\xi = .1000$.

Source: Repr. from X. Giné and R. M. Townsend, 'Evaluation of Financial Liberalization: A General Equilibrium Model with Constrained Occupation Choice', *Journal of Development Economics*, 74 (2004), 269–307. Copyright 2004 with permission from Elsevier.

the best possible fit to five 'macro' time-series variables z^{ec}: GDP growth, inequality, the savings rate, the time-varying fraction of entrepreneurs, and labor share. The mean square error criterion for best fit is the squared difference between the model estimated $zsim$ and actual economy zec variables z, normalized by actual means μ_z. That is the calibration metric is

$$C = \sum_{s=1}^{5} \sum_{t=1976}^{1996} w_{st} \left[\frac{z_{st}^{sim} - z_{st}^{ec}}{\mu_z} \right].$$

Table 6.1 displays the set of estimated parameters from the Townsend Thai and SES data, as well as those obtained when all parameters are calibrated. The standard error bands indicate the potential range of parameter values at a 95 per cent confidence interval, obtained from bootstrap estimation, drawing the sample repeatedly from an urn with replacement.

The LEB model is simulated using the computer programs of Giné and Townsend 2004. At every date there is a distribution of beginning-of-period wealth, presumed to lie on some a priori grid. Guessing a wage, along with using the estimated parameters of technology, the regions of the occupation partition are pinned down. The distribution of talent then determines the fractions of the population choosing to be workers, subsisters, or entrepreneurs at each level of wealth. Adding up over all wealth levels, these population fractions should sum up to one, and otherwise the labor market does not clear. This procedure is repeated to find an equilibrium wage in a bisection algorithm. The end-of-period wealth is determined.

A fraction $\overline{\omega}$ of this wealth is saved, and this determines next period's distribution of beginning-of-period wealth. The distribution of set-up cost for entrepreneurs adds additional diversity. The lower endpoint of the wealth distribution is the wealth of the household in the previous period who had least beginning-of-period wealth and the lowest talent (highest set-up cost), and the upper endpoint is associated with the household in the previous period who had the highest beginning-of-period wealth and the highest talent (lowest set-up cost). The initial condition of the model is the estimated initial distribution of wealth. Here we take the 1976 SES wealth distribution, scaled by the chosen wealth scale for converting Thai baht into model units, s, determined also in the estimation, as the initial wealth distribution for simulation. One period in the simulation corresponds to one year in the data.

The model without a financial sector fails to explain much of the data even when ω, γ_{gr} and η are calibrated to allow the model to do as well as possible. As illustrated in the figure for the parameters estimated from SES data, the model's growth rate is low, virtually zero. The savings rate matches better, via calibration. Labor share is rising, as it does eventually in the data, but it is too low. The fraction of entrepreneurs and the Gini measure of inequality are both low as well, and the latter decreases in the model simulation, unlike the data. Behind the scenes, the model is converging to one with many people in subsistence agriculture with common earnings.

In contrast, suppose we allow the intermediated sector, with perfect credit markets, to expand at exactly the rate we see in the SES participation data. Then the model at both point estimates and standard error bands does well with the observed time varying growth of GDP, particularly the upturn in 1986 when the financial sector expanded dramatically (see Figure 6.2(a)–(e)). The savings rate and labor share are reasonably well matched. Note that the point estimates of labor share first decrease and then increase, as in the data, and the Gini measure of inequality first increases and then decreases, as in the data. The wider confidence intervals

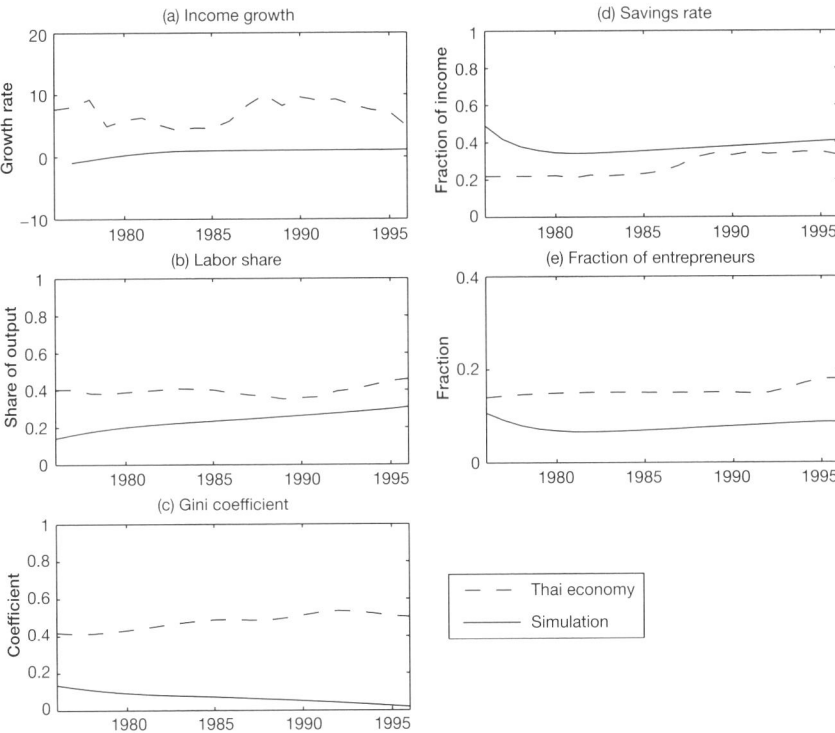

Fig. 6.2(a)–(e). *Benchmark model best overall fit (Socio-economic Survey data)*

Source: Giné and Townsend 2003.

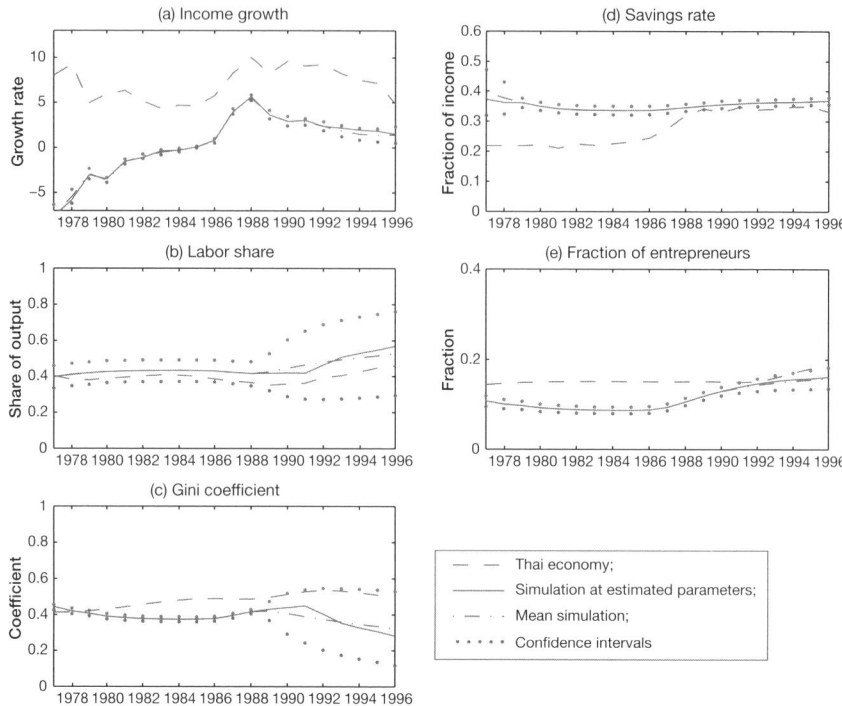

Fig. 6.3(a)–(e). *Intermediated model (Socio-economic Survey data)*

Notes: $\eta=0.026$, $\omega=0.321$, $\gamma_{gr}=0$.

Source: Repr. from X. Giné and R. M. Townsend, 'Evaluation of Financial Liberalization: A General Equilibrium Model with Constrained Occupation Choice', *Journal of Development Economics*, 74 (2004), 269–307. Copyright 2004 with permission from Elsevier.

have to do with the undesirable knife-edge property of the model: the wage does not increase until the farm sector is depleted, and the timing of that event varies with parameter values. The fraction of predicted entrepreneurs is low but increasing, as in the data (see Figure 6.3(a)–(e)).

6.1.3. Distribution of Gains and Losses

The distinct paths of the Thai economy with and without intermediation allow us to estimate at the micro, household level the distribution of gains (and potential losses) from the observed expansion/liberalization of the financial sector. Essentially, one can overlap the occupation-choice diagrams of the non-intermediated and intermediated sectors. The figure above shows estimated parameters for the simulated year 1979 with both

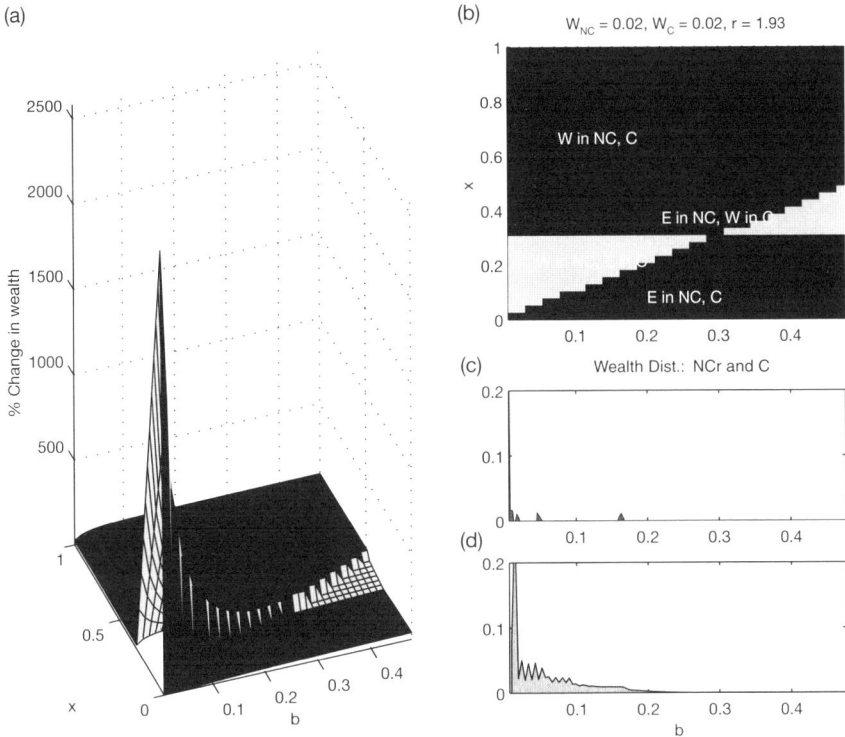

(a)

(b) $W_{NC} = 0.02$, $W_C = 0.02$, $r = 1.93$

W in NC, C

E in NC, W in C

E in NC, C

x

(c) Wealth Dist.: NCr and C

(d)

b

Fig. 6.4(a)–(d). *Welfare comparison in 1979 (Townsend Thai data) (See color version at the end of the book).*

Source: Giné and Townsend 2004.

sectors. Of great interest is the region of those who establish enterprise in the economy with some intermediation and would not do so in the economy without intermediation. As the wage is the same in both economies in 1979, this is simply a comparison across sectors in 1979 of otherwise identical households with and without access to banks. Of interest also are those who would set up firms in the non-intermediated sector but who save their money in the bank in the intermediated sector. The associated differences in end-of period wealth, that is, the 'static' welfare gains, are depicted in Figure 6.4(a)–(d). These in turn can be weighted by the fractions of the population imagined to be at various *wealth = b*, *cost = x* combinations, according to the estimated distribution of costs *x* and various assumptions about what the distribution of wealth *b* would look like in the non-intermediated and intermediated economies.

Apparent are the extraordinary gains for talented, poor households. There are other interesting features of the graph, such as the gain for high-cost, high-wealth households who abandon the inefficient enterprises they would have been running. Related is financial income; wealth increases savings that can be put into the bank. Note, however, that those who would be wage earners in either sector do not experience any welfare gain. Again, in 1979 the wage is the same in the two economies. Likewise, no one can experience a welfare loss. As prices have not moved, the choice of every household is the same or less restricted than what it would have been without Figure 6.3(a)–(e) intermediation.

By 1996, however, the wage in the Thai economy is higher than it would have been without intermediation. That means that a (b, x) household running a firm in the actual, intermediated economy has lower profits (see Figure 6.5(a)–(d)) than they would have had if running a firm in the associated non-intermediated economy at a lower wage. One can no longer compare across intermediated and non-intermediated sectors in the actual Thai economy. Difference in earnings due to differences in access do not pick up the general equilibrium wage effect. We can still calculate, however,

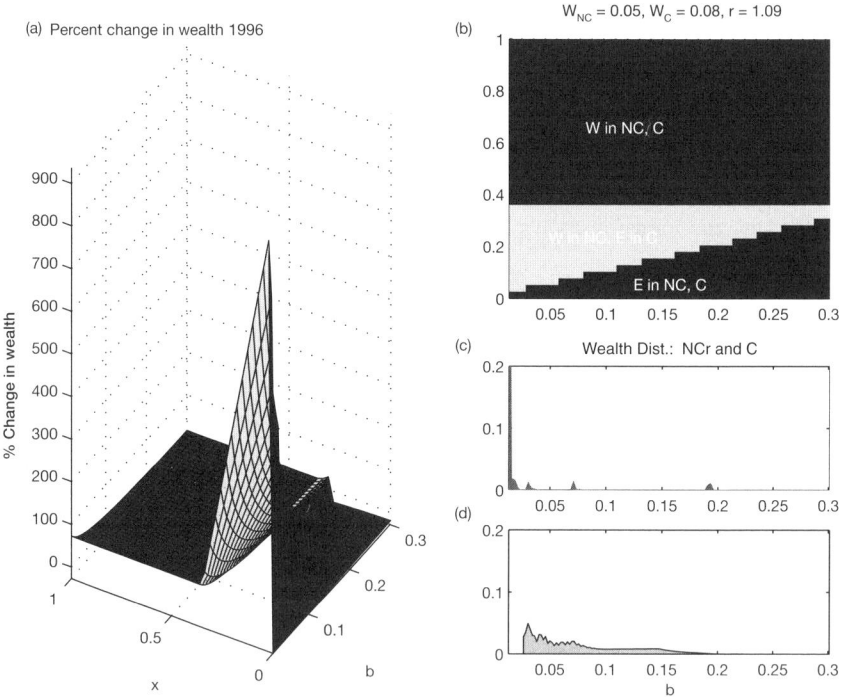

Fig. 6.5(a)–(d). *Welfare comparison in 1996 (SES data) (See color version at the end of the book).*

Source: Giné and Townsend 2004.

from the structure of the model, the differences in earnings of those wage earners at (b,x) points who would be wage earners in the non-intermediated economy but set up firms by borrowing from banks in the intermediated economy. These gains are still quite large. But now those who would be wage earners in the economy without intermediation and remain wage earners in the economy with intermediation also experience the gain of an increased wage. As mentioned, those who would be firms in the non-intermediated economy and in the intermediated economy if given access may well experience losses due to the increase in the wage (though excess savings can be put in the bank at interest). For previously constrained firms, in the economy without intermediation, enhanced access allows them to operate at a more efficient scale. Higher wage effects and increased efficiency compete with one another.

Table 6.2 (from Giné and Townsend 2004), summarizes the distribution of gains and losses to expansion of the financial sector. As anticipated, average,

Table 6.2. *Welfare gains and losses*

	Intermediated economy		Wealth distribution	Non-intermediated economy		Wealth distribution
	1997 baht	dollar	percentage of income	1997 baht	dollar	percentage of income
Townsend Thai data, 1979						
Welfare gains						
Mean	82,376	3,295	200.93	61,582	2,463	150.21
Median	22,839	914	55.71	3,676	147	8.97
Mode	7,779	311	18.97	6,961	278	16.98
Percentage of population		100			100	
Townsend Socio-economic Survey data, 1996						
Welfare gains						
Mean	76,840	3,074	100.54	83,444	3,338	109.18
Median	25,408	1,016	33.24	20,645	826	27.01
Mode	25,655	1,026	33.57	18,591	744	24.32
Percentage of population		86			95	
Welfare losses						
Mean	117,051	4,682	107.59	115,861	4,634	106.50
Median	113,705	4,548	104.51	112,097	4,484	103.04
Mode	117,486	4,699	107.99	118,119	4,725	108.57
Percentage of population		14			5	

Source: Repr from X. Giné and R. M. Townsend, 'Evaluation of Financial Liberalization: A General Equilibrium Model with Constrained Occupation Choice', *Journal of Development Economics*, 74 (2004), 269–307. Copyright 2004 with permission from Elsevier.

median, and modal gains can be substantial in the various years, from 17 per cent to 201 per cent of average Thai household income. The skewness of gains is what makes the three measures so different from one another. Welfare losses are also substantial, at approximately 104 per cent to 109 per cent of average income (the overall average, not the income of entrepreneurs). The fraction of losers varies from 5 per cent to 14 per cent of the population.

6.1.4. Some Structure Policy Experiments

The structure of the model at estimated parameter values also allows us to assess the impact of foreign capital inflows. Recall that there is increased domestic use of the banking system at almost the same time as increased

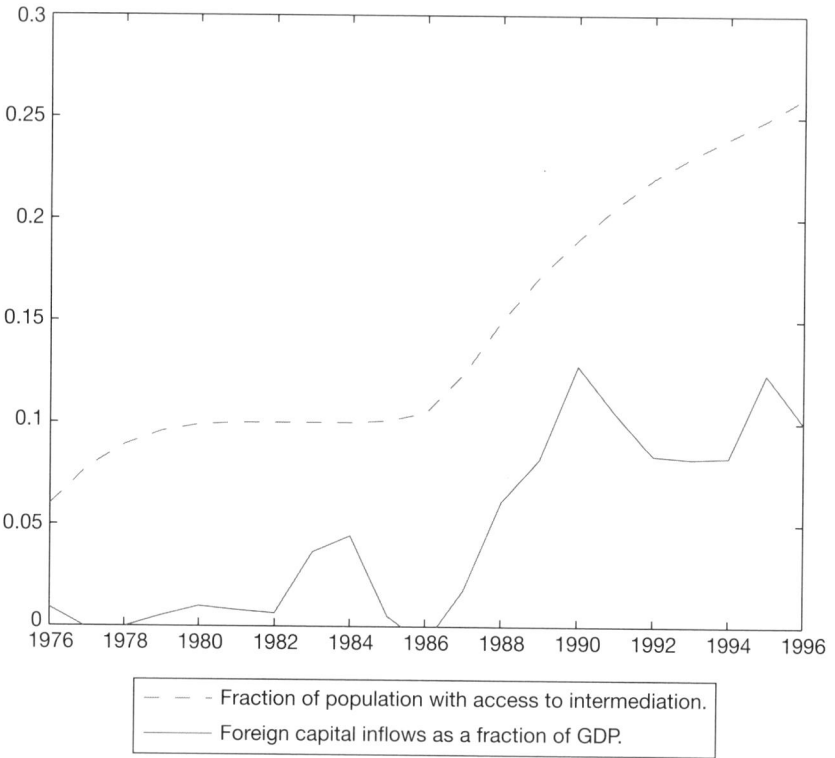

Fig. 6.6(a). *Foreign capital inflows and financial liberalization, 1976–96*

Source: Repr. from X Giné and R. M. Townsend, 'Evaluation of Financial Liberalization: A General Equilibrium Model with Constrained Occupation Choice', *Journal of Development Economics*, 74 (2004), 269–307. Copyright 2004 with permission from Elsevier.

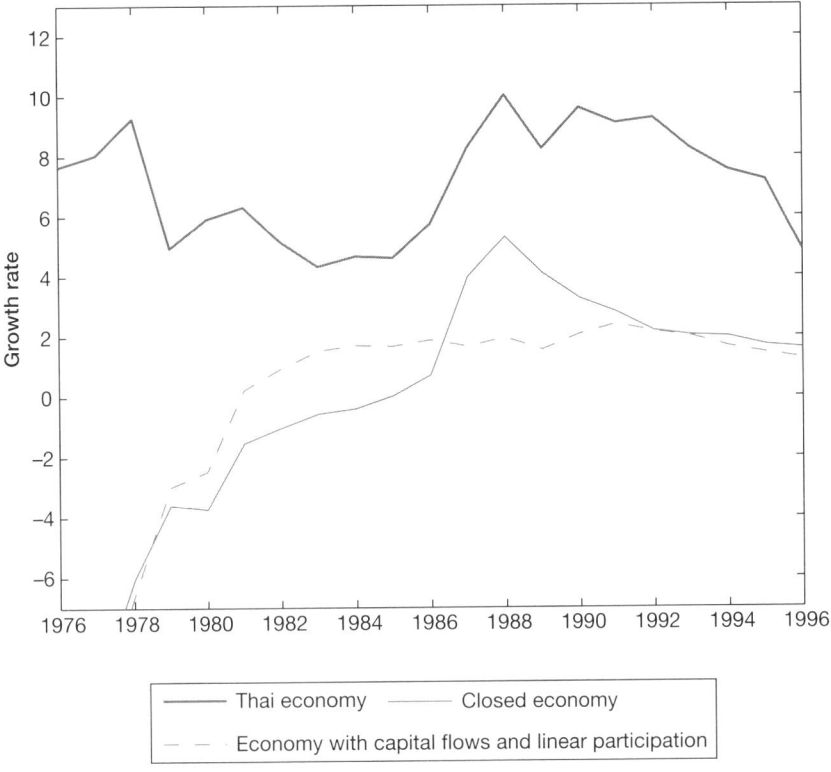

Fig. 6.6(b). *Access to capital and foreign capital, 1976–96 (Socio-economic Survey data)*

Source: Repr. from X Giné and R. M. Townsend, 'Evaluation of Financial Liberalization: A General Equilibrium Model with Constrained Occupation Choice', *Journal of Development Economics*, 74 (2004), 269–307. Copyright 2004 with permission from Elsevier.

foreign inflows. We linearize the observed trend of increasing access to the domestic financial system, eliminating the 'S' upturn that we suspect is behind the accelerated growth. At the same time, we allow augmented savings (investment) from foreign sources and the associated decreased domestic interest rate. The wage is also endogenous. Featured in Figures 6.6(a), 6.6(b), and 6.6(c) are three paths: the growth path of the actual Thai economy; the former predicted, simulated path of the closed economy (with its acceleration); and the newly predicted path. The last at the estimated SES and Townsend Thai parameters is essentially flat. Foreign capital inflows did not cause the accelerated growth, apparently.

We conduct another experiment, allowing some measure of informal credit for those outside the formal sector. Specifically, borrowers who

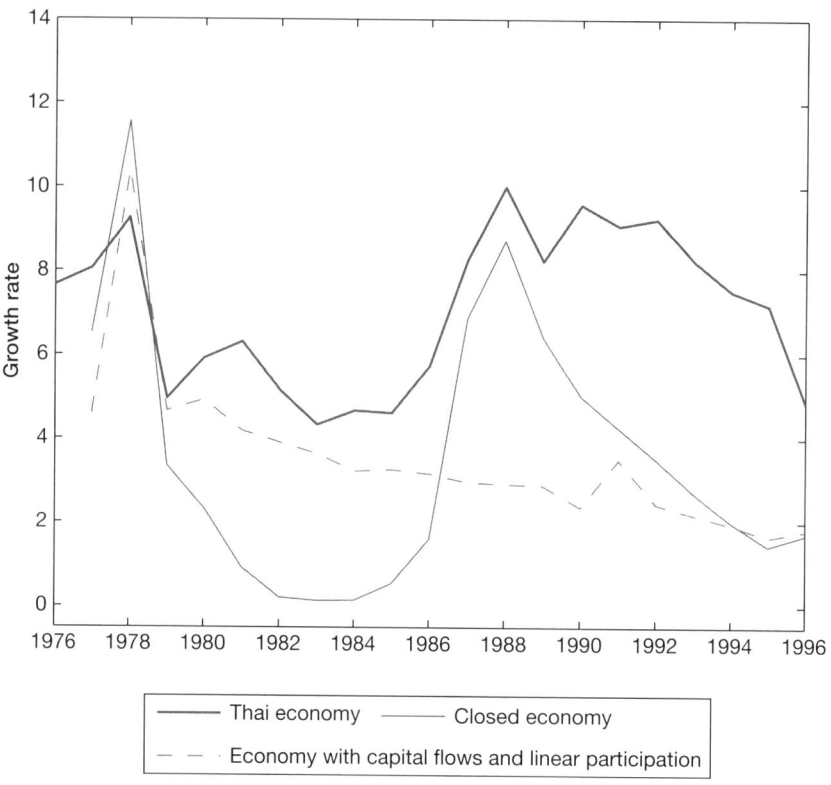

Fig. 6.6(c). *Access to capital and foreign capital 1976–96 (Townsend Thai data)*

Source: Repr. from X Giné and R. M. Townsend, 'Evaluation of Financial Liberalization: A General Equilibrium Model with Constrained Occupation Choice', *Journal of Development Economics*, 74 (2004), 269–307. Copyright 2004 with permission from Elsevier.

renege on a loan contract are apprehended with probability p and though they can hide their income they receive a punishment with additive disutility d and lose their wealth. This is weighed against repaying loans L. Specifically, borrowers will renege if $rb + pd < rL$, so loan size is bounded; that is, $L \leq b + \Delta$ where $\Delta = pd/r$. Setting r at 1 and calibrating Δ to best fit the observed dynamics gives most scope for the informal sector to have impact. The calibrated Δ turns out to be consistent with informal borrowing to wealth ratios as in the Townsend Thai data. Wages increase earlier than before, but the path of the economy is not much altered from the economy without informal credit. The welfare gains from an expansion of the formal sector are similar to the earlier calculations without informal credit.

6.1.5. TFP Due to Financial Deepening

As we may recall from the earlier figure, Thai TFPG, as measured by the standard Solow residual (SR), also shoots up during the period when the domestic financial system expanded, 1986–90 (see Figure 6.7).

The structure of the micro-based occupation-choice model allows us to disentangle the differences in output across sectors and over time that give rise to measured TFPG. Specifically, output from firms in the intermediated sector, say sector 2, Y_2^m consists of output under production function $f(k,l)$ with inputs $k^*(w,r)$ and $l^*(w,r)$ at wage w and interest rate r. The integral over the sources of heterogeneity, wealth b and talent x, delivers output of the representative firm (firms are all identical) multiplied times the fraction of entrepreneurs in the population:

$$Y_2^m = H(\tilde{x}(w,r))f[k_2^*(w,r), l_2^*(w,r)] = G_2(w,r). \qquad (6.1.5.1)$$

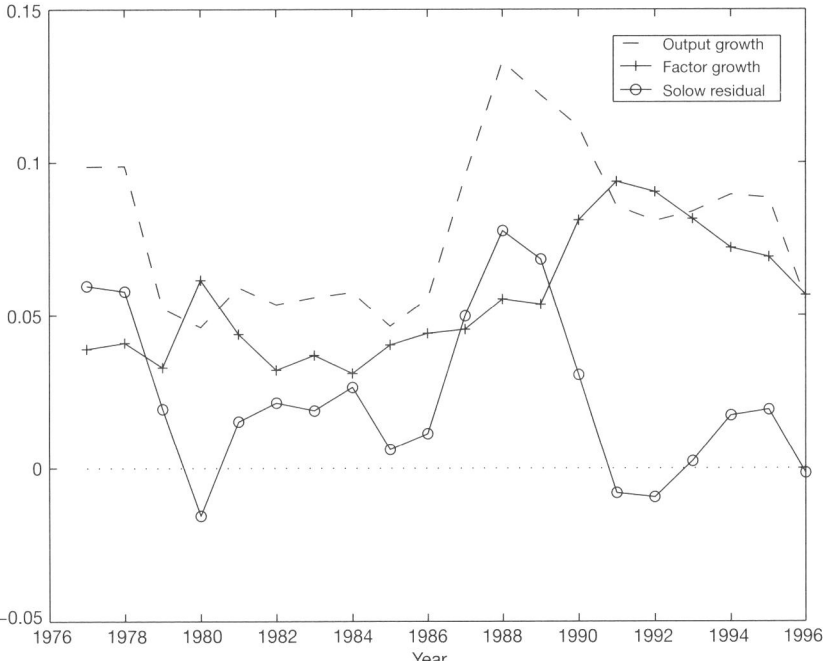

Fig. 6.7. *Standard growth accounting in Thailand, 1976–96*

Source: Jeong and Townsend 2007.

This is per capita GDP from manufacturing (better put, GDP minus agriculture). The growth of output can vary if changing wages and interest rates change the fraction of firms in the population, even adjusting for changes in the measured inputs, capital, and labor. But per capita GDP in manufacturing from firms without access Y_1^m is a complicated weighted average of firms run by constrained households of varying wealth b, distributed according to $\Psi_1(b)$, and talent x distributed according to $H(x)$:

$$Y_1^m = \int_0^\infty \int_0^{x^e(b,w)} f[k_1(b,x,w), l_1(b,x,w)] dH(x) d\psi_1(b) = G_1(w,\psi). \quad (6.1.5.2)$$

We will have to work further to get a decomposition. Persistent algebra breaks aggregate TFPG into four key components.

$$TFPG = TFPG\_SSR + TFPG\_ACH + TFPG\_OCCS + TFPG\_FIN. \quad (6.1.5.3)$$

The first term,

$$TFPG\_SSR \equiv (1-p)\tilde{s}_{y_1} SR_1 + p\tilde{s}_{y_2} SR_2 \quad (6.1.5.4)$$

is the Solow residual SR_j in each of the two sectors, $j=1,2$, weighted by the proportion of output in the two sectors the $s_{Y_j}, j=1,2$ and weighted in turn by the fraction p of the population in the intermediated sector and $(1-p)$ in the non-intermediated sectors. Here, output consists not only of that produced but also that coming from subsistence agriculture. There is a second capital adjustment component in the first, non-intermediated sector:

$$TFPG\_ACH \equiv (1-p)\tilde{s}_{y_1} s_{k_1} g_{k_1} \quad (6.1.5.5)$$

as standard TFP calculations assume, incorrectly, that all capital is priced at its rental rate r. The change in capital g_{k_1} in the non-intermediated sector is weighted by fraction of the population $(1-p)$ in the non-intermediated sector, the share $\tilde{s}_{Yj}$ of output coming from that sector, and also the share of capital s_{k_1} in factor payments in that sector. The third component is a pure occupation shift effect from those moving out of subsistence and/or wage labor into enterprise:

$$TFPG\_OCC \equiv (1-p)\bar{s}_{y_1}(-s_{L_1} g_{L_1}) + p\bar{s}_{y_2}(-s_{L_2} g_{L_2}). \quad (6.1.5.6)$$

Here $-g_{L_j}$ is weighted at labor shares s_{L_j}, the fraction of total output, and the population fraction p and $(1-p)$ in the intermediated and non-intermediated sectors, respectively. The negative sign occurs because the fraction still in subsistence is not helping overall productivity; it is the fraction *leaving* which helps. The final, fourth component is the direct financial deepening effect:

$$TFPG\_FIN = \left[\tilde{S}_{Y_2} \frac{\Pi_2}{Y_2} - \tilde{S}_{Y_1} \frac{\Pi_1}{Y_1} \right] pg_p. \qquad (6.1.5.7)$$

Much in the spirit of the earlier Theil decompositions, this is the ratio of total profits to total output differenced across the two sectors, presumably higher in the intermediated sector, though weighted by the proportion of total output coming from the non-intermediate sector. The impact on productivity comes from the shift in the population pg_P into the intermediated sector.

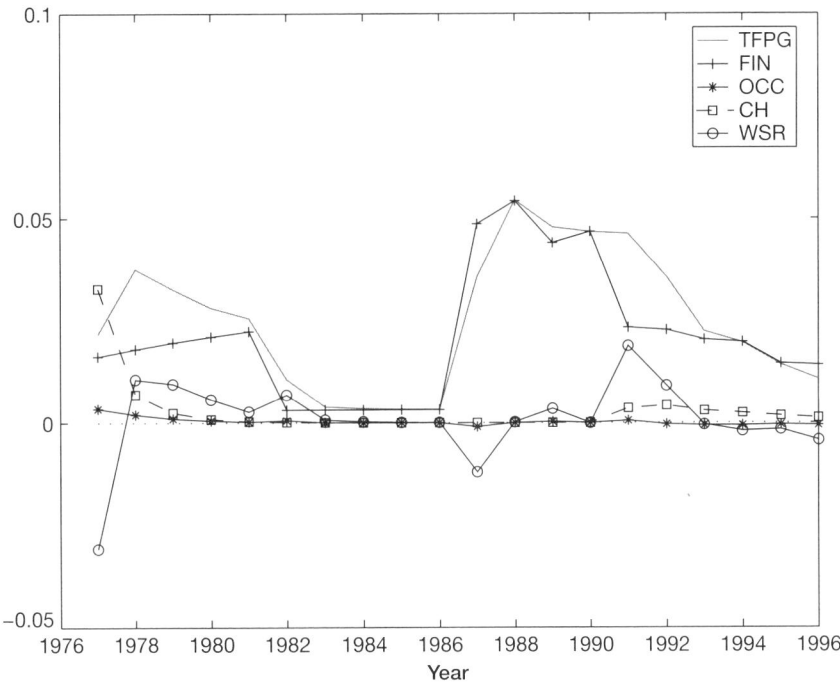

Fig. 6.8(a). *Decomposition of standard total-factor productivity growth*

Note: TFPG: TFP Growth in equation (27); FIN: financial-deepening effect in equation (38); OCC: occupational-shift effect in equation (39); CH: capital-heterogeneity effect in equation (40); WSR: within-sector Solow residual in equation (41).

Source: Jeong and Townsend 2007.

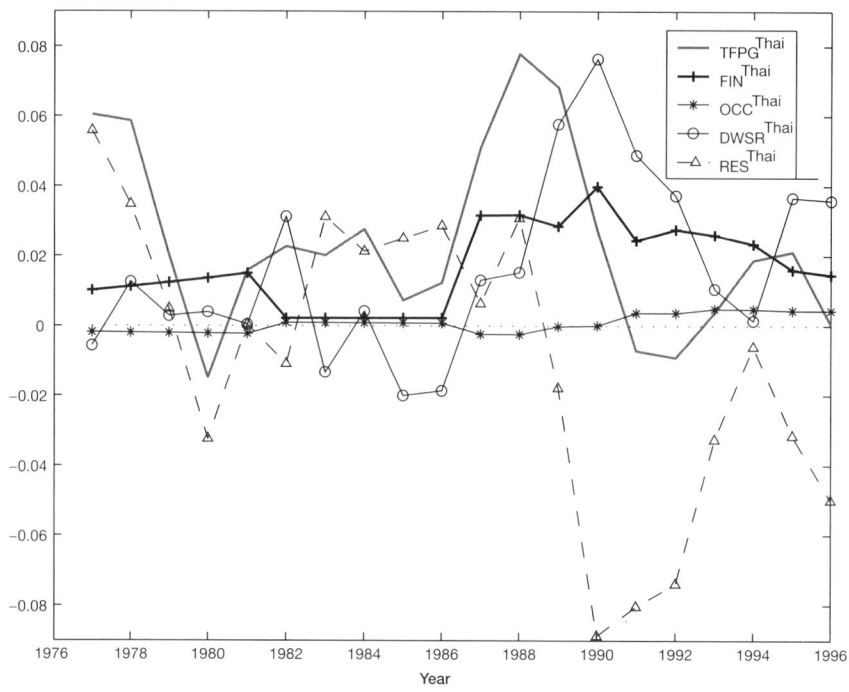

Fig. 6.8(b). *Decomposition of actual Thai total-factor productivity growth*

Notes: TFPG^{Thai}: TFP growth in equation (46); FIN^{Thai}: financial-deepening effect in equation (38); OCC^{Thai}: occupational-shift effect in equation; DWSR^{Thai}: dual within-sector Solow residual in equation (47); RES^{Thai}: residual TEP growth in equation (48).
Source: Jeong and Townsend 2007.

The decomposition of TFPG in the model and in the data reveals a striking success of the modeling effort. Measured Thai TFPG moves with the financial deepening effect not only in the model but also in the data. In both there is a 'repression' effect through the early to mid-1980s and then a dramatic surge from 1986 to 1990. This continues in the model through the late 1990s but drops in the data. A residual in the Thai data that we cannot decompose also goes negative in the 1990s. Both may presage the financial crisis. In the model and the data, the occupation effect and Solow residual (SR) effects are smaller, though the SR effect is much larger in the data than in the model.

Some of the key ingredients in the model simulation, at calibrated values, and in the Thai economy, are displayed in these figures. Movements of wages and interest rates are in the top panels. As has been anticipated repeatedly, wage rates are more or less steady until the 1990s, both in the model and in the data. The wage is measured as the average earnings of full-time wage households, excluding part-time income. The interest rate naturally declines in the model and may be badly measured in the data, especially initially where all we see is the regulated rate. The occupation effect is determined by Figure 6.9 (d) and (e) for the model, and Figure 6.10 (d) and (e) for the data. These are the fraction of firms and sector wage shares, respectively. In the model, as in the data, the fraction of firms are higher in intermediated sector 2, and the wage share is lower there, but the differences across sectors are too large in the model relative to the data. Likewise, the financial-deepening effect is determined by the

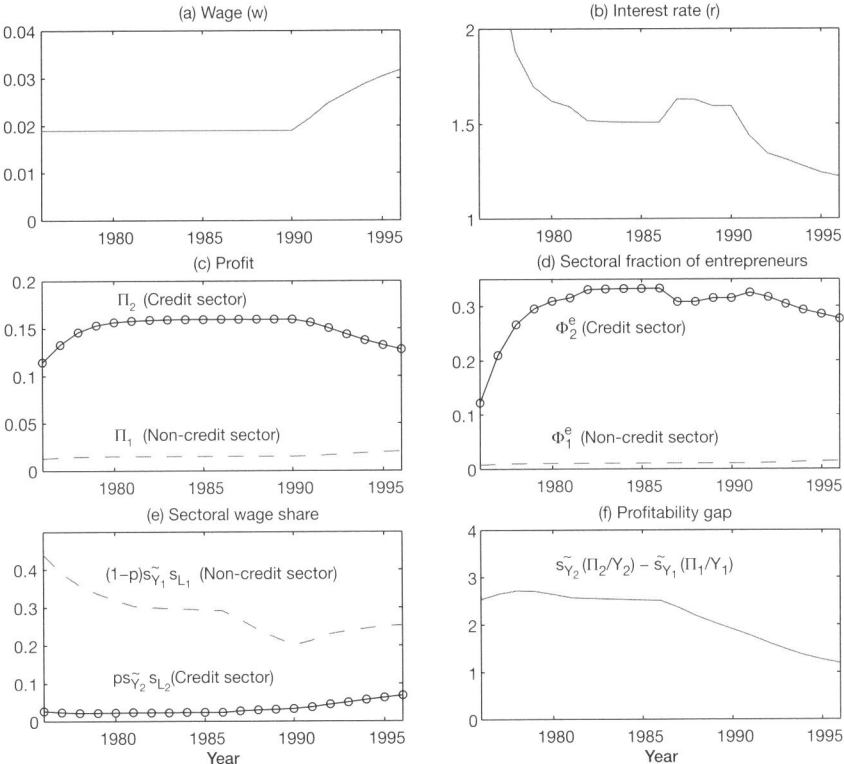

Fig. 6.9(a)–(f). *Underlying variables for simulated total-factor productivity growth*

Source: Jeong and Townsend 2007.

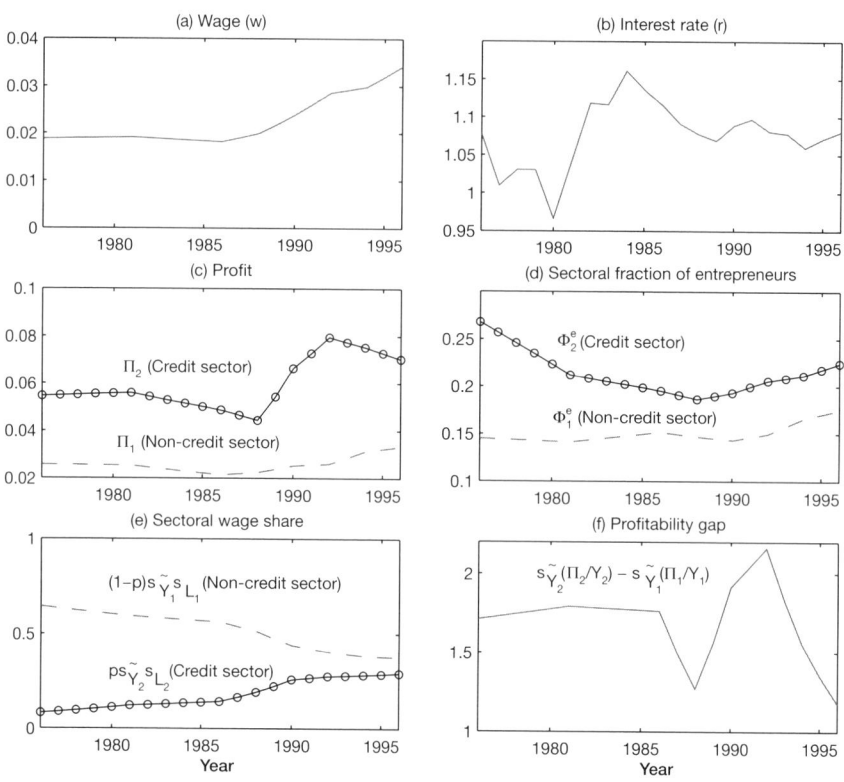

Fig. 6.10(a)–(f). *Underlying variables for Thai total-factor productivity growth*

Source: Jeong and Townsend 2007.

variables (c) and (f) for the data. Again, the rank ordering is correct, but the differences are accentuated in the model relative to the data. (Note the differences in scale in the Figures.) Also in the data is an upturn in absolute profits and an upturn in the profitability gap not predicted by the model (see Figure 6.11).

Figure 6.12 (a)–(b) summarizes the main conclusions: the actual financial-deepening effect in the data is much like the financial-deepening-effect model. That effect plus the substantial growth in capital are what contributed to the increase in Thai GDP.

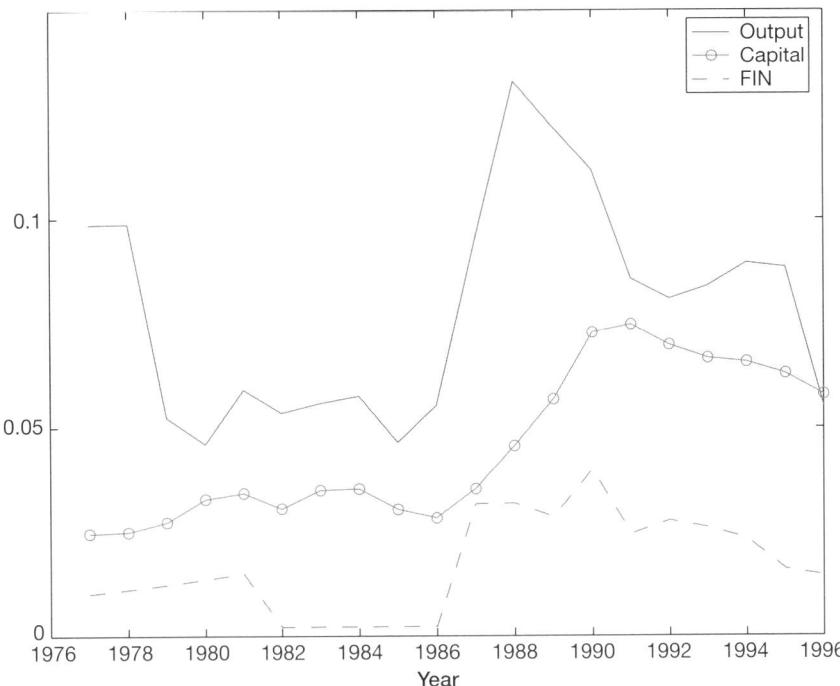

Fig. 6.11. *Capital deepening vs financial deepening*
Source: Jeong and Townsend 2007.

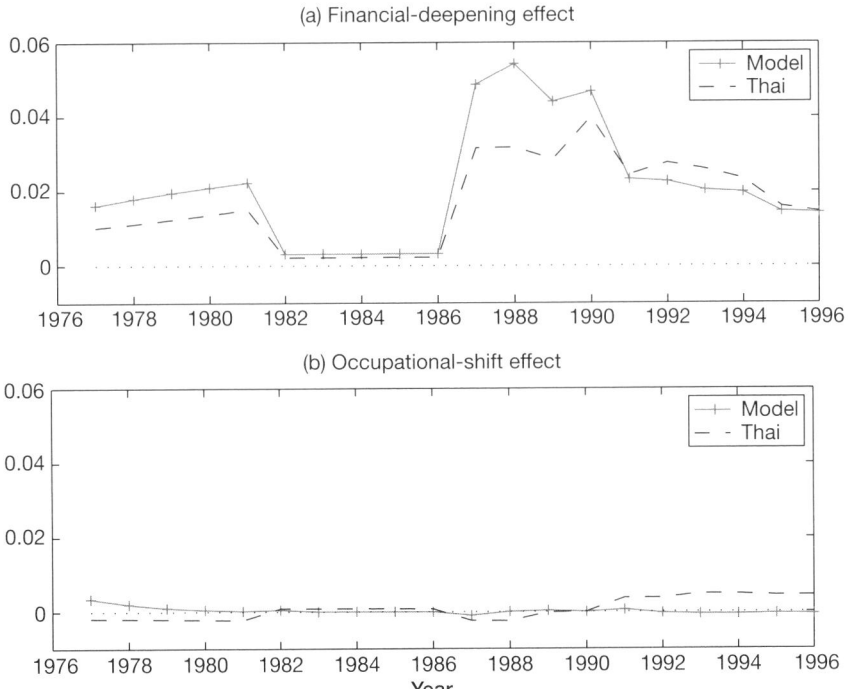

Fig. 6.12(a)–(b). *Sources of total-factor productivity growth*
Source: Jeong and Townsend 2007.

6.2. Access Choice: Financial Sector Endogenous

6.2.1. Review

The motivation for the second model comes from our earlier review of the essential facts. Thailand experienced growth with increasing inequality, financial deepening, varying cycles with a difference between the maximum and minimum growth rate of 10 per cent, large idiosyncratic shocks relative to macro aggregate shocks, low levels of inequality in agriculture relative to non-farm entrepreneurs, increasing wealth to access transition profiles, and financial-sector providers with operating systems which would allow the amelioration of idiosyncratic shocks (schemata).

6.2.2. The Model

The model follows Greenwood and Jovanovic 1990 and the earlier literature, as modified by Townsend and Ueda 2006. The model features risk and the reallocation risk, though savings rates and activities are also endogenous. Specifically, the typical household is imagined to be risk averse and to maximize discounted expected utility

$$E_1\left[\sum_{t=1}^{\infty} \beta^{t-1} u(c_t)\right] \tag{6.2.2.1}$$

with contemporaneous utility is $u(c) = \frac{c^{1-\gamma}}{1-\gamma}$. Households are risk averse, so $\gamma > 0$. When in autarky, not connected to the formal financial sector, the household chooses the amount to save s_t; the fraction ϕ_t of that to put in a risky activity, with a linear return per unit capital of δ; and residual fraction $1 - \phi_t$ in a safe activity with a linear return per unit capital $\theta_t + \epsilon_t$. Here the aggregate shock is θ_t and the idiosyncratic, household/firm specific risk ϵ_t. The realization of macro and idiosyncratic shocks takes place after investment, between periods t and $t+1$. As a first approximation, ϕ_t can be taken to be household resources devoted to farming and the residual to non-farm business. The law of motion for wealth is simply

$$k_{t+1} = s_t\left(\phi_t(\theta_t + \varepsilon_t) + (1 - \phi_t)\delta\right) \tag{6.2.2.2}$$

where wealth k_t is entirely fungible (like putty), either consumed in amount c_t, or saved in amount s_t, as stated earlier.

There are advantages to being in the formal financial system—namely, the sharing of idiosyncratic risks. But this comes at a cost. There is competition among potential intermediaries who form mutual funds and charge fees to cover the costs. The earlier model of Townsend 1978, though static with idiosyncratic shocks, is illustrative, so we cover that part here.

Let I denote the set of agents. It is assumed here that I is countable infinite. Each agent $j \in I$ is endowed with a quantity of the unique factor of production of the model, the capital good k^j. The endowments of this capital good are identical for all agents and perfectly divisible. Each agent is also endowed with a stochastic technology which transforms the capital good into a distribution of the unique consumption good of the model. Each of these technologies or investment projects displays constant return to scale. Let λ^j denote the output of the consumption good per unit of the capital input y_j in project j. Each λ^j is a random variable and the λ^j, $j \in I$ are assumed to be independent and identically distributed. A state of the economy subsequent to the realization of the shocks is a complete specification of the value of each of the λ^j, $j \in I$. The set of all possible states will be denoted Ω with typical element ω. Let $\mu(\omega)$ denote the probability that state ω will occur. Each agent tries to maximize expected utility, so that each has objective function

$$W^j(c^j) = \int_{\omega \in \Omega} \mu(\omega) U[c^j(\omega)]. \qquad (6.2.2.3)$$

Here, of course, $c^j(\omega)$ is the consumption of agent j in state ω.

Exchange in the model is assumed to be costly. For each bilateral deal a fixed cost of $2a$ units of the capital good is incurred, a per agent. This gives rise to intermediaries, to economize on these costs.

A market M is defined to be the smallest set of agents for which every agent of the set deals with other agents of the set and with no agent outside that set. Let $\eta(M)$ denote the number of bilateral exchanges in a market M with $\#M$ participants. Hence,

$$(\#M - 1) \le \eta(M) \le (\#M)(\#M - 1)/2. \qquad (6.2.2.4)$$

Then an allocation $\{c^j, y^j; j \in M\}$ is said to be feasible for market M if the reallocation of the capital good is feasible, net of transactions costs,

$$\sum_{j \in M}(k^j - y^j) \ge (2\alpha)\eta(M) \qquad (6.2.2.5)$$

and there is enough output to meet consumption demands,

$$\sum\nolimits_{j \in M} \lambda^j(\omega) y^j \geq \sum\nolimits_{j \in M} c^j(\omega), \quad \omega \in \Omega. \tag{6.2.2.6}$$

An allocation $\{c^j, y^j; j \in C\}$ is said to be *feasible for a coalition C* if there exists a set of markets, A such that $\cup_{M \in A} M = C$ and the allocation $\{c^j, y^j; j \in M\}$ is feasible for each market $M \in A$. The *core* for the economy I is the set of allocations which are feasible for the entire economy I and which are not blocked by any coalition. An allocation $\{c^j, y^j; j \in I\}$ is said to be *blocked* by a coalition B if there exists an allocation $\{c^j_*, y^j_*, j \in B\}\}$ which is feasible for B such that $W^j(c^j_*) > W^j(c^j)$ for each agent $j \in B$.

In the cooperative version of this economy specified agents are designated as intermediaries. Each intermediary selects a group of agents for projects in his portfolio. These sets are assumed to be disjoint so that in effect intermediaries are forming markets M. Each agent in a market agrees to sell shares in his project to the intermediary for a price of one in terms of the capital good, and the intermediary sells shares in his portfolio for a price of one in terms of the capital good. In effect, shares are exchanged one for one. A share in the output of project j entitles the holder to λ^j units of the consumption good. A share in the portfolio of an intermediary of market M entitles the holder to $\sum_{i \in M} \lambda^i / \#M$ units of the consumption good. All transactions costs are shared equally by all agents in a given market. With $(\#M - 1)$ as the minimum number of bilateral exchanges in M, these transactions costs will be $(\#M - 1)(2a)$. In these circumstances agents in a market will trade shares with the intermediary on a one-to-one basis up to the limits of their initial endowments, less transactions costs. Each intermediary determines the number of agents in his market, and each will act to maximize the utility function of a representative consumer,

$$EU\left\{ \left[k^j - \frac{(2\alpha)(\#M - 1)}{\#M} \right] [\sum\nolimits_{i \in M} \lambda^i / \#M] \right\} \tag{6.2.2.7}$$

with respect to $\#M$. Core allocations are equivalent to the equilibrium allocations of a non-cooperative game.

In the non-cooperative game the determination of who is to act as an intermediary, and under what terms, is endogenous. Each agent is free to announce any intermediation strategy, and it is assumed that each selects a strategy in such a way as to maximize expected utility. This strategy is the market proposed by agent h as intermediary, the yield in terms of the consumption good for one share in the portfolio of agent h; a price in terms of the capital good at which agent h is willing to buy an unlimited number of shares in any project j of its market, a fixed fee in terms of the capital good for the purchase of shares in the portfolio of agent h by agent j, and a price in terms of the capital good at which agent h is willing to sell an unlimited number of shares in his portfolio to agents j. Agents must act on the strategies prior to the realization of the state. Once the state has occurred, agents make the transfers of the consumption good required to honor claims issued. Given that intermediaries have been selected in some way, all other agents regard the strategies as parameters and maximize expected utility. An intermediary who is active for his proposed market will have expected utility that is determined by the residual consumption left over after completing all trades.

An agent b may find it is in his *own* interest to announce a blocking strategy. In the process of undercutting an active intermediary of a specified market or in the process of forming a new market, all the agents with whom agent b deals are made better off than initially. Roughly speaking agent b may be viewed as a firm who is aware of demand curves and seeks to exploit profitable markets. This type of free entry will be crucial in determining the allocation of resources. A non-cooperative equilibrium is described in part as an allocation for which there exist no blocking strategies for any agent.

In an equilibrium: (i) any agent who is not an active intermediary maximizes expected utility by choosing an intermediary with whom to trade, the number of shares in his own project to be sold to that intermediary, the number of shares in the portfolio of that intermediary to be purchased, and the amount to invest in his own project, regarding as parameters the announced intermediation strategies of all other agents; (ii) agents partition themselves into markets—for each market there is one active intermediary with a strategy and a maximizing input choice, which support the maximizing choices of inactive agents; (iii) free entry condition is the motivated above with the discussion of blocking.

The equivalence of core allocations and equilibrium allocations can be established. In particular, if there exists an equilibrium, the equilibrium allocation is in the core. All core allocations can be supported as equilibria. These are the analogues of the two fundamental welfare theorems. Finally, note that with free entry intermediaries have zero profits in the sense that their utility is drawn down to that of non-intermediated customers.

As incorporated in Greenwood and Jovanovic (GJ), there is a continuum of agents in the financial sector, a kind of limit in the above model, and all idiosyncratic shocks are shared completely by members/customers of the associated financial institution, so there is no residual idiosyncratic risk for these households. This could be accomplished by having loan repayment vary with idiosyncratic shocks ϵ_t, as in the BAAC implicit insurance, risk-contingency system. Thus, in principle, all projects are evaluated at their expected returns. A second advantage to the formal financial system here is advanced information on forthcoming aggregate shocks, as if experienced loan officers were advising clients. Thus the mutual fund yield is

$$r(\theta_t) = \gamma \max[\theta_i, \delta] \qquad (6.2.2.8)$$

where γ is the return left over after proportional transaction costs $1 - \gamma$. Here, then, even the choice between risky and safe technologies is without risk. This is a bit overdone.

In sum, in the present model the advantages of the formal financial sector are imagined to go to extremes: full risk-sharing and complete advanced information. The advantages of the financial sector must be weighed against two costs. One is the marginal cost $1 - \gamma$, a spread between borrowing and lending rates. A second cost is a fixed cost q for entering the financial system. The latter is a stylized version of the earlier model of costly bilateral exchange and captures the cost of financial infrastructure, branch banks, roads, and household learning.

The solution technique for the dynamic model is summarized by a pair of value functions. Let $V(k)$ denote the discounted expected utility value of being in the financial system today with wealth k, and $W(k)$ is the value for those currently not in the financial system at wealth k. Those having decided not to enter today at date t face the choice again next period, so

$$W(k_t) = \max_{s_t, \phi_t} u(k_t - s_t) + \beta \int \max\{W(k_{t+1}), V(k_{t+1} - q)\} dH(\eta_t)$$

$$(6.2.2.9)$$

where at the time of entry fixed cost q is subtracted from wealth. Shock $\eta_t \equiv \theta + \epsilon_t$, and the law of motion for capital was given earlier in equation 6.2.2.2. Once households enter they will never exit, and the value function $V(k)$ is

$$V(k_t) = \max_{s_t} u(k_t - s_t) + \beta \int V(k_{t+1})\} dF(\theta_t) \qquad (6.2.2.10)$$

with law of motion of capital, $k_{t+1} = s_t r = (\theta_t)$, and investment return given earlier in equation 6.2.2.8. There is also a counterfactual lower bound, the value for those never ever allowed to enter the financial system,

$W_o(k_t) = \max_{s_t, \phi_t} u(k_t - s_t) + \beta \int W_o(k_{t+1}) dH(\eta_t)$ subject to 6.2.2.2. The advantage of this formulation is that one can obtain closed-form solutions for V

and W_o, and hence trap function W between them, that is, $W_o(k_t) \leq W(k_t)$ $< V(k_t)$. The savings and portfolio policies s and ϕ under W_o also offer an interesting benchmark.

Example value functions $V(k), V(k-q), W(k)$, and $W_0(k)$ are all depicted for selected parameter values, along with the savings and portfolio decisions under W and W_O (see Figure 6.13(a)). The savings rate under W_O and V is 0.96 out of wealth k and the fraction ϕ put in risky activities is 0.4. Key to the model dynamics: there is a critical level of wealth, here $k^* = 15$, below which a household will not (yet) enter the financial system and above which the household will enter and stay. Also, the savings rate rises the nearer is the household to that critical value of wealth k^*, to finance q at the time of entry. Surprisingly, the portfolio share into risky activities is also higher than under permanent autarky, W_0, and rises as the household approaches the same critical value of wealth k^*. This is because the utility frontier is otherwise not concave.

The savings and portfolio decisions of those in temporary autarky reflect the probability of future entry. Otherwise, those without access are

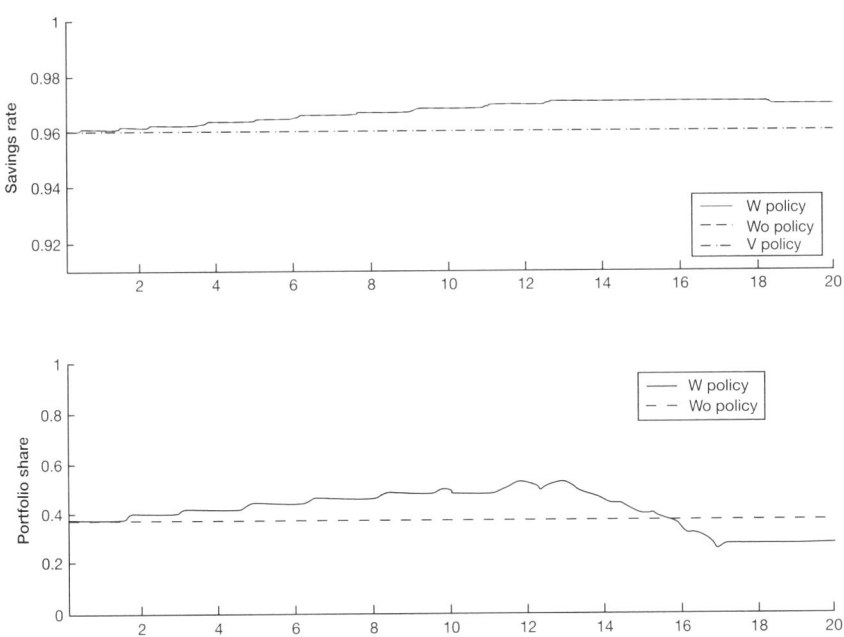

Fig. 6.13(a). *Policy functions*

Source: Townsend and Ueda 2006.

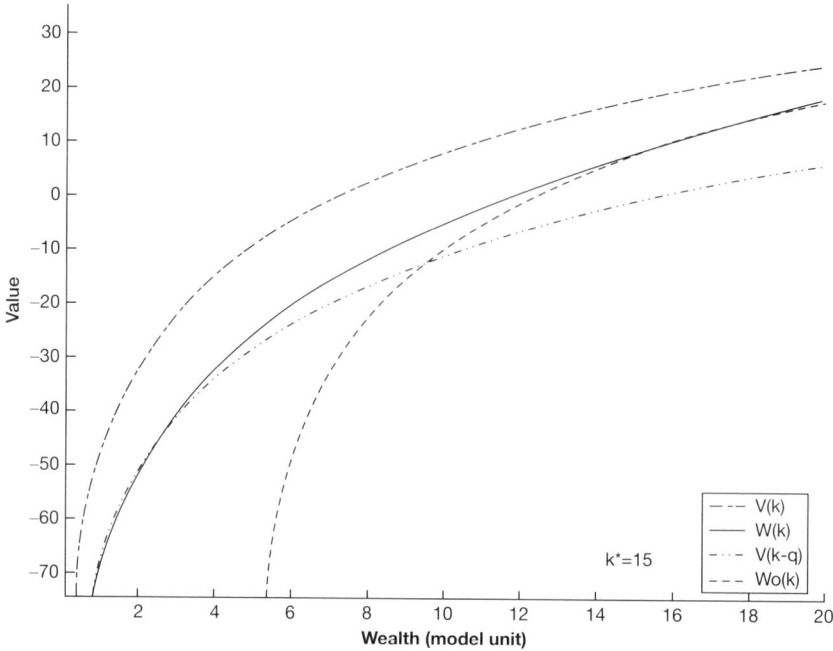

Fig. 6.13(b). *Value functions*

Source: Townsend and Ueda 2006.

essentially in a savings-only regime and can be expected to display a kind of buffer stock behavior. Both consumption and investment will move with today's realized income.

Parameters of preferences and technology can be calibrated. Alternatively, they can be estimated with micro data via an explicit likelihood function. Both methods will be described in more detail momentarily. As is evident from Table 6.3(a)–(b), the two methods yield strikingly similar conclusions: risk aversion, close to the log utility; rate of return on the safe technology at about 5 per cent; the range of macro shocks from ±10 per cent to 15 per cent; the range of idiosyncratic shocks (ROA holding θ constant, from ±60 per cent to ±100 per cent; preference discount rate β at 0.96, and zero marginal transaction costs γ). The fixed cost q varies across specifications, but it will be rescaled relative to the estimated initial empirical distribution of wealth.

For calibration, we set the technology parameters using Townsend Thai data. We use income to capital ratios to estimate the technology parameters for those not in the financial system. The survey shows that the net return from capital investment in subsistence agriculture, which we regard here as a crude approximation to the safe project δ, at 5.4 per cent in 1997. For the

Table 6.3. *Calibration/data sources*

(a) Benchmark parameter values calibrated, as real business cycle (RBC)						
σ	q	δ	θ	ϵ	β	$1-\gamma$
1	5	1.054	[1.047, 1.147]	[−0.6, 0.6]	0.96	0

(b) Maximum-likelihood estimated Greenwood–Jovanovic parameters: micro data						
σ	q	δ	$\underline{\theta}, \bar{\theta}$	$\bar{\epsilon}$	β	$1-\gamma$
0.9946	0.5021	1.0479	[1.0470, 1.1905]	[−0.9954, 0.9954]	0.9627	0
[0.0926]	[0.0482]	[0.0064]	[0.0451, 0.0514]	[0.0355]	[0.0061]	[0.0000]

Sources: (a) Townsend and Ueda 2006; (b) Jeong and Townsend 2003.

idiosyncratic shocks in the risky project, we also use income to capital ratios, but for those in non-agricultural business, and set the support of idiosyncratic shocks ϵ as $\epsilon = [-0.6, +0.6]$. This is the range of returns or income to capital ratios in the cross-section from the bottom 1 per cent to the top 99 per cent.

Pinning down the parameters on aggregate shocks turned out to be somewhat difficult. We know that the difference between the minimum and maximum real per capita growth rate from 1976 to 1996 is 8.7 per cent. According to the model with projects selected by the financial sector, underlying variation of the aggregate shocks would be yet larger. Thus we assume the *range* for the aggregate shocks θ at 10 per cent. We vary the *mean* of θ and pick the support of θ as (1.047, 1.1471) to minimize sum of squared (production) errors of the actual GDP growth rate versus the model prediction. This is the only part of calibration which uses dynamic data. This is our benchmark.

The fixed cost q is a free parameter, and we take it to be $q = 5$ in model units of capital. By comparing the critical capital level k^* in the model units and k^* in the actual data in Thai baht, we find a scalar or 'exchange rate' between the model units and the actual Thai baht. The critical capital level in model units is obtained by computing the value function—namely, $k^* = 15$ under the benchmark parameter values. The critical capital level in the actual data is estimated using the SES and the observed fraction participating in 1976. That is, we use the actual wealth distribution of 1976 from SES of Thailand as the initial condition (in 1990 baht, following Jeong 2000). We also use the information about participation in the financial system from the same SES. According to that survey the fraction of the population who had access to the financial system was 6 per cent in 1976. The estimated cumulative distribution of wealth in 1976 shows that people who had wealth of more than 220,000 baht were 6 per cent of the population in 1976. To generate the observed 6 per cent participation in 1976 with the critical level of the model at $k^* = 15$, we set the scalar or 'exchange rate' at about 15,000 baht per model unit per model unit capital.

Likelihood methods for estimation require the probability that a household j with initial wealth $k_{j,t-1}$ at period $t-1$ would be observed to participate, $d_{jt} = 1$, in the formal financial system at date t, and $d_{jt} = 0$ otherwise. That is,

$$d_{jt} = 1, if \ V(k_{jt} - q) \geq W(k_{jt})$$
$$= 0, if \ V(k_{jt} - q) < W(k_{jt}).$$

Equivalently,

$$d_{jt} = 1, if \ \ k_{jt} \geq k^*$$
$$= 0, if \ \ k_{jt} < k^*$$

We imagine in the SES cross-section for young households we are seeing wealth at the beginning of the period and the participation decision at the end of the period. Critical wealth k^* can be determined numerically, given an initial guessed parameter vector, denoted PM, for utility and technology. We determine the probability that saving (investment) at $k_{j,t-1}$, with fraction ϕ_{t-1} of that savings invested in the risky activity, delivers wealth k_j above (not less than) the threshold k^*. Expressions for the critical value of composite shocks $\eta_t \equiv \theta_t + \epsilon_t$, coming from the law of motion in 6.2.2 are given as

$$d_{jt} = 1, \ if \ \ \eta_{jt} \geq \eta \times (k_{j,t-1}, PM)$$
$$= 0, \ if \ \ \eta_{jt} < \eta \times (k_{j,t-1}, PM)$$

where

$$\eta^*(k_{j,t-1}, PM) \equiv \frac{1}{\phi(k_{j,t-1}, PM)} \left[\frac{k^*(PM)}{s(k_{j,t-1}, PM)} - (1 - \phi(k_{j,t-1}, PM))\delta \right].$$

Summing over all periods for a specified draw of shocks θ_t over the sample period, then weighting by the probability of those shocks, delivers the overall likelihood for each household j.

The driving underlying force in the model is the endogenous and evolving distribution of wealth. Again, the initial condition at 1976 comes from the SES data and Jeong's principal components measure of wealth. Figure 6.14 makes clear the tendency for those with access, with wealth above k^*,

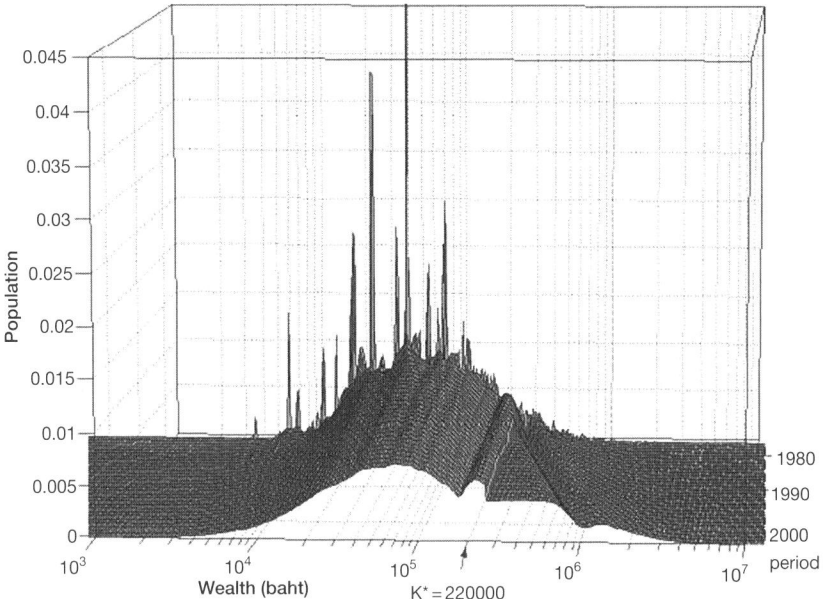

Fig. 6.14. *Wealth evolution*

Source: Townsend and Ueda 2006.

to take off from the rest of the distribution. One of the ridges is created by the assumption of uniform transactions costs q incurred at k^* (to be explored further below).

The trends for growth, financial participation, and inequality delivered by the model, averaging over 1,000 random draws for the aggregate shocks, are displayed in Figures 6.15 (a)–(c) and 6.15 (d)–(f). A variance–co-variance weighted mean squared error criterion minimizing the distance between a given simulation and the actual data delivers a 'best fit' path, also displayed. Specifically, the metric is

$$\psi_s \equiv (x_s - x_0)' b_0^{-1} (x_s - x_0),$$

where x_s is the simulated data, and x_0 is the Thai actual path. Matrix b_0 is estimated by the simulated sample analogue

$$\frac{1}{S} \sum_{s=1}^{S} (x_s - x_0)' (x_s - x_0).$$

Evidently, the model delivers a trend for financial participation that goes right though the middle of the Thai data. The model's Theil inequality measure coincides with the Thai data initially and then, after 1992, stays above the decreasing Thai level. The growth rate of the model is on average low and less volatile than GDP in the actual data. Note in particular the model with its entirely endogenous financial deepening misses the surge in the financial system and upturn in growth around 1986 that we have previously associated with financial liberalization. This gives credence to the view that the deviation above trend was indeed policy induced.

There is empirical literature connecting growth and inequality to financial deepening, arguing, for example, that more liberal systems and those with low inequality parameters grow faster. We need to try to compare this literature to the model at hand. Specifically, we conduct an experiment: we fix the benchmark economy, populate it with 1,002 households respecting the initial 1976 Thai wealth distribution, and then draw idiosyncratic shocks in the population and aggregate temporal shocks for thirty years. We do this experiment 1,000 times, with different shocks, generating in

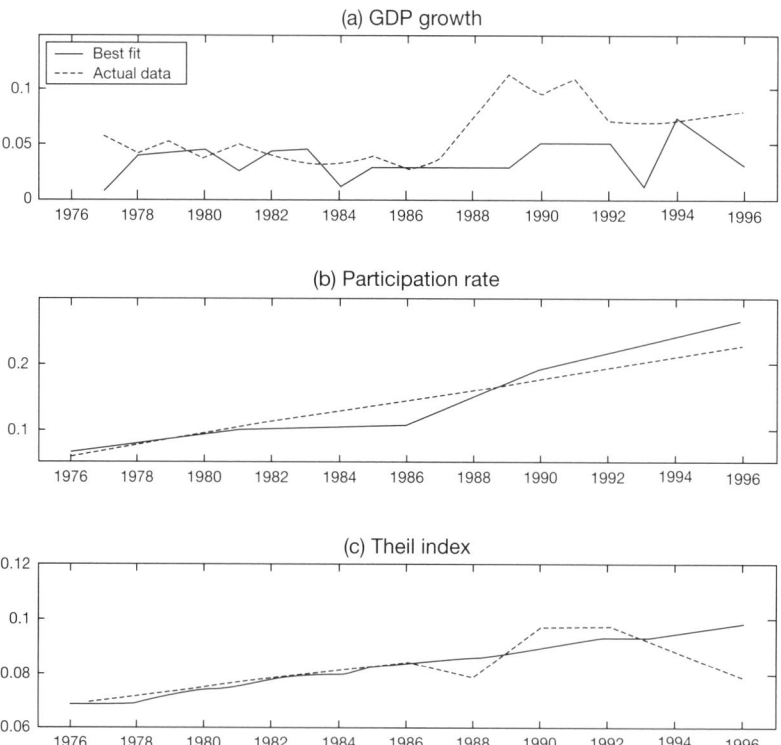

Fig. 6.15(a)–(c). *Benchmark, best fit*

Source: Townsend and Ueda 2006.

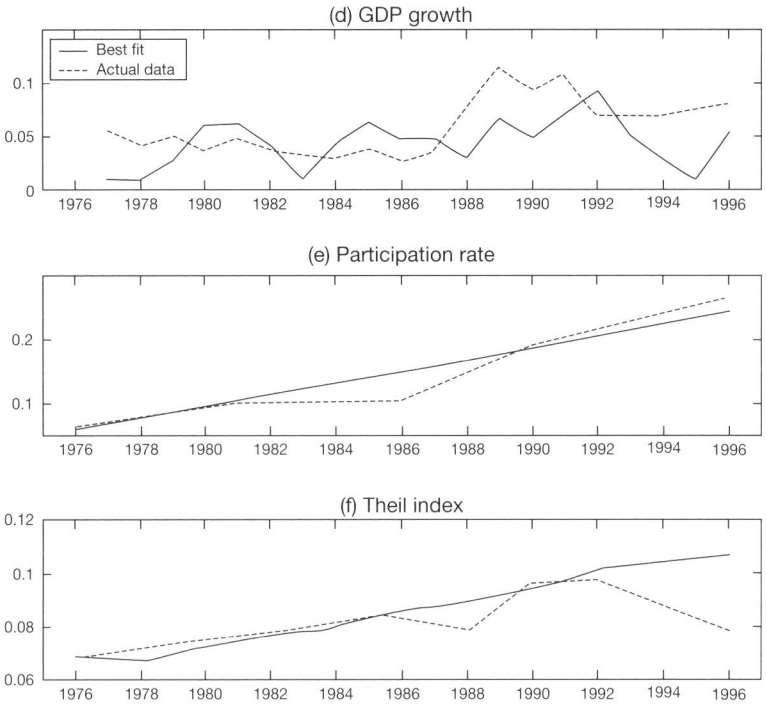

Fig. 6.15(d)–(f). *Higher θ variance, best fit*

Source: Townsend and Ueda 2006.

effect panel data for 1,000 (artificial) countries. We then revisit these countries after 1976 to examine their status in later years.

The advantage of any formal, structural model of growth is that the mechanism or 'drivers' are made clear. Here, for example, given common initial inequality in the wealth distribution and the parameters of technology and preferences, the drivers are the realized draws of idiosyncratic and aggregate shocks. There are stationary aspects to the model: household savings and portfolio decisions at date t; hence the likelihood of financial participation at date $t+1$ are all determined by current wealth and current participation status. But aggregate growth, inequality, and overall financial deepening are not stationary time series even after taking logs and lags. They are all endogenous and all determined by these underlying shocks and decisions in complex and non-linear ways. Note that these complex dynamics are not only found in our canonical model, but also in many other theoretical models that depict endogenous financial deepening, inequality, and growth.

King and Levine (1993) report that there is a robust positive relationship between 'initial' 1960 financial depth and subsequent growth, averaged over 1960 to 1989. They conclude that financial services stimulated growth. Here we regress twenty-year average growth rates on the 'initial' 1985, or 1980, level of financial depth, controlling for the initial log level of GDP (as created by five or ten years of early model history). Likewise, Forbes (2000) replicates a typical finding in the empirical literature: a robust negative relationship between 'initial' inequality in 1965 and average growth from 1965 to 1990. Here we regress twenty-year average growth rates on initial 1985, or 1980, levels of inequality.

What shows up in the regression results appear to be determined by initial conditions and the history of shocks, rather than the structure of the model. There is an extreme, if easy, way to make this point. Suppose we had taken 1976 as an 'initial' period. Then, all 1,000 simulations share the same wealth distribution in 1976, and hence the same levels of inequality and financial depth. In other words, the true initial condition is the same for all 1,000 simulated economies, meaning there would not exist any meaningful relationship between initial financial depth or initial inequality and subsequent growth. The fact that this is less true over time does not mitigate the point that a regression of growth onto financial depth and inequality is a questionable way to think about the data and possible structural models.

Forbes (2000) estimated a robust positive relationship between lagged inequality and five-year average growth rates over 1965 to 1995, contrary to her long-run regressions. We construct medium-term, five-year average variables and conduct panel estimation of the effect of lagged financial deepening and inequality on the GDP growth rate, controlling for country fixed effects, time dummies, and the lagged GDP levels in logarithms. While the sign on inequality is now positive in some instances, consistent with the results of Forbes 2000, the sign is negative in other instances, depending apparently on sampling and data availability, as it were, and inequality is never significant. Indeed, none of the regressors is significant. We conclude that regressions are not an effective way to examine the data from economies in transition. We need to use the structure of the presumed, trial model to assess the impact of inequality and financial reforms.

6.2.3. Distribution of Gains from Liberalization

If, as does seem evident from the model simulations, the Thai economy suffered from policy distortions, then we can ask what the welfare gains from liberalization were relative to a continued repression. In model terms,

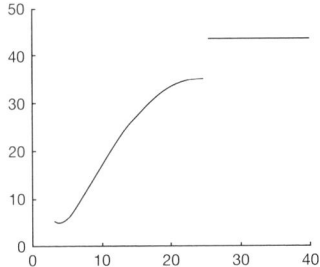

Fig. 6.16(a). *Welfare gains from reduction of marginal costs (wealth compensation %)*
Source: Townsend and Ueda 2008.

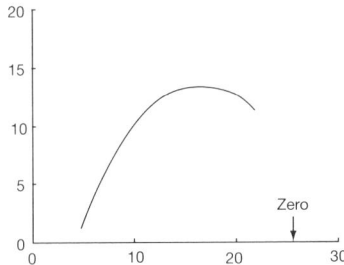

Fig. 6.16(b). *Welfare gains from reduction in entry costs (wealth compensation %)*
Source: Townsend and Ueda 2008.

we vary the marginal costs of banking in proportion to an increasing share of government directed lending, as calibrated from actual data, raising this in the financial repression of the early 1980s—then lower in the liberalization period. We do the same in another experiment for the cost of entry q. We then compute the (discounted expected) utility gain and its consumption equivalent for the liberalization. The distribution of gains is evident in Figures 6.16(a) and 6.16(b). The average gain is about 8 per cent, and 27 per cent for the reduction in transaction cost, a large number. The average gain for the reduction in entry costs is 2 per cent. This is the group, otherwise near the threshold, which would have been willing to pay transactions costs to enter the financial system and could not when there is an artificial restriction effectively raising that cost. But, though the welfare gains are large, the effect on growth is negligible.

With heterogeneity in mind, we have conducted a preliminary sensitivity analysis, specifically allowing variation in the entry cost q over different education and geographic groups, utilizing additional information in SES.

Fortunately, the model with its linear returns (and no endogenous prices) allows us to calibrate and simulate for various key education and geographic groups, one at a time. For example, we can distinguish SES households by the completed level of education of the head (elementary and advanced secondary). We continue to fix technology and preference parameters at their benchmark values, including the model version of q, hence k^*. But for each group separately we center the initial (SES estimated) wealth distribution so that the initial participation rates of the Thai data match the predictions of the model (on the false assumption that everyone above the threshold was participating). Those initial participation rates in 1976 were 5 per cent and 20 per cent for the two chosen education groups (again, elementary and advanced secondary) and 5 per cent and 16 per cent for rural and urban households, respectively. We then simulate the model economy from 1976 to 1996 one group at a time. The model substantially over-predicts access for the educated and urban households. The inference is that these households were suffering from implicit policy restrictions.

6.3. Occupation Choice and Financial Access at the Provincial/Village Levels

The occupation-choice and financial-access-choice models can each be taken to a more local, provincial context, as in the work done with Felkner (Felkner and Townsend 2007). Specifically, villages within four provinces have been geo-located and vectorized in a GIS. Thus, data such as those from the CDD village census can be displayed on the maps and used in analysis. The four provinces are those of the original Townsend Thai Survey, with two provinces in the Central region near Bangkok: Lop Buri and Chachoengsao, and two in the poorer Northeast: Buriram and Sisaket. As anticipated earlier, wealth and commercial bank access vary across provinces in the obvious way. The point here is that these and other variables vary within each province.

Roads, district center, and all transport systems can also be vectorized and used in analysis (see Figure 6.17). Time to a major highway and to the intersections of major highways are computed and can be shown to bear some relationship to wealth, financial access, frequency of enterprise, and other variables.

The earlier models are initialized and then simulated using the within-province village data. The financial-access model uses exactly the same parameters that were calibrated for the work of Townsend and Ueda (2006)

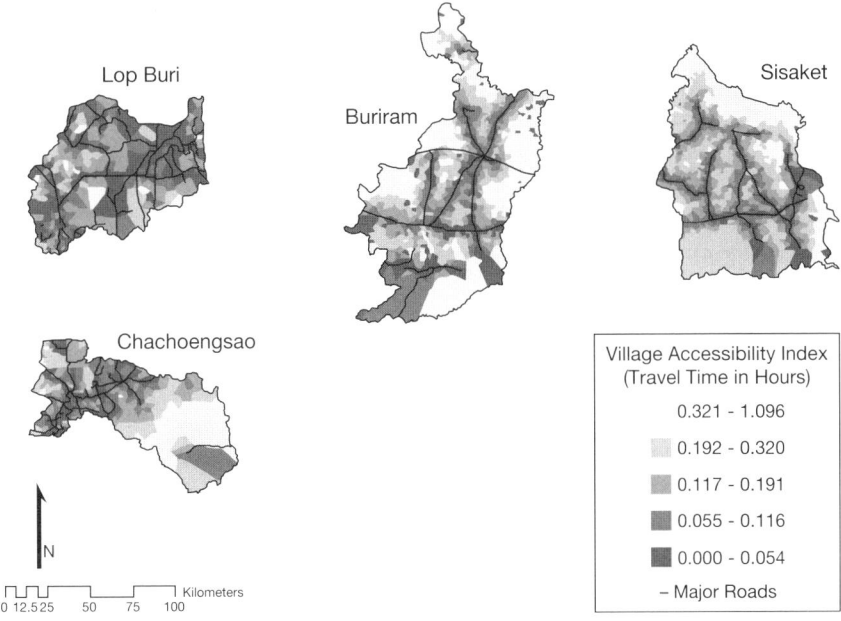

Fig. 6.17. *Community Development Department village and amphoe district center locations, with distance–cost variable (travel time to major roads)*

at the national level, using the Townsend Thai data. The occupation-choice model starts with the parameters that were used in the work with Giné and Townsend (2004), and also Jeong and Townsend (2003) using the SES data. Most of these parameters remain fixed throughout the analysis below (see Table 6.4). However, the key cost skewness parameter m, was calibrated to best fit to the CDD village data. Specifically the end-of-period, 1996 model simulation of frequency of enterprise, sorting by village was calibrated against the actual frequency allowing parameter m to vary by bins, according to their distance from major intersections. Strikingly, the greater the distance from major intersections, the higher these estimated set up costs.

As earlier, but here with village-level data, the time series generated from the two models, occupation-choice and financial-access choice, are close to the actual data (see Figures 6.18, 6.19, and 6.20). For the occupation-choice model the model-simulated enterprise variable is above the data, as in actuality the measured enterprise variable in the CDD data is quite low. But the simulated variable has the same trend and moves up and down almost exactly as in the data. The average simulation of the financial-access model hits the trend in access very well and only under-predicts slightly, for

Table 6.4. Within-province village data financial-access model

LEB-estimated parameters

| Parameters | α | Alowed To Vary | | | | ρ | σ | γ | g_γ | ξ |
		β	ω	η	m					
Initial values (from Jeong and Townsend 2003 for Socio-economy Survey data)	1.0011	0.0940	0.2400	0.0000	-1.0000	0.0033	0.0000	0.0120	0.0020	0.0566
Estimated values for community development department	0.9186	0.0910	0.2727	0.0208	-0.0004					

Estimated LEB M parameter: distance modified LEB simulation

	Bin1	Bin2	Bin3
Sample divided into 3 bins by equal distance	-0.2143	0.3612	0.2659

Estimated LEB M parameter: distance modified LEB simulation

	Bin1	Bin2	Bin3	Bin4	Bin5
Sample divided into 5 bins by equal number of villages	-1.0000	-1.0000	-0.1587	0.3978	0.4256

GJ-estimated parameters

Parameters	σ	q	δ	θ	ε	β	γ
Initial values (from Townsend and Ueda 2006 for Townsend Thai data)	1.000	5.000	1.054	[1.047,1.147]	[-0.600,0.600]	0.960	0.000

Source: Felkner and Townsend 2004.

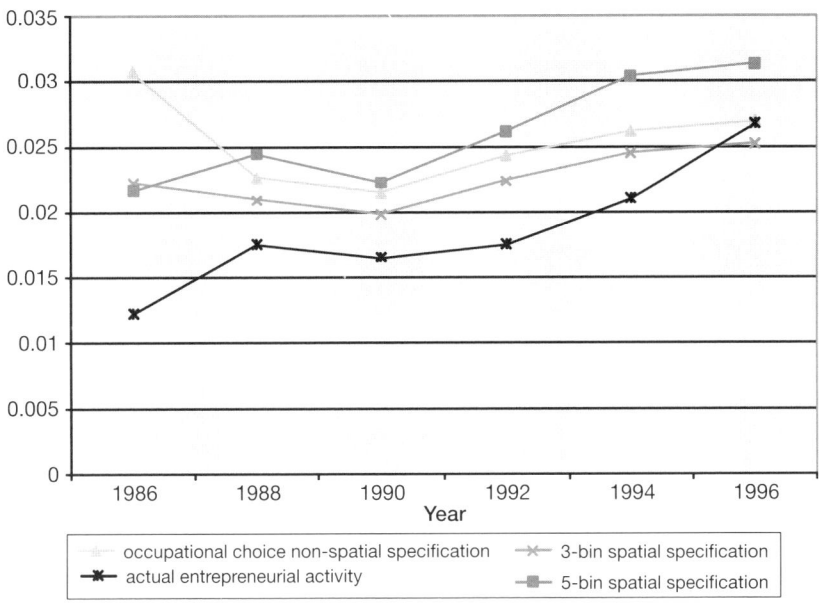

Fig. 6.18. *Occupational choice simulated vs actual means*

Source: Felkner and Townsend 2004.

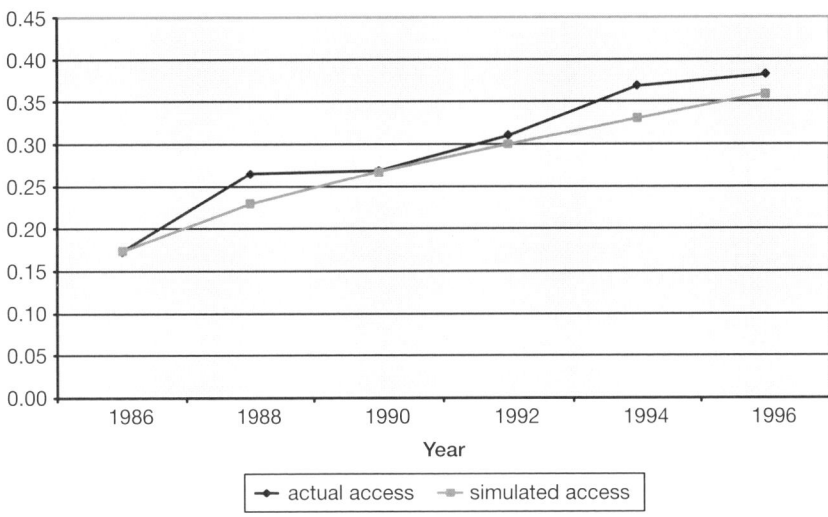

Fig. 6.19. *Financial-deepening simulation: actual vs simulated financial credit access*

Source: Felkner and Townsend 2007.

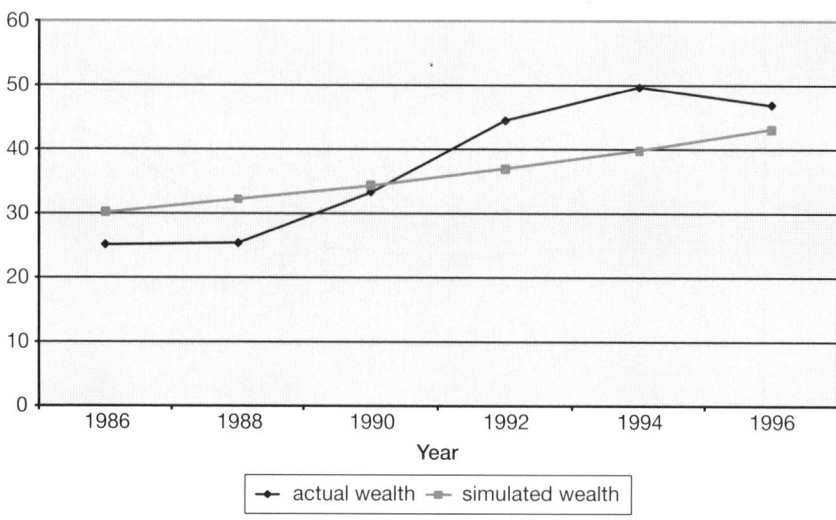

Fig. 6.20. *Financial-deepening simulation: actual vs simulated wealth*
Source: Felkner and Townsend 2007.

the 1986–8 and 1990–6 periods. The model predicts an increase in village wealth, as in the data. But here, using wealth data, not income data, it is clear that the model under-predicts the observed, dramatic increase in the wealth of villages. (In the SES, wealth growth is also much higher than income growth, but income is better measured in the SES. Income is in turn measured poorly in the CDD data.)

The occupation-choice model also does well spatially. Geographic prediction errors for the end of the sample year, 1996, that is model-predicted minus actual frequency of enterprise, display some clustering initially, in Figure 6.24, but these correlated error areas virtually disappear in Figure 6.25 when allowing cost parameter m to vary with distance, as indicated earlier. Varying costs are important as a determinant of who goes into business.

Indeed, the impact of road construction is evident through the lens of the model. In a simulation we moved the location of roads with their major intersections into agricultural areas. The frequency of business enterprise jumps up dramatically (see Figures 6.21–6.23).

Spatially, the financial-access model does less well, though this could be anticipated from the earlier work with Ueda and the reduced-form regressions. Prediction errors for financial access show *significant clustering, with model over-prediction* in and around the red hot spots of initial concentration near the intersections of major roads and district centers and green

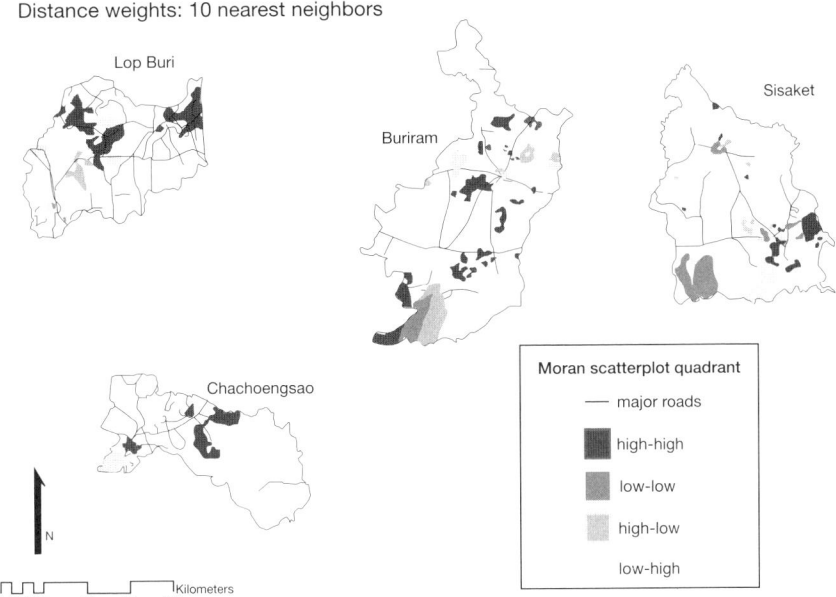

Fig. 6.21. *Lloyd-Ellis–Bernhardt (LEB) simulation residuals non-spatial specification: global m parameter (local moran map at P=0.05 cut-off value)*

Source: Felkner and Townsend 2007.

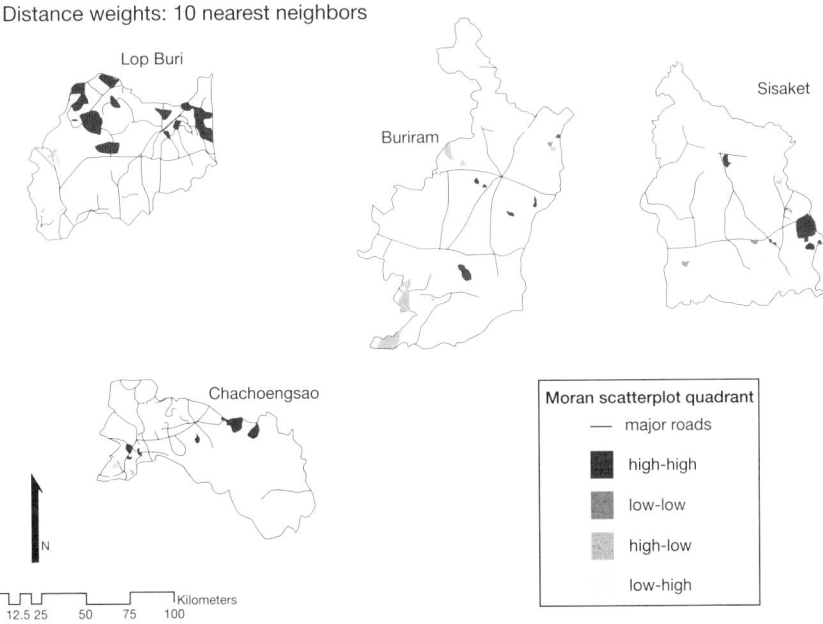

Fig. 6.22. *Lloyd-Ellis–Bernhardt (LEB) distance-modified (5-bin) simulation residuals spatial specification (5-bin) simulation residuals: m parameter varies with space (local moran map at P=0.05 cut-off value)*

Source: Felkner and Townsend 2007.

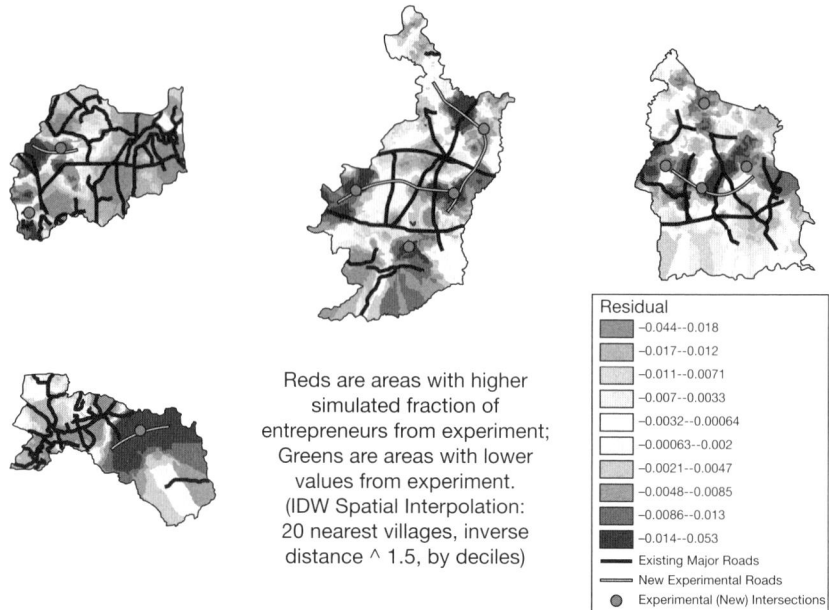

Reds are areas with higher simulated fraction of entrepreneurs from experiment; Greens are areas with lower values from experiment. (IDW Spatial Interpolation: 20 nearest villages, inverse distance ^ 1.5, by deciles)

Residual
- −0.044--0.018
- −0.017--0.012
- −0.011--0.0071
- −0.007--0.0033
- −0.0032--0.00064
- −0.00063--0.002
- −0.0021--0.0047
- −0.0048--0.0085
- −0.0086--0.013
- −0.014--0.053
— Existing Major Roads
— New Experimental Roads
● Experimental (New) Intersections

Fig. 6.23. *Residuals from entrepreneurial choice experiment: effect of adding new (hypo-thetical) road intersections (See color version at the end of the book).*

Source: Felkner and Townsend 2007.

cool spots of *model under-prediction* in the less-developed areas of eastern Chachoengsao and the more-rural areas of Sisaket and Buriram. The prediction errors for wealth display a similar, if even more salient, pattern. Wealth grew considerably more than predicted off the main roads and away from towns (see Figures 6.24 and 6.25).

Multivariate regressions of the prediction errors confirm these patterns. The spatially calibrated occupation-choice model has prediction errors which are not correlated with distance to major roads, major intersections, or district centers, nor with wealth, education, or financial access. Being in a 1986 agglomeration hot spot, or distance to the center of such hot spots, is rarely significant, or of the wrong sign, as in Lop Buri (see Tables 6.5 and 6.6).

In contrast, the financial-choice model over-predicts for villages near major roads, the intersections of major roads, or district centers, and over-predicts with increasing levels of education and wealth. Being in a 1986 agglomeration hot spot is highly correlated with the model's over-prediction of financial access, and distance to the center of such spots is a significant negative covariate for the prediction error in access almost all the time. The same pattern emerges with wealth.

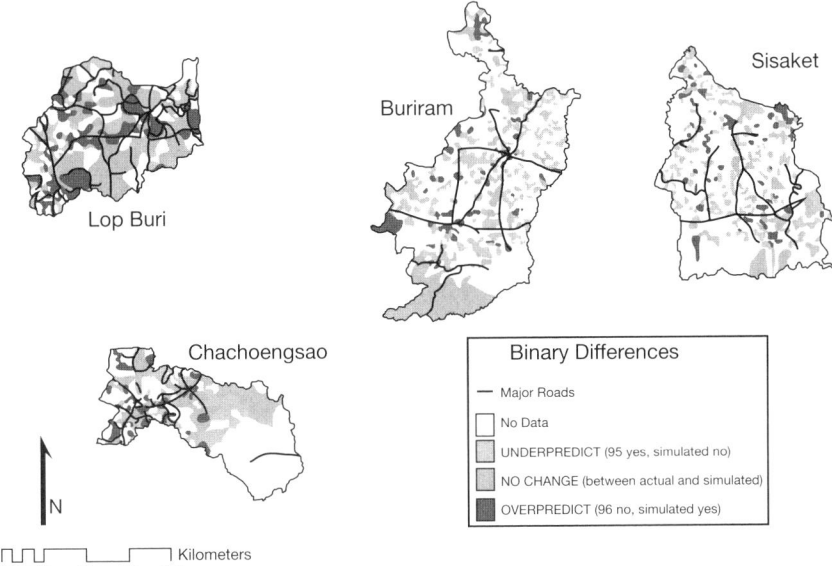

Fig. 6.24. *1996 Greenwood–Jovanovic (GJ) access index simulation differences: binary values, 1996 (See color version at the end of the book).*

Notes: Differences are between actual and simulated. Reds are areas of model overprediction, greens are areas of model underprediction.
Source: Felkner and Townsend 2007.

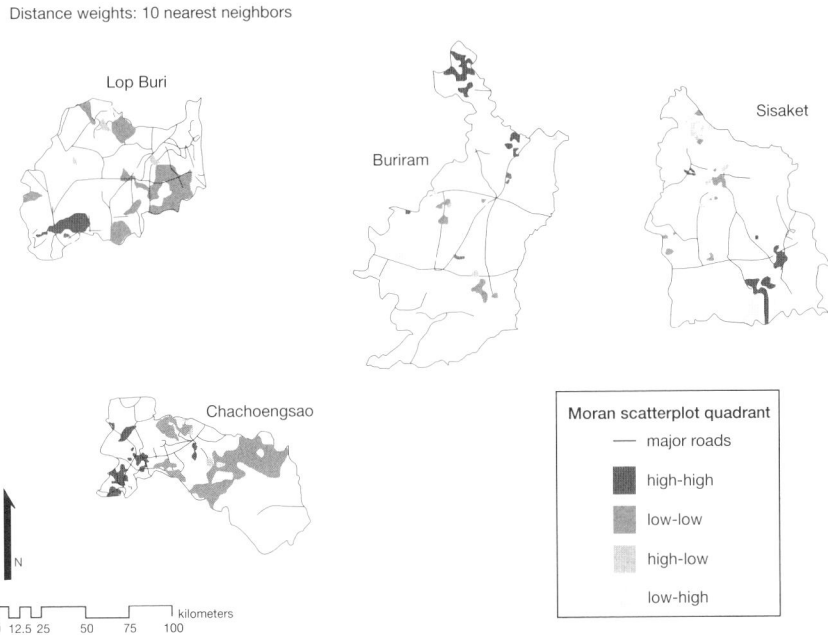

Fig. 6.25. *Greenwood–Jovanovic (GJ) wealth simulation residuals (local moran map at P=0.05 cut-off value).*

Source: Felkner and Townsend 2007.

Table 6.5. *Lloyd-Ellis–Bernhardt (LEB) and Greenwood–Jovanovic (GJ) 1996 simulation differences regressed onto distance variables*

Coefficient values in bold, probability values in italics

Independent variables	*Dependent variable:* **LEB simulation 1996 residuals**		
	Distance to major roads	*Distance to major intersections*	*Distance to district centers*
Distance	**0.0033**	**0.0001**	**0.0285**
	0.8925	*0.0986*	*0.2589*
Intermediation index	**0.0431**	**0.0427**	**0.0426**
	0.0001	*0.0001*	*0.0001*
Education	**−0.0030**	**−0.0003**	**−0.0026**
	0.9060	*0.9921*	*0.9183*
Wealth	**−0.0002**	**−0.0001**	**−0.0002**
	0.2793	*0.4016*	*0.3703*
R-squared	**0.0686**	**0.0700**	**0.0703**

Independent variables	*Dependent variable:* **LEB distance-modified 3-bin simulation residuals**		
	Distance to major roads	*Distance to major intersections*	*Distance to district centers*
Distance	**−0.0044**	**0.0001**	**0.0166**
	0.8621	*0.9947*	*0.5301*
Intermediation index	**−0.0089**	**−0.0089**	**−0.0091**
	0.2460	*0.2486*	*0.9504*
Education	**0.0013**	**0.0014**	**0.0017**
	0.9611	*0.9582*	*0.9504*
Wealth	**−0.0001**	**−0.0001**	**−0.0001**
	0.6719	*0.6880*	*0.7598*
R-squared	**0.0331**	**0.0330**	**0.0336**

Independent variables	*Dependent variable:* **LEB distance-modified 5-bin simulation residuals**		
	Distance to major roads	*Distance to major intersections*	*Distance to district centers*
Distance	**−0.0207**	**0.0001**	**0.0164**
	0.4312	*0.1518*	*0.5441*
Intermediation index	**−0.0024**	**−0.0016**	**−0.0025**
	0.7578	*0.8403*	*0.7486*
Education	**0.0244**	**0.0206**	**0.0251**
	0.3723	*0.4529*	*0.3594*
Wealth	**−0.0002**	**−0.0002**	**−0.0001**
	0.3810	*0.2615*	*0.4732*
R-squared	**0.0230**	**0.0250**	**0.0227**

(continued)

Table 6.5. (*Continued*)

Independent variables	Dependent variable: **GJ wealth simulation 1996 residuals**		
	Distance to major roads	Distance to major intersections	Distance to district centers
Distance	−17.4512	−0.0008	−31.5170
	0.0002	0.0001	0.0001
Intermediation index	2.1993	2.8967	2.1405
	0.1376	0.0462	0.1448
Education	34.6477	30.5663	33.3364
	0.0001	0.0001	0.0001
R-squared	0.3051	0.3320	0.3171

Independent variables	Dependent variable: **GJ credit intermediation simulation 1996 residuals**		
	Distance to major roads	Distance to major intersections	Distance to district centers
Distance	−0.7028	−0.0001	−0.6625
	0.0000	0.0000	0.0002
Education	0.0027	0.0024	0.0024
	0.0002	0.0009	0.0006
Wealth	1.1009	1.0195	1.1015
	0.0000	0.0000	0.0000
R-squared	0.5853	0.5863	0.5844

Source: Felkner and Townsend 2004.

These patterns hold for many of the principal financial-sector providers, with the telling exception of the BAAC in the central areas provinces. We now turn our attention to this.

The financial-access model can be initialized and simulated separately for each financial-sector provider, again respecting distance from major intersections. For bin 1, villages close to the intersections of major roads, the model under-predicts somewhat the expansion of the BAAC and over-predicts substantially the expansion of commercial banks. This would be consistent with the expansion of the BAAC, targeting outlying provinces like those far away from Bangkok, also consistent with restrictions, or a political economy motive, that might have impeded the expansion of commercial banks in areas they might otherwise be more prone to serve the educated middle class (see Figure 6.26).

Related, if we take high-wealth villages from bin 1, near the main roads, and redistribute them to bin 3, far from main roads, the model predicts that commercial bank expansion in bin 1 would be much as we see it in the data

Table 6.6. Summary of Lloyd-Ellis–Bernhardt (LEB) and Greenwood–Jovanovic (GJ) simulation residuals onto spatial heterogeneity variables

Coefficient values in bold, probability values in italic. Regressions include controls for wealth and education.

Independent variables	LEB-dependent variables				GJ-dependent variables				
	LEB residuals	LEB 3-bin residuals	LEB 5-bin residuals	GJ access index	GJ wealth residuals	GJ БAAC residuals	GJ commercial banks	GJ suppliers credit	GJ village savings
Sisaket									
North–South regimes	**−0.0194**	**−0.0026**	**−0.0050**	**0.3106**	**1.2029**	**0.1092**	**0.3978**	**0.3426**	**0.0925**
	0.0460	*0.7882*	*0.6205*	*0.0000*	*0.5861*	*0.0050*	*0.0000*	*0.0000*	*0.1001*
Two–clusters regimes	**0.0082**	**0.0134**	**0.0255**	**0.2683**	**13.0947**	**0.1339**	**0.2929**	**0.3656**	**0.1061**
	0.3998	*0.1677*	*0.0100*	*0.0001*	*0.0000*	*0.0008*	*0.0001*	*0.0000*	*0.0658*
Three–clusters regimes	**−0.0105**	**−0.0054**	**0.0093**	**0.3176**	**12.8600**	**0.1450**	**0.3072**	**0.4186**	**0.1405**
	0.2792	*0.5816*	*0.3526*	*0.0000*	*0.0000*	*0.0002*	*0.0000*	*0.0000*	*0.0122*
Distance to two–clusters	**−0.0001**	**−0.0001**	**−0.0001**	**−0.0001**	**−0.0003**	**−0.0001**	**−0.0001**	**−0.0001**	**−0.0001**
	0.0419	*0.0157*	*0.0005*	*0.0567*	*0.0001*	*0.0013*	*0.0130*	*0.0001*	*0.8211*
Distance to three–clusters	**0.0000**	**−0.0001**	**−0.0001**	**−0.0001**	**−0.0003**	**−0.0001**	**−0.0001**	**−0.0001**	**−0.0001**
	0.9034	*0.8430*	*0.1437*	*0.0005*	*0.0001*	*0.0001*	*0.0006*	*0.0000*	*0.3732*
Buriram									
Distance to three–clusters	**0.0000**	**−0.0001**	**−0.0001**	**−0.0001**	**−0.0004**	**−0.0001**	**−0.0001**	**−0.0001**	**−0.0001**
	0.6099	*0.5685*	*0.8250*	*0.1974*	*0.0000*	*0.0128*	*0.0197*	*0.0003*	*0.0058*
Distance to four–clusters	**0.0000**	**0.0000**	**−0.0001**	**−0.0001**	**−0.0004**	**−0.0001**	**−0.0001**	**−0.0001**	**−0.0001**
	0.3582	*0.4936*	*0.5871*	*0.1595*	*0.0000*	*0.0332*	*0.0285*	*0.0005*	*0.0525*
Lop Buri									
East–West regimes	**−0.0370**	**−0.0310**	**−0.0209**	**0.1665**	**20.5449**	**−0.0446**	**0.2929**	**0.2857**	**0.1034**
	0.0105	*0.0440*	*0.2057*	*0.1342*	*0.0001*	*0.3278*	*0.0014*	*0.0004*	*0.2128*
Distance to one–clusters	**0.0000**	**0.0000**	**0.0000**	**−0.0001**	**−0.0004**	**−0.0001**	**−0.0001**	**−0.0001**	**−0.0001**
	0.0059	*0.0792*	*0.4588*	*0.0207*	*0.0000*	*0.7083*	*0.0014*	*0.0000*	*0.2001*
Distance to two–clusters	**0.0000**	**0.0000**	**−0.0001**	**−0.0001**	**−0.0010**	**−0.0001**	**−0.0001**	**−0.0001**	**−0.0001**
	0.0730	*0.3756*	*0.8741*	*0.0002*	*0.0000*	*0.5291*	*0.0149*	*0.0000*	*0.0884*
Chachoengsao									
East–West regimes	**−0.0219**	**−0.0139**	**0.0067**	**0.2589**	**30.9920**	**0.0500**	**0.1995**	**0.2330**	**0.1616**
	0.4981	*0.6627*	*0.8324*	*0.0005*	*0.0000*	*0.1047*	*0.0026*	*0.0031*	*0.0664*
West cluster	**−0.0086**	**−0.0005**	**0.0151**	**0.2181**	**29.8703**	**0.0286**	**0.1472**	**0.1738**	**0.1610**
	0.7754	*0.9865*	*0.6055*	*0.0052*	*0.0000*	*0.3779*	*0.0338*	*0.0345*	*0.0784*

Source: Felkner and Townsend 2004.

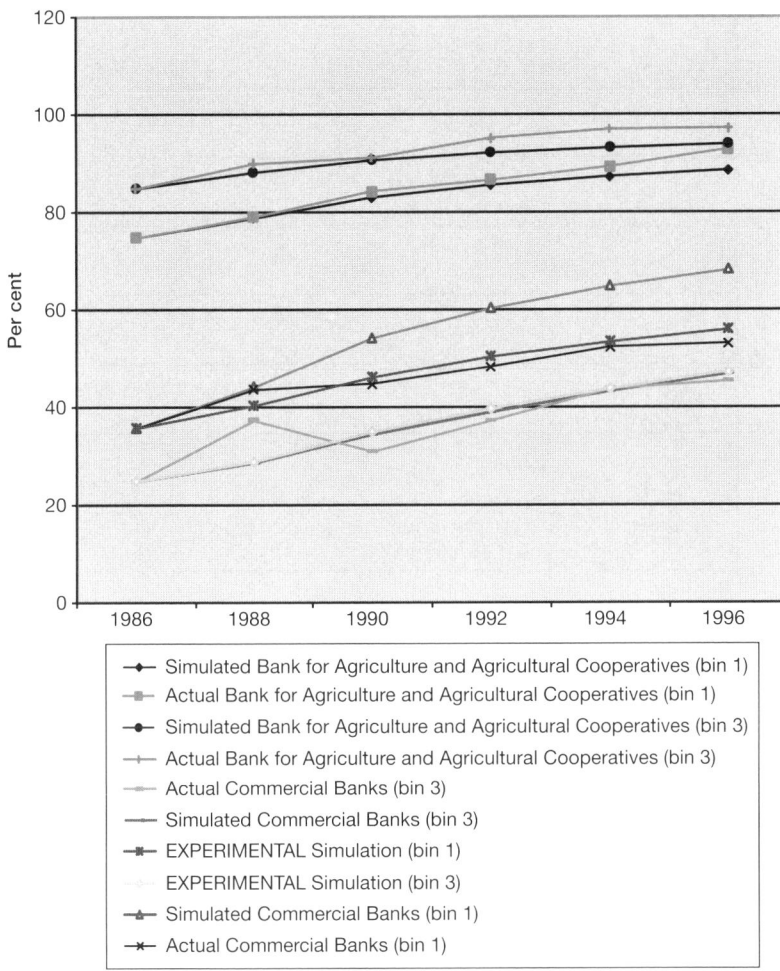

Fig. 6.26. *Spatially specified financial-deepening results by distance-bins*

Source: Felkner and Townsend 2004.

(only slightly higher). The distribution of wealth in the model has an impact on growth and financial deepening. This particular experiment moves villages away from a key threshold in the high-growth urban sector to a more-rural sector where they are already over the threshold, hence no subsequent transition effects through the extensive margin.

Indeed, the structure of the model can be used to rationalize the data we see, not by moving wealth but by varying the supposed transaction cost (see Figure 6.27). Consistently, costs are lower for the BAAC. But for both

243

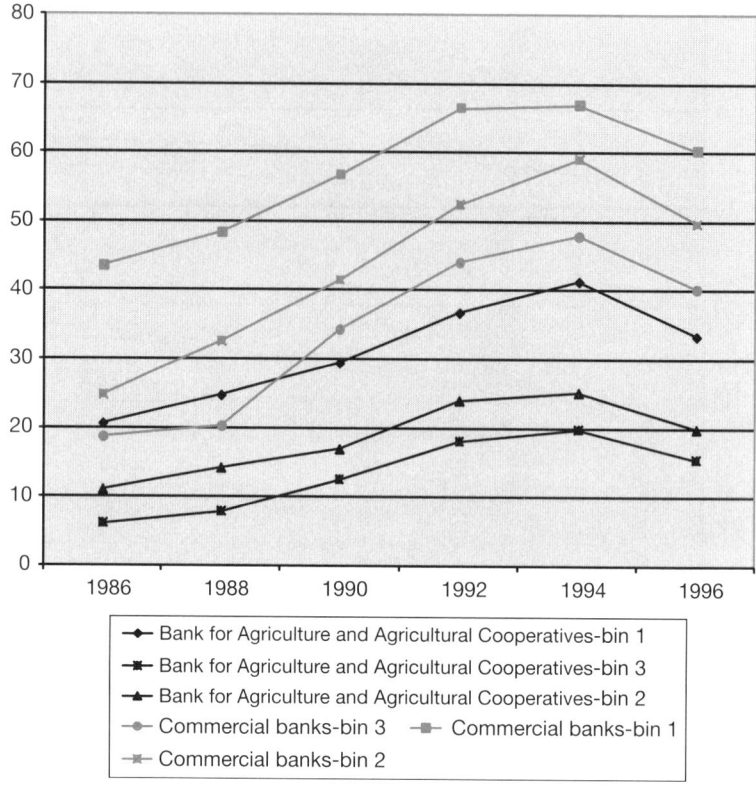

Fig. 6.27. *Financial deepening simulation—k^ defined by actual wealth distribution and participation rate*

Source: Felkner and Townsend 2007.

the BAAC and commercial banks costs are *higher* for those *closer* to the intersection of major roads.

If, however, wealth were measured inaccurately, and had more mass in the right tail than in measured reality, then these estimates could be off. Likewise, the redistribution of wealth away from high-wealth areas in the earlier experiment might only be capturing a measurement error correction.

6.4. Disaggregated to the Household Levels: Successes and Anomalies

The two models can also be taken to household level data. First, as described earlier, both the occupation-choice model and financial-access-choices model are estimated against the SES using the likelihoods of the cross-sectional data for young households, aged less than 30. Here, moreover, we disaggregate into sectors.

The goal is to try to understand the patterns in growth and inequality that were described earlier—namely, high-composition effects for financial access and high-income effects for occupation.

Specifically, the occupation-choice model (LEB) at estimated parameter values delivers repeated cross-sections of household data, as in the SES, and so the model's predictions for the growth of income and inequality can be compared to growth and inequality in the SES data. As is obvious from Table 6.7, for growth, the composition effects of population shifts into non-farm business are positive in the model, as in the data, but the effect is much larger in the model, which apparently overdoes the occupation dichotomy. Keeping track of financial access as another category, jointly, moves the model closer to the data, but the gap remains substantial.

Similarly, the occupation-choice models gets correct the sign of each of the terms in the change in inequality: positive for the two composition effects and negative for the income-convergence effect. But these are much

Table 6.7. *Growth decompositions*

| | By Occupation | | |
	Subgroup	Composition	Total
Thailand	0.867	0.032	0.899
LEB	0.115	0.754	0.869

| | By Financial Participation | | |
	Subgroup	Composition	Total
Thailand	0.580	0.319	0.899
LEB	0.413	0.456	0.869

| | By Joint Category | | |
	Subgroup	Composition	Total
Thailand	0.573	0.326	0.899
LEB	0.141	0.728	0.869

Source: H. Jeong and R. M. Townsend, 'Growth and Inequality: Model Evaluation Based on an Estimation-Calibration Strategy', *Macroeconomic Dynamics Special Issue on Inequality*, 12 (2008), 231–84. Copyright 2008 Cambridge University Press. Reproduced with permission.

Table 6.8. *Decomposition of aggregate inequality change in Lloyd-Ellis–Bernhardt (LEB)*

| | By Occupation | | | | |
| | Within-group | | Across-group | | |
	Subgroup	Composition	Income gap	Composition	Total
Thailand	0.524	0.001	−0.051	0.010	0.483
LEB	0.042	0.022	−1.056	1.881	0.338

| | By Financial Participation | | | | |
| | Within-group | | Across-group | | |
	Subgroup	Composition	Income gap	Composition	Total
Thailand	0.304	0.032	0.015	0.133	0.483
LEB	−0.177	0.189	−0.066	0.439	0.338

| | By Joint Category | | | | |
| | Within-group | | Across-group | | |
	Subgroup	Composition	Income gap	Composition	Total
Thailand	0.340	0.028	−0.003	0.120	0.483
LEB	0.015	0.053	−0.750	1.371	0.338

Source: H. Jeong and R. M. Townsend, 'Growth and Inequality: Model Evaluation Based on an Estimation-Calibration Strategy', *Macroeconomic Dynamics Special Issue on Inequality*, 12 (2008), 231–84. Copyright 2008 Cambridge University Press. Reproduced with permission.

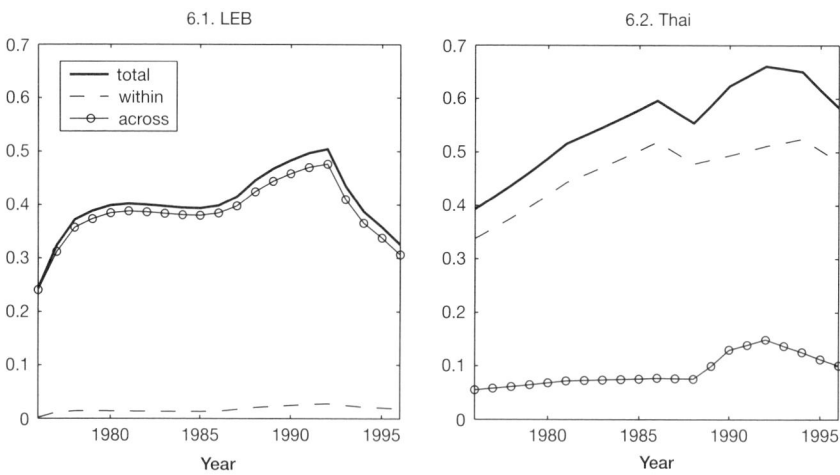

Fig. 6.28. *Within vs across inequality decomposition*

Source: H. Jeong and R. M. Townsend, 'Growth and Inequality: Model Evaluation Based on an Estimation-Calibration Strategy', *Macroeconomic Dynamics Special Issue on Inequality*, 12 (2008), 231–84. Copyright 2008 Cambridge University Press. Reproduced with permission.

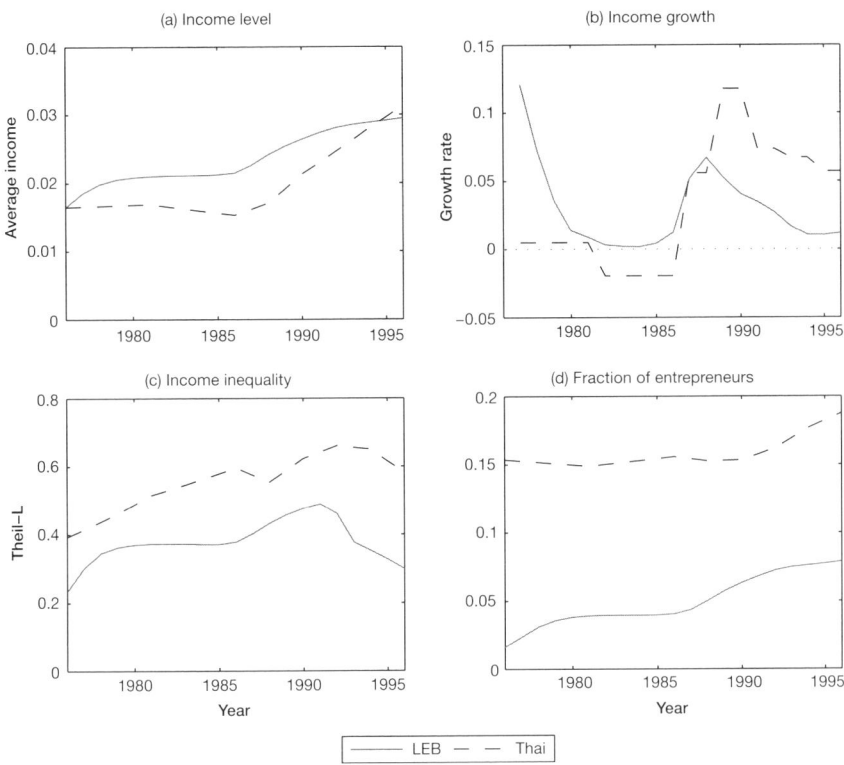

Fig. 6.29(a)–(d). *Lloyd-Ellis–Bernhardt (LEB) aggregate dynamics*

Source: H. Jeong and R. M. Townsend, 'Growth and Inequality: Model Evaluation Based on an Estimation-Calibration Strategy', *Macroeconomic Dynamics Special Issue on Inequality*, 12 (2008), 231–84. Copyright 2008 Cambridge University Press. Reproduced with permission.

smaller in the data, while the 'unexplained' within-group effect is much larger in the data (see Figure 6.28). Financial-access and occupation categories jointly again allow the model to do better (see Table 6.8).

These successes and anomalies are related to the degree of sector aggregation, more or less successful for aggregated data and less satisfactory for the data disaggregated into specific sectors. As anticipated earlier in the work in Giné and Townsend (2004), the occupation-choice model does reasonably well with the change in income levels, particularly the upturn associated with liberalization. It also delivers paths for inequality and the fraction of entrepreneurs which are lower than the data but move in tandem with the data (see Figure 6.29(a)–(d)).

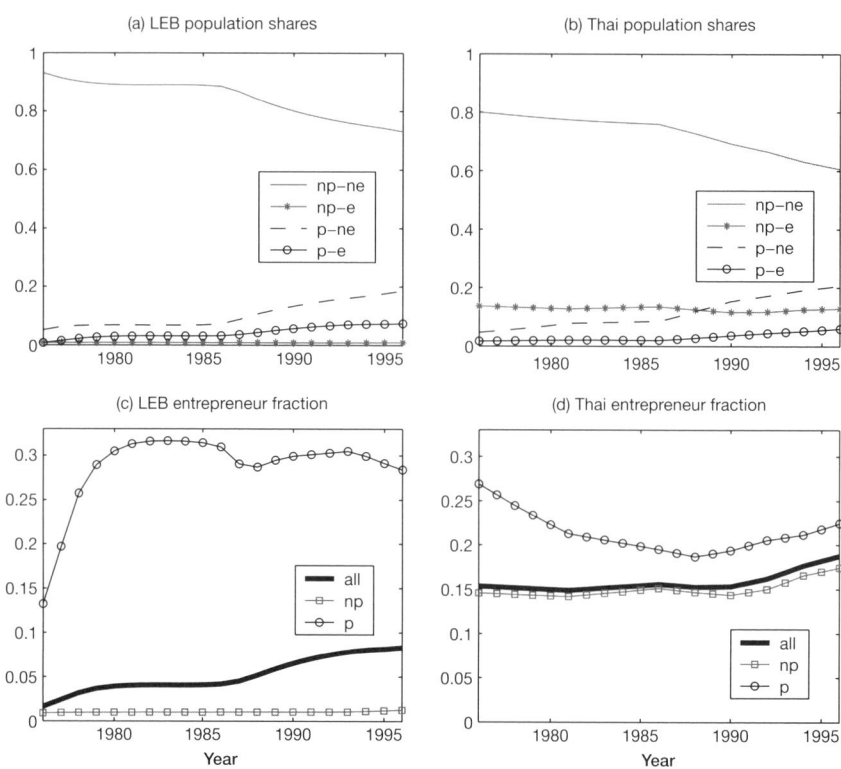

p=participant np=non-participant e=entrepreneur ne=non-entrepreneur

Fig. 6.30(a)–(d). *Lloyd-Ellis–Bernhardt (LEB) population dynamics*

Source: H. Jeong and R. M. Townsend, 'Growth and Inequality: Model Evaluation Based on an Estimation-Calibration Strategy', *Macroeconomic Dynamics Special Issue on Inequality*, 12 (2008), 231–84. Copyright 2008 Cambridge University Press. Reproduced with permission.

The model also gets right the falling trend of non-participant wage-earners/farmers and the rising trend of participant entrepreneurs and participant wage-earners/farmers. But the model misses the higher level, and falling trend, of non-participant entrepreneurs. In the model, among all entrepreneurs there are too few without transactions in the financial sector and too many with financial transactions relative to the data (see Figure 6.30 (a)–(d)).

Likewise, income differences, of entrepreneurs relative to wage-earners/ farmers, are far too large in the model at the current set of parameter values. In the model, entrepreneurs earn more than farmers/wage-earners (regardless of financial participation), and non-participant entrepreneurs earn the

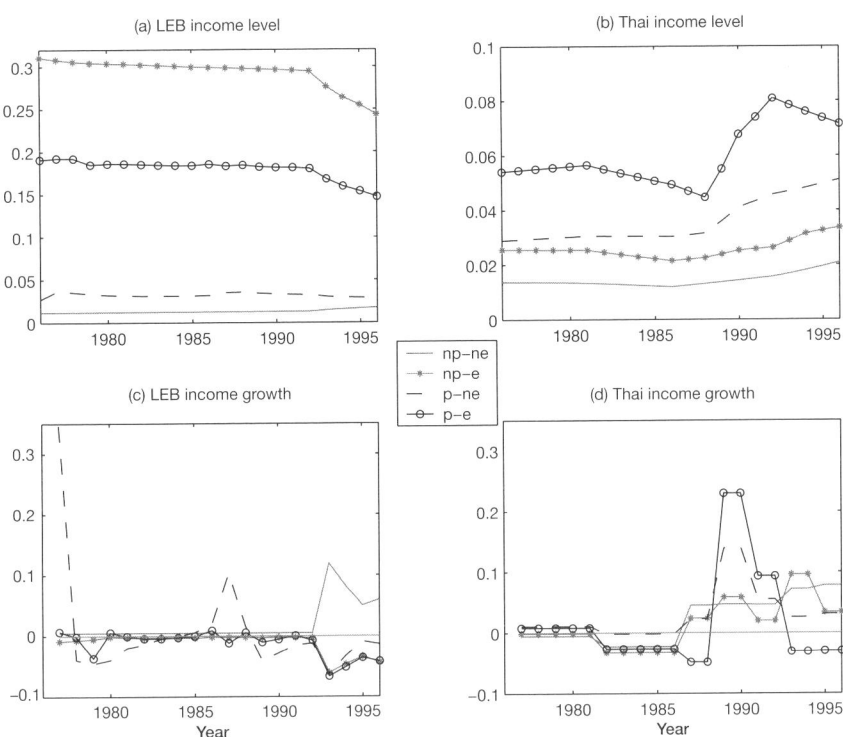

p=participant np=non-participant e=entrepreneur ne=non-entrepreneur

Fig. 6.31(a)–(d). *Lloyd-Ellis–Bernhardt (LEB) subgroup growth dynamics*

Source: H. Jeong and R. M. Townsend, 'Growth and Inequality: Model Evaluation Based on an Estimation-Calibration Strategy', *Macroeconomic Dynamics Special Issue on Inequality*, 12 (2008), 231–84. Copyright 2008 Cambridge University Press. Reproduced with permission.

most. In the SES data, financial-sector participants earn more than non-participants (regardless of occupation), and participant entrepreneurs earn the most. Entrepreneurs in the model tend to have decreasing incomes, due to diminishing returns, but in the data all categories tend to have increasing incomes. More generally, there is much more co-movement in the data across groups/categories, whereas in the model increasing wages causes divergence. Wage-earners benefit and entrepreneurs suffer. Revealing, perhaps, the income of participant entrepreneurs in the data most closely matches aggregate GDP statistics though their numbers in household surveys are low. The household data may be underestimating their true number (see Figure 6.31 (a)–(d)).

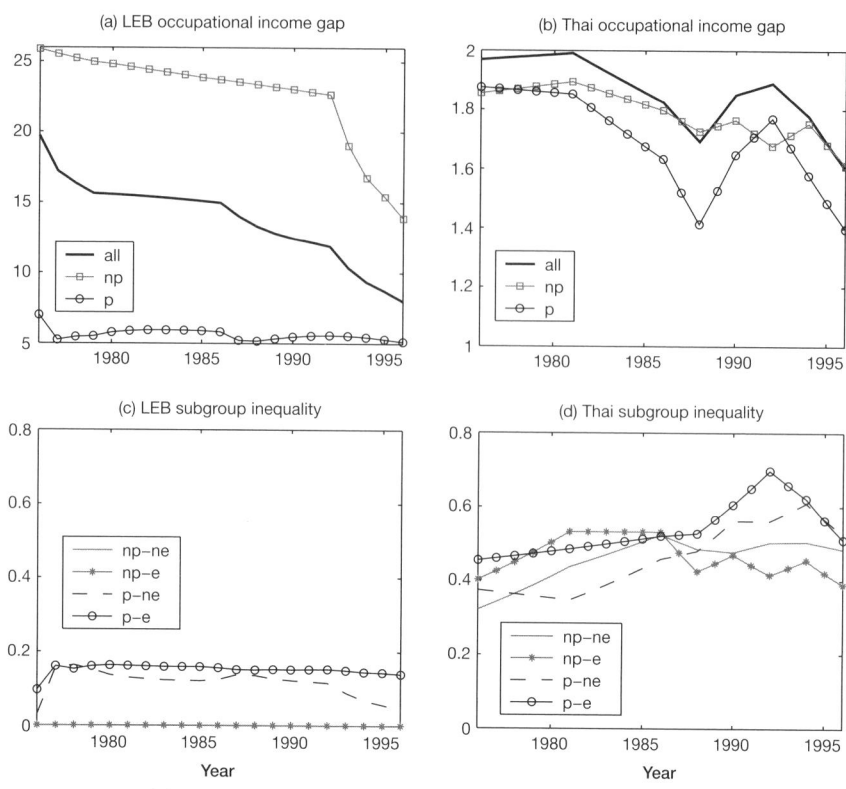

Fig. 6.32(a)–(d). *Lloyd-Ellis–Bernhardt (LEB) subgroup inequality dynamics*

Source: H. Jeong and R. M. Townsend, 'Growth and Inequality: Model Evaluation Based on an Estimation-Calibration Strategy', *Macroeconomic Dynamics Special Issue on Inequality*, 12 (2008), 231–84. Copyright 2008 Cambridge University Press. Reproduced with permission.

The overestimation in the occupation-choice model of the composition effect in inequality is intimately related to the overestimation of income gaps of entrepreneurs over wage-earners/farmers. The model does, however, get right the decline over time of the income gap and the fact that the gap is smaller for participants, as barriers to entry are reduced. The model thus seems to be overstating the magnitude efficiency of the intermediated sector, but gets right the improvement over time. Related, there is high inequality among participant entrepreneurs in the model, as a participating low-cost household can borrow at high interest and have low net earnings after subtracting financing costs. In the data, participant entrepreneurs

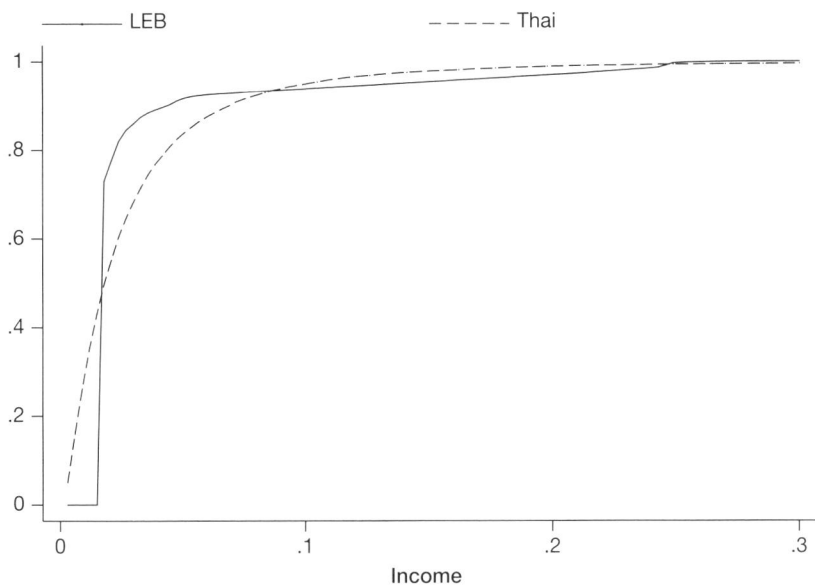

Fig. 6.33. *Cumulative distribution function (CDF) of income distribution, 1996 (prediction)*

Source: H. Jeong and R. M. Townsend, 'Growth and Inequality: Model Evaluation Based on an Estimation-Calibration Strategy', *Macroeconomic Dynamics Special Issue on Inequality*, 12 (2008), 231–84. Copyright 2008 Cambridge University Press. Reproduced with permission.

have the highest inequality only after the liberalization of the mid-1980s (see Figure 6.32 (a)–(d)).

The occupation-choice model's prediction for the income distribution misses much variation on the low end and some variation on the high end. The model does not have diversity created by education, for example. Thus the low-skilled labor force of the model earns a common low wage. There is also a small fraction of the population in the data who seem to have very high incomes, more so than in the model (see Figure 6.33).

The financial-access model, when estimated via maximum likelihood in the SES data for those under 30, does a reasonable job in matching the composition of population shifts across access/no-access categories (see Tables 6.9 and 6.10). This is true in both the change of income and the Kuznets effect in the change in inequality. The model gets correct also the sign in inequality change of the income divergence effect but gets incorrect the residual composition effect in inequality. More telling, there remains much more inequality within the access/no-access subgroups in the data than in the model (see Figure 6.34).

Table 6.9. *Decomposition of aggregate income growth in Greenwood–Jovanovic (GJ)*

	Subgroup	Composition	Total
Thailand	0.580	0.319	0.899
GJ	0.184	0.654	0.838

Source: H. Jeong and R. M. Townsend, 'Growth and Inequality: Model Evaluation Based on an Estimation-Calibration Strategy', *Macroeconomic Dynamics Special Issue on Inequality*, 12 (2008), 231–84. Copyright 2008 Cambridge University Press. Reproduced with permission.

Table 6.10. *Decomposition of aggregate inequality change in Greenwood–Jovanovic (GJ)*

	Within-group		Across-group		
	Subgroup	Composition	Income gap	Composition	Total
Thailand	0.304	0.032	0.015	0.133	0.483
GJ	−0.014	−0.085	0.295	0.338	0.575

Source: H. Jeong and R. M. Townsend, 'Growth and Inequality: Model Evaluation Based on an Estimation-Calibration Strategy', *Macroeconomic Dynamics Special Issue on Inequality*, 12 (2008), 231–84. Copyright 2008 Cambridge University Press. Reproduced with permission.

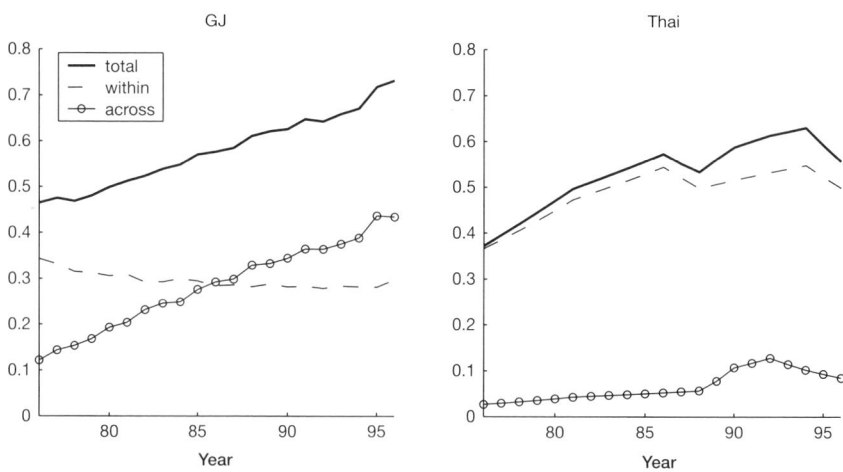

Fig. 6.34. *Within vs across inequality decomposition*

Source: H. Jeong and R. M. Townsend, 'Growth and Inequality: Model Evaluation Based on an Estimation-Calibration Strategy', *Macroeconomic Dynamics Special Issue on Inequality*, 12 (2008), 231–84. Copyright 2008 Cambridge University Press. Reproduced with permission.

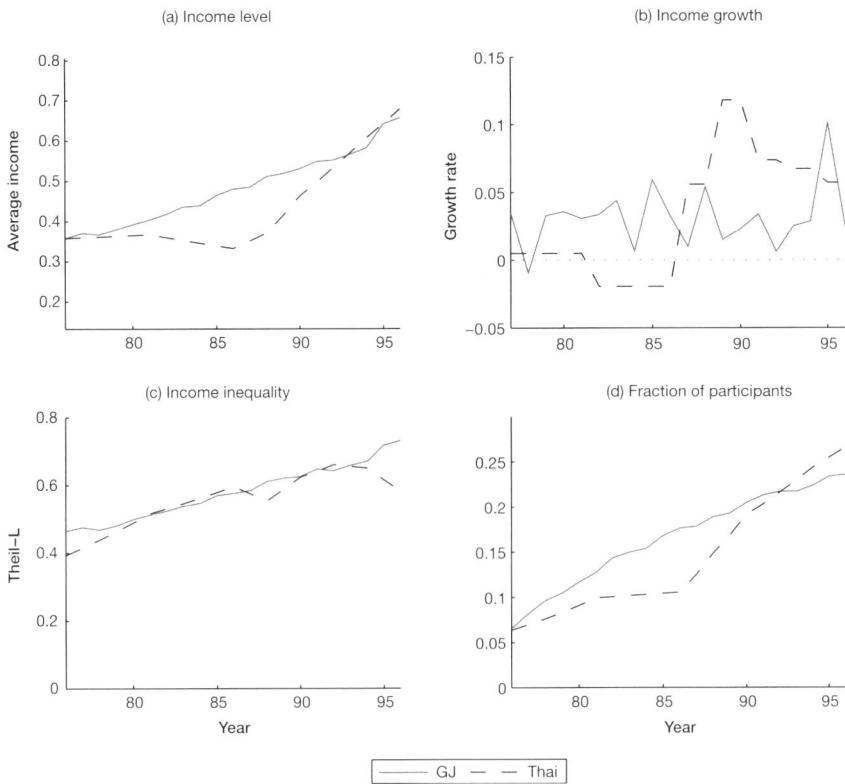

Fig. 6.35(a)–(d). *Greenwood–Jovanovic (GJ) aggregate dynamics*

Source: H. Jeong and R. M. Townsend, 'Growth and Inequality: Model Evaluation Based on an Estimation-Calibration Strategy', *Macroeconomic Dynamics Special Issue on Inequality*, 12 (2008), 231–84. Copyright 2008 Cambridge University Press. Reproduced with permission.

Simulations over time reveal familiar patterns. The model misses the surge in household income from the mid-1980s and the increase in participation at that time. But the match to inequality is quite good, except for the eventual decrease in inequality in the data (see Figure 6.35(a)–(d)).

One success story for the model is the predicted increase in the income of financial-sector participants, and the gap over non-participants, though the model misses the fact that income increases for non-participants also. Likewise, there is co-movement in incomes in the data, whereas in the model participant income is more volatile than the relatively flat non-participant income (see Figure 6.36(a)–(d)).

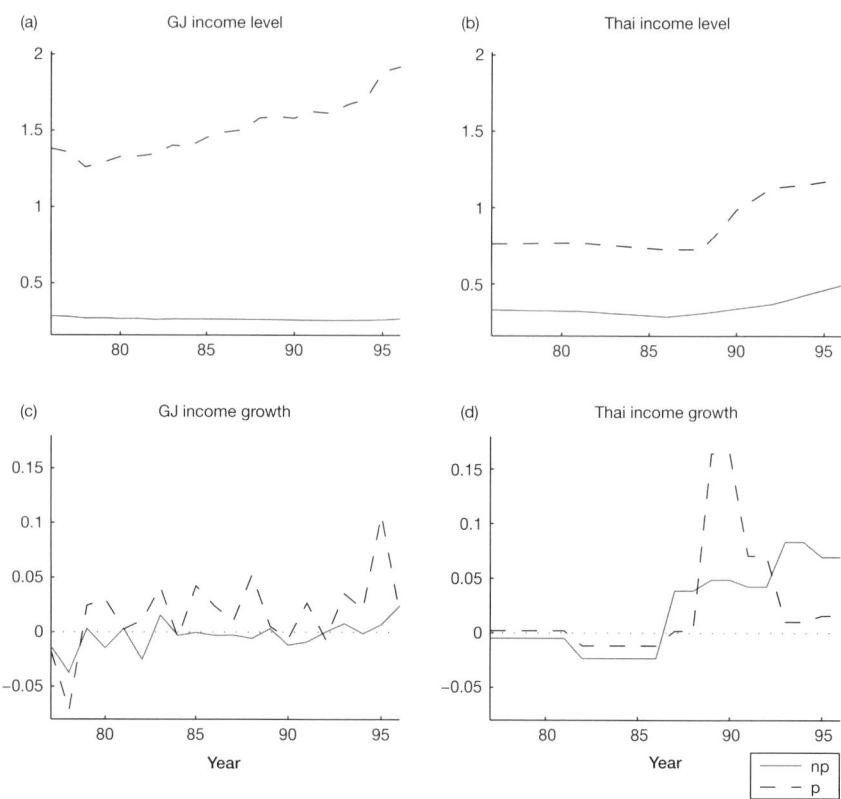

Fig. 6.36(a)–(d). *Greenwood–Javanovic (GJ) subgroup growth dynamics*

Source: H. Jeong and R. M. Townsend, 'Growth and Inequality: Model Evaluation Based on an Estimation-Calibration Strategy', *Macroeconomic Dynamics Special Issue on Inequality*, 12 (2008), 231–84. Copyright 2008 Cambridge University Press. Reproduced with permission.

Again, the model widely over-predicts the gaps in income between participants and non-participants. Inequality is increasing for participants in the model, as in the data, but inequality among non-participants is decreasing in the model while increasing overall in the data. The biggest discrepancy, perhaps, is the low level of income inequality among participants relative to non-participants in the model, relative to the data. This is symptomatic of the assumed perfect risk-sharing among financial-sector participants. The actual financial system seems imperfect (see Figure 6.37 (a)–(d)).

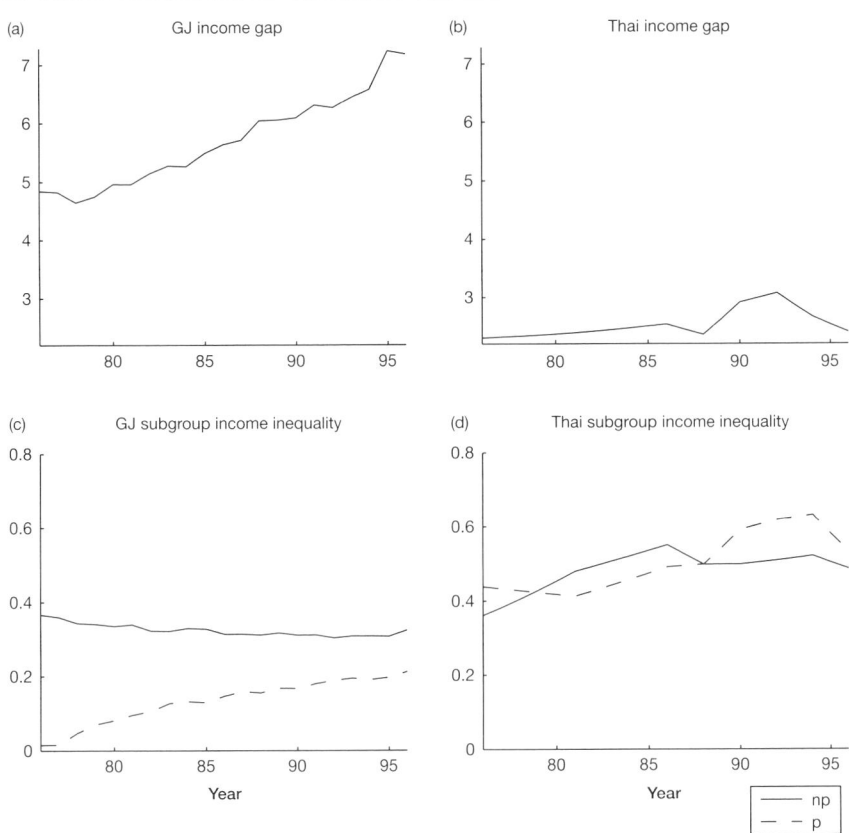

Fig. 6.37. *Greenwood–Jovanovic (GJ) subgroup inequality dynamics.*

Source: H. Jeong and R. M. Townsend, 'Growth and Inequality: Model Evaluation Based on an Estimation-Calibration Strategy', *Macroeconomic Dynamics Special Issue on Inequality*, 12 (2008), 231–84. Copyright 2008 Cambridge University Press. Reproduced with permission.

Overall, the financial-access model does quite well in predicting the end-of-sample, 1996, distribution of income. It cannot be statistically distinguished from the actual data according to a Kolmorgorov–Smirnov (KS) test. The model is still missing variety among the relatively poor, missing the very rich that exist in the SES data, and missing the single-peaked modal value of the data. This last effect can be attributed, as noted earlier, to the (false) assumption that all households have common access costs (see Figure 6.38).

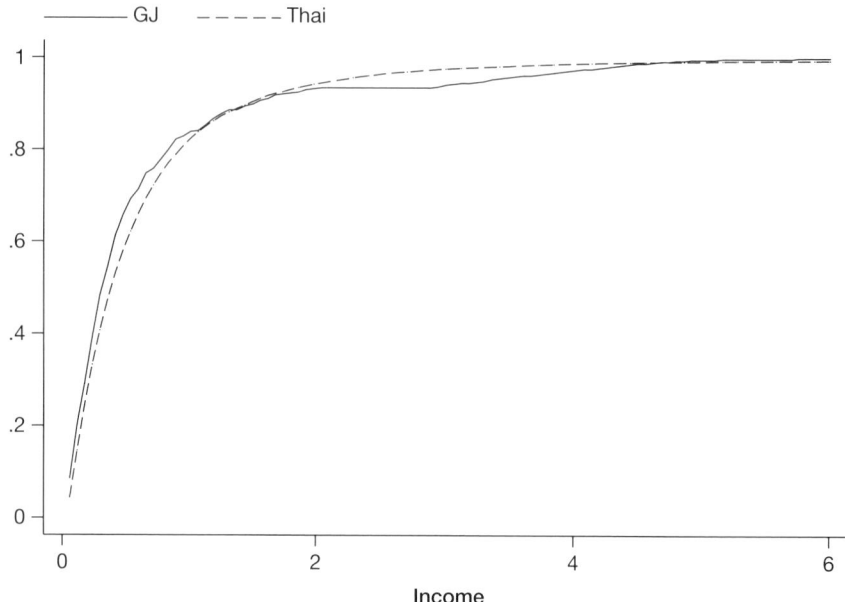

Fig. 6.38. *Cumulative distribution function (CDF) of income distribution, 1996 (end of sample)*

Source: H. Jeong and R. M. Townsend, 'Growth and Inequality: Model Evaluation Based on an Estimation-Calibration Strategy', *Macroeconomic Dynamics Special Issue on Inequality*, 12 (2008), 231–84. Copyright 2008 Cambridge University Press. Reproduced with permission.

7

Neoclassical Benchmarks and Anomalies for Those with Access

If markets and institutions were perfect, and there were no policy distortions, then certain benchmark standards would be implied. This was apparent from the earlier models—for example, ideal financing across firms, efficient occupation choice, no one constrained, and pooling of idiosyncratic risk. Relative to these benchmarks, there are many anomalies in the Thai economy, even for those using formal credit and savings instruments, unlike the dual-sector models. Initial wealth facilitates entry into business and facilitates investment for those in business. Many households and businesses appear to be constrained in occupation choice and investment. Estimated rates of return are high for constrained low-wealth households and, equally telling, low for unconstrained high-wealth households. Poor households and SMEs are particularly vulnerable in consumption and investment to variation in income and cash flow. Some villages and family-related industrial groups offer protection. But some insurable shocks such as movement in international rubber prices are not covered.

7.1. Finance

Paulson and Townsend (2004) use the Townsend Thai Project data to examine the relationship between transitions into business and covariates such as wealth, education, demographics, and financial access. As anticipated, prior 1992, wealth is a consistent positive and significant covariate in probits of those going into business between 1992 and 1997 (see Table 7.1). The effect may decline with increasing wealth, suggesting diminishing returns. Years of schooling of the head is significant overall and in the Northeast, though curiously not in the Central region. Demographic effects such as

Table 7.1. *Probit estimates of having started a business in last 5 years*

	Whole sample		Northeast		Central region	
	dF/dx*	Z-statistic	dF/dx*	Z-statistic	dF/dx*	Z-statistic
Age of head	−0.0105	−3.18	−0.0106	−3.01	−0.0111	−1.84
Age of head squared	0.0001	2.52	0.0001	2.68	0.0001	1.21
Years of schooling (head)	0.008	3.01	0.0102	3.74	0.0034	0.67
Number of adult females in household	0.0013	0.15	0.0089	0.96	−0.0131	−0.85
Number of adult males in household	0.0158	2.03	0.0013	0.16	0.0345	2.41
Number of children (<18 years) in household	0.0045	−0.79	−0.0115	−1.8	0.0103	0.99
Wealth 6 years ago[†]	0.0276	3.25	0.0861	2.15	0.0246	2.82
Wealth squared[‡]	0.0000	−1.78	0.0000	−1.2	0.0000	−0.79
Member/customer in organization/institution 6 years ago						
Formal financial institution	0.0199	1.1	0.004	0.19	0.0314	1.03
Village institution/ organization	−0.0224	−1.05	−0.04	−1.96	0.0239	0.55
Agricultural lender	0.0278	1.39	0.0145	0.67	0.0511	1.4
BAAC group	0.0397	1.72	0.0519	2.06	0.0084	0.2
Moneylender	0.0014	0.04	0.013	0.36	−0.0176	−0.31
Observed frequency	0.1407		0.0915		0.207	
Predicted frequency at mean of X	0.1105		0.0699		0.172	
Log likelihood	−860.30		−363.62		−488.65	
X² for significance of fixed effects	152.96		28.83		85.69	
Prob > X²	0.00		0.19		0	
Pseudo R-squared (percentage)	14.14		10.87		15.59	
Number of observations	2467		1333		1135	

Notes: Probit estimates of having started business between 1992 and 1997.
The sample excludes the top 1% of households by wealth.
* dF/dx is equal to the infinitesimal change in each continuous independent variable. For dummy variables, it is equal to the discrete change in probability when the dummy variable changes from 0 to 1. Dummy variables are marked by an asterisk.
[†] Wealth 6 years ago is made up of the value of household assets, agricultural assets, and land. Number in table is estimated coefficient multiplied by 1,000,000.
[‡] Number in table is estimated coefficient multiplied by 1,000,000.
Source: Anna L. Paulson and R. M. Townsend, 'Entrepreneurship and Financial Constraints in Thailand', *Journal of Corporate Finance*, 10 (2004), 229–62. Copyright 2004; reproduced with permission from Elsevier.

the number of male family members are, on the other hand, significant overall and in the Central region, but not in the Northeast.

Access/use of the formal financial sector via the BAAC appears helpful overall (see again Table 7.1). However, given that a household is in a BAAC joint-liability group in the Northeast, increased household wealth is somewhat helpful at marginal significance levels as in Table 7.2 (but negative for the formal sector otherwise). This contradicts the prediction that occupation

Table 7.2. *Probit estimates of having started a business in last 5 years (with wealth+inheritance)*

	Whole sample		Northeast		Central region	
	dF/dx*	Z-statistic	dF/dx*	Z-statistic	dF/dx*	Z-statistic
Age of head	−0.0106	−3.2	−0.0107	−3.03	−0.0112	−1.85
Age of head squared	0.0001	2.56	0.0001	2.71	0.0001	1.25
Years of schooling (head)	0.0080	3	0.0101	3.68	0.0035	0.68
Number of adult females in household	0.0009	0.11	0.0088	0.95	−0.0145	−0.93
Number of adult males in household	0.0154	1.96	0.0017	0.2	0.0336	2.3
Number of children (<18 years) in household	−0.0035	−0.61	−0.0114	−1.79	0.0121	1.15
Wealth 6 years ago‡	0.0279	3	0.0856	2.03	0.022	2.17
Wealth squared‡	0.0000	−1.74	0.0000	−0.98	0.0000	−0.63
(Wealth + inheritance) X member/customer in organization/institution 6 years ago						
Formal financial institution‡	−0.0126	−1.76	−0.0275	−0.66	−0.0098	−1.26
Village institution/ organization‡	0.0055	0.48	0.0287	0.53	−0.0020	−0.12
Agricultural lender‡	0.0085	1.07	−0.0292	−0.71	0.0082	1
BAAC group‡	0.0068	0.7	0.0207	0.49	0.0204	1.49
Moneylender‡	−0.0235	−1.09	−0.0041	−0.06	−0.0282	−0.93
Member/customer in organization/institution 6 years ago						
Formal financial institution*	0.0394	1.85	0.0198	0.65	0.0553	1.56
Village institution/ organization*	−0.0270	−1.18	−0.0477	−1.76	0.0186	0.39
Agricultural lender*	0.0161	0.72	0.0304	0.99	0.0350	0.93
BAAC group*	0.0320	1.24	0.0387	1.17	−0.0269	−0.56
Moneylender*	0.0210	0.56	0.0156	0.32	0.0145	0.22
Observed frequency	0.1407		0.0915		0.2070	
Predicted frequency at mean of X	0.1105		0.0695		0.1729	
Log likelihood	−856.43		−363.01		−484.71	
X^2 for significance of fixed effects	154.69		28.79		87.93	
Prob > X^2	0.00		0.19		0.00	
Pseudo R-squared (percentage)	14.53		11.02		16.27	
Number of observations	2467		1333		1135	

The sample excludes the top 1% of households by wealth.

* dF/dx is equal to the infinitesimal change in each continuous independent variable. For dummy variables, it is equal to the discrete change in probability when the dummy variable changes from 0 to 1. Dummy variables are marked by an asterisk.

‡ Number in table is estimated coefficient multiplied by 1,000,000.

Notes: *Business starts; wealth X access, significant.*

Source: Anna L. Paulson and R. M. Townsend, 'Entrepreneurship and Financial Constraints in Thailand', *Journal of Corporate Finance*, 10 (2004), 229–62. Copyright 2004; reproduced with permission from Elsevier.

Table 7.3. *Constraints and wealth access*

	Whole sample		Northeast		Central region	
	dF/dx*	Z-statistic	dF/dx*	Z-statistic	dF/dx*	Z-statistic
Age of head	−0.0035	−0.21	0.0854	2.45	−0.0272	−1.37
Age of head squared	0.0000	−0.11	−0.0008	−2.62	0.0002	1.05
Years of schooling (head)	0.0099	0.78	−0.0117	−0.47	0.0165	1.03
Number of adult females in household	0.0766	1.77	−0.0058	−0.06	0.1038	2.07
Number of adult males in household	−0.0216	−0.53	−0.104	−1.17	0.0257	0.55
Number of children (<18 years) in household	0.0157	0.53	−0.0087	−0.12	0.0201	0.60
Wealth 6 years ago[‡]	−0.0027	−0.08	−0.0829	−0.18	0.0056	0.23
Wealth squared[‡]	0.0000	0.49	0.0000	0.38	0.0000	−0.34
(Wealth + inheritance) X member/customer in organization/institution 6 years ago						
Formal financial institution[‡]	−0.0316	−1.07	0.7040	1.87	−0.0186	−1.08
Village institution/ organization[‡]	0.0393	0.84	0.2510	0.43	0.0382	1.63
Agricultural lender[‡]	0.0188	0.56	−0.4900	−1.20	−0.0099	−0.54
BAAC group[‡]	−0.0212	−0.61	−0.0729	−0.18	0.0068	0.32
Moneylender[‡]	−0.4040	−1.37			−0.335	−1.15
Member/customer in organization/institution 6 years ago						
Formal financial institution*	−0.0435	−0.48	−0.4472	−1.93	0.0038	0.04
Village institution/ organization*	−0.0467	−0.35	0.2861	0.80	−0.1745	−1.20
Agricultural lender*	0.1353	1.15	0.0600	0.22	0.2696	1.99
BAAC group*	−0.0454	−0.37	0.1485	0.52	−0.147	−1.03
Moneylender*	0.4438	2.00			0.4191	1.51
Observed frequency	0.5131		0.5870		0.4732	
Predicted frequency at mean of X	0.5131		0.6091		0.4461	
Log likelihood	−185.18		−51.17		−131.38	
X^2 for significance of fixed effects	32.00		9.26		26.11	
Prob > X^2	0.70		0.9		0.16	
Pseudo R-squared (percentage)	12.65		17.95		15.21	
Number of observations	306		92		224	

The sample excludes the top 1% of households by wealth.

* dF/dx is equal to the infinitesimal change in each continuous independent variable. For dummy variables, it is equal to the discrete change in probability when the dummy variable changes from 0 to 1. Dummy variables are marked by an asterisk.

[‡] Number in table is estimated coefficient multiplied by 1,000,000.

Notes: Wealth and constraints are related and anticipate Giné.

Source: Anna L. Paulson and R. M. Townsend, 'Entrepreneurship and Financial Constraints in Thailand', *Journal of Corporate Finance*, 10 (2004), 229–62. Copyright 2004; reproduced with permission from Elsevier.

Table 7.4. *Median initial investment in business by wealth and education*

	Wealth			
	Lowest quartile	Second quartile	Third quartile	Fourth quartile
Whole sample				
Business	17,053	12,317	16,917	30,585
Constrained	13,494	12,317	25,644	30,905
Unconstrained	20,257	12,536	11,658	29,636
Central				
Business	22,562	14,147	15,727	32,478
Constrained	13,603	18,191	19,130	43,000*
Unconstrained	38,504	10,926	13,970	28,695+
Northeast				
Business	12,732	12,313	5,205	21,705
Constrained	12,732	7,617	4,856	15,720
Unconstrained	11,614	21,202	5,877	33,343

	Education		
	0–3 years	4 years	5–16 years
Whole Sample			
Business	15,420	18,401	18,674
Constrained	9,920	25,664	14,211
Unconstrained	36,263	14,147+	23,467
Central			
Business	15,727	30,905	18,218
Constrained	7,710	32,478##	10,419#
Unconstrained	44,398	15,942++	33,478
Northeast			
Business	15,329	10,063	26,677
Constrained	12,131	11,600	30,844
Unconstrained	15,420	5,615	16,917#

Notes: *, **, *** indicate the significance of the difference in median initial investment for businesses, constrained businesses, or unconstrained businesses when the lowest wealth quartile is compared to the highest wealth quartile at the 10%, 5%, and 1% levels, respectively. #, ##, ### indicate the significance of the difference in median initial investment for businesses, constrained businesses, or unconstrained businesses when the wealth quartile, or the education category, indicated in the column heading is compared to the next-lowest wealth quartile, or the next-lowest education category, at the 10%, 5% and 1% levels, respectively. +, + +, + + + indicate the significance of the difference in median returns to investment, within the category indicated by the column heading, for constrained businesses and unconstrained businesses at the 10%, 5%, and 1% levels, respectively.

Source: Paulson and Townsend 2004.

choice should be free from wealth effects for those with financial access. Evidently, we need both a model of imperfect credit access and selection of occupation and finance. Strange at first sight in the tables is the negative effect of village financial institutions onto business transitions in the Northeast. This too begs the issue of selection: those with access to and use of village funds may have other household/village characteristics negatively associated with business—for example, village funds exist in predominantly rural, agricultural areas where there is less likely to be a subsequent transition.

Table 7.5. *Regression estimates of initial investment in business (business started in the last 5 years)*

	Whole sample		Northeast		Central region	
	Coefficient	T-statistic	Coefficient	T-statistic	Coefficient	T-statistic
Age of head	−0.0132	−0.23	−0.0261	−0.27	−0.0577	−0.83
Age of head squared	−0.0001	−0.15	0.0000	0.01	0.0003	0.54
Years of schooling (head)	0.1208	3.13	0.1376	2.36	0.1321	2.67
Number of adult females in household	0.1250	0.89	0.2621	1.06	0.0810	0.52
Number of adult males in household	0.2007	1.55	0.3608	1.48	0.1212	0.81
Number of children (< 18 years) in household	−0.0318	−0.34	−0.0497	−0.26	−0.0144	−0.14
Wealth 6 years ago[†]	0.3390	3.13	−0.3100	−0.31	0.1230	1.68
Wealth squared[‡]	0.0000	−2.51	0.0000	1.24	0.0000	−1.82
Constant	10.2197	6.71	9.6242	3.87	11.8264	6.31
Adjusted R-squared (percentage)	8.52		11.77		5.38	
Number of observations	252		83		177	

Notes: The sample excludes the top 1% of households by wealth and initial investment.
[†] Wealth 6 years ago is made up of the value of household assets, agricultural assets and land. Number in table is estimated coefficient multiplied by 1,000,000.
[‡] Number in table is estimated coefficient multiplied by 1,000,000.

Source: Anna L. Paulson and R. M. Townsend, 'Entrepreneurship and Financial Constraints in Thailand', *Journal of Corporate Finance*, 10 (2004), 229–62. Copyright 2004; reproduced with permission from Elsevier.

Households in the Townsend Thai Project were also asked if they believe they could make more money if their business or farm could be expanded. Though an affirmative response would not be possible in a neoclassical world with perfect credit markets, if the question were correctly interpreted, an affirmative response is typical, for about half of the household sample. As for the individual financial-sector providers, those borrowing from a moneylender are more likely to report being constrained, but given that they borrow, increases in wealth reduce constraints (see Table 7.3). The pattern is the opposite for those borrowing from the formal sector—that is, they are less likely to report being constrained but, given that they borrow, increases in wealth seem to increase constraints. There is variation in these patterns by region. All these responses beg again selection issues and causality. For example, those borrowing from the informal sector may be more productive, hence constrained, given their level of credit, though this is reduced with use of own wealth. Customers who borrow from commercial banks are ones who may have achieved lower rates of return,

Table 7.6 *Financial demand by the amount of fixed assests*

			Paid-up capital					
		Total	≤10m baht	11–50m baht	51–100m baht	101–200m baht	201–500m baht	NA
Yes, urgently	N	61	48	6	4	1	1	1
	percentage	6.5	11.9	4.4	10.5	5.8	25	2.2
Yes, urgently	N	186	122	39	14	5		6
	Percentage	28.9	30.2	28.8	36.8	29.4		13.3
No	N	394	232	90	20	11	3	38
	Percentage	61.3	57.5	66.6	52.6	64.7	75	84.4
No answer	N	1	1					
	Percentage	0.1	0.2					
Base all respondents		642	403	135	38	17	4	45

			Paid-up capital				
		Total	≤10m baht	11–50m baht	51–100m baht	101–200m baht	NA
Yes, urgently	N	61	24	17	9	3	8
	%	9.5	10	10.8	20.4	7.3	5
Yes, urgently	N	186	77	46	12	11	40
	%	28.9	32	29.3	27.2	26.8	25
No	N	394	139	94	23	26	112
	%	61.3	57.9	59.8	52.2	63.4	70
No answer	N	1				1	
	%	0.1				2.4	
Base all respondents		642	240	157	44	41	160

Note: The smaller the assets, the greater the demand.

Source: Japan Bank for International Cooperation.

though the higher their wealth is, the more productive (and constrained) they may be. Needed, of course, are further models to get beneath the observed correlations and conjectures. The point here is only that the world is not neoclassical, not even for those with access/use.

Related also, those who report themselves as constrained in running businesses in the Central region tend to have investment in business start-ups that is increasing in wealth (see Table 7.4). This would be consistent with some of the simple models of imperfect credit, both as described earlier and as modified below. More generally, business start-ups are related to wealth in the Central region and whole sample, and related to education, presumably an indicator of talent. Likewise, according to the JBIC survey, many SMEs are constrained in the sense that they would like more credit for working capital and equipment (see Table 7.5).

Table 7.7. *Median returns to business investment in business by wealth and education (%)*

	Wealth			
	Lowest quartile	Second quartile	Third quartile	Fourth quartile
Whole sample				
Business	56.7	38.4	20.7	16.2**
Constrained	96.9	67.2	13.8	16.4***
Unconstrained	10.5++	31.2	32.3	16.1
Central				
Business	80.8	48.8	39.1	16.0***
Constrained	98.2	79.3	28.2	14.4***
Unconstrained	48.0	34.8	56.6	21.0
Northeast				
Business	21.2	12.7	6.6	10.0
Constrained	57.9	35.7	23.2	17.1
Unconstrained	4.0+	8.9	3.2	0.0

	Education		
	0–3 years	4 years	5–16 years
Whole sample			
Business	5.80	28.54	22.77
Constrained	32.59	30.44	25.63
Unconstrained	2.90	28.46	19.37
Central			
Business	6.42	38.99	25.63
Constrained	21.84	37.84	25.63
Unconstrained	6.42	43.89	24.98
Northeast			
Business	4.10	12.71	21.40
Constrained	35.59	18.69	26.52
Unconstrained	−5.43++	4.32	4.53

Notes: Rates of returns decline with wealth for constrained business (percentage). *, **, *** indicate the significance of the difference in median initial investment for businesses, constrained businesses or unconstrained businesses when the lowest wealth quartile is compared to the highest wealth quartile at the 10%, 5%, and 1% levels, respectively. +, + +, + + + indicate the significance of the difference in median returns to investment, within the category indicated by the column heading, for constrained businesses and unconstrained businesses at the 10%, 5%, and 1% levels, respectively.

Source: Anna L. Paulson and R. M. Townsend, 'Entrepreneurship and Financial Constrints in Thailand', *Journal of Corporate Finance*, 10 (2004), 229–62. Copyright 2004; reproduced with permission from Elsevier.

This declines apparently with size (the value of fixed assets). In sum, smaller businesses in both the household and SME surveys seem to be more constrained (see Table 7.6).

In the household enterprise data, as in Table 7.7, rates of return do seem to decline with wealth or size. For constrained households, as wealth increases from the lowest to the highest quartile, income-to-asset ratios decline. Strikingly, the rates of return on apparently constrained businesses

Table 7.8(a)–(b) *Performance*

(a) Return on assets

	First Quartile	Fourth Quartile
All observations		
Number of observations	604	563
Production (millions)		
Mean	9.31	241
Standard deviation	1.28	612
Sales (millions)		
Mean	11.5	308
Standard deviation	16.4	764
Domestic sales (percentage of total sales)		
Mean	89.95	60.59
Standard deviation	27.06	37.59
Profit Margin (percentage): *profit to cost of production ratio*		
Mean	45.95	64.53
Standard deviation	203.40	334.03
ROA (percentage)		
Mean	32.51	13.26
Standard deviation	434.90	237.90
Truncated sample (only firms with positive equities)		
Number of observations	497	484
Production (millions)		
Mean	9.44	248
Standard deviation	1.33	609
Sales (millions)		
Mean	1.14	317
Standard deviation	1.53	740
Domestic sales (percentage of total sales)		
Mean	89.62	58.86
Standard deviation	27.48	37.80
Profit margin (percentage): *profit to cost of production ratio*		
Mean	36.51	69.65
Standard deviation	120.72	359.06
ROA (percentage)		
Mean	43.48	13.39
Standard deviation	105.40	256.51

(b) Regressions of return on assets on firm's size

Dependent variable: ROA	All firms			Truncated sample (only firms with positive equities)	
Total assets (million baht)	Not significant (p = 0.997)	Not significant (p = 0.82)	—	Not significant (p = 0.98)	—
Total asset quartile (1, 2, 3, or 4)	—	—	−0.12* (p = 0.06)	—	−0.13** (p = 0.03)
Industry fixed effects	Not controlled	Controlled	Controlled	Controlled	Controlled
Number of observations	2.352	2.352	2.352	1,989	1,989

Notes: Significance levels * = 10%; ** = 5%; and *** = 1%.

Source: Adapted from Thai Ministry of Industry data, with Samphantharak tabulations.

reaches 96.9 per cent in the low-wealth quartile, declining to 16.4 per cent in the high-wealth quartile. Rates of return within each wealth quartile are with rare exception higher for the constrained households than for unconstrained households. Rates of return for unconstrained high-wealth households are among the lowest in the sample, especially in the Northeast, as if alternative use of funds were restricted. A related regional disparity: rates of return are higher in the Central region.

From the income and balance sheets of households in the monthly micro-project data we surmise that rates of return on household wealth and on assets are non-trivial. There are preliminary indications that ROA declines with wealth and also declines with debt. They appear unrelated to underlying risk.

Similarly, rates of return on assets among firms in a Ministry of Industry survey decline with asset quartile, significantly, though it is necessary to control for industry type (see Table 7.8(a)–(b)). In addition, larger firms in an IMF study often have proportionately more debt, and ROA declines with

Table 7.9. *Fixed-effect panel model results*

	(1)	(2)	(3)	(4)
Dependent variable	Net ROA	Net ROA	Gross ROA	Gross ROA
Independent variables				
Log (sales)	0.007	0.006	0.014	0.008
	(3.16)	(3.68)	(8.09)	(5.81)
Debt/assets	−0.026	−0.03	−0.012	−0.018
	(−17.05)	(−3.25)	(−10.38)	(−1.98)
Short-term liabilities/Total liabilities	−0.017	0.0001	0.016	0.018
	(−2.27)	(0.02)	(2.88)	(3.43)
Market share	0.114	−0.0002	0.094	−0.002
	(4.6)	(−0.02)	(4.90)	(−0.20)
Current ratio	0.002	0.002	0.0007	0.001
	(2.35)	(2.29)	(1.35)	(1.87)
Input cost ratio	−0.004	−0.005	−0.003	−0.005
	(−4.01)	(−3.05)	(−3.88)	(−2.79)
Constant	−0.071	−0.054	−0.177	−0.091
	(−2.42)	(−2.21)	(−7.85)	(−3.96)
Number of firms	362	362	362	362
Total number of observations	13.720	13.720	13.720	13.720
Number of quarters (average)	37.9	37.9	37.9	37.9
R-squared	0.04	0.05	0.03	0.04
Hausman test (p-value)	110.10		175.41	
	(0.00)		(0.00)	
Breusch Pagan Lagrange Multiplier test (P-value)	16.71		57.68	
	(0.00)		(0.00)	

Note: t-ratios in parentheses.

Source: Haskar and Kongsamut 2003.

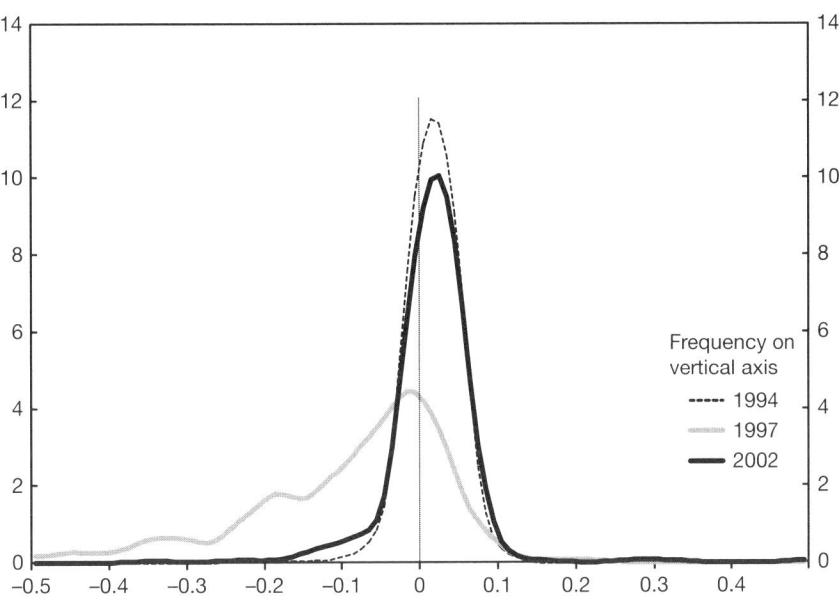

Fig. 7.1. *Kernel estimate of distribution of return on assets, 1994–2002*

Source: Haksar and Kongsamut 2003.

debt. But, again, the direction of causality is not clear (see Table 7.9). One hypothesis is that the financial system may be 'over-lending' to the larger firms, driving down their rates of return relative to 'underfinanced' smaller firms with little debt. This happens in the dual-sector models as firms without debt tend to be constrained, hence high rates of return. It will happen below in models with limited liability even for those with access to loans. As wealth increases, so do loans, driving down rates of return. There are other explanations: despite early indications, risk may be higher for smaller firms, so that higher average returns come with higher risk of default that lenders seek to avoid. But the relationship of loan size to risk can be complicated. In various models below, higher loans lead to higher risk, not lower, as borrowers choose riskier projects, for example. In an adverse selection model below, the riskier households are more likely to be borrowing, and those with no loans are the safest type.

The role of supply-side distortions and the hypothesis of 'over-lending' are given some credence in recent history. That is, there are indicators in an IMF study of increasing inefficiency in the banking system prior to the financial crisis. The histogram of ROA among firms' shifts left rather dramatically from 1994 to 1997 (see Figure 7.1).

7.2. Risk-sharing

The benchmark standard for the optimal allocation of risk in an economy, or risk-sharing group, can be derived from the sub-problem of maximizing a λi-weighted sum of discounted expected utilities of individuals in the risk-sharing group, by choice of state-contingent consumption $c_t^i(\varepsilon_1, \ldots, \varepsilon_t)$ and leisure $l_t^i(\varepsilon_1, \ldots, \varepsilon_t)$.

$$\max \sum_{i=1}^{N} \lambda^i \sum_{t=1}^{T} \beta^t \sum_{\varepsilon_1 \ldots \varepsilon_t} \text{prob} \, (\varepsilon_1, \ldots, \varepsilon_t) W^i \left[c_t^i(\varepsilon_1, \ldots, \varepsilon_t), l_t^i(\varepsilon_1, \ldots, \varepsilon_t), A_t^i \right]$$

$$(7.2.1)$$

subject to constraints defining aggregate group-consumption and leisure.

$$\sum_i c_t^i \, (\varepsilon_1, \ldots, \varepsilon_t) \leq \bar{c}_t \, (\varepsilon_1, \ldots, \varepsilon_t) \forall t, \varepsilon_1, \ldots, \varepsilon_t \qquad (7.2.2)$$

$$\sum_i l_t^i \, (\varepsilon_1, \ldots, \varepsilon_t) \leq \bar{l}_t \, (\varepsilon_1, \ldots, \varepsilon_t) \forall t, \varepsilon_1, \ldots, \varepsilon_t. \qquad (7.2.3)$$

The term A_t^i is a household i demographic, age, and gender index over number of household members. Now, let $h_t = (\varepsilon_1, \ldots, \varepsilon_t)$ denote the history of shocks before t and the realized shock ε_t at t. These include shocks to production and technology. The maximum problem thus delivers familiar first-order conditions

$$\lambda^i W_c^i \left[c_t^i(h_t), l_t^i(h_t), A_t^i \right] = \lambda^j W_c^j \left[c_t^j(h_t), l_t^j(h_t), A_t^j \right] = \mu_c(h_t) \; \forall i, j \quad (7.2.4)$$

and

$$\lambda^i W_l^i \left[c_t^i(h_t), l_t^i(h_t), A_t^i \right] = \lambda^j W_l^j \left[c_t^j(h_t), l_t^j(h_t), A_t^j \right] = \mu_l(h_t) \; \forall i, j \quad (7.2.5)$$

where $\mu_c(h_t)$ and $\mu_l(h_t)$ are common Lagrange multipliers on constraints 7.2.2 and 7.2.3, respectively. Note in particular that $\mu_c(h_t)$ is the common marginal utility of aggregate consumption from 7.2.2 and this will play a salient role below. Suppose further that Wi is separable in consumption and leisure, and utility of consumption is exponential.

$$U(c_i) = -\frac{1}{\gamma_i} \exp \left(-\gamma_i \frac{c_i}{a_i} \right) \qquad (7.2.6)$$

and each member k of household j has identical absolute risk aversion γ_i. Then we get the risk-sharing rule

$$\frac{\sum_{k=1}^{N_t^i} c_t^k}{\sum_{k=1}^{N_t^i} A_t^k} = \frac{1}{\sigma}\left(\log(\lambda^j) - \frac{1}{N}\sum_{i=1}^{N}\log(\lambda^i)\right)$$

$$-\frac{1}{\sigma}\left[\frac{\sum_{k=1}^{N_t^i} A_t^k \log(A_t^k)}{\sum_{k=1}^{N_t^i} A_t^k} - \frac{1}{N}\sum_{i=1}^{N}\frac{\sum_{k=1}^{N_t^i} A_t^k \log(A_t^k)}{\sum_{k=1}^{N_t^i} A_t^k}\right] \quad (7.2.7)$$

$$+\frac{1}{N}\sum_{i=1}^{N}\frac{\sum_{k=1}^{N_t^i} c_t^k}{\sum_{k=1}^{N_t^i} A_t^k}$$

Evidently, household j per capita adjusted consumption is determined by the log Pareto weight of household j relative to group, its demographics related to the group, and average per capita adjusted consumption of the entire group. The Pareto weight will be the inverse of the marginal utility of wealth in the decentralized problem.

First differences over time of 7.2.7 eliminate the household-specific fixed effect. A common time dummy captures the movement of *average* consumption. The inclusion of household income should not be significant. More specifically, a standard econometric specification is

$$\Delta c_{t,t+1}^j = \beta_{t,t+1}^j D_{t,t+1}^j + \delta\,\Delta\bar{A}_{t,t+1}^j + \eta\,\Delta hs_{t,t+1}^j$$
$$+\mu X_{j96} + \xi\,\Delta Y_{t,t+1}^j + v\,\Delta Y_{t,t+1}^j X_{j96} + u_{t,t+1}^j. \quad (7.2.8)$$

The time difference removes the household fixed effect. A term $\Delta hs_{t,t+1}^j$ is added for changing household size to reflect economies of scale in household food consumption, as is standard. The relative demographic change is $\Delta\bar{A}_{t,t+1}^j$. Average consumption change in the group is replaced by a time-varying fixed effect, $D_{t,t+1}^j$. The alternative hypothesis is the household-specific income change $\Delta Y_{t,t+1}^j$ will influence household consumption change, $\Delta c_{t,t+1}^j$. By further interacting $\Delta Y_{t,t+1}^j$ with characteristics X_{j96} at some initial date, say, 1996, one can gauge which groups in the population might be especially vulnerable, with uncovered risk. The X_{j96} are put in as further controls. Random variable $u_{t,t+1}^j$ can be interpreted as consumption-measurement error.

More generally, the risk-sharing and production problem can be embedded in the larger group or in small open-economy problems. For simplicity, we suppress labor supply. Then, maximize λ-weighted discounted expected household utilities W_i by choice of not only consumption but also productions q, costly investments I_t, determining capital stock k_{t+1} subject to a budget (resource) constraint for the group, that the sum of consumption plus investment cannot exceed aggregate output less the costs of hiring labor, less the costs of capital adjustment, plus new loans, less the repayment of debt with interest at the outside rate of $r_{t-1}(h_{t-1})$.

$$\max \sum_i \lambda^i \sum_{t=1}^{T} \sum_{h_t} \text{prob}\,(h_t)\,\beta^t W_i\,[c_{it}\,(h_t)] \tag{7.2.9}$$

subject to the Lagrange multiplier

$$\sum_i c_{it}\,(h_t) = \bar{c}_t\,(h_t)\,\forall h_t \lambda_t\,(h_t) \tag{7.2.10}$$

and budget constraint

$$\sum_i q^i\left(k_t^i(h_{t-1}), \varepsilon_t\right) - \sum_i C^i\left(k_t^i(h_{t-1}), \varepsilon_t, I_t^i(h_t)\right)$$
$$-\left(1 + r_{t-1}(h_{t-1})\right)L_{t-1}(h_{t-1}) + L_t(h_t) \tag{7.2.11}$$
$$= \bar{c}_t(h_t) + \sum_i I_t^i(h_t)$$

and the law of motion for capital

$$k_{t+1}^i = (1-\gamma)k_t^i(h_{t-1}) + I_t^i(h_t). \tag{7.2.12}$$

Among the familiar first-order conditions are those for investment

$$\lambda_t(h_t)\left[1 + \frac{\partial C^i\left(k_t^i(h_{t-1}), I_t^i(h_t)\right)}{\partial I_t^i(h_t)}\right] = \tag{7.2.13}$$

$$\sum_{\varepsilon_{t+1}} \lambda_{t+1}(h_t, \varepsilon_{t+1})\left[\frac{\partial q^i\left(a_{it+1}(h_{t+1}), k_{t+1}^i(h_t)\varepsilon_t\right)}{\partial k_{t+1}^i} + \frac{\partial C^i\left(k_{t+1}^i(h_t), I_{t+1}(h_{t+1}, \varepsilon_{t+1})\right)}{\partial k_{t+1}^i(h_t)}\right]$$

so that the marginal cost of investment at current marginal utility 'prices' equals the future net marginal revenue product. The $\lambda_t(h_t)$ here plays the same role as the $\mu_t(h_t)$ earlier, though the aggregate budget constraint is a bit more complicated.

Indeed, to decentralize, let $P_{ct}(h_t)$ denote the price of an Arrow–Debreu security giving a unit pay-off under history $h_t = (\varepsilon_1, \ldots, \varepsilon_t)$. Then the household i would maximize discounted expected utility at date 0, by choice of state-contingent consumption and leisure, as well as the individual level variables mentioned earlier at the aggregate level (investments, hires, subsidized loans, etc.). In sum,

$$\max \sum_{t=1}^{T} \sum_{h_t} \text{prob}\,(h_t)\beta^t W_i\left[c_{it}\,(h_t)\right] \tag{7.2.14}$$

subject to *one* single date $t=0$ budget constraint,

$$\sum_t \sum_{h_t} P_{ct}(h_t)c_{it}(h_t) + \sum_t \sum_{h_t} P_{ct}(h_t)I_t^i(h_t)$$

$$= \sum_t \sum_{h_t} \begin{bmatrix} P_{ct}(h_t)q^i\left(c_{it}(h_t), k_t^i(h_{t-1})\varepsilon_t\right) \\ -C\left(k_t^i(h_{t-1}), I_t^i(h_t)\varepsilon_t\right) \\ -\left(1 + r_{t-1}(h_{t-1})L_{t-1}^i(h_{t-1})\right) + L_t^i(h_t) \end{bmatrix} \tag{7.2.15}$$

Among other things, we get a familiar first-order degree condition for investment,

$$P_{ct}(h_t)\left[1 + \frac{\partial C^i\left(k_t^i(h_{t-1}), I_t^i(h_t)\varepsilon_t\right)}{\partial I_t^i(h_t)}\right]$$

$$= \sum_{\varepsilon_{t+1}} P_{ct}(h_t, \varepsilon_{t+1})\left[\frac{\partial q^i\left(a_{it+1}(h_{t+1}), k_{t+1}^i(h_{t+1})\varepsilon_{t+1}\right)}{\partial k_{t+1}^i(h_t)}\right] \tag{7.2.16}$$

which is quite similar to 7.2.13, the marginal cost of investment and the future revenue product. Logically, 'firms' face no risk in this perfect market, as all output which is contingent on future shocks is sold forward in advance, in the contingent claims market at known prices. This is virtually identical to the Euler equation in a risk-neutral firm, where the probabilities of that problem are incorporated into the prices here.

The standard result of that financial literature with quadratic equations, as seen in Gilchrist and Himmelberg or Samphantharak, after linearizing the approximations, is

$$
\frac{I_{i,t}}{K_{i,t}} = \alpha_0 + f_i + \alpha_1 Q_{i,t}^{FIN} + \sum_{J=1}^{N} (\gamma_{0,t}^J d_{i,t}^J + \gamma_{1,t}^J d_{i,t}^J Q_{i,t}^{FIN})
$$
$$
+ \alpha_3 Q_{i,t}^{MPK} + \varepsilon_{i,t}; E[\varepsilon_{i,t}] = 0. \tag{7.2.17}
$$

where $Q_{it}^{F_{in}}$ is the set of financial characteristics of firm i, $Q_{it}^{F_{in}}$ is the set of financial characteristics that determine *group* borrowing rates and other group constraints in the outside market. Q_i^{MPK} is the firm i, the specific productivity term capturing future profitability—that is, Tobin's q, as it is referred to in the literature. Again, the inclusion in 7.2.17 of firm i cash-flow characteristics should not be significant. A time dummy might pick up group-specific aggregate system effects.

More specifically, again, under various approximations, and retaining a parallel with 7.2.8, there is an investment equation,

$$
\frac{I_t^i}{k_t^i} = \beta_{t,t+1}^j D_{t,t+1}^j + \delta \Delta \bar{A}_{t,t+1}^j + \eta \Delta hs_{t,t+1}^j
$$
$$
+ \mu X_{j96} + \xi \Delta \gamma_{t,t+1}^j + \nu \Delta \gamma_{t,t+1}^j X_{j96} + u_{t,t+1}^j \tag{7.2.18}
$$

such that household/firm investment per unit capital be determined by time-specific fixed effects and not by household-specific cash flow or income change. The cash flow change variable can be interacted with X_{j96} characteristics. As noted, the version of this in the finance literature tests for whether investment is sensitive to cash flow, over and above the correlation of cash flow with future productivity.

Townsend Thai Panel data indicate, as in Table 7.10, that households in the Central region's consumption was vulnerable to idiosyncratic fluctuations, especially during the crisis 1997–9, and households in the Northeast seem to smooth risk better, on average. But, households in the Northeast were vulnerable in investment, especially in the recovery period, between 1999 and 2001 (see Table 7.11). There are few consistent patterns for supposedly vulnerable groups such as the elderly, female-headed households, and those with low education. There is, however, a very consistent pattern in wealth—the poor households, those with few assets, are more vulnerable. (Related high-wealth households can pass tests for permanent income hypothesis but the poor do not.) Financial markets seem far from perfect for this low-wealth group. Stratifications by primary occupation,

Table 7.10. *Consumption smoothing and target groups*

Change in consumption onto change in income (levels); incremental effect.

	Overall	Central	Northeast	Central crisis	Recovery	Northeast crisis	Recovery
Overall	0.057***	0.109***	0.004	0.112***	0.082***	0.013	0.003
	(0.000)	(.000)	(.832)	(.000)	(.001)	(.675)	(.919)
Age	0.047***	0.019	0.291***	0.019	0.012	0.254***	0.391***
	(.001)	(.257)	(.000)	(.499)	(.620)	(.000)	(.000)
Female	0.014	−0.065	0.315**	−0.193	0.091	0.227	0.815***
	(.849)	(.468)	(.031)	(.178)	(.437)	(.252)	(.001)
Education	−0.009	−0.001	−0.070***	0.007	0.011	−0.046***	−0.121***
	(.206)	(.894)	(.000)	(.663)	(.452)	(.017)	(.000)
Wealth	−1.3e−12***	−7.8e−07***	−6.3e−06***	−1.1e−06**	−7.3e−07	−5.4e−06***	−8.8e−06***
	(.000)	(.013)	(.000)	(.021)	(.135)	(.000)	(.000)

Notes: The table reports the coefficient of income change interacted with household characteristics in Equation (4) of the original text. Line 1, (Overall) reports the coefficients from OLS regression and lines 2–5 report the coefficient from Median regressions with age, female, education, and wealth run jointly. Tambon-specific fixed effects are included in the regression equations. *** indicates 1% significant level; ** 5%; and * 10%. P-values in parenthesis.

Source: Alem and Townsend 2006.

Table 7.11. *Investment sensitivity*

	Overall	Central	Northeast	Central crisis	Recovery	Northeast crisis	Recovery
Overall	2.28***	0.068***	2.84***	0.103***	0.068***	0.044	2.84***
	(0.000)	(0.000)	(0.000)	(0.000)	(0.000)	(0.193)	(0.000)
Age	−0.980** *	−0.083***	−0.624***	−0.080***	−0.091***	−0.049**	−0.649***
	(0.000)	(0.000)	(0.000)	(0.000)	(0.000)	(0.040)	(0.000)
Female	−1.80***	0.048	−1.96***	−0.185***	0.183***	−0.856***	−2.23***
	(0.000)	(0.201)	(0.000)	(0.000)	(0.005)	(0.000)	(0.000)
Education	0.229***	−0.042***	−0.265***	−0.008	−0.052***	0.050***	−0.350***
	(0.000)	(0.000)	(0.000)	(0.619)	(0.000)	(0.006)	(0.000)
Wealth	−5.7e−05***	−4.1e−06***	−2.1e−05***	−3.5e−06***	−2.1e−06	−1.1e−05***	−1.5e−05**
	(0.000)	(0.000)	(0.000)	(0.001)	(0.043)	(0.000)	(0.044)

Notes: The table reports the coefficient of income change interacted with household characteristics in Equation (5) of the original text. Line 1, Overall, reports the coefficients from OLS regression and lines 2-5 report the coefficient from Median regressions with age, female, education and wealth run jointly. Tambon-specific fixed effects are included in the regression equations. *** indicates 1% significant level; ** 5%; and * 10%. P-values in parenthesis. The shaded row highlights that the poor are vulnerable.

Source: Alem and Townsend 2006.

Table 7.12. *Consumption and investment*

	Overall	Central	Northeast	Central crisis	Recovery	Northeast crisis	Recovery
Consumption							
By income source							
Agriculture	0.597***	0.059	0.857***	−0.007	0.157	0.768***	0.069
Fish farmers	0.264**	0.310**	0.172	0.368	0.186	−0.874	−0.242
Wage	1.12***	1.29***	0.343	1.71***	0.425	0.103	0.808
Business	−0.317***	−0.245**	−0.242***	−0.186	−0.238*	−0.530***	−0.022
Investment							
By income source							
Agriculture	−2.64***	0.201***	−2.49***	0.475***	0.181***	1.13***	−2.47***
Fish farmers	−1.64*	0.791*	1.93	−2.21*	0.920*	10.0	−2.98
Wage	6.90***	0.203**	7.03***	0.504***	0.221*	0.475	7.03***
Business	−0.059	0.302***	2.31***	0.016	0.666***	−0.092	2.70***

Notes: The table reports the coefficient of income change variable by source in Equations (4) and (5) of the original text. Tambon-specific fixed effects are included in the regression equations. *** indicates 1% significant level, ** 5%; and * 10%. P-values in parenthesis. The table highlights that businesses are better covered, either by networks or formal finance.

Source: Alem and Townsend 2006.

Table 7.13. *Investment cash-flow sensitivity*

	All	1st quartile	4th quartile
Simple regression			
Beta	0.039***	0.09***	.008**
t-stat	5.19	9.79	1.79
Number of observations	1,476	284	406
Controlled for industry fixed effects (captured profitability)			
Beta	0.039***	0.078***	0.007
t-stat	5.02	7.45	1.63
Number of observations	1,476	284	406

Notes: Regression: investment = alpha + beta*cash flow + epsilon; investment = change in fixed assets/beginning fixed assets; cash flow = (net profit + depreciation)/beginning fixed assets; ***, **, * indicate significance levels of 1%, 5%, and 10% respectively. Controlling for capital structure (debt-to-asset ratios), size (total assets), and ownership (Thai vs foreign) does not change the results. These control variables are not statistically significant.

Source: Samphantharak and Townsend 2009.

and by income source, indicate that wage-earners and those in agriculture in the Northeast are vulnerable to shocks. Surprisingly, business-owners do seem to manage to smooth consumption, but investment is sensitive to cash flow (see Table 7.12). A conjecture: a rise in income may lead to a more than proportionate increase in investment as consumption leads to a drop in financial investment activities. This seems not to happen for the other occupation groups.

Likewise, in the Ministry of Industry data in Table 7.13, normalized investment is sensitive to cash flow, and this is more salient for smaller firms. Controlling for industry fixed effects, the lowest quartile firms are vulnerable and the highest are not.

7.3. Disaggregation and Risk-sharing Groups

The entire economy may not be the appropriate level of aggregation. The economy under consideration might consist of a collection of family-related firms in an industrial conglomerate, or a family dynasty in a village, if not the entire village itself. Various illustrations of this were given earlier in Chapter 2 (Figure 2.10 for networks in villages, and 2.13 for industrial groups). See Figures 7.2(a)–(d) and 7.3.

Samphantharak (2002) shows that the sensitivity to cash flow is much reduced for family-related industrial groups, reduced to such an extent that

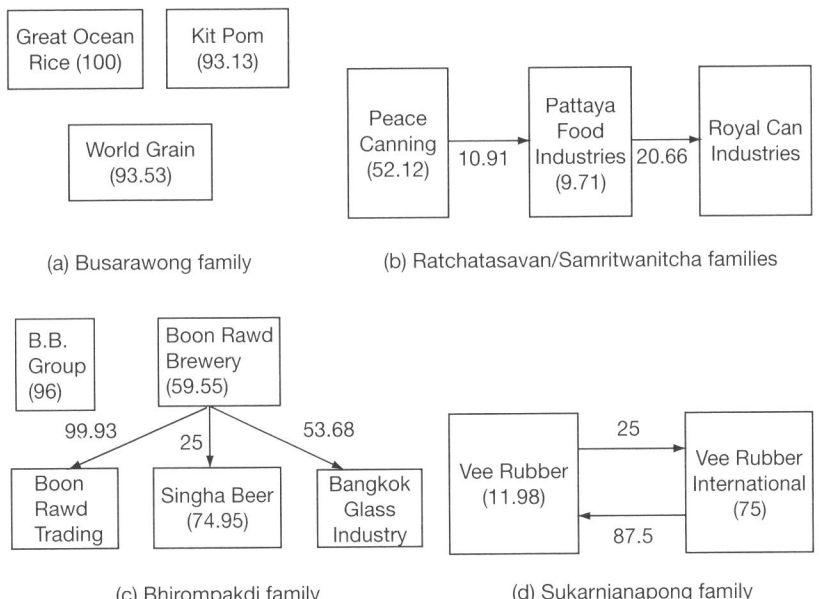

Fig. 7.2(a)–(d). *Family-related firms (part 1)*

Source: Samphantharak 2002.

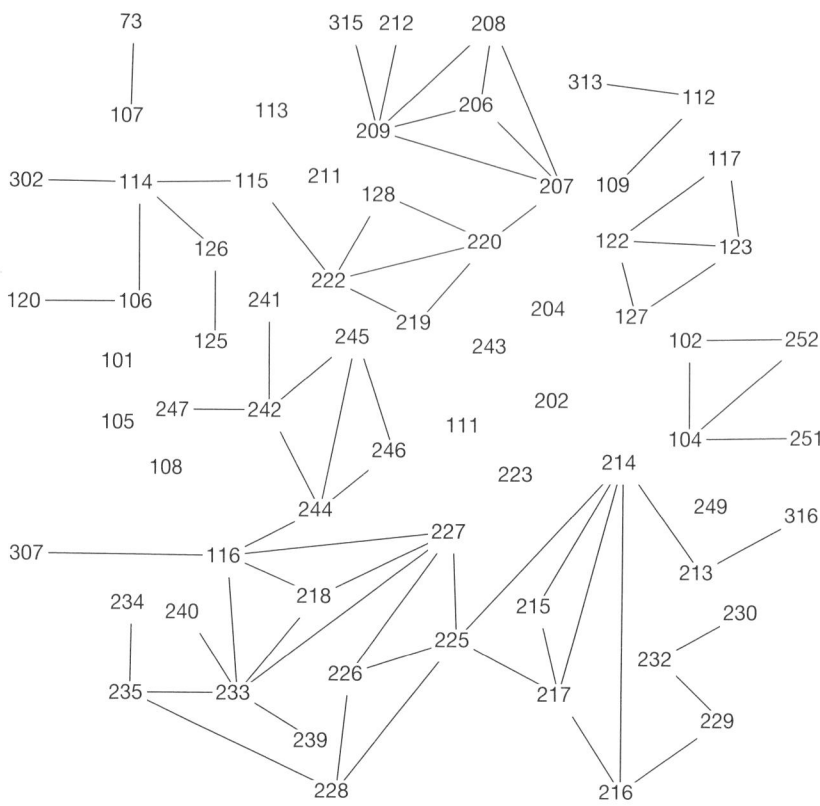

Fig. 7.3. *Family-related firms (part 2)*

Source: Samphantharak 2002.

the magnitude of vulnerability is almost zero. Attributes of the group which are especially helpful are number of members, not being listed on the stock exchange, and the existence of a financial intermediary in the group itself (see Table 7.14(a)–(b)).

Chiappori, et al. (2006) consider efficient risk-sharing and heterogeneous preferences. We start from the usual procedure in the literature: assume $u_i(c)=c^{1-\gamma}/(1-\gamma)$ (identical CRRA preferences). Then, as earlier for efficient allocations:

$$\log c_{it} = \alpha_i + \delta_t \tag{7.3.1}$$

Table 7.14(a) *Regressions of investment on cash flow and Q for non-group firms and group firms.* **(b)** *Effects of group size and composition on investment (cash-flow sensitivity of group firms)*

(a)		
Dependent Variable: Investment capital	(1)	(2)
Cash flow/capital	0.124***	0.412***
	(0.015)	(0.033)
Group vs non-group dummy* (cash flow/capital)		−0.350***
		(0.037)
Group vs non-group dummy	Not Included	Included
Industry average Q	0.012	0.012*
	(0.078)	(0.007)
Adjusted R^2	0.022	0.115

(b)				
Dependent Variable: Investment capital	(1)	(2)	(3)	(4)
Cash flow/capital	0.176***	0.222***	0.309***	0.341***
	(0.023)	(0.026)	(0.034)	0.038
Group's number of firms* (cash flow/capital)	−0.004**	−0.055***	−0.035***	−0.041***
	(0.002)	(0.015)	(0.010)	(0.011)
Group's number of industries * (cash flow/capital)		0.003	−0.023	−0.016
		(0.003)	(0.017)	(0.017)
Group's number of listed firms* (cash flow/capital)			0.092***	0.081***
			(0.024)	(0.025)
Group's number of within-* group intermediaries (cash flow/capital)				−0.047*
				(0.026)
Individual group-year dummies	Included	Included	Included	Included
Industry average Q	0.024**	0.025**	0.026***	0.025**
	(0.010)	(0.010)	(0.010)	(0.010)
R^2	0.138	0.155	0.171	0.175

Remarks: All regressions include firm fixed effects, firm size, and year effects. Standard errors are in parentheses. ***, **, and * indicate that the estimate is significant at 1%, 5%, and 10%, respectively.
Source: Samphantharak (2002).

which is the log analogue. a_i is the household fixed effect and δ_t is the common time dummy. But, what if $u_i(c) = c^{1-\gamma_i}/(1 - \gamma_i)$, heterogeneity in risk aversion. Then, for efficient allocations:

$$\log c_{it} = \alpha_i + \delta_t/\gamma_i. \tag{7.3.2}$$

If we maintain hypothesis of efficiency, we can use a likelihood ratio to test identical preferences 7.3.1 versus heterogeneity as in 7.3.2. Or, we can test for efficiency with heterogeneous preferences by seeing whether income is

Table 7.15. *Test of efficient risk-sharing using income*

heterogeneous risk aversion?		N	Y	N	Y
heterogeneous time preference?		N	N	Y	Y
Changwat	Village	P-values			
Chachoengsao	1	0.09	0.01	0.41	0.23
	2	0.04	0.03	0.05	0.03
	3	0.97	0.68	0.69	0.46
	4	0.04	0.13	0.19	0.05
Buriram	1	0.002	0.003	0.04	0.03
	2	0.92	0.65	0.99	0.84
	3	0.05	0.10	0.15	0.26
	4	0.000	0.000	0.001	0.000
Lop Buri	1	0.60	0.26	0.28	0.29
	2	0.14	0.12	0.05	0.05
	3	0.10	0.03	0.02	0.03
	4	0.22	0.20	0.24	0.09
Sisaket	1	0.48	0.44	0.47	0.40
	2	0.61	0.57	0.55	0.34
	3	0.003	0.004	0.003	0.002
	4	0.08	0.03	0.10	0.02

Source: Chiappori, Samphantharak, Schulhofer-Wohl, and Townsend 2006.

Table 7.16. *Test of homogeneous vs heterogeneous risk aversion*

		test of H_0: identical risk aversion		
Changwat	Village	χ^2	d.f.	P-value
Chachoengsao	3	111.54	29	1e–11
Buriram	2	124.03	13	3e–20
Lop Buri	1	64.28	34	0.00129
	4	69.90	30	0.00005
Sisaket	1	74.63	37	0.00024
	2	110.81	41	2e–8

Notes: Must maintain the hypothesis of perfect risk-sharing to perform this test, so we test for identical preferences only in villages where we cannot reject perfect risk-sharing. Based on 52 months of data on per capita consumption per household; test assumes identical time preference.

Source: Chiappori, Samphantharak, Schulhofer-Wohl, and Townsend 2006.

significant in 7.3.2. We can add heterogeneous rates of time preference as well, so that

$$\log c_{it} = \alpha_i + \rho_i t - \delta_t / \gamma_i. \qquad (7.3.3)$$

Parameters can be found by minimizing a mean square error criterion. In ongoing work, Chiappori, Schulhofer-Wohl, and Samphantarak examine the villages of the Townsend Thai monthly surveys for variation in risk aversion and time preferences, as well as Pareto weights.

Approximately half the villages pass tests for full insurance (Table 7.15), with heterogeneous preferences within them (Table 7.16).

7.4. By Shock: Rain and Rubber Prices

The analyst can also assess vulnerability, and a residual need for insurance, against specific shocks. When provincial GDP is regressed onto rainfall, controlling for year and region effects, the results indicate that mean per capita provincial GDP would increase by 17 per cent if rainfall were one standard deviation above the mean. This regression has an adjusted R^2 of 57 per cent. Using the same rainfall data, but with observations on household income from the Thai SES, Paxson (1992) finds roughly the same relationship between rainfall and the income of rice farmers: their income would increase by 13 per cent if rainfall were one standard deviation above the mean from April to June.

Evident from the graph shown in Chapter 3 (Figure 3.16), and as shown in Table 3.12(a)–(b), rubber price shocks are quite persistent, with a half-life of about three and a half years. Real prices have drifted downward on average over the sample period (driven in substantial part by increasing competition from synthetic rubber substitutes). Similarly, households are potentially vulnerable to movements in international rubber prices. For areas of potential vulnerability, especially those in the South, see Chapter 3 (Figure 3.21).

The permanent income standard can be used as a measure of insurance. The difference between the permanent income, perfect credit markets model, and the full insurance model is that the household does its smoothing by borrowing and lending against a given interest rate, typically assumed to be less than or equal to the rate implicit in the time discount rate. Depending on the model, idiosyncratic shocks may not be completely smoothed—some portion of a shock may enter into consumption, the rest into saving. For example, if credit is limited, or there is no borrowing at all, then households save at relatively high rates on average. They accumulate buffer stocks in anticipation of future shortfalls. Consumption moves even more with current income when buffer stocks are low.

The difference between the full risk-sharing model and the permanent-income model becomes more apparent when shocks have a persistent component. A shock to permanent income moves consumption in the full risk-sharing model only if the persistent component is common across households. Consider an infinitely lived household with an exponential utility function maximizing

$$U_t = -\frac{1}{\gamma} E_t \left[\sum_{t-1}^{\infty} \beta^t \exp\left(-\gamma c_{it}\right) \right]$$

and income stream following an $AR(1)$ process: $y_t = \bar{y} + \rho y_{t-1} + \epsilon_t$ where ϵ_t is normally distributed $(0, \sigma^2)$. Denote the household's wealth at the time t by W_t, and assume the household can borrow and lend at interest rate $r = \frac{1-\beta}{\beta}$. Under these special conditions, the current-period consumption of the household is given by the simple linear form,

$$c_t = \underbrace{\mu + (1-\beta)W_t}_{\substack{\text{permanent income} \\ \text{component}}} \qquad \underbrace{+\frac{1-\beta}{1-\rho\beta}[y_t - \mu]}_{\substack{\text{current income: deviation from} \\ \text{long-run average}}} \qquad \underbrace{-\frac{\beta}{1-\beta}\cdot\frac{1}{2}\sigma^2\gamma}_{\substack{\text{precautionary savings} \\ \text{component}}}$$

where $\mu = \frac{\bar{y}}{1-\rho}$ is the unconditional mean of y_t. The current period saving of the household is given by:

$$s_t = -(1-\beta)W_t + \frac{\beta(1-\rho)}{1-\rho\beta}[y_t - \mu] + \frac{\beta}{1-\beta}\frac{1}{2}\sigma^2\gamma.$$

As $\rho \to 1$ (i.e., as the shock comes close to being permanent), a unit shock to income y_t results in a unit change in c_t, leaving saving unchanged. Conversely, as $\rho \to 0$, only the fraction $1-\beta$ is consumed, and typically this is close to zero.

If rainfall shocks are entirely transitory, as they seem to be in the data, then the income process is autoregressive with parameter ρ close to zero. The coefficient on income in the consumption equation should be of the order of magnitude of the size of the interest rate $\frac{r}{1-r}$, and the coefficient on savings should be $\beta = \frac{1}{1+r}$, close to one, as if all transitory income were saved. Thus income and saving should respond equally to exogenous shocks.

If rubber price shocks are persistent, as they seem to be in the data, then ρ is far from zero, and consumption should move with income, in the order of magnitude $\frac{1-\beta}{1-\rho\beta}$.

Paxson cannot reject in cross-sectional SES data that various (imperfect) measures of saving move one to one with rainfall related income (see Table 7.17). A guess from the thesis work of Paulson (2001) is that remittances are helping to smooth shocks, especially in the Northeast.

Table 7.17. *Response of savings to transitory income*

Variable	Income Estimate	t	Save1 Estimate	t	Save2 Estimate	t	Save3 Estimate	t
Intercept	2,455.6	(16.30)	767.30	(2.88)	1,062.0	(4.03)	358.38	(1.06)
Year = 1981	301.68	(6.39)	44.774	(0.54)	37.450	(0.45)	121.57	(1.15)
Year = 1986	−402.26	(4.85)	−616.08	(4.20)	−725.18	(5.00)	−229.02	(1.23)
Rainfall variables								
(R_1-R_1)	1.9093	(2.52)	3.238	(2.42)	2.9861	(2.26)	2.6737	(1.58)
$(R_2-R_1)^2$	−0.0450	(3.99)	−0.0654	(3.28)	−0.0493	(2.50)	−0.0388	(1.54)
(R_2-R_2)	1.2502	(5.55)	1.2077	(3.03)	1.2888	(3.27)	1.2698	(2.52)
$(R_2-R_2)^2$	0.2282	(1.00)	−0.7973	(1.98)	−0.6963	(1.75)	0.6231	(1.23)
(R_3-R_3)	0.2282	(1.00)	−0.7973	(1.98)	−0.6963	(1.75)	0.6231	(1.23)
$(R_3-R_3)^2$	0.0004	(0.62)	0.0008	(0.63)	0.0009	(0.72)	0.0011	(0.66)
(R_4-R_4)	1.6097	(2.57)	0.5466	(0.49)	0.6314	(0.58)	2.7626	(1.97)
$(R_4-R_4)^2$	−0.0095	(2.85)	−0.0090	(1.53)	−0.0087	(1.50)	−0.0170	(2.29)
Sex/age/education variables								
Number of people aged 0–5	37.693	(1.73)	−43.168	(1.12)	−56.465	(1.48)	26.942	(0.55)
Number of males aged 6–11	59.730	(2.29)	13.313	(0.29)	37.334	(0.82)	20.976	(0.36)
Number of females aged 6–11	79.547	(3.16)	9.2344	(0.21)	20.577	(0.47)	−74.5333	(1.32)
Number of males aged 12–17	220.57	(8.11)	−32.445	(0.68)	38.508	(0.81)	32.678	(0.54)
Number of females aged 12–17	192.98	(7.80)	−19.965	(0.41)	40.598	(0.85)	60.605	(1.00)
Number of males aged 18–64								
Primary school or less	349.38	(13.14)	41.919	(0.89)	95.070	(2.04)	30.400	(0.51)
Secondary school	765.72	(8.20)	−131.55	(0.80)	76.724	(0.47)	−318.86	(1.53)
Post-secondary school	1042.9	(7.69)	23.487	(0.10)	302.51	(1.27)	−185.55	(0.60)
Number of females aged 18–64								
Primary school or less	62.306	(1.62)	31.259	(0.46)	43.890	(0.65)	292.07	(3.39)
Secondary school	345.63	(2.59)	−257.59	(1.09)	−43.456	(0.19)	210.00	(0.70)

(continued)

Table 7.17. (*Continued*)

	Income		Save1		Save2		Save3	
Post-secondary school	676.93	(3.32)	186.11	(0.52)	277.2	(0.78)	−429.96	(0.94)
Number of males aged 65 or more	135.52	(1.99)	−5.1721	(0.04)	−32.04	(0.27)	−48.097	(0.32)
Number of females aged 65 or more	159.68	(2.60)	−91.856	(0.85)	−53.10	(0.50)	27.394	(0.20)
Landownership dummies (omitted category is owns 40 rai or more)								
Renter	−1,338.8	(18.93)	−742.32	(5.93)	−938.24	(7.58)	−297.15	(1.88)
Owns less than 2 rai	−1,699.6	(5.46)	−281.72	(0.51)	−588.17	(1.08)	−24.900	(0.04)
Owns 2–4 rai	−1,769.4	(16.32)	−707.31	(3.69)	−924.65	(4.87)	−479.16	(1.98)
Owns 5–9 rai	−1,583.2	(20.97)	−641.01	(4.80)	−850.34	(6.44)	−440.61	(2.61)
Owns 10–19 rai	−1,368.3	(21.11)	−695.45	(6.07)	−841.95	(7.42)	−382.71	(2.64)
Owns 20–39 rai	−1,008.3	15.99	−559.39	(5.01)	−685.25	(6.21)	−367.25	(2.60)
R^2	0.34		0.03		0.04		0.02	
F tests:[a]								
Test 1	0.0001		0.0008		0.0016		0.0090	
Test 2			0.4044		0.6180		0.9049	
Test 3			0.0001		0.0001		0.1432	

Notes: The numbers in parentheses are t statistics. The table shows ordinary least-squares estimates of income and savings equations. The number of observations is 4,855. In addition to the variables listed, the regression included dummy variables for twenty regions over two years. Definitions of variables: SAVE1 is income minus expenditure on all goods; SAVE2 is income minus expenditure on non-durable goods; SAVE3 is the change in assets.

[a] Table entries for F tests are P values. Test 1: rainfall variables jointly insignificant. Test 2: effect of rain on income equals effect of rain on savings. Test 3: landownership variables jointly insignificant.

Table 7.18(a)–(b). *Basic results*

	(a) Least squares		
Dependent variable	Household income	Household saving	Household consumption
rubber_prop	−938.642 (465.414)**	−371.956 (440.771)	−566.686 (265.694)**
rubber_prop*time	73.314 (52.758)	16.958 (50.310)	56.356 (31.439)*
rubber_prop*rubber_price	521.445 (131.282)***	37.741 (149.130)	483.703 (124.259)***
Number of observations	44009	44009	44009
R∧2	0.15	0.04	0.18

	(b) Median regression		
Dependent variable	Household income	Household saving	Household consumption
rubber_prop	−139.344 (163.798)	−254.458 (112.071)**	−219.973 (128.721)*
rubber_prop*time	28.714 (19.532)	40.280 (13.361)***	4.586 (15.353)
rubber_prop*rubber_price	243.363 (62.091)***	15.499 (42.473)	231.589 (48.823)***
Number of observations	44009	44009	44009

Notes: Estimation by least square (first part of table) and median regression (second part of table). Robust standard errors. Regression also includes a constant and: (i) 8 dummies for the sex and education level of household head; (ii) controls for number of children in 5 different sex–age categories; (iii) dummies for changwat (province) location of household; (iv) dummies for the year-quarter the household was surveyed; (v) 8 dummies for the socio-economic class of the household head; (vi) 13 dummies for the type of enterprise the household head was primarily occupied with. *, **, *** – significant at 10%, 5%, and 1% respectively.

Source: Vickery 2004.

But virtually identical tests in Vickery and Townsend 2004 find that consumption moves with rubber-price-related income more than would be predicted by the permanent income model (see Figure 7.3). Specifically, as earlier, let the income of household be expressed as

$$y_{it} = \alpha_0 + X_{it}\alpha_1 + \alpha_2 E_{it}R_t + \varepsilon_{it} \qquad (7.4.1)$$

where R_t is the rubber price at t and E_{it} is a measure of the intensity of rubber farming in the village of household i at date t. The X_{it} are controls. The consumption specification is

$$c_{it} = \delta_0 + X_{it}\delta_1 + \delta_2 E_{it}R_t + u_{it}. \qquad (7.4.2)$$

Turning to column 1, of Table 7.18(a)–(b), a_2, the coefficient on $E_{it}R_t$ as a determinant of household income has the expected positive sign: when rubber prices are high (low), households in villages with a high proportion of rubber tappers ('rubber villages', for short) experience an increase (decrease) in income relative to other households. A one-standard-deviation fall in rubber prices reduces income in rubber villages by 521 baht; this corresponds to 7.7 per cent of average household income. This estimate is statistically significant at the 1 per cent level (z-stat = 3.9). Rubber villages have a somewhat (938 baht) lower income on average compared to non-rubber villages.

Columns 2 and 3 present estimates of the effect of rubber-price shocks on household savings and consumption respectively—only one of these is independently estimated; since we define consumption identically as $c_{it} = y_{it} - s_{it}$ any one of columns 1, 2, or 3 is a linear combination of the other two. The results suggest that little of the rubber-price-induced change in income is absorbed by borrowing and saving. The point estimate of $a_2 - \delta_2$ from column 2 (i.e., the coefficient on $E_{it}R_t$) implies that a one-standard-deviation fall in rubber prices reduces saving for households in rubber villages by only 38 baht relative to non-rubber households (6 per cent of the estimated change in income, and in fact not statistically distinguishable from zero). The remainder (483 baht) is reflected in a change in consumption. That is, our point estimate of the marginal propensity to consume out of rubber-price-induced changes in income is 0.94.

A simple permanent income model can account for part of the divergence of the results from the previous literature, simply because rubber price shocks are quite persistent, and thus have large effects on permanent income. As a rough guide, we take Cashin, Liang, and McDermott's (1999) estimate of an autocorrelation parameter of 0.82, assume an interest rate of 0.10, and apply these to the CARA-normal permanent-income model. This yields a marginal propensity to consume of $\frac{1-\beta}{1-\rho\beta} = 0.38$. But our estimated marginal propensity to consume of 0.94 is economically and statistically higher than this number.

Related, savings, credit, and remittances change little with rubber-price movements, especially in the South. Thus, parts of the Thai economy seem to suffer from incomplete insurance.

8

Impacts: Experimental and Econometric Program Evaluations

If markets were incomplete, or were suffering from the effects of policy distortions, then exogenous variation in access to intermediation and government program innovations could have non-trivial impacts on both households and businesses. The key is to come up with policy variation that does not suffer from selection effects—that is, to find instruments for temporal variation, or cross-sectional variation, that are related to access/use of a program and unrelated to the unobserved variables driving impact in other ways. The new 1 Million Baht Village-Funds Program seems to have increased consumption, agricultural investment, and total borrowing above and beyond village-fund credit, while also raising default rates and interest rates and lowering assets/savings. Running in reverse, a BAAC debt-moratorium program has had a neutral if not negative impact. Arguably, exogenous variation in villages funds by policy (emergency services, training, monitoring, pledged saving) and by type (rice bank, buffalo bank, production credit group, women groups) implies variation in impact (asset accumulation, risk-sharing, occupation-choice, and reliance on moneylenders). Many of these impact variables are related to the key variables of the earlier models. Instrumented variation in access allows an assessment of financial institutions (commercial banks, BAAC, village funds, informal sector) and, in effect, provides a score-card/rating-system for the impact on clients' consumption and investment smoothing.

8.1. Million-baht Village Funds

In 2002, the government of Thailand transferred 1 million baht, or approximately $25,000, to every village in Thailand for the purpose of establishing a new village borrowing fund. Ironically, the number of households in a village varies considerably around the average of 173, from a minimum of thirty households per village to a maximum of 3,194 households, so the potential availability of credit varied greatly. The higher the number of households in a village, the less credit there is available for each household. Figure 8.1 shows that total short-term village-fund credit moved positively in the cross-section of villages in the Townsend Thai data with the inverse of the number of households in a village.

The order of magnitude of this 'quasi experiment' becomes clear from the evident deviation in the time trend of the expansion of formal-sector borrowing (see Table 8.1). Recall the earlier numbers, according to the SES, that formal-sector access increased from 6 per cent in 1976 to 26 per cent in 1996. Including village funds with BAAC and commercial banks as part of the formal sector, the fraction of households in the Townsend Thai Panel using formal sources for borrowing was 30.8 per cent in 1998 and 36.7 per cent in 2001. But this jumps to 69 per cent, almost doubling with village-fund innovation, in 2002. We thus have the opportunity to see directly in the panel the impact of this intervention.

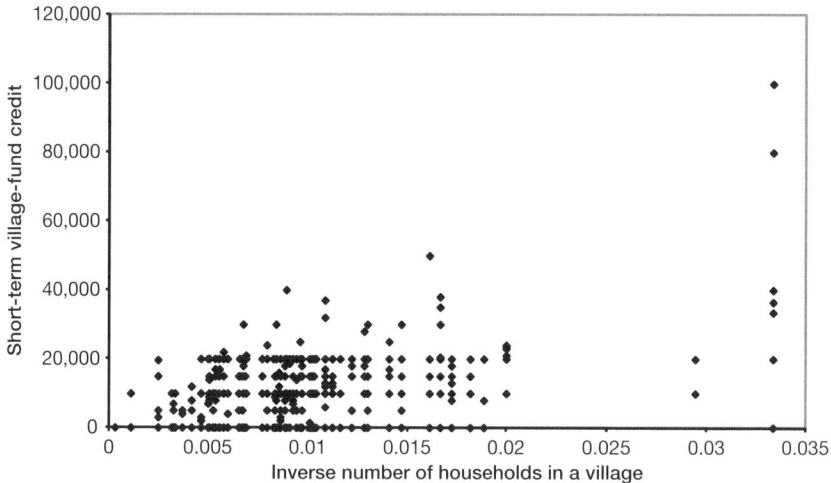

Fig. 8.1. *Short-term village-fund credit vs inverse village size in 2002*

Note: Each dot represents a household.

Source: Kaboski and Townsend 2007.

Table 8.1. *Expansion of formal-sector borrowing*

Central Northeast	1998	1999	2000	2001	2002	2003	2004
Capital markets	32.80%	29.80%	24.80%	24.30%	22.60%	37.50%	45.30%
Formal borrowings	30.80%	34.50%	36.60%	36.70%	69.00%	74.20%	74.70%
Borrowing from BAAC	23.20%	25.70%	28.40%	27.20%	20.20%	20.70%	25.40%
Informal borrowings	35.80%	41.50%	36.00%	32.80%	30.50%	25.60%	24.50%
Chachoengsao	**1998**	**1999**	**2000**	**2001**	**2002**	**2003**	**2004**
Capital markets	28.00%	47.50%	36.90%	38.60%	27.80%	26.10%	29.60%
Formal borrowings	25.50%	33.30%	37.80%	38.20%	62.20%	66.40%	68.30%
Borrowing from BAAC	20.90%	27.10%	30.70%	29.50%	18.70%	17.80%	26.70%
Informal borrowings	19.70%	26.70%	32.80%	32.00%	24.10%	19.10%	22.50%
Buriram	**1998**	**1999**	**2000**	**2001**	**2002**	**2003**	**2004**
Capital markets	36.40%	24.70%	12.90%	12.90%	19.60%	53.30%	60.80%
Formal borrowings	39.70%	37.70%	44.60%	40.00%	79.20%	82.10%	82.90%
Borrowing from BAAC	36.40%	33.90%	40.40%	32.50%	26.70%	31.30%	37.10%
Informal borrowings	39.30%	44.80%	40.00%	35.00%	37.90%	35.40%	35.40%
Lop Buri	**1998**	**1999**	**2000**	**2001**	**2002**	**2003**	**2004**
Capital markets	48.30%	25.00%	25.90%	27.20%	23.80%	20.40%	44.60%
Formal borrowings	12.10%	24.60%	24.70%	33.50%	70.80%	75.00%	73.80%
Borrowing from BAAC	2.90%	10.40%	11.30%	17.20%	13.80%	12.90%	16.70%
Informal borrowings	46.30%	51.30%	30.50%	31.40%	28.80%	22.90%	17.50%
Sisaket	**1998**	**1999**	**2000**	**2001**	**2002**	**2003**	**2004**
Capital markets	18.40%	22.10%	23.30%	18.30%	19.20%	50.00%	46.30%
Formal borrowings	46.00%	42.50%	39.20%	35.00%	63.80%	73.30%	73.80%
Borrowing from BAAC	32.60%	31.30%	31.30%	29.60%	21.70%	20.80%	21.30%
Informal borrowings	38.10%	43.30%	40.60%	32.90%	31.30%	25.00%	22.50%
Yala	**1998**	**1999**	**2000**	**2001**	**2002**	**2003**	**2004**
Capital markets						2.50%	
Formal borrowings						9.20%	
Borrowing from BAAC						5.80%	
Informal borrowings						5.80%	
Satun	**1998**	**1999**	**2000**	**2001**	**2002**	**2003**	**2004**
Capital markets						5.80%	5.80%
Formal borrowings						13.30%	20.80%
Borrowing from BAAC						9.20%	5.80%
Informal borrowings						3.30%	1.70%

Sources: Townsend Thai Panel data; work with Esteban Puentes.

We use several specifications in thinking about the impact of village-fund credit (*VFCR*) on dependent variables $y_{n,t}$, for household n at date t. In the first specification, current credit has a level effect on the outcome measure and the history of credit is not relevant:

$$y_{n,t} = \sum_{i=1}^{I} \alpha_i X_{i,n,t} + \beta VFCR_{n,t} + u_{n,t} \tag{8.1.1}$$

The $X_{i,n,t}$ for $i=1,2\ldots,I$ are a set of control variables for household n: number of adult males, number of adult females, number of children, a dummy for male head of household, age of household head, age of head squared, years of schooling of head, gross assets, gross assets squared, and income. The time-differenced version of the equation is

$$y_{n,t} - y_{n,t-1} = \sum_{i=1}^{I} \alpha_i \left(X_{i,n,t} - X_{i,n,t-1} \right)$$
$$+ \beta \left(VFCR_{n,t} - VFCR_{n,t-1} \right) + \left(u_{n,t} - u_{n,t-1} \right) \tag{8.1.2}$$

where below $\Delta VFCR_{n,t}$ is the time change in village-fund credit in this equation.

For certain outcome variables we might expect a delayed effect. Village-fund credit may have impacts on the future levels of assets and income both because of the transfer of resources over time, and the investments that it might facilitate. Other outcome measures where the delayed effects of credit are of particular interest are outcomes that measure borrowers' *ex post* ability to repay loans, amount of short-term credit in default, amount of total credit in default, fraction of short-term credit in default, amount of credit from informal sources, and average interest rates. Thus we use *lagged* village-fund credit for these variables. That is,

$$y_{n,t} = \sum_{i=1}^{I} \alpha_i X_{i,n,t} + \beta VFCR_{n,t-1} + u_{n,t} \tag{8.1.3}$$

Differencing this equation yields the analogous expression in changes:

$$y_{n,t} - y_{n,t-1} = \sum_{i=1}^{I} \alpha_i \left(X_{i,n,t} - X_{i,n,t-1} \right)$$
$$+ \beta \left(VFCR_{n,t-1} - VFCR_{n,t-2} \right) + \left(u_{n,t} - u_{n,t-1} \right) \tag{8.1.4}$$

where below $\Delta VFCR_{n,t-1}$ is the lagged time change in village-fund credit in this equation.

Rather than use the level, $VFCR$, or the change, $\Delta VFCR$, directly in these impact equations, we use a measure that we can more safely attribute to the intervention. The key instrument: the inverse number of households in the village of household n interacted with dummy variables for the years of the intervention—2002 and 2003 (unless the lagged specification removes 2003). A reduced-form equation for village-fund credit also allows that variable to reflect the characteristics of the household $X_{i,n,t}$, common time effects θ_t, common village effects θ_n for household n, and the (inverse) size of the village of household n directly without interaction (in addition to the instrument). Specifically, for contemporaneous effects,

$$VFCR_{n,t} = \sum_{i=1}^{I} \delta_i X_{i,n,t} + \theta_t + \theta_n + \lambda_1 invHH_{t,n}$$
$$+ \lambda_2 invHH_{t,n} * \chi_{t=2002} + \lambda_3 invHH_{t,n} * \chi_{t=2003} + e_{n,t} \tag{8.1.5}$$

for changes,

$$\Delta VFCR_{n,t} = \sum_{i=1}^{I} \delta_i \Delta X_{i,n,t} + \theta_t + \theta_n + \lambda_1 invHH_{t,n}$$
$$+ \lambda_2 invHH_{t,n} * \chi_{t=2002} + \lambda_3 invHH_{t,n} * \chi_{t=2003} + e_{n,t} \tag{8.1.6}$$

and for the lagged effects,

$$VFCR_{n,t-1} = \sum_{i=1}^{I} \delta_i X_{i,n,t} + \theta_t + \theta_n + \lambda_1 invHH_{t,n}$$
$$+ \lambda_2 invHH_{t,n} * \chi_{t=2002} + e_{n,t} \tag{8.1.7}$$

and lagged changes,

$$\Delta VFCR_{n,t-1} = \sum_{i=1}^{I} \delta_i \Delta X_{i,n,t} + \theta_t + \theta_n + \lambda_1 invHH_{t-1,n}$$
$$+ \lambda_2 invHH_{t-1,n} * \chi_{t=2002} + e_{n,t} \tag{8.1.8}$$

Table 8.2 gives an example of one full-regression result. The example shows both stages of the regression of the level of total new short-term

Table 8.2. *Sample regression: two-stage fixed-effect estimate of the impact of current level of village-fund credit on level of total new short-term credit*

	Coefficient	Standard error	t-statistic
First stage: village-fund credit on instruments			
Constant (1997 dummy excluded)	−5778**	2693	−2.07
Year=1998 dummy	27	310	0.09
Year=1999 dummy	42	318	0.13
Year=2000 dummy	32	328	0.10
Year=2001 dummy	−5	336	−0.01
Year=2002 dummy	1978**	467	4.24
Year=2003 dummy	3540**	474	7.46
Number of adult males in household	82	137	0.60
Number of adult females in household	516**	156	3.31
Number of children (< 18 years) in household	204	107	1.91
Male head of household	1499**	451	3.32
Head of household's primary occupation is farming	45	217	0.21
Age of head	174	95	1.84
Age of head squared	−1.71**	0.84	−2.05
Years of education—head of household	−0.99	70.27	−0.01
Wealth	−2.40e−5	4.45e−5	−0.54
Wealth squared	3.31e−13	4.90e−13	0.67
Income	5.08e−4	4.99e−4	1.02
Inverse village size (invHH)	−84,371	46,394	−1.82
Interaction of inverse village size and year=2002 dummy	759,701**	31,805	23.89
Interaction of inverse village size and year=2003 dummy	577,203**	32,226	17.91
Number of observations/groups			5472/800
R^2—within			0.5328
R^2—between			0.1430
R^2—overall			0.4731
Second stage: total new credit on predicted village-fund credit			
Constant (1997 dummy excluded)	20,453	21,115	0.97
Year=1998 dummy	4267	2419	1.76
Year=1999 dummy	2463	2480	0.99
Year=2000 dummy	9140**	2542	3.60
Year=2001 dummy	9338**	2624	3.56
Year=2002 dummy	4008	3770	1.06
Year=2003 dummy	1557	3764	0.41
Number of adult males in household	2586**	1072	2.41
Number of adult females in household	291	1218	0.24
Number of children (< 18 years) in household	288	835	0.35
Male head of household	7536**	3542	2.13
Head of household's primary occupation is farming	263	1694	0.16
Age of head	−667	742	−0.90
Age of head squared	4.12	6.56	0.63
Years of education—head of household	−54	548	−0.10
Wealth	1.32e-3**	3.47e-4	3.80

Wealth squared	−1.43e–11**	3.82e–12	−3.74
Income	3.27e–2**	3.90e–3	8.38
Inverse village size (invHH)	−136,455	366,912	−0.37
Village fund credit (predicted)	1.61**	0.28	5.67
Number of observations/groups			5472/800
R²—within			0.0851
R²—between			0.1235
R²—overall			0.1025

** indicates significance at the 5% level.

Source: Kaboski and Townsend 2004.

credit from all sources relative to previous year levels on the predicted level of village-fund credit relative.

In the first stage, we see that we are able to explain about half of the variation in village-fund credit. Inverse village size does not in general play a large or significant role in village credit. However, in post-program years (2002–3) the inverse of village size is a strong and significant predictor of the level of village-fund credit. The coefficient of 760,000 on the 2002 instrument compares well with average amount of total credit that the village funds themselves reported offering in 2002, about 900,000 baht. The somewhat smaller coefficient of 577,000 baht in 2003 reflects some reduced lending in the second year of the program (village-fund short-term credit fell from an average of 9,600 baht/household in 2002 to 9,100 baht in 2003).

Tables 8.3–8.5 give examples of the results. There are five specifications each for levels and lag regressions: a normal regression, one with 1 per cent outliers removed, 5 per cent removed, a binary dummy variable for a positive value for the dependent variable (e.g., have formal credit) and a dummy for the village-fund credit on the right hand side, and finally a dummy when the dependent variable is above the all-household average and a dummy for credit on the right hand side above the village average.

The tables of results can be summarized, although only levels are shown here in Tables 8.3–8.5: total credit and credit from other sources such as commercial banks seems to increase with village-fund intervention. This point is important for it indicates that increases in village-fund credit did not simply substitute for a decrease in other (potentially higher cost) sources (see Banerjee and Duflo 2004). Agricultural investment increased, though business investment and the number of new businesses did not; conversely, business income increased while agricultural income

Table 8.3. *Impact of village-fund credit on other credit: levels regressions*

Response variable	Other credit sources				Stated reasons for borrowing				Credit market indicators	
Technique	New short-term credit	BAAC/Agricultural Cooperative Credit	Commercial bank credit	Informal credit†	Credit for agricultural investment	Credit for business investment	Credit for fertilizers, pesticides, etc.	Credit for consumption	Average short-term credit interest rate†	Amount of short-term credit in default†
Baseline regression	1.6056** (0.2832)	0.4488** (0.1779)	0.2506** (0.0454)	−0.0296 (0.2424)	0.0665 (0.0633)	−0.0192 (0.2072)	0.8748** (0.1596)	0.8095** (0.1194)	2.80e-6* (1.49e-6)	0.3735 (0.3827)
Regression without 1% outliers	1.3798** (0.1767)	0.2446** (0.1184)	0.0480 (0.0322)	0.0846 (0.1798)	0.0753 (0.0542)	−0.0335 (0.1608)	0.5947** (0.1208)	0.6989** (0.0998)	2.48e-6** (1.30e-6)	0.7087** (0.2633)
Regression without 5% outliers	1.0081** (0.1369)	0.1844* (0.0968)	−0.0494* (0.0288)	0.1102 (0.0866)	0.0821* (0.0430)	0.0685 (0.0962)	0.2722** (0.1037)	0.3471** (0.0809)	1.43e-6 (8.95e-7)	0.4935** (0.1580)
Regression with DVs for positive response value and village-fund credit	0.3597** (0.1035)	0.0700 (0.0858)	−0.0013 (0.0164)	0.2394** (0.1046)	0.1079** (0.0525)	0.0036 (0.0489)	0.1384 (0.0943)	0.3324** (0.1021)	−0.1606 (0.1721)	0.1960** (0.0848)
Regression with DVs for above-average response value and village-fund credit	0.8114** (0.1090)	0.1340 (0.0878)	−0.0037 (0.0155)	0.2320** (0.0983)	0.0986** (0.0502)	0.0268 (0.0466)	0.1495 (0.0925)	0.4152** (0.0978)	0.1800 (0.2972)	0.2061** (0.0821)

**Significant at 5% level; *Significant at 10% level.
The independent variables are year dummies, household fixed effect dummies, male head of household dummy, number of adult males, number of adult females, number of kids, age of head and age of head squared, years of schooling of head, gross assets and gross assets squared, income, and inverse number of households in village. The treatment variable is the level of short-term village fund credit. The additional instruments in the first-stage are the inverse village size interacted with a dummy variable for year=2002 and year=2003. The fertilizer credit regressions also contain the area of cultivated land as an explanatory variable. Standard errors for the binomial regressions are not corrected for heteroskedasticity.
† Regressions are based on specification (3), where the treatment variable is the level of *lagged* village credit.

Source: Kaboski and Townsend 2004.

Table 8.4. *Impact of village-fund credit on consumption: levels regressions*

Response variable						Components of consumption								
Technique	Total	Education	Grain	Dairy	Meat	Alcohol home	Alcohol out	Fuel	Tobacco	Ceremony	House repair	Vehicle repair	Clothes	Eating out
Baseline regression	2.1048** (.6159)	.0624 (.0594)	.0200 (.0829)	.0606** (.0290)	.0328 (.0313)	.0203 (.0296)	.0221 (.0199)	.0829 (.0718)	.0195 (.0176)	−.0415 (.0987)	.6115** (.2822)	.1465** (.0587)	.0143 (.0133)	−7.27e-4 (.0279)
Regression without 1% outliers	1.1384** (.3662)	.0304 (.0404)	.0094 (.0277)	.0443** (.0204)	.0169 (.0203)	.0469** (.0198)	.0223** (.0107)	.0816** (.0370)	.0032 (.0106)	−.0505 (.0354)	.1360 (.0928)	.0300 (.0203)	.0143 (.0091)	−.0125 (.0185)
Regression without 5% outliers	1.0320** (.2486)	.0094 (.0267)	.0069 (.0213)	.0370** (.0132)	.0050 (.0158)	.0267** (.0115)	.0064 (.0058)	.0704** (.0213)	−.0005 (.0061)	−.0269 (.0194)	−.0009 (.0376)	.0186 (.0125)	.0144* (.0075)	−.0009 (.0096)
Regression with DVs for positive response value and village-fund credit	‡	−.0664 (.0781)	−.0035 (.0120)	.0821 (.1080)	.0071 (.0442)	.1445 (.0997)	.2160** (.0975)	.1404* (.0744)	−.1151 (.0837)	−.0437 (.0447)	.0633 (.1054)	.2270** (.0996)	−.0472 (.0854)	.0021 (.0958)
Regression with DVs for above-average response value and village-fund credit	.4744** (.1289)	−.1507 (.1202)	.0865 (.1228)	.0826 (.1161)	−.0584 (.1274)	.1637 (.1069)	.1931** (.0954)	.3356** (.1154)	−.0299 (.1130)	−.0025 (.1216)	.1163 (.0958)	.1937* (.1146)	.1595 (.1259)	−.0329 (.1244)

** Significant at 5% level; * Significant at 10% level.

The independent variables are year dummies, household fixed effect dummies, male head of household dummy, number of kids, age of head and age of head squared, years of schooling of head, gross assets and gross assets squared, income, and inverse number of households in village. The treatment variable is the change in short-term village fund credit. The additional instruments in the first-stage are the inverse village size interacted with a dummy variable for year=2002 and year=2003.

‡ Regression could not be run because all values were positive.

Source: Kaboski and Townsend 2005. Copyright 2005 European Economic Association.

Table 8.5. *Impact of village-fund credit on outcome measures: levels regressions*

Response variable	Net income				Investment and input uses				Gross farming income		
Technique	Farm profits	Business profits	Wage and salary	Wage income paid	Number of new businesses	Business investment	Agricultural investment	Fertilizers, pesticides, etc. expenditures	Gross income from rice farming	Gross income from other crops	Gross income from livestock
Baseline regression	−3.94e-5 (0.0003)	3.91e-6 (6.33e-6)	4.91e-6** (1.60e-6)	−0.2451 (0.1594)	1.47e-6 (1.84e-6)	−0.0436 (0.3146)	−0.0763 (0.2150)	−0.2208* (0.1245)	−1.72e-6 (1.43e-6)	−1.95e-6* (1.09e-6)	5.48e-7 (9.28e-7)
Regression without 1% outliers	−5.11e-6** (2.25e-6)	4.05e-7 (1.29e-6)	4.91e-6** (1.60e-6)	−0.1744 (0.1453)	††	−0.0288 (0.1375)	−0.0433 (0.1404)	−0.0454 (0.0656)	−1.53e-6 (1.39e-6)	−2.04e-6* (1.08e-6)	3.43e-7 (7.93e-7)
Regression without 5% outliers	−3.23e-6* (1.92e-6)	1.64e-6* (8.72e-7)	4.09e-6** (1.52e-6)	††	††	−1.51e-4 (0.0673)	0.0723 (0.0790)	−0.1240** (0.0484)	−1.80e-6 (1.22e-6)	−5.50e-7 (1.04e-6)	−1.55e-7 (4.75e-7)
Regression with DVs for positive response value and village-fund credit	−0.1180 (0.0912)	0.1482** (0.0864)	0.0737 (0.0966)	0.0635 (0.0395)	0.0544 (0.0563)	−0.0067 (0.0605)	0.2176** (0.0718)	−0.0782 (0.0673)	−0.0646 (0.0667)	−0.2009** (0.0819)	0.0418 (0.1004)
Regression with DVs for above-average response value and village-fund credit	−0.1404 (0.1280)	0.1441 (0.0900)	0.2383* (0.1264)	0.0881** (0.0377)	0.0518 (0.0540)	0.0206 (0.0570)	0.1658** (0.0656)	−0.1372 (0.1214)	−0.1487 (0.1166)	−0.0701 (0.1015)	0.0731 (0.0986)

** Significant at 5% level; * significant at 10% level.

The independent variables are year dummies, household fixed effect dummies, male head of household dummy, number of kids, age of head and age of head squared, years of schooling of head, gross assets and gross assets squared, income, and inverse number of households in village. The treatment variable is the level of short-term village fund credit. The additional instruments in the first-stage are the inverse village size interacted with a dummy variable for year=2002 and year=2003. The fertilizer expenditure regressions also contain the area of cultivated land as an explanatory variable. Standard errors for the binomial regressions are not corrected for heteroskedasticity.

†† Outliers could not be eliminated because of large mass points (i.e., either >5% or >1%, respectively) at the boundaries of the empirical distribution.

Source: Kaboski and Townsend 2005. Copyright European Economic Association.

did not. Even more so, labor-market incomes increase and from the monthly Townsend Thai data it seems wage rates for unskilled labor in the villages increased. Consumption and expenditures more generally also increased, although some of these are automobile and other repairs consistent with investment. Household assets decreased as buffer stocks. Both the level and fractions of credit in default went up, as did some interest rates.

8.2. BAAC Debt Moratorium

A related way to assess the impact of credit interventions is to take advantage of knowledge of participation rules, as in the thesis by Suchanan Tambunlertchai (2004). In 2002, the government asked the BAAC to suspend payment of client loans due for three years. To be eligible to participate in this debt-moratorium program (DMP), a farm household needed to have been a member of the BAAC in 2001 and have outstanding loans not exceeding 100,000 baht. Potential and actual participation can be compared, as in Table 8.6. Actual DMP participation is thus regressed onto DMP eligibility E and demographic control variables X, to create an instrumented version of participation, as in

$$DMP_n = \sum_{i=1}^{l} \delta_i X_{i,n} + \delta E_n + \xi_n \tag{8.2.1}$$

Eligibility is statistically significant. The impact equation is

$$y_n = \sum_{i=1}^{l} \alpha_i X_{i,n} + \beta DMP_n + \mu_n \tag{8.2.2}$$

The impact variables include consumption growth, asset growth, and savings growth.

Impact regressions analogous to Table 8.7 show that there were few benefits that were statistically significant. Indeed, agricultural investment

Table 8.6. *Debt-moratorium program participation*

Debt-moratorium program-eligible	Yes	No	Total
Yes	136	193	329
No	0	591	591
Total	136	784	920

Source: Tambunlertchai 2004.

Table 8.7. *Agricultural asset accumulation*

	−1	−2	NE	CEN
Debt-moratorium	−15,136.32	−17,043.04	54.944	−31,583.53
program	[11,262.784]	[11,411.904]	[7,506.471]	[24,151.358]
Number of household	−194.156	−170.508	585.618	157.401
members	[1,322.979]	[1,327.139]	[980.709]	[2,479.249]
Age of head	439.942*	425.569*	246.981	317.384
	[240.712]	[240.317]	[182.046]	[435.044]
Female head	6,797.34	7,227.94	−3,437.79	15,659.59
	[5,155.663]	[5,154.517]	[3,798.927]	[9,572.604]
Amount of cultivated	711.276***	697.182***	130.065	746.038***
land (rai)	[80.612]	[81.665]	[95.326]	[115.670]
Children living away	−3,683.335***	−3,460.810***	−2,684.624***	−3,222.74
	[1,313.600]	[1,309.932]	[943.326]	[2,492.727]
Northeast	3,301.38	3,190.62	0	0
	[5,328.688]	[5,266.877]	[0.000]	[0.000]
(Change)	−0.005			
outstanding	[0.030]			
(Change) debt–	13,345.909***	11,906.517***	2,642.95	17,229.692***
income ratio	[2,183.160]	[2,006.672]	[1,740.647]	[3,348.777]
(Change) Number of	2,557.18			
businesses	[3,291.019]			
(Change) Net income	−0.006	−0.008	0.005	0.001
	[0.012]	[0.012]	[0.009]	[0.020]
BAAC savings	−0.378**	−0.382**		
	[0.170]	[0.173]		
Occupation: shrimp	392.636	−980.664		
farmer	[31,477.334]	[31,220.011]		
Occupation: rice	1,377.87	2,690.10		
farmer	[5,535.824]	[5,532.751]		
Occupation:	−3,956.49	−13,142.31		
professional	[12,555.081]	[12,950.994]		
Amount outstanding		0.038***	−0.022*	0.063***
		[0.015]	[0.013]	[0.023]
Number of businesses		−3,353.51	−1,539.14	−3,484.60
		[2,477.348]	[1,872.011]	[4,495.189]
(Change) BAAC		0.066	0.583	−0.024
savings		[0.216]	[0.462]	[0.289]
Constant	−21,271.18	−20,846.64	2,082.76	−23,199.91
	[13,483.472]	[13,565.492]	[9,874.113]	[24,556.219]
Observations	768	768	399	369
R-squared	0.16	0.17	0.05	0.22

Standard errors in brackets; * significant at 10%; ** significant at 5%; *** significant at 1%.
Source: Tambunlertchai 2004.

may have actually declined as a result of the program (at 15 per cent, the significance levels are marginal). This would be consistent with running the village-fund program in reverse, so to speak, if somehow villagers felt there was an aspect of compulsion in the program. The key then is induction into the program and how this was determined.

8.3. Crises, Wealth Loss, and Commercial Banks

Given the multifaceted nature of an economic system, it is sometimes difficult to sort out the actual impact a financial institution has. Chue and Cook (2004) and others have argued that financial institutions in the Asia crisis were forced to disintermediate—that is, to reduce loans outstanding, or even close, if they had suffered exchange-rate losses due to dollar-denominated international debt, both short- and long-term. Otherwise they may have been in reasonable shape. The ratio of exchange losses relative to assets in 1997 is used as an instrument in probits and OLS regressions. Evidently, lending was reduced, though we do not have results specific to Thailand.

In more detail, then, Chue and Cook study East Asian financial intermediaries, including Thailand. By and large, these institutions had borrowed heavily in international markets before the 1997 currency crisis. Thailand was quite salient in this. During the crisis, financial institutions' stock market values declined sharply, many curtailed lending, and several closed. Specifically, those with higher international debt, especially short-term debt, suffered a more severe contraction in assets and liabilities.

The results are obtained using the following specification. Let r_j denote loss of equity as measured by the change in the domestic currency value of equity divided by the initial value of equity. This is positively related to a key variable, $\frac{FXLOSS_j}{CAP_j}$, foreign exchange losses relative to pre-crisis stock market capitalization.

$$r_j = \alpha + \beta \frac{FXLOSS_j}{CAP_j} + X_j\gamma + \varepsilon_j \qquad (8.3.1)$$

The 'control' variables X_j in equation 8.3.1 include overall leverage—that is, the liability-to-asset ratios, so that we can distinguish the effects of international debt from other debt; financial value relative to book value—that is, the value-to-asset ratio, in order to control for pre-crisis expectations; the share of assets that is loans—that is, the loan/asset ratio; and the share of assets that consists of securities to control for riskiness of assets. Another key set of equations is

$$BSE \quad GROWTH_j = \alpha + \beta \frac{FXLOSS_j}{BSE_j} + X_j\gamma + \varepsilon_j \qquad (8.3.2)$$

where *BSE GROWTH* is the growth in balance sheet line items such as on-lending, between 1996 and 1998, and $\frac{FXLOSS_j}{BSE_j}$ is foreign exchange loss

Table 8.8. *Change in availability of bank credit during the crisis*

	(1) baseline specification	(2) parsimonious	(3) Korea only	(4) Thailand only
Relationship variables				
log(1+relationship length)	−0.168 (0.055)***	−0.148 (0.054)***	−0.192 (0.079)**	−0.170 (0.111)
log(1+no. of relationships)	0.182 (0.069)***	0.214 (0.065)***	0.147 (0.089)*	0.268 (0.120)**
Controls				
log(1+firm age)	−0.181 (0.098)*	−0.150 (0.091)*	−0.252 (0.323)	−0.151 (0.120)
log(total assets)	0.031 (0.024)	0.040	0.007 (0.036)	(0.030)
log(total employment)		0.005 (0.031)		
profit / assets	11.396 (14.245)		−29.057 (31.584)	20.927 (14.140)
liabilities / assets	19.199 (8.311)**		19.882 (11.695)	16.467 (11.052)
industry*country dummies: F-test	0.0132**	0.0014***	0.0034***	0.701
Pseudo R2	0.0327	0.028	0.0193	0.0226
Number of observations	1057	1140	685	372

Notes: Dependent variable is answer to the question: 'How has the availability of credit from domestic banks changed since the onset of the crisis?' Integer between 1 (much less restrictive) and 5 (much more restrictive). Estimation is by ordered probit. Robust standard errors. Coefficients represent the rate of change in the expected value of the dependent variable following a small change in the right-hand-side (RHS) variable for each observation in the dataset. ***, **, and * represent two-sided statistical significance at 1%, 5%, and 10% levels, respectively.
Source: Vickery 2004.

normalized by initial balance sheet level. Equations 8.3.1 and 8.3.2 are both corrected for selection effects, that some institutions may not be in existence due to the same foreign exchange losses.

Vickery (2004) argues in a related context, and for Thailand separately, that credit reductions were less likely if the firm had been an exclusive customer of the bank for some time (see Table 8.8). Of course, a model of exclusive vs multiple relations with supply-side variation would be a logical next step.

8.4. Village Funds

To determine the effect of financial intermediation, one would like to turn such intermediation off and on exogenously and track the impact on households and businesses. Something like this is made possible with the variation in village-fund policies that were evident in the 1997

Table 8.9. *Impact estimates by policies of institution*

Presence of institution with policy	Number of observations	Asset growth	Reducing consumption or input use in bad year	Starting a business	Changing jobs	Becoming money-lender customer
		Outcome variable growth/failure related policies				
Baseline	2858	0.0296	0.0914	0.0161	0.0050	−0.0821
		(0.0521)	(0.0227)	(0.0153)	(0.0186)	(0.0151)
Offer lending services	716	−0.1332	−0.0041	−0.0477	0.0145	0.0333
		(0.1186)	(0.0550)	(0.0367)	(0.0457)	(0.0305)
Savings used to evaluate loan applicants	731	−0.0979	−0.1792	−0.0209	−0.0351	−0.0381
		(0.0960)	(0.0468)	(0.0322)	(0.0359)	(0.0283)
Offer emergency services	672	−0.0604	−0.2005	−0.0996	−0.0693	0.0118
		(0.1690)	(0.0826)	(0.0447)	(0.0623)	(0.0451)
Provide training or advice	674	0.2605	−0.0993	−0.0175	−0.0094	−0.0087
		(0.1125)	(0.0555)	(0.0327)	(0.0459)	(0.0319)
Offer saving services	731	0.2546	−0.1344	0.0068	−0.0063	−0.0268
		(0.0996)	(0.0464)	(0.0273)	(0.0371)	(0.0289)
Offer pledged savings accounts	688	0.3183	−0.1155	0.0670	0.1305	−0.0671
		(0.1274)	(0.0672)	(0.0427)	(0.0539)	(0.0339)
Offer traditional savings accounts	731	−0.1433	−0.2946	−0.1058	−0.2644	0.0663
		(0.2533)	(0.1149)	(0.0890)	(0.1009)	(0.0749)
Savings is optional to members	716	−0.0735	−0.1201	−0.0450	−0.0373	−0.0291
		(0.1079)	(0.0515)	(0.0316)	(0.0412)	(0.0284)
Savings requires minimum deposit	688	0.1057	−0.1496	−0.0286	−0.0424	0.0162
		(0.1015)	(0.0499)	(0.0307)	(0.0389)	(0.0296)
		Impact variable traditional microfinance policies				
Baseline	2858	0.0296	0.0194	0.0161	0.0050	−0.0821
		(0.0521)	(0.0227)	(0.0153)	(0.0186)	(0.0151)
Collateral required	552	0.1230	0.0776	−0.0182	−0.0266	−0.0348
		(0.1728)	(0.0744)	(0.0496)	(0.0690)	(0.0487)
Guarantor required	582	0.0318	0.0268	0.0044	0.0464	−0.0054
		(0.1176)	(0.0533)	(0.0352)	(0.0458)	(0.0367)
Frequent payments	537	−0.0279	0.0233	−0.0237	0.0105	0.0150
		(0.1909)	(0.0834)	(0.0629)	(0.0738)	(0.0548)
Frequent monitoring	375	0.2253	0.0018	−0.0071	−0.0149	−0.0077
		(0.1850)	(0.0758)	(0.0510)	(0.0613)	(0.0563)
Everyone monitored	360	−0.1971	−0.1256	−0.0024	0.0103	−0.0215
		(0.1643)	(0.0762)	(0.0465)	(0.0570)	(0.0400)

Notes: Light shading indicates significance at 5% level; dark shading indicates significance at the 10% level. Impact estimates are the ordinary least squares (OLS) estimate of the coefficient on the dummy variable for all institutions in the village in 1990 having/not having the relevant policy. 'Outcome variables' are the dependent variables. The other independent variables are the list of controls variables.

Source: Kaboski and Townsend 2005. Copyright 2005 European Economic Association.

retrospective institutional Townsend Thai Survey. Note that this is prior to the crisis and prior to the 1 Million Baht Fund and other government policies. As noted in Table 5.20, village funds varied considerably in saving, lending, application, training, and monitoring policies. Different government ministries promoted funds with different policies. Some of these policies are positively correlated with intermediation: increased numbers of members, savings, and lending. However, others are negatively correlated. That shrinking or failing institutions continue to appear in the data is the odd part of the story of their promotion from various ministries that do not have monitoring/evaluation systems in place.

In Kaboski and Townsend 2005, we run a regression

$$y_n = \sum_{i=1}^{I} \alpha_i X_{i,n} + \sum_{j=1}^{J} \tau_j Z_{j,n} + \beta M_n + u_{y,n} \tag{8.4.1}$$

where the binary instrument M_n for intermediation is whether or not a household n resides in a village where there is a fund with a given policy. The X_i and Z_j are additional household and village controls for $i=1,2,\ldots,I$ and $j=1,2,\ldots,J$ (see more below). This parameter β captures ideally the average treatment effect of a fund with specified policy not only directly on members in the village but also indirectly on non-members in the village. The latter seems a plausible indirect effect of intermediation, though this is not modeled.

As anticipated, some of the policies which are proxies for helpful intermediation (as in Table 5.20) also seem to have a direct positive impact on households, as in Table 8.9. Offering pledged saving accounts facilitates the changing of occupations, reduces reliance on moneylenders (apparently reduces constraints), and makes it less likely a household would have to reduce consumption and material inputs in a low-income year. The last is the most common effect for other policies: savings used in the evaluation of loan customers provides training to members, offers pledged, and minimum balance savings. (Flexible savings accounts are also helpful in this instance, in the provision of insurance, despite the wrong sign on intermediation.) Monitoring loan customers also facilitates insurance, a policy emphasized in the microfinance literature but not correlated with success or failure in the bottom half of Table 8.9.

More generally, an evaluation requires both statistical controls and some variable which is an instrument for access—that is, a variable which is correlated with membership and uncorrelated with the error terms in the impact equation. Again, let y_n be the outcome variable and M_n the membership variable for household n:

$$y_n = \sum_{i=1}^{I} \alpha_i X_{i,n} + \sum_{j=1}^{J} \tau_j Z_{j,n} + \beta M_n + u_{y,n} \tag{8.4.2}$$

$$M_n = \sum_{i=1}^{I} \gamma_i X_{i,n} + \sum_{j=1}^{J} \phi_j Z_{j,n} + \delta I_n + u_{m,n} \tag{8.4.3}$$

Membership, M_n, affects outcomes y_n additively in 8.4.2 and the presence of the institution in the village, I_n, affects membership additively in 8.4.3. The $X_{i,n}$ are sets of household specific variables and $Z_{j,n}$ are sets of village-specific variables for household n.

We assume that $u_{y,n}$ and $u_{m,n}$ are independent of $X_{i,n}$ for all i. We are interested in the parameter β in equation 8.4.2 as our measure of membership impact, and since membership M_n may be potentially endogenous and correlated with $u_{y,n}$, the presence of an institution is the key instrument for membership in the membership equation 8.4.3. Although institutions may also be present in a biased set of villages, we assume that our observable village characteristics $Z_{j,n}$ control for this village selection bias. That is, given the village-level observables, we assume I_n is uncorrelated with $u_{y,n}$ and is therefore a valid instrument for two-stage least squares estimation.

One problem with two-stage least squares estimation is that it assumes linearity of relationships that are clearly non-linear. For example, the membership variable M_n is binary, but first-stage estimation will give us intermediate values and memberships are not necessarily probabilities. Asset growth and some other outcome variables are not binary as well. Given this, we use a second model specification that allows us to account for these non-linearities, though it requires us to assume a (normal) distribution for the errors terms.

Let the binary variables $D_{y,n}$ and $D_{m,n}$ be determined by continuous latent indices y_n^* and M_n^*, respectively:

$$D_{y,n} \begin{cases} 0, & \text{for } y_n^* \leq 0 \\ 1, & \text{for } y_n^* > 0 \end{cases} \tag{8.4.4}$$

and

$$D_{m,n} \begin{cases} 0, & \text{for } M_n^* \leq 0 \\ 1, & \text{for } M_n^* > 0 \end{cases} \tag{8.4.5}$$

We assume linear empirical relationships for these two latent unobserved indices and avoid imposing linear relationships for the binary outcome variable and membership variable themselves:

$$y_n^* = \sum_{i=1}^{I} \alpha_i X_{i,n} + \sum_{j=1}^{J} \tau_j Z_{j,n} + \beta M_n + u_{y,n} \qquad (8.4.6)$$

$$M_n^* = \sum_{i=1}^{I} \gamma_i X_{i,n} + \sum_{j=1}^{J} \phi_j Z_{j,n} + \delta I_n + u_{m,n} \qquad (8.4.7)$$

Again, both $u_{y,n}$ and $u_{m,n}$ are assumed independent of the $X_{i,n}$ and $Z_{j,n}$. But, we allow the dependence of membership M_n and $u_{y,n}$ through (an estimated) correlation between $u_{m,n}$ and $u_{m,n}$. That is, we assume a joint normal distribution of $u_{y,n}$ and $u_{m,n}$ with a correlation of ρ:

$$(u_{m,n}, u_{y,n}) \sim \text{Bivariate Standard Normal } (0, 0; \rho) \qquad (8.4.8)$$

The normalization of variances to unity is possible since y_n^* and M_n^* are unobserved indices, with zero being the only critical value. Equations 8.4.4 to 8.4.7 can be estimated as a system of simultaneous equations with the village variable I_n playing the role of an exclusion restriction (instead of as an instrument in the two-stage least squares).

The instruments are more likely to be uncorrelated with the error term in the impact equation with the inclusion of village-level characteristics $Z_{j,n}$. Here we utilize subsets of the many possible relevant variables in the CDD data base: travel time to market, number of households, economic status of the village, etc. (see Table 8.10 for a more comprehensive list).

Various candidates are available for instruments. Among these is whether the institution of a specified type was operating in the village in 1992, according to the 'Key Informant' interviews with the headman. (The dependent variables are changes or events between 1992 and 1997.) Another is the local or neighborhood average of the prevalence of that type of institution according to CDD data. Figure 8.2(a)–(b) displays a measure of local intensity which comes from averaging availability of that type of institution over all villages in a 10 km radius of every pixel, with weights that decline linearly with distance from the pixel. That 'propensity' score is assigned to villages in the Townsend Thai household data. Note in Figure 8.2(a)–(b) the potential difference between the point responses and the GIS assignment. Plausibly, the GIS measure picks up the activities of particular government officers or other exogenous supply-side variables. A third

Table 8.10. *Summary statistics of relevant Community Development Department village-level data*

	No. of obs.	Mean or fraction	Stand. dev.
Community Development Department village controls‡			
Municipal location*	174	0.017	0.131
Typical travel time to district office (in minutes)	172	38.67	22.82
Typical travel time to market (in minutes)	171	40.56	27.42
Number of households	176	121.7	146.7
Economic status of village relative to other villages in subdistrict (1,2,3)**	178	2.06	0.52
Development level of village relative to other villages in the district (1,2,3)**	177	2.08	0.518
Fraction of households with piped water supply*	176	0.049	0.179
Fraction of households with state-supplied electricity*	178	0.076	0.300
Fraction of households with members working in agriculture only	178	0.333	0.360
Fraction of households with members working in multiple occupations	178	0.504	0.367
Fraction of households engaged in cottage industries	178	0.001	0.012
Fraction of rice-farming households using government-promoted varieties	178	0.497	0.398
Households migrate from the village for labor*	175	0.943	0.233
Fraction of households with members working outside the subdistrict	173	0.290	0.237
Fraction of households that are members of an agricultural bank/cooperative	178	0.807	0.394
Use of a commercial bank	178	0.236	0.423
Use of the Agricultural Bank (BAAC)	178	0.865	0.343
Level of government aid relative to other villages in district (1,2,3)**	177	2.10	0.49
Village has assembly hall*	178	0.390	0.488
Community Development Department data institutional presence			
Village has rice bank*	177	0.232	0.422
Village has buffalo bank*	178	0.146	0.353
Village has production cooperative group*	178	0.112	0.316
GIS-predicted institutional presence			
Probability of village having rice bank	192	0.210	0.354
Probability of village having buffalo bank	192	0.134	0.299
Probability of village having production cooperative group	192	0.125	0.281

Notes: * Binary variable; ** qualitative variable with 1 = above average, 2 = average, and 3 = below average; ‡ from over 650 variables, these 19 village control variables were examined. All variables are for the year 1990.
Source: Kaboski and Townsend 2005. Copyright 2005 European Economic Association.

candidate for an instrument takes the opposite tack: the 'surprise' variable which indicates that a village has a particular type of institution though others nearby do not, or vice versa. This specification allows the GIS average to be included in village controls $Z_{j,n}$ so that, in effect, only the surprise is the excluded or instrumental variable.

(a) Community Development Department Villages in 1990

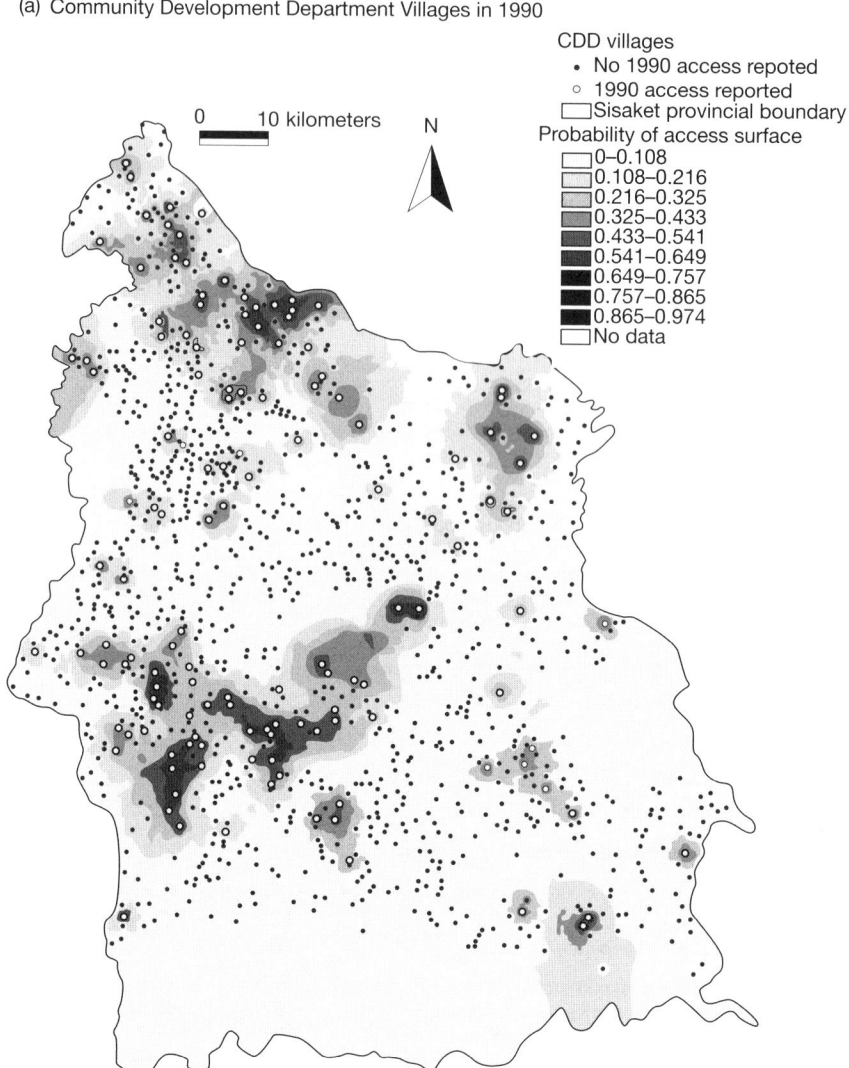

Fig. 8.2(a–b). *Maps of surveyed villages in 1990*

Notes: Color-coded by those reporting access to village savings funds overlaid on top of interpolated probability surface.

Source: Kaboski and Townsend 2005. Copyright 2005 European Economic Association.

(b) Townsend Thai Survey Villages in 1990

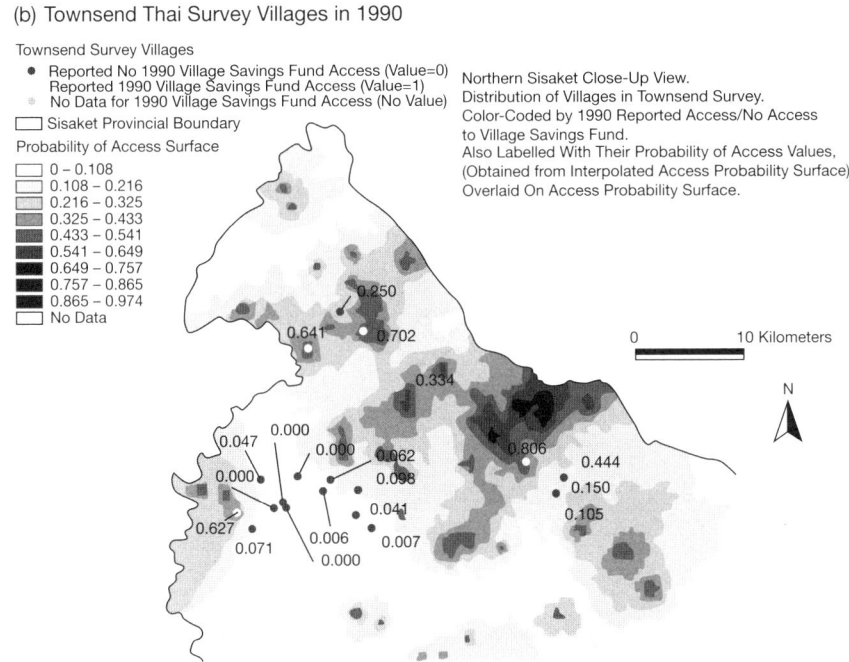

Townsend Survey Villages
- • Reported No 1990 Village Savings Fund Access (Value=0)
  Reported 1990 Village Savings Fund Access (Value=1)
- ⊙ No Data for 1990 Village Savings Fund Access (No Value)

Sisaket Provincial Boundary

Northern Sisaket Close-Up View.
Distribution of Villages in Townsend Survey.
Color-Coded by 1990 Reported Access/No Access
to Village Savings Fund.
Also Labelled With Their Probability of Access Values,
(Obtained from Interpolated Access Probability Surface).
Overlaid On Access Probability Surface.

Probability of Access Surface
- 0 – 0.108
- 0.108 – 0.216
- 0.216 – 0.325
- 0.325 – 0.433
- 0.433 – 0.541
- 0.541 – 0.649
- 0.649 – 0.757
- 0.757 – 0.865
- 0.865 – 0.974
- No Data

0   10 Kilometers

N

Fig. 8.2(a–b). *Continued (See color version at the end of the book).*

Table 8.11 is an illustration of the results. Village institution (not distinguishing type) tends to encourage asset growth and lessen reliance on moneylenders. By type, production credit groups, and especially women groups, are helpful. Rice banks and buffalo banks do not seem helpful: they actually seem to have perverse effects. Again, these are promoted by various ministries.

8.5. Evaluation with Panel

Similarly, one can make use of panel data to estimate the impact of commercial banks, BAAC, village funds, agricultural cooperatives, informal credit, and informal savings (rice in storage). The relevant equations are modified versions of the safety net specification given earlier; here with idiosyncratic income change interacted with an instrumented version of membership.

Table 8.11. *Membership estimates using Townsend Thai key informant data, by type of institution*

Outcome variable

Membership by institution type	Number of members	Asset growth	Reducing consumption or input use in bad year	Starting a business	Changing jobs	Becoming moneylender customer
Any village institution	367	0.2175	0.1693	0.1238	0.0408	−0.6338
2SLS		(0.3998)	(0.1993)	(0.1187)	(0.1529)	(0.1335)
Any village institution	367	1.7037	0.7098	−0.0302	0.0183	−1.3903
Simultaneous MLE		(0.0678)	(0.3493)	(0.3725)	(0.4216)	(0.1161)
Rice bank	107	−0.3157	0.2815	0.1112	0.0608	−0.0517
2SLS		(0.3398)	(0.1516)	(0.1020)	(0.1233)	(0.1192)
Rice bank	107	−0.7212	0.7917	0.3430	0.5320	1.3191
Simultaneous MLE		(0.2051)	(0.3117)	(0.4231)	(0.6036)	(0.6506)
Buffalo bank	13	−1.3584	2.2932	0.3474	1.0805	1.4900
2SLS		(1.8823)	(1.3029)	(0.6836)	(0.8022)	(1.1835)
Buffalo bank	13	−2.0419	1.4777	1.8044‡	−1.0918‡	−1.1848‡
Simultaneous MLE		(0.4190)	(0.4332)	(0.5217)	(0.2281)	(0.2194)
PCG	68	0.7178	0.0058	0.0236	−0.2944	−0.0903
2SLS		(0.6119)	(0.3099)	(0.1866)	(0.2140)	(0.1607)
PCG	68	1.7798	0.1671	0.4082	−0.4873	−0.6680
Simultaneous MLE		(0.1183)	(0.5641)	(0.6244)	(0.8814)	(0.5120)
Women's group	54	4.9670	−18.1780	1.5768	1.4076	−4.2552
2SLS		(6.0915)	(59.5241)	(2.4794)	(4.2478)	(3.0400)
Women's group	54	1.8805	2.0672‡	−0.0142	2.1976	−1.5887
Simultaneous MLE		(0.1132)	(0.1057)	(1.2957)	(0.7468)	(0.1285)

Notes: Shading indicates significance at 5% level. ‡ Estimate is significant, but maximum likelihood estimation (MLE) yielded an insignificant error correlation that approached perfect positive or negative correlation. The impact estimate is the coefficient on the membership variable in 1990. 'Outcome variables' are the dependent variables in the outcome equation. Impacts are measured from 1991 to 1997. Other independent variables used as controls are head of household characteristics (age; age squared; years of education, sex); household characteristics (numbers of adult males, adult females, and children; total assets, total assets squared; membership/customer of commercial bank, agricultural bank, money lender); and village characteristics (average wealth; average wealth squared; average years education of household heads; fraction of households in rice farming as primary occupation, in multiple occupations, and in agriculture only; presence of a hall for village assembly; economic status relative to other villages in the *tambon*/subdistrict; and the relative level of government assistance that the village receives). In addition the 'asset growth' and 'reducing consumption' equations contain occupation dummies for the household head. The 'becoming moneylender customer' excludes customer of moneylender as a right-hand side regressor. The wealth controls for 'starting a business' use non-business wealth. The membership equation contains all of the control variables in the outcome equation as well as a dummy variable for the presence of the institution in the village in 1990 from the Townsend data.
Source: Kaboski and Townsend 2005. Copyright 2005 European Economic Association.

$$\Delta c^{j}_{t,t+1} = \beta_{t,t+1} D_{t,t+1} + \delta \bar{A}^{j}_{t,t+1} + \eta \Delta hs^{j}_{t,t+1} + \xi \Delta Y^{j}_{t,t+1}$$
$$+ \psi Z_{ji96} + \gamma X_{j96} + \mu \Delta Y^{j}_{t,t+1} * Z_{ji96} \qquad (8.5.1)$$
$$+ v \Delta Y^{j}_{t,t+1} * X_{j96} + \rho \Delta Y^{j}_{t,t+1} * M_{j96} + u^{j}_{t,t+1}$$

$$\Delta I^{*j}_{t,t+1} = \beta_{t,t+1} D_{t,t+1} + \delta \bar{A}^{j}_{t,t+1} + \eta \Delta hs^{j}_{t,t+1}$$
$$+ \xi \Delta Y^{j}_{t,t+1} + \psi Z_{ji96} + \gamma X_{j96} + \mu \Delta Y^{j}_{t,t+1} * Z_{ji96} \qquad (8.5.2)$$
$$+ v \Delta Y^{j}_{t,t+1} * X_{j96} + \rho \Delta Y^{j}_{t,t+1} * M_{j96} + e^{j}_{t,t+1}.$$

The membership equation in this notation is:

$$M_{j96} = \psi X_{j96} + \theta Z_{ji96} + \delta I_{j96} + \varsigma_{mj}. \qquad (8.5.3)$$

Geographic surprise:

$$Mj_{j} = \psi X_{j(96)} + \theta Z_{ji(96)} + \delta I^{*}_{j(96)} + \gamma \xi_{j} + \varsigma_{mj}. \qquad (8.5.4)$$

Table 8.12. *Correlation of 1996 instruments with subsequent frequency of use*

	HEAD*	P-value	TIME	P-value	GIS	P-value	Surprise	P-value
BAAC								
- Borrowing	.0869	(.0050)	.0675	(.0307)	.2115	(.0000)	.1363	(.0000)
- Savings	.0667	(.0313)	.0602	(.0540)	.2140	(.0000)	.1589	(.0000)
Commercial banks								
- Borrowing	−.0209	(.4995)	−.0795	(.0108)	.0977	(.0016)	.0808	(.0090)
- Savings	.0558	(.0714)	−.0988	(.0015)	.0889	(.0041)	.0479	(.1222)
Agricultural Cooperatives								
- Borrowing	.1062	(.0006)	.0045	(.8847)	.1818	(.000)	−.0518	(.0945)
- Savings	.1527	(.0000)	−.0013	(.9678)	.1897	(.000)	−.0379	(.2212)
PCG								
- Borrowing	.2186	(.0000)	−.0961	(.0020)	.1312	(.0000)	.0885	(.0042)
- Savings	.1943	(.0000)	−.0930	(.0028)	.1668	(.0000)	.0875	(.0047)
Informal sector								
- Borrowing	NA	—	.0174	(.5770)	.0098	(.7522)	.0988	(.0014)
- Savings (rice)	NA	—	.1228	(.0001)	.0696	(.0244)	.0605	(.0506)

Notes: Surprise represents the Geographical Surprise instrument; GIS is the Geographical Information System instrument; TIME measures the travel time from the village to the district center; and HEAD is the response of the Headman to questions about institutional presence. Frequent use is a dummy variable indicating whether the household had a particular type of transaction in 3 out of the 4 years in the panel.

Source: Alem and Townsend 2006.

Table 8.13. *Coefficients of instruments in the membership equation*

Instruments	BAAC	CBANK	AGCOOP	PCG	INFBOR	INFSAV
OVERALL						
- Headman	.139***	.080	.158***	.173***	–	–
- GIS	.432***	.184**	.285***	.219***	−.222***	.020
- Time	.004***	.000	−.002*	−.002**	−.003*	.000
- Surprise	.245***	.095***	.179***	.363***	−.125***	.015
CENTRAL						
- Headman	.265***	−.006	.156***	.209***	–	–
- GIS	.379***	.094	.222***	.382**	−.277***	−.058**
- Time	.008***	.003	−.002	.000	−.008***	−.001
- Surprise	.300***	.163**	.102	.323***	−.184***	−.013
NE						
- Headman	.025	dropped	.110**	.193***	–	–
- GIS	.861***	.523***	.263***	.121	−.087	.187***
- Time	.006**	.003	−.007***	−.002	−.003	.002*
- Surprise	.202*	.086	.165***	.444***	−.175**	.110***

Notes: *** indicates 1% significant level, ** 5%, and * 10%, respectively. Surprise represents the Geographical Surprise instrument; GIS is the Geographical Information System instrument; Time measures the travel time from the village to the district center; and Headman is the response of the Headman to questions about institutional presence. BAAC is the Bank of Agriculture and Agricultural Cooperatives; CBANK is commercial banks; AGCOOP is Agricultural Cooperatives; PCG is village funds; INFBOR is informal borrowing; and INFSAV is rice storage.

Source: Alem and Townsend 2006.

The instruments dated 1996 are time to the district center, the GIS average, the GIS surprise, and the headman response. These can be shown to have desirable properties. Many are significant in the membership equation (Table 8.13) and are correlated with measured, subsequent use of the institution in the panel—that is, there are changes in borrowing and/or saving in that institution or mechanism, 1997–2001 (Table 8.12). If neither criterion is satisfied, the instrument is dropped.

Table 8.14(a)–(b) summarizes the tendency of PCGs and the informal sector to ameliorate income shocks, a negative coefficient with other things being equal, and Table 8.15 is a scorecard, rating various financial institutions.

8.6. A Structural Model of Credit Constraints and Impact of Village Funds

To reiterate, the Thai economy is not neoclassical and the ability to achieve benchmark standards is facilitated by the availability of financial institutions. But policy interventions do not completely overcome underlying obstacles. A structural model with credit constraints, with Joe Kaboski

Table 8.14(a)–(b). *Income shocks*

(a) Change in consumption on to (level) change in income (incremental effect of PCG)

	Overall	Region central	North-east	Period during crisis	After crisis	Central during crisis	After crisis	Northeast during crisis	After crisis
Naive	-0.119	-0.206	-0.828***	0.117	-0.287	-0.335	0.008	-0.671	-0.867**
GIS Select	7.20***	-1.28	—	6.00**	13.0***	-2.72	-1.65	—	—
Headman	-2.79***	-1.60**	-4.81***	-3.42***	-2.12***	-2.83**	-0.052	-4.69***	-2.99*
Time to Center	-1.65	—	—	-4.86*	-7.81***	—	—	—	—
Surprise	-2.50***	-1.19	-2.00	-2.98***	-3.86***	-0.976	-0.234	-2.35	-2.28

Note: The table reports the coefficient of income change interacted with instrumented membership in equation (7). *** indicates 1% significant level, ** 5%, and * 10% respectively.

(b) Investment change on to income change (scaled) (incremental effect of the PCG)

	Overall	Region central	North-east	Period during crisis	After crisis	Central during crisis	After crisis	Northeast during crisis	After crisis
Naive	1.55***	0.773***	1.36*	-0.595***	1.51***	-0.129	0.759***	-0.098	1.36
GIS Select	-16.6***	-12.4***	—	-2.26*	-10.0***	-2.99	-9.43***	—	—
Headman	6.33***	2.00***	8.45**	-3.02***	5.55***	-1.34*	3.11***	-0.794	9.77*
Time to Center	12.5***	—	—	-1.90	9.50*	—	—	—	—
Surprise	1.54**	1.87***	5.00*	-2.51***	2.37***	-2.38**	1.82**	-0.498	5.22

Notes: The table reports the coefficient of income change interacted with instrumented membership in equation (8). *** indicates 1% significant level, ** 5%, and * 10% respectively.

Source: Alem and Townsend 2006.

Table 8.15. *Rating financial institutions*

Alem scorecard

Different lenders are different: plus depend on region/time

Commercial Bank	Consumption → not helpful
	Investment → helps overall and after crisis, 'hurt' during
BAAC	Consumption → helps overall, Northeast, Northeast during crisis
	Investment → hurts NE, Central after crisis, NE after crisis
Agricultural	Consumption → helps Northeast, Northeast after crisis
Cooperative	Investment → helps overall, Central, Northeast—but helps DURING but not after
Production cooperative	Consumption → helps Northeast after, Northeast after
group	Investment → hurts overall, Central, Northeast, but helps DURING but not after, especially Central
Informal Debt	Consumption → helps Northeast, after crisis, after Northeast
	Investment → helps during Northeast, but pretty uniformly helps in Central
Rice	→ helps consumption in Northeast, not Central

Source: Alem, unpublished.

(Kaboski and Townsend 2007), provides some interpretation of observed impact, and some caveats for the reduced-form analysis of this chapter.

Our interpretation of the impact of the 1 Million Baht Program is that investment projects come in potentially large indivisible sizes, that with the introduction of the program some households borrow more to finance them, and that many reduce consumption. But, for others not near a threshold, increased liquidity (a weakened borrowing constraint) means increased consumption and potentially lower savings (credit lowers the need for a buffer stock). Following Gourinchas and Parker (2002), imagine a Zeldes (1989)-like model but with investment—that is, permanent income has a component which is increased with investment but is subject to drift and a stochastic term, that the permitted size of investment is random, that the upper bound on borrowing is related to permanent income, that there are as well transitory shocks to current income, and that liquid resources today are the sum of current income and past savings (if any). We conjecture that the effect of the village-fund program can be captured by a surprise increase in the credit limit. That is, we use pre-intervention data to estimate the parameters of this structural model, then compare predictions to what actually happened. Consumption expenditures increase in the model, similar to the data, and more than the increase in per capita credit. This is evidence of credit constraints. Investment also increases, though this effect is less salient and is sensitive to sample size and outliers.

We do presume, however, that investment size and the other shocks are unobserved to the econometrician. There is heterogeneity in impact—that is, non-linearities and non-monotonicities, unlike the presumed linear homogenous econometric treatment effect models with instruments which focus on an impact parameter. Of course, the structural model does allow the analyst to understand this diversity and trace out the underlying distribution of gains.

8.7. Measuring the Impact of Financial Intermediation: Linking Theory to Econometric Policy Evaluation

Likewise, potential instruments such as distance to commercial bank branches, or even randomized trials which give some people access do not necessarily have the presumed econometric properties in the context of modified structural models with unobserved heterogeneity. For example, in joint work with Sergio Urzua, we show that the models of occupation choice with an intermediated and non-intermediated sector, as detailed earlier, may have this property. Easier access may cause some but not all households to go out of business, as the not-so-talented but wealthy house-holds find they have higher returns in the bank. Exogenous variation in treatment, or binary near-far categories, allow instrumented impact equations to give the local average treatment effect on income, the incremental income gain coming solely from those newly participating in the program. See Heckman and Vytlacil 2001, Imbens and Angrist 1994, Heckman, Urzua, and Vytlacil 2006, and Rubin 1974. But without further instruments for the other margins of choice we cannot also get the income gain solely from occupation switches induced by the program. The homogeneous-treatment-effect models either assume this kind of selection is negligible or that there are sufficient household and village observables to control for this selection. With this in mind, we turn next to structural models with obstacles to trade and conduct policy experiments in that context.

9

Obstacles to Trade, Enhanced Models of Selection, and the Impact of Policy Variation

This chapter uses structural models and data on the choice of occupation, source of funds, type of loan contract, and loan default to discern that moral hazard, limited commitment, transaction costs, and other obstacles to trade are salient features of the Thai financial landscape. This chapter tests one financial regime against another to judge which obstacle, or set of obstacles, is most important. There is regional variation. There is also evidence of incomplete markets over and above the impact of the obstacles. Policy variation and financial regime change and have rich implications in partial and general equilibrium settings for the distribution of gains and losses as well as for macro dynamics.

The model of occupational choice with heterogeneous talent is modified to make endogenous the choice of whether or not to borrow. This new model also allows investment, ROA, and insurance to be limited even for those with access to it. Various possible financial regimes are tested with the micro data in this partial-equilibrium static context, taking interest rates and wages as given. Specifically, unobserved effort (moral hazard), the possibility of default (collateral-/wealth-backed loans), both problems together simultaneously, and exogenously limited regimes (savings only, borrowing and lending with bankruptcy but incomplete risk-sharing) are each taken to the micro data on (predetermined) wealth and occupation transitions. The underlying parameters of preferences (risk aversion, work aversion), technology (marginal productivity of capital), and talent (relation to education and wealth) are estimated for each regime, and the best fit is determined from non-nested likelihood comparisons. That and auxiliary data on borrowing as a function of wealth are consistent in the prediction that either moral hazard alone or moral hazard with limited liability account well for the overall data. In the Central region, moral hazard is more clearly the dominant concern. The financial regime is less well characterized in the Northeast, and may include, for example, only liability.

Experiments with policy variation allow computation of the distribution of gains and losses to exogenous variation in (regulated on-lending) interest rates, losses (wealth transfers) to branch banks, enhanced collateral (larger borrowing limit), and movement from limited to more complete regimes (e.g., from moral hazard to full information, to be balanced by monitoring costs). The distribution of gains may be high for low-wealth, talented households, as in the earlier occupation-choice dual-sector model, but orders of magnitude at estimated parameter values depend on the experiment and impediment to trade. For example, interest-rate subsidies can yield surprisingly high gains for a few poor talented households if there is a moral hazard problem, and smaller gains for a larger group when limited liability is the problem. Still, this is not the ideal way to help the poor. In an expanded, general-equilibrium context, one wants to move along a Pareto frontier, and this corresponds with direct lump-sum wealth transfers, for example, allowing local banks to make losses with compensation via tax revenue from the government. To facilitate computation we imagine a small open economy in which wages and interest rates are fixed. The larger gains do come from changed access on the extensive margin—that is, placement of funds which allow movement out of autarky, or out of savings only, into an imperfect financial regime.

One cannot distinguish in the data an information-constrained moral-hazard regime from one with more-limited insurance—that is, borrowing and lending with bankruptcy. A savings-only regime fits the partial equilibrium, cross-sectional data best in the distant past, suggesting that financial regimes have become more sophisticated over time. There is some success with the partial-equilibrium life-cycle predictions; those who will eventually set up enterprises in the data save at higher rates and enter business at limited scales. Ironically, the observed wealth-to-occupation transition is shown in this context to be a downward-biased estimate of the gains to wealth transfers or the weakening of collateral constraints. But the models as they stand without transaction costs (or policy restrictions) do not do well with historical macro paths. That is, when limited only by wealth interacted with the constraints, these specific models with information problems or legal impediments tend to go to steady states (without growth) much too quickly.

313

Selection across formal and/or informal lenders can also help to quantify the importance of underlying impediments to trade and help to assess various policy options. Suppose households vary in underlying characteristics: productivity, potential scale of enterprise, wealth, and the availability of collateral. The first two are unobserved by the econometrician, as was talent earlier. Borrowing from formal lenders is at a relatively low interest rate but entails transaction costs and limited, asset-backed loans. Borrowing from informal lenders is at a high interest rate but without enforcement problems. This structural model of selection is estimated via maximum likelihood methods. At estimated parameter values, transaction costs are low for the informal sector. Likewise, the most effective policies involve enhanced collateral or weakened default possibilities. This dominates placement of village funds (lower transaction costs) and interest subsidies (which induce selection into business of less than talented people). But the transaction costs as estimated here are substantially lower than those which rationalized slow transition paths in the earlier endogenous financial-access model.

Households can borrow as a group from the BAAC. Data on repayment rates in these joint-liability groups allow, with explicit choice-based partial-equilibrium static models, an assessment of the importance of obstacles to trade. There is another dimension of the moral hazard problem not mentioned earlier—joint-liability partners may jointly select without outside knowledge the risk of their projects. This might be mitigated by monitoring of non-borrowing members, but there is an incentive constraint which equates the reduced likelihood of joint-liability payment with the increased cost of effort. Another version of the limited-commitment problem not mentioned earlier—borrowers in a joint-liability group may play a strategic game in the decision of whether or not to repay, with the outcome determined as Nash equilibrium. Alternatively, there may be a cooperative, collusive solution against the lender. An additional information problem is adverse selection—that is, at given interest rates, households with safer projects decide not to borrow, depending on outside options. In all these models an increase in the (administered) interest rate lowers repayment rates while an increase in productivity (education) raises them. There are also data relevant to one model at a time: whether or not there is screening of customers, the cost of monitoring, and the magnitude of official penalties. But more often sign restrictions distinguish the models. The key dependent variable is a default rate, specifically whether the BAAC has raised its interest rate on borrowing groups. The right hand side variables include data on the magnitude of joint-liability payments, correlation across project returns, cooperative behavior, loan size, and the prevalence of additional credit options. Again, the information models fit best in the Central region, and, overall and more salient now, the strategic-default model fits best in the Northeast.

Likewise, there are policy implications. Under certain conditions, joint-liability lending Pareto dominates individual lending, if the interest rate is allowed to clear the market. Enhanced penalties for default can be helpful, but if they are from the informal sector households have to be willing to carry out *ex ante* threats to impose them. Likewise, cooperation among borrowers *ex post* can lower welfare. Lowered correlation can lower repayments in the moral hazard project selection model, a caution. Increased credit limits can also cause eventual decreases in repayment, as could the presence of additional outside lenders. This suggests a distinction between *ex ante* and *ex post* competition and the need for long-term contracts and commitment.

Enhanced models of selection focus on insurance and the choice of individual versus joint-liability loans. These offer tests of the presumption of moral hazard. The BAAC offers both individual as well as joint-liability loans. Mutual loans and village funds allow borrowing with co-signers. We observe in the data, borrower choices over these as a function of wealth and inequality. As wealth increases in the cross-section, or with outsiders making larger losses, the prevalence of group loans first decreases and then increases, as in a model comparing relative performance versus group regimes. Likewise, disparity of wealth among potential joint-liability borrowers increases the prevalence of joint-liability loans, as in that model comparison. Note that wealth emerges again as the key state variable here, for choice of financial regime. Inequality and the distribution of wealth matter as well. Under some conditions the risk-sharing group has perfect arrangements internally but limited arrangements externally, as anticipated earlier in the discussion of sub-aggregation.

Related again is the adverse selection model and the decision of whether or not to borrow at all. One measure of a project/household type's risk conforms to the model's prediction—safe types are less inclined to borrow. Another measure that conforms is the cross-sectional relationship with the correlation of project returns—high correlation across projects of members enhances joint-liability loans. 'One Household' and Community Development Department (CDD) covariates and the earlier supply-side instruments are entered here as additional controls. While they are significant, the earlier results are robust. A conjecture is that the conclusions regarding adverse selection and participation on the extensive margin, as well as moral hazard and the selection into and across contracts on the intensive margin, will be robust to (exogenous) variation in financial infrastructure.

Finally, wealth, poverty, inequality, networks, and the organization of industry are co-determined with optimal financial contracts in these models. Imagine in a general equilibrium context that households can borrow or enter into insurance arrangements either as individuals or as groups. Production with a supervisor as in a credit cooperative may alleviate the moral hazard problem. All households are endowed with capital and may vary in talent for the worker or supervisory positions. Interest rates and wages (skill prices) are endogenous in a competitive equilibrium which determines the number and type of firms as well as borrowing/insurance arrangements. Supervision eliminating the moral hazard problem is costly in this model. Rather than exogenously remove the moral hazard problem, its magnitude is determined in equilibrium. Some moral hazard may or may not remain. The higher the economy-wide capital is, the scarcer labor is and the less likely it is to be used up in supervision. There can be limited commitment, the possibility of running off with financed capital. Likewise, there are welfare and impact implications for alleviating this—more inequality (or more transfers/taxes), higher firm values, lower interest rates or prices for capital, and increased wages. Moving along the Pareto frontier via wealth transfers from rich to poor makes individual production and teams with homogenous agents more likely.

Both the level of wealth and the distribution of wealth matter for equilibrium configurations. These would vary over time in a dynamic model with bequests, giving once again the dynamics of growth with inequality and poverty. More generally, networks are endogenous in these types of models. Transition from the relative performance to the group regime tends to occur when rewards exacerbate inequality, while transition from groups to relative performance tends to come with a decrease in utility promise. Thus financial contracts, networks, and industrial organization will evolve optimally in the economy; otherwise the economy will enter suboptimal states.

9.1. Distinguishing Obstacles to Trade from Occupation Choice

The prototypical moral hazard model assumes both consumption c and effort z enter into the contemporary utility function $U(c,z)$ according to

$$U(c, z) = \frac{c^{1-\gamma_1}}{1 - \gamma_1} - \kappa \frac{z^{\gamma_2}}{y_2}. \tag{9.1.1}$$

Household risk aversion is increasing in γ_1; with $\kappa > 0$ and $y_2 > 0$, effort z is painful, giving the household a desire to shirk. Output of a project or business run by the household yields output $q = \theta$ with a probability of success which is increasing in effort z and also increasing in (positive) capital k, according to a Cobb–Douglas specification,

$$P(q = \theta | z, k > 0) = \frac{k^\alpha z^{1-\alpha}}{1 + k^\alpha z^{1-\alpha}}. \tag{9.1.2}$$

Otherwise, $q = 0$ and the project fails with the residual probability. Thus expected output has the usual features. Coefficient θ is meant to capture the underlying talent of the household, as in

$$\ln \theta = \delta_0 + \delta_1 \ln(A) + \delta_2 \ln(1 + S) + \eta \tag{9.1.3}$$

where 1 is added to prevent the log of zero.

In this static specification talent is allowed to be correlated with wealth A and schooling S, as predetermined variables. In a larger, more-dynamic setting these would be endogenous.

The alternative to running a business is to be a wage worker, where $k = 0$, with success of employment at wage w related again to effort,

$$P(q = w | z, k = 0) = \frac{z}{1 + z}. \tag{9.1.4}$$

As anticipated, the household decides on its occupation, as earlier, but here also on the level of finance. In sum, the choice problem is:

$$\max \begin{cases} \max_{z} w \dfrac{z}{1+z} - \kappa \dfrac{z^{\gamma_2}}{\gamma_2} + rA \quad \text{if} \quad k = 0 (\text{wage worker}) \\[2ex] \max_{z,k} \theta \dfrac{k^\alpha z^{1-\alpha}}{1 + k^\alpha z^{1-\alpha}} - \kappa \dfrac{z^{\gamma_2}}{\gamma_2} + r(A - k) \\[1ex] \text{if} \quad k > 0, \quad k \leq A(\text{entrepreneur, net saver}) \\[2ex] \max_{z,k} \theta \dfrac{k^\alpha z^{1-\alpha}}{1 + k^\alpha z^{1-\alpha}} - \kappa \dfrac{z^{\gamma_2}}{\gamma_2} - r(A, \theta)(k - A) \dfrac{k^\alpha z^{1-\alpha}}{1 + k^\alpha z^{1-\alpha}} \text{if} \quad k > 0, \\[1ex] k > A(\text{entrepreneur, net borrower}) \end{cases}$$

$$\tag{9.1.5}$$

For clarity, we focus first on finance and introduce insurance subsequently. If the decision is to be a worker, then wealth A can be put into savings at gross interest rate $r = (1+\hat{r})$. If the decision is to set up a firm, then there are two possibilities: self-finance with the excess put in savings accounts, or borrow at rate schedule $r(A, \theta)$, where repayment is possible only if the firm does not fail. The latter creates a potential divergence of incentives between borrower and lender. Lenders maximize profits, but free entry is imagined to push expected profits to zero for each wealth and talent group, on the assumption the lender has perfect information on wealth and talent. This yields:

$$r(A, \theta) \frac{k^\alpha z^{1-\alpha}}{1 + k^\alpha z^{1-\alpha}} = r, \; for \; \forall k > A, \forall \theta, \forall A. \qquad (9.1.6)$$

More generally, with risk aversion, let $c(q)$ denote the final consumption of the borrower. Then, the lender breaks even. Constraint for each (z,k) firm unit rate for a household of wealth A:

$$\sum_q \left[q - \left(c(q) \right) \right] P(q \,|\, z, k) = r(k - A). \qquad (9.1.7)$$

Thus, the cost of funds at exogenous outside interest rate r must be covered by an insurance premium and loan repayment, unless the institution takes a government subsidy (which can be analyzed by creating a gap of various sizes). The market will in effect maximize the utility of each household type (A, θ).

There are potential additional constraints on the problem. The lender may be concerned about repayment and only lend up to a proportion of wealth. Suppose, for example, as in Banerjee 2003 (and the earlier discussion of informal credit) that the borrower is tempted to default but if he were to do so he would be captured with a specified probability and forced to pay a penalty. This would yield $k \leq \lambda A$ as a possible constraint, as is assumed in Evans and Jovanovic 1989. Alternatively, effort z may be unobserved, in which case the borrower will choose z to solve its own sub-problem, with first-order condition

$$[\theta - r(A, \theta)(k - A)] \left[\frac{(1 - \alpha)k^\alpha z^{-\alpha}}{(1 + k^\alpha z^{1-\alpha})^2} \right] - \kappa z^{y_2 - 1} = 0. \qquad (9.1.8)$$

The more-general specification, allowing risk aversion, is the standard incentive compatibility constraint,

$$\sum_q U[c(q), z]P(q \mid z, k) \geq \sum_q U[c(q), z']P(q|z', k) \text{ for all } z', k > 0.$$

(9.1.9)

In the analysis here we turn each constraint off and on, to discuss various financial regimes: limited liability/default alone, moral hazard alone, or both in combination.

Figure 9.1 indicates both the objective function and set of potential constraints for the case of risk neutrality, $\gamma_1=0$, at parameters close to those estimated in the data (see below). Utility for the household decreases as one moves away from the first best, the solution without constraints. This appears as a satiation or 'bliss' point in the space of k,z combinations in the diagram. The moral hazard constraint 9.1.8 is a set of (k,z) pairs which satisfy the first-order condition and the solution to the moral hazard

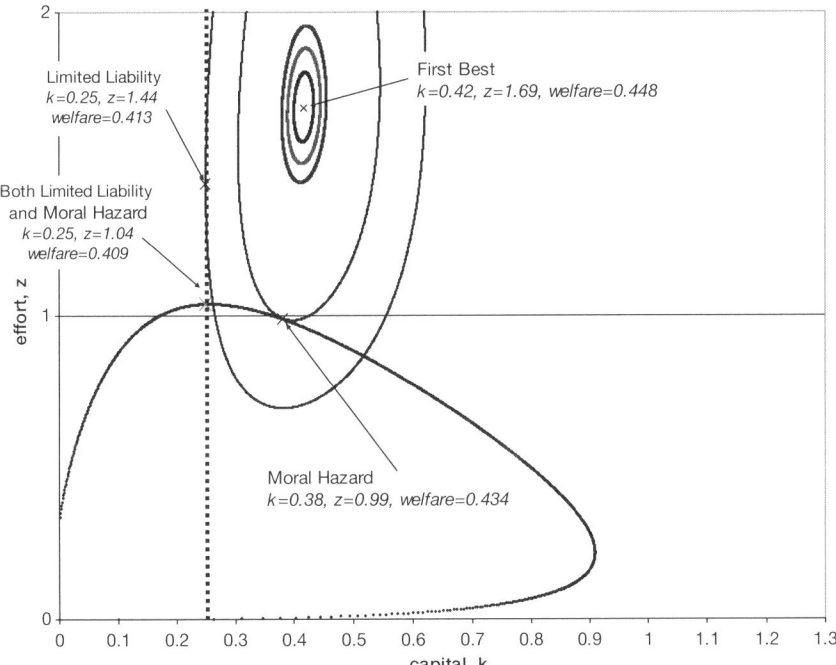

Fig. 9.1. *Configuration of constraints*

Notes: Assignments of capital (k) and effort (z) for the entrepreneurs in the risk-neutral-model: moral hazard, limited liability, and both moral hazard and limited liability. Assumptions: $\theta=2.56$, A=0.10, $a=0.78$, k=0.08, $Y^2=1.00$, r=1.10, $\lambda=2.50$

Source: Paulson, Townsend, and Karaivanov 2006.

problem is the tangency of an indifference curve with that locus. Note the relatively low effort and high capitalization. The limited liability constraint set $k \leq \lambda A$ is on or to the left of the vertical line segment, and the limited liability solution is indicated as well; higher z and lower k. Potentially, both constraints are binding, where the two loci intersect, and in this case preferences do not matter. Increases and wealth A in the cross-section move constraints northeast.

The risk-neutral model described above includes special cases which have been studied in the literature. For example, Evans and Jovanovic 1989 can be derived by first eliminating a role for entrepreneurial effort by setting z to 1 and setting the disutility of effort, k, to 0. Next, assume that output is a deterministic function of capital, k, so that $q = \theta k^{\alpha}$ and that loans must be fully repaid in the amount rk, no matter what. The maximum loan size is determined by the limited liability constraint, at equality—namely, $k = \lambda A$ so maximum debt is $(\lambda - 1)A$, where $\lambda \geq 1$. Apart from the normalized probabilities, these assumptions deliver exactly the limited liability model of Evans and Jovanovic. The likelihood of becoming an entrepreneur is increasing in wealth and entrepreneurial talent. Holding wealth fixed, more talented entrepreneurs are more likely to be constrained. Entrepreneurial households who face a binding limited liability constraint will borrow and invest more when wealth increases.

We can also use our framework to generate the model of Aghion and Bolton (1997). Assume that capital k can be either 0 or 1. In other words, firms must be capitalized at $k=1$. Eliminate any role for entrepreneurial talent by setting θ equal to 1, and assume that the income of wage workers is unaffected by effort, or equivalently assume that $z=1$ for wage workers. Finally, assume that γ_2 is equal to 2, so that the disutility of effort is quadratic. Apart from the normalized probabilities, these assumptions deliver exactly the model of Aghion and Bolton. As they stress, effort, z, which must be incentive compatible, will be a monotonically increasing function of wealth. As wealth increases, the probability of entrepreneurial success thus increases, which means that wealthier households will face lower interest rates. On the other end, low-wealth households face such high interest rates that they may choose not to borrow, they become wage-workers rather than entrepreneurs. Entrepreneurial households with wealth less than 1 must borrow an amount equal to $1-A$ to finance their firm, which, as noted, must be capitalized at $k = 1$. These households are subject to a binding incentive compatibility constraint. In contrast to the limited-liability models of Evans and Jovanovic 1989, when wealth increases for these constrained households, they will borrow *less* (and by construction continue to invest the same amount in their firms).

More generally, solutions to the various financial regimes can be determined numerically by a linear programming problem which assigns consumption $c \in C$, output $q \in Q$, effort $z \in Z$, and capital $k \in K$ according to probability $\pi(c,q,z,k)$. This formulation allows for risk aversion. The objective function for a household of talent θ, wealth A, and schooling S is

$$\max_{\pi(c,q,z,k) \geq 0} \sum_{c,q,z,k} \pi(c,q,z,k)U(c,z). \qquad (9.1.10)$$

A constraint

$$\sum_c \pi(c,\bar{q},\bar{z},\bar{k}) = \tilde{p}(\bar{q} \mid \bar{z},\bar{k}) \sum_{c,q} \pi(c,q,\bar{z},\bar{k}) \text{ for all } \bar{q},\bar{z},\bar{k} \qquad (9.1.11)$$

ensures that what appears to be an endogenous likelihood of output q is in fact consistent with the technology in nature, $\tilde{p}(\bar{q} \mid \bar{z},\bar{k})$; that is, if $k>0$, $q = \theta'$ for firms, and $q=w$ for wage earners. Also,

$$\sum_{c,q,z,k} \pi(c,q,z,k)(c-q) = r \sum_{c,q,z,k} \pi(c,q,z,k)(A-k) \qquad (9.1.12)$$

is again the zero profit or break-even constraint for the financial sector. Again,

$$\sum_{c,q} \pi(c,q,z,k)U(c,z) \geq \sum_{c,q} \pi(c,q,z,k)\frac{\tilde{p}(q|z\prime,k)}{\tilde{p}(q|z,k)} U(c,z\prime) \text{ for all } k > 0 \; z, z\prime$$

$$(9.1.13)$$

is the moral hazard constraint where the household contemplates various alternative (lower) efforts z'. The limited-liability constraint is imposed by varying the grid of possible capital assignments k given wealth A and specified parameter λ. Technological probability $\tilde{p}(q \mid z, k)$ comes from the earlier specification—that is, if positive, $q=\theta$ for firms and $q=1$ for wage earners.

The various regimes are estimated with the Townsend Thai 1997 retrospective data (see Table 9.1), utilizing observed-occupation transitions into business, initial wealth A, and schooling S as in the earlier occupation-choice model. The underlying parameters are found as those that maximize the likelihood of the data, as created by solution to program. The likelihood function uses the optimal contract $\pi^*(c,q,z,k \mid \theta,A,S)$, computed by calling to the linear-programming commercial library CPLEX. We obtain the probability of being an entrepreneur—namely, those with positive k,

Table 9.1. *Whole sample structural estimates*

	Moral hazard	Limited liability	Both
1. Risk aversion, talent (income)			
γ_1	0.0985	0.0982	0.1025
	(0.0125)	(0.0003)	(0.0046)
γ_2	2.1007	1.1713	2.4753
	(0.3216)	(0.0037)	(0.1797)
κ	0.1257	0.1079	0.1190
	(0.0227)	(0.0003)	(0.0062)
a	0.7775	0.6937	0.7208
	(0.0325)	(0.0165)	(0.0108)
λ	—	22.9885	20.8082
		(0.0727)	(1.4882)
Log likelihood	−0.4038	−0.4706	−0.4683
2. Risk neutral, talent (income)			
γ_2	1.5801	1.3475	1.5511
	(0.0243)	(0.0167)	(0.0171)
κ	0.0530	0.0675	0.0789
	(0.0009)	(0.0009)	(0.0008)
a	0.7700	0.6800	0.6902
	(0.0099)	(0.0273)	(0.0043)
λ	—	24.5000	28.3848
		(0.3307)	(0.3095)
Log likelihood	−0.4104	−0.4608	−0.4372
3. Risk aversion, talent (percentage entrepreneur)			
γ_1	1.0737	0.0668	0.7781
	(0.0123)	(0.0004)	(0.0035)
γ_2	1.0000	1.0000	1.0000
	(0.0192)	(0.0141)	(0.0105)
κ	0.0904	0.0722	0.1219
	(0.0001)	(0.0001)	(0.0016)
a	0.9780	0.9702	0.5062
	(0.0032)	(0.0003)	(0.0066)
λ		10.7281	1.9014
		(0.0305)	(0.0042)
Log likelihood	−0.4590	−0.7514	−0.6064
4. Risk aversion, estimated talent			
γ_1	0.5753	0.0957	0.1002
	(0.0175)	(0.0002)	(0.0005)
γ_2	1.0494	1.2314	1.0939
	(0.0171)	(0.0120)	(0.0061)
κ	1.2312	0.9889	1.0022
	(0.0649)	(0.0049)	(0.0065)
a	0.7931	0.2283	0.7985
	(0.0148)	(0.0030)	(0.0188)
δ_0	1.0175	0.8853	0.1002
	(0.0464)	(0.0108)	(0.0007)
δ_1	0.0604	0.0285	0.0503
	(0.0218)	(0.0002)	(0.0004)
δ_2	0.0516	−0.2226	0.3005
	(0.0053)	(0.0046)	(0.0018)
λ	—	21.0118	5.0088
		(0.2223)	(0.0970)
Log likelihood	−0.3996	−0.4134	−0.4035

Bootstrap standard errors are in parentheses. Parameter estimates allow various specification talent/income.
Source: Paulson, Townsend, and Karaivanov 2006.

$$\pi^E(\theta, A, S) \equiv \sum_{c,q,z,k} \pi^*(c, q, z, k | \theta, A, S, k > 0). \tag{9.1.14}$$

The probability of being a worker is simply $1 - \pi^E(\theta, A, S)$. Talent shock η is not seen by the econometrician, so a function $\bar{\pi}^E(A,S)$ is computed as integral, taking expectations over 9.1.14 using 9.1.3. We also compute only at twenty grid points for wealth A and separately estimate a relationship between wealth and schooling. To get the probability for all data points, we use a cubic spline interpolation of $\bar{\pi}^E(A,S)$. In sum, the probability of being an entrepreneur given wealth A_i and schooling S_i for household i in the data is denoted by $\bar{H}^E(A_i, S_i \mid \psi)$, where $\psi \equiv (\gamma_1, \gamma_2, \kappa, a, \delta_0, \delta_1, \delta_2, \lambda)$ is the vector of model parameters: risk aversion, curvature in effort, work aversion, productivity, talent parameters $\delta_0, \delta_1, \delta_2$, and limited-liability parameter λ, if estimated. Let E_i be a binary variable, which takes the value of 1 if agent i becomes an entrepreneur in the data, and 0 otherwise. The log-likelihood function $L(\psi)$ for n households is given by:

$$L(\psi) = \frac{1}{n} \sum_{i=1}^{n} E_i \ln H(A_i, S_i | \psi) + (1 - E_i) \ln \left(1 - H(A_i, S_i | \psi) \right). \tag{9.1.15}$$

Various alternative assumptions are made about talent, to match either observed income differentials, as begged from the earlier discussion, or the average number of firms in the data (again, something which the likelihoods may miss) (see Table 9.1). For the most part, the parameters make sense, with (modest) amounts of risk aversion, relatively high marginal productivities of capital, and so on. The parameter λ is occasionally in the range of two, as theory might suggest. Talent is estimated to increase with wealth and schooling.

Beneath these estimated parameters lie the assignments of capital, effort and consumption, and their variation with wealth, according to which constraint or constraints might be causing problems (see Figure 9.2 (a)–(f)). For example, with limited liability, capital increases with wealth but the opposite is true under moral hazard.

A Vuong (1989) likelihood ratio test for non-nested models provides the key measure of which financial regime is closest to the actual data. Moral hazard is by and large the financial regime which does best, both overall and without exception, in the Central Region. Limited liability alone cannot explain the data overall, but it may act in combination with moral hazard, and may be of greater importance in the Northeast (see Table 9.2 (a)–(f)).

An auxiliary implication of the model is that credit should be increasing with wealth, and net savings decreasing with wealth, for constrained

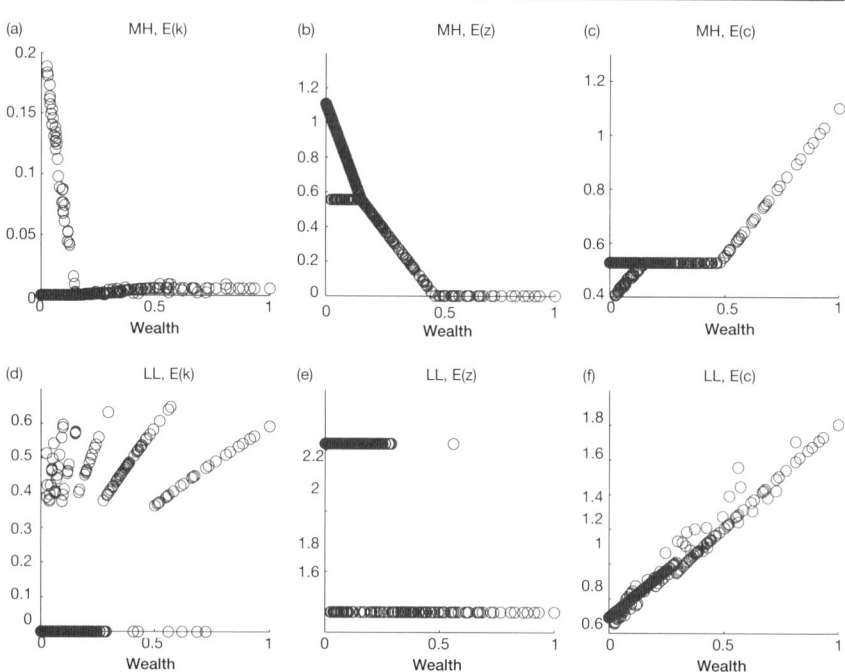

Fig. 9.2(a)–(f). *Assignments of capital, effort, and consumption, and their variation with wealth*

Notes: MH = moral hazard; LL = limited liability, $E(k)$, $E(z)$, $E(c)$ are expected utilities of capital, effort, and consumption.

Source: Karaivanov unpub. research note.

households in the limited-liability regime. On the other hand, higher wealth would allow greater self-finance, which is a good thing in the moral hazard regime when the incentive constraint is binding—only constrained households should be borrowing. The evidence is consistent with moral hazard in the Central region. Net savings is increasing in non-financial wealth for constrained households overall and in the Central region (bottom, Table 9.3 (a)–(b)) and being constrained is an indicator of borrowing there. These results are robust to demographic controls.

The variation in regional results begs an explanation. It may have something to do with the varying mix of lenders. In the Central region, BAAC, commercial banks, and the informal sector all provide services and potentially compete with one another. Recall the earlier figures. In the Northeast, the BAAC is the dominant provider. It is as yet unclear, however, why information would be the major obstacle in the Central region and a willingness to default the major obstacle in the Northeast.

Table 9.2(a)–(c) *Comparison of financial regimes, Vuong test results*

	MH v. LL	MH v. Both	LL v. Both	Best Overall Fit
A. Whole sample				
Risk aversion, talent (income)	MH***	MH***	Both	MH
	(0.0000)	(0.0001)	(0.8866)	
Risk neutral, talent (income)	MH***	MH**	Both***	MH
	(0.0010)	(0.0252)	(0.0033)	
Risk aversion,	MH***	MH***	Both***	MH
talent (percentage entrepreneur)	(0.0000)	(0.0000)	(0.0000)	
Risk aversion, estimated talent	MH***	MH	Both***	MH or Both
	(0.0046)	(0.3402)	(0.0046)	
B. Northeast				
Risk aversion, talent (income)	MH***	MH*	Both***	MH
	(0.0071)	(0.0519)	(0.0081)	
Risk neutral, talent (income)	MH***	MH***	Tie	MH
	(0.0073)	(0.0073)	(0.1018)	
Risk aversion,	MH***	MH***	Both***	MH
talent (percentage entrepreneur)	(0.0000)	(0.0012)	(0.0000)	
Risk aversion, estimated talent	MH	Both	Both	MH, LL or
	(0.4213)	(0.3718)	(0.1846)	Both
C. Central				
Risk aversion, talent (income)	MH***	MH***	Both	MH
	(0.0003)	(0.0008)	(0.1897)	
Risk neutral, talent (income)	MH***	MH**	Both**	MH
	(0.0007)	(0.0263)	(0.0133)	
Risk aversion, talent (high)	MH***	MH***	Both***	MH
	(0.0000)	(0.0000)	(0.0027)	
Risk aversion, estimated talent	MH***	MH**	Both	MH
	(0.0004)	(0.0426)	(0.1342)	

Notes: MH = Moral Hazard; LL = Limited Liability; Both = Moral Hazard and Limited Liability. The abbreviation for model which best fits the data in the pairwise comparison is reported. The P-value for the Vuong tests are in parentheses. *** indicates significance at at least the 1% level; ** at at least the 5% level; and * at at least the 10% level.

Source: Paulson, Townsend, and Karaivanov 2006.

These structural models allow a quantification of the gains and losses to various possible policy interventions, moving from the contemporary situation at estimated parameter values for each potential regime. Suppose we were able to lower the borrowing/lending rate in this partial equilibrium setting from 1.10 to 1.05. This has a different effect depending on the regime. There is a tendency for talented poor borrowers to gain, but in the moral hazard regime the gains can be higher than under limited liability. Still, the number of winners overall is higher under limited liability. In both regimes, there are some high-wealth losers. In both financial regimes, the number of entrepreneurs increases. Under the first, best interest rate effects exist, but are not so dramatic (see Figure 9.3 (a)–(f)).

Table 9.3(a)–(b). *Probit estimates of being a net borrower and regression estimates of net savings, business households*

(a) Probit estimates of being a net borrower

	Whole sample		Northeast		Central region	
	dF/dx*	Z-statistic	dF/dx*	Z-statistic	dF/dx*	Z-statistic
Constrained (=1 if constrained, 0 otherwise)*	0.0849	1.55	−0.0491	−0.48	0.1321	1.97
Wealth six years ago[†]	−0.0013	−0.24	0.1880	1.75	0.0007	0.12
Age of head	−0.0115	−0.82	−0.0149	−0.58	−0.0116	−0.67
Age of head squared	0.0001	0.65	0.0001	0.47	0.0001	0.49
Years of schooling (head)	0.0049	0.47	−0.0027	−0.16	0.0010	0.07
♯ of Adult females in household	0.0494	1.37	0.1320	1.81	0.0268	0.62
♯ of Adult males in household	−0.0701	−2.05	−0.1838	−2.64	−0.0334	−0.82
♯ of Children (<18 years) in household	0.0344	1.47	0.1338	2.63	0.0059	0.21
Observed Frequency	0.5457		0.6066		0.5146	
Predicted Frequency at mean of X	0.5483		0.6367		0.5153	
Log Likelihood	−237.02		−70.50		−158.47	
Pseudo R-squared	4.70%		13.79%		4.28%	
Number of observations	361		122		239	

(b) Regression estimates of net savings, business households

	Whole sample		Northeast		Central region	
	Coeff.	T-statistic	Coeff.	T-statistic	Coeff.	T-statistic
Wealth six years ago (constrained business)[†]	0.048	4.32	−0.004	0.05	0.048	3.63
Wealth six years ago (unconstrained business)[†]	0.012	1.42	0.383	3.31	0.012	1.19
Age of head	9592.724	0.52	5639.596	0.29	15814.300	0.60
Age of head squared	−93.922	−0.56	−71.272	−0.41	−161.393	−0.68
Years of schooling (head)	−23179.890	−1.67	−12283.410	−0.96	−28433.790	−1.35
♯ of Adult females in household	−105875.200	−2.18	−133223.000	−2.59	−104812.200	−1.56
♯ of Adult males in household	108636.700	2.37	60962.520	1.22	140117.500	2.22
♯ of Children (<18 years) in household	37710.180	1.21	−60660.900	−1.68	64761.760	1.54
Constant	−234535.400	−0.48	121595.300	0.25	−461081.300	−0.65
Adjusted R-squared	7.86%		9.94%		8.71%	
Number of observations	361		122		239	

Notes: Net savings is defined to be financial assets plus loans owned to household minus debt. Dummy variables are marked by an asterisk. [†]Wealth six years ago is made up of the value of household assets, agricultural assets, and land. Number in table is estimated coefficient multiplied by 1,000,000. The sample excludes the top 1% of households by wealth. The estimates also include controls for past membership/patronage of various financial institutions and organizations.

Source: Paulson, Townsend, and Karaivanov 2006.

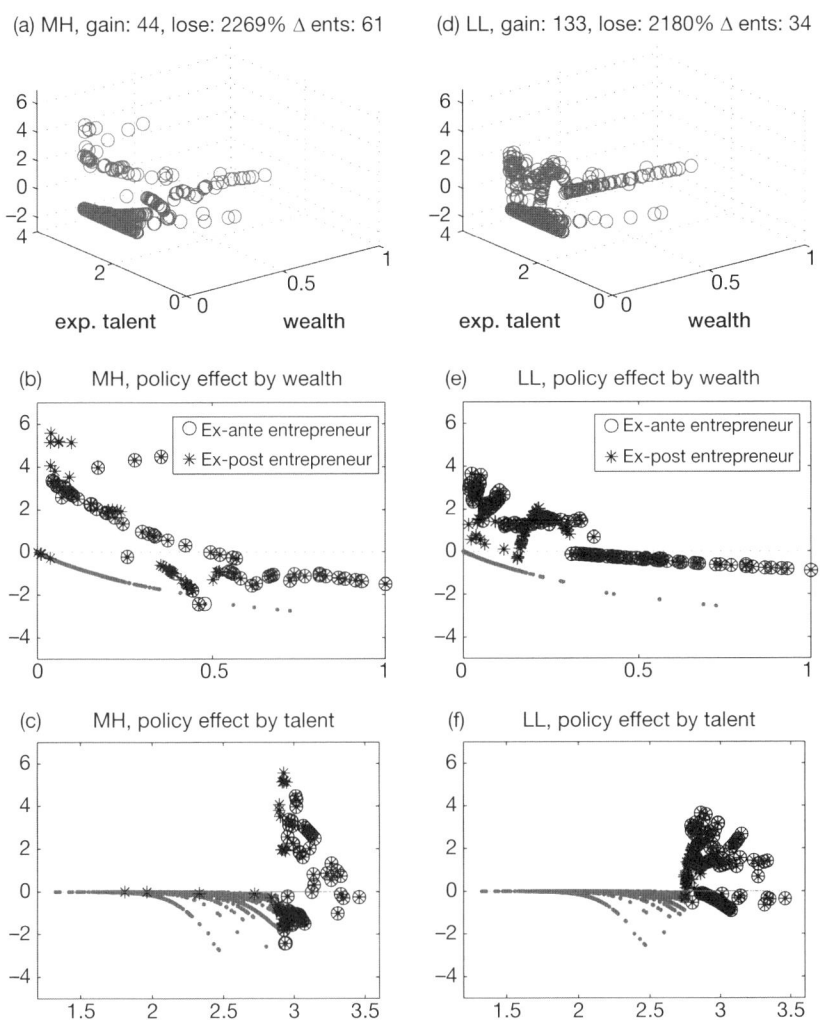

Fig. 9.3(a)–(f). *Quantification of the gains and losses to various possible policy interventions*

r = 1.05 (down/consumption supplements)
Notes: MH = moral hazard; LL = limited liability. Ex-ante E denotes someone who was an entrepreneur before the policy change, ex-post E is someone who shifts into business as a result of policy change.
Source: Karaivanov unpub. research note.

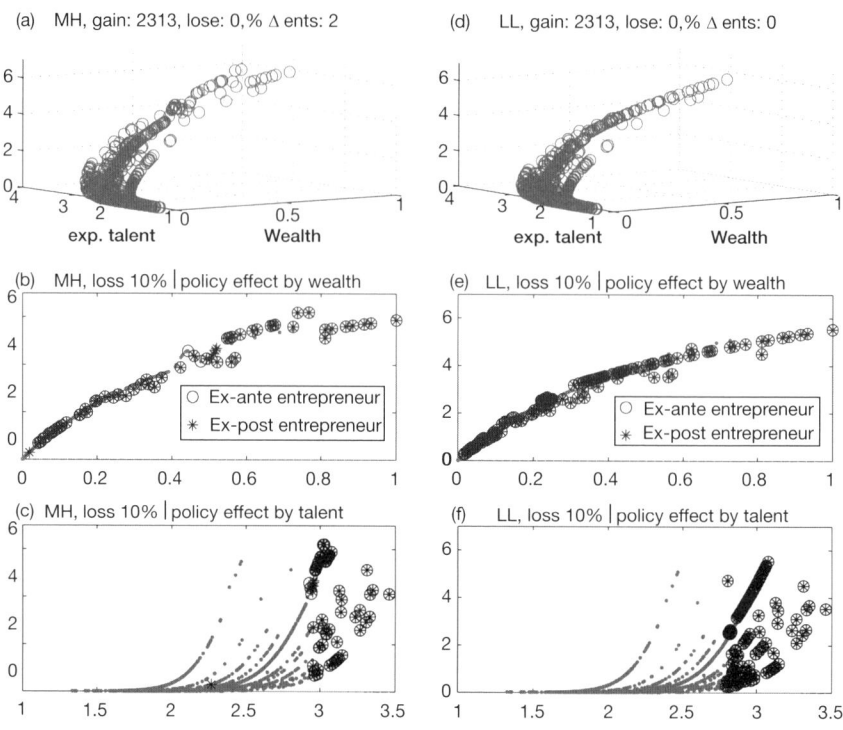

Fig. 9.4(a)–(f). *Consumption supplements*

Notes: MH = moral hazard; LL = limited liability. Ex-ante E denotes someone who was an entrepreneur before the policy change, ex-post E is someone who shifts into business as a result of policy change.

Source: Karaivanov unpub. research note.

Holding the interest rate fixed, we allow lump sum transfers in the sense of allowing banks to make losses (10 per cent). This is potentially more efficient, and consumption equivalent gains are larger. Again, the gains are larger for the moral hazard regime relative to limited liability. In neither regime is there any substantial change in the number of entrepreneurs (see Figure 9.4(a)–(f)).

Likewise, eliminate moral hazard or limited liability. A move from moral hazard to full information again benefits the talented poor and is substantial enough that costly monitoring in terms of lost output might be justified. Of course, in the model the talent is known by the bank, which is unrealistic. Changes in the limited liability parameter down (or up) are associated with gains (or losses) particularly for the talented poor as well.

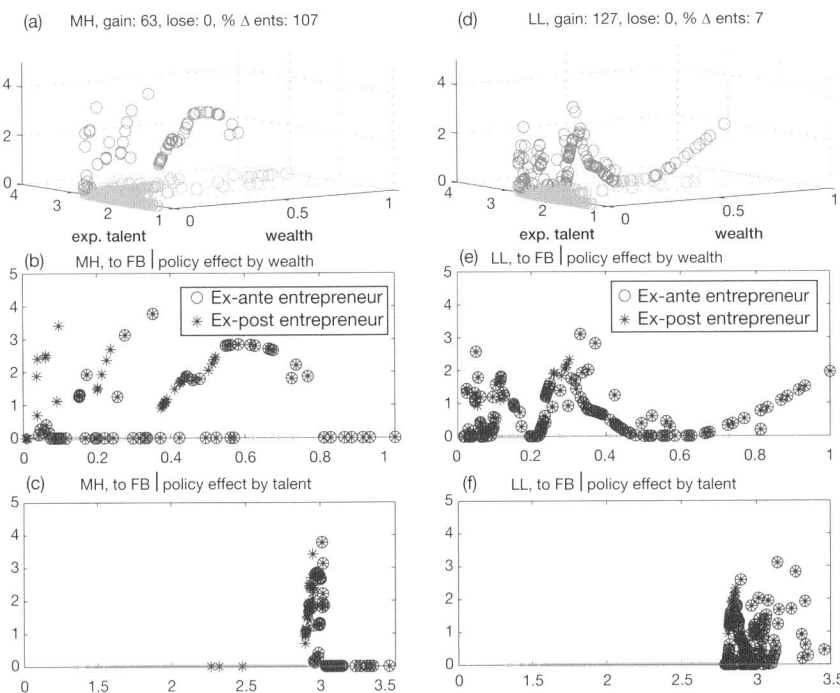

Fig. 9.5(a)–(f): *Moral hazard or limited liability eliminated*

Notes: MH = moral hazard; LL = limited liability. Ex-ante E denotes someone who was an entrepreneur before the policy change, ex-post E is someone who shifts into business as a result of policy change.

Source: Karaivanov unpub. research note.

The fraction of households as firms can vary considerably (e.g., up 75 per cent) (see Figure 9.5(a)–(f)).

9.2. Exogenous Incomplete Markets

Various incomplete regimes can be considered; here we report on Karaivanov (2005). In somewhat similar notation, let $p^e(z,k)$ denote the probability for an entrepreneur of successful outcome $q_h = \theta$, and the residual be the probability of failure, $q_l = 0$. $p^w(z)$ is the associated probability for a worker of getting paid a high wage, w_h, otherwise it is zero.

Under savings, only the difference between wealth A and capital k is if any is put in the bank at interest rate r. Workers have nothing to finance and save A automatically. Thus, the problem for entrepreneurs is:

$$\max_{z,k} \; p^e(z,k)U(c_h, z) + \left(1 - p^e(z,k)\right)U(c_l, z)$$

$$
\begin{aligned}
s.t. \quad & c_h = \theta + r(A - k) \\
& c_l = r(A - k) \\
& 0 \leq k \leq A
\end{aligned}
\tag{9.2.1}
$$

and for wage-earners it is:

$$\max_{z,k} \; p^w(z)U(c_h, z) + (1 - p^w(z))U(c_l, z)$$

$$
\begin{aligned}
s.t. \quad & c_h = w_h + rA \\
& c_l = rA
\end{aligned}
\tag{9.2.2}
$$

The borrowing/lending regime with bankruptcy is similar except that when investment k is greater than wealth A, the interest rate R is adjusted so that the bank breaks even: $R = \dfrac{r}{p^e\left(z(R), k(R)\right)}$. The borrower takes the rate $R = R(A, \theta)$ as given, but the modeler must solve for the rate as part of the equilibrium specification. This was considered before under risk neutrality, but if imposed under risk aversion, and contingencies are not added to the loan contract, then the financial regime is limited and exogenously incomplete. In sum, the problem is:

$$\max_{z,k} \; p^e(z,k)U(c_h, z) + (1 - p^e(z,k))U(c_l, z)$$

$$
\begin{aligned}
s.t. \quad & c_h = \theta - R(k - A) \\
& c_l = 0
\end{aligned}
\tag{9.2.3}
$$

An information-constrained moral hazard regime was considered previously, as in Paulson, Townsend, and Karaivanov 2006 (PTK). For numerical examples we let preferences and technology be as in PTK and derive a likelihood which depends on parameters ϕ and on the financial regime.

Again, consumption, the degree of insurance over success and failure states, effort, borrowing, investment, and the probability of being an entrepreneur all vary with wealth (see Figures 9.6 and 9.7). The profiles depend on the financial regime. Effort is generally higher in the incomplete regimes and rises quickly with wealth, as these provide less insurance and greater incentives to be diligent, even for the poor. Insurance, the difference in consumption between high and low states, increases as one moves from savings only to borrowing/lending only to the moral hazard insurance regime. Primarily, the increased insurance comes from a diminished consumption premium for success. Borrowing rises with wealth in the borrowing/lending-only regime at very low levels of wealth because investment is

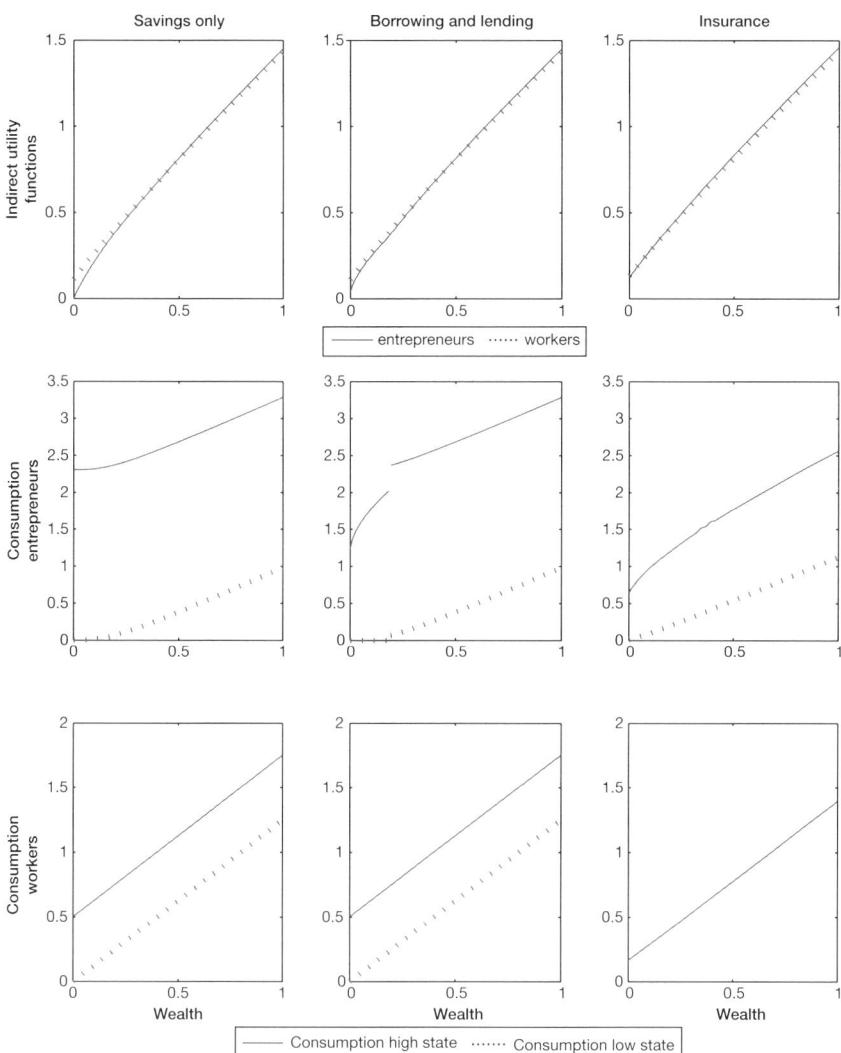

Fig. 9.6. *Static model implications 1*

Source: Karaivanov 2003.

increasing with wealth there, but then at higher wealth, and as in the other models, borrowing declines with wealth (investment increases at a slow rate, and so savings increases and borrowing drops dramatically). The sharpest rise in the enterprise transition wealth diagram comes with the endogenously incomplete regime, so evidently this is a distinction which matters in the estimates with the data. *Ex ante* wealth lotteries allow for

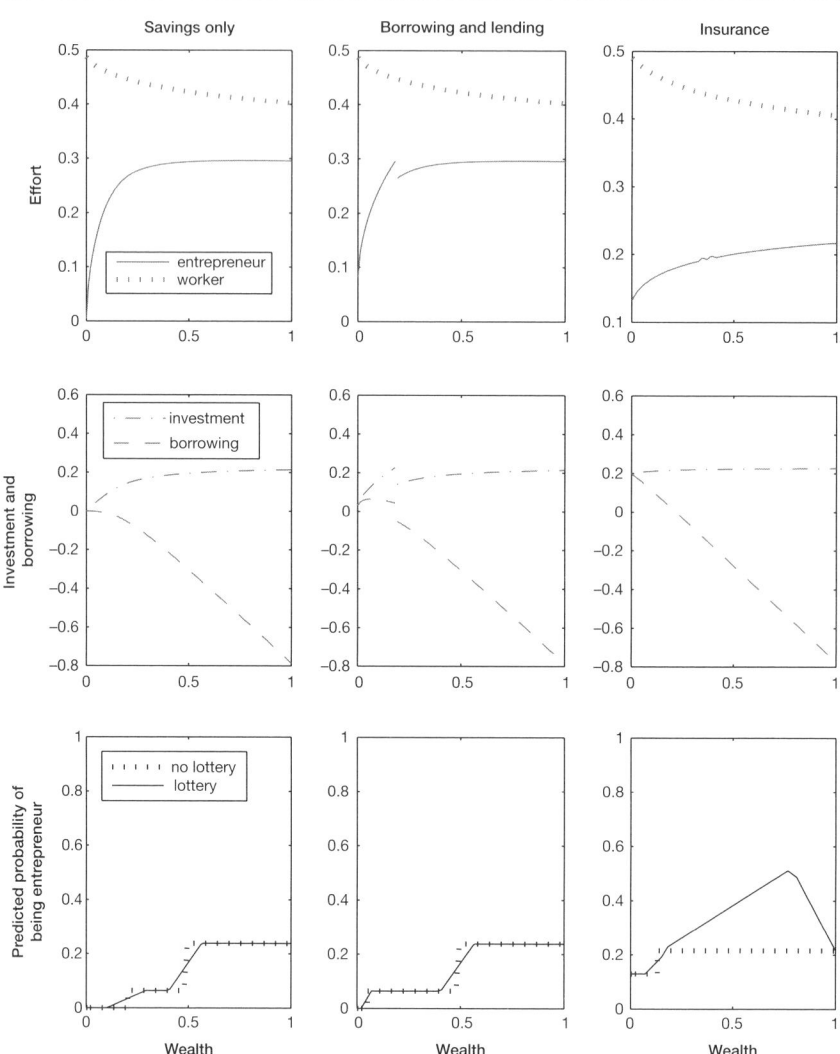

Fig. 9.7. *Static model implications 2*

Notes: See Table 9.4 for parameter values. Parameter, = 0.1012, = 1.5167, = 0.3934, = 0.8088, = 1.0017, = 2.3000, = 0.5034, = 0.2500. * The interest rate *r* is exogenously determined in the dynamic simulations.

Source: Karaivanov 2003.

early gains in all regimes, and smooth out the enterprise wealth transition diagram.

The savings-only regime is typically rejected in the Townsend Thai data (see Table 9.4). But it is difficult to distinguish the limited borrowing/

Table 9.4. *Savings-only regime*

N	(percentage) Business	Stratification	Comparison Z-statistics					
			Contracts without lotteries			Contracts with lotteries		
			SNL v BNL	SNL v INL	BNL v INL	SL v BL	SL v IL	BL v IL
2313	13.8	Whole sample	-4.1471**	-3.8197**	0.9661	-2.5688**	-1.9946**	0.9102
1091	19.2	Central	-1.5358	-1.6860*	-0.6282	-1.7124*	-0.7806	1.1583
1222	9.1	Northeast	-1.1582	-1.2779	-0.1041	-0.6869	-2.0217**	-0.2764
1157	12.6	Wealth below median	-0.1354	-0.1906	-0.1849	0.0357	-0.9423	-1.0632
1156	15.1	Wealth above median	-0.5959	0.3785	0.3952	-0.2858	0.5400	0.5503
455	9.0	Education < 4 yrs	-0.6780	-0.5392	-0.1611	-0.1069	-0.0424	0.0920
1554	13.8	Education = 4 yrs	-4.1975**	-4.2849**	0.9752	-2.1029**	-1.7535*	0.8791
304	21.1	Education > 4 yrs	0.1908	0.3121	0.0463	0.3138	0.4651	0.2171
1927	12.8	No formal credit	-3.9320**	-3.2705**	0.4407	-0.6726	0.3766	1.7073*
386	19.2	Formal credit	-0.5545	-0.7354	-0.1882	-0.1079	0.0152	0.1033
1388	16.1	Any debt	-3.1712**	-3.2053**	0.3873	-1.8734*	-1.2939	0.9408
925	10.4	No debt	-0.6656	-0.2876	0.9157	-0.3331	-1.2774	-0.4402
231	15.1	Northeast, BAAC	-1.1406	-0.5817	-0.2598	-0.2440	-1.2935	-0.5956
150	26.0	Central, BAAC	-2.8807**	-2.4783**	-0.6522	0.5397	0.6003	-0.1715

Notes: S = saving; B = borrowing; I = endogenous incomplete insurance; NL = no lottery; L = lottery; negative value indicates second regime dominates in the comparison.

Source: Karaivanov 2003.

lending, *b-l* with bankruptcy regime from the endogenous insurance, moral hazard regime. In this sense, the data provide (weak) evidence that contemporary financial regimes may be incomplete. One exception may be revealing. Limiting attention to those who do not borrow formally (only borrow informally), the *b-l* limited regime fits best. This suggests that informal markets are not a good substitute for a more-sophisticated formal financial market.

9.2.1. Welfare Experiments and the Dynamics of Financial Regimes

Historically, using the SES cross-section for the young in 1976, Karaivanov finds the more-limited savings-only regimes fit best (see Table 9.5). This indicates more decisively the relatively low level or incompleteness of the formal and informal markets early on. As indicated, there are also gains from going from limited regimes such as savings only to more complete regimes, as if incomplete markets were filled in, in some way. But by far the largest gains come from moving from financial autarky to moral hazard or from financial autarky to limited liability regimes. If the move is from 'savings only' to constrained borrowing/lending, then the range of gains is considerably less. These results suggest that access on the extensive margin may yet be the primary determinate of the distribution of welfare gains. Implicitly, obstacles to movement on the extensive margin are going to have to be large to rationalize the data.

Likewise, these occupation-choice financial regimes can be appended to a dynamic model and time paths examined. Given an initial distribution and parameters also from the SES, one can allow an end-of-period myopic savings rule, to link one period to the next, as in earlier occupation-choice dual model. The interest rate and degree of financial deepening are endogenous too. But the dualism is attenuated. The credit market within each period is now not perfect for those with access, though access is now endogenous (i.e., autarky is self-determined).

Table 9.5. *Model comparisons, 1979 Socio-Economic Survey, Young Household Data*

Stratification	BL v SL	SL v IL	BL v IL
Whole sample	−0.2297*	0.7722	0.5865
Wealth below median	−0.4875	0.3914	0.1179
Wealth above median	−1.1841	0.3729	−0.7878

* The reported values are Z-statistics.

Source: Karaivanov 2003.

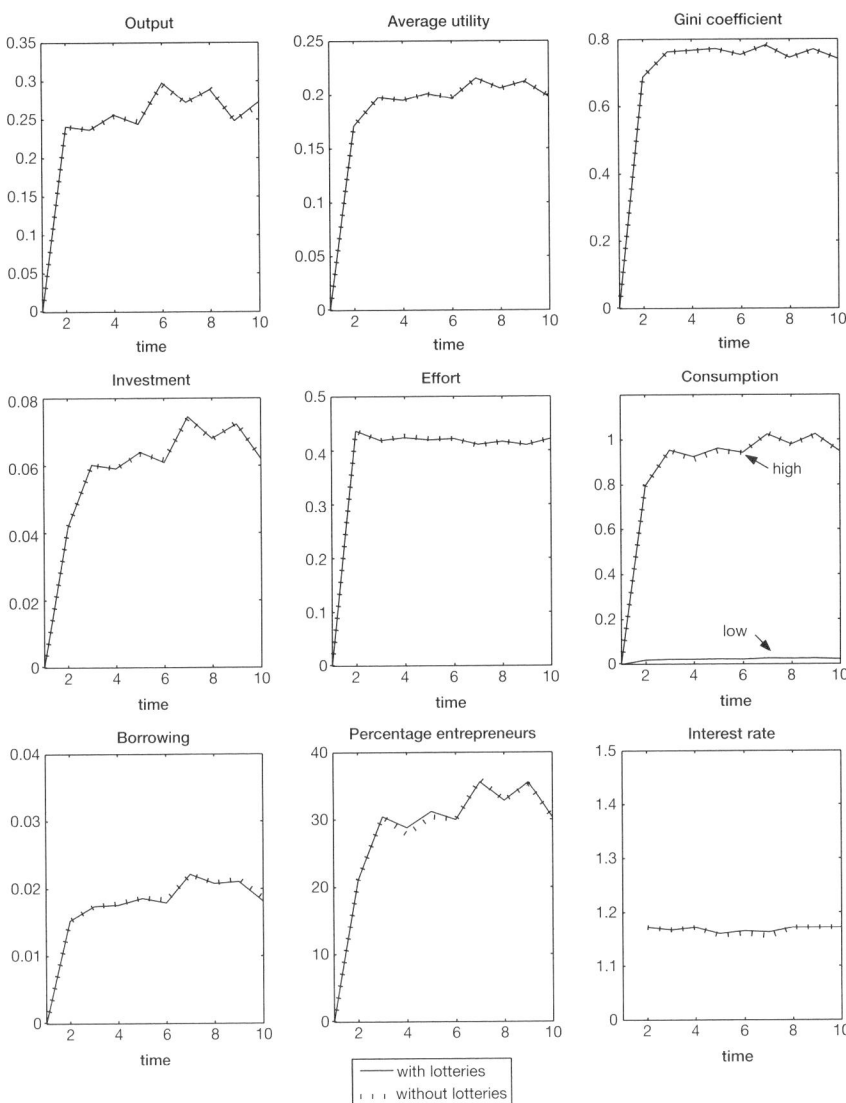

Fig. 9.8. *Dynamic model implications, borrowing and lending*

Notes: See Table 9.4 for Parameter values.

Source: Karaivanov 2003.

Unfortunately, these various formal regimes converge to a steady state too fast relative to the slower transition in the data. The borrowing lending regime in Figure 9.8, at estimated parameter values denoted earlier, is an illustrative simulation starting from a degenerate distribution of wealth.

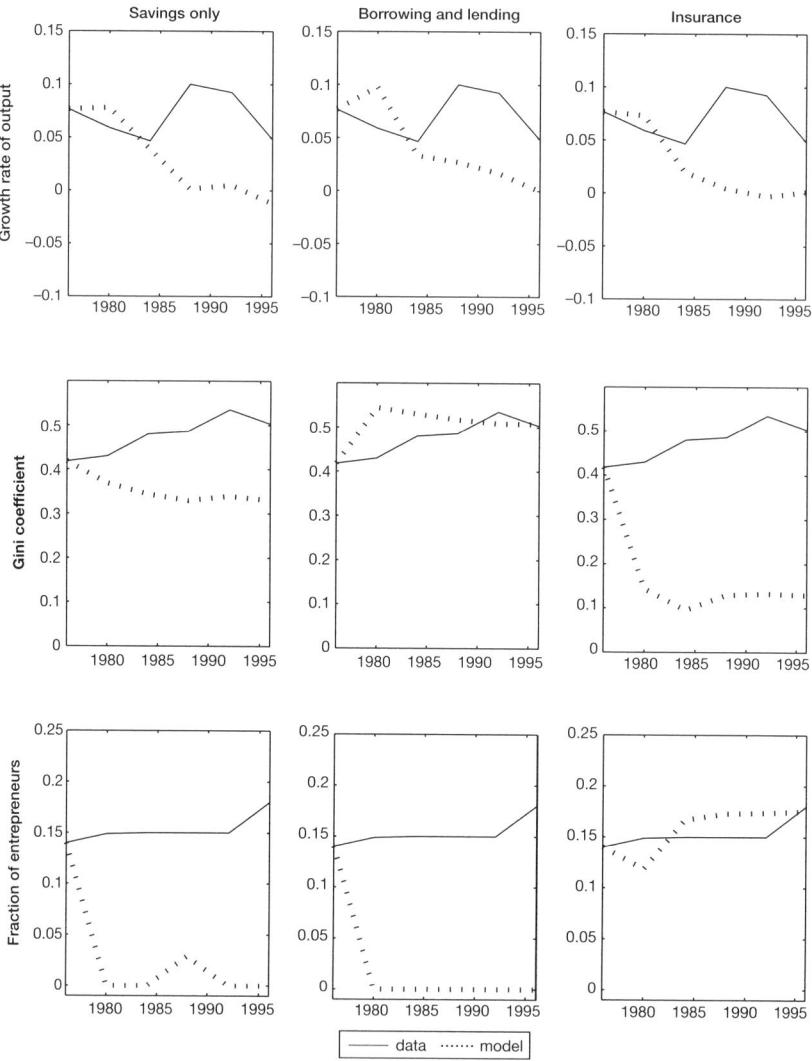

Fig. 9.9. *Model calibration, SES data (best overall fit)*

Source: Karaivanov 2003.

More generally, we can simulate from the 1976 initial distribution of wealth. The savings rate is calibrated at about 0.25 as generating the best overall fit to historically observed paths (see Figure 9.9). The micro parameters are as before. Again, the interest rate is endogenous, equalizing the supply and demand for funds. The moral hazard regime is most consistent with the observed path of entrepreneurs and the b-l-with-bankruptcy regime most consistent with the observed path of inequality. None of the models does well with output growth, as each predicts a growth slowdown that is not apparent in the data. We conclude from this that we have not yet hit on a compelling combination of obstacles.

9.3. Life-cycle and Occupation Choice with Limited Credit

More successful are life-cycle predictions. As in Buera 2003, forward-looking behavior makes savings, hence wealth, endogenous. In his model savings, occupation transitions, the size and growth of firms, and ROA are related to each other and to talent. A typical household is imagined to maximize discounted expected utility:

$$\max_{c(t),\theta,a(t),k(t)\geq 0} \int_0^\infty e^{-\rho t} U\Big(c(t)\Big) dt \qquad (9.3.1)$$

where

$$U(c) = \frac{c^{1-\gamma}}{1-\gamma}. \qquad (9.3.2)$$

$$\dot{a}(t) = y\Big(\theta, a(t)\Big) - c(t) \qquad (9.3.3)$$

where $p \leq r$ is the inter-temporal discount rate. To be determined is the choice of savings (change in wealth) at each data, with occupation choice contributing to earnings y, specifically,

$$y\Big(\theta, a(t)\Big) = \max\Big\{y^e\Big(\theta, a(t)\Big), y^w\Big(a(t)\Big)\Big\} \qquad (9.3.4)$$

by choice of entrepreneurs, branch e or wage workers branch w, gives wealth $a(t)$ and given firm talent θ. A savings-only prototype with exogenous interest r is easiest to envision, but one can allow credit (below $k \leq \lambda a$ with $\lambda > 1$).

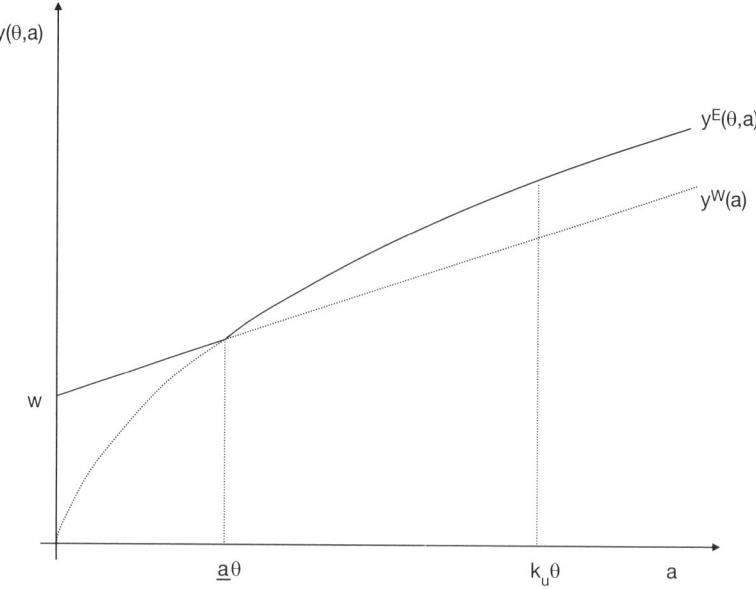

Fig. 9.10. *Technologies available to households*

Source: Buera 2003.

The choice of occupation and earnings $y(\theta, a)$ is simply the choice at *any* given date which maximizes total income plus end-of-period wealth, much as in the occupation-choice model discussed earlier.

$$
y(\theta, a) = \begin{cases}
w + ra & \text{if } a \in \left[0, \underline{a}(\theta)\right) \\
\max_{k \leq a} f(\theta, k) - r(k - a) & \text{if } a \in \left[\underline{a}(\theta), k_u(\theta)\right) \\
f\left(\theta, k_u(\theta)\right) + r\left(a - k_u(\theta)\right) & \text{if } a \in \left[k_u(\theta), \infty\right)
\end{cases}
$$

Again, in the examples, Buera sets $k \leq \lambda a$ with $\lambda = 1$. There is a wealth threshold. If wealth is less than $\underline{a}(\theta)$ then wage earnings dominate, though this depends on talent θ. Interestingly, this model carries a rate of return implication for firms. A household may find total end-of-period wealth greater as an entrepreneur but with limited wealth may be restricted in the scale k of the enterprise to something less than the efficient scale, $k_u(\theta)$ (which would obtain for a firm under perfect credit an interest rate r) (see Figure 9.10). The range between $\underline{a}(\theta)$ and $k_u(\theta)$, and the degree of excess returns, depend on talent θ and the exact form of the production function f.

Suppose that the production is

$$f(\tilde{\theta}, k) = A\tilde{\theta}^{1-\alpha}k^{a}.$$

Dividing by the wage w, profits relative to the wage thus define the relative gain to becoming an entrepreneur. Wealth to the wage becomes the current key state. It is convenient to normalize the ability to correspond to the net profits an entrepreneur would make if able to borrow at rate r and hence is unconstrained:

$$\theta = \max_{k}\{A\tilde{\theta}^{1-\alpha}k^{\alpha} - rk\}.$$

This gives the $f(\theta,k)$ of the earlier notation.

A standard Euler Equation describes the optimal consumption path,

$$-\frac{U''(c)c}{U'(c)}\frac{\dot{c}}{c} = \begin{cases} r - \rho & \text{if} \quad a \in [0, \underline{a}(\theta)) \\ f_{k}(\theta, k) - \rho & \text{if} \quad a \in [\underline{a}(\theta), k_{u}(\theta)), \\ r - \rho & \text{if} \quad a \in [k_{u}(\theta), \infty). \end{cases}$$

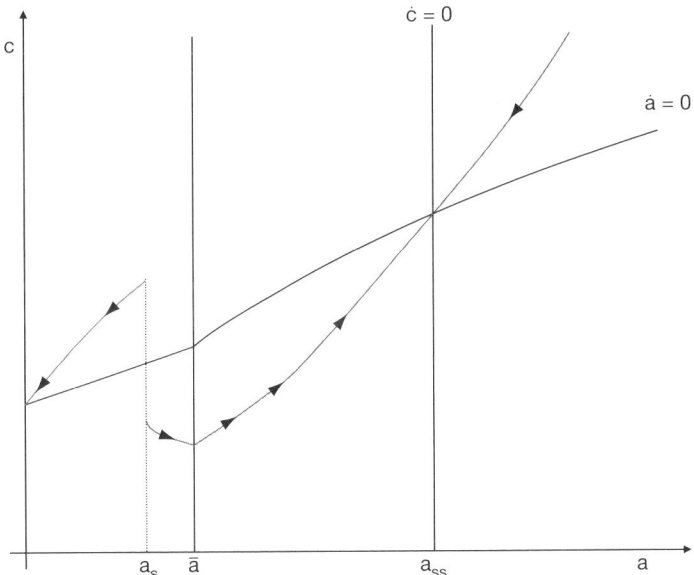

Fig. 9.11. *Optimal trajectories (intermediate ability)*

Source: Buera 2009.

The marginal rate of substitution should equal the marginal rate of transformation. Again, the law of motion for wealth is simply $\dot{a} = y(\theta,a)-c$.

Buera describes the steady states in Figure 9.11. If, for given talent θ, wealth is less than yet another, lower, critical value $a_s(\theta)$, the household will plan to stay a worker and converge to one possible steady state with zero wealth and consumption equal to the wage. Parameter $a_s(\theta)$ is a poverty trap threshold. For slightly higher wealth, the household will work toward another steady state (a_{ss},c_{ss})—that is, will plan to set up a firm eventually and save now at a relatively high rate. Once wealth is high enough, greater than $\underline{a}(\theta)$, that household will become an entrepreneur, though constrained and with a high ROA. Finally, the household reaches the position of being an unconstrained entrepreneur (see Figure 9.12).

The implication of higher savings rates for eventual will-be-entrepreneurs is borne out in the Townsend Thai data. Eleven years prior to the survey, the median wealth of households that started a business in the five years prior to the survey was only 58 per cent of that of households who never started a business. However, six years prior to the survey, the median wealth of business households was 152 per cent the median wealth of non-business households.

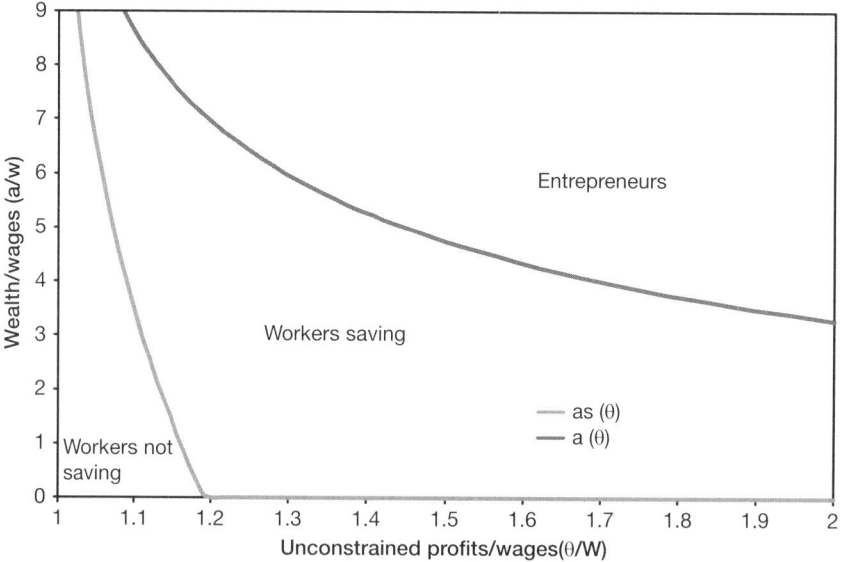

Fig. 9.12. *Poverty trap*

$\alpha=0.05$

Source: Buera 2008.

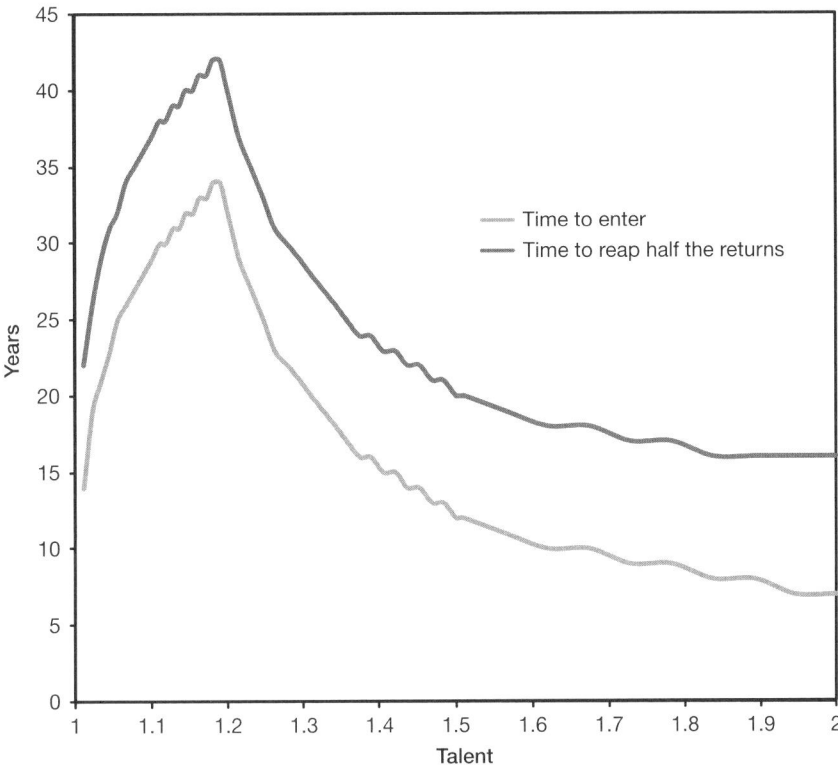

Fig. 9.13. *Time to entry and time to reap half the unconstrained returns starting from the poverty trap threshold*

Source: Buera 2008.

It may take time to become an entrepreneur. For example, at calibrated parameters that match the US data, the upper bound on the time to enter varies from zero to eighteen years, depending on talent. This calculation assumes the household starts just above the 'poverty trap', $a_s(\theta)$, the critical value of wealth below which they would decide to become a worker forever. Note that this poverty trap depends on talent, and is decreasing in talent, so as talent increases in Figure 9.13, the starting-point of wealth is lower. Initially this means it takes longer to reach the point of entry. On the other hand, higher talent raises the entrepreneur earnings profile in the figure, making the switch to business at a given wealth earlier. This effect dominates after talent greater than 1.15. One can similarly plot the time to reach efficient scale. The difference between these two curves tells the analyst how many years to expect small but growing firms to be operating with high ROA.

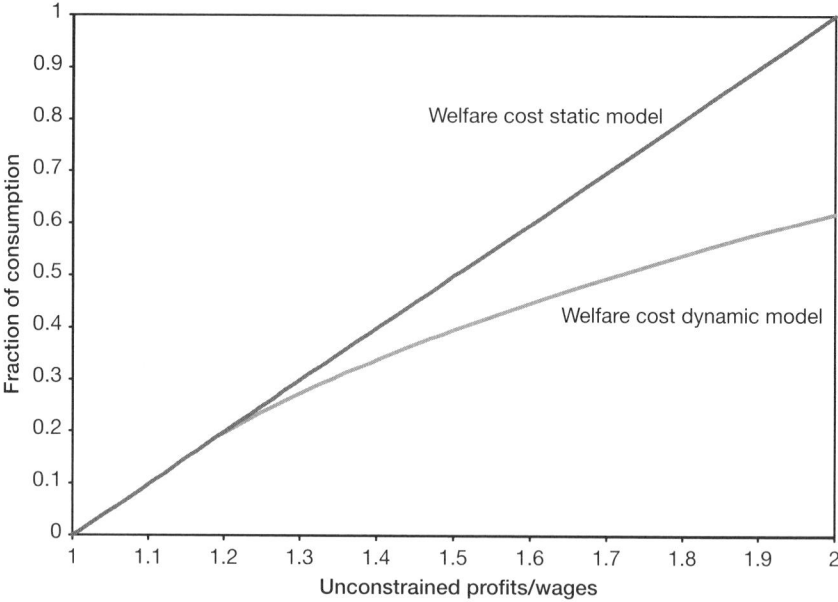

Fig. 9.14. *Consumption equivalent compensation for people who start with zero wealth*
Source: Buera 2008.

If it were possible to eliminate the credit constraint, there would be a welfare gain, for each wealth and talent combination. As earlier, this can be converted to an equivalent consumption gain. This depends on whether the model is static, or, as here, dynamic. Endogenous savings does help talented households enter business but does not overcome the welfare loss to restricted credit markets (see Figure 9.14). The diagram depicts the difference in welfare gain between the static and dynamic models for those households starting at the poverty trap, again featuring gains by talent.

The magnitude of the gain depends as earlier not only on ability but also on wealth. By restricting attention to the ability distribution for those planning to become entrepreneurs, the median household in ability and normalized wealth gains 18 per cent (see Table 9.6). Less-talented, wealthier households gain little. The distribution of gains is skewed toward low-wealth, high-talent households, reaching 56 per cent.

Buera also makes a comparison between cross-sectional relations in wealth and the effect of wealth transfers. On the one hand, he studies the relation between transitions into business in time interval Δ for agents observed at chronological date t (e.g., $t = 0$) who have wealth a as observed

Table 9.6. *Distribution of welfare cost*

	Zero wealth	25th percentage wealth/wage	median of wealth/wage	75th percentage wealth/wage
25th percentage entrants' ability	0.02	0.01	0.01	0.01
Median entrants' ability	0.24	0.23	0.18	0.10
75th percentage entrants' ability	0.56	0.49	0.34	0.19

Source: Buera 2003.

in the cross-section, as compared to the agents with higher wealth $\tilde{a}$ nearby. On the other hand, he studies transition into business in time interval Δ for agents at date $t = 0$ who have wealth a in the cross-section, as compared to what such a household would do if given a policy-induced exogenous increment in wealth $\tilde{a}$, say via some transfer. The cross-sectional profile and its derivative underestimates the impact of lump-sum wealth transfers. This is due to a negative selection effect. At higher wealth in the cross-section, the fraction that will make the transition may be going down because more talented agents have already entered business (see Figure 9.15). The larger point is that impact coefficients from a reduced form model may not provide reliable answers to policy questions.

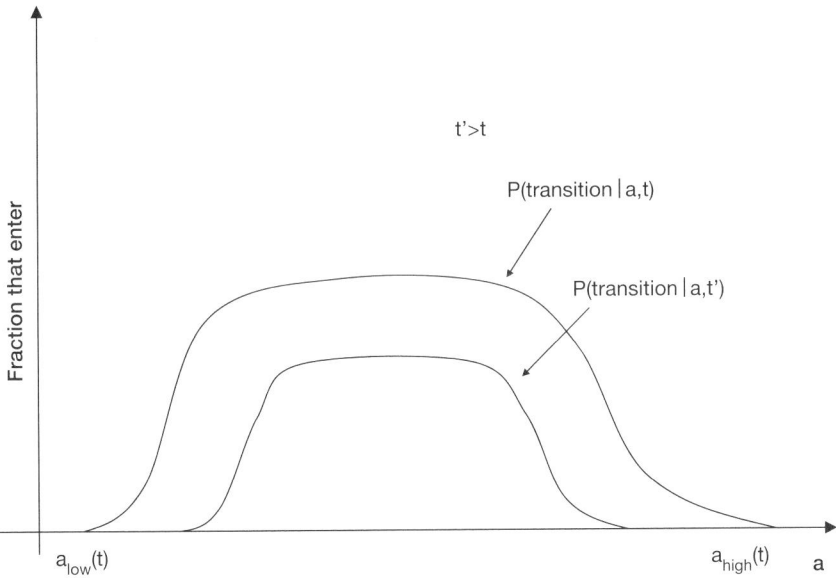

Fig. 9.15. *Transition into entrepreneurship as a function of wealth and age*
Source: Buera 2009.

343

9.4. Projects and Choice among a Combination of Lenders

We turn next, as in Giné 2005, to this issue of borrowing in setting up a business and in particular whether to borrow from the formal or the informal sector, or both, in setting up a business. This will allow a further assessment of limited commitment with transaction costs.

Suppose a household is endowed with initial, predetermined wealth A, ability z, maximum scale of project K, and the fraction of capital η which as working capital cannot be used as collateral to secure loans. Only wealth A and collateral $(1-\eta)A$ are observed to the econometrician, but there is no uncertainty on the part of the household or lender.

The timeline of the model is depicted in Figure 9.16. First, wealth b and ability z are given as predetermined; then project characteristics, fraction of required working capital η and scale K are determined in the cross-section as if drawn from a probability distribution. Then there is a financial decision to be described momentarily—namely, how much to save and from whom to borrow. Then, fixed capital $(1-\eta)k$ is supposed to be invested in the project. Commercial bank clients decide to invest the remainder working capital or to default on the contract. Otherwise, households repay loans and consume.

The technology of the household as entrepreneur is:

$$f(z, k, K, \eta) = zk + \hat{\delta}(1 - \eta)k \quad \text{s.t.} \quad k \leq K. \qquad (9.4.2)$$

Here direct output is the sum of zk, a linear function of capital multiplied by talent, plus depreciated collateral capital, which can be sold. Parameter $\hat{\delta}$ is one minus the rate of depreciation.

In his paper, Giné refers to a constrained household as one which invests below maximum capacity, $k < K$. Essentially, with the linearity, if a project is undertaken and the household is not indifferent, then one would expect maximum capacity, with $k = K$. Otherwise, some financial constraint must be limiting investment.

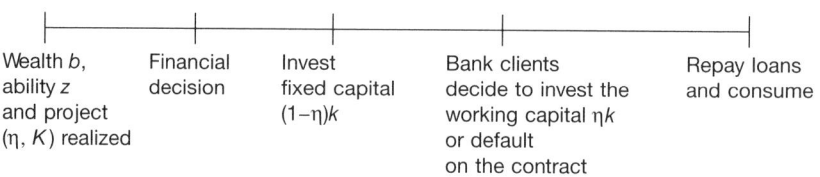

Wealth b,   Financial   Invest   Bank clients   Repay loans
ability z decision   fixed capital   decide to invest the   and consume
and project $(1-\eta)k$ working capital ηk
(η, K) realized   or default
         on the contract

Fig. 9.16. *Timeline of the model*

Source: Giné 2005.

If the entrepreneur decides to self-finance he will obtain a net income of

$$Y_s(z, b, K, \eta) = \max_k zk + \delta k + (b - k)r_D$$

$$\text{s.t. } k \leq b, \quad k \leq K$$

(9.4.3)

where r_D denotes the opportunity cost of using own funds—namely, the deposit rate. We simplify notation by letting $\delta = \hat{\delta}(1 - \eta)$. Since the technology is linear, we write the optimal choice of capital as

$$k_s(z, K, \eta) = \begin{cases} K \text{ if } z \geq r_D - \delta \quad \text{and } b \geq K, \\ b \text{ if } z \geq r_D - \delta \quad \text{and } b < K, \\ 0 \text{ if } z < r_D - \delta \end{cases}$$

In other words, the entrepreneur will invest K if it is profitable and there is enough wealth, and he will invest total wealth b if the maximum scale K is larger than his wealth b, and will not invest at all if the return on the investment is lower than the interest the bank pays for deposits.

If the entrepreneur goes to the bank (B), net income can be written as

$$Y_B(z, b, K, \eta) = \max_k zk - (k - b)r_B + \delta k - \Gamma_B$$

$$\text{s.t. } k \leq K$$

(9.4.4)

$$zk - (k - b)r_B + \delta k \geq \eta k$$

(9.4.5)

The interest rate r_B denotes the cost of borrowing and the parameter Γ_B captures the fixed transaction cost of dealing with a bank. This cost parameter captures all expenses related to obtaining the loan: trips to the bank, bank fees, and due diligence to assess the repayment capacity of the borrower. By having the borrower pay Γ_B, the bank learns the borrower's characteristic (z,b,K,η).

A key constraint, 9.4.5, captures the enforcement disadvantage that banks face. Before producing, bank clients can 'run away' with the working capital advanced, at the cost of losing all the previously deposited wealth as well as the fixed capital scrap value, both seized by the bank. Implicitly, we assume that although banks may fully observe their borrowers' actions, they have no legal mechanisms to prevent a borrower from 'consuming' the working capital. The optimal choice of capital for the entrepreneur depends on whether or not the enforcement constraint is binding. If it binds, the maximum amount of capital that the bank is willing to lend is given by:

$$k^c = \frac{br_B}{\eta - (z + \delta - r_B)}. \tag{9.4.6}$$

The above expression is found using the enforcement constraint 9.4.5 at equality and solving for k. Notice that there will be fewer constraints if the project is more productive (ability z is high), the entrepreneur is richer, or he operates a technology with relatively more fixed assets (lower η). If the constraint does not bind, entrepreneurs earn net income,

$$Y_{BU} = (z + \delta - r_B)K + r_B b - \Gamma_B \tag{9.4.6}$$

whereas, if it does bind,

$$Y_{Bc} = \eta k^c - \Gamma_B. \tag{9.4.7}$$

Figure 9.17 plots the optimal investment k as a function of ability z. When the return on the investment $z + \delta$ is lower than the deposit rate r_D, it pays to keep the money in the bank. When ability is higher than the

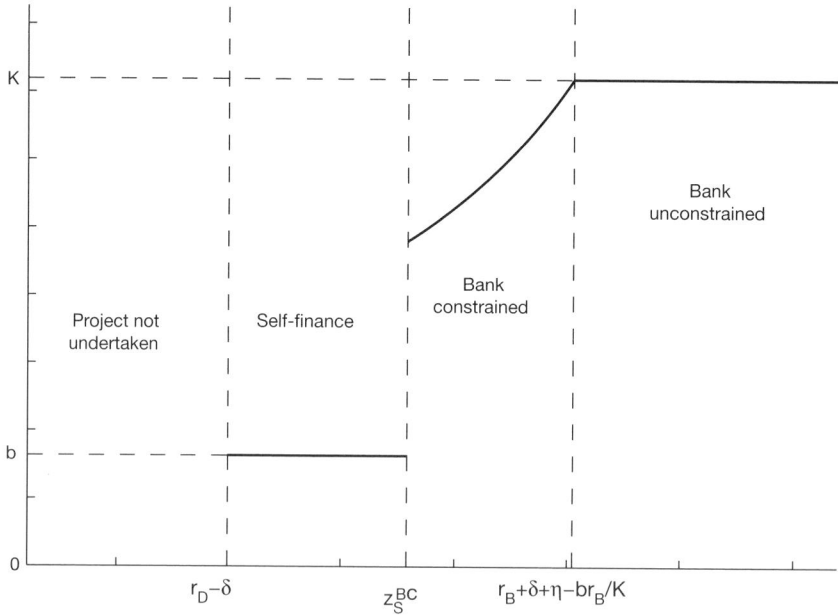

Fig. 9.17. *Optimal investment k*

Notes: X-axis indicates ability z; Y-axis indicates investment k.
Source: Giné 2005.

cut-off $r_D-\delta$ but lower than some level z_s^{Bc}, the agent self-finances, investing her total wealth b. The cut-off ability z_s^{Bc} is found by equating the net incomes from self-financing Y_S with that of resorting to a bank but being constrained, Y_{BC}. The gross capital expenses are larger than wealth b because the fixed cost Γ_B of transaction with the bank must be forgone. Notice that investment must be large enough so that returns cover fixed costs. In the segment above z_s^{Bc}, investment is an increasing function of ability z at least until the capacity constraint K is reached. For higher-ability values, the agent will be at capacity K.

Now, suppose that the household resorts to a moneylender alone. The amount borrowed is denoted $k-b$ and income becomes:

$$Y_M(z, b, K, \eta) = \max_k \; zk - (k - b)r_M + \delta k - \Gamma_M$$
$$\text{s.t.} \;\; k \leq K \tag{9.4.9}$$

where r_M denotes the interest rate charged by the moneylender, and it is assumed that $r_M > r_B$. The moneylender is not subject to enforcement problems and will therefore advance the loan $k-b$ so that the entrepreneur operates the project at maximum capacity.

Finally, the entrepreneur may find it of interest to resort to both a bank and a moneylender (BM). This case will arise if the bank offers too little capital due to enforcement problems: the project may be intensive in working capital (high η) or the entrepreneur may not be talented enough to convince the bank that she will not default on the loan contract and run away with the working capital. Since the interest rate charged by the moneylender is higher than that of the bank, the agent borrows from the bank as much as the bank is willing to lend $l_B=k^c-b$ and will then turn to the moneylender to finance $l_m=K-k^c$, the remaining capital investment. Net income can be written as total revenues from investing the maximum scale minus loan repayments and fixed costs. More formally:

$$Y_{BM}(z, b, K, \eta) = zK - (k^c - b)r_B - (K - k^c)r_M + \delta K - \Gamma_B - \Gamma_M. \tag{9.4.10}$$

We can distinguish households in the data by their choices of lender. Figure 9.18 is illustrative. Low-skill households will self-finance, as will those with low capacity. This is the region S in the figure. For given scale K, the higher is, the more likely is the household to finance in some way. There are two distinct 'moneylender' M-only regions in Figure 9.18. When the scale K is relatively low and wealth is close to that scale, and talent is high, it is not economic for the household to borrow from the bank despite

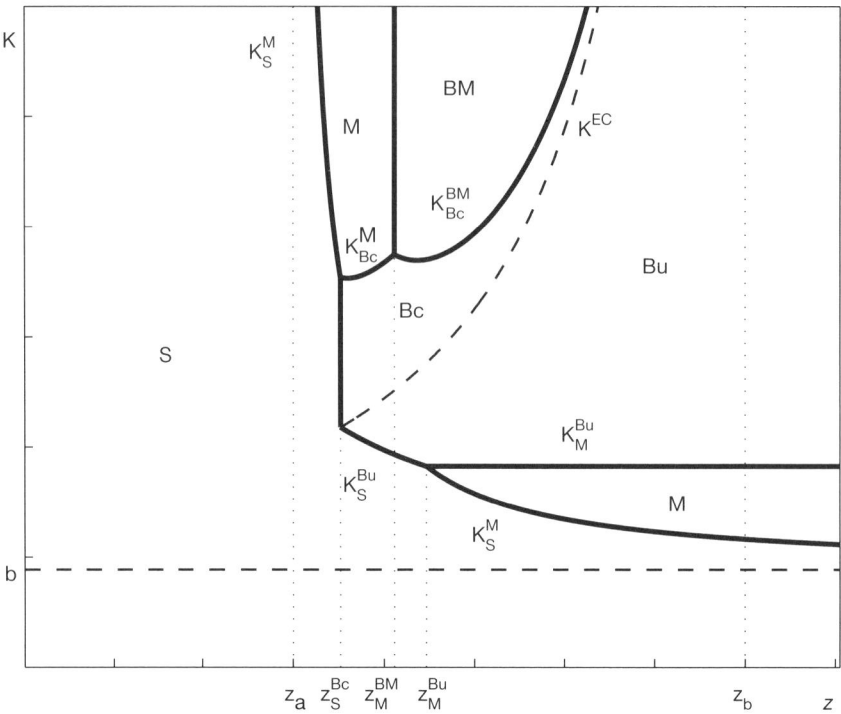

Fig. 9.18. *Financial choice map*

Notes: solid, thick lines mark the different financial choices, S, M, B, BM. X-axis indicates ability, z; Y-axis indicates investment, K. The horizontal dashed line indicates the level of wealth, b.
Source: Giné 2005.

lower interest payments to the bank, due to the fixed bank transaction costs. When the scale K is high, but talent is relatively low, the amount that can be borrowed from the bank is low, due to the enforcement constraint 9.4.5, and the firm also turns to moneylenders.

However, in this second M region, at the higher scale K, if talent z is a bit higher, then the household borrows both from the bank up to the maximum and then also from the moneylender, region *BM*. At yet, even higher values for talent, or more-modest scales, the household will borrow from the bank and be constrained, B_c. Finally, at highest talent and high scale, the household is unconstrained in borrowing from the bank, the region B_U.

The key observables to us are wealth b and the value of collateral assets. Realized project size K, talent z, transaction costs for the formal sector Γ_B, transaction costs for bank Γ_M, and the value of default $v = \eta k^c$ are the key unobserved variables. Note the latter is simply the working capital portion of a firm operating at constrained capital level k^c. Two different specifications for fixed costs and the value of default are considered: homogeneity— that is, uniformity across households versus heterogeneity, variety across households. Specifically, the log of transaction costs and the log of the value of default are normally distributed with means possible functions of observables X_j for household j and a residual, orthogonal error term. The error terms are possibly correlated. Interest rates for the formal and informal sector are pinned down at their sample means, abstracting from the identity of individual providers, and $r_M > r_B > r_D$. Talent z and capacity K are drawn from a joint normal distribution with means M_S, M_K, variance δ_S, δ_K and covariation c. Thus, the model at fixed parameters delivers the likelihood of falling into the various regions of the figure. In a sense, the parameters moving in the likelihood estimation try to capture as much of the observed frequencies in the data as possible.

The scale K is estimated to have a mean of 3.9 million baht and high variance of 220 million baht. This is higher but comparable to mean household wealth. Recall the discussion of the size of business assets earlier in this book. There is a negative correlation between scale K and talent z (i.e. the highest talent households are not running the largest businesses, as was also conjectured in the earlier discussion). The (common) fixed costs are estimated at between 311 to 685 baht, depending on the specification. This is a low number, roughly 2 per cent of the average loan size—and much less than the fixed costs in the transaction costs model with endogenous financial deepening. Education, ties to the village committee, and the presence of a formal institution, each lower the cost of formal finance. Thus, the new 1 million baht funds would help (but see below). Having savings with a formal institution and borrowing from the formal sector in the past also lowered the fixed formal costs (but not the informal). Transaction costs for the informal sector are virtually zero: 11 baht. Education and male household head increase the value of default (being more constrained in the sense of Evans and Jovanovic 1989). Households in villages with more formal connections are less likely to be constrained, consistent with results earlier.

Both transaction costs and limited enforceability are needed. If transaction costs were zero (or equal) for banks and moneylenders, then the households would go first to the bank, and if constrained then to the moneylender. We would never observe households borrowing from a moneylender alone, region BM as in the data. If enforcement were perfect, then the region BM disappears also as the decision to go to the bank, or the

Table 9.7. *Maximum likelihood estimates*

	Common default value				Differentiated default value			
	Common cost		Differential cost		Common cost		Differential cost	
Variable	Coefficient	Southeast	Coefficient	Southeast	Coefficient	Southeast	Coefficient	Southeast
Distribution								
$\mu\,\zeta$	−0.191	0.0125	−0.221	0.0123	−0.139	0.0128	−0.165	0.0124
$\mu\,\kappa$	0.981	0.0199	1.012	0.0197	0.895	0.0226	0.916	0.0220
$\sigma\,\zeta$	0.969	0.0062	0.953	0.0061	0.966	0.0063	0.945	0.0059
$\sigma\,\kappa$	1.561	0.0129	1.543	0.0127	1.610	0.0147	1.572	0.0140
ρ	−0.870	0.0038	−0.868	0.0038	−0.844	0.0052	−0.849	0.0049
Formal access								
Constant (in baht)	685.1	6.4	1,896.5	52.8	311.3	2.4	1,643.5	118.7
Formal institution in village	—		0.369	0.0131	—		0.592	0.0243
Past member (formal institution)	—		0.800	0.0516	—		0.669	0.0490
Past member (informal institution)	—		1.741	0.2289	—		1.033	0.1912
Member of village community	—		1.275	0.1092	—		0.844	0.0834
Education		—	1.030	0.0052		—	0.968	0.0082
Savings in formal institution		—	0.260	0.0099		—	0.255	0.0128
Region		—	0.992	0.0222		—	1.022	0.0501
Informal access								
Constant (in baht)	0.1	6.4	9.0	5.6	4.8	2.7	10.8	3.0
Enforcement constraint								
Constant		—		—	0.898	0.0018	0.917	0.0129
Number of formal institution in village		—		—	0.985	0.0024	0.985	0.0031
Member of village community		—		—	1.005	0.0076	0.993	0.0076
Sex of head (male)		—		—	1.085	0.0028	1.072	0.0133
Education		—		—	1.019	0.0003	1.024	0.0011
Region (Northeast)		—		—	1.006	0.0033	0.984	0.0069
Number of observations	2,270		2,270		2,270		2,270	
Likelihood	−51,647.04		−45,899.40		−43,284.36		−42,056.29	

Source: Giné 2005.

moneylender, is determined by the trade-off between interest rates and transaction costs, depending on scale.

The model can rationalize some of the facts in the data presented earlier. High-wealth households are likely to have high collateral, hence borrow from commercial banks. The data confirm that land and a few capital assets that serve as collateral in the data are more prevalent for the rich. Some high-wealth households are not so talented, and will self-finance. Other things equal, self-finance increases with wealth. This makes wealth higher for those who self-finance relative to those who borrow from the informal sector. In this model, expected income is higher for those who borrow informally because they do not suffer the loss of transaction costs. This is one interpretation of the higher-income/capital ratios for constrained borrowers. In fact, the model offers some findings for who is likely to report being constrained, specifically those who borrow from both sources, as well as those who borrow exclusively from the formal sector.

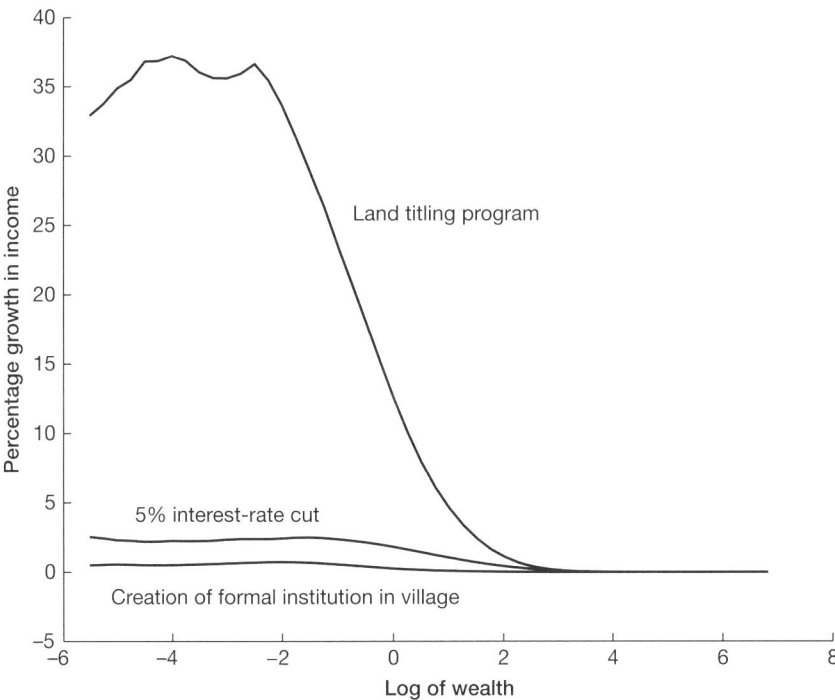

Fig. 9.19. *Percentage income growth from different policies*

Source: Giné 2005.

Table 9.8. *Percentage growth in income and investment*

	Investment	Income
Relevance of market imperfections		
Limited enforcement, no transaction costs	0.1	0.2
Perfect enforcement, transaction costs	25.4	347.6
Perfect enforcement, no transaction costs	25.7	348.8
Policy analysis		
5 per cent cut in formal interest rate	1.4	1.2
Creation in formal institution in village	0.1	0.1
Land-titling program	15.2	201.5

Notes: For each household, 1,000 (z, K) pairs are simulated from the estimated distribution. Using each household's vector of characteristics and estimated parameters, the investment and income are computed under each scenario. Growth rates for each household and simulation are computed and the overall mean is reported.

Source: Giné 2005.

Comparative static policy exercises are revealing. A cut in the interest rates formal banks charge leads to a decrease in self-finance and a decrease in borrowing from moneylenders but an increase in bank and bank money-lender finance (see Table 9.8). There would be modest increases in investment and income, as in Table 9.7, and the distribution gains in terms of income growth are fairly uniform up to middle-income borrowers, as in Figure 9.19. This policy is inefficient in that it attracts low-talent borrowers to business. The creation of formal institutions in villages does not create this distortion. However, it does not alleviate enforcement problems either. Lower transactions costs accomplish little here. Thus, more households would report themselves constrained. Those borrowing from a moneylender decreases, as in the data, but those borrowing from both banks and moneylender increases. The distribution of gains in terms of income growth is flat and relatively low on all dimensions for these two policies (see Figure 9.19). On the other hand, a land-titling program changing at the estimated parameter values dramatically increases investment, and especially net income. Those borrowing from a bank increase dramatically, while self-finance and other sources of finance, M and BM, all decline. The distribution of gains is high and peaked for relatively low-wealth households.

9.5. Distinguishing Obstacles from Repayment Data

We return to the issue of identifying the key obstacles to trade, allowing both limited commitment and moral hazard. But, rather than focus on choice of occupation and wealth, or method of finance, we turn as in the

Table 9.9. *Percentage changes in predicted probabilities of financial choices*

	S	B	M	BM
5 per cent cut in formal interest rate	−0.92	2.92	−2.49	0.49
Creation of formal institution in village	−0.46	1.39	−2.38	1.45
Land-titling program	−1.06	15.87	−2.32	−12.49

Notes: Financial choices are self-finance (S); bank (B); moneylender (M); and bank and moneylender (BM).

Notes: Table reports the percentage changes in the predicted fraction of households making each financial choice for each policy considered relative to the benchmark estimation.

Source: Giné 2005.

work in Ahlin and Townsend 2004 that uses data on loan defaults from BAAC households in joint-liability groups (with cosigned loans) (see Table 9.9).

The models considered are representative of the literature. In Stiglitz 1990, households choose among safe and risky projects, something not observed by the lender. In Banerjee, Besley, and Guinnane 1994, the choice of project type is monitored at a cost by a second non-borrowing partner. Both these models have a moral hazard problem. In Besley and Coate 1995, the problem is repayment and strategic default. Repayment may not happen. In Ghatak 2000 there is an adverse selection problem.

The models have in common that an increase in the interest rate reduces repayment and increases the productivity of borrowers, which leads to an increase in a project's repayment. There are also implications specific to the individual models. Lowering monitoring costs increases repayment in Banerjee, Besley, and Guinnane 1994, higher official and/or unofficial penalties increase repayment in Besley and Coate 1995, and enhanced ability by the bank to screen outside customers raises repayment in Ghatak. More interesting are implications which distinguish the models. Cooperation raises repayment in Stiglitz and lowers it in two other models. The informal market may have this limit. Covariance in returns raises repayment in two of the information models but lowers it in Besley and Coate 1995. More generally, see Table 9.10 for a summary.

In the Stiglitz model of joint liability, each of two partners chooses the riskiness of projects, either safe S with probability of success p_s or risky R with probability of success p_R. Output upon success depends on risk type $i = R,S$ written $Y(p_i,L)$ where L is loan size. Output under failure is 0, and the borrower must default. Amount rL is repayment of principal and interest upon success—r is the gross rate inclusive of principal. If one borrower pays for another, the amount of payment is qL, and it is assumed that $q < r$. Utility $U(c)$ is concave in consumption c. Higher loan size L carries with it an implicit commitment for more effort and hence, via a separable negative

Table 9.10. *Repayment implications*

		Effect on repayment		
Variable	Stiglitz	Banerjee, Besley, and Guinnane	Besley and Coate	Ghatak
interest rate r	↓	↓	↓	↓
loan size L	↓	↓‡	no pred.	⌒‡
liability payment q	↓⁴	↑	no pred.	↓
productivity H	↑‡	↑‡	↑‡	↑‡
screening	no pred.	no pred.	no pred.	↑
positive correlation	↑‡	no pred.	↓‡⁵	↑‡
cost of monitoring	no pred.	↓	no pred.	no pred.
cooperative behavior	↑‡	↓‡⁶	↓‡⁷	—
outside credit options	↓‡	no pred.	no pred.	no pred.
official penalties	no pred.	no pred.	↑	no pred.
unofficial penalties	no pred.	no pred.	↑	no pred.

Notes: List of possible control/policy experiments; change in interest rate; loan size; liability payment; encourage screening; cooperation; allow more lenders/competition; increase official penalties; facilitate monitoring. Entries with a ‡ are the result of our own extensions of the authors' original models.

Source: Ahlin and Townsend 2004.

term, disutility $W(L)$. In sum, the expected utility to a borrower who chooses technology risk i while his partner chooses technology j (while loan size is L regardless):

$$V_{ij}(r, L, q) = p_i p_j U[Y(p_j, L) - rL] + p_i(1 - p_j)U[Y(p_i, L) \\ - rL - qL] - W(L), i, j \in \{R, S\}$$

(9.5.1)

To illustrate the determination of the signs of derivatives of repayment with respect to cross-group characteristics, restrict attention for the moment to three variables: interest rate r, loan size L, and joint-liability payment q (all of which arguably the BAAC has under its control as policy variables). If the borrowing pair cooperate and choose the same level of risk, either S or R, then the observed probability of success, and the fractions of non-default in the population, would be determined by a simple indicator function of whether V_{SS} dominates V_{RR}:

$$p = p_R + (p_S - p_R)1\{V_{SS}(r, L, q) \geq V_{RR}(r, L, q)\}.$$ (9.5.2)

Thus, the derivative of $V_{RR} - V_{SS}$ with respect to covariates is the key to whether defaults should be more prevalent in the data. Consider the curves of indifference, as between L and r in Figure 9.20, with q held fixed. Increases in r and/or L push borrowers up into the region of risky project choice. Increases in q can be shown to move the entire line down. Non-cooperation among borrowers, as in a Nash equilibrium of project

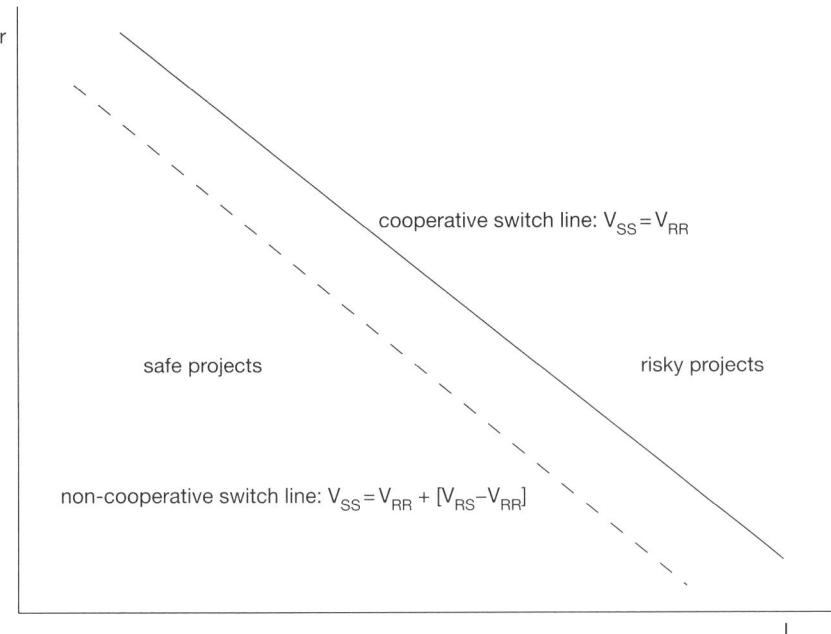

Fig. 9.20. *Stiglitz model: switch line*

Notes: To the left of the solid line, safe projects are chosen; to the right, risky ones. The dashed line is the switch line for graps acting non-cooperatively.

Source: Ahlin and Townsend 2007b.

choice, also moves the line down. More comprehensively, see Table 9.10 and the 'Stiglitz' column; see Ahlin and Townsend 2004 for details of the derivation.

In Banerjee, Besley, and Guinnane 1994 one cooperative-saving member or partner is a monitor on a second borrowing partner. Both are risk neutral. The first partner guarantees the loan of the second. Thus, there is a first-order condition for monitoring. This equates the gain from an incremental movement or derivative with respect to the probability of success p—namely, the reduced probability of paying q, to the cost of securing p—namely, the derivative of the monitoring costs $M(c)$ with respect to p where $M(c) = M(c(p,r))$. Here c is the penalty that can be inflicted on the borrower for deviation from p, and $c(p,r)$ is the critical c which ensures incentive compatible choice of project risk p when the interest rate is r. That is, let $E(p)$ denote the expected pay-off when the risk is p. The incentive constraint is $E(p) - pr \geq E(\underline{p}) - \underline{p}r - c$, where $\underline{p}$ is the riskiest behavior which the borrower

355

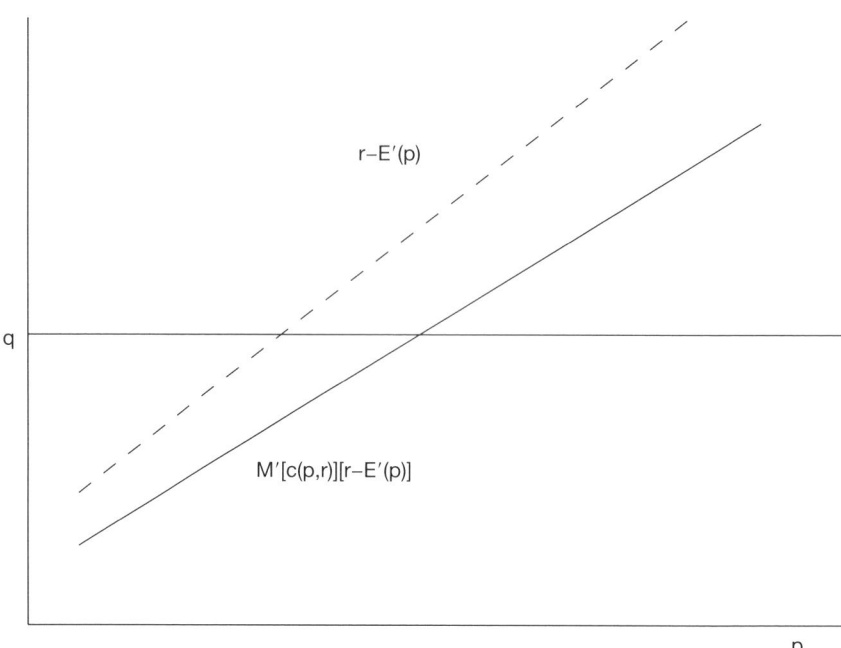

Fig. 9.21. *Determination of* p *under costly monitoring (solid line) and costless operation (dashed line)*

Source: Ahlin and Townsend 2007b.

can resort to, and the penalty for deviation is c. This defines c as $c(p,r) \equiv E(p) - E(\underline{p}) + r(p - \underline{p})$. In sum, the first-order monitoring equation is thus

$$q = M'[c(p, r)]c_p(p, r). \tag{9.5.3}$$

Essentially, total differentiation of 9.5.3 determines how repayment rate p varies with key covariates. Illustrative in the p,q space of Figure 9.21 is the intersection of the horizontal q line, the left hand side of 9.5.3, with the up-sloping right hand side of 9.5.3. The intersection determines project type, and the risk/probability of p. An increase in the interest rate r will shift the up-sloping line vertically upwards, so that p will go down. Under certain assumptions, cooperation also yields an alternative right hand side schedule that is shifted up, reducing repayment. For further details of the derivation, see Ahlin and Townsend 2004, and the column in Table 9.10 labeled 'Banerjee, Besley, and Guinnane'.

In Besley and Coate 1995, borrowers can default but penalties can be imposed, and these are increasing in project output. The two borrowers' returns are drawn independently from distribution $F(Y)$, with support

356

[0,Y$_{\max}$]. Repayment decisions are then made non-cooperatively. Joint liability here implies that if the lender does not receive the full repayment amount of the group, $2r$, he imposes an *official penalty* of $C^0(Y_i)$ on each borrower $i \in \{1,2\}$. It is assumed that $C^0(Y)$ is continuous, strictly increasing, unbounded, and that $C^0(Y) < Y$ when $Y > 0$. In other words, the lender penalizes more severely when output is higher, but never as severely as outright confiscation. It is useful to define a cut-off output function $\underline{Y}(r)$, such that $C^0[\underline{Y}(r)] = r$ via the inverse function C:

$$\underline{Y}(r) \equiv (C^0)^{-1}(r). \tag{9.5.4}$$

By construction, then, when weighing repaying r against incurring penalties $C^0(Y)$, repayment is weakly more attractive if $Y \geq \underline{Y}(r)$ and default is more attractive if $Y < \underline{Y}(r)$. The properties of $C^0(Y)$ imply that $\underline{Y}(r)$ is strictly increasing in r.

Similarly, let $C_1^u(Y_i, \Lambda_j)$ denote the unofficial penalty on a delinquent borrower i who realized output Y_i and this default decreases his partner j's

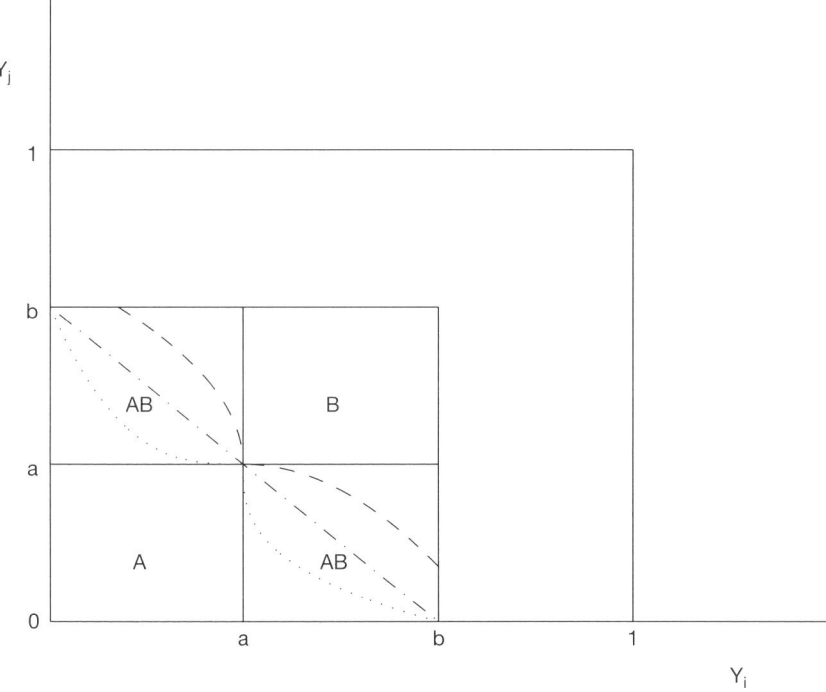

Fig. 9.22. *The Besley–Coate (BC) model: default region*

Source: Ahlin and Townsend 2007b.

pay-off by Λ_j, either through r if partner j pays i's loan, or the official penalty if partner j now defaults also.

The function $\hat{\underline{Y}}(r,Y_j)$ is defined to satisfy $r = C^0(\hat{Y}) + C^u[\hat{Y},\Lambda(r,Y_j)]$. Thus, when Y is between $\underline{Y}(r)$ and $\underline{Y}(2r)$ the borrower finds it attractive to pay his own loan when the other is paying also, but to default if he is also liable for the other's payment, r. This is the region where strategic default and the non-cooperative game come into play. There is another region where each would default regardless by virtue of his personal loan itself, when $Y<\underline{Y}(r)$.

Figure 9.22 describes the Besley–Coate (BC) Default Region (where $a \equiv \underline{Y}(r)$, $b \equiv \underline{Y}(2r)$, and Y_{max} is normalized to one). Default in the non-cooperative game occurs if joint-output realizations fall in box A, or in boxes AB below the dashed curve $\hat{\underline{Y}}(r,y)$ determining the critical value of output for Y_2 given Y_1. (The curve through the upper AB box must be its reflection above the

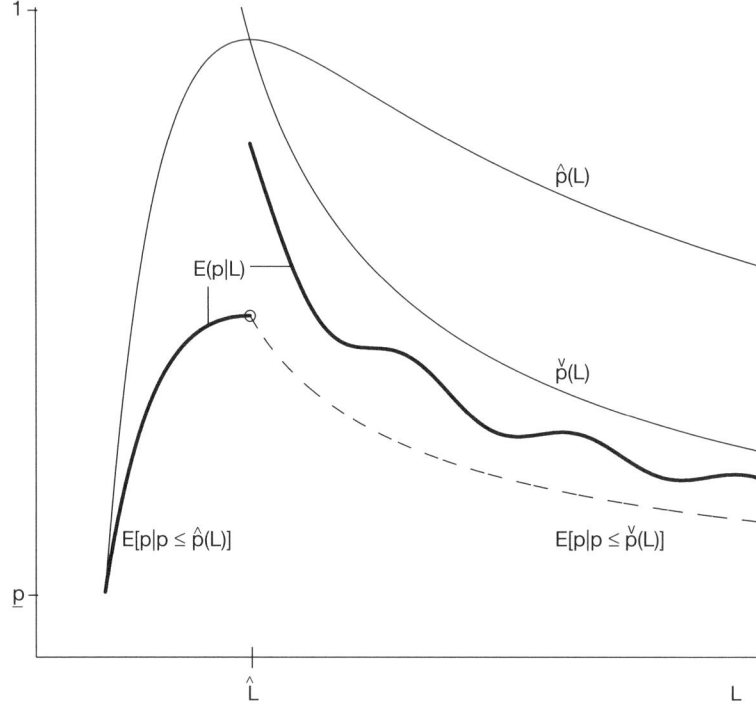

Fig. 9.23. *The Ghatak model: how p varies with L*

Note: When L is small enough–specifically, below $\hat{L} \equiv r^{-1}([u-EF(0)]/E]$)—then $\hat{p}(L) < \check{p}(L)$ and E(p|L) follows $E[p|p \le \hat{p}(L)]$. For $L \ge \hat{L}$, P(L) and E(p|L) is a carvex combination of $\check{p}(L)$ and $E[p|p \le \check{p}(L)]$.

Source: Ahlin and Townsend 2007b.

Table 9.11. *Independent variables*

Variable	Description	Mean	(σ)
Productivity			
AVGLAND	Average landholdings of group members (rai)	23.6	(15.7)
EDCATION	Index of group average education levels	3.1[a]	(0.32)
Screening			
SCREEN	Do some want to join this group but cannot?	0.39	
KNOWTYPE	Do group members know the quality of each other's work?	0.94	
Covariance			
COVARBTY*	Measure of coincidence of economically 'bad' years across villagers	0.28	(0.16)
HOMOCCUP[†]	Measure of occupational homogeneity within the group	0.87	(0.24)
Cost of monitoring			
LIVEHERE	Percentage of group living in the same village	0.88	(0.22)
RELATPCT[†]	Percentage of group members having a close relative in the group	0.58	(0.36)
Cooperation			
SHAREREL	Measure of sharing among closely related group members	2.1	(1.6)
SHAREUNR	Measure of sharing among unrelated group members	1.5	(1.4)
BCOOPPCT*	Percent in tambon naming this village best in the tambon for 'cooperation among villagers'	0.25	(0.11)
JOINTDCD	Number of decisions made collectively	0.37	(0.91)
Outside credit options:			
PCGMEM*[‡]	Percentage in village claiming Production Credit Group membership	0.08	(0.16)
CBANKMEN*	Percent in village claiming to be clients of a commercial bank	0.28	(0.18)
Penalties for default			
BINSTPCT*[‡]	Percentage in tambon naming this village best in the tambon for 'availability and quality of institutions'	0.27	(0.19)
SNCTIONS*	Percent of village loans where default is punishable by informal sanctions	0.10	(0.11)

Notes: Variables marked with an asterisk are taken or constructed from the household-level survey (HH). All others are from the group-level survey (BAAC). Variables marked with a † might also be included under the next set of variables; variables marked with a ‡ might also be included under the previous set.

[a] See text for the interpretation of this education index.

Source: Ahlin and Townsend 2004.

45-degree line, due to borrower symmetry. Default under cooperation occurs below the dash-dotted line, for example, and under the non-cooperative game and severe unofficial penalties (including being positive even at $Y_i = 0$) below the dotted curve.) In sum, the repayment rate p is 1 minus the regions of default:

$$p = 1 - [F(\underline{Y}(r))]^2 - 2\int_{\underline{Y}(r)}^{\underline{Y}(2r)} F(\hat{\underline{Y}}(r, Y))\,dF(Y). \qquad (9.5.5)$$

Derivatives of the right hand side of 9.5.5 with respect to r determine the response of repayment rates to the interest rate, for example. Cooperation

Table 9.12. *Independent variables and controls*

Variable	Description	Mean	(σ)
Control			
LNYRSOLD	Number of years group has existed (Log)	11.4[a]	(8.5)
VARIBLTY*	Village average coefficient of variation for next year's expected income	0.30	(0.09)
WEALTH*	Village average wealth (million 97 Thai baht)	1.1	(2.1)
MEMBERS	Number of members in the group	12.3	(5.1)
Fundamentals			
r	Average interest rate faced by the group	10.9	(2.0)
L	Average loan size borrowed by the group (thousand 97 Thai baht)	18.7	(18.3)
q	Percent landless in the group	0.06	(0.15)

Notes: Variables marked with an asterisk are taken or constructed from the household-level survey (HH). All others are from the group-level survey (BAAC).

[a] Here the mean and standard deviation are for age, not log of age.

Source: Ahlin and Townsend 2004.

mitigates the use of unofficial penalties, changes the critical output levels, and delivers the changed regions of the graph. Other experiments are possible. Other implications from Ahlin and Townsend are marked in Table 9.10, marked 'Besley and Coate'.

Under adverse selection, as in Ghatak 2000, agent types vary exogenously—that is, there are risky types and safe types, the riskiest type being $p > 0$. Agents choose to borrow if the pay-off to borrowing is greater than the supposed outside pay-off $\underline{U}$. Some of the characteristics which determine $\underline{U}$ are observable. It can be established that agent types will choose to pair with one another homogenously, p to p. Intuitively, high p safe types are desirable partners, especially so for higher p who are likely not to default and thus may have to pay off the partner's loan. In Ghatak, the expected project return E is held constant, so, ideally, we need to control for this in the data. The marginal borrowing type, just indifferent to choosing to borrow at all, is the type with $p = \hat{p}$ which solves

$$E(p) - pr - p(1 - p)q = U. \qquad (9.5.6)$$

This is the selection equation. One can show that if $q \leq r$, the borrowing pay-off, the left hand side of 9.5.6 is decreasing in p. Thus, safe agents with type $p > \hat{p}$ prefer not to borrow, while risky agents with $p < \hat{p}$ prefer to borrow. The exclusion of safe agents from the borrowing pool stems from the inability of the bank to observe borrower risk; it cannot vary the contract by risk-type.

Table 9.13. *Univariate mean comparisons*

	Percent of tests significant at 90%, with sign						Total tests		
	Northeast groups		Central groups		All groups		Northeast groups	Central groups	All groups
Control	(+)	(−)	(+)	(−)	(+)	(−)			
LNYRSOLD	0%	83%	0%	90%	0%	85%	18	20	26
VARIBLTY	3%	3%	8%	0%	0%	0%	73	50	140
WEALTH	5%	0%	0%	49%	0%	12%	73	51	139
MEMBERS	0%	0%	0%	50%	0%	53%	9	14	17
Fundamentals									
r	0%	5%	0%	0%	0%	28%	20	16	29
L	0%	3%	0%	0%	0%	9%	37	24	55
q	0%	0%	0%	95%	0%	96%	5	20	27
Productivity									
AVGLAND	0%	0%	68%	0%	11%	0%	29	34	46
EDCATION	30%	0%	7%	0%	18%	0%	23	14	44
Screening									
SCREEN	0%	0%	0%	0%	0%	0%	1	1	1
KNOWTYPE	—	—	—	—	0%	0%	0	0	1
Covariance									
COVARBTY	0%	8%	38%	0%	10%	0%	49	32	71
HOMOCCUP[†]	0%	0%	0%	0%	0%	0%	11	28	46
Cost of monitoring									
LIVEHERE	0%	0%	20%	0%	38%	0%	13	30	42
RELATPCT[†]	0%	2%	0%	18%	0%	35%	44	39	57
Cooperation									
SHAREREL	0%	0%	0%	25%	0%	0%	5	4	5
SHAREUNR	0%	0%	0%	67%	0%	50%	4	3	4
BCOOPPCT	0%	3%	0%	0%	0%	2%	60	38	108
JOINTDCD	33%	0%	—	—	100%	0%	3	0	3
Outside credit options									
PCGMEM[‡]	0%	100%	0%	0%	0%	55%	9	6	11
CBANKMEM	0%	0%	0%	0%	0%	20%	13	9	20
Penalties for default									
BINSTPCT[‡]	0%	0%	8%	0%	0%	0%	63	37	108
SNCTIONS	55%	0%	0%	0%	0%	0%	33	25	51

Notes: Variables that could be included in the next group are denoted by a †; in the previous group by a ‡.
Source: Ahlin and Townsend 2004.

The selection equation 9.5.6 determines repayment rate by considering the mix of households in the borrowing pool. We can show, for example, that positive correlation in project returns reduces the probability of off-diagonal, success–failure events $p(1-p)$, raises the pay-off on the left hand side of the selection equation, raises the cut-off $\hat{p}$, and so safer borrowers are drawn into the pool. This takes advantage of the fact that BAAC interest

Table 9.14. *Logit results*

	Northeast groups	Central groups	All groups
	N=130	N=89	N = 219
Control			
LNYRSOLD	−1.54 (.488)***	−1.61 (.701)***	−0.958 (.282)***
VARIBLTY	1.41 (4.40)	−10.1 (5.82)**	−3.47 (2.66)
WEALTH	1.00 (1.29)	0.125 (.117)	0.026 (.083)
MEMBERS	−0.014 (.089)	0.113 (.079)	0.034 (.047)
Fundamentals			
r	−0.056 (.142)	−0.385 (.299)	−0.119 (.101)
L	20.4 (48.3)	187.4 (99.8)**	32.9 (30.8)
L^2	−0.319 (.409)	−2.39 (1.42)**	−0.463 (.335)
q	−4.69 (6.76)	−7.69 (3.31)***	−3.65 (1.51)***
Productivity			
AVGLAND	−0.013 (.026)	−0.007 (.023)	−0.006 (.013)
EDCATION	1.88 (.935)***	0.949 (1.25)	1.28 (.698)**
Screening			
SCREEN	−0.950 (.624)*	1.17 (.876)	−0.364 (.402)
KNOWTYPE	−1.38 (1.23)	2.24 (2.12)	−0.139 (.773)
Covariance			
COVARBTY	1.66 (2.13)	1.82 (4.03)	2.05 (1.39)*
HOMOCCUP[†]	1.39 (1.45)	0.061 (1.69)	0.220 (.858)
Cost of monitoring			
LIVEHERE	−0.694 (1.84)	1.01 (1.26)	0.879 (.831)
RELATPCT[†]	−1.29 (.925)	−0.574 (1.21)	−0.590 (.573)
Cooperation			
SHAREREL	0.491 (.417)	0.375 (.487)	0.382 (.250)*
SHAREUNR	−0.497 (.410)	−0.586 (.558)	−0.553 (.266)***
BCOOPPCT	−6.65 (3.53)**	−5.12 (5.97)	−2.30 (2.40)
JOINTDCD	0.317 (.358)	1.58 (.765)***	0.499 (.265)**
Outside credit options			
PCGMEM[‡]	−6.56 (1.98)***	−2.98 (3.42)	−3.81 (1.18)***
CBANKMEM	−2.07 (2.39)	0.206 (2.34)	0.288 (1.21)
Penalties for default			
BINSTPCT[‡]	3.42 (1.91)**	5.24 (3.81)	2.10 (1.36)*
SNCTIONS	12.1 (4.34)***	−1.04 (3.55)	3.18 (1.95)*

Source: Ahlin and Townsend 2004.

rates are administered, not designed to clear the market, and so *r* can be used as constant in the experiment. Other derivations are in Ahlin and Townsend 2004 and are summarized in Table 9.10, marked 'Ghatak'. We now give one more example.

Suppose loan size is determined exogenously in random offers from the lender. Using separability assumptions, expected output is $EF(L)$, where L is loan size. We make typical assumptions on function F, including strict concavity, Inada conditions, and that $F(0)=0$. Define $Z(p) \equiv pr + p(1-p)q$

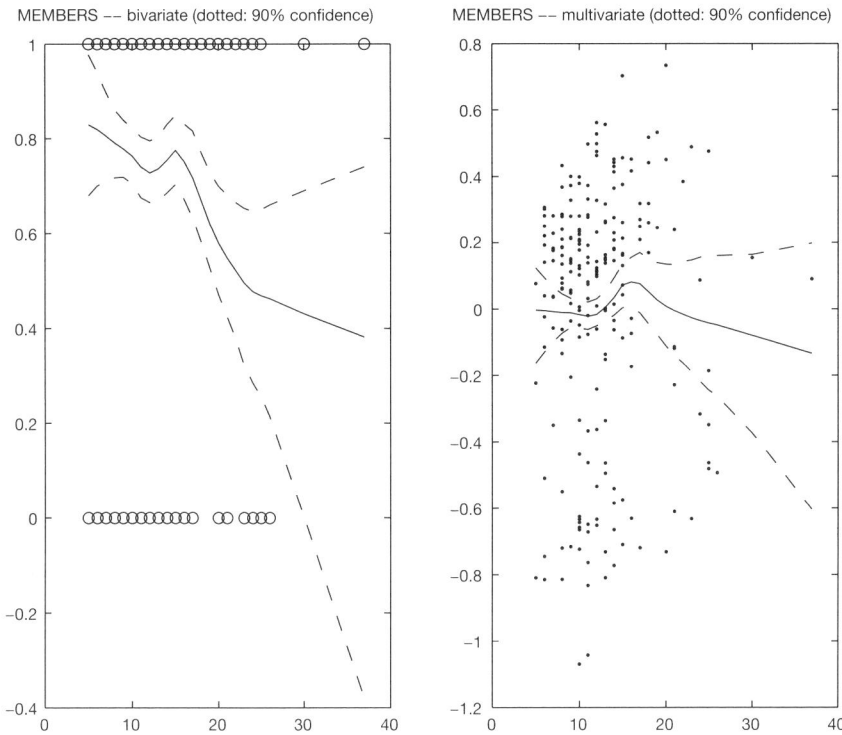

Fig. 9.24. *Number of members against repayment in a bivariate locally linear regression and in a partially linear regression*

Source: Ahlin and Townsend 2004.

as the (expected) unit borrowing cost of a type-p agent. The borrower pay-off, under symmetric loan sizes, is then

$$EF(L) - prL - p(1-p)qL = EF(L) - Z(p)L. \qquad (9.5.7)$$

Observing an agent borrowing L establishes two facts. First, it must be that $EF(L) - Z(p)L \geq \underline{U}$. Otherwise, the agent would choose the outside option. Rearranging,

$$Z(p) \leq [EF(L) - \underline{U}]/L. \qquad (9.5.8)$$

Since $Z(p)$ is increasing in p, this implies that $p \in [\underline{p}, \hat{p}(L)]$, where $\hat{p}(L)$ solves the selection equation 9.5.7 at equality. One can also show that the right hand side of inequality 9.5.8 first increases, then decreases in L, implying that $\hat{p}(L)$ does the same (see Figure 9.22). Second, assuming the borrower can always borrow less (if not more) than the lender's offer, the borrower's pay-off cannot be decreasing in loan size. Otherwise, the borrower could

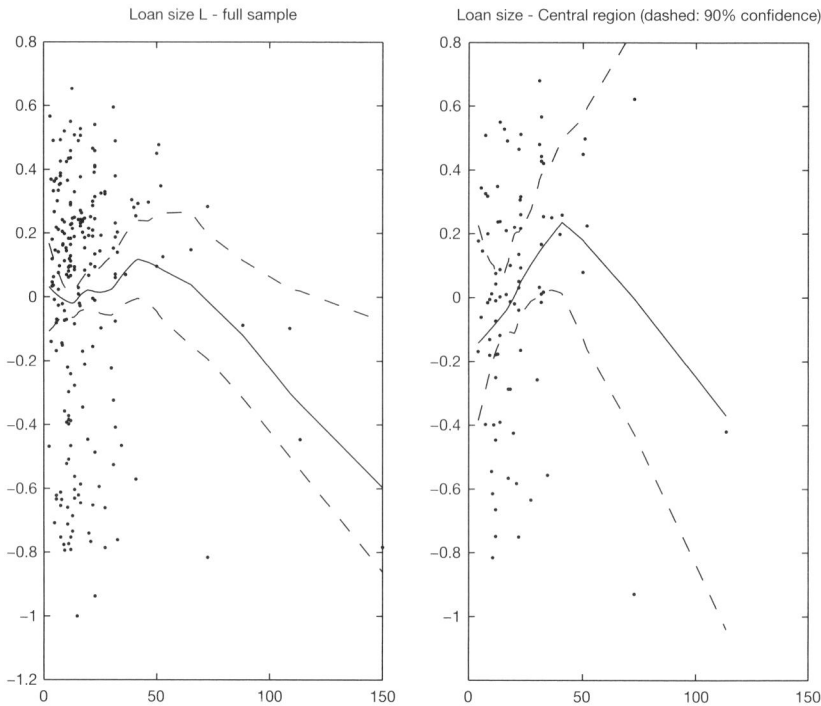

Fig. 9.25. *Partially linear regressions: loan size against repayment for the whole sample and the central region only*

Source: Ahlin and Townsend 2004.

have refused some of the loan and increased his pay-off. Applying this to pay-off function 9.5.7 gives

$$EF'(L) - Z(p) \geq 0 \quad \text{or} \quad Z(p) \leq EF'(L). \tag{9.5.9}$$

This guarantees that $p \in [\underline{p}, \check{p}(L)]$, where $\check{p}(L)$ solves relation 9.5.9 at equality. The larger L, the tighter the bound of inequality 9.5.9, and hence the lower $\check{p}(L)$ (again, see Figure 9.22). Intuitively, larger loans signal a lower (expected) cost of capital, which is true of more risky groups.

In sum, observing L tells us that $p \in [\underline{p}, \min\{\hat{p}(L), \check{p}(L)\}]$. Manipulating inequalities 9.5.8 and 9.5.9 makes it clear that the former bound is tighter, implying $\hat{p}(L) < \check{p}(L)$, if

$$\Gamma(L) \equiv F(L) - LF'(L) < \underline{U}/E \tag{9.5.10}$$

$\Gamma(L)$ is increasing from 0 as L increases, so condition 9.5.10 holds when loan sizes are small enough, as in Figure 9.23. When it does, the marginal borrower is credit-constrained. Thus, a higher loan size means higher pay-offs and borrowers being drawn from a larger, safer pool.

When the observed L is large enough so that the reverse of inequality 9.5.10 holds, $\check{p}(L) \leq \hat{p}(L)$ and thus the group type is in $[\underline{p}, \check{p}(L)]$. However, the expected repayment rate is not simply $E[p \mid p \leq p(L)]$, where the expectation is with respect to density of types denoted $g(p)$. The reason is that there is essentially a mass point at type $\check{p}(L)$ corresponding to all groups of type $\check{p}(L)$ who were offered more than L, but only accepted L, their optimal amount.

The expected repayment rate is a convex combination of $\check{p}(L)$ and $E[p \mid \check{p} \leq p(L)]$ as in Figure 9.23. Both of these terms are declining in L and approach $\underline{p}$, but the combination may be non-monotonic if the weights shift. In sum, one can anticipate from this model that defaults should be decreasing and then increasing in loan size.

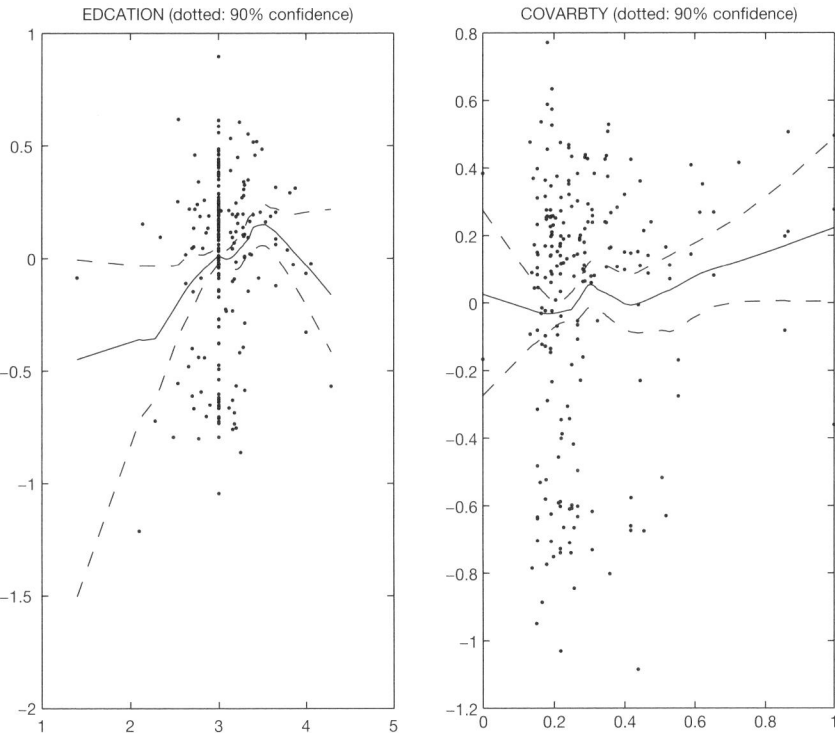

Fig. 9.26. *Partially linear regressions: group average education, village covariability against repayment*

Source: Ahlin and Townsend 2007b.

Our measure of default is a binary dummy from the BAAC survey, which equals one if the BAAC has ever, in the history of the group, raised the interest rate as a penalty for late payment. Twenty seven per cent of the groups responded affirmatively. This relatively high figure should not be taken as a mark against the BAAC lending program. Annual default rates are much lower, whereas this measures default over the entire history of the group (median group age is ten). Further, imposing an interest-rate penalty is one of the first remedial actions in a dynamic process the BAAC uses with delinquent-group-guaranteed borrowers, as discussed in section 2.1; repayment ultimately may have occurred. For the empirical tests, we recode this variable to let 0 represent default and 1 represent repayment.

The key covariates for empirical work of all four theories are listed in Table 9.11, grouped by the subject to which they are related: productivity, screening, covariance, cost of monitoring, cooperation, outside credit options, and penalties for default. The controls are the number of years the group has existed, the village average coefficient of variation for the next year's expected income, village average wealth, and number of members of the group. We proceed with three types of statistical tests.

First, for each independent, right hand side variable, the sample was partitioned into two subsamples as many ways as possible, satisfying the requirements (1) no subsample had less than fifteen groups and (2) each subgroup in one subsample had strictly higher values for the independent variable than each group in the other subsample. For each partition, a significant difference in the mean of the dependent variable across subsample was tested at the 90 per cent level. The table lists the percentage of partitions for a given independent variable producing significant mean differences across the two subsamples, with the sign indicating a positive or negative relationship.

Second, a multivariate logit allows the inclusion of all covariates at the same time. The results are summarized in Table 9.14. Standard errors are in parentheses; significance at 5 per cent, 10 per cent, and 15 per cent denoted by ***, **, and *, respectively.

Third, non-parametric regressions indicate the role of controls, such as number of members and loans size, as well as potentially non-linear relations with the key covariates, such as education, covariance, outside credit, and sanctions. The left hand sides of Figures 9.24–9.27 are sample univariate relations, and the right hand sides with both dependent and right hand sides purged of the other covariates.

The findings are, with rare exceptions, consistent with there being an information problem in the Central region and overall, though this can be

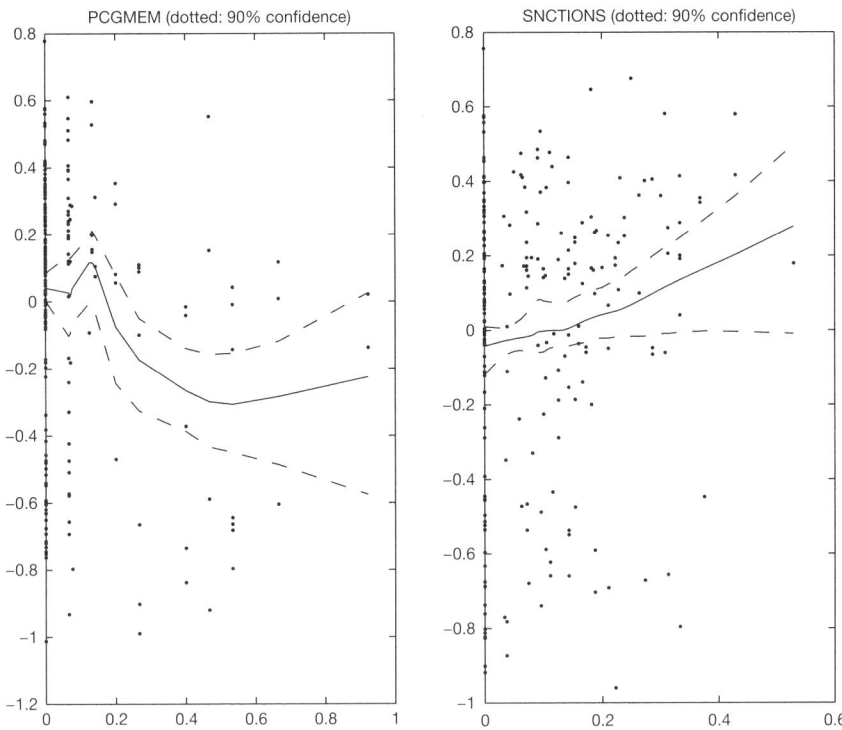

Fig. 9.27. *Partially linear regressions: production credit group prevalence, village sanctions against repayment*

Source: Ahlin and Townsend 2007b.

mixed on occasion with a default, strategic problem. The latter is clearly more predominant in the Northeast.

Specifically, moving down the rows of Table 9.15, the non-monotone derivative with respect to loan size in the adverse selection model of Ghatak is found in the Central region and in the full sample. The negative sign with respect to the joint-liability payment of the moral model of Stiglitz, and the model of Ghatak, is found in the Central region and overall. The sign-on screening is counter to the Ghatak model is the Northeast and overall. Covariance raises repayment as in the two information models in the Central region and overall. Ease of monitoring reducing moral hazard and raising repayment is found in the Central region and overall under one of the two variables. Cooperation lowers repayment in Banerjee, Besley, and Guinnane and Besley and Coate, and this is typical of most of the data,

Table 9.15. *Summary of results*

Variable	Northeast	Central	Full sample	Stiglitz	BBG	BC	Ghatak
	(Non-parametric, Logit)			Theoretical predictions			
Control							
LNYRSOLD	↓↓↓,↓↓↓	↓↓↓,↓↓↓	↓↓↓,↓↓↓				
VARIBLTY	ø,↓↓	ø,↓↓	ø,↓↓				
VILGWLTH	ø,ø	↓,ø	ø,↓				
MEMBERS	ø,ø	↓↓,ø	↓↓,ø				
Fundamentals:							
r	ø,ø	ø,ø	↓,↓	↓	↓	↓	↓
L	ø,ø	ø,↑↑↓↓	ø,↑↓	↓	↓		∧
q	ø,ø	↓↓↓,↓↓↓	↓↓↓,↓↓↓	↓	↑		↓
Productivity				↑	↑	↑	↑
AVGLAND	ø,ø	↑↑,ø	ø,ø				
EDCATION	↑,↑↑↑	ø,ø	ø,↑↑↑				
Screening							↑
SCREEN	ø,↓	ø,ø	ø,ø				
KNOWTYPE	ø,ø	ø,ø	ø,↓				
Covariance				↑	↑		↓
COVARBTY	ø,ø	↑,ø	ø,↑↑				
HOMOCCUP†	ø,ø	ø,ø	ø,ø				
Ease of Monitoring:					↑		
LIVEHERE	ø,ø	↑,ø	↑,↑↑				
RELATPCT†	ø,ø	ø,ø	↓,↓↓				
Cooperation				↑	↓	↓	
SHAREREL	ø,ø	↓,ø	ø,↑				
SHAREUNR	ø,ø	↓↓,ø	↓↓,↓↓↓				
BCOOPPCT	ø,↓↓	ø,ø	ø,ø				
JOINTDCD	↑,ø	ø,↑↑↑	↑↑↑,↑				
Outside credit options				↓	↓		
PCGMEM‡	↓↓↓,↓↓↓	ø,ø	↓↓,↓↓↓				
CBANKMEM	ø,ø	ø,ø	↓,↓↓				
Penalties for default							
BINSTPCT‡	ø,↑↑	ø,ø	ø,↑↑			↑	
SNCTIONS	↑↑,↑↑↑	ø,ø	ø,↑↑			↑	

Notes: Dependent Variable = 1 if BAAC has never raised the interest rate as a penalty, 0 if it has, significance in the logit regression at 15, 10, and 5% denoted by one, two, and three arrows, respectively; significant mean differences at the 10% level in 20, 50, and 80% of the non-parametric, univariate tests denoted by one, two, and three arrows, respectively. Variables that could be included in the next group are denoted by a †; in the previous group by a ‡.
Source: Ahlin and Townsend 2004.

with the exception for cooperation in decision-making, which has a positive sign in the moral hazard model of Stiglitz, and especially in the Central region and overall. Outside credit should lower repayment in the moral hazard models, and this is found overall but also in the Northeast. Sanctions for strategic default are especially effective in the Northeast.

9.6. Selection into and across Credit Contracts

We can test for the prevalence of moral hazard and adverse selection in models which focus on the method of borrowing, or whether to borrow at all. Here we follow closely Holmström and Milgrom 1990. Output or public-project yields are linearly related to private household effort and an array of potentially correlated but unobserved shocks. Specifically, there are two agents, or borrowers, indexed by i. Each produces output q_i as a function of his effort e_i and some random shock ε_i. One could think of output q_i as varying with loan size also, but the latter is regarded as fixed and dropped from the notation. Output is then an addition of effort and shock:

$$q_i = e_i + \varepsilon_i, \quad i = 1, 2. \tag{9.6.1}$$

The ε_i's are distributed joint-normally with a means of zero and a variance-covariance matrix,

$$\sum \equiv \begin{bmatrix} \sigma_1^2 & \sigma_{12} \\ \sigma_{12} & \sigma_2^2 \end{bmatrix}. \tag{9.6.2}$$

Thus, higher-effort e_i makes higher-output q_i more likely, but there is noise and the returns may be correlated. Note also that the projects may differ in risk σ_i^2 and we control for variance of output in some empirical specifications. Let q and e be the column vectors $[q_1, q_2]^T$ and $[e_1, e_2]^T$, respectively. Since only the q_i's are publicly observed, borrower pay-offs must be in terms of them. Attention is restricted to contracts giving agent i consumption c_i as a linear function of output:

$$c_i(q; \kappa_{i0}, \kappa_i) = \kappa_{i0} + \kappa_i^T q, \quad i = 1, 2 \tag{9.6.3}$$

where the column vector $\kappa_i = [\kappa_{i1} \ \kappa_{i2}]^T$. Further, κ is just the collection of all the compensation parameters; let $\kappa \equiv \{\kappa_{ij}\}$, for $i = 1, 2$ and $j = 0, 1, 2$.

In this model, we consider preferences in which the disutility of effort can be measured in consumption units by $C_i(e_i)$, a strictly convex function. We also assume that agents maximize expected utility, where the utility function over consumption is exponential with a coefficient of absolute risk aversion $r_i > 0$. Then, given effort choices e_1 and e_2, the certainty equivalent (CE) for agent i of contract κ has an analytic form:

$$CE_i(e; \kappa) = \kappa_{i0} + \kappa_i^T e - C_i(e_i) - \left(\frac{1}{2}\right) r_i \kappa_i^T \sum \kappa_i, \quad i = 1, 2 \qquad (9.6.4)$$

where $\kappa_i^T \sum \kappa_i = \kappa_{i1}^2 \sigma_1^2 + \kappa_{i2}^2 \sigma_2^2 + 2\kappa_{i1}\kappa_{i2}\sigma_{12}$ is the variance of i's compensation. Note that diversity in cost of effort and risk aversion is allowed, though we cannot control for these in the data beyond using education and demographic and occupational variables. The lender is assumed risk neutral and thus has certainty equivalent utility,

$$CE_p(e; \kappa) = e_1 + e_2 - (\kappa_1 + \kappa_2)^T e - \kappa_{10} - \kappa_{20}. \qquad (9.6.5)$$

Suppose, first, that the lender can deal with each borrower individually—the borrowers do not observe each others' actions or outcomes and cannot conduct side-contracts. Then the lender sets both contracts to maximize his pay-off subject to the agents' participation constraints and incentive compatibility constraints. Since the model exhibits transferable utility, the optimal contract maximizes total surplus (the sum of all pay-offs) subject to the incentive compatibility constraints only. Thus, at the optimum, κ_1 and κ_2 solve

$$\max_{\kappa_1, \kappa_2} \quad e_1 + e_2 - C_1(e_1) - C_2(e_2) - \frac{1}{2} r_1 \kappa_1^T \sum \kappa_1 - \frac{1}{2} r_2 \kappa_2^T \sum \kappa_2 \qquad (9.6.6)$$

subject to the first-order conditions for household i's effort: $C'_i(e_i) = \kappa_{ii}$, $i = 1, 2$.

Total surplus equals expected output (the first and second terms in the maxim) minus the costs of effort (the third and fourth terms) and risk costs (the fifth and sixth terms). The optimal contract satisfies

$$\kappa_{ii} = \frac{1}{1 + r_i \sigma_i^2 (1 - \rho^2) C''_i}, \kappa_{ij}$$
$$= -\kappa_{ii}\sigma_{12}/\sigma_j^2; \quad i = 1, 2, j = 1, 2, j \neq i \qquad (9.6.7)$$

where $\rho \equiv \sigma_{12}/\sigma_1\sigma_2$ is the correlation coefficient for noise in project return ε_i. Note that the direct, own-production term κ_{ii} decreases in σ_i^2 and r_i as is natural with risk aversion. The cross term κ_{ij} varies inversely with the technological correlation σ_{12} and with the risk of the other borrower σ_j^2. The overall risk cost can be calculated:

$$(1 - \rho^2) \frac{r_1 \kappa_{11}^2 \sigma_1^2 + r_2 \kappa_{22}^2 \sigma_2^2}{2}. \qquad (9.6.8)$$

If $\rho=1$ then relative performance evaluation works perfectly well: all deviations in effort are detectable, and the lender offers full insurance. The risk-sharing occurs because the correlation between shocks mitigates the principal's lack of information about the agents' efforts.

Suppose next that the two borrowers *can cooperate*, as is presumably easier within a joint-liability group. Specifically, they do observe each other's actions and can commit to transfers with each other conditional on observed actions and outcomes. The principal still sees output only. This allows the group mutually to reinsure each other and to coordinate to an agreed upon set of actions. The side contracts they can write will be of the form

$$\tau(e,q) = \gamma^T q + \tau(e_1 + e_2), \tag{9.6.9}$$

where $\tau(\boldsymbol{e},\boldsymbol{q})$ gives the net transfer from agent 1 to agent 2 as a result of actions e and output realizations q. The function $\tau(\boldsymbol{e},\boldsymbol{q})$ allows the pair to enforce any set of actions as a Nash equilibrium. The mutual insurance agreements, for which coefficient γ denotes the vector $[\gamma_1 \; \gamma_2]^T$, are restricted to being linear in output, as above.

Holmström and Milgrom (1990) assume the pair will choose $\tau(\boldsymbol{e},\boldsymbol{q})$ and γ to reach a Pareto optimal set of actions and transfers. Again, given transferable utility, which can be done within the group using $\tau(\bullet)$, this implies the pair will maximize joint surplus. Given the external borrowing contract with its incentive κ, the two borrowers thus choose $(\boldsymbol{e},\boldsymbol{\gamma})$ to maximize

$$(\kappa_1 + \kappa_2)^T e - C_1(e_1) - C_2(e_2) - (r_1/2)(\kappa_1 - \gamma)^T \sum (\kappa_1 - \gamma) \\ -(r_2/2)(\kappa_2 + \gamma)^T \sum (\kappa_2 + \gamma). \tag{9.6.10}$$

As before, the principal can be thought of as choosing (κ_1,κ_2) to maximize total surplus, constrained, however, by what the group is doing:

$$\max_{\kappa_1,\kappa_2} \quad e_1 + e_2 - C_1(e_1) - C_2(e_2) \\ -(r_1/2)(\kappa_1 - \gamma)^T \sum (\kappa_1 - \gamma) - (r_2/2)(\kappa_2 + \gamma)^T \sum (\kappa_2 + \gamma). \tag{9.6.11}$$

subject to: $(\boldsymbol{e},\boldsymbol{\gamma})$ maximizes 9.6.10 given κ.

Holmström and Milgrom 1990 proves, as in Wilson 1968, that the lender's optimal design coincides with that for a single ('syndicate') borrower whose effort-cost function satisfies $C(e_1,e_2)=C_1(e_1)+C_2(e_2)$ and absolute risk aversion coefficient r satisfies $1/r=1/r_1+1/r_2$. In other words, the risk tolerance coefficient of the syndicate borrower is greater than the risk tolerance of each individual borrower. This corresponds to a lower total risk cost to the pair, due to internal risk sharing.

Now the principal is reduced from four degrees of freedom or parameters to two, since what matters is not κ_1 and κ_2 individually, but the sum $\kappa_1+\kappa_2$. So, without loss of generality, assume $\kappa_{12}=\kappa_{21}=0$. Given $(\kappa_{11}, \kappa_{22})$, the total overall risk cost is

$$(1/2)r[\kappa_{11}^2\sigma_1^2 + \kappa_{22}^2\sigma_2^2 + 2\kappa_{11}\kappa_{22}\rho\sigma_1\sigma_2]. \tag{9.6.12}$$

This expression is increasing in ρ.

Here, as in the relative performance regime, actions will be chosen that equate κ_{ii} and $C'_i(e_i)$. Thus, any pair of actions (e_1,e_2) must be implemented by the same contract parameters $(\kappa_{11},\kappa_{22})$ in both regimes. This enables us to determine easily which regime delivers higher total surplus when implementing a given set of actions. For a given set of actions, the only part of total surplus that varies by regime is the risk cost, given in expressions 9.6.8 and 9.6.12, respectively. These risk costs are easily compared, for a given set of actions, since $(\kappa_{11},\kappa_{22})$ are the same in both regimes.

It can be verified that at $\rho=0$ the risk cost of implementing any set of actions e is lower under the cooperative regime. It follows that at $\rho=0$, the cooperative regime gives higher total surplus than the individualistic regime. Similarly, at $\rho=1$, the risk cost of implementing any set of actions e is lower under the individualistic regime, and thus the individualistic relative performance regime gives higher total surplus. Further, as ρ increases, the cost of implementing every set of actions in the cooperative regime is increasing (see expression 9.6.12), which implies that maximized surplus under this regime is decreasing in ρ. The cost of implementing every set of actions in the individualistic regime is strictly decreasing in ρ (see expression 9.6.8), which implies that the maximized surplus under this regime is strictly increasing in ρ.

In summary, holding risk aversion and other parameters constant, the pay-off is strictly increasing in ρ under relative performance and decreasing in ρ under cooperation. At $\rho=0$, the cooperative regime dominates, while at $\rho=1$, the relative performance regime dominates. This proves that there is a cut-off, $\bar{\rho}\in(0,1)$, above which the individualistic regime dominates and below which the cooperative regime does. The intuition is that when correlation is high, the scope for internal risk-sharing is low, while the lender is able to offer significant insurance through relative performance comparisons. When correlation is low there is great need for internal insurance and relative performance works poorly.

More generally, following Prescott and Townsend (2002), we need not assume constant absolute risk aversion, nor particular forms for production. Optimal contracts can be determined by the linear programming methods described earlier. That is, let the utility function of agent i be $U_i(c_i) + V_i(T_i - e_i)$ where T_1 is the total time endowment, c_i is consumption and e_i is effort. The principal or insurer is risk neutral. Let c denote the consumption row vector $c = (c_1, c_2)$, q the vector of outputs $q = (q_1, q_2)$, e_i denotes the vector of efforts over two projects $e_{i\bullet} = (e_{i1}, e_{i2})$, (though typically we imagine household i only works on his own project). Likewise, let a denote the vector of efforts over the two projects $a = (a_1, a_2)$ (though typically these are agent specific efforts (e_1, e_2)). The technology of production is described by the probability that output vector is q given effort vector a— namely, $p(q \mid a)$.

The programming problem for the determination of the relative performance regime searches over the policy probability $\pi(c, q, e_1, e_2)$. The optimal contract is found by maximizing surplus

$$\sum_{c,q,e_{1\bullet},e_{2\bullet}} \pi(c, q, e_{1\bullet}, e_{2\bullet})(q_1 + q_2 - c_1 - c_2) \qquad (9.6.13)$$

subject to promise keeping for the group at Pareto weight λ_i:

$$\sum_{c,q,e_{1\bullet},e_{2\bullet}} \pi(c, q, e_{1\bullet}, e_{2\bullet}) \sum_i \lambda_i [U_i(c_i) + V_i(T_i - e_i)] \geq \bar{G}, \qquad (9.6.14)$$

technological probability

$$\sum_c \pi(c, \bar{q}, \bar{e}_{1\bullet}, \bar{e}_{2\bullet}) = p(\bar{q} | \bar{e}_{1\bullet} + \bar{e}_{2\bullet}) \sum_{c,q} \prod (c, q, \bar{e}_{1\bullet}, \bar{e}_{2\bullet}), \forall \bar{q}, \bar{e}_{1\bullet}, \bar{e}_{2\bullet}$$

$$(9.6.15)$$

individual incentive constraints for agent 1

$$\sum_{c,q,e_{2\bullet}} \pi(c, q, e_{1\bullet}, e_{2\bullet})[U_1(c_1) + V_1(T_1 - e_1)] \geq$$

$$\sum_{c,q,e_{2\bullet}} \pi(c, q, e_{1\bullet}, e_{2\bullet}) \frac{p(q | \hat{e}_{1\bullet} + e_{2\bullet})}{p(q | e_{1\bullet} + e_{2\bullet})} [U_1(c_1) + V_1(T_1 - \hat{e}_1)], \quad \forall e_{1\bullet}, \hat{e}_{1\bullet}$$

$$(9.6.16)$$

and individual incentive constraint for agent 2

$$\sum_{c,q,e_{2\bullet}} \pi(c, q, e_{1\bullet}, e_{2\bullet})[U_2(c_2) + V_2(T_2 - e_2)] \geq$$

$$\sum_{c,q,e_{2\bullet}} \pi(c, q, e_{1\bullet}, e_{2\bullet}) \frac{p(q|e_{1\bullet} + \hat{e}_{2\bullet})}{p(q|e_{1\bullet} + e_{2\bullet})}[U_2(c_2) + V_2(T_2 - \hat{e}_2)], \quad \forall e_{2\bullet}, \hat{e}_{2\bullet}$$

$$(9.6.17)$$

Of course, the contract must also satisfy probability measure constraints

$$\pi(c, q, e_{1\bullet}, e_{2\bullet}) \geq 0, \quad \forall c, q, e_{1\bullet}, e_{2\bullet} \qquad (9.6.18)$$

for each

$$\sum_{c,q,e_{1\bullet},e_{2\bullet}} \pi(c, q, e_{1\bullet}, e_{2\bullet}) = 1. \qquad (9.6.19)$$

Again, this formulation of the problem maximizes the 'surplus' of the principal subject to a reservation utility constraint. The first constraint ensures a given (λ_i-weighted) amount of utility for the pair. Note that, as $\bar{G}$ increases, in effect the wealth of each borrower increases. Parameter $\bar{G}$ can be varied parametrically as in partial equilibrium comparative statics. Equivalently, one can maximize a weighted sum of utilities subject to a minimum surplus or 'wealth' constraint for the outsider.

Again, a joint-liability contract allows the two agents to enter into a risk-sharing group agreement with internal rules $c_i(c_g, \mu)$ where $\mu = (\mu_1, \mu_2)$ are the within-group Pareto weights, μ_i the Pareto weight of agent i, and consumption c_i of agent i as a function of group consumption c_g. We make a similar substitution for leisure/effort $e_i(a_g, \mu)$ where a_g is total effort $a_1 + a_2$, or for ease of notation $e_i(a, \mu)$.

The programming problem for the determination of the group regime searches over policy probability $\pi(c_q, \boldsymbol{q}, \boldsymbol{a}, \mu)$. It should maximize surplus

$$\sum_{c_g,q,a,\mu} \pi(c_g, q, a, \mu)(q_1 + q_2 - c_g) \qquad (9.6.20)$$

subject to reservation utility of the group, and technology constraint

$$\sum_{c_g,q,a,\mu} \pi(c_g, q, a, \mu) \sum_i \lambda_i [U_i\left(c_i(c_g, \mu)\right) + V_i\left(T_i - e_i(a, \mu)\right)] \geq \bar{G},$$

$$(9.6.21)$$

technological probability

$$\sum_{c_g} \pi(c_g, \bar{q}, \bar{a}, \bar{\mu}) = p(\bar{q}|\bar{a}) \sum_{c_g, q} \prod (c_g, q, \bar{a}, \bar{\mu}), \quad \forall q, \bar{a}, \bar{\mu}, \qquad (9.6.22)$$

and group incentive constraint

$$\sum_{c_g, q} \pi(c_g, q, a, \mu) \sum_i \mu_i [U_i \Big(c_i(c_g, \mu) \Big) + V_i \Big(T_i - e_i(a, \mu) \Big)] \geq$$

$$\sum_{c_g, q} \pi(c_g, q, a, \mu) \frac{p(q|\hat{a})}{p(q|a)} \sum_i \mu_i \Big[U_i \Big(c_i(c_g, \mu) \Big) + V_i \Big(T_i - e_i(\hat{a}, \mu) \Big) \Big] \quad \forall a, \hat{a}, \mu.$$

$$(9.6.23)$$

The last constraint is the group incentive to take action vector a over $\hat{a}$ given internal weight μ. The degree of internal inequality μ is endogenous here and may differ from the objective weights λ because of this group incentive constraint. The difficulty of incentives is linked to the distribution of income. Typically, though, in the example solutions below we do not distinguish μ from λ.

For certain classes and technologies, we know that weights μ and λ must be equal. Assume that sets of feasible consumption and efforts are continua, just as we did in the analysis of internal group-sharing rules, but retain the constant relative risk aversion (CRRA) preference specification. These preferences aggregate in the sense of Gorman 1954. Then, varying the weights within the group will not affect the group's schedule of payments to the outsider in any way. It is as if the outsider were facing a single agent who has the choice of effort over the two technologies. The consumption and labor allocation to this 'single agent' is determined as in the well-understood, classic, principal–agent model.

Suppose, in particular, that preferences do not aggregate. Specifically, individuals are required to work their own technologies. Suppose further, for example, that projects either succeed or fail. Then there are four possible outputs, reflecting all the different combinations of high or low outputs on the two technologies. Figure 9.28, from Prescott and Townsend 2002, describes which of the four lines corresponds to which output combination. Not shown in the figure is the optimal labor assignment, but here for the full range of $\lambda_1 \in [0.0, 0.5]$ both agents are assigned the high labor effort.

Starting from the left side of the graph, at $\lambda_1 = 0.0$, agent 1 receives no weight within the group. Not shown in the graph is individual consumption. Of course, at $\lambda_1 = 0.0$ agent 1's consumption is 0 for all outputs, while agent 2 consumes the entire group consumption c_g. Low consumption and high effort for agent 1 have little consequence for group utility because

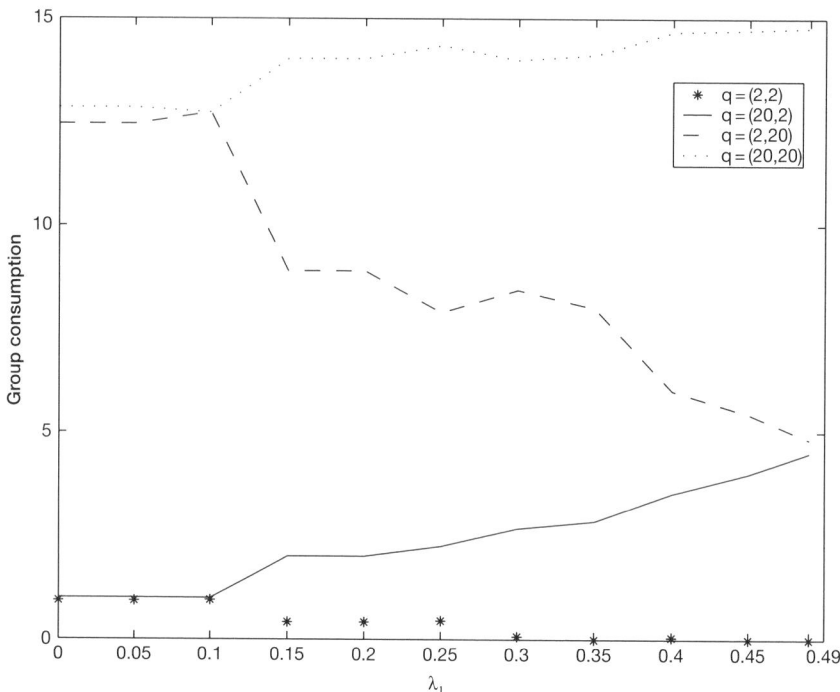

Fig. 9.28. Group consumption sharing rules for various λ_1

Source: Prescott and Townsend 2002.

agent 1 has low weight. Essentially, agent 1 is a 'serf'. Internally, having agreed on the distribution of welfare implicit in λ, agent 1 abides by the agreement, which is to work hard and to consume little or nothing. That is, $c_g(q_1,q_2)$ lines for $(q_h,q_h)=(20,20)$ and $(q_l,q_h)=(2,20)$ nearly coincide in Figure 9.28 at $\lambda_1=0.0$ (any difference is due to numerical approximation). Coincident also are the lines for $(q_l,q_l)=(2,2)$ and $(q_h,q_l)=(20,2)$. Thus, group consumption does not depend on output from the technology utilized by agent 1. The risk-neutral principal provides full insurance on technology 1 because internal monitoring and perfect commitment take care of potential incentive problems for agent one.

In contrast, agent 2, the so-called 'lord' of the group, has the high λ_2 weight. At and near $\lambda_1=0.0$, and λ_2 near 1.0, the 'mongrel consumer's' utility is nearly identical to that of agent 2. Since the mongrel consumer cares (mostly) about the effort of agent 2, the group must be given incentives to make him work hard. Thus, group consumption and agent 2's consumption vary positively with the output of agent 2 on technology 2.

This logic prevails more generally, as λ_1 increases toward the symmetric weight $\lambda_1 = 0.5$. Over this range, group consumption c_g depends primarily on output of agent 2 from technology 2—namely, q_2, as he is most inclined to shirk. Though output q_1, of agent 1 from technology 1 becomes increasingly important. In sum, for $0.0 < \lambda_1 < 0.5$, group consumption c_g is ordered with technology output:

$$c_g(q_1 = 2, q_2 = 2) < c_g(q_1 = 20, q_2 = 2) < c_g(q_1 = 2, q_2 = 20)$$
$$< c_g(q_1 = 20, q_2 = 20).$$

The dominance of one financial regime over another in this context is a function of the Pareto weight λ, which determines where agents 1 and 2 lie on the utility possibilities frontier and the utility $\bar{W}$ of the principal (see Figure 9.29(a)–(d)). (Variation $\bar{W}$ is achieved by varying parameter $\bar{G}$ in the program: the higher $\bar{W}$ is, the lower $\bar{G}$ is.) If the utilities U_1, U_2 of the agents lie on or close to the 45-degree line in utility space—that is, the agents are to be treated more or less equally, then the relative performance regime dominates the group insurance regime. Thus, utility dispersion is a force for groups. Note also that as the utility of the principal is varied, groups emerge and disappear again.

Now, imagine a variety of local economies k which vary in the preferences $U_{ki}(c_i) + V_{ki}(T_{ki} - e_i)$, technologies $p(q| e_{1\bullet} + e_{2\bullet})$, and Pareto weights $(\lambda_{k1}, \lambda_{k1})$ of local residents. Then contract regimes could vary across these local economies k, especially with the degree of local inequality. Indeed, with a continuum of economies of each type, we can let a_k be the relative number of economies of type k, and let ρ_k be the relative Pareto weight of local economy k. One can then write down a mechanism design problem similar to the earlier programs, but here for the larger single economy. We would maximize the ρ_k weighted sums of type k utilities subject to a single economy-wide resource constraint, that the surplus when added across all small economies be no less than zero. In effect, the utility $\bar{W}$ of a single risk neutral principal would be at least zero.

The solution, when reinterpreted, does allow interactions among the local economies. In principle, transfers *across* economies of *different* types are allowed, though the natural benchmark would be no transfers across types. Key is the provision of insurance for local fluctuations among local economies of the same type. When there are non-trivial lotteries for an economy of a given type, then the extended model predicts coexistence of

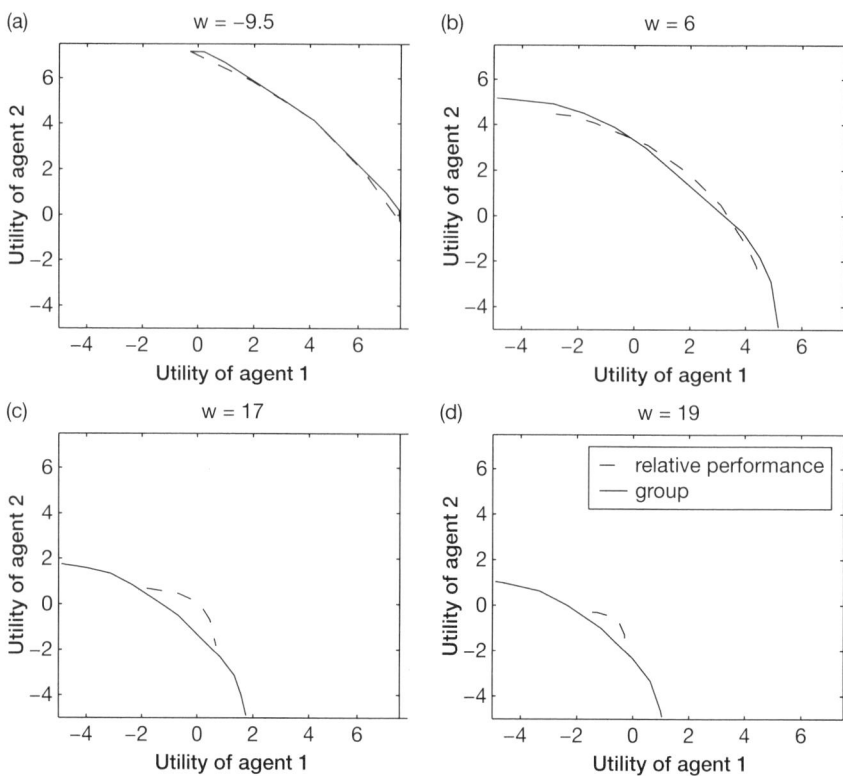

Fig. 9.29(a)–(d). *Slices of Pareto frontier*

Source: Prescott and Townsend 2002.

regimes, as observed in the data. Note the non-convexities in the outer envelope of the utilities frontier in Figure 9.29(a)–(d).

There is, in fact, a decentralization of the large economies in which each local economy (with its own level of inequality) interacts in larger, economy-wide markets. The advantage of that decentralization is that it sets the surplus of each economy type to zero endogenously. But, also, as in the second welfare theorem, there are possible wealth reallocations across economy types as ρ_k is varied. There would, of course, be an overall restriction, zero net resource use across all economies, so that intermediary losses in subsidies to one group are financed by taxes on other groups.

Later, we shall discuss making the local Pareto weights $(\lambda_{k1}, \lambda_{k1})$ endogenous, as well. They will be determined naturally enough by the endogenous value of individual endowments evaluated at equilibrium prices. These connections underlie our interchangeable use of Pareto weights and wealth—that is, asymmetric Pareto weights are equivalent with high wealth dispersion in the local economy, and low weight ρ_k in the local economy with low average wealth.

To test these credit-selection models, Ahlin and Townsend (2004) use the data from the BAAC and households instruments of the Townsend Thai Survey. As described earlier, some households have entered into group-guaranteed loans and others into individual loans. We also broaden the categories to include loans from village funds. We have these data for each loan and each individual. The dependent variables that we use are dummies reflecting whether the household has taken out a group-guaranteed loan from a lending institution in the past year. There are two versions of this variable. The first, BAGPLOAN, restricts attention to group-guaranteed loans from the BAAC. As noted, this government institution is the primary institutional lender in rural Thailand: for example, 64 per cent of institutional loans in our sample are from the BAAC. The BAAC offers both individual loans, which must be guaranteed by some form of collateral, usually land, and joint-liability loans. To receive the latter, one must form or join an official BAAC-registered borrowing group and enter into a joint-liability arrangement. BAGPLOAN equals one if the household has had an outstanding loan from the BAAC in the past year and lists the collateral for this loan as either none, a single guarantor, or multiple guarantors. About 23 per cent of the household sample has such a loan.

The second version of the dependent variable is GRUPLOAN, which incorporates group-guaranteed loans from the BAAC and other institutions. These others are typically smaller institutions such as agricultural cooperatives and often village-based ones such as production credit groups (PCGs), but they also include commercial banks. Using this broader definition increases the proportion of the sample that qualifies as having a group-guaranteed loan to about 30 per cent. However, the institutions incorporated are diverse in size and practice, which makes isolating contracts that are clearly group contracts more imprecise. We report specifications using both BAGPLOAN and GRUPLOAN. Two analogous variables measure whether the household has an individual loan contract from a lending institution. BAIDLOAN and INDLOAN correspond to BAGPLOAN and GRUPLOAN, respectively, in the lenders they cover. The criterion for a loan counting as an individual loan is that the collateral used was land, savings, current or future crops, and other collateral such as a house or boat. BAIDLOAN is positive for about 13 per cent of the population, INDLOAN for about 22 per cent. Neither of these will be used directly in regressions, but will at times be used to limit the sample to only those households having secured either an individual or a group loan.

Let $\overline{WEALTH}$ denote average village wealth. To measure wealth dispersion, labeled WLTHDSPR in the logits, we use the following function of household wealth and village average wealth.

$$WLTHDSPR = \left[1 - \frac{WEALTH}{\overline{WEALTH}}\right]^{1/2}.$$

This is similar to a simple distance function, $[\overline{WEALTH}\text{--}WEALTH]$. The differences are that we divide by $\overline{WEALTH}$, which makes it a scale-free measure, and we take a square root which dampens the effect of $WEALTH$'s long right tail. To check robustness relative to functional form, we will also use a non-parametric regression technique on

$$\frac{WEALTH}{\overline{WEALTH}}$$

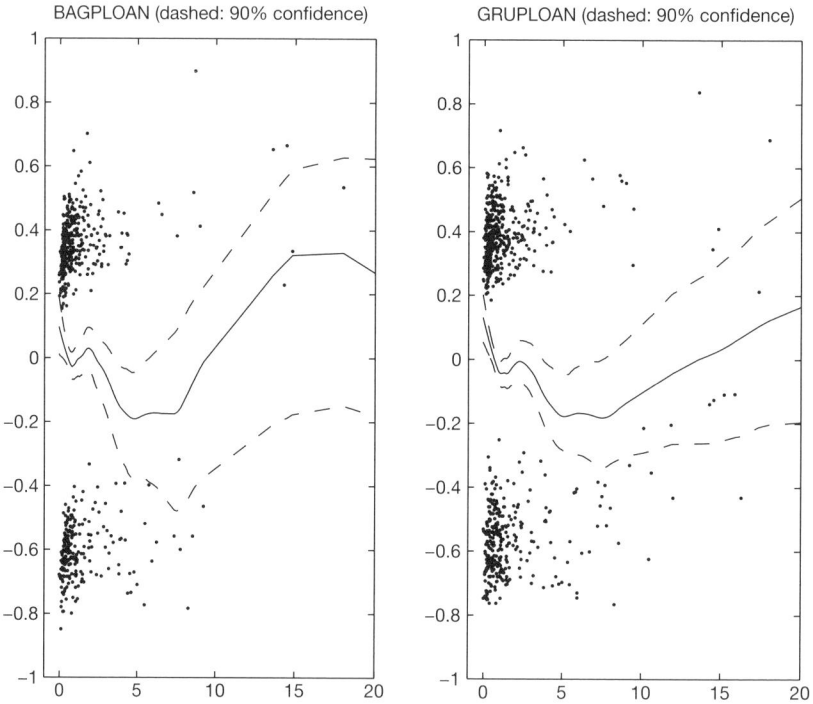

Fig. 9.30. *Wealth as a predictor of having a group loan*

Repr. from C. Ahlin and R. M. Townsend, 'Selection into and across Credit Contracts: Theory and Field Research', *Journal of Econometrics* (2007), 136: 665–98. Copyright 2007; reproduced with permission from Elsevier.

itself. Inequality matters for prediction of whether we should see joint-liability or individual loan contracts, assuming there are no policy restrictions.

The multivariate logit examines the prevalence of group-guaranteed, joint-liability loans with wealth, wealth squared, wealth spread, titled land with a linear and quadratic term, and some other controls (expected income, Northeast, in agriculture, land owned, education, male head). We also examine the implication of correlation in project returns by including various measures one at a time: the fractions of the household among village respondents for whom the best year in the last five was the same year, the fraction for whom the worst year was the same, and a measure which counts identical responses across both good and bad years.

The best indicator we have of the wealth of the potential group is the wealth of the household itself. One can see from non-parametric regression Figure 9.31 and the logits in Table 9.16, both with multivariate controls,

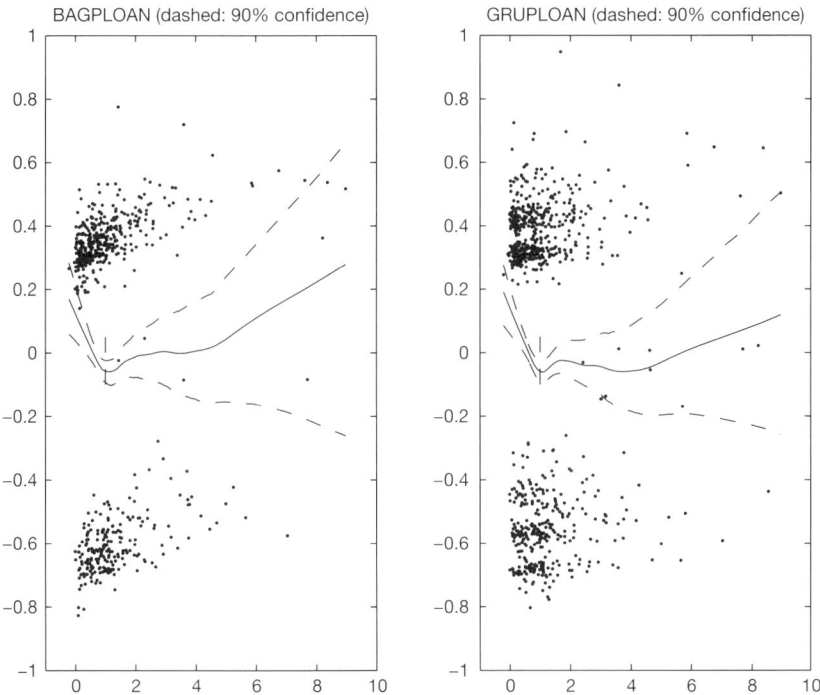

Fig. 9.31. *Relative wealth: household wealth divided by the village mean as a predictor of having a group loan*

Repr. from C. Ahlin and R. M. Townsend, 'Selection into and across Credit Contracts: Theory and Field Research', *Journal of Econometrics* (2007), 136: 665–98. Copyright 2007; reproduced with permission from Elsevier.

Table 9.16. *Restricted samples: restricted only to those borrowers having either a group-guaranteed loan or an individual loan*

	BAGPLOAN			GRUPLOAN		
WEALTH	−.417	−.418	−.418	−.174	−.173	−.175
	(.169)***	(.169)***	(.169)***	(.096)**	(.097)**	(.097)**
WEALTHSQ	3.24E-8	3.28E-8	3.26E-8	1.03E-8	1.03E-8	1.02E-8
	(1.73E-8)**	(1.72E-8)**	(1.73E-8)**	(4.91E-9)***	(4.98E-9)***	(4.94E-9)***
WLTHDSPR	.696	.686	.695	.505	.500	.509
	(.253)***	(.254)***	(.254)***	(.217)***	(.217)***	(.217)***
TITLE	.213	.219	.216	−.053	−.043	−.046
	(.164)	(.165)	(.165)	(.090)	(.090)	(.090)
TITLESQ	−3.14E-8	−3.21E-8	−3.17E-8	−8.14E-9	−8.19E-9	−8.10E-9
	(1.70E-8)**	(1.70E-8)**	(1.70E-8)**	(4.63E-9)**	(4.71E-9)**	(4.66E-9)**
PROBHI	.023	.017	.029	−.139	−.124	−.123
	(.353)	(.354)	(.353)	(.308)	(.308)	(.308)
SAMEBEST	.176			.549		
	(.401)			(.350)*		
SAMEWRST		−.190			−.059	
		(.407)			(.367)	
SAMEITHR			.009			.482
			(.513)			(.471)
INCOME	.312	.335	.310	.075	.082	.037
	(.877)	(.882)	(.876)	(.738)	(.735)	(.727)
EXINCOME	−.732	−.771	−.734	−.090	−.102	−.042
	(1.10)	(1.11)	(1.10)	(.943)	(.938)	(.928)
NRTHEAST	−.368	−.344	−.355	−.223	−.191	−.222
	(.214)**	(.213)*	(.214)**	(.176)	(.176)	(.177)
AGRYES	−.538	−.537	−.530	.003	.040	.021
	(.522)	(.522)	(.522)	(.354)	(.353)	(.353)
AGRNO	−.804	−.802	−.798	−.415	−.387	−.403
	(.531)*	(.532)*	(.531)*	(.361)	(.360)	(.361)
OWNSBSNS	−.116	−.125	−.117	−.512	−.521	−.508
	(.225)	(.226)	(.226)	(.189)***	(.189)***	(.189)***
LANDOWND	−7.28E-3	−7.21E-3	−7.25E-3	−6.21E-3	−6.22E-3	−6.27E-3
	(4.12E-3)**	(4.12E-3)**	(4.11E-3)**	(3.45E-3)**	(3.45E-3)**	(3.44E-3)**
EDYEARH	.030	.029	.030	.010	.007	.010
	(.042)	(.042)	(.042)	(.033)	(.033)	(.033)
MALEH	.437	.446	.445	.628	.644	.632
	(.243)**	(.243)**	(.243)**	(.208)***	(.208)***	(.208)***
N	573	573	573	736	736	736

Notes: Standard errors in parentheses; significance at 5, 10, and 15% denoted by ***, **, and *, respectively.

Source: C. Ahlin and R. M. Townsend, 'Selection into and across Credit Contracts: Theory and Field Research', *Journal of Econometrics*, 136 (2007), 665–98. Copyright 2007; reproduced with permission from Elsevier.

that an individual is more likely to be in a joint-liability group as a U-shaped function of wealth. The initial negatively sloped part is especially prominent.

There may be other explanations for such a relationship. Chief among these could be a story revolving around collateralizable wealth: since individual loans require collateral, we would expect them to be more prevalent at higher wealth levels, at the expense of group loans. This story, however, does not immediately make clear why the relationship should turn up again to deliver a U-shape. Further, we separate out and control for the part of wealth that is most commonly used and accepted as collateral, TITLE and TITLESQ, and still find the U-shaped relationship between total wealth and being in a group contract. Thus, the collateral story does not seem to be driving the results.

One might also think that poor households borrow in groups, moderately wealthy households borrow as individuals, and the wealthiest households take out both kinds of loans since their demand for credit is higher. This would produce a U-shape relationship between wealth and having a group loan. But, note that this explanation is ruled out since the sample includes households with one or the other kind of loan, but not both.

We do not have group-level wealth, only wealth of households. Another approach would be to proxy group wealth for a given household as the average between that household's wealth and the average household wealth level in the village (or among villagers who borrow). The inverted-U shape loses significance in the majority of specifications under this approach. This need not be due to a deficiency of the model, but rather an imperfect proxy for group wealth.

A strong and statistically significant result is that group borrowing is more likely the higher the spread in wealth. The non-parametric regressions in Figure 9.30 using the simple measure $\frac{WEALTH}{WEALTH}$ show that prevalence of the group reaches its minimum almost precisely when individual wealth equals the village mean. Here the declining portion is most significant, within tight standard error bands, though the upturn is evident locally as well.

The theory was not designed to capture supply-side variation. But, households who borrow from the BAAC have made a broader decision as to whether to borrow at all, in turn a function of the availability or ease of use of BAAC facilities. Though we do not expand in this section the selection model, we conduct a robustness check. We include in the logits the variables we had used earlier as supply-side instruments, such as headman responses on the use of the BAAC and other institutions in the village, time to the district center, various GIS averages, as well as a batch of CDD village-level characteristics. Many of the covariate's controls and (former) instruments are significant. Remarkably, though, the featured significant variables, wealth and wealth spread remain (see Table 9.17).

Table 9.17. *Selection with supply-side variation: moral hazard*

Variable	Original•	New ••
WEALTH	−416845.45***	−462334.08***
WEALTHSQ	.0324**	.0345*
WLTHDSPR	.6962***	.6609***
TITLE	213194.59	313053.16**
TITLESQ	−.0314**	−.0336*
PROBHI	0.0233	−.1441
% OF OTHER RESPS.	0.1755	0.4329
INCOME	0.3122	0.6668
EXINCOME	−.7318	−1.1167
NRTHEAST	−.3677**	−.5586**
AGRYES	−.5382	−.6078
AGRNO	−.8035*	−.7778
OWNSBSNS	−.1163	−0.1166
LANDOWND	−.0073**	−.0063
EDYEARH	0.03	0.0148
MALEH	.4371**	0.3906
AGRI ONLY		−1.3951
CDD MULTIPLE Occ.		−1.3545
ASSEMBLY HALL CDD		.7180***
ECON STATUS CDD		−.4465**
HELP FROM GOVT		−.4435**
TIME TO DIST. CENTER		−.0095
USE OF BAAC		−.4268
COMMUNITY BANK		0.1961
HAS RICE BANK		−.3657
HAS BUFFALO BANK		−.0811
COTTAGE IND.		−30.1780***
PREDIC. lb 5		−.3723
PREDIC. Rb 5		0.9221**
PREDIC. vf 5		0.004
CONSTANT	0.8436	2.6715***
N	573	501

Legend: * p<.15; ** p<.10; *** p<.05. • Original variables (Table 9.1.3);
•• New variables (including Community development department).
Source: Puentes and Townsend research note 2006.

Moral hazard is not the only possible information problem. The adverse selection model of Ghatak was described earlier. The key selection equation as in 9.5.6 earlier is:

$$E(p) - pr - p(1 - p)q = \underline{U}.$$

The key variable to measure is the risk-types of the borrower. We do so using subjective income assessments, taking Ghatak 2000 quite literally. Specifically, each household was asked what their income would be in the coming year if it were a good year (Hi), what their income would be if it was a bad year (Lo), and what they expected their income to be (Ex). We assume the income distribution is binomial over the high and low states, as in Ghatak 2000. The probability of success, *PROBHI*, is then calculated to be

$$PROBHI = \frac{Ex - Lo}{Hi - Lo}$$

using the fact that *PROBHI**Hi+(1− *PROBHI*)*Lo=*Ex*.

The full sample, including, of course, those not borrowing, and those borrowing with individual collateral, is used to determine whether borrowing in a group is a function of risk, or other variables such as the correlation of returns (see Table 9.18). Under the theory, low-risk, high-*p* types should not be borrowing. Strikingly, in multivariate logits with a binary 1, zero variable for the use of joint liability, the higher is the probability of success p, the less likely is a household to borrow under joint liability (we also include individual loans in the dependent variable as a robustness check so that the alternative is not borrowing at all). Risk-type appears as an important variable in virtually all specifications, at varying levels of significance. It seems evident that there is an adverse selection problem in the provision of insurance.

Note that we have not identified adverse selection vis-à-vis moral hazard. A moral hazard interpretation of the data could be that risk was endogenous to having a group loan; that is, having the loan was causing the borrower to operate with more risk, rather than vice versa. In order to identify a pure adverse selection effect, we make use of the fact that some of the loans in our data have already been repaid (usually within the last few months). Under adverse selection, those who took a loan but have already repaid it would still be forecasting low probabilities of success, since they are inherently more risky. Under moral hazard, the incentives for risk-taking from having a limited-liability loan vanish when the loan is repaid, so those who have already repaid their loan should look no different from those who never had a loan. We run the logits again after eliminating all households with a group loan that has not yet been repaid. Unfortunately, this leaves less than 20 per cent of the households who had group loans. In all specifications, the coefficient actually increases noticeably in magnitude (i.e., becomes more negative), but so do the standard errors. In the three specifications using BAGPLOAN, PROBHI remains significant, twice at the 10 per cent level and once at the 15 per cent level. In the specifications using GRUPLOAN, the estimates drop just beyond conventional significance levels (15 per cent to 30 per cent). This may be expected from the significant drop in sample size. We interpret these results as suggestive that adverse selection specifically is occurring in this credit market.

Table 9.18. Full samples: the full sample is used in each of these regressions

	BAGPLOAN			GRUPLOAN		
WEALTH	−.077	−.077	−.077	.016	.016	.015
	(.078)	(.078)	(.078)	(.067)	(.068)	(.068)
WEALTHSQ	1.08E-9	1.04E-9	1.08E-9	−1.37E-9	−1.48E-9	−1.43E-9
	(2.81E-9)	(2.84E-9)	(2.81E-9)	(2.85E-9)	(2.96E-9)	(2.91E-9)
WLTHDSPR	.119	.130	.123	−.098	−.078	−.084
	(.176)	(.176)	(.176)	(.164)	(.165)	(.165)
TITLE	.017	.014	.014	−.125	−.124	−.127
	(.110)	(.110)	(.110)	(.071)**	(.071)**	(.071)**
TITLESQ	−3.30E-9	−3.09E-9	−3.16E-9	2.21E-9	2.30E-9	2.29E-9
	(6.06E-9)	(6.06E-9)	(6.04E-9)	(2.80E-9)	(2.90E-9)	(2.84E-9)
PROBHI	−.460	−.431	−.448	−.386	−.344	−.353
	(.235)***	(.236)**	(.235)**	(.218)**	(.219)*	(.218)**
SAMEBEST	−.008			.370		
	(.269)			(.251)**		
SAMEWRST		.351			.408	
		(.289)			(.272)*	
SAMEITHR			.331			.784
			(.367)			(.346)***
INCOME	.611	.605	.603	.049	.042	.035
	(.559)	(.562)	(.560)	(.508)	(.513)	(.511)
EXINCOME	−.578	−.565	−.563	.066	.075	.087
	(.672)	(.674)	(.672)	(.591)	(.596)	(.594)
NRTHEAST	.618	.603	.600	.317	.326	.301
	(.133)***	(.133)***	(.134)***	(.122)***	(.121)***	(.122)***
AGRYES	1.03	1.03	1.02	1.16	1.17	1.15
	(.244)***	(.244)***	(.244)***	(.214)***	(.213)***	(.214)***
AGRNO	.761	.753	.752	.737	.735	.725
	(.251)***	(.251)***	(.252)***	(.221)***	(.221)***	(.221)***
OWNBSNS	.280	.294	.287	.079	.093	.093
	(.152)***	(.153)**	(.153)**	(.141)	(.142)	(.142)
LANDOWND	4.21E-3	4.13E-3	4.19E-3	4.17E-3	4.01E-3	4.09E-3
	(2.68E-3)*	(2.67E-3)*	(2.67E-3)*	(2.36E-3)**	(2.36E-3)**	(2.35E-3)**
EDYEARH	.037	.038	.038	.056	.057	.057
	(.024)*	(.024)*	(.024)*	(.023)***	(.023)***	(.023)***
MALEH	.510	.508	.504	.468	.476	.467
	(.168)***	(.168)***	(.168)***	(.152)***	(.152)***	(.152)***
N	1666	1666	1666	1602	1602	1602

Notes: Standard errors in parentheses; significance at 5, 10, and 15% denoted by ***, **, and *, respectively.

Source: C. Ahlin and R. M. Townsend, 'Selection into and across Credit Contracts: Theory and Field Research', *Journal of Econometrics*, 136 (2007), 665–98. Copyright 2007; reproduced with permission from Elsevier.

Correlation in returns also enters with the predicted, positive sign. It is interesting to distinguish here the contrasting results across the two selection models. Correlation of returns is helpful in drawing in safer borrowers in the joint-liability adverse selection model of Ghatak. But, correlation of returns should have made relative performance more prevalent than group loans in the regime comparison model of HM. This is true even though we act as if those borrowing under individual liability (or relative performance) were not borrowing at all. Apparently, the correlation force is greater on the extensive margin.

Table 9.19. *Selection with supply-side variation: adverse selection*

Variable	Original •	New ••
WEALTH	−76698.667	−127602.89
WEALTHSQ	0.0011	0.0008
WLTHDSPR	0.119	0.1218
TITLE	17421.048	45550.29
TITLESQ	−.0033	−.0026
PROBHI	−.4599***	−.5131***
% OF OTHER RESPS.	−.0085	0.221
INCOME	0.6113	1.589**
EXINCOME	−.5781	−1.6910**
NRTHEAST	0.6175***	.4896***
AGRYES	1.033***	.8278***
AGRNO	.7609***	.5311***
OWNSBSNS	.2804**	0.1852
LANDOWND	.0042*	.0072***
EDYEARH	.0370*	0.0266
MALEH	.5102***	.4783***
AGRI ONLY		−.3080
CDD MULTIPLE Occ.		−.0931
ASSEMBLY HALL CDD		.4841***
ECON STATUS CDD		−.2419*
HELP FROM GOVT		0.1553
TIME TO DIST. CENTER		−.0013
USE OF BAAC		.7030***
COMMUNITY BANK		.3306**
HAS RICE BANK		0.0217
HAS BUFFALO BANK		0.1382
STATE ELECTRICITY		0.2402
COTTAGE IND.		−19.4008**
PREDIC. lb 5		0.0402
PREDIC. Rb 5		−.0804
PREDIC. vf 5		−.1815
CONSTANT	−2.8114***	−3.2150***
N	1666	1430

Legend: * p<.15; ** p<.10; *** p<.05. • Original variables (Table 9.16); •• New variables (including Community development department).

Source: Puentes and Townsend research note 2004.

Evident also from the regression is the significance of many covariates which might well help to determine the reservation, alternative utility $\underline{U}$. Households were asked whether or not they engage in agricultural activity and, if so, whether or not they would like to expand their operations. From these questions we derive two dummy variables, AGRYES and AGRNO. AGRYES (AGRNO) equals 1 for the 46 per cent (33 per cent) of households that engage in agricultural activity and would (would not) like to expand their activity. The remaining 21 per cent of households for whom neither equals 1 are those who do not engage in agricultural activity. It is crucial to control for occupation, since the BAAC and several other institutional lenders targeted agricultural activities exclusively at the time of the survey. One further proxy for desirability of a loan is the dummy variable OWNSBSNS, which equals 1 for the 21 per cent of households that own a business. Consistent with the discussion, these are much more likely to appear when the choice is on the extensive margin than when examining, as earlier, how to borrow—that is, individual versus joint liability.

Including CDD controls as in the earlier analysis does not alter these conclusions; indeed, it enhances them in some instances (see Table 9.19). Adverse selection remains even when there is plausible variation on the supply side. The risk-type variable remains negative and significant. Likewise, the former instruments which determined membership in financial institutions are significant here in determining the prevalence of joint-liability loans. Some variables, such as expected income, required by the theory, are now significant also. On the other hand, the correlation result is slightly weakened.

9.7. Endogenous Industrial Organization

Likewise, there are general equilibrium forces which make the organization of industry and financial contracts endogenous. Suppose households are not stuck in villages but rather can migrate and either work alone, as in single proprietorships, or pair with households in worker–supervisory relationships as in an industrial group.

There is a continuum of agents of measure 1. All agents have the same preferences over consumption $c \in C$, effort $a \in A$, and job $j \in J = \{w_1, w_2, s\}$. Consumption is bounded below by zero. Job $j = w_1$ means that the agent is the first worker, job $j = w_2$ means that he is the second worker, and job $j = s$ means that he is the supervisor. If there is only one worker in the firm, we drop the subscript and refer to the worker by $j = w$. If these are only a worker or supervisor, we let $j=w_1,s$. We express the utility function over consumption, effort, and job as $U(c,a,j)$. It is strictly increasing in c and decreasing in a.

There is a finite number I of agent types in the economy. We denote an agent's type by $i \in \{1, \dots, I\}$. For each type i the number of agents is a positive fraction $\alpha_i > 0$ of the population. Types only differ in their non-negative endowment of capital κ_i. The total endowment of capital is $\kappa = \sum_i \alpha_i \kappa_i$. This capital is divisible, and it is the fundamental ingredient into creating the capital input k.

There is a production technology f, freely available to all agents, that produces output $q \in Q$ as a stochastic function of workers' efforts and capital input $k \in K$. As earlier in the moral-hazard model of occupation choice, we assume that Q can only take on a finite number of values.

A self-employment firm consists of one unsupervised agent, who is treated as a worker for utility purposes. With no supervisor, the effort of the single working agent is private information. A self-employment contract is an n-tuple $(c(q),a,k)$.

An incentive-compatible self-employment contract is one that satisfies the constraints that the actual action a be the same as the one recommended in the contract, that is,

$$\sum_q f(q\,|\,a,k)U\Big(c(q),a,w\Big) \geq \sum_q f(q\,|\,\hat{a},k)U\Big(c(q),\hat{a},w\Big), \quad \forall \hat{a} \in A.$$

$$(9.7.1)$$

The utility an agent receives from choosing one such contract is his expected utility,

$$u(b_1) = \sum_q f(q\,|\,a,k)U\Big(c(q),a,w\Big). \qquad (9.7.2)$$

Contracts use resources. Expected net consumption of a $b_1=[(q),a,k]$ self-employment firm is

$$r_{c-q}(b_1) = \sum_q f(q\,|\,a,k)\Big(c(q) - q\Big), \qquad (9.7.3)$$

and its usage of the capital input is

$$r_k(b_1) = k. \qquad (9.7.4)$$

Each $b_1=(c(q),a,k)$ indexes a different self-employment contract or firm. Thus, a self-employment firm is indexed by all of its characteristics: the capital input k it uses, the effort a of its member, and the schedule $c(q)$ used to determine final consumption. If capital, effort, or consumption can take on a continuum of values, then there is an infinite number of possible types of self-employment firms, a set B_1.

The second type of organization we consider is a two-agent firm with a worker who operates the technology and a supervisor who monitors him. We assume that the supervision process makes the worker's effort public, though it is easy enough to relax this assumption so the supervisor sees only a correlated signal, as in Holmström (1979). A supervisor–worker contract b_2 is an n-tuple $(c_w(q), c_s(q), a_w, a_s, k)$.

The monitoring technology requires that supervisory effort equals worker effort so only contracts that satisfy $a_w = a_s$ are feasible. There are no incentive constraints in this type of firm. Again, we define each agent's utility directly in terms of the contract, though now utility also depends on the job. Utility is

$$u(b_2, j) = \sum_q f(q|a_w, k) U(c_j(q), a_j, j), \quad j = w, s. \tag{9.7.5}$$

Consumption resource usage is

$$r_{c-q}(b_2) = \sum_q f(q|a_w, k)\left(c_w(q) + c_s(q) - q\right) \tag{9.7.6}$$

and the usage of the capital input is

$$r_k(b_2) = k. \tag{9.7.7}$$

In this two-agent worker–supervisor firm, the object b_2 is a contract that specifies joint usage of the capital input, coordinates efforts, and gives each member's output-dependent consumption. It is joint consumption and production features that make these contracts club goods. B_2 is the set of all b_2 firms.

For simplicity, here we limit consideration to these two types of firms. Still, agents can be in only one firm at a time, so the commodity space needs to respect this feature. One method for handling this problem is to let agents choose indicator functions over the types of firms, the b_1, b_2, and in the case of the multi-agent firms, their job j as well.

To decentralize, let $p(b_1)$ denote the price of a unit of a b_1 self-employment firm, $p(b_2, j)$ the price of a unit of a b_2 firm jointly with the decision to be the worker $j=w$ or the supervisor $j=s$.

Let $x_i(b_i)$ denote type-i's purchase of probability of being assigned to a b_1 firm and let $x_i(b_2,j)$ be the purchase of job j in a type-b_2 firm.

The problem for a type-i consumer is then

$$\max \sum_{b_1} x_i(b_i)u(b_1) + \sum_{b_2,j} x_i(b_2,j)u(b_2,j) \tag{9.7.8}$$

subject to $x_i \in X$, the space of lotteries, and the budget constraint

$$\sum_{b_1} x_i(b_i)p(b_1) + \sum_{b_2,j} x_i(b_2,j)p(b_2,j) \le p_k k_i \tag{9.7.9}$$

where the capital endowment, κ_i, is sold for income at price p_k. This is the key wealth variable. Price p_k can be taken as the measure and set at unity.

The intermediation sector carries out several activities. It converts the capital stock endowments into the capital input, it supplies the capital input to firms, it intermediates state-contingent consumption across agents, and it staffs the firms. In performing these activities, the intermediation sector is creating firms. There are constant returns to scale in these activities, so it does not matter how many profit-maximizing entities there are, and profits will be zero in equilibrium.

For convenience, we will refer to a single such representative intermediary; and to distinguish it from the firms of our theory, we will refer to this entity as the production sector. Denote $\delta(b_i)$ as the number of b_1 firms produced. The first constraint is a resource constraint on the capital input.

$$\sum_{l=1,2} \sum_{b_l} \delta(b_l)r_k(b_l) + y_k \le 0 \tag{9.7.10}$$

so that capital input used in creating the firms is less than or equal to the capital endowment purchased. In creating the firms, the production sector also provides insurance via firms' compensation schedules to individuals. It collects consumption from some firms and transfers it to others. These transfers, analogous to premiums and indemnities, need to sum to zero. The net consumption resource constraint is

$$\sum_{l=1,2} \sum_{b_l} \delta(b_l)r_{(c-q)}(b_l) \le 0. \tag{9.7.11}$$

In creating two-agent firms—the b_2—the production sector staffs positions in them. Each of these firms requires two members. Let $y(b_2,w_1)$ be the number of b_2 firms with a worker and let $y(b_2,s)$ be the number of b_2 firms with a supervisor. Thus, fully to staff a firm,

$$\forall b_2, \delta(b_2) = y(b_2, w_1) = y(b_2, s). \tag{9.7.12}$$

Given prices, the production sector's maximization problem is

$$\max_{y(b_1), y(b_2, j), \delta(b_1)} \sum_{b_1} p(b_1) y(b_1) + \sum_{b_2, j} p(b_2, j) y(b_2, j) + p_k y_k \tag{9.7.13}$$

subject to $y \in Y$.

A competitive equilibrium in this economy is a (x^*, y^*, p^*) such that:

1. $\forall i, x_i^*$ solves the consumer's problem;
2. y^* solves the production sector's problem;
3. markets clear.

Both welfare theorems hold for this economy: competitive equilibria are Pareto optimal and Pareto optimum can be supported as competitive equilibria. Thus, as is standard, a Pareto program will be useful for analyzing prices and for developing an algorithm for computing competitive equilibria. Let λ_i denote the Pareto weight on type-i agents. Using the market-clearing constraints to substitute out for production y, the Pareto program is

$$\max_{x_i > 0, \delta \geq 0} \sum_i \lambda_i \alpha_i \left(\sum_{b_1} x_i(b_1) u(b_1) + \sum_{b_2, j} x_i(b_2, j) u(b_2, j) \right) \tag{9.7.14}$$

subject to the probability measure constraints,

$$\forall i, \sum_{b_1} x_i(b_i) + \sum_{b_2} x_i(b_2, j) = 1, \tag{9.7.15}$$

The club or matching constraints are

$$\forall b_1, \delta(b_1) = \sum_i \alpha_i x_i(b_1), \tag{9.7.16}$$

$$\forall b_2, \delta(b_2) = \sum_i \alpha_i x_i(b_2, w) = \sum_i \alpha_i x_i(b_2, s), \tag{9.7.17}$$

The resource constraint on net consumption is

$$\sum_{l=1,2} \sum_{b_l} \delta(b_l) r_{(c-q)}(b_l) \leq 0 \tag{9.7.18}$$

and the resource constraints on capital, where again κ is the aggregate capital endowment,

$$\sum_{l=1,2}\sum_{b_l}\delta(b_l)r_k(b_l) \leq \kappa. \tag{9.7.19}$$

A key result here is a monotonic relationship between the λ_i in the Pareto program and the k_i in the competitive equilibria.

By framing the formation of firms as an activity in the production set, prices of firms follow naturally. Let $\mu_{(c-q)}$ be the shadow price of consumption and let μ_k be the shadow price of the capital input. At a competitive equilibrium, these are the prices of consumption and capital. These μ_k and the associated interest rates are endogenous. The price of firms are determined by their costs,

$$p(b_1) = \mu_{(c-q)}\sum_q f(q|a,k)\Big(c(q) - q\Big) + \mu_k k, \tag{9.7.20}$$

$$\begin{aligned} p(b_2,w) + p(b_2,s) = \mu_{(c-q)}\sum_q f(q|a_w,k)\Big(c_w(q) + c_s(q) - q\Big) \\ + \mu_k k, \end{aligned} \tag{9.7.21}$$

with an inequality when a firm does not exist—that is, prices do not cover cost.

The wage, or price of jobs, are also endogenous to the equilibrium. Let $\Delta U \equiv u(b_2,s) - u(b_2,w)$, and $\Delta P \equiv p(b_2,s) - p(b_2,w)$. Suppose, for example, an agent type-i is indifferent to purchasing an additional unit of probability of being a worker or a supervisor, then

$$\lambda_i \Delta U = \Delta P. \tag{9.7.22}$$

Since agent type-i is indifferent on the margin, the price differential is precisely the utility differential, scaled by the Pareto weight (again, the inverse of his marginal utility of wealth).

Figure 9.32 describes the occurrence of supervisor–worker firms as a function of the wealth level and the wealth distribution (as measured by the Pareto weights). A (1,1) supervisor–worker firm means that both members are type-1 agents. A (1,2) supervisor–worker firm means a type-1 agent is the worker and a type-2 agent is the supervisor. Note that in the figure the existence of a supervisor–worker firm does not preclude the existence of a self-employment firm.

The particular optimum that will prevail depends on the Pareto weights λ_i and on the amount of economy-wide capital κ, or equivalently the distribution of wealth, the k_i. As an example, suppose there are only two types— the rich and the poor. The figure describes parameter values for which

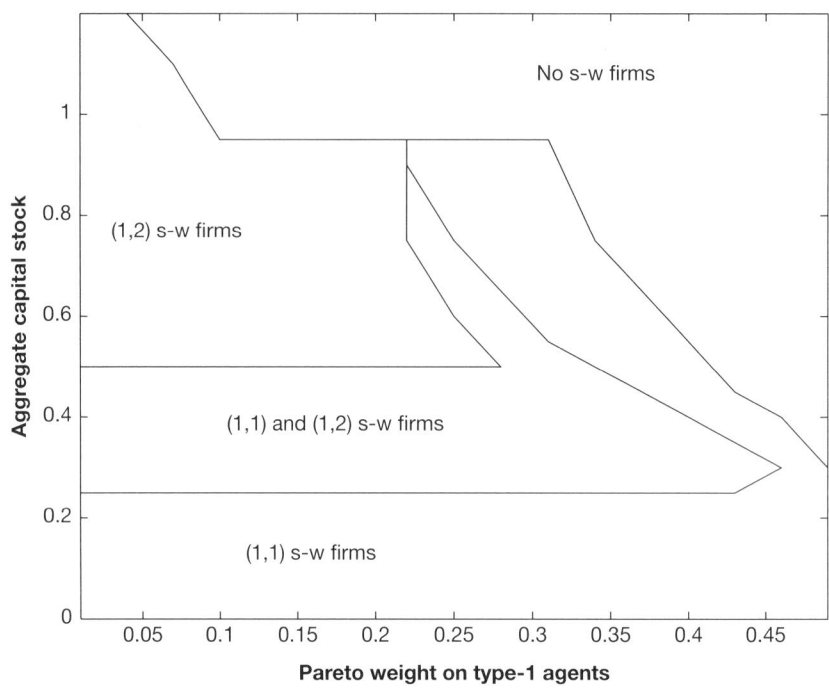

Fig. 9.32. *The occurrence of supervisor–worker firms as a function of the wealth level and the wealth distribution*

Source: Prescott and Townsend 2006.

supervisor–worker firms occur in equilibrium. For high-aggregate-capital levels and relatively equal Pareto weights (the upper right hand corner of Figure 9.32) all firms are single proprietorships.

As the aggregate-capital level declines and the Pareto weights become more unequal, supervisor–worker firms begin to appear. The composition of these two-agent firms varies with the parameters. At high capital levels but relatively unequal Pareto weights (the upper left hand side of Figure 9.32) all the supervisor–worker firms consist of a type-1 as the worker and a type-2 as the supervisor. Capital is plentiful and labor is scarce in these economies, so it is worthwhile to use the high Pareto weight (type-2) agents as a supervisor. At low capital levels but relatively equal Pareto weights (the lower right hand side of Figure 9.32), the program assigns the low Pareto weight (type-1) agents to supervise their fellow type-1 workers. For the remaining parameter values both types of supervisor–worker firms are observed in equilibrium.

Some forms of limited commitment can be incorporated. Let $d \in D=\{0,1\}$, where $d=0$ means the agent stays in the firm and does not run off with the capital. Conversely, $d=1$ means the agent runs off with the capital. If an agent runs off with the capital, he converts it into consumption at some exogenous rate $\tilde{r}$ with no effort supplied. Define the value of default as $V(k, d=1)\equiv U(\tilde{r}k,0,j)$. The utility from staying $d=0$ is unchanged from before. Thus, a self-employment contract under limited commitment when $d=0$ is an n-tuple $(c(q),a,d,k)$ such that:

$$\sum_q f(q|a,k)U\Big(c(q),a,w\Big) \geq V(k,d=1) \qquad (9.7.23)$$

'rogeneity' in agents' abilities can also be incorporated into our framework.

This framework allows us better to conceptualize policy advice and the meaning of previous policy experiments. First, any given equilibrium is unlikely to deliver the first best, or, if it does, it is only by diverting considerable resources to monitoring. Otherwise, from capitalization, ROA and induced effort can all be expected to vary in an observed cross-section. Second, movements along the Pareto frontier are associated with redistribution of wealth k_i, as if varying the right hand side of the household's budget constraint with lump-sum taxes and subsidies. Note that, overall, the intermediation sector still makes zero profits and satisfies overall resource and other constraints. Third, prices such as interest rates and job premiums can vary as one moves along the frontier. Without the general equilibrium it is hard to allow for this. Fourth, removal in some way of the limited-commitment constraint, as if going from one economy to the other, also has these indirect effects. In computed examples, industrial organization, job assignment, inequality, and the price of firms and capital all move with the distribution of wealth, and with whether or not default is allowed.

If at the end of the period households had myopic savings rates, then one can imagine the evolution of the economy over time. There would be a tendency for economy-wide wealth to increase as in the neoclassical growth model, and the path of inequality would be determined as well.

9.8. Dynamic Village Networks

The possibilities for dynamics with inequality and organization become clear with explicit examples. For this purpose we return to the discussion of individual, relative-performance regimes versus risk-sharing, joint-liability groups as in section 9.6, but imagine there are two periods. The second period is as described earlier; static problem and the financial organization results are the same. In somewhat simplified notation, let $\pi^r(c,q,e)$ denote the probability of the relative-performance regime with allocation (c,q,e) and $\pi^g(c,q,e,\mu)$ those of the group regime. The maximum surplus that can be obtained in the second period given a utility pair (w_1,w_2) is thus given by Program 1:

$$S^2(w_1, w_2) = \max_{\pi^r, \pi^g} \sum_{c,q,e} \pi^r(c, q, e)[q_1 + q_2 - c_1 - c_2]$$
$$+ \sum_{c,q,e,\mu} \pi^g(c, q, e, \mu)[q_1 + q_2 - c_1 - c_2] \tag{9.8.1}$$

$$w_i = \sum_{c,q,e} \pi^r(c, q, e)[U(c_i) + V(e_i)]$$
$$+ \sum_{c,q,e,\mu} \pi^g(c, q, e, \mu)[U(c_i) + V(e_i)], \tag{9.8.2}$$

for $i = 1,2$

$$\sum_{c,q,e} \pi^r(c, q, e) + \sum_{c,q,e,\mu} \pi^g(c, q, e, \mu) = 1; \pi^r, \pi^g > 0. \tag{9.8.3}$$

Here π^g satisfies technological and group constraints like 9.6.22 and 9.6.23 for all values of μ in M and π^r satisfies technological and incentive constraints 9.6.15–9.6.17 earlier. The surplus is maximized conditional on the incentive and technological constraints and on the utility level of individuals—implied by equation 9.8.2. Equation 9.8.3 implies that the choice of the planner is a probability distribution.

The dynamic problem is solved in the first period. The planner makes all the contingent plans at this period. The surplus function $S^2(w_1,w_2)$ is essential because the planner can use the first and the second period to achieve desired initial utility pairs for the individuals, and the surplus function defines the effect on the objective function of assigning utility pairs (w_1,w_2) in the second period. The planner can assign to each individual a utility level in the second period belonging to the set W. The possible outcomes are consumption, output, and effort vectors in the first period; the type of organization that they are part of in the first period; and again the utility pairs for the second period. The distribution of effort, consumption, output, and the type of organization in the second period is implied by the choices of w_1 and w_2 as noted above.

The incentive constraints for the relative performance regime in the first period are

$$
\begin{aligned}
&\sum_{c,q,e_2,w} \pi^r(c,q,e_1,e_2,w)[U(c_1) + V(e_1) + \beta w_1] \\
&\geq \sum_{c,q,e_2,w} \pi^r(c,q,e_1,e_2,w) \frac{p(q|\hat{e}_1,e_2)}{p(q|e_1,e_2)}[U(c_1) + V(\hat{e}_1) + \beta w_1],
\end{aligned}
\tag{9.8.4}
$$

and

$$
\begin{aligned}
&\sum_{c,q,e_2,w} \pi^r(c,q,e_1,e_2,w)[U(c_2) + V(e_2) + \beta w_2] \\
&\geq \sum_{c,q,e_2,w} \pi^r(c,q,e_1,e_2,w) \frac{p(q|e_1,\hat{e}_2)}{p(q|e_1,e_2)}[U(c_2) + V(\hat{e}_2) + \beta w_2],
\end{aligned}
\tag{9.8.5}
$$

$\forall e_2, \hat{e}_2$, where $\pi^r(c,q,e,w)$ is the probability that individuals are assigned to the relative-performance regime; and the vector of consumption, outputs, efforts, and promised utilities is (c,q,e,w). Notice that these conditions are similar to the static problem above, but here the distribution of promised utilities in the second period can also be used as an incentive tool. The technological constraint is similar to equation 9.8.3:

$$
\sum_{c,w} \pi^\tau(c,\tilde{q},\tilde{e},w) = p(\tilde{q}|\tilde{e}) \sum_{c,q,w} \pi^\tau(c,q,\tilde{e},w), \quad \forall \tilde{q}, \tilde{e}.
\tag{9.8.6}
$$

The incentive constraint for a group in the first period with Pareto weights (μ_1, μ_2) is:

$$
\begin{aligned}
&\sum_{c,q,w} \pi^g(c,q,e,w,\mu) \sum_i \mu_i[U(c_i) + V(e_i) + \beta w_i] \\
&\geq \sum_{c,q,w} \pi^g(c,q,e,w,\mu) \frac{p(q|\hat{e})}{p(q|e)} \sum_i \mu_i[U(c_i) + V(\hat{e}_i) + \beta w_i],
\end{aligned}
\tag{9.8.7}
$$

$\forall e, \hat{e}$ where $\pi^g(c,q,e,w,\mu)$ represents the probability that individuals are assigned to a group and the vector of consumption, outputs, efforts, and promised utilities for the second period is (c,q,e,w). The technological constraints analogous to equation 9.8.5 are:

(a) u = (1.5738, −1.5738)

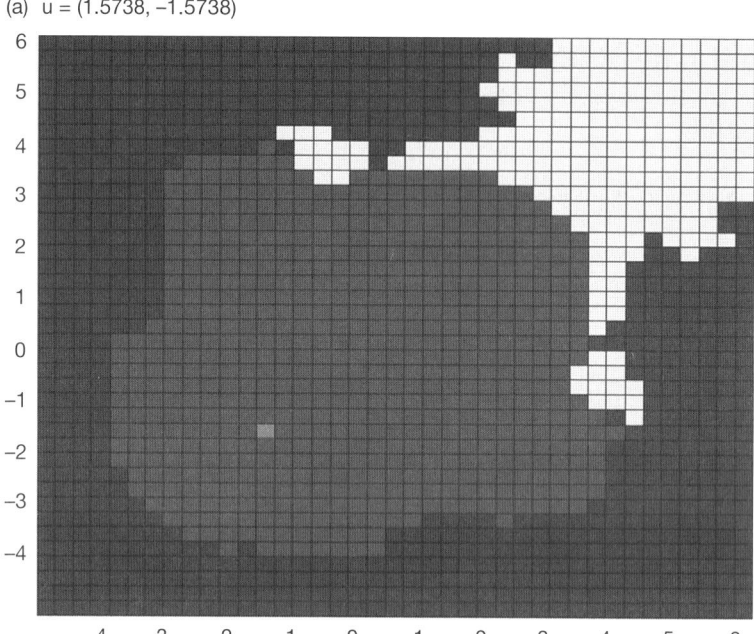

(b) u = (4.3169, 0.6703)

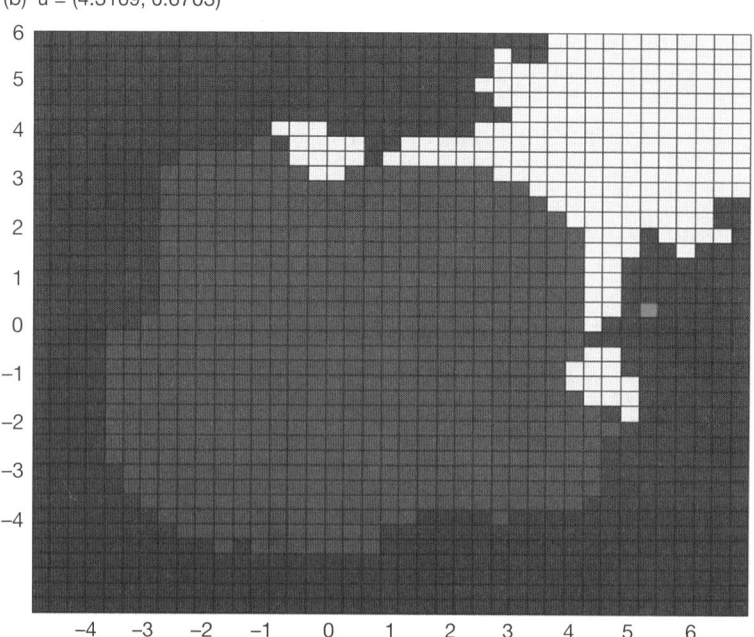

Fig. 9.33(a)–(d). *See over*

(c) u = (3.4754, −2.6959)

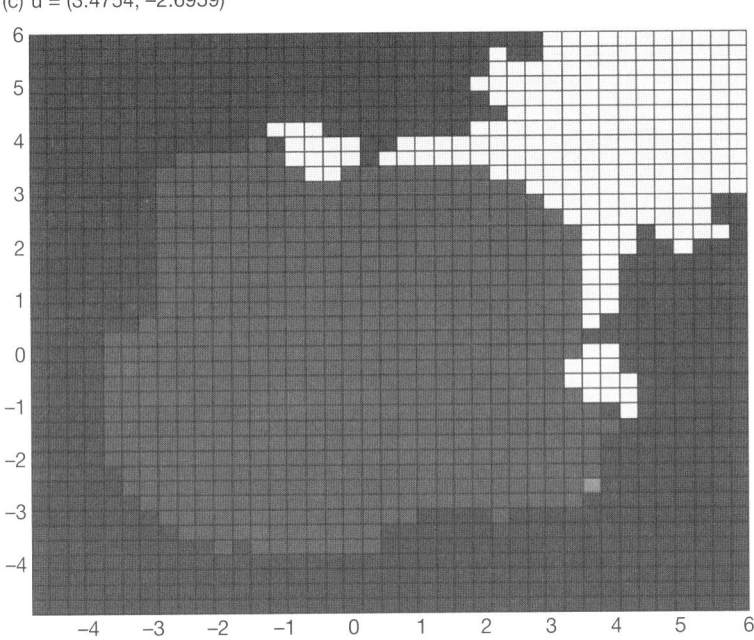

(d) u = (2.0728, −3.8179)

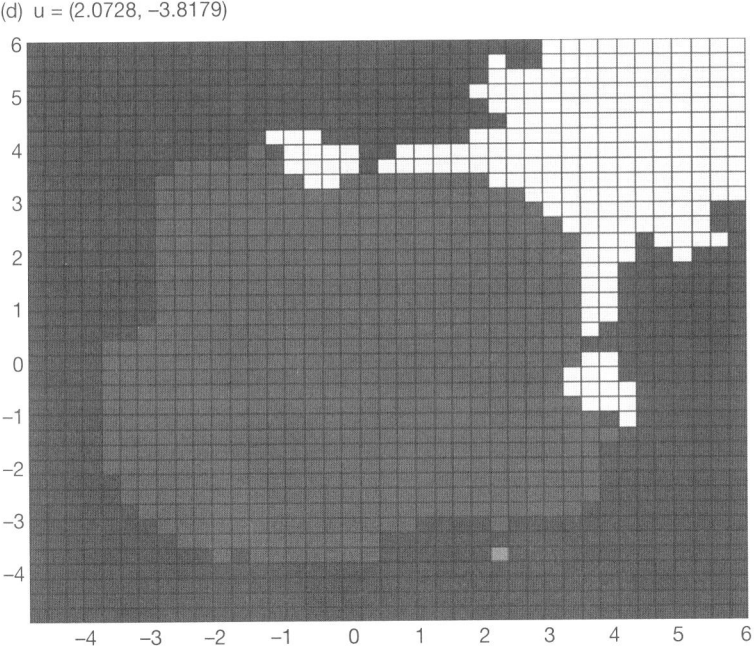

Fig. 9.33(a)–(d). *Utility pairs studied, transition from T–1 to T*

Source: G. A. Madeira and R. M. Townsend research note 2007.

$$\sum_{c,w} \pi^s(c,\tilde{q},\tilde{e},w,\tilde{\mu}) = p(\tilde{q}|\tilde{e}) \sum_{c,q,w} \pi^s(c,q,\tilde{e},w,\tilde{\mu}),$$

$$\forall \tilde{q},\tilde{e}. \sum_{c,w} \pi^s(c,\tilde{q},\tilde{e},w,\tilde{\mu}) \tag{9.8.8}$$

$$= p(\tilde{q}|\tilde{e}) \sum_{c,q,w} \pi^s(c,q,\tilde{e},w,\tilde{\mu}), \quad \forall \tilde{q},\tilde{e}.$$

The first period Pareto problem is thus:
Program 2

$$S^1(u_1,u_2) = \max_{\pi^r,\pi^s} \sum_{c,q,e,w} \pi^r(c,q,e,w)[q_1 + q_2 - c_1 - c_2 + \beta S^2(w)]$$

$$+ \sum_{c,q,e,w,\mu} \pi^s(c,q,e,w,\mu)[q_1 + q_2 - c_1 - c_2 + \beta S^2(w)] \tag{9.8.9}$$

st.

$$\sum_{c,q,e,w} \pi^r(c,q,e,w)[U(c_i) + V(e_i) + \beta w_i]$$

$$\geq \sum_{c,q,e,w,\mu} \pi^s(c,q,e,w,\mu)[U(c_i) + V(e_i) + \beta w_i] \geq u_i \tag{9.8.10}$$

A numerical example makes clear that entry into joint-liability or risk-sharing groups, and exit from them, can depend on the history of performance as well as assigned wealth or utilities. This is summarized in Figures 9.33(a)–(d), 9.34(a)–(b), and 9.35(a)–(b) and the paths of transition in various starting-points. If, initially. two households are similar in wealth or promises, then relative performance is optimal, as earlier. But, if outcomes in the current period are not similar—if, for example, one project succeeds while another fails, then the two households will be treated differently not only in current compensation, as earlier, but in next periods' promises/wealth. Heterogeneous wealth is a force for groups, so one thus sees a group forming over time. Likewise, those in a group in the current period which does well should be rewarded not just in terms of higher consumption but higher utility next period. The latter can send them down the U-shaped group-prevalent profile, and thus exit them for joint liability. The steady-state distribution of utility pairs for the infinite horizon

(a)

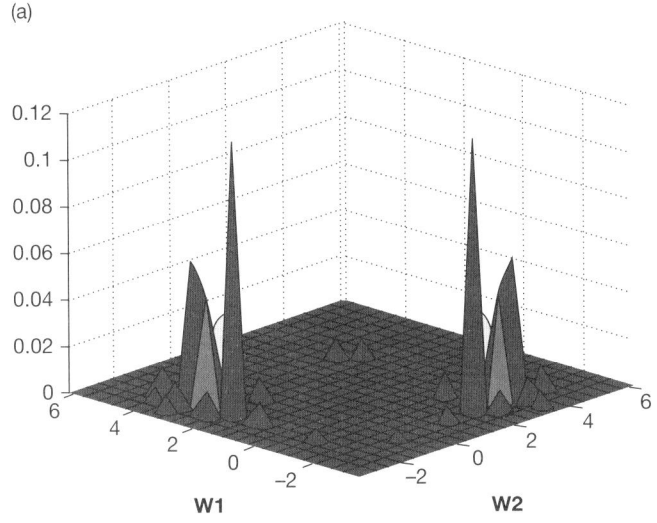

(b)

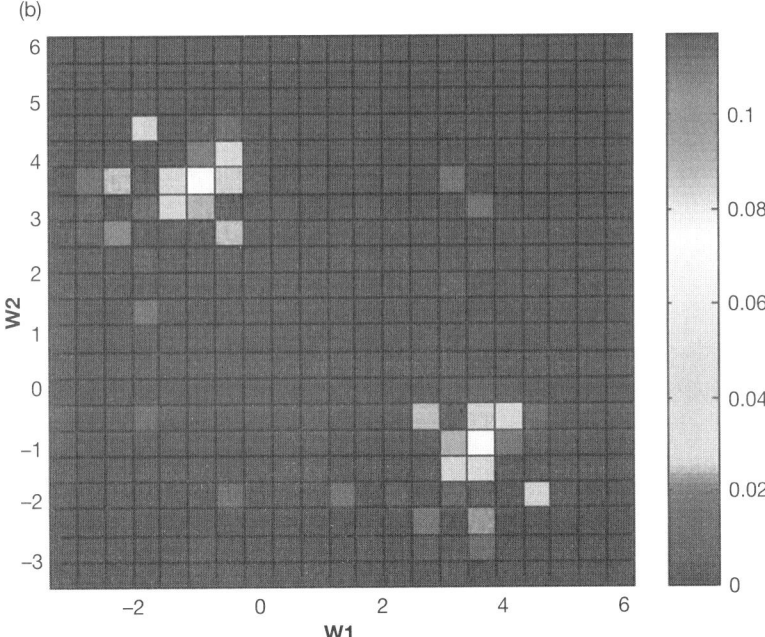

Fig. 9.34(a)–(b). *Distribution of pairs switching from groups to RP (See color version at the end of the book).*

Source: G. A. Madeira and R. M. Townsend research note 2007.

(a)

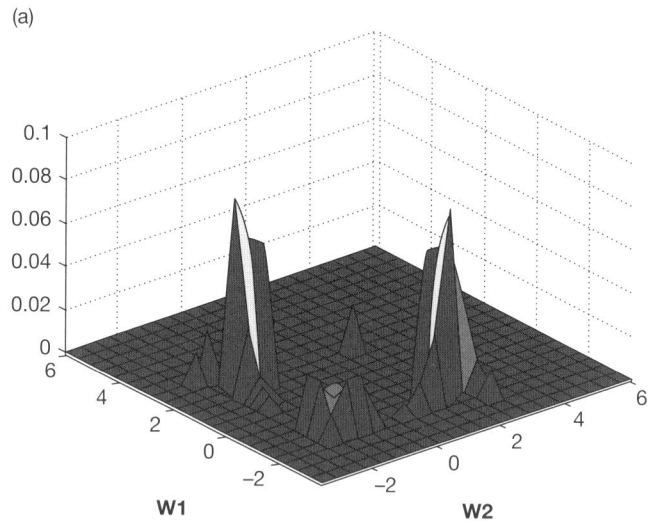

(b)

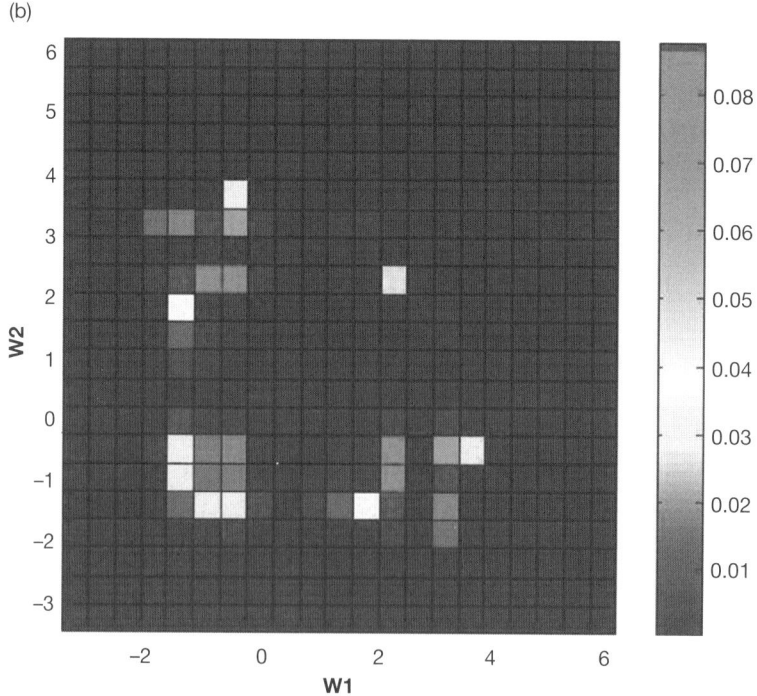

Fig. 9.35(a)–(b). *Distribution of pairs switching from RP to groups (See color version at the end of the book).*

problem is depicted earlier in the figures. The point is that joint liability, within-village networks, industrial conglomerates, and other types of groups are endogenous and we would expect to see their evolution over time. Alternatively, if there were policy restrictions, this could lead to welfare losses and inefficiency.

10
Summary and Conclusions

The data used in this manuscript come from a variety of sources. A comprehensive database research archive facilitates access to and use of Bank of Thailand macro data, provincial product data, a Community Development Department village census, Socio-Economic Income and Expenditure Surveys, Labor Force Surveys, the Population Census, as well as surveys of firms: Japanese JBIC, Stock Exchange of Thailand, World Bank, Ministry of Industry, and special efforts. GIS functionality allows these data to be displayed at the plot (household, farm, and firm), village, amphoe, and province level, depending on the identifiers and the original coding. Thus, one can pick a key variable such as income and display it across the various datasets. Or, one can pinpoint an area of interest and zoom in and out at various levels of geographic aggregation, extracting data from the various surveys. Theorists inevitably need key variables with no counterparts in existing data, and this motivates acquisition of new data, as in the Townsend Thai initial 1997 survey, the 1997–2010 annual panel, and the 1998–2010 monthly micro panel. More specifically, many of the theories of occupation choice and risk-sharing were reviewed, as were existing data and standardized LSME, Family Life, and other questionnaires. Key variables not typically gathered and used in many of the analyses are highlighted in the text: for example, penalties for default, whether or not borrowers cooperate in production decisions, measures of sharing in informal networks, the existence of monitoring, screening, and the riskiness of the borrower. In practice, the power of this emerging database research archive is that it facilitates using various datasets in combination, as illustrated in various subsections.

Quite apart from theory, the measurement of variables and their interpretation should be consistent with standard accounting frameworks. This

404

is emphasized in Chapter 2. A bonus of the approach is that it makes the micro and macro frameworks consistent with one another and with the general economic equilibrium—National Income and Product Accounts come from the income, balance sheet, and cash flow statements of firms as in corporate finance. One obvious benefit of the accounting framework is that double-entry book keeping, cross checks, and the need for consistency across the accounts create better measurement of variables or reveal short-comings. The Townsend Thai monthly data are being organized in this way. Likewise, one is more sensitive to the timing of variables in the theories themselves, the distinction between stocks (assets, net indebtedness) and flows (cash flow, income), or the distinction between performance and liquidity. Unfortunately, putty-putty models (i.e., where capital is malleable, easily combined with income, and potentially consumed) are much in use here as elsewhere, and make the distinction less important in theory than it seems to be in practice. Inequality in wealth and inequality in income are quite distinct from one another, for example. Indicators of financial access benefit from the distinction between stocks and flows as well, as the patterns are different from one another and different from more conventional stereotypical measures of access.

There are various 'false' or misleading dichotomies that do not come from the accounts per se but are sometimes mistakenly associated with them. One such dichotomy that comes from the national income accounts is the distinction between households as consumers and suppliers of factor inputs and firms as producers and sources of factor income. Households in developing countries are both consumers and producers. Fortunately, the financial and national income accounts do not require the distinction. One can do the requisite unified measurement of households as firms. Indeed, there is information on households as firms in standard income and expenditure surveys—information which is not inconsistent with the importance of non-farm proprietorships in the national accounts. This is featured in the material on occupation choice as a driving factor. Put bluntly, one can use household-based surveys to understand GDP. Perhaps the most dramatic example of this is the model of TFP using SES data. Households are not simply a source of aggregate demand or the beneficiaries/victims of wealth effects.

Another dangerous label is the distinction between formal and informal (underground) economies—often informal means unmeasured or unconnected to recognized institutions. Commercial banks are in the measured, formal sector, at least at an aggregated level for deposits and lending. Commercial banks appear to dominate other financial institutions in access, stocks, and flows. Yet, the distinction between formal and informal vanishes with measurement as in the Townsend Thai and other surveys, and with the recognition of important social structures: the family, family-related conglomerates, trading and joint-liability partners, or networks. These are documented as playing relatively large roles. Again, none of that is inconsistent with the construction and use of financial and national product accounts; still, there is ample scope for improved survey design and for sampling which combines 'households' with 'firms', as the terms are typically understood. Policy recommendations ought to include the design and implementation of not only standard but also more imaginative, innovative surveys.

The first few chapters of this book are thus intended to be a picture of Thailand as in operational general equilibrium models; thus the movement is from macro to micro and back again, repeatedly, and in various ways. Key facts at the outset are macro GDP growth, inequality recognizing uncertainty and heterogeneity, and poverty recognizing the evident distinction among income, consumption, and wealth, with wealth as a predetermined constraint. The exposition in these early chapters deliberately features the facts and not methodological issues. Chapter 2 features the usefulness of spatial disaggregation, taking growth, inequality, and poverty as well as other topics/facts from the national level down to the provinces, to villages within provinces, to households within villages, to individuals within households, and then back to a Mekong basin in a cross-country comparison. Still, some level of organization and interpretation of the facts is required as a starting point for the choice of actual models. Both micro Kuznets decompositions and Macro TFP decompositions as in Chapter 4 are enormously useful guides for what to put into the models. In Thailand, this highlights education, occupation choice/sector, and financial access as key driving forces of the dynamic general equilibrium. Chapter 5 does the same in a less structured fact-finding mission: it takes the driving forces behind growth, inequality, and poverty decompositions—namely, levels of education, financial sector access/use, and occupation choice/sector—and examines them one at a time at the national, province, village, and household level. Financial deepening and financial institutions are featured in these early sections, both as facts to be incorporated in the models and to set the stage for a rigorous financial sector analysis.

Benchmarks from the Baseline Neoclassical model are featured midway through the book, in Chapter 7, after the initial facts and two initial dual-sector models. However, in a policy-motivated research algorithm, tests of the benchmark standards might well come first. The point is that the tests can be carried out with relatively little data; thus the general equilibrium standard becomes operational quickly. If there were no major holes or imperfections, or the orders of magnitude of distortions were small, then there would be no reliable basis for policy remedies other than redistribution. There are two obvious points to stress in this context. First, even those without financial sector access may do well: lack of access does not create a prima facie case for intervention. Second, if there are distortions or gaps then it is important to know for whom. There may be gaps not only for those without financial sector access, potentially, but also for those with access as well. Gaps may have a rationale in obstacles to trade, or in policy distortions. The distinction is crucial as the latter are more easily remedied (apart from political considerations). Thus both of these hypotheses, distortions from obstacles versus distortions from policy, need to be brought into the research/policy algorithm. But first things first: are there gaps, how big are the gaps, and for whom?

Under the neoclassical standard, business starts and choice of economic sector should not be related to initial predetermined wealth, controlling for talent. It is not difficult to get wealth and occupation histories even in a one-time-only, cross-sectional survey. The Townsend Thai 1997 questions ask the household if each of many possible assets is held, if so, when acquired, and the value at that time. Earlier purchases still held can be depreciated. Land purchases and sales are memorable and easily tracked, though here one can estimate the contemporary value as the resale value. Likewise, households remember well the year of change of crop or change of primary activity of the head. Thus, one ends up with a retrospective panel on wealth and on occupation transitions. Other household surveys such as those of IADB ask about the contemporary value of existing assets. One can also use a principal component's measure of responses to simple, yes/no ownership-of-assets questions, as in the Thai SES survey, to create a latent variable for wealth (unobserved factor) which best explains the cross-sectional ownership variance.

For the test of neoclassical separation, one can run a probit of transition into business over an interval of time onto pre-existing, initial wealth and other characteristics, such as education and family composition. More non-parametric are the methods of Adonis Yatchew. In Thailand, wealth in the probit is positive and significant and the standard error band for the slope coefficients of the locally linear regressions is up-sloping and narrow. Wealth matters and the distortion are substantial, apparently. There are worries that wealth, though taken as predetermined, is endogenous in a larger dynamic problem. But we know from Francisco Buera that the cross-

407

sectional transitional gradient only understates the prevalence of credit constraints. Talented households may have more wealth prior to entry, but that is because credit constraints generate a demand for higher saving. The latter implication is also tested.

Those with access to the financial system might be presumed to be more likely to reach the neoclassical standard, that business starts and sector of occupation be unrelated to initial wealth. Here one equates financial access with measured use, momentarily. (In the choice model below, access and use are not equivalent.) In the Townsend Thai survey instrument, one asks questions about borrowing and saving with informal and formal financial service providers, as in some but not all existing surveys. The surveys also ask about whether the farm or enterprise could make more money and if so whether credit access is the problem. Then, either stratify the data into access/no-access groups, or append as an additional variable the interaction of wealth with an indicator of being a customer or member of a financial institution, possibly by type. In Thailand wealth facilitates access. For Bank for Agriculture and Agricultural Cooperative (BAAC) joint-liability groups, wealth makes a borrower less likely to be constrained. Thus Thailand is not neoclassical even for those with access. The credit market either suffers from a distortion or some obstacles to trade make wealth a key variable.

Likewise, initial investment in a business should be unrelated to initial wealth, overall and for those with access. In the Townsend Thai data, we ask simply what the initial investment in the business was. Pre-existing wealth is significant both before and after the financial crisis (but not during), in ordinary least squares regression equations for business investment. Histograms reveal that the distribution of initial business assets is shifted to the right for firms using the financial system.

Rates of return on assets (ROA) are another potential indicator of constraints. Marginal ROAs should be equated across households and technologies; otherwise there is a violation of the neoclassical standard. A simple measure of ROA is an income to wealth ratio. Income data is asked in an abbreviated way in the Townsend Thai survey, and wealth in that survey was discussed earlier. The ratio is an average rather than a marginal return, so some caution is in order. But in Thailand, the range of returns is so large, from almost zero to 90 per cent, that adjustments with additional controls for type of firm and with possible ranges for a capital share parameter, as in the Cobb Douglas production specification, are unlikely to overturn the dramatic results: low-wealth households that say they could profit if able to expand their business have rates of return that are quite high, and high wealth households who say they are not constrained have rates of return that are quite low. A redistribution of resources from the latter group as lenders to the former group as borrowers would allow large gains, apparently. The gap is of course the obvious measure of insufficient intermediation. Similarly, one can use the income and balance sheet statements of firms, as in the Ministry of Industry survey, to compute the standard ROA ratios. Controlling for industry type, ROA is declining in firm size, measured by the value of fixed assets. Note also that the income measure used here is accrued income, not cash flow, a better measure of underlying, true performance.

For firms listed on the Stock Exchange of Thailand, ROA is also declining in debt. Thus debt alone, as an indicator access, does not make firms alike, of equal marginal return, as in the neoclassical model. The second, larger point is that the current financial system appears to direct credit to larger and less efficient firms, though other hypotheses are being explored. The political economy of this has yet to be determined.

When there is uncertainty, the neoclassical complete markets standard implies that household consumption should move with aggregate consumption of the risk-sharing group and not with household specific income. It is as if all income were pooled, aggregating up idiosyncratic and aggregate shocks, so that only aggregate shocks remain. Aggregate consumption, after auxiliary smoothing, for example, borrowing and lending with those outside the group, should then be distributed in the group population according to Pareto weights or wealth, and these are not functions of contemporary income/shock conditions. Aggregate consumption can be replaced in a regression by a time dummy, picking up the common aggregate shocks. Household consumption can be measured comprehensively as in an income expenditures survey. In the SES, this is administered in a morning. Or, as in the Townsend Thai survey, information on a few key items is ascertained in a few minutes, specifically, twelve items which when weighted explain up to 70 per cent of non-durable expenditures in the SES. Likewise, household investment should move with aggregate shocks and not with household specific cash flow. Investment in the panel is created by keeping track of household assets and their changes.

In Thailand, the benchmark risk-sharing standard is rejected overall in household data. Vulnerability of consumption to income shocks appears more salient during the financial crisis in the Central region, and sensitivity of investment to cash flow shocks is a chronic problem in the Northeast. But households with low education, households with female heads, and the elderly do not seem more sensitive to idiosyncratic shocks than are other households. This is of enormous importance to policymakers who tend to single out these types of households as likely targets for safety net funding, either in emergencies or as long-term structural alleviation strategies. There is, however, a salient and important exception: low-wealth households are consistently more vulnerable in both consumption and investment to adverse shocks across regions and time periods. Among these are poor farmers and wage earners. Thus, it seems policymakers might redouble efforts to put in place social insurance and security systems for these households (though obstacles to trade as an explanation are explored below).

Data for firms from the Ministry of Industry tell a similar story. Controlling for sector, small and medium firms are much more likely to display sensitivity of investment to cash flow. Evidently, the SME programs already in place in Thailand, the SME bank and Small Industry Credit Guarantee Corporation, are not sufficient, though this finding is typical to most countries.

The permanent income standard is similar to the full risk-sharing standard and uses identical data. Transitory shocks should be saved; for example, though income might move with a rainfall shock, consumption should not. The Thai SES data indicate that rainfall shocks are well covered. More persistent shocks such as slow-moving rubber prices should show up in consumption, but the permanent income models tell us how much. The Thai SES data indicate rubber shocks are not well covered for all income groups.

The buffer stock, savings model is related—households can save but have limited borrowing. This raises the overall level of savings for low-wealth households, though consumption remains more sensitive to drops in income. The buffer stock model, when it fits well, is indicative of constraints on borrowing.

The point here is that consumption and income data are being used to judge the efficiency of the financial system; whether or not households borrow, the amount of their savings, and whether they have access/use of the financial system are at best proximate if not misleading criteria. Likewise, as with savings for households, capital asset ratios for financial institutions tell us little about overall efficiency. Likewise, as with debt and repayment for households, the amount of lending and even loan recovery for financial institutions is not equivalent with overall efficiency. (Bankruptcy is treated as a transfer payment in national income accounts.) Some non-payment as a contingency in a loan contract can be a good thing for the household and well understood by an insuring institution. Existing standardized debt contacts with high repayment may not span the space of returns: it may be incomplete. Welfare may be gained for some, potentially by the introduction of new securities, for example, partial credit guarantees, or reinsurance. More generally, when an exogenously incomplete regime is tested and found to fit the data better than an endogenously incomplete regime, then there can be gains toward making the contracts/markets more complete. But steps in that direction may alter the distribution of income and so require potential compensation.

The BAAC has in place an operating system which allows some insurance. This insurance is distinguished from strategic default and litigation arrears, in which case a penalty of 3 per cent is charged. Farmers experiencing natural disasters, other adverse events in nature (drought, flood, crop disease), and household-specific shocks (illness, fire) can request that the BAAC defer repayment of their loan. On occasion, with large regional shocks (such as the floods of 1995 and 1997) interest and some principal are forgiven. A credit officer must go into the field and verify damage—a version of costly monitoring. In principle, adverse events are coded and computerized, though we have yet to secure these data. Related would be BAAC flow of funds by branch and province, that is, BAAC net financial flows as a 'response' to real shocks as measured in secondary data.

The BAAC shortfall in revenue is paid by the government to the BAAC on behalf of the farmer clients. It appears in the accounts as an income-recompense transfer. Unfortunately, a single line item in the income statement mixes these insurance transfers with subsidies for targeted government projects. Robert Townsend and Amir Yaron were able to confirm for specific years that income-recompense transfers were substantially greater than transfers for government projects. In any event, the overall magnitude of the sum of the two was quite large: without it, reported BAAC profits would have been negative. More generally, the BAAC is on-lending to farmers at rates of 1–2 per cent below the market, so naturally it has losses. As Yaron has recommended, market prices for sources of funds should be used to make a realistic assessment of the actual costs to society of running the Bank. Likewise, loans with slow repayment should be provisioned according to historical arrears data, not via the mechanistic formula currently in use and recommended by international organizations during the crisis (essentially, straight-line provisions as a function of number of years in arrear). Use of historical arrears would also give a more realistic estimate of current costs and overall performance. This should be done, moreover, by branch and type of event.

Adjusted, market-based costs should then be compared to the net benefit farmers receive from the insurance implicit in the operating system. If farmers were willing to pay that net benefit to the bank in fees, and neither the BAAC nor customers altered their behavior, then the BAAC would in effect be breaking even. That is, the BAAC should exist if it passes this cost/benefit test, and should be shut down otherwise. Existence is not necessarily inconsistent with the receipt of a subsidy indirectly distributed by BAAC to client farmers. In some models, it would be as if the lump sum subsidy went to farmers directly, with farmers then paying this back to BAAC in premia and fees. (However, a farmer would not have to use the bank to collect the subsidy, which in some instances can be a better arrangement as there is no distortion). In sum, the Thai economy with institutions such as the BAAC may simply be at a point on the Pareto frontier, a competitive equilibrium with taxes/transfers. As for commercial banks and other financial institutions, we lack data from Thailand to get this far.

The discussion thus far has focused on the correlation of household/firm budget/cash flow deficits with financing devices. That is, the discussion featured correlation of new borrowing or failure to repay old debt with a shortfall between consumption and income, or a shortfall between investment and cash flow from operations (or for household/businesses essentially the sum of the two).

But caution is in order. A high correlation between a deficit and financing devices does not tell us if the movement of the financial instrument is sufficient to reach the benchmark consumption or investment standard. On the other hand, not using a financial instrument or mechanism may indicate only that the household or firm is using yet some other, alternative device. The goal, then, is to come up with a score card which tells us whether a particular instrument or institution is truly helpful. In the language of counterfactuals, we want to know whether a household or firm would suffer if the institution or its contracts disappeared. In other words: does the household/firm participate because there is a net gain? Would households/firms not currently participating benefit if they were given access?

Fortunately, we have data from some quasi-experiments exogenously varying intermediation that come about from financial sector policy changes. In some of these experiments, there is an element of compulsion or, in the language of experiments and trials, unavoided treatment. In others, there are selection issues, but, under some assumptions, instrumental variables allow determination of the average treatment effect. Granted that the choice problems that generate participation and subsequent actions need to be modeled, as in other chapters; this part of the manuscript should be taken as akin to tests of the neoclassical standard. A positive impact on production/investment/occupation from intervention is akin to the existence of a prior neoclassical anomaly.

A reading of the history of the Thai financial system generates the ideas that lie behind many of the policy changes and the availability of potential instruments. Financial sector reforms were implemented starting in 1986 or so, after some difficulties. These included the opening of new branches, the removal of interest rate restrictions on savings and on loans, and limits to existing social targeting. This is a classic financial liberalization period. The government, however, continued to play a role: the BAAC expanded, and village-level funds were promoted by various independent ministries. While overall this was a period of very high growth, not everyone benefited equally, as we have seen from the inequality story. Next comes the financial crisis and the contraction of commercial banks. Wealth losses, or their proxies, provide instruments for evaluation of impact of commercial banks lending. But again the government continued to play a role. The BAAC continued to expand, though selected client farmers were given the option of joining a debt moratorium program. (Program eligibility creates the instrument in this case.) Post crisis, the government has played an increasing role in the financial system. The million baht village-fund program is a prominent example: $25,000 was placed in each of 72,000 villages. Households in villages with fewer household units were more likely to receive new loans, and these new loans appear not to have been substitutes for existing loans. Short-term village-fund credit is thus instrumented with the inverse of village population size and binary time dummies indicating the dates of intervention.

In fact, the instruments are most obvious when we proceed in reverse chronological order. The inverse of population size is a control in periods before the village-fund intervention and seems, in any event, unrelated to things that were happening before the intervention. It is likely uncorrelated with the error terms in the impact equation, especially if household and village controls capturing key heterogeneities are used as well. If it is presumed in addition that the error term in the impact equation for participants and non-participants are identical or, more weakly, of constant average difference, then the IV-estimated parameter on the treatment variable in the second stage OLS regression is a measure of the local average gain (of those induced to receive the treatment who would not have been involved otherwise).

The impact/outcome variables in the million baht fund program are consumption, income, overall short-term debt, assets, agricultural investment, business formation, number of households in business, levels and per cent of loan over due, and interest rates. There seem to be real consequences over and above what would happen in the neoclassical with a lump sum transfer of wealth; though consumption goes up, net savings (in terms of physical assets) goes down while agricultural investment goes up. There is seemingly little impact in terms of number of households making a transition to business, but the number of households that remain in business may have increased as does business profits. The number of loans in default, and the fraction of loans in default, also increase, as does the interest rate.

The government did implement a BAAC debt moratorium program post crisis. Though long-term client farmers with less than 100,000 baht in debt could then delay payment of existing loans without penalty, farmers participating in the program could not take out new loans. A binary variable for eligibility is the instrumental variable, regressed onto actual participation in a two-stage least squares procedure. Impact assessment shows that most effects were neutral or statistically insignificant. But the point estimate on agricultural investment is troublesome. It is negative, the opposite of the positive coefficient for the expansionary village-fund program. It is as if there was some compulsion in the decision to participate in the BAAC debt moratorium even though it may not have been beneficial. More generally, the debt moratorium sets a bad precedent if it creates an expectation on the part of farmers that they need not pay off BAAC debt generally, regardless of their underlying situation. This shortcoming is especially salient when compared with the BAAC traditional risk contingent operating system.

Banks, finance companies, and other formal intermediaries with dollar-denominated loans experienced losses in the financial crisis from the exchange-rate devaluation, losses not related per se to their own idiosyncratic situation. The pre-crisis level of dollar-denominated loans relative to total liabilities is in effect the instrument. This exogenous right hand side variable has a significant negative sign in a regression onto the volume of on-lending. There are indications of Vickery that long-term customers suffered less from the associated contraction. However, as informative as such episodes might be to an assessment of the role of financial institutions, they do beg for an explanation of the inefficiencies that brought on the crisis and for enhanced political economy models.

The village-fund programs prior to the crisis were administered by various independent government ministries and NGOs such as Catholic Relief Services. The Townsend Thai 1997 survey elicited responses from all existing (and some past) institutions operating in the 192 sampled villages and

414

secured the institutions' record books. The institutions are quasi-formal; they do keep records and often have bank accounts, but do not in general have their own offices. Many institutions received initial funding from parent sources, and these same government and non-government organizations offer advice, training, and end-of-year accounting assistance.

PCGs are the most common type of institution. They are often promoted by the Community Development Department which calls them 'village savings funds' because they aim to promote 'good savings habits' within the village. Members of PCGs are relatively less likely to be the poorest in the village and are more likely to be women. The second most common village institution is a rice bank, which usually makes small, short-term emergency consumption loans. These loans are in rice and at high interest. Rice banks are promoted by the Department of Agriculture and used as vehicles for the introduction high yield varieties of seed. Members are generally required to donate a given amount of rice at the founding of the institution, hopefully as a self-sustaining fund. Women's groups are distinguished more by their female membership than financial activities. Some promote new occupations such as silk weaving in the Northeast. Buffalo banks lend cattle, with the loan repaid when the initial buffalo gives birth. If the buffalo dies or does not give birth, no further loans can be made.

The outcome variables are the ones emphasized in the theories: transition to business, occupation change, risk-sharing, alleviation of constraints, and asset growth. Specifically, we can gauge the average impact on the whole village population by regressing outcome variables onto whether or not there was a fund in the village with a certain policy. Some policies such as training and savings plans are shown to promote intermediation: growth in membership, in funds mobilized, and on lending. Other policies such as lending in kind are shown to lead to disintermediation and potential failure. We do not distinguish for this part who in the village is a member or participant, as this allows non-participants to benefit indirectly, a local equilibrium effect. To get treatment on the treated from certain types of funds, we regress outcomes onto an instrumented version of whether the village likely had the type of fund in question in a given year. Instruments are created by the headmen responses to retrospective questions eliciting history, CDD data indicating hot spots of likely activity of credit officers/ministries, and surprising instances in which a village is predicted to have a fund of a given type but did not and vice versa.

We find evidence in support of the theory for positive impacts of village institutions on asset growth. Institutions which seem to succeed in

415

membership, savings mobilization, and lending are institutions that have higher positive impact. Cash loans are associated with stability and expansion of services, while rice-lending institutions and buffalo banks are associated with contraction and failure. Three specific policies associated with institutional success in intermediation (offering training services, savings services, and pledged savings accounts) were each individually associated with 5–6 per cent faster asset growth. Institutions with emergency services, flexible savings accounts were 10–29 percentage points less likely to reduce consumption and/or key inputs in a year with a bad income shock. There is more evidence in support of job mobility than in constrained occupation choice per se. Women's groups and pledged savings accounts increase the probability of switching jobs. But emergency services lower the probability of starting a business. The most robust result is that institutions which intermediate successfully help reduce by 8 per cent the reliance on money lenders, our indirect measure of being constrained.

The bottom-line policy recommendations from this analysis are straightforward but of some consequence. Rice bank, buffalo banks, and funds making in-kind loans should be presumed not helpful and, unless local analysis indicates otherwise, shut down. Initial training in non-agricultural activities is to be encouraged. Training in accounting was requested by numerous committees on site visit. Having application forms is helpful, as is expanding membership beyond the village. Surprisingly, apart from emergency funds, optimal and flexible savings plans are not helpful, while time deposits and pledged savings accounts are a good thing. On-lending helps as does using savings information as a consideration in lending. Many but not all of these policies were part of the relatively new million baht fund program.

A similar evaluation procedure can be applied to the 1997–2002 annual panels in an evaluation not only of village funds, but also the BAAC, Agricultural Cooperatives, commercial banks, money lenders, and informal savings in rice. Instruments for being a member or customer in 1996, in addition to those discussed earlier, include distance to the district center. The further the distance, the less likely a household will be a member or customer of an Agricultural Cooperative or Production Credit Group, or use informal trade credit, but the opposite is true for the BAAC and for use of rice in storage (in the Northeast). It is more difficult to find instruments for commercial banks use. Controlling for observed household and village characteristics, the propensity scores for most of the financial institutions are positively related to subsequent use in the panel of the institution in savings and/or borrowing.

The bottom-line score card from this evaluation is that the BAAC and Agricultural Cooperatives are helping in the smoothing consumption from idiosyncratic shocks, but less so the smoothing of investment from variation in cash flow. The opposite is true of commercial banks, more helpful in investment than consumption. PCGs help in both consumption and investment smoothing in the Northeast. The informal sector helps both also, in both regions. Rice storage is helpful in the smoothing of consumption in the Northeast. Some of the policy conclusions are novel for Thailand. The stated objective of eliminating money lenders and the informal sector would at best seem premature. Existing formal intermediaries are only hitting limited segments of the market and only for some functions, but we do not know if this is about the operating systems, regulation, or the obstacles.

The net effect of the 1986 financial liberalization was to allow the formal financial system to expand rather dramatically. Unfortunately, we lack detailed knowledge of the implementation of the program and so far have had trouble securing historical records. So, at a crude level, for the analysis here, we take the expansion to be exogenous and assess impact via the dual-sector structural models, described again below.

In sum, variation coming from inter-temporal shocks (growth and crisis), the political economy of segmented markets, or preconceived government programs can give us useful instruments. They leave little doubt that financial sector innovations promoting intermediation in Thailand have been helpful. Unfortunately, we still lack crucial knowledge about operating systems and exogenous supply-side variation for certain financial institutions such as commercial banks. We also lack the details of some specific government policies. More on the legal system and how disputes are adjudicated—bankruptcy and collateral—would also be helpful.

To move beyond neoclassical anomalies and the impact of innovations, we need to discover how choices are made and the nature of constraints. We need to know whether or not there are obstacles to trade, document their type, and measure their severity. We need to assess in this context the distribution of gains, and potential losses, to financial sector policy change.

Models of occupation choice are modified to allow moral hazard, potential default, or a combination of the two. No obstacles, that is, the full-information, full-commitment model is embedded as an alternative for sake of comparison. Most obstacles deliver an up-sloped schedule of wealth to business transition. But these models with their various combinations of impediments to trade differ quantitatively and are tested against one another. In these models, a household can decide how much to borrow and/or save. The different qualitative implications are checked in the data as well. Finally, investments in the business, effort, ROA, and the degree of insurance are endogenous within some of the models. For example, financial institutions take into account the possibility of project failure, and an endogenous interest rate bears a default premium relative to fixed costs of outside funds. Wealth is endogenous and related to talent. There is limited commitment, and this is what restricts the level of loans. But households are forward looking and can choose the level of pre-business savings. The model determines as well the speed of entry, the size and growth of new firms, and consumption jumps. Implications of endogenously incomplete contracts (e.g., limited only by moral hazard) are compared to exogenously limited incomplete regimes (e.g., a borrowing and lending regime with bankruptcy or a savings-only regime). One tests again for statistically significant differences. In one of the models, households decide whether to borrow formally, informally, or in combination. Limited commitment from the borrower for formal sector loans limits loan size, while there is full commitment for loans from the informal sector but a higher interest rate. There are potential transaction costs in both sectors. The maximum likelihood routine in effect searches over regions where one, another, both, or neither obstacles may be present in an attempt to fit the combination-of-lender data.

We discover from this work that credit markets are imperfect. More specifically, moral hazard is a problem overall and particularly in the Central region, and limited liability is a problem, especially in the Northeast. This may help fine-tune policy initiatives directed at improvement: monitoring would appear to have a payoff in the Central region and asset collateralization or enhanced penalties for default more critical in the Northeast. The contemporary financial system may be incomplete in lacking risk contingencies, as was anticipated earlier. More surely the financial system was incomplete in the past, approximately a savings-only regime. There is direct evidence for limited commitment overall in pre-business saving rates and in households that are constrained yet use money lenders, only or in combination with the formal system. The legal system deserves closer scrutiny. Transaction costs appear to play some role. These are positive for commercial banks access, so universal access would seem an inappropriate goal. But transaction costs are smaller, virtually zero, for the informal sector. Still, even the formal sector costs are low in comparison with those estimated from dynamic models of transition. This may indicate that there have been policy distortions.

Models of joint liability and data on repayment problems also tell us something about constraints. Note that default rates are used here to determine the prevalence and type of obstacles. Tested are models of whether there is joint determination of project risk when outsiders are uninformed, whether a borrowing member is monitored internally by a non-borrowing member, whether there can be strategic default despite formal and informal penalties, and whether there is adverse selection so that the riskier potential customers are the ones actually borrowing. Decisions include type of project, effort in projects, monitoring, and strategic default. Insights come from the models' predictions for correlations of repayment with co-movement of project returns, loans size, interest rate, and productivity, the existence of screening, cost of monitoring, cooperative behavior among borrowers, outside credit options, and official and unofficial penalties. Methods are largely non-parametric, with sign restrictions coming from concavity and so on. It is found again, in this alternative model with different data, that moral hazard is a problem overall and especially in the Central region, and limited liability a problem overall and especially in the Northeast.

The model of whether to borrow under joint liability or as an individual in a relative performance regime assumes that moral hazard is the underlying problem. Groups facilitate risk-sharing, as in the neoclassical full-commitment, full-information model, but this comes with a distortion created by moral hazard—collusion in choice of effort against a poorly informed outsider. In an individualistic relative performance regime, the outsider can give borrowing members high-powered incentives to work hard, so they repay, but in this financial regime insiders are presumed to suffer from moral hazard as well. Likewise, collusion among insiders is mitigated but only a cost. The insight provided by this comparison of regimes is that the level of wealth and the distribution of wealth among potential joint-liability customers determine the optimal choice of loan contract. Low wealth and wealth inequality are forces for group joint-liability loans. This is supported in the data; implicitly, then, the premise of moral hazard is supported as well. Likewise, the implication of the adverse selection model is that safer types are not borrowing. Covariation in project returns also makes a household less likely to borrow. Both these implications are supported in the data. Policymakers should be aware in making complaints about limited access that lenders may be coping with an adverse selection problem.

Each of the models with obstacles takes as given a price or policy variable. These can be altered in policy experiments at estimated parameter values. We can thus back out the distribution of gains, or losses. We can assess the

419

likely impact of policies typically considered elsewhere or evaluate policies which are already part of the Thai financial scene. Specifically examined are further reductions and increases in an on-lending rate. The impact of potential remedies for the limited commitment, default problem are captured albeit crudely by weakening the borrowing constraint parameter as in allowing other aspects of wealth to serve as collateral. The welfare gain from alleviating the moral hazard problem is examined (to be compared with a cost of doing so). Direct wealth transfers and wealth transfers via bank losses are examined. A reduction in transaction costs or nearer access to financial institutions or agglomeration centers is examined as is the gain of going from autarky to an otherwise incomplete regime.

The overall conclusion is that the distribution of gains of many of these policy changes is skewed toward low-wealth high talent households. Which particular policy instrument is most effective seems to depend on the underlying impediment to trade. Interest rate subsidies have a big impact on some of the talented poor if there is moral hazard, but interest rate subsidies reaches more households with a lower average impact when there is limited liability. The point is that different households suffer differently from the impact of alternative constraints. One way to see this is to go from moral hazard as a constraint to limited liability as a constraint. Moral hazard is the more damaging constraint for some of the poorest households. In an interesting comparison, Xavier Giné finds enhanced enforcement to be more effective than interest rate subsidies and which are in turn more effective than nearby branches and the creation of village funds.

Virtually all of these results use the full structure of the presumed models. Curiously, the impact of bank placement and the lowering of transaction costs might be assessed via instrument variables and two-stage least squares, as in the earlier impact studies. The conditions for a valid instrument, that it facilitate access and not alter outcomes or relative gains, are satisfied in some of the models under specified assumptions. On the other hand, those conditions can be violated, even in the partial equilibrium context. More generally, the equilibrium consequence of wealth redistributions and collateral policies include movements in the prices of assets, the prices of firms, and again in wages. Unfortunately, these are not picked up in difference-in-difference or other IV specifications.

Dynamic mechanism design models have both positive and normative implications. Poverty and wealth inequality are endogenously determined in models of selection across methods of borrowing. The more general point is that with moral hazard, incentives to work hard in order to ensure project success are marshaled not only with contemporary outcomes but also with future promises and threats. Thus, an unsuccessful outcome comes with lower future wealth. If projects fail together, then local wealth is decreased but its dispersion in the population remains. Conversely, if one project succeeds while another fails, inequality should increase. Low wealth and increased inequality are forces for group lending. Conversely, initial homogeneity and uniform success are forces for the individualistic relative performance regime. Thus, networks are endogenous and evolving—as should be the method of lending. No single policy is always best.

Models with long-run transition dynamics take us back to the heart of the manuscript. A financial liberalization which (exogenously) extends access in the population to formal financial institutions can explain growth with increasing and then decreasing inequality. An evolving distribution of wealth and endogenous prices are key. Such models can also explain the movement in TFP and the decline in observed rates of poverty. A welfare analysis compares the gains and losses in end-of-period wealth across economies with and without the financial liberalization. Unfortunately, in this model with myopic savings and bequests, there is no natural overall utility metric. Here instead the wealth and income gain for the talented poor is computed for various years one at a time, and shown to be quite large. Transition dynamics also puts the focus back on poverty and inequality. Poverty is reduced over time through access to the financial system, in the short and medium run, and increases in the (unskilled) wage, in the longer run. Likewise, financial access creates inequality as at first only a few of the poor can gain from profitable businesses, but eventual increases in the wage reduces profits and increases the incomes of those without access, in effect, a big catch-up effect. The models also establish that there can be losses for some with increases in the wage, again, a political economy motive for financial repression. Difference-in-difference comparisons within a given economy for those with access and those without would not pick this up. Instrumental variable assessment of impact in an economy without price changes may yield the desired treatment on the treated, but the necessary assumptions are restrictive. Structural models can also be used to examine the impact of international capital flows and of an expanded informal sector. Neither matter much under current estimates. On the other hand, an improved transportation system which increases proximity to agglomeration hot spots has a large impact.

A second transition model with transaction costs is forward looking. Again the evolving endogenous distribution of wealth is key. This model picks up large transaction costs for the educated and urban segments of the potential market, as if there were a policy distortion. How the political economy of repression and segmentation might have created this distortion is a story yet to be told. Evidently the gains from liberalization fall largely on the middle class—those that would be glad to enter and pay transaction costs but apparently were not allowed to do so. In this context, surprise wealth redistributions from rich to poor can slow down subsequent growth. But if wealth redistributions or bank branch expansions are anticipated, and enter nonlinearly, then the instruments which work well in static contexts have an impact on outcomes in the dynamic setting, negating their use.

The version of this model which best tracks the average trend of inequality, growth, and financial deepening has transaction costs which are estimated to be quite large. The problem of the model with lower costs is that the transition happens too quickly. Thus, estimates of transaction costs in static choice models with micro data can be in conflict with what is needed for the dynamic macro transition models. This is exemplary of the kinds of tensions which are explored openly throughout the manuscript. Another is the need to reconcile the apparent role of aggregate shocks in the macro economy with the plethora of much larger idiosyncratic shocks in the micro data. Still, the manuscript never claims to have all the answers. Rather, it seeks to display via well-worked examples methods for integrated research, of micro with macro and of models with data. That is, the purpose of the manuscript is to put existing pieces together into a coherent whole. This naturally creates new, unanswered questions and orders the priorities for the continuing research in Thailand and in other countries.

Bibliography

Abiad, A., N. Oomes, and K. Ueda (2004) 'The Quality Effect: Does Financial Liberalization Improve the Allocation of Capital?', IMF Working Paper No. 04/112,
Washington, DC. IMF.

Acemoglu, D., and F. Zilibotti (1997) 'Was Prometheus Unbound by Chance?: Risk,
Diversification, and Growth', *Journal of Political Economy*, 105: 709–51.

Aghion, P., and P. Bolton (1997) 'A Theory of Trickle-down Growth and Development', *Review of Economic Studies*, 64: 151–72.

—— and P. Howitt (1995) 'Technical Progress in the Theory of Economic Growth'. In
J.-P. Fitoussi (ed.), *Economics in a Changing World: Proceedings of the Tenth World
Congress of the International Economic Association*, v. London: Macmillan: 101–22.

Ahlin, C., and R. M. Townsend (2004) 'Using Repayment Data to Test Across Models
of Joint Liability Lending'. Bureau for Research and Economic Analysis of Development Working Paper No. 072. <http://ipl.econ.duke.edu/bread/papers/work
ing/072.pdf>.

—— —— (2007a) 'Selection into and across Credit Contracts: Theory and Field
Research', *Journal of Econometrics*, 136: 665–98.

—— —— (2007b) 'Using Repayment Data to Test Across Models of Joint Liability
Lending', *Economic Journal*, 117/517: F11–F51.

Alem, M., and R. M. Townsend (2006) 'An Evaluation of Safety Nets and Financial
Institutions in Crisis and Growth'. <http://cier.uchicago.edu/papers/2006/
alem-townsend-0804.pdf>.

Assunção, J., S. Mityakov, and R. M. Townsend (2008) 'Commercial vs. Government
Development Banks: Heterogeneous Spatial Expansion Patterns'. Paper presented
at Innovations in Development Theory and Survey Data: Implications for Policy
Conference, Bangkok, 4–6 Aug. 2008.

Banerjee, A. (2003) 'Contracting Constraints, Credit Markets and Economic Development', Massachusetts Institute of Technology Department of Economics Working Paper No. 02–17. Cambridge, Mass.: MIT.

—— T. Besley, and T. W. Guinnane (1994) 'Thy Neighbor's Keeper: The Design of a Credit
Cooperative with Theory and a Test', *Quarterly Journal of Economics*, 109: 491–515.

—— and E. Duflo (2003) 'Inequality and Growth: What Can the Data Say?', *Journal
of Economic Growth*, 8: 267–99.

Banerjee, A., and E. Duflo (2004) 'Growth Theory through the Lens of Development Economics', Massachusetts Institute of Technology Department of Economics Working Paper No. 05–01. Cambridge, Mass.: MIT.

—— and K. Munshi (2004) 'How Efficiently is Capital Allocated?: Evidence from the Knitted Garment Industry in Tirupur', *Review of Economic Studies*, 71: 19–42.

—— and A. Newman (1993) 'Occupational Choice and the Process of Development', *Journal of Political Economy*, 101: 274–98.

Bank of Thailand (2003) 'National Statistical Office Annual Economic Report 2003', Bangkok. <http://www.bot.or.th/English/ResearchAndPublications/Report/DocLib_AnnualEconReport/Annual-03.pdf>.

Bank of Thailand Money and Finance Section (1997) 'Financial Institutions and Markets in Thailand'. Bangkok : Bank of Thailand Economic Research Department Report.

Barro, R. J. (2000) 'Inequality and Growth in a Panel of Countries', *Journal of Economic Growth*, 5: 5–32.

—— and X. Sala-i-Martin (2004) *Economic Growth*. 2nd edn. Cambridge, Mass.: MIT Press.

Beck, T., R. Levine, and N. Loayza (2000) 'Finance and the Sources of Growth', *Journal of Financial Economics*, 58: 261–300.

Bencivenga, V. R., and B. D. Smith (1991) 'Financial Intermediation and Endogenous Growth', *Review of Economic Studies*, 58: 195–209.

Berglof, E., and S. Claessens (2004) 'Corporate Governance and Enforcement', Policy Research Working Paper No. 3409, Washington, DC.

Bertrand, M., P. Mehta, and S. Mullainathan (2002) 'Ferreting Out Tunneling: An Application to Indian Business Groups', *Quarterly Journal of Economics*, 117: 121–48.

—— A. Schoar, and D. Thesmar (2004) 'Banking Deregulation and Industry Structure: Evidence from the French Banking Reforms of 1985', Centre for Economic Policy Research Discussion Paper No. 4488. London: CEPR.

Besley, T., and S. Coate (1995) 'Group Lending, Repayment Incentives and Social Collateral', *Journal of Development Economics*, 46: 1–18.

Binford, M. W., T. Jeong Lee, and R. M. Townsend (2004) 'Sampling Design for an Integrated Socio-economic and Ecologic Survey Using Satellite Remote Sensing and Ordination', *Proceedings of the National Academy of Sciences*, 101: 11517–22.

Blundell, R., L. Pistaferri, and I. Preston (2004) 'Consumption Inequality and Partial Insurance', Institute for Fiscal Studies Working Paper No. W04/28. London: IFS.

Bond, P. (2004) 'Bank and Nonbank Financial Intermediation', *Journal of Finance*, 59: 2489–529.

Bourguignon, F. (1979) 'Decomposable Income Inequality Measures', *Econometrica*, 47: 901–20.

—— and F. H. G. Ferreira (2004) 'Decomposing Changes in the Distribution of Household Incomes: Methodological Aspects'. In F. Bourguignon, F. H. G. Ferreira, and N. Lustig (eds), *The Microeconomics of Income Distribution Dynamics in East Asia and Latin America*. Washington, DC: World Bank: 17–47.

Bourguignon, F., and C. Morrisson (2002) 'The Size Distribution of Income among World Citizens: 1820–1990'. World Bank. manuscript. <http://siteresources.worldbank.org/INTDECINEQ/Resources/bourguignon.pdf>.

Browning, M., and P.-A. Chiappori (1998) 'Efficient Intra-household Allocations: A General Characterization and Empirical Tests', *Econometrica*, 66: 1241–78.

Buera, F. (2003) 'A Dynamic Model of Entrepreneurial Choice with Borrowing Constraints'. University of Chicago. manuscript. <http://cier.uchicago.edu/papers/students/pacothesis.pdf>.

——(2008) 'Persistency of Poverty, Financial Frictions and Entrepreneurship'. Northwestern University. Manuscript. <http://www.econ.ucla.edu/fjbuera/papers/paper120071217.pdf>.

——(2009) 'A Dynamic Model of Entrepreneurship with Borrowing Constraints: Theory and Evidence', *Ann. Finance*, 5: 443–64.

Burgess, R., and R. Pande (2005) 'Do Rural Banks Matter?: Evidence from the Indian Social Banking Experiment', *American Economic Review*, 95: 780–95.

Caballero, R. J. (2007) 'Specificity and the Macroeconomics of Restructuring'. Cambridge, Mass.: MIT Press.

—— T. Hoshi, and A. K. Kashyap (2006) 'Zombie Lending and Depressed Restructuring in Japan', National Bureau of Economic Research Working Paper No. W12129, Cambridge.

Cagetti, M., and Mariacristina De Nardi (2005) 'Wealth Inequality: Data and Models'. Federal Reserve Bank of Chicago Working Paper No. 2005–10.

Cashin, P., H. Liang, and C. John McDermott (1999) 'How Persistent are Shocks to World Commodity Prices?' IMF Working Paper No. 99/80. Washington, DC.: IMF.

Chiappori, P. A., K. Samphantharak, S. Schulhofer-Wohl, and R. M. Townsend (2006) 'Heterogeneity and Risk Sharing in Thai Villages'. mimeo.

Chue, T., and D. Cook (2004) '*Sudden Stops and Liability Dollarization: Evidence from East Asian Financial Intermediaries*'. Far Eastern Meetings 646. Econometric Society.

Colander, D. C. (2004) *Macroeconomics*, 5th edn. New York: McGraw-Hill.

—— (2007) *Macroeconomics*, 7th edn. New York: McGraw-Hill.

Cunha, F., and J. J. Heckman (2008) 'A New Framework for the Analysis of Inequality', *Macroeconomic Dynamics*, 12 (Suppl. 2): 315–54.

De Nardi, M., and M. Cagetti (2008) 'Wealth Inequality: Data and Models', *Macroeconomic Dynamics*, 12 (Suppl. 2): 285–313.

Deaton, A. (1997) 'The Analysis of Household Surveys: A Microeconometric Approach to Development Policy'. Baltimore, Md.: Johns Hopkins University Press for the World Bank.

—— (2005) 'Measuring Poverty in a Growing World (or Measuring Growth in a Poor World)', *Review of Economics and Statistics*, 87: 1–19.

Demirgüç-Kunt, A., and V. Maksimovic (1998) 'Law, Finance and Firm Growth', *Journal of Finance*, 53: 2107–37.

Doepke, M., and R. M. Townsend (2006) 'Dynamic Mechanism Design with Hidden Income and Hidden Auctions', *Journal of Economic Theory*, 126: 235–85.

Bibliography

Dollar, D., and M. Hallward-Driemeier (1998) 'Crisis, Adjustment, and Reform: Results from the Thailand Industrial Survey', Conference on Thailand's Dynamic Economic Recovery and Competitiveness, National Economic and Social Development Board of Thailand/World Bank, Bangkok, May.

—— and A. Kraay (2001) 'Growth is Good for the Poor', World Bank Policy Research Working Paper No. 2587, Washington, DC.

—— —— (2002) 'Spreading the Wealth', *Foreign Affairs*, 81: 120–76.

Duflo, E. (2003) 'Grandmothers and Granddaughters: Old Age Pension and Intrahousehold Allocation in South Africa', *World Bank Economic Review*, 17: 1–25.

—— and C. Udry (2004) 'Intrahousehold Resource Allocation in Côte d'Ivoire: Social Norms, Separate Accounts and Consumption Choices', National Bureau of Economic Research Working Paper No. 10498. Cambridge.

Evans, D. S., and B. Jovanovic (1989) 'An Estimated Model of Entrepreneurial Choice under Liquidity Constraints', *Journal of Political Economy*, 97: 808–27.

Fafchamps, M., and S. Lund (2000) 'Risk-sharing Networks in Rural Philippines', Economics Working Papers in Oxford Department of Economics Series 10. Oxford.

Faust, K., B. Entwisle, R. R. Rindfuss, and Y. Sawangdee (1999) 'Spatial Arrangement of Social and Economic Networks among Villages in Nang Rong District, Thailand', *Social Networks*, 21: 311–37.

Fazzari, S. M., R. G. Hubbard, and B. Petersen (2000) 'Investment Cash Flow Sensitivities are Useful: A Comment', *Quarterly Journal of Economics*, 115: 695–705.

Felkner, J. S. (2000) 'A Digital Spatial Predictive Model of Land-use Change Using Economic and Environmental Inputs and a Statistical Tree Classification Approach: Thailand, 1970s–1990s'. DDes. dissertation, Harvard University. In *ABI/INFORM Proquest Complete* [database on-line] <http://www.proquest.com> (publication No. AAt 9988860).

Felkner, J., and R. M. Townsend (2004) 'The Wealth Villages: An Application of GIS and Spatial Statistics to Two Structural Economic Models', Social Science Computing Services, University of Chicago. Unpub.

—— —— (2007) 'Enterprise and the Wealth of Villages'. Working Paper. <http://cier.uchicago.edu/papers/2006/felkner_townsend_2006.pdf>.

—— and Q. Youliang (2006) 'A Distributed Semantic GIS Metadata Framework', 2006 Environmental Systems Research Institute (ESRI) Conference, 7–11 Aug. 2006, San Diego, Calif.

Ferreira, F. H. G., P. G. Leite, and J. A. Litchfield (2007) 'The Rise and Fall of Brazilian Inequality: 1981–2004', *Macroeconomic Dynamics*, 12 (Suppl. 2): 199–230.

Forbes, K. J. (2000) 'A Reassessment of the Relationship between Inequality and Growth', *American Economic Review*, 90: 869–87.

Foster, A. D., and M. R. Rosenzweig (1996) 'Comparative Advantage, Information and the Allocation of Workers to Tasks: Evidence from an Agricultural Labour Market', *Review of Economic Studies*, 63: 347–74.

Foster, A. D., and M. R. Rosenzweig (2000) 'Financial Intermediation, Transfers, and Commitment: Do Banks Crowd Out Private Insurance Arrangements in Low-income Rural Areas?'. In A. Mason and G. Tapinos (eds), *Sharing the Wealth: Intergenerational Economic Relations and Demographic Change*. New York and Oxford: Oxford University Press.

Galbraith, J. K. (2002) 'By the Numbers', *Foreign Affairs*, 81: 178–83.

Galor, O., and J. Zeira (1993) 'Income Distribution and Macroeconomics', *Review of Economic Studies*, 60: 35–52.

Ghatak, M. (2000) 'Screening by the Company You Keep: Joint Liability Lending and the Peer Selection Effect', *Economic Journal*, 110: 601–31.

Giné, X. (2005) 'Access to Capital in Rural Thailand: An Estimated Model of Formal Versus Informal Credit', World Bank Policy Research Working Paper No. WPS 3502. Washington, DC.

—— and R. M. Townsend (2003) 'Evaluation of Financial Liberalization: A General Equilibrium Model with Constrained Occupation Choice'. IMF Policy Research Working Paper No. WPS 3014. Washington, DC: IMF.

—— —— (2004) 'Evaluation of Financial Liberalization: A General Equilibrium Model with Constrained Occupation Choice', *Journal of Development Economics*, 74: 269–307.

Goldstein, M., and C. Udry (1999) 'Gender and Land Resource Management in Southern Ghana'. Working Paper. <http://www.econ.yale.edu/~cru2//pdf/soilpap2.pdf>.

Gollin, D. (2002) 'Getting Income Shares Right', *Journal of Political Economy*, 110: 458–74.

Gorman, W. M. (1953) 'Community Preference Fields', *Econometrica*, 21: 63–80.

Gourinchas, P.-O., and J. A. Parker (2002) 'Consumption over the Life-cycle', *Econometrica*, 70: 47–89.

Greenwood, J., and B. Jovanovic (1990) 'Financial Development, Growth, and the Distribution of Income', *Journal of Political Economy*, 98: 1076–107.

Guiso, L., P. Sapienza, and L. Zingales (2006) 'The Cost of Banking Regulation'. National Bureau of Economic Research Working Paper No. 12501. Cambridge.

Haksar, V. (2000) 'Financial Sector Restructuring in Thailand: Selected Issues', IMF Staff Country Report Number 00/21. Washington, DC: IMF.

—— and P. P. Kongsamut (2003) 'Dynamics of Corporate Performance in Thailand'. IMF Working Paper No. 03/214. Washington, DC: IMF.

Heaton, J., and D. Lucas (2000) 'Portfolio Choice and Asset Prices: The Importance of Entrepreneurial Risk', *Journal of Finance*, 55: 1163–98.

Heckman, J. J., and E. Vytlacil (2001) 'Local Instrumental Variables'. In C. Hsiao, K. Morimune, and J. L. Powell (eds), *Nonlinear Statistical Modeling: Proceedings of the Thirteenth International Symposium in Economic Theory and Econometrics: Essays in Honor of Takeshi Amemiya*. Cambridge and New York, Cambridge University Press: 1–46.

—— —— (2005) 'Structural Equations, Treatment Effects and Econometric Policy Evaluation', *Econometrica*, 73: 669–738.

Bibliography

Heckman, J. J., L. J. Lochner, and C. Taber (1998a) 'Explaining Rising Wage Inequality: Explorations with a Dynamic General Equilibrium Model of Labor Earnings with Heterogeneous Agents', *Review of Economic Dynamics*, 1: 1–58.

—— —— —— (1998b) 'General Equilibrium Treatment Effects: A Study of Tuition Policy', *American Economic Review*, 88: 381–6.

—— S. Urzua, and E. Vytlacil (2006) 'Understanding Instrumental Variables in Models with Essential Heterogeneity', *Review of Economics and Statistics*, 88: 389–432.

Holmström, B., and P. Milgrom (1990) 'Regulating Trade Among Agents', *Journal of Institutional and Theoretical Economics*, 146: 85–105.

Hook, J., S. Novak, and R. Johnston (2003) *Social Atlas of the Lower Mekong Basin.* Phnom Penh: Mekong River Commission.

Imbens, G. W., and J. D. Angrist (1994) 'Identification and Estimation of Local Average Treatment Effects', *Econometrica*, 62: 467–75.

International Monetary Fund (2003) 'Tanzania: Financial System Stability Assessment, including Reports on the Observance of Standards and Codes on Banking Supervision'. IMF Country Report No. 03/241, prepared by the Monetary and Financial Systems and the African Departments. Washington, DC: IMF.

Jeong, H. (2000) 'Sources of Kuznets Dynamics in Thailand'. University of Chicago PhD thesis.

—— (2008) 'Assessment of Relationship between Growth and Inequality: Micro Evidence from Thailand', *Macroeconomic Dynamics* (spec. issue on inequality), 12: 155–97.

—— —— (2007) 'Sources of TFP Growth: Occupational Choice and Financial Deepening', *Economic Theory*, 32: 179–221.

—— —— (2008) 'Growth and Inequality: Model Evaluation Based on an Estimation-Calibration Strategy', *Macroeconomic Dynamics Special Issue on Inequality*, 12: 231–84.

Juhn, C., K. M. Murphy, and B. Pierce (1993) 'Wage Inequality and the Rise in Returns to Skill', *Journal of Political Economy*, 101: 410–42.

Kaboski, J. P., and R. M. Townsend (1998) 'Borrowing and Lending in Semi-urban and Rural Thailand'. University of Chicago. manuscript.

—— —— (2004) 'The Impact of Credit: An Early Evaluation of a Large-scale Government Credit Injection'. Chicago: University of Chicago. mimeo.

—— —— (2005) 'Policies and Impact: An Analysis of Village-level Microfinance Institutions', *Journal of the European Economic Association*, 3: 1–50.

—— —— (2007) 'Consumption Investment and Saving Under Credit Constraints: Testing Structural Theory Using a Large-scale Micro Finance Experiment'. unpub. <http://cier.uchicago.edu/papers/2006/buffstock-assa010306.pdf>.

Kaplan, S. N., and L. Zingales (1997) 'Do Investment-Cash Flow Sensitivities Provide Useful Measures of Financing Constraints', *Quarterly Journal of Economics*, 112: 169–215.

—— —— (2000) 'Investment Cash Flow Sensitivities are Not Valid Measures of Financing Constraints', *Quarterly Journal of Economics*, 115: 707–12.

428

Karaivanov, A. (2001) 'Computing Moral Hazard Programs with Lotteries Using Matlab'. manuscript. <http://www.sfu.ca/~akaraiva/MHmatlab.pdf>.

—— (2003) 'Financial Contracts and Occupational Choice'. University of Chicago PhD thesis.

Kehoe, T. J., and E. C. Prescott (2002) 'Great Depressions of the Twentieth Century', *Review of Economic Dynamics*, 5: 1–18.

Kermel-Torrès, D. (2004) *Atlas of Thailand: Spatial Structures and Development*. Paris and Chiang Mai: IRD Editions/Silkworm Books.

Kilenthong, W. (2005) 'Collateralized Contracts as a Risk Sharing Mechanism'. <http://economics.uchicago.edu/download/job_market.pdf>.

King, R. G., and R. Levine (1993) 'Finance and Growth: Schumpeter Might be Right', *Quarterly Journal of Economics*, 108: 717–37.

Koriyama, Y., and R. M. Townsend (2008) 'Dynamic Poverty Mapping in Thailand: A Spatial Kuznets Analysis'. Working Paper. <http://www.yatsuke.gr.jp/~korbie/KoriyamaTownsend2008SpatialKuznetsALL.pdf>.

Legros, P., and A. F. Newman (1996) 'Wealth Effects, Distribution, and the Theory of Organization', *Journal of Economic Theory*, 70: 312–41.

Lehnert, A., E. Ligon, and R. M. Townsend (1999) 'Liquidity Constraints and Incentive Contracts', *Macroeconomic Dynamics*, 3: 1–47.

Levine, R. (1997) 'Financial Development and Economic Growth: Views and Agenda', *Journal of Economic Literature*, 35: 688–726.

Lim, Y., and R. M. Townsend (1998) 'General Equilibrium Models of Financial Systems: Theory and Measurement in Village Economies', *Review of Economic Dynamics*, 1: 59–118.

Lloyd-Ellis, H., and D. Bernhardt (2000) 'Enterprise, Inequality and Economic Development', *Review of Economic Studies*, 67: 147–68.

Lucas Jr, R. E. (1993) 'Making a Miracle', *Econometrica*, 61: 251–72.

—— (2004) 'The Industrial Revolution: Past and Future'. 2003 Annual Report Essay. Minneapolis, Minn.: Federal Reserve Bank of Minneapolis.

McKenzie, D., and C. Woodruff (2003) 'Do Entry Costs Provide an Empirical Basis for Poverty Traps? Evidence from Mexican Microenterprises', BREAD Working Paper No. 020. Boston, Mass.: Bureau for Research and Economic Analysis of Development.

Madeira, G. A., and R. M. Townsend (2008) 'Endogenous Groups and Dynamic Selection in Mechanism Design', *Journal of Economic Theory*, 142: 259–93.

Maksimovic, V., A. Demirgüç-Kunt, and T. Beck (2002) 'Financial and Legal Constraints to Firm Growth: Does Size Matter?', IMF Policy Research Working Paper No. WPS 2784. Washington, DC: IMF.

Mallikamas, R. P., Y. Thaicharoen, and D. Rodpengsangkaha (2003) 'Investment Cycles, Economic Recovery and Monetary Policy'. Paper presented at Bank of Thailand Symposium 2003, Bank of Thailand, Bangkok, Aug. 2003.

Matsuyama, K. (2001) 'On the Rise and Fall of Class Societies', CIRJE-F-173, Tokyo: CIRJE, Faculty of Economics, University of Tokyo.

Mookherjee, D., A. Banerjee, and R. Benabou (eds) (2006) *Understanding Poverty*. New York: Oxford University Press.

National Account Division (1999) '1999 Thailand per Capita Gross Provincial Product (GPP)'. Bangkok: Office of the Thai National Economic and Social Development Board.

National Statistical Office (2000) 'Preliminary Report: The 2000 Population and Housing Census', Office of the Prime Minister of Thailand, Bangkok. <http://web.nso.go.th/eng/en/pop2000/prelim_e.htm>.

—— (2003) 'Thailand Development Report Indicators 2003'. Bangkok: Statistical Office Report.

—— (2007) 'The 1960–2000 Population and Housing Census'. Bangkok: National Statistical Office of Thailand. <http://web.nso.go.th/census/poph/prelim_e.htm>.

Okuda, H., and F. Mieno (1999) 'What Happened to Thai Commercial Banks in the Pre-Asian Crisis Period: Microeconomic Analysis of the Thai Banking Industry', *Hitotsubashi Journal of Economics*, 40: 97–121.

Orozco, M., and R. Fedewa (2006) 'Leveraging Efforts on Remittances and Financial Intermediation'.Working Paper 24, Inter-American Development Bank, Washington, DC.

Paulson, A. L., and R. M. Townsend (2004) 'Entrepreneurship and Financial Constraints in Thailand', *Journal of Corporate Finance*, 10: 229–62.

—— —— (2005) 'Financial Constraints and Entrepreneurship: Evidence from the Thai Financial Crisis', *Federal Reserve Bank of Chicago Economic Perspectives*, 29: 34–48.

—— —— and A. Karaivanov (2006) 'Distinguishing Limited Liability from Moral Hazard in a Model of Entrepreneurship', *Journal of Political Economy*,114: 100–44.

Paxson, C. H. (1992) 'Using Weather Variability to Estimate the Response of Savings to Transitory Income in Thailand', *American Economic Review*, 82: 15–33.

Phelan, C., and R. M. Townsend (1991) 'Computing Multi-period, Information-constrained Optima', *Review of Economic Studies*, 58: 853–81.

Piketty, T. (1997) 'The Dynamics of the Wealth Distribution and the Interest Rate with Credit Rationing', *Review of Economic Studies*, 64: 173–89.

Pitts, J. W. (2002) 'Inequality is No Myth', *Foreign Affairs*, 81: 178–83.

Prasad, E., K. Rogoff, Shang-Jin Wei, and M. Ayhan Kose (2003) 'Effects of Financial Globalization on Developing Countries: Some Empirical Evidence'. IMF Occasional Paper No. 220. Washington, DC: IMF.

Prescott, E. S. (1999) 'A Primer on Moral-hazard Models', *Federal Reserve Bank of Richmond Economic Quarterly*, 85: 47–78.

—— and R. M. Townsend (2002) 'Collective Organizations versus Relative Performance Contracts: Inequality, Risk Sharing, and Moral Hazard', *Journal of Economic Theory*, 103: 282–310.

—— —— (2006) 'Firms as Clubs in Walrasian Markets with Private Information', *Journal of Political Economy*, 114: 644–71.

Quah, D. (1993) 'Empirical Cross-section Dynamics in Economic Growth', *European Economic Review*, 37: 426–34.

Radelet, S., and J. D. Sachs (1998) 'The Onset of the East Asian Financial Crisis'. National Bureau of Economic Research Working Paper No. W6680. Cambridge.

Rajan, R. G., and L. Zingales (1998) 'Financial Dependence and Growth', *American Economic Review*, 88: 559–86.

Research Institute for Development and Finance (2001) 'Issues of Sustainable Development in Asian Countries: Focused on SMIs in Thailand'. Japan Bank for International Cooperation Research Paper No. 8–1. Tokyo: JBIC.

Rodrik, D. (1999) 'Determinants of Economic Growth'. Washington, DC: Overseas Development Council.

Rosenzweig, M. R., and K. I. Wolpin (2000) 'Natural "Natural Experiments" in Economics', *Journal of Economic Literature*, 38: 827–74.

Rubin, D. B. (1974) 'Estimating Causal Effects of Treatments in Randomized and Non-randomized Studies', *Journal of Educational Psychology*, 66: 688–701.

Samphantharak, K. (2002) 'Internal Capital Markets in Business Groups'. University of Chicago PhD thesis.

—— and R. M. Townsend (2009) *Households as Corporate Firms: An Analysis of Household Finance Using Integrated Household Surveys and Corporate Financial Accounting*. Econometric Society Monographs. Cambridge: Cambridge University Press.

Schulhofer-Wohl, S. (2004) 'Testing for Credit Constraints in Entrepreneurship'. University of Chicago. manuscript. <http://economics.uchicago.edu/download/ssw_applications_20050207.pdf>.

—— (2007) 'Heterogeneity, Risk Sharing and the Welfare Costs of Risk'. University of Chicago PhD thesis.

Seiler, E., and R. M. Townsend (1998a) 'Assets in Semi-urban and Rural Thailand'. University of Chicago. manuscript.

—— —— (1998b) 'Saving in Rural Thailand'. Chicago: University of Chicago. mimeo.

Shapiro, E., and W. J. Baumol (1970) *Macroeconomic Analysis*. 2nd edn. New York: Harcourt, Brace and World.

—— and S. Balbirer (1999) *Modern Corporate Finance: A Multidisciplinary Approach to Value Creation*. Englewood Cliffs, NJ: Prentice Hall.

Smith, A. (1776) *An Inquiry into the Nature and Causes of the Wealth of Nations*. London: W. Strahan and T. Cadell.

Stiglitz, J. E. (1990) 'Peer Monitoring and Credit Markets', *World Bank Economic Review*, 4: 351–66.

Suehiro, A. (1989) *Capital Accumulation in Thailand, 1855–1985*. Bangkok: Silkworm Books.

—— (1999) 'The Road to Economic Re-entry: Japan's Policy toward Southeast Asian Development in the 1950s and 1960s', *Social Science Japan Journal*, 2: 85–105.

Suri, T. (2005) 'Spillovers in Village Consumption: Testing the Extent of Partial Insurance'. New Haven, Conn.: Yale University. mimeo.

Tambunlertchai, S., and C. Loohawenchit (1988) *Rural Industries in Thailand*. Bangkok.

Tambunlertchai, S. (2004) 'The Government's Helping Hand: A Study of Thailand's Agricultural Debt Moratorium'. Harvard University Senior Honors thesis.

Thaicharoen, Y., K. Ariyapruchya, and T. Chucherd (2004), 'Rising Thai Household Debt: Assessing Risks and Policy Implications', Bank of Thailand Symposium 2004, 6–7 Sept. 2004, Bangkok.

Tinakorn, P., and C. Sussangkarn (1998) 'Total Factor Productivity Growth in Thailand: 1980–1995', Thailand Development Research Institute research report submitted to the National Economic and Social Development Board. Bangkok: TDRI.

Townsend Project, Thailand Database Research Archive (1997–2005) Monthly Surveys and Annual Resurveys. <http://cier.uchicago.edu/townsend_thai/townsendproj.htm>.

Townsend Thai Socio-economic Survey (1957–2000), National Opinion Research Center, University of Chicago. <http://cier.uchicago.edu/reldata/ses/ses.htm>.

Townsend, R. M. (1978) 'Intermediation with Costly Bilateral Exchange', *Review of Economic Studies*, 45: 417–25.

—— (1994) 'Risk and Insurance in Village India', *Econometrica*, 62: 539–91.

—— (1995a) 'Consumption Insurance: An Evaluation of Risk-bearing Systems in Low-income Economies', *Journal of Economic Perspectives*, 9: 83–102.

—— (1995b) 'Financial Systems in Northern Thai Villages', *Quarterly Journal of Economics*, 110: 1011–46.

—— and K. Ueda (2006) 'Financial Deepening, Inequality, and Growth: A Model-Based Quantitative Evaluation', *Review of Economic Studies*, 73: 251–93.

—— —— (2008) 'Welfare Gains from Financial Liberalization'. Working Paper. <http://cier.uchicago.edu/papers/Ueda/Welfare.pdf>.

—— and J. I. Vickery (2004) 'Commodity Price Shocks, Consumption and Risk Sharing in Rural Thailand'. In J. I. Vickery, 'Essays in Banking and Risk-Management'. Massachusetts Institute of Technology PhD thesis: 121–8.

—— and J. Yaron (2001) 'The Credit Risk Contingency System of an Asian Development Bank', *Federal Reserve Bank of Chicago Economic Perspectives*, 25: 31–48.

United Nations Development Programme (2003) 'Thailand Human Development Report 2003'. <http://hdr.undp.org/en/reports/nationalreports/asiathepacific/thailand/thailand_2003_en.pdf>.

Urzua, S. S. (2004) 'Poverty and Inequality: A Review'. University of Chicago. manuscript.

—— and R. M. Townsend (2006) 'Occupational Choice with Financial Intermediation: Linking Mechanism Design with Heterogeneity to Econometric Policy Evaluation'. University of Chicago. manuscript.

US Department of Commerce and Bureau of Economic Analysis (1985) 'An Introduction to National Economic Accounting'. Methodology Paper Series MP-1, Washington, DC. Bureau of Economic Analysis.

Vanitcharearnthum, V. (1986–1996) 'Recent Development in Poverty, Risk-Sharing and Social Safety Nets in Thailand'. Working Paper. Bangkok: Thammasat University Community Development Department data set, Rural Development Committee, Thai Ministry of the Interior.

Vickery, J. I. (2004) 'Essays in Banking and Risk Management'. Massachusetts Institute of Technology PhD thesis.

Vuong, Quang H. (1989) 'Likelihood Ratio Tests for Model Selection and Non-nested Hypotheses', *Econometrica*, 57: 307–33.

Wilson, R. (1968) 'The Theory of Syndicates', *Econometrica*, 36: 119–32.

Yang, L. (2002) 'The Dynamics of Provincial Income Distribution in Thailand'. Working Paper. University of Chicago.

—— (2004) 'Unequal Provinces but Equal Families? An Analysis of Inequality and Migration'. In L. Yang, 'Thailand in Essays on the Determinants and Consequences of Internal Migration'. University of Chicago Department of Economics thesis.

Yaron, J., M. P. Benjamin, and G. Piprek (1997) 'Rural Finance: Issues, Design and Best Practices'. Environmentally and Socially Sustainable Development Studies and Monographs Series 14. Washington, DC: World Bank.

Young, A. (1995) 'The Tyranny of Numbers: Confronting the Statistical Realities of the East Asian Growth Experience', *Quarterly Journal of Economics*, 110: 641–80.

Zeldes, S. (1989) 'Consumption and Liquidity Constraints: An Empirical Investigation', *Journal of Political Economy*, 97: 305–46.

Index

Index

initial wealth 198, 201, 226, 321
  business starts and sector of occupation
    unrelated to 407
  entry into business facilitated by 2, 257
  initial investment in business should be
    unrelated to 408
  occupation choice and 200
instrumental variables 14, 303, 413, 414, 421
insurance vii, 315, 316, 318, 377
  based on incentives 175
  endogenous 334
  full 371, 376
  incomplete 284
  increased 330
  internal 372
  markets for 1
  mutual agreements 371
integrated micro-macro models 195–256
interest rates 280
  adjusted 330
  attractive vi
  average 159, 288
  BAAC 314, 361–2, 366
  best effects 325
  ceilings lifted 31
  cut in 352
  decreased 209
  dispersed 13, 15
  endogenous 196, 316, 334, 337, 393, 418
  equilibrium 195, 316
  exogenous 313, 318
  fixed viii, 313, 328
  heterogeneous 13
  high(er) vi, 15, 314, 320, 418
  implicit zero net 199
  imposing a penalty 160
  increase in 353, 356, 414
  lowered 5, 314, 316, 320
  market clearing 200, 315
  outside 175, 318
  raised 160, 285, 314, 366
  removal of restrictions 413
  response of repayment rates to 359
  subsidies 5, 313, 314, 420
  trade-off between transaction costs and 351
  variation in 159, 313
  see also real interest rates
intermediation 1, 158, 204, 206, 207, 220, 221, 311, 391
  effects of 298, 300
  exogenous variations in access to 2, 285
  extent of 29, 165
  institutional success in 416
  insufficient 409

low level of 138
perfect 195
policies positively correlated with 300
promoting 178, 415, 417
quasi-experiments exogenously
  varying 412
restricted by financial crisis 3
unnatural variation in 178
zero profits 395
international markets 297
intra-group effect 132
inventories 48, 53
investment vi, 4, 5, 12, 13, 16, 38, 47, 48, 102, 138, 165, 209, 222, 226
  agricultural 295
  capital 224, 347
  constant return to scale 219
  consumer durables classified as 57
  financial 275
  financial constraint limiting 344
  frequency of viii
  high rates v
  increasing with wealth 330–1
  initial 142
  initial wealth facilitates 257
  large enough that returns cover fixed
    costs 347
  marginal cost of 271
  more than proportionate increase in 274
  must be covered by cash flow 167
  optimal 346
  realization of macro and idiosyncratic
    shocks takes place after 218
  size of 310–11
  smoothing 2
  start-up 153
  variability of 55
  see also FDI; over-investment; private
    investment
irrigation 64, 121
Islamic provinces 67
Italy 13

Japan 9, 12
JBIC (Japan Bank for International
  Cooperation) 9, 141, 160, 165, 263, 404
Jeong, H. 22, 24, 28, 131, 134–6, 225, 226, 233
joint liability viii, 6, 138, 258, 357, 385, 399, 403
  disparity of wealth among potential
    borrowers 315
  entry and exit 400
  individual versus 315, 388, 419

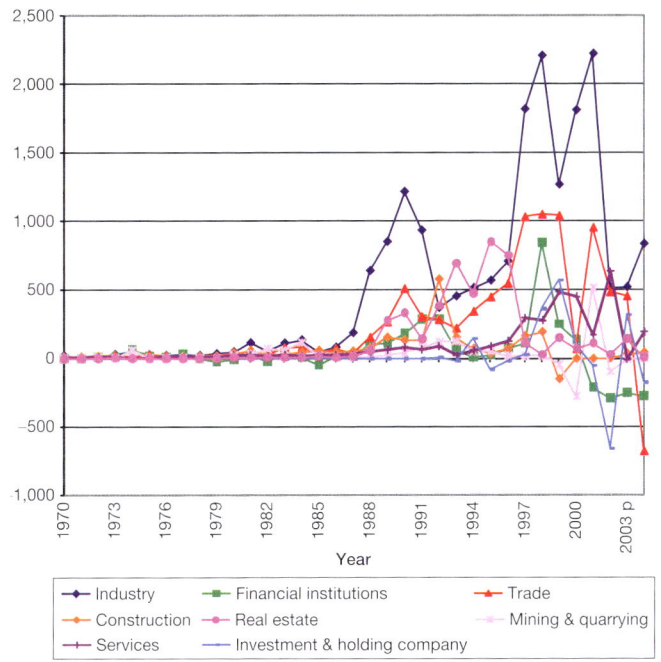

FIG. 2.6. Net flow of FDI by sector, 1970–2004p (See p. 46)

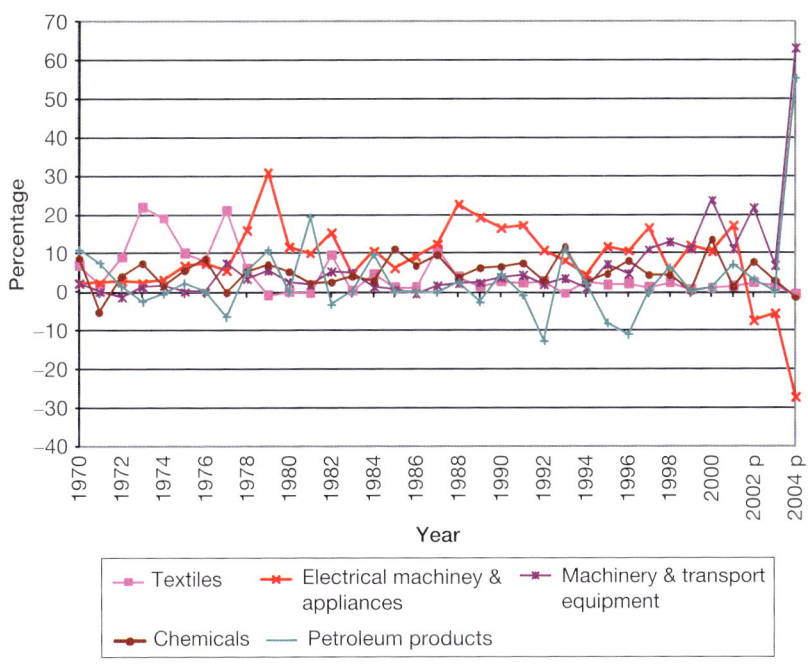

FIG. 2.7. FDI in industry at disaggregate level (percentage of total FDI) (See p. 47)

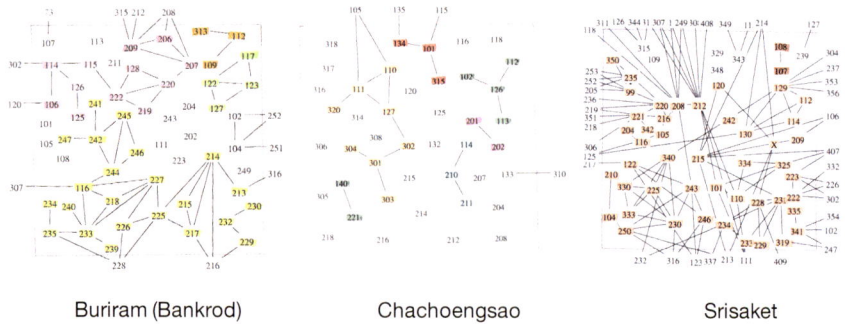

Buriram (Bankrod)   Chachoengsao   Srisaket

FIG. 2.10. Family networks in villages (See p. 58)

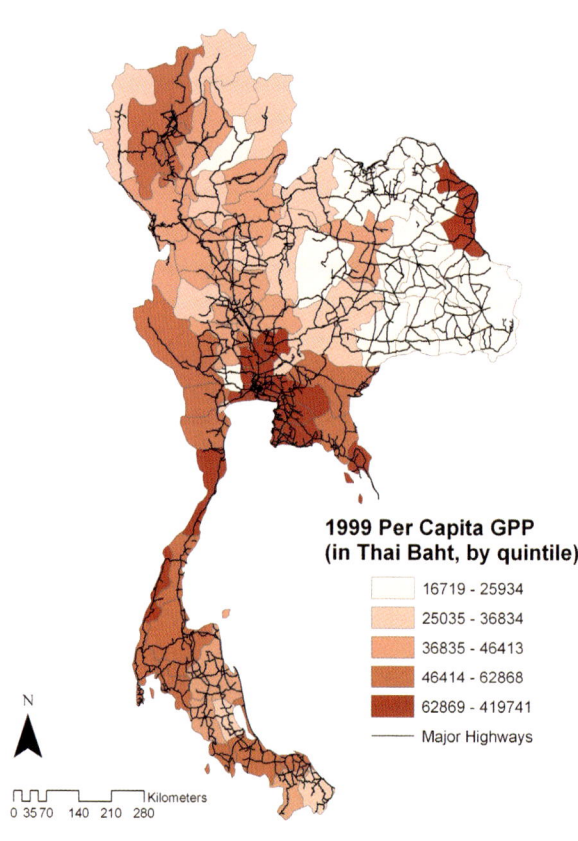

FIG. 3.1. 1999 Thailand per capita gross provincial product
(in Thai baht, by quintile) (See p. 66)

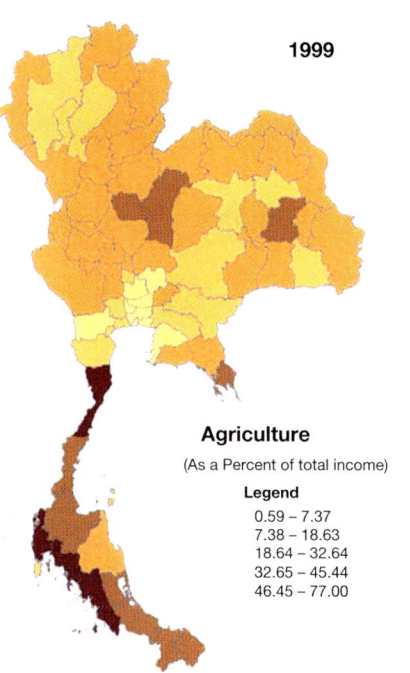

1999

Agriculture

(As a Percent of total income)

Legend

0.59 – 7.37
7.38 – 18.63
18.64 – 32.64
32.65 – 45.44
46.45 – 77.00

FIG. 3.2 (a)
Agriculture in Thailand as a
percentage of total income, 1999
(See p. 67)

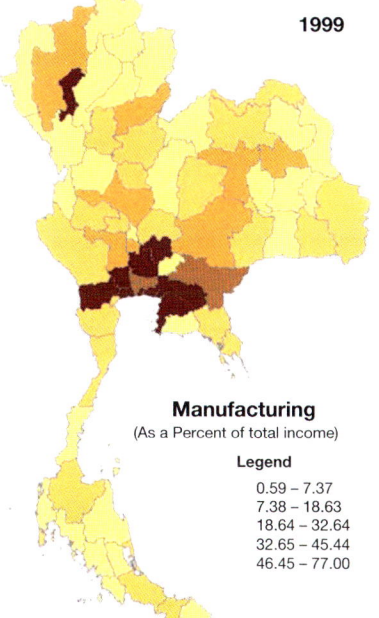

1999

Manufacturing

(As a Percent of total income)

Legend

0.59 – 7.37
7.38 – 18.63
18.64 – 32.64
32.65 – 45.44
46.45 – 77.00

FIG. 3.2 (b)
Manufacturing in Thailand as a
percentage of total income, 1999
(See p. 67)

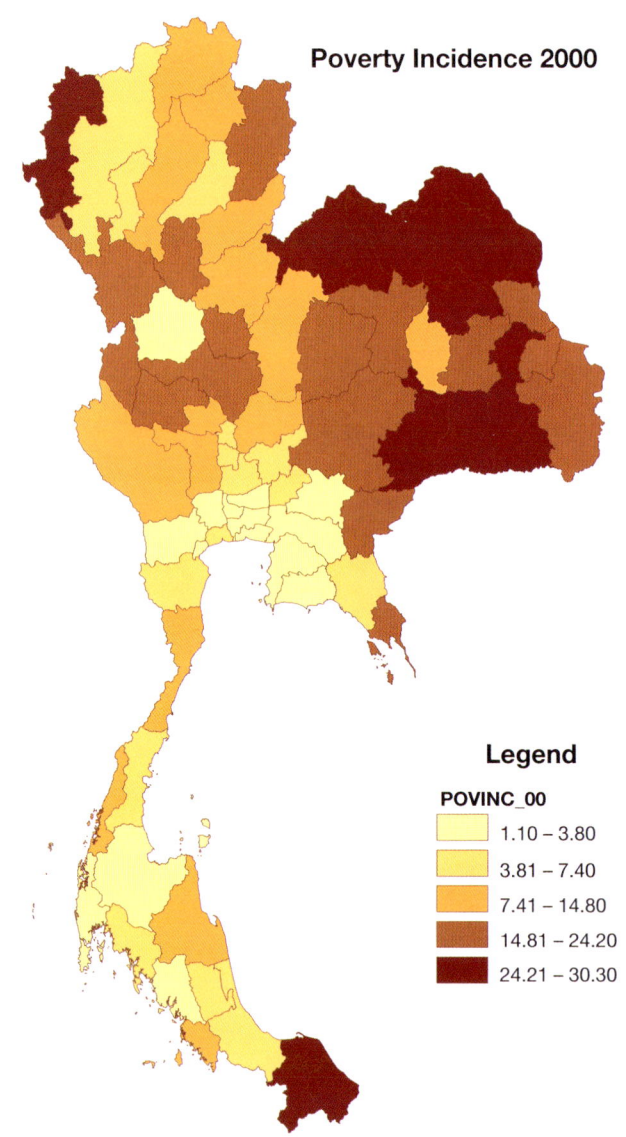

FIG. 3.3. Poverty incidence in Thailand, 2000 (See p. 68)

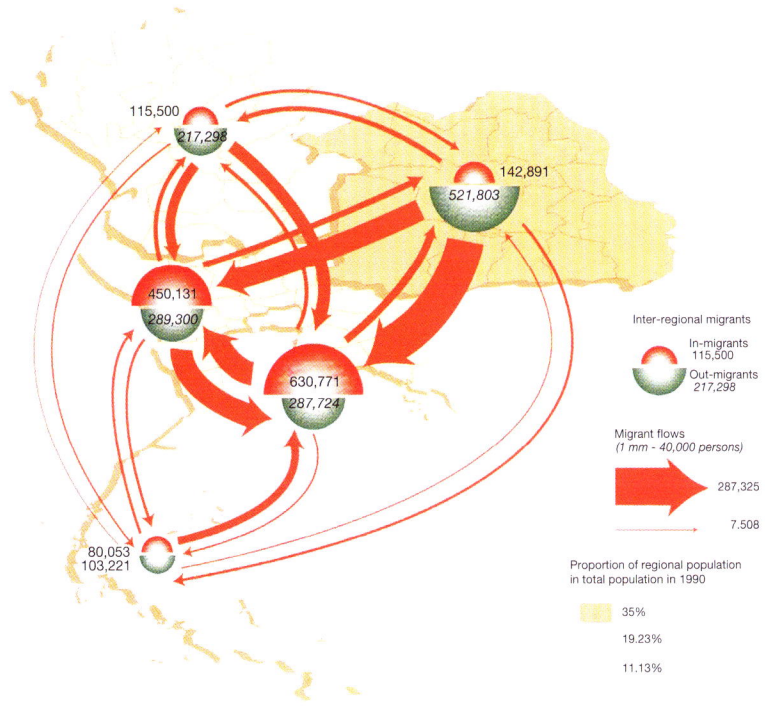

FIG. 3.6. Inter-regional migrations, 1985–90 (See p. 72)

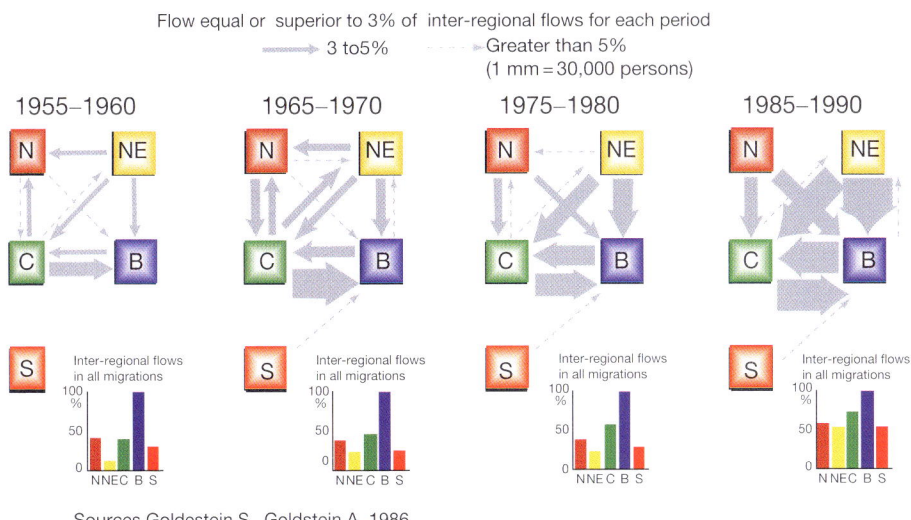

Flow equal or superior to 3% of inter-regional flows for each period
3 to5%   Greater than 5%
(1 mm = 30,000 persons)

Sources,Goldestein S., Goldstein A.,1986
NSO, 1990

FIG. 3.7. Variation in inter-regional migrations, 1955–1990 (See p. 72)

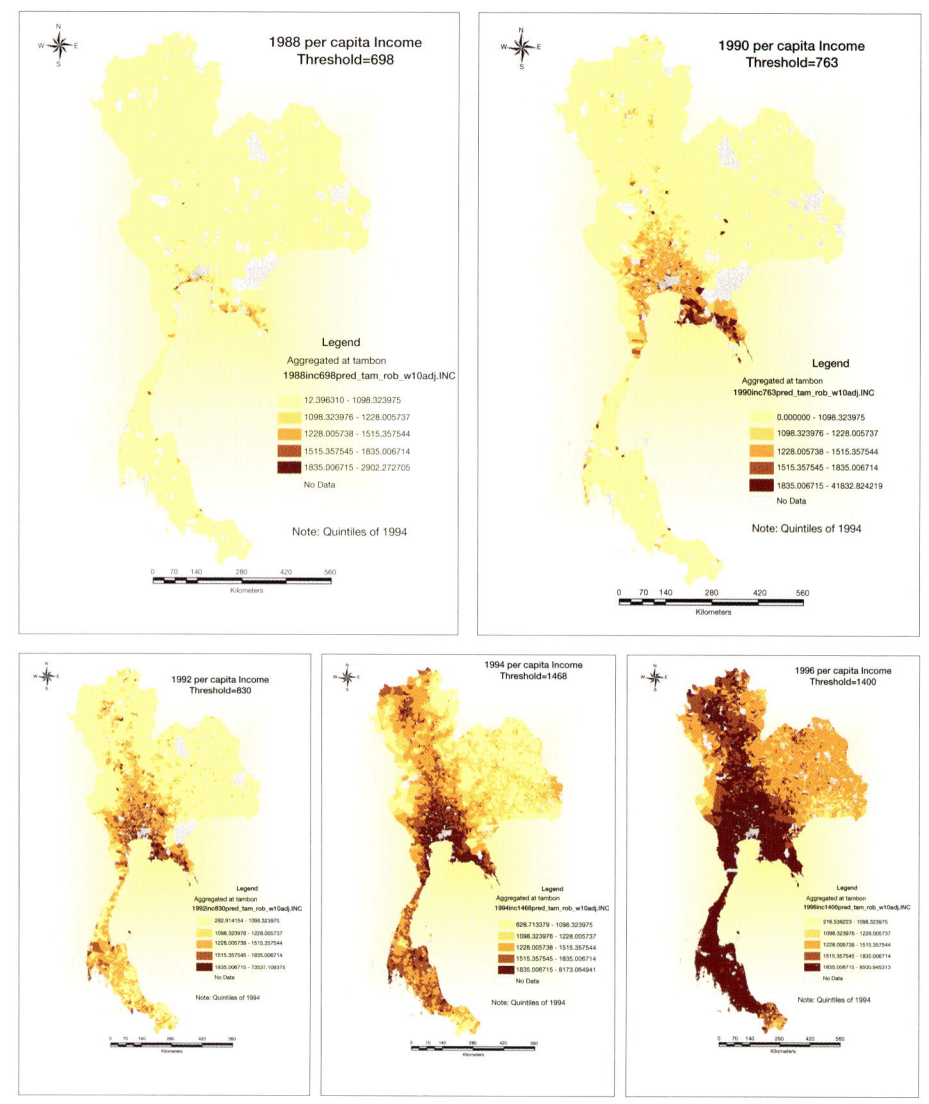

FIG. 3.9 (a–e) *Top left to lower right*
Per capita income, 1988–1996 (See pp. 77–81)

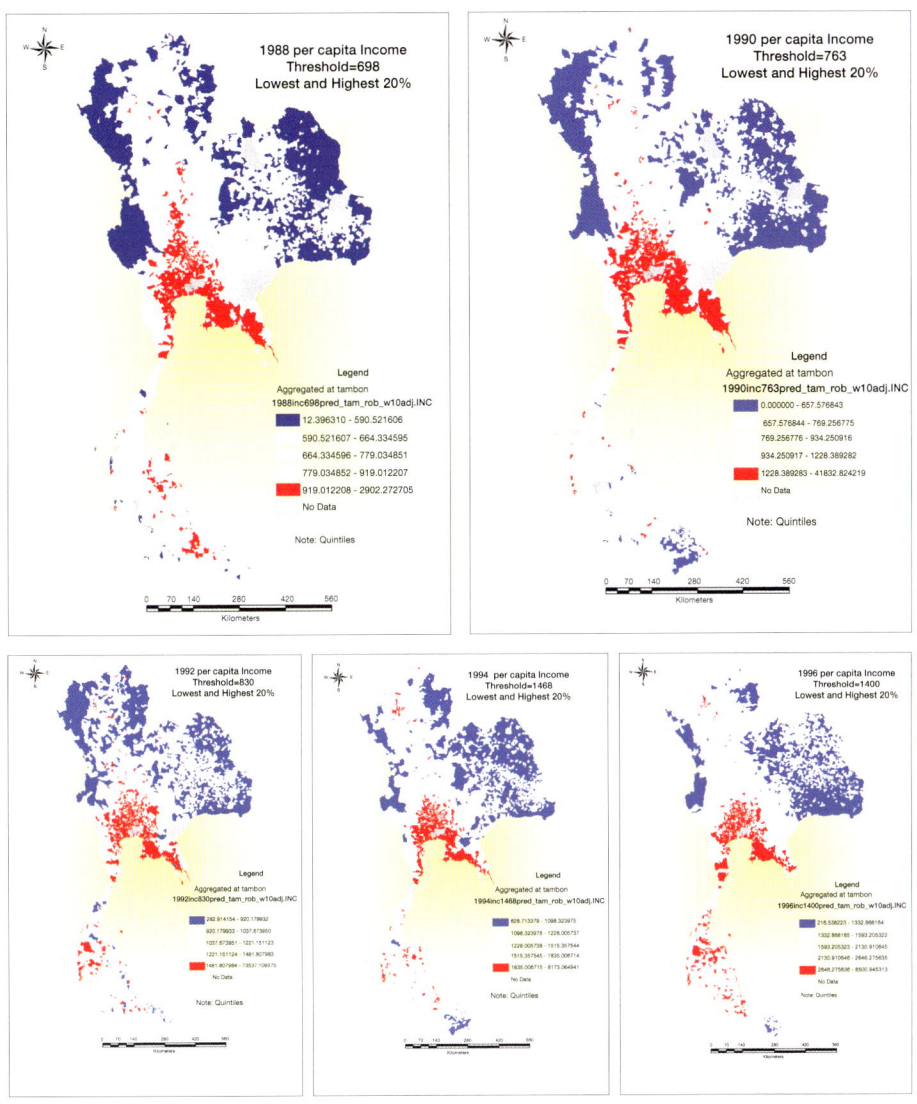

FIG. 3.10 (a–e) *Top left to lower right*
Wealth index, 1988–96, principal component of 3 assets (lowest 20 per cent)
(See pp. 82–86)

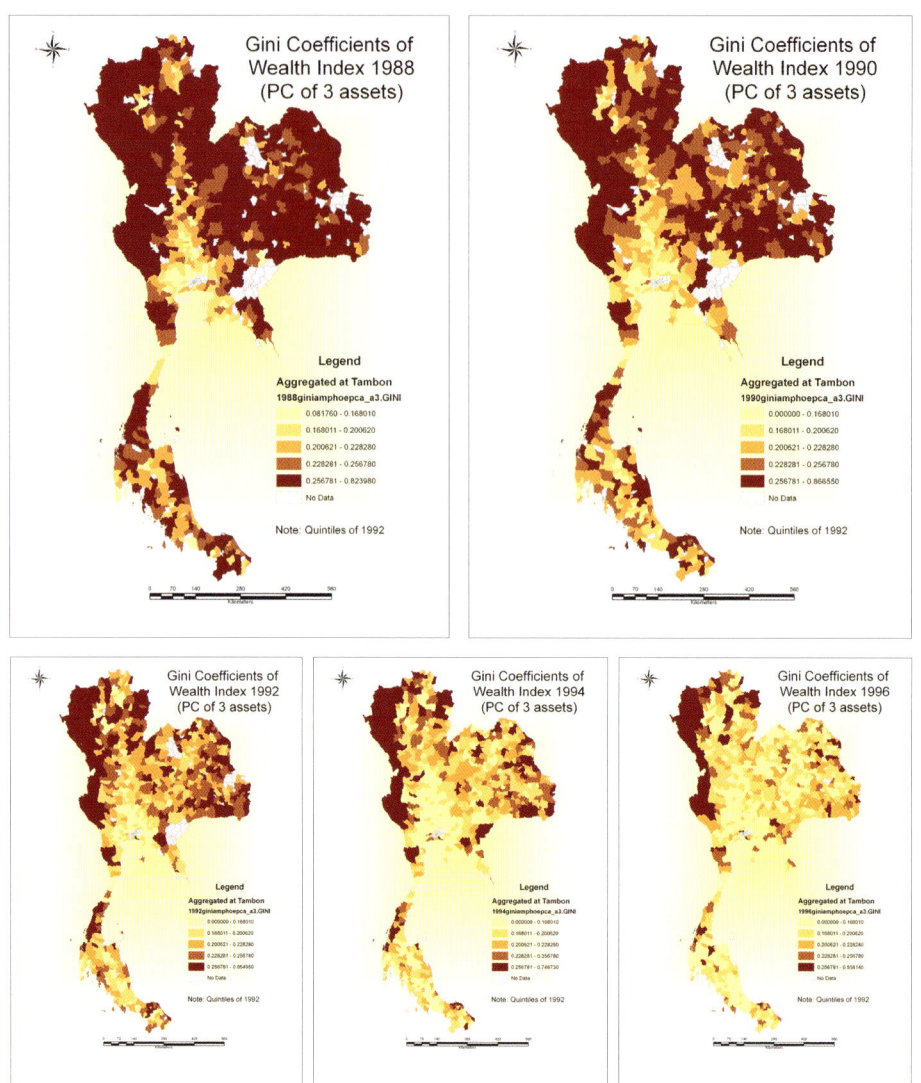

FIG. 3.11 (a–e) *Top left to lower right*
Gini coefficients of wealth index, 1988–96, principal component of 3 assets
(See pp. 87–91)

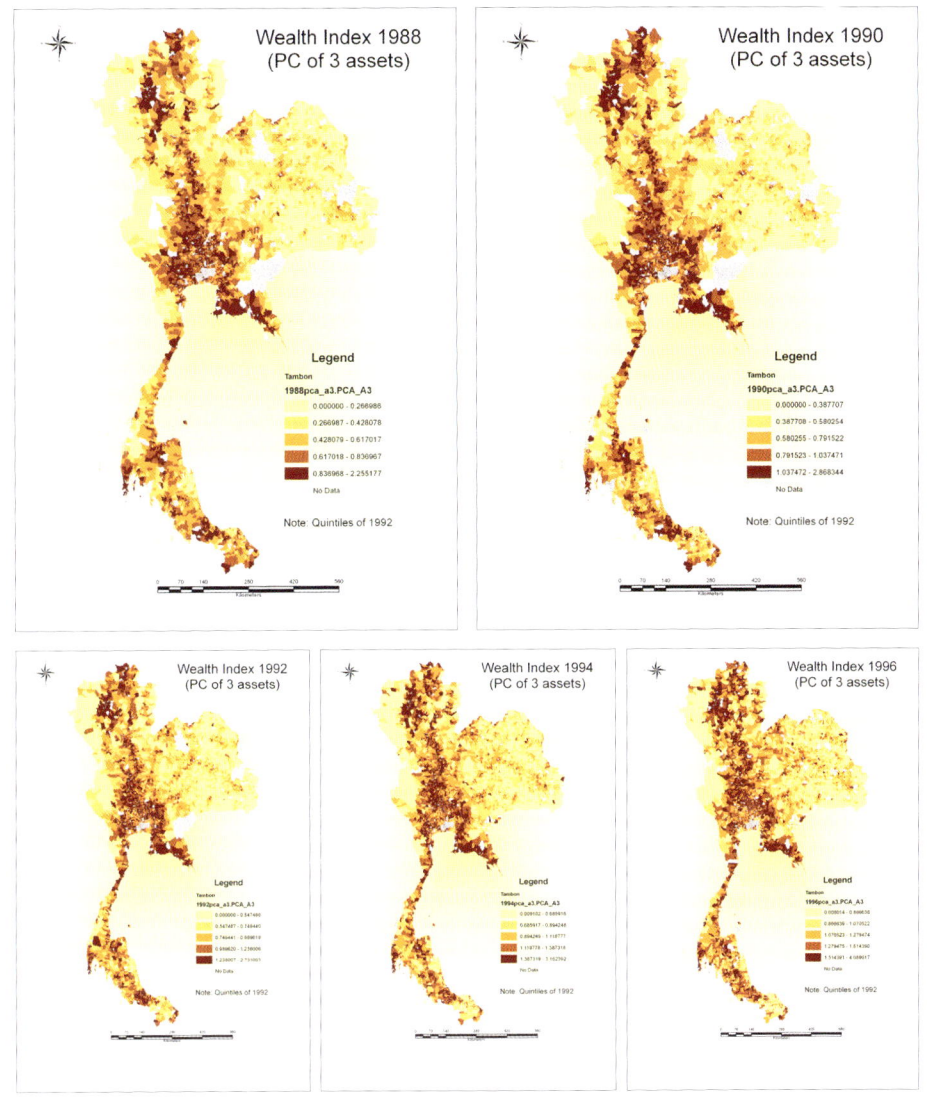

FIG. 3.12 (a–e) *Top left to lower right*
Wealth index, 1988–96, principal component of 3 assets (See pp. 92–96)

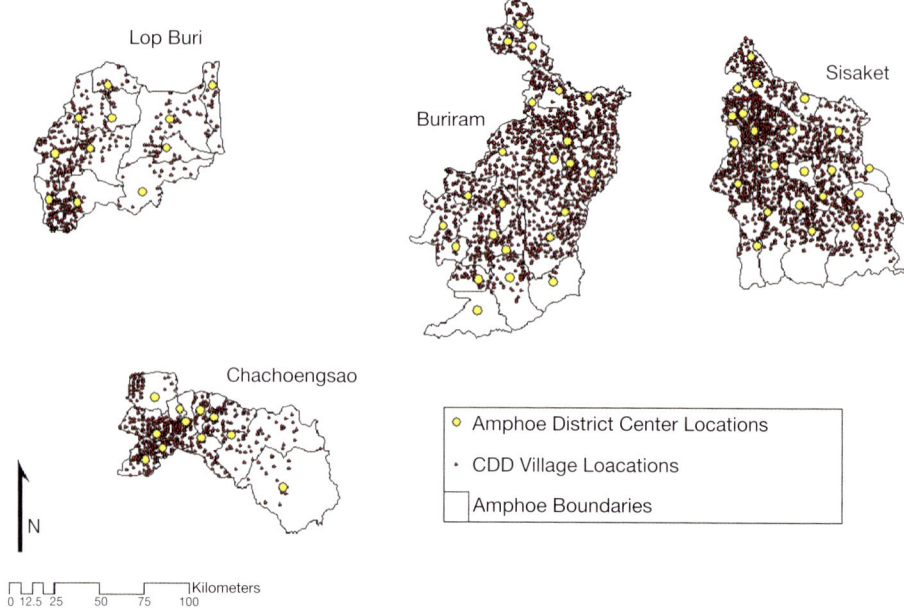

FIG. 3.13. Community development department village
and amphoe district center locations (See p. 98)

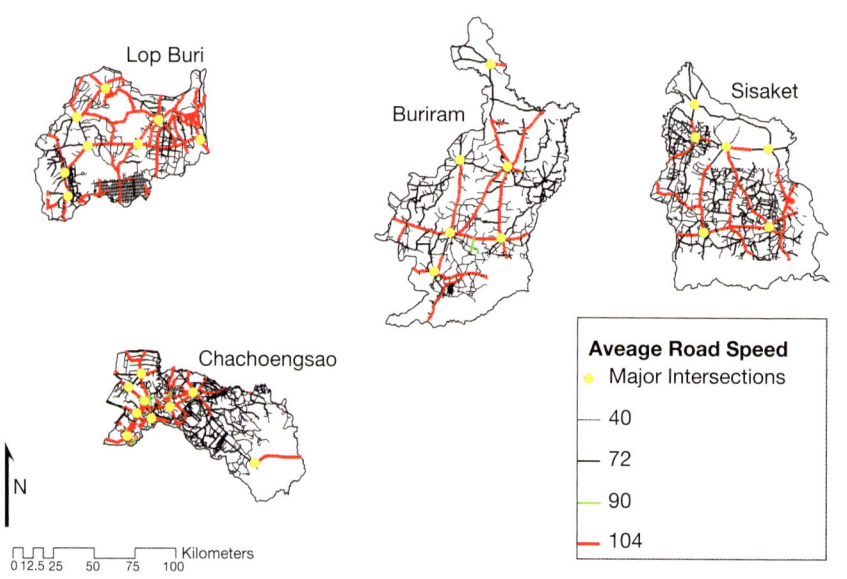

FIG. 3.14. Road networks and major intersection locations, with average road speeds
(See p. 98)

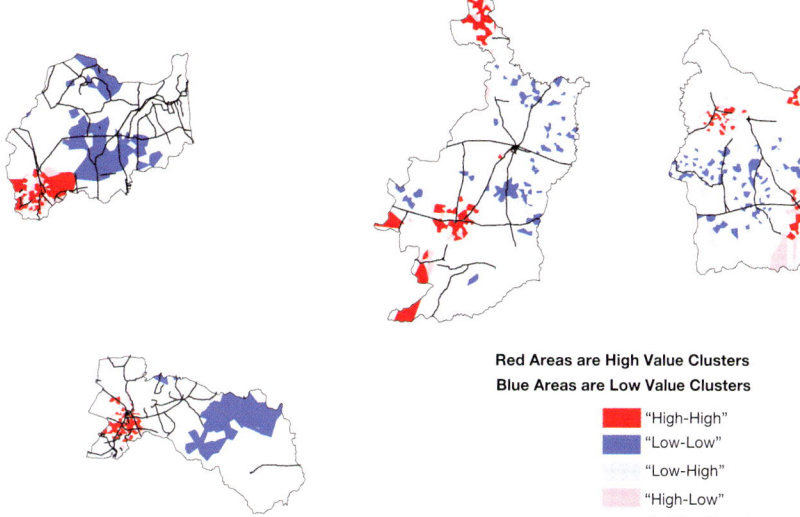

1986 Wealth Spatial Clusters
Local Moran Map: Clusters Statistically
Significant at p = .05
Distance Weights: 10 Kilometers

Red Areas are High Value Clusters
Blue Areas are Low Value Clusters

- ■ "High-High"
- ■ "Low-Low"
- "Low-High"
- "High-Low"
- Not Significant
- —— Major Roads

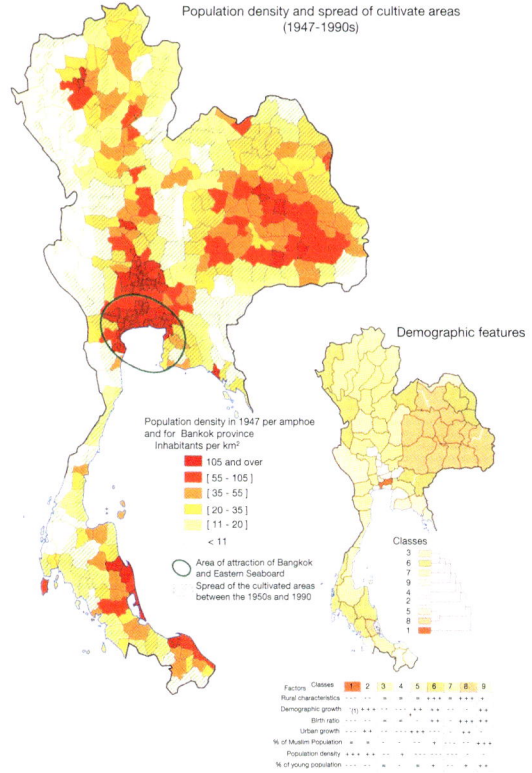

Population density and spread of cultivate areas
(1947-1990s)

Demographic features

Population density in 1947 per amphoe
and for Bankok province
Inhabitants per km²

- ■ 105 and over
- ■ [55 - 105]
- ■ [35 - 55]
- ■ [20 - 35]
- [11 - 20]
- < 11
- ◯ Area of attraction of Bangkok
  and Eastern Seaboard
  Spread of the cultivated areas
  between the 1950s and 1990

Classes
3
6
7
9
4
2
5
8
1

Factors	Classes	1	2	3	4	5	6	7	8	9
Rural characteristics		- - -	- -	=	=	=	+++	++	+++	++
Demographic growth		(1) +++	- - -	- - -	+++	++	- -			++
Birth ratio		- - -	- -	=	=	+	++	+++	+++	
Urban growth		- - -	++	- -	=	+++	- - -	++	++	-
% of Muslim Population		=	=	- -	- -	- -	+	- - -	+++	+++
Population density		+++	+++	+	=	- -	- -	- -		
% of young population		- - -	- -	=	=	+	+	+	+++	

(1) High for 1970-1990, near stagnation for 1990-2000

FIG. 3.15. *Above*
Wealth index, 1986 (See p. 99)

FIG. 3.17. Population distribution
and demographic features
(See p. 100)

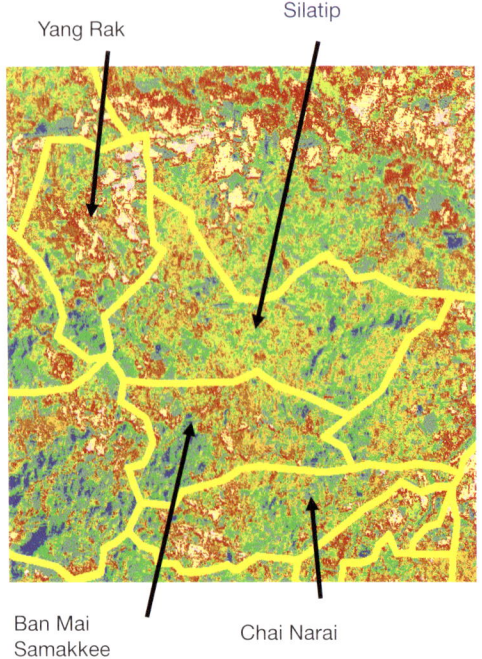

Yang Rak

Silatip

Ban Mai
Samakkee

Chai Narai

FIG. 3.18 (a) Variation in land cover in Lop Buri (See p. 107)

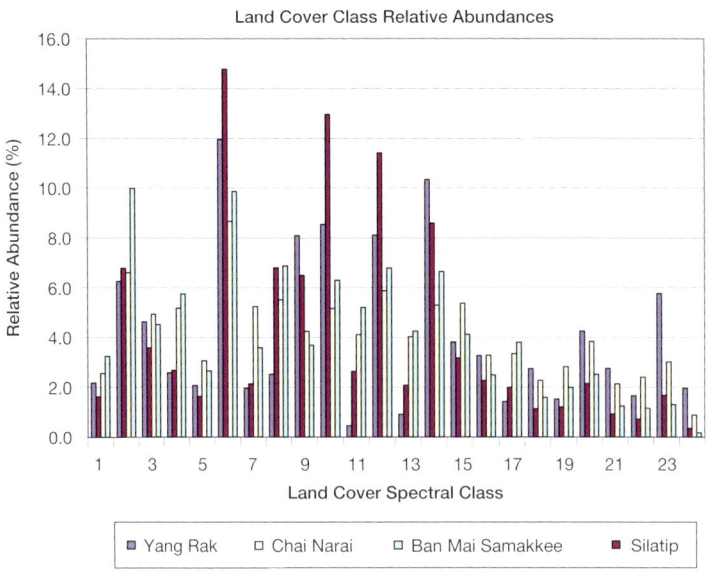

FIG. 3.18 (b) Histogram of land-cover class-relative abundances
for 4 tambons in Lop Buri (See p. 107)

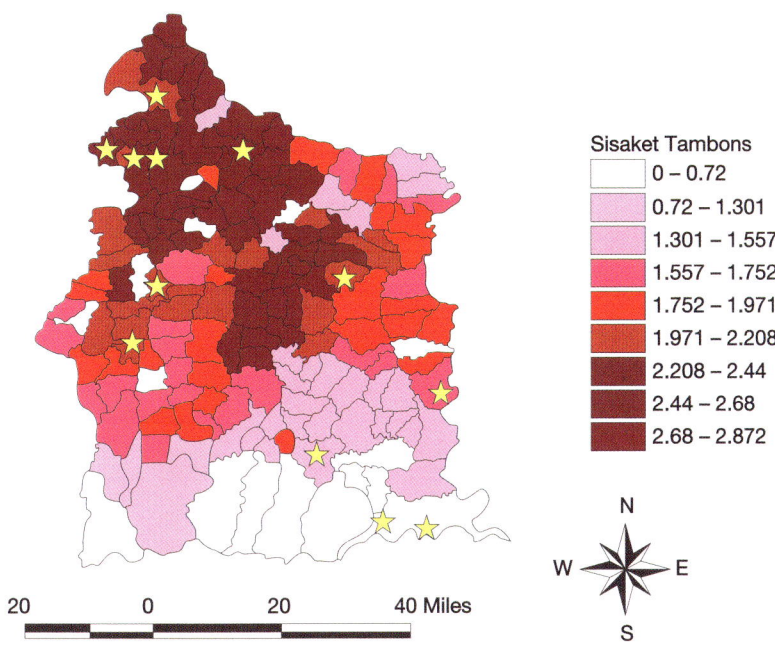

Sisaket Tambons
- 0 – 0.72
- 0.72 – 1.301
- 1.301 – 1.557
- 1.557 – 1.752
- 1.752 – 1.971
- 1.971 – 2.208
- 2.208 – 2.44
- 2.44 – 2.68
- 2.68 – 2.872

FIG. 3.19 (a) Sisaket tambon detrended correspondence analysis scores (See p. 108)

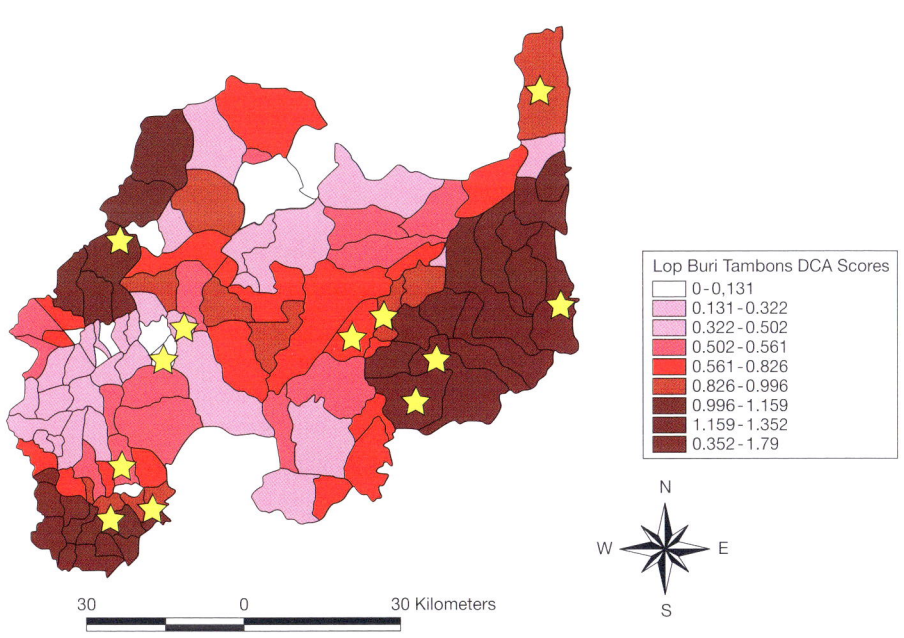

Lop Buri Tambons DCA Scores
- 0 – 0,131
- 0.131 – 0.322
- 0.322 – 0.502
- 0.502 – 0.561
- 0.561 – 0.826
- 0.826 – 0.996
- 0.996 – 1.159
- 1.159 – 1.352
- 0.352 – 1.79

FIG. 3.19 (b) Lop Buri tambon detrended correspondence analysis scores (See p. 109)

FIG. 3.21 Number of households engaged in growing rubber trees, 1999 (See p. 113)

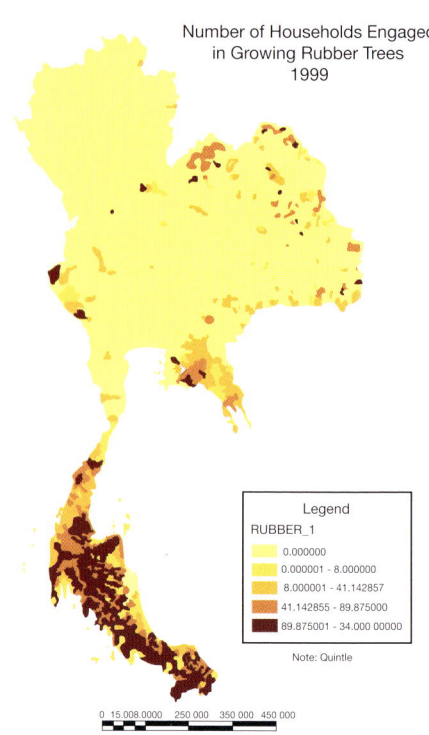

Number of Households Engaged
in Growing Rubber Trees
1999

Legend
RUBBER_1
0.000000
0.000001 - 8.000000
8.000001 - 41.142857
41.142855 - 89.875000
89.875001 - 34.000 00000

Note: Quintle

0 15.008.0000   250 000   350 000   450 000

FIG. 3.23 Average rainfall in Thailand (See p. 114)

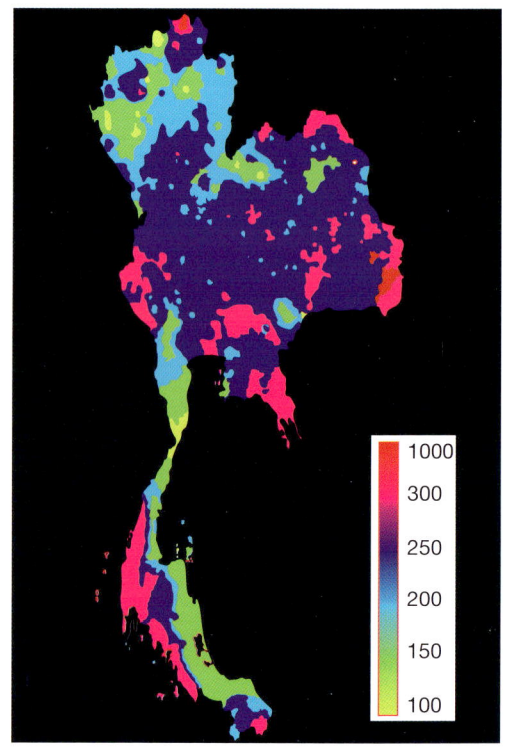

1000
300
250
200
150
100

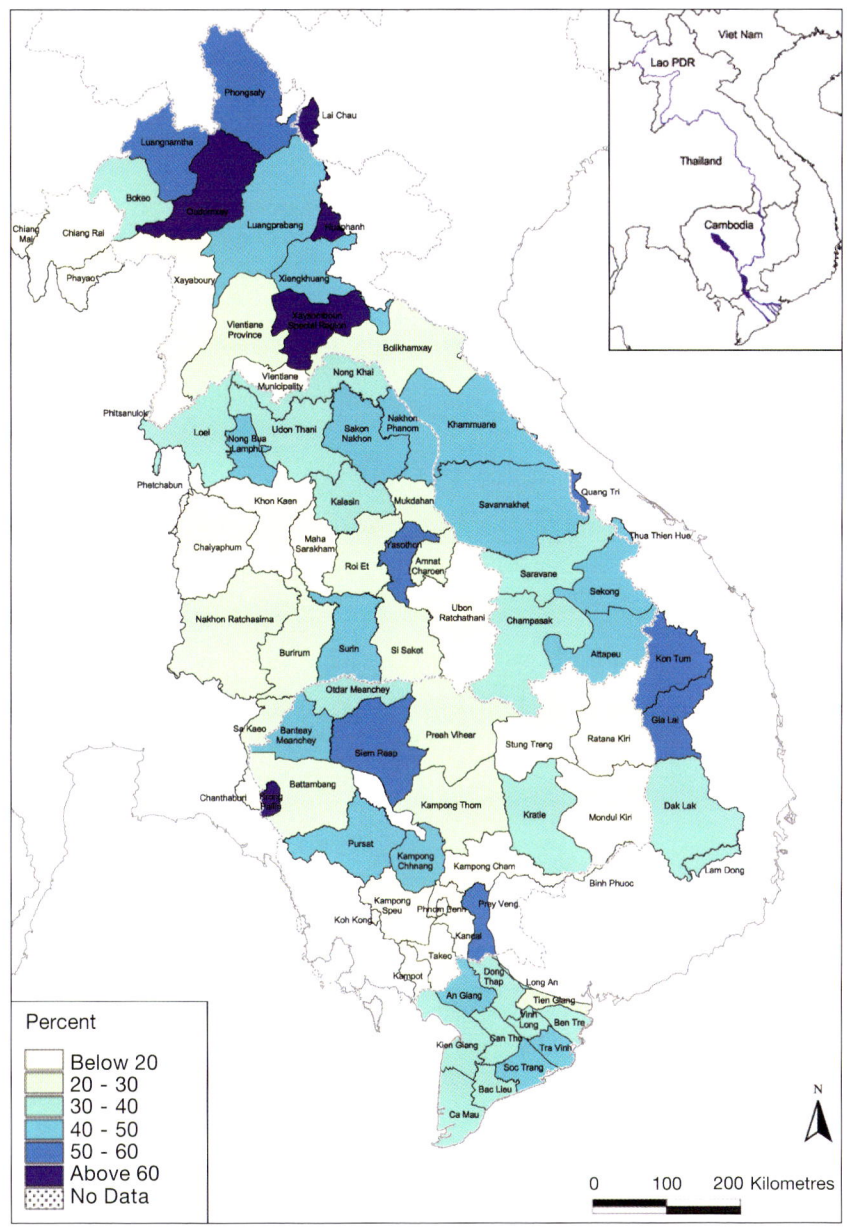

FIG. 3.26 Proportion of people living below the consumption-based poverty line
(See p. 117)

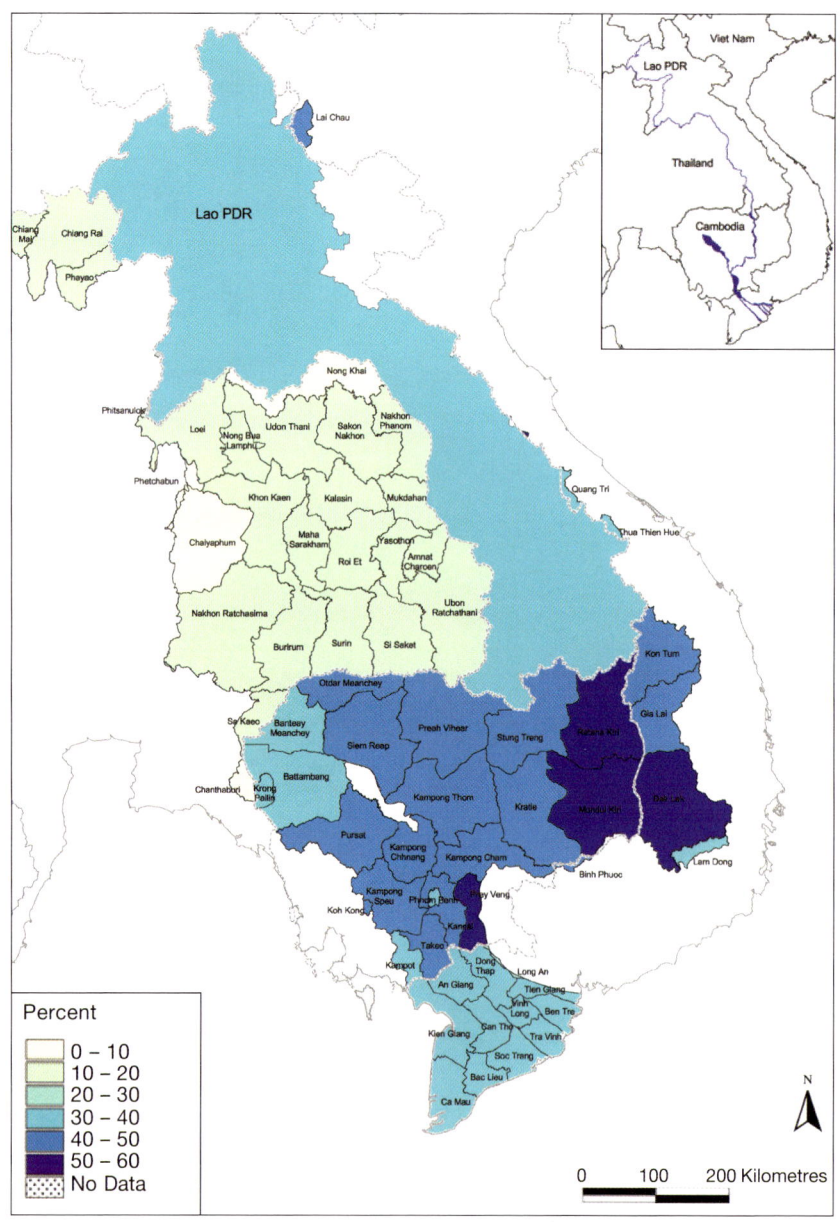

FIG. 3.27 Proportion of children underweight for age (See p. 118)

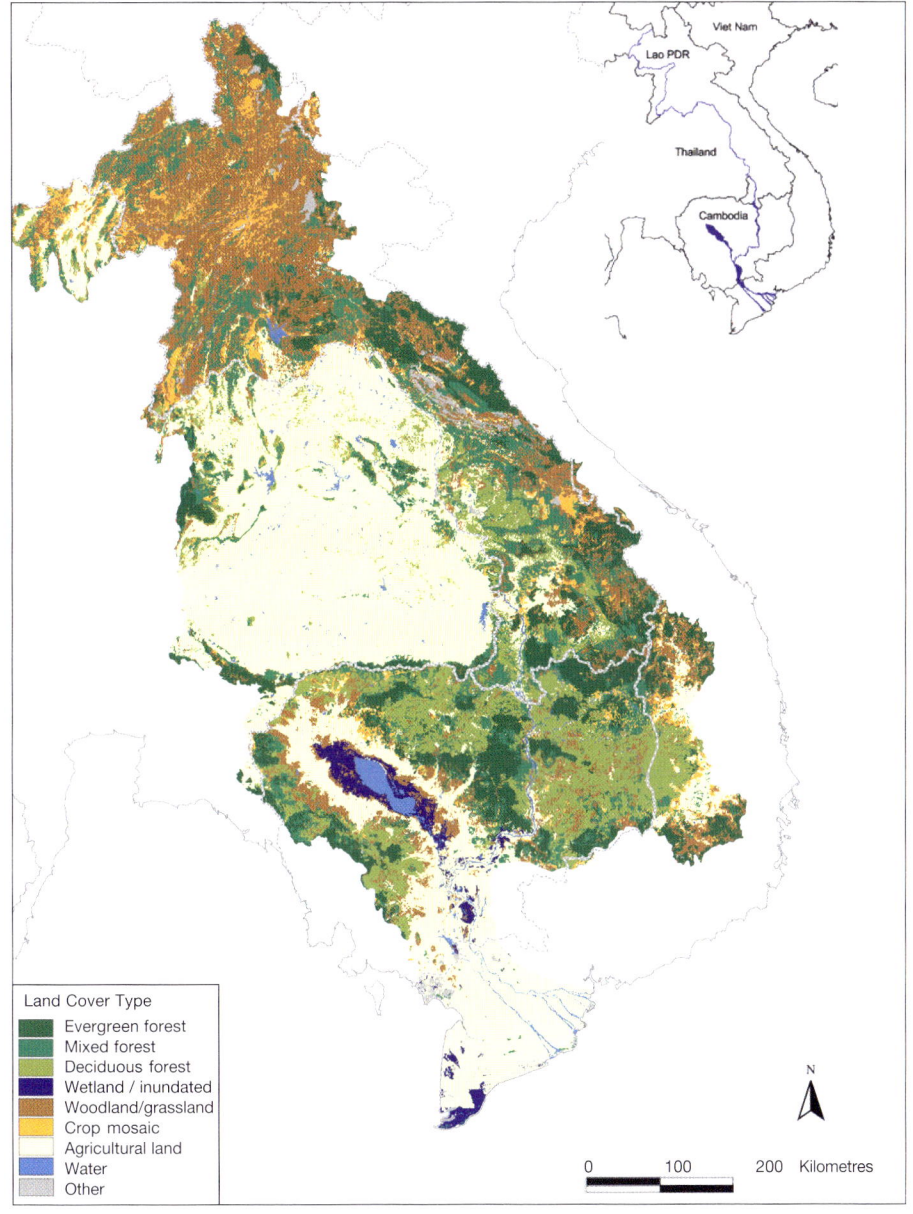

Land Cover Type
Evergreen forest
Mixed forest
Deciduous forest
Wetland / inundated
Woodland/grassland
Crop mosaic
Agricultural land
Water
Other

0   100   200   Kilometres

FIG. 3.28 Major land cover categories (See p.119)

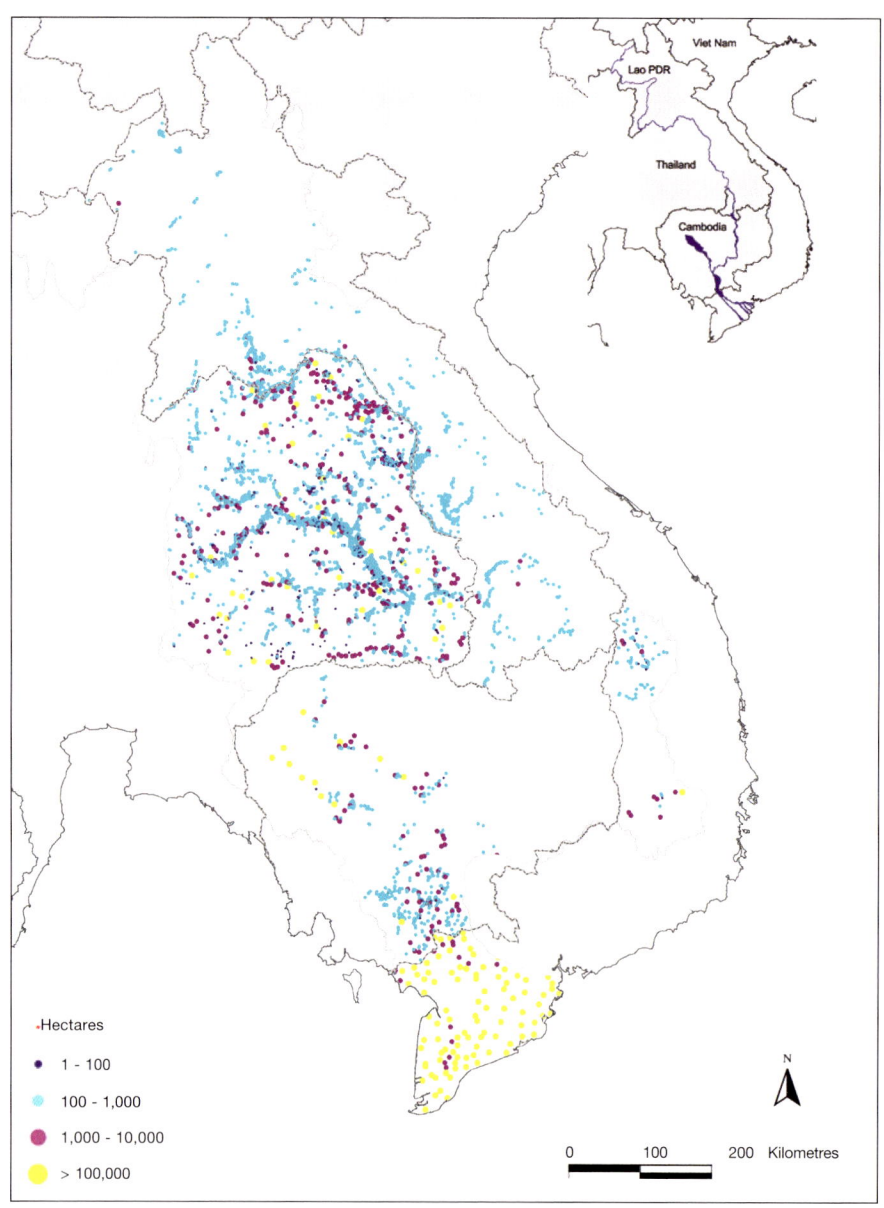

FIG. 3.29 Size of irrigation areas (See p. 120)

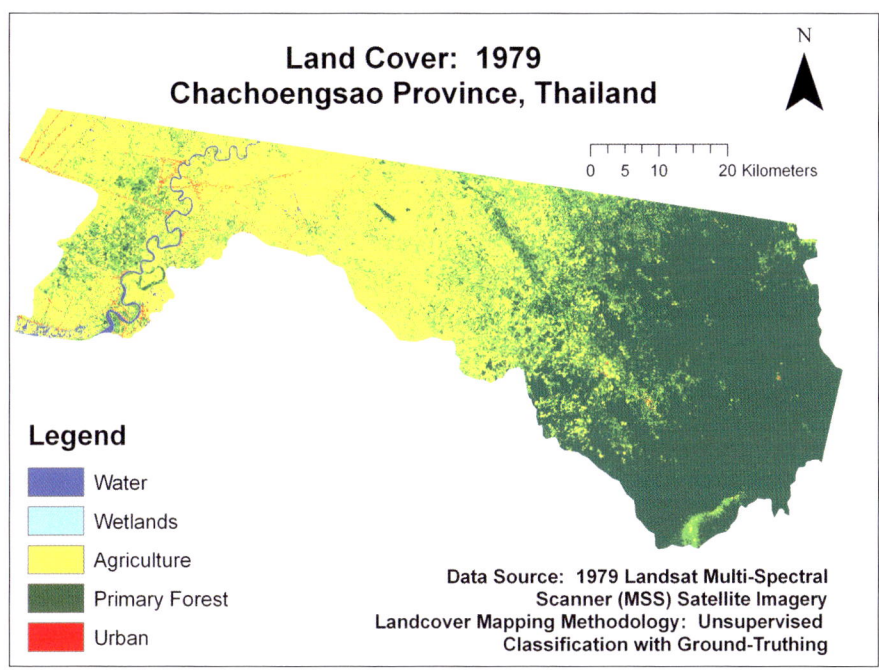

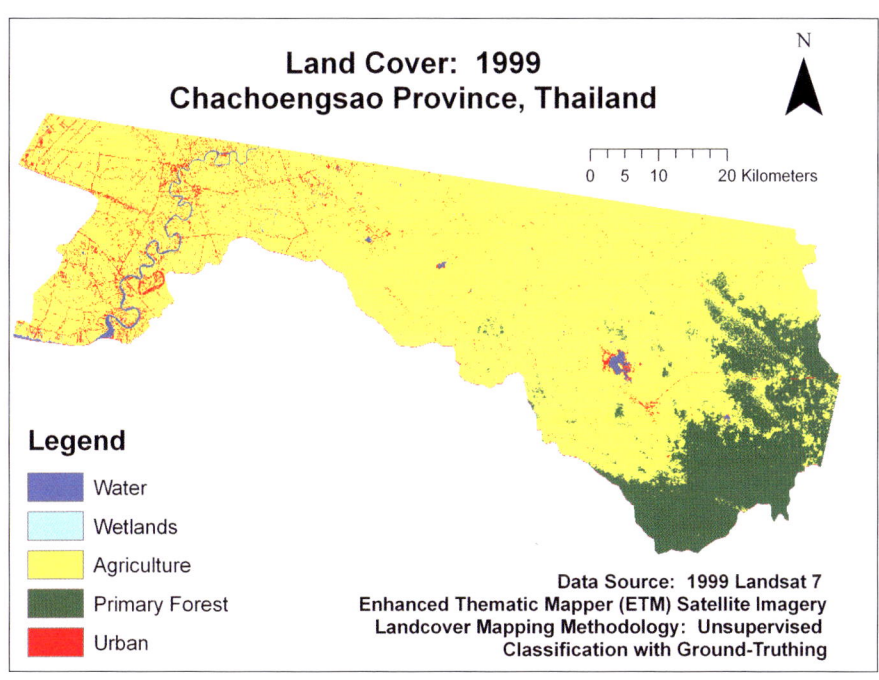

FIG. 5.3 (a–b) Satellite view of the industrialization of Thailand (See p. 149)

FIG. 5.12 (a)
Use of commercial bank
credit facility, 1986
(See p. 181)

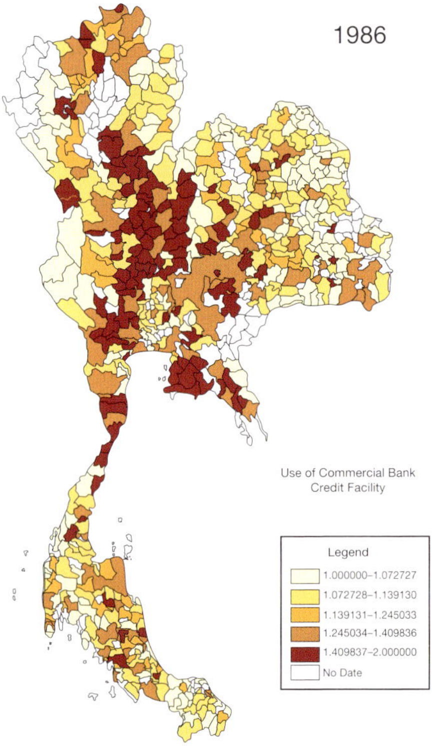

1986

Use of Commercial Bank
Credit Facility

Legend
1.000000–1.072727
1.072728–1.139130
1.139131–1.245033
1.245034–1.409836
1.409837–2.000000
No Date

FIG. 5.12 (b)
Use of commercial bank
credit facility, 1994
(See p. 182)

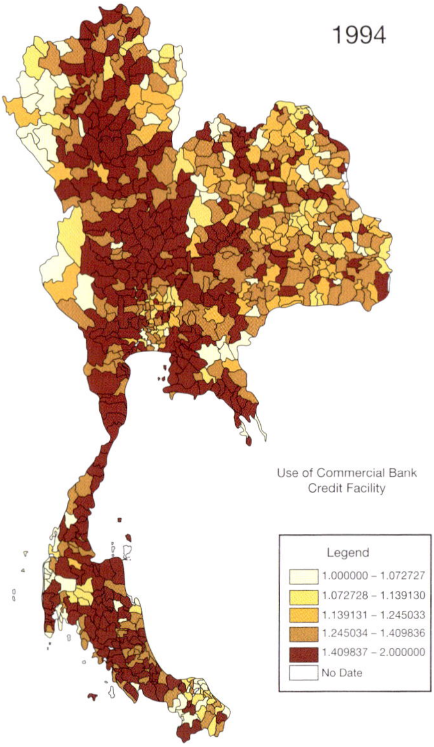

1994

Use of Commercial Bank
Credit Facility

Legend
1.000000 – 1.072727
1.072728 – 1.139130
1.139131 – 1.245033
1.245034 – 1.409836
1.409837 – 2.000000
No Date

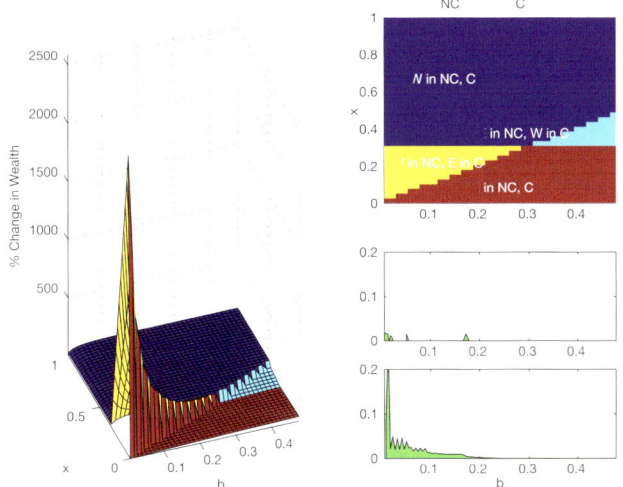

FIG. 6.4 (a–d)
Welfare comparison in 1979 (Townsend Thai data) (See p. 205)

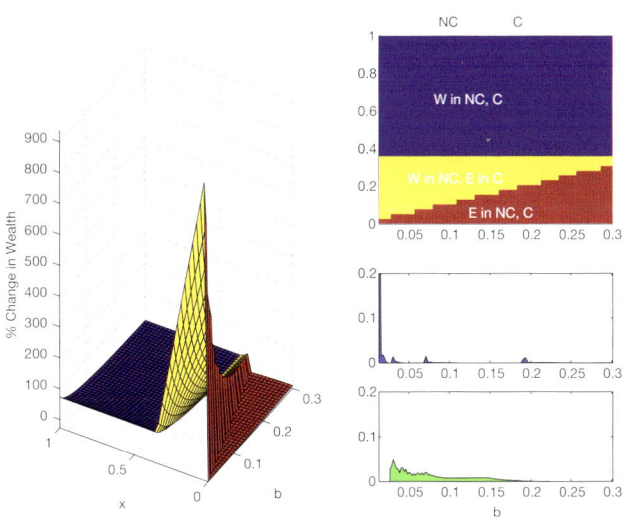

FIG. 6.5 (a–d)
Welfare comparison in 1996 (Townsend Thai data) (See p.206)

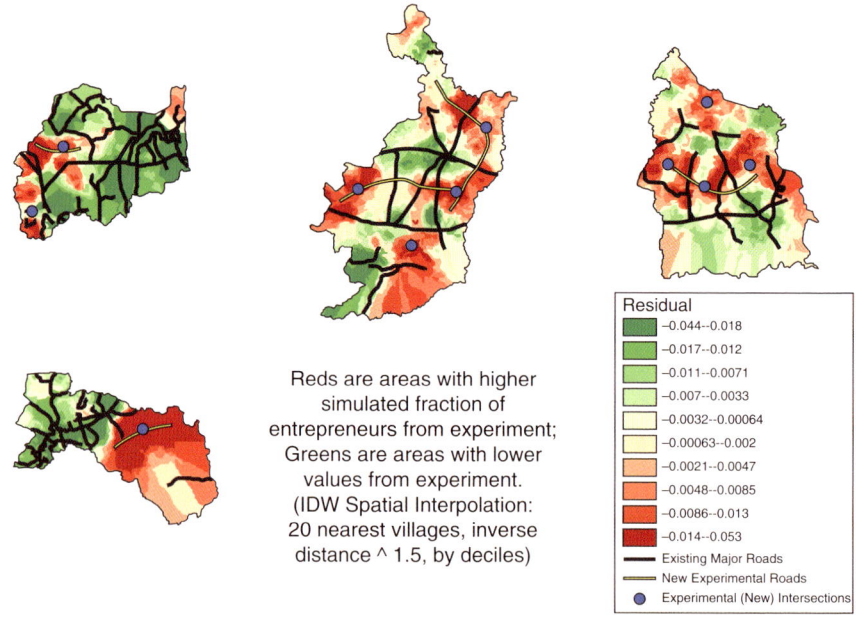

Reds are areas with higher
simulated fraction of
entrepreneurs from experiment;
Greens are areas with lower
values from experiment.
(IDW Spatial Interpolation:
20 nearest villages, inverse
distance ^ 1.5, by deciles)

Residual
- −0.044–−0.018
- −0.017–−0.012
- −0.011–−0.0071
- −0.007–−0.0033
- −0.0032–−0.00064
- −0.00063–−0.002
- −0.0021–−0.0047
- −0.0048–−0.0085
- −0.0086–−0.013
- −0.014–−0.053
—— Existing Major Roads
—— New Experimental Roads
● Experimental (New) Intersections

FIG. 6.23 Residuals from entrepreneurial choice experiment: effect of adding new
(hypothetical) road intersections (See p. 238)

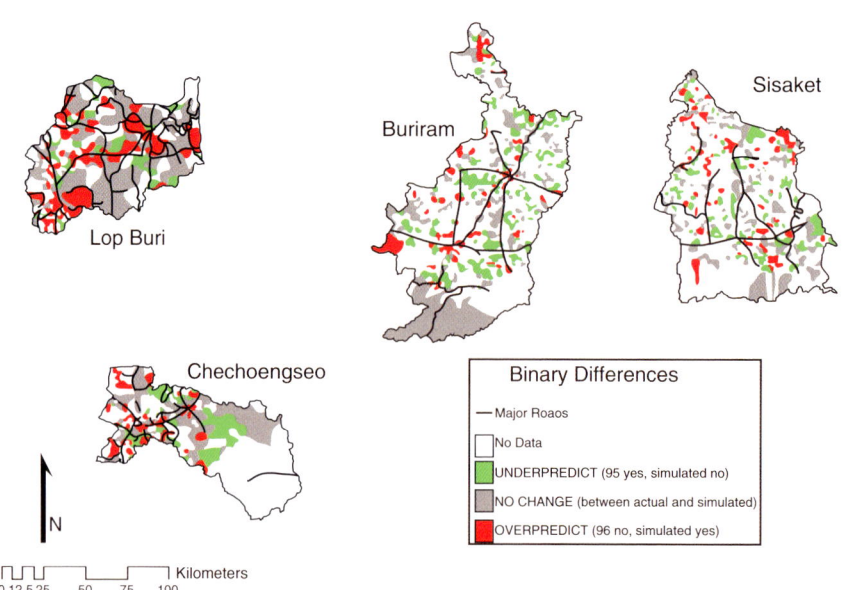

Binary Differences
—— Major Roaos
□ No Data
■ UNDERPREDICT (95 yes, simulated no)
■ NO CHANGE (between actual and simulated)
■ OVERPREDICT (96 no, simulated yes)

FIG. 6.24 1996 Greenwood and Jovanovic (GJ) access index simulation differences:
binary values, 1996 (See p. 239)

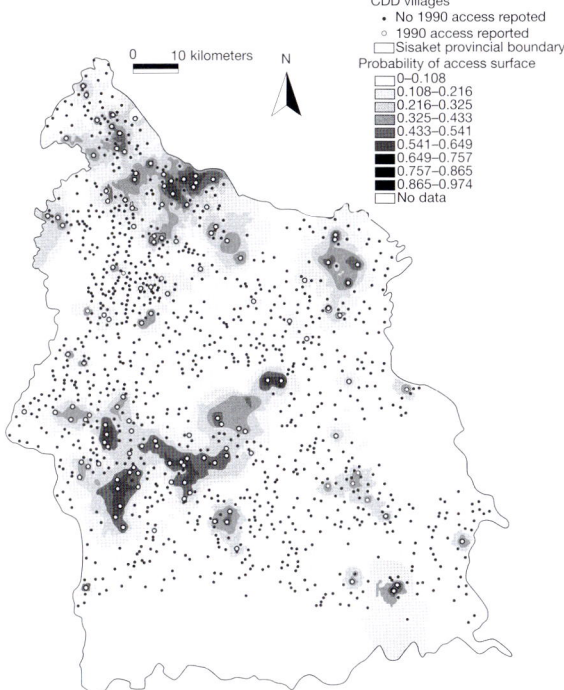

FIG 8.2 (a) Community Development Department Villages in 1990 (See p. 304)

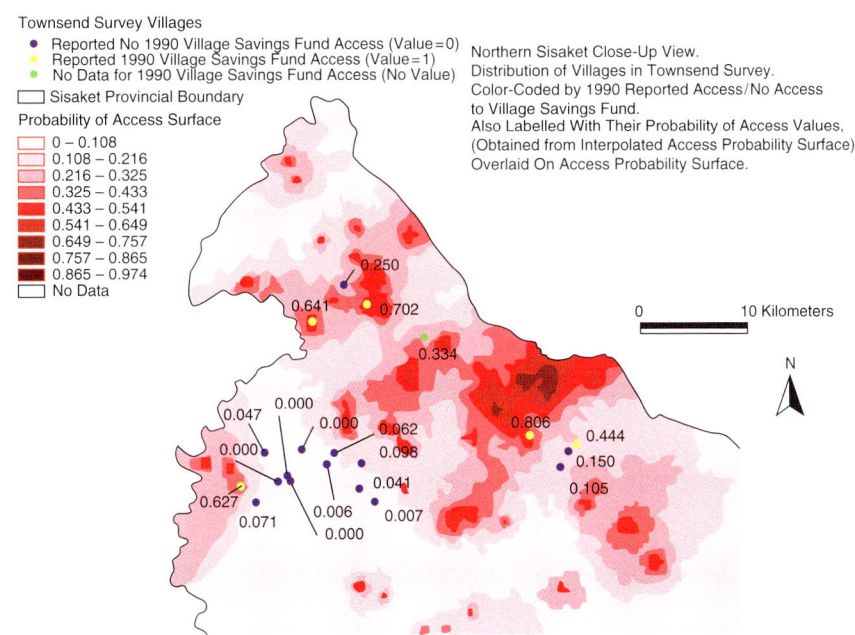

FIG. 8.2 (b) Townsend Thai Survey Villages in 1990 (See p. 305)

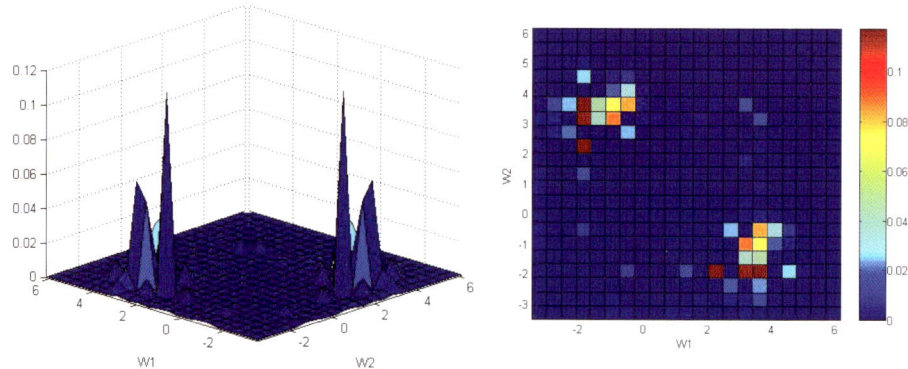

FIG. 9.34 (a–b) Distribution of pairs switching from groups to RP (See p. 401)

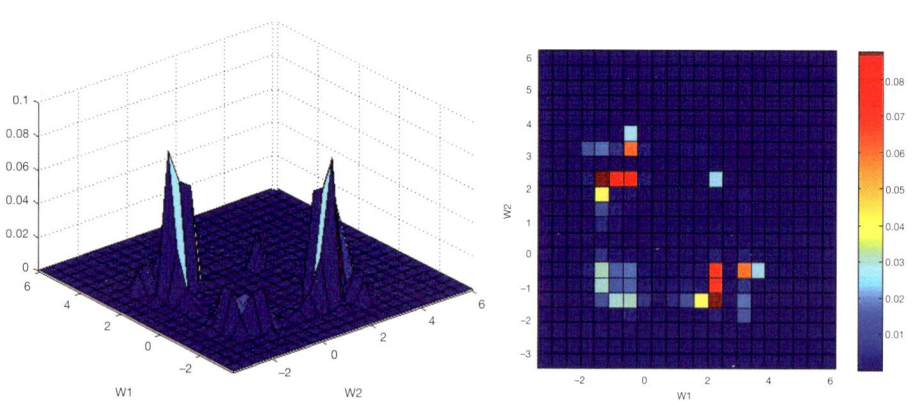

FIG. 9.35 (a–b) Distribution of pairs switching from RP to groups (See p. 402)